By the same author

FICTION

March Violets
The Pale Criminal
A German Requiem

EDITOR

The Penguin Book of Lies

THE PENGUIN BOOK OF

FIGHTS, FEUDS AND HEARTFELT HATREDS

AN ANTHOLOGY OF ANTIPATHY

Edited by Philip Kerr

VIKING

For my sister
Caroline
with love

VIKING

Published by the Penguin Group
Penguin Books Ltd, 27 Wrights Lane, London W8 5TZ, England
Penguin Books USA Inc., 375 Hudson Street, New York, New York 10014, USA
Penguin Books Australia Ltd, Ringwood, Victoria, Australia
Penguin Books Canada Ltd, 10 Alcorn Avenue, Toronto, Ontario, Canada M4V 3B2
Penguin Books (NZ) Ltd, 182–190 Wairau Road, Auckland 10, New Zealand

Penguin Books Ltd, Registered Offices: Harmondsworth, Middlesex, England

First published 1992
1 3 5 7 9 10 8 6 4 2
First edition

Copyright © Philip Kerr, 1992

Typeset by DatIX International Limited, Bungay, Suffolk
Set in 12/14pt Lasercomp Garamond
Printed in England by Clays Ltd, St Ives plc

A CIP catalogue record for this book is available from the British Library

ISBN 0–670–84020–3

Contents

Contents

Introduction

In coming to the idea for a book on Antipathy it seemed to me that the other side of feeling's coin, Sympathy, had received an undue share of scholarly attention. There had been numerous books to do with love, friendship, likes and attractions, but nothing on the subject of who and what people hate. I found this odd as the greater part of man's history consists in recurring manifestations of hatred.

As a title, however, *The Penguin Book of Antipathy* seemed rather too esoteric, where *The Penguin Book of Fights, Feuds and Heartfelt Hatreds* had at least the twin merits of accessibility and the promise of something more deliciously humorous besides the many colder dishes of pure hatred. So *The Penguin Book of Fights, Feuds and Heartfelt Hatreds* it is, with 'antipathy' on board as an all-embracing subtitle.

But what do I mean by fights, feuds and heartfelt hatreds? For that matter, how do I define antipathy?

This book is concerned with fights: antipathies between people which manifest themselves in violence, such as the duel fought between Pushkin and D'Anthès; it is concerned with feuds: mutual antipathies which exist for a long period of time, such as that which existed between Bette Davis and Joan Crawford; and it is concerned with heartfelt hatreds: antipathies between people, and between people and things which need be neither active nor mutual, such as Robert Lynd's hatred of insects.

They are by no means exclusive. A hatred might become a feud, and a feud might eventually manifest itself in a fight as happened with the feud between Aaron Burr and Colonel Hamilton. But the essential factor is antipathy.

Antipathy means having a strong feeling against someone or

something, an aversion which can be constitutional or settled. Not all fights are included, however. That German and British soldiers of the First World War could leave their trenches on a Christmas Day and play football in no man's land seems to illustrate the point that, at the level of ordinary soldier, wars need not always take place in circumstances of hatred or ill-will. Similarly with boxers, who often embrace one another at the end of a bloody and apparently arduous contest. It goes without saying that many wars and a good few boxing matches are fought with considerable hatred and ill-will, but quite a few lack the element of real antipathy, and since war and boxing are already the subjects of many excellent anthologies they are therefore excluded from this book.

Antipathy, where it takes the form of religious and racial hatred, is no less common than it has always been. It is sad to reflect that today there are Catholics and Protestants who hate each other as much as they did on St Bartholomew's Day in 1572, when French Roman Catholics murdered hundreds of French Protestants. Martin Dillon's chilling account of Northern Ireland's Shankill butchers reminds us, as Swift says, that 'we have just enough religion to make us hate, but not enough to make us love one another'. And Vitali Vitaliev shows us that 'Soviet' Jews are blamed for that country's modern problems just as Jews were blamed for the poisoning of wells during the Black Death of 1349.

Antipathy of a personal nature – where it takes the form of a feud between two people – is perhaps less destructive than it was. During the age of duelling, enmities between public figures such as Aaron Burr and Colonel Hamilton were often settled fatally on the 'field of honour'. It is no bad thing that honour is no longer held in such high regard. These days when men of letters have a falling out it is unlikely to result in anything more fatal than a slap in the mouth.

It would be hard to imagine that antipathy could ever find much of an excuse. However everyone finds it easy to under-stand people who claim a constitutional aversion to snakes or spiders; a settled antipathy to other people is no less common. The poet Horace: 'I hate the unholy masses and keep away from them'; and another poet, Walter Savage Landor: 'I know not whether I am proud, / But this I know, I hate the crowd.' For that matter the Duke of Wellington, like King George I before him, hated people like Horace and Walter Savage Landor: 'I hate the whole race. There is no believing a word they say – your professional poets, I mean – there never existed a more worthless set than Byron and his friends for example.' We can even excuse an antipathy towards that which we normally love where it is expressed with the wit of W. C. Fields: 'Any man who hates dogs and babies can't be all bad.'

There are antipathies in which we can take some vicarious satisfaction. For example, here is Dr Johnson describing Lord Bathurst: 'Dear Bathurst was a man to my very heart's content: he hated a fool and he hated a rogue; and he hated a whig; he was a very good hater.'

Equally there are occasions when it seems positively enjoyable to hate someone, as the poet Thomas Moore seems to suggest: 'To love you was pleasant enough. And oh! 'Tis delicious to hate you!'

There is a sense in which life would be very dull indeed without our antipathies. Antipathy is the touchstone of our opinions. I hate rap music just as I love a Haydn string quartet. I have an aversion to the paintings of Jackson Pollock just as I adore the work of David Hockney. How else are we to measure the strength of what we enjoy and admire if not by that which we hate and despise? Here is Henry David Thoreau: 'It were treason to our love / And a sin to God above / One iota to abate / Of a pure impartial hate.'

The Book of Common Prayer asks the Good Lord to deliver us 'from envy, hatred and malice, and from all uncharitableness'. Yet history would seem to show that there is only one thing more corrupting to the human soul than being universally hated, and that is being universally loved. Was ever a person so adored as the hugely corrupted Elvis Presley? A good measure of antipathy towards ourselves helps to remind us of our own failings and thereby to keep a sense of proportion. And how else but by overcoming antipathy and adversity can we measure our own worth? If we need enemies (and yes let us love them as St Luke exhorts us to do) then it follows that we ought to perform the same service for other people. With this in mind it is useful to consider the advice of Oscar Wilde in respect, that 'a man cannot be too careful in his choice of enemies'.

Antipathy finds its best excuse as something existential, as a satisfying and extreme form of freedom, with each of us having to answer our own conscience as to the choice that is made and how it is acted upon.

During the preparation of this book I have received assistance from Jane Thynne, Christopher Silvester, Tony Lacey, Judith Flanders, and Nicholas Wetton, who cleared the permissions. I hope they will accept a general but heartfelt thank you for their patience and help.

Caesar and Pompey

PLUTARCH

Theirs was one of the most famous feuds of ancient times. Like many feuds, the participants had once been friends. In 69 BC it had been Caesar who helped Pompey to obtain the supreme command for the war in the East. It was Caesar who, in 60 BC, organized the First Triumvirate, made up of Pompey, commander-in-chief of the army; Marcus Licinius Crassus, the wealthiest man in Rome; and Caesar himself. With the death of Crassus, in 53 BC, the First Triumvirate came to an end, and set Pompey and Caesar at each other's throat. Caesar finally defeated Pompey at the battle of Pharsali in 48 BC, after which Pompey fled to Egypt, where he was killed. Here Plutarch describes the early stages of the feud and attempts to explain its origins.

Caesar had long ago decided that Pompey must be removed from his position of power; and Pompey, for that matter, had come to just the same decision about Caesar. Crassus, who had been watching their struggle, ready to take on the winner himself, had been killed in Parthia; so that now the field was clear. The man who wanted to be on top had to get rid of the one who at present held that position: the man who was for the moment on top had, if he wished to stay there, to get rid of the man he feared before it was too late. It was only recently that Pompey had come to fear Caesar. Up till this time he had despised him. It was through his influence, he thought, that Caesar had grown great, and it would be just as easy to put him down as it had been to raise him up. But Caesar's plan had been laid down from the very beginning. Like an athlete he had, as it were, withdrawn himself from the ring and, in the Gallic wars, had undergone a course of training. In these wars he had brought his army into perfect condition and had won such fame for himself that he had now reached a height where his own achievements could challenge comparison with the past successes of Pompey. He made use too of every argument and circumstance that was to his advantage. Some of these were given to him by Pompey himself, some by the general state of affairs and by the collapse of good government in Rome. Here things had gone so far that candidates for office quite shamelessly bribed the electorate, actually counting out the money in public, and the people who had received the bribes went down to the forum not so much to vote for their benefactors as to fight for them with bows and arrows and swords and slings. Often, before an election was over, the place where it had been held was stained with blood and defiled with dead bodies, and the city was left with no government at all, like a ship adrift with no one to steer her. The result was that intelligent people could only be thankful if, after such a mad and stormy period, things ended in nothing worse than monarchy. In fact there were many people who actually ventured to declare in public that there was now no other possible remedy for the disease of the state except government by one man, that this remedy was available from the gentlest of physicians (meaning Pompey) and ought to be taken. As for Pompey, so far as words went he put on a show of declining the honour, but in fact did more than anyone else to get himself made dictator. Cato was able to grasp the situation and persuaded the senate to appoint Pompey as sole consul, hoping that he would be satisfied with this more legal form of monarchy and not grasp the dictatorship by force. At the same time the senate voted that his period of government over his provinces should be prolonged. He had two provinces – Spain and all Africa. These were governed by officers appointed by him and he maintained armies in both provinces for which he received a thousand talents a year from the treasury.

Caesar now sent to Rome asking to be allowed to stand for a consulship and to have his own provincial commands prolonged also. At first Pompey himself did not declare himself either way; but Marcellus and Lentulus opposed Caesar's requests. They had always hated Caesar and they now used every means, fair or foul, to dishonour and discredit him. For instance, they took away the rights of Roman citizenship from the people of Novum Comum, which was a colony recently established by Caesar in Gaul; and Marcellus, during his consulship, had a senator from Novum Comum who had come to Rome beaten with rods. 'I am putting these marks on you,' he said, 'to prove that you are not a Roman. Now go away and show them to Caesar.'

However, by the time that the consulship of Marcellus was over Caesar was already in a most lavish way making available to public figures in Rome the wealth which he had won in Gaul. He paid the enormous debts of the tribune Curio; and he gave the consul Paulus fifteen hundred talents with which he added to the beauty of the forum by building the famous Basilica which was erected in place of the one known as 'the Fulvia'. Pompey now became alarmed at the party which was forming and came into the open. Both he and his friends began to work for having Caesar replaced by a successor in his provincial command, and he sent to him to ask for the return of the troops whom he had lent to him for the war in Gaul. Caesar sent the soldiers back, after giving each man a present of 250 drachmas. The officers who brought these troops back to Pompey publicly spread rumours about Caesar which were in themselves neither likely nor true, but which had the effect of warping Pompey's judgement and filling him with false hopes. It was Pompey, according to these officers, who was really the idol of Caesar's army, and while Pompey, because of the festering disease of envy in Roman politics, was having some difficulty in controlling things in Rome, the army in Gaul was there, ready for him to use, and, if it once crossed over into Italy, would immediately come over to him, so unpopular had Caesar become because of his innumerable campaigns and so greatly was he suspected of planning to seize supreme power for himself. All this fed Pompey's vanity. On the assumption that he had nothing to fear, he took no measures for the raising of troops, and imagined that he was winning the war against

Caesar by speeches and by resolutions of the senate, though in fact all these resolutions meant nothing to Caesar at all. It is said that one of Caesar's centurions, who had been sent by him to Rome, was standing outside the senate house and, when he was told that the senate would not give Caesar an extension of his command, he clapped his hand on the hilt of his sword and said: 'This will give it to him all right.'

Yet the demands made by Caesar certainly looked fair enough. What he suggested was that he should lay down his arms and that Pompey should do the same thing; they should then both, as ordinary private individuals, see what favour they could find from their fellow citizens. He argued that those who wanted him to be disarmed while Pompey's own forces were strengthened were simply confirming one man in the tyranny which they accused the other one of aiming at.

•

First feuds

MAX GLUCKMAN

The anthropologist Max Gluckman describes the historical and anthropological roots of the feud and shows that peace remains implicit in the very notion of the feud.

In their great *History of English Law* Pollock and Maitland wrote that in Anglo-Saxon times 'personal injury was in the first place a cause of feud, or private war, between the kindreds of the wrongdoer and of the person wronged'. The *Shorter Cambridge Mediaeval History* says that feud 'produced a state of incessant private warfare in the community, and divided the kindreds themselves when the injury was committed by one member against another of the same group'. I doubt this. The Anglo-Saxon vengeance group, called the *sib*, which was entitled to claim blood-money for a dead man, was composed of all his kindred, through males and females, up to sixth cousins. But the group which resided and worked together seems to have been some form of patriarchal joint family: again we find that the vengeance group did not coincide with the local group. And if you trace each man's kin up to his sixth cousins, they form a widely scattered grouping which could not mobilize. Each man, with only his full-brothers and full-sisters, was the centre of his own sib; and every individual was a member of the sibs of many other people. Indeed, I venture to suggest that in a long-settled district, where there had been much intermarrying, almost everyone would have been a member of everyone else's sib. Hence where vengeance had to be taken, or redress enforced, some people would have been members of both plaintiff and defendant sibs. They would surely have exerted pressure for just settlement. This is the position among the Kalingas of the Philippine Islands who have a similar kinship system. Feuds may have been prosecuted between sibs in separated districts, or as battles between local communities mobilized behind noble families. But we must not take sagas and tales of feuding as evidence, for they may, like the tales of the Nuer* 'man of the earth's' curse, stand as warnings. Or even as historical records they may have been better warnings. There was only one lot of Hatfields and McCoys in the Kentucky and Virginia hills. Generally, over a limited area, there is peace as well as war in the threat of the feud.

This peace arises from the existence of many kinds of relationships, and the values attached to them all by custom. These ties divide men at one point; but this division in a wider group and over a longer period of time leads to the establishment of social order. In separated districts men can quarrel. The smaller the area involved, the more numerous the social ties. But as the area narrows the occasions which breed quarrels between men multiply; and here it is that their conflicting ties both draw them apart and bring them into relationship with other people

* A Sudanese tribe.

who see that settlement is achieved. In this way custom unites
where it divides, co-operation and conflict balancing each other.
At the widest range, cohesion is stated in ritual terms – supported by mystical retribution – where values are unquestioned
and axiomatic. Hence ritual reconciliation and sacrifice often
follow the settlement of a quarrel, and ritual methods are used
to reach adjustment.

The social process of the feud and threat of feud may seem
very distant from us, but in fact it is present on our doorsteps.
The application of this analysis to international affairs would
overlook many complicating factors: is there a single moral
order, for example, as among the Nuer? Can nations allow their
members to recognize external conflicting ties or loyalty? There
is clearly, as in Nuerland, an increasing technological necessity
for some kind of peace over all the world. That I leave aside. I
would, however, argue that it is useful to look at our own
national life in these terms. If we examine the smaller groups
which make up our vast and complex society, it is easy to see that
divisions of interest and loyalties within any one group prevent
it from standing in absolute opposition to other groups and to
the society at large. For men can only belong to a large society
through intermediate smaller groups, based on technical process,
on personal association, on locality, on sectarian belief within a
larger cult, and so forth. Schools which are organized in houses
cutting across forms, and Universities which have colleges
cutting across departments and faculties, exhibit more cohesion
than amorphous schools and universities. Tight loyalties to
smaller groups can be effective in strengthening a larger community if there are offsetting loyalties.

The feud is, according to the dictionary, 'a lasting state of
hostility'. There is no society which does not contain such states
of hostility between its component sections; but provided they
are redressed by other loyalties they may contribute to the peace
of the whole. One group of workers, bound together in a
particular process and not immediately involved in a dispute
with a factory's employers, may oppose another group's going

on strike. Indeed, there is a conflict in the loyalties which operate on each worker and each working-group because of familial and national ties, so that man and group are inhibited from moving into violent action. Every worker has an interest in keeping the factory working at all costs, in addition to an interest in getting as high wages as he can. Or if work stops, he wants it to begin again. Similar divisions exist between employing-groups, and within the ranks of management inside a factory. Nowadays the significant groups in British political life are largely functional groups – trade unions, employers' and trade associations, educational interests, religious sects, and the like. It is these which exert pressure on Parliament, but it is not interest-groups which elect members to Parliament. We therefore get a high degree of national representation because most members of Parliament are elected by amorphous constituencies which contain many of these interest-groups. The Member of Parliament is supposed to represent all his constituents, whatever their party affiliation; and this system of representation cuts clean across the important political pressure groups. He is like the Nuer 'man of the earth'.

Again, I am not suggesting that divided loyalties and interests will always prevent a dispute arising, or prevent social dislocation and change. Loyalties and interests are not thus beautifully balanced. What I am saying is that these conflicting loyalties and divisions of allegiance tend to inhibit the development of open quarrelling, and that the greater the division in one area of society, the greater is likely to be the cohesion in a wider range of relationships – provided that there is a general need for peace, and recognition of a moral order in which this peace can flourish.

I have hinted at where the process of the feud, with its war and its peace, can be detected in Britain. Many people have so detected it; but as many are reluctant to accept the reality of social life – that quarrels and conflicts exist in all groups and cannot be wished out of existence. They must be redressed by other interests and other customary loyalties, so that the individual is led into association with different fellows. The more his ties require that his opponents in one set of relations are his allies in another, the greater is likely to be the peace of the feud.

•

A duel with a dog

LEWIS MELVILLE AND REGINALD HARGREAVES

At the close of the thirteenth century, Philip the Fair, having justly entertained at that early period a refined sense of the evil attending the judicial combat, used his best means to put a restraint on its practice. But the state of the times militated so much against his good intention that all he was able to effect was the publication of an edict of regulation, whereby nothing was to be brought to that bloody issue which could be determined by any other means. In consequence of this was adopted that singular ordeal, for want of other evidence, which took place in the Isle of Notre Dame, in the reign of Charles V of France.

The Chevalier Maquer, in the sight of all Paris, entered the lists, with a dog, in mortal combat. The spot which was the scene of this singular encounter is still shown. The following are the circumstances that gave rise to it. Aubry Mondidier, whilst taking a solitary walk in the neighbourhood of Paris, was murdered and buried under a tree. His dog, which he had left at home, went out at night to search for his master, whom at length he traced to the forest, and discovered his grave. Having remained some days in the spot, till hunger compelled him to return to the city, he hastened to the Chevalier Ardilliers, a friend of the deceased, and by his melancholy howling gave him to understand that their common friend was no longer in existence. Ardilliers offered the dog some food, and endeavoured to quiet him by caresses; but the distressed animal continued to howl pitiably, and laying hold of his coat led him significantly towards the door.

Ardilliers at length complied with the dog's apparent request, and was led by the sagacious and affectionate animal from street to street, and conducted from the city to a large oak in the forest, where he began to howl louder and to scratch the earth with his feet. Aubry's friend could not help surveying the spot with melancholy foreboding, and desired the servant who accompanied him to fetch a spade and dig up the earth – when, in a short time, he discovered the body of his murdered friend.

Some time after, the dog accidentally met the murderer of his master, barked, rushed upon him, and attacked him with such ferocity that the spectators could not, without great difficulty, extricate him. The same circumstance occurred several times. The faithful animal, which was in general as quiet as a lamb, became like a raging tiger every time he saw the person who had murdered his master.

The circumstance excited great astonishment, and strong suspicions having arisen, it was remembered that Maquer on several occasions had betrayed symptoms of enmity against Aubry; and various other circumstances being combined, brought the matter almost to a certainty. The King hearing of this affair, was desirous of being convinced with his own eyes whether or not the dog was in the right. The parties were brought before him; the dog fawned upon everybody else, but attacked Maquer with the utmost violence as soon as he saw him enter. The King, considering this to be a fair occasion for the ordeal – which was at the time customary upon less important occasions – ordered the fate of Maquer to be determined by single combat with the dog. Charles instantly appointed the time and place. Maquer entered the list armed with his lance; the dog was let loose upon him, and a most dreadful contest ensued. Maquer made a thrust, but the dog springing aside, seized him by the throat, and threw him down. Thereupon the villain confessed his crime, and Charles, in order that the remembrance of the faithful animal might be handed down to posterity, caused to be erected to him in the forest where the murder was committed, a marble monument, with a suitable inscription.

... it may be remarked that Maquer had a great advantage over the dog in being armed with a lance, so that the encounter was ten to one in his favour. On the other hand, it by no means follows that Maquer, unarmed, would have had no chance with the dog. This would depend entirely on the kind of man and kind of dog. Some dogs would be an overmatch for most men; but some men unarmed in any manner would be an overmatch for *any* dog. An instance of this, among many others that might be mentioned, occurred in the city of Londonderry. A man undertook to fight a very fierce and powerful bulldog merely for a trifling bet. The place appointed was in the Diamond – a square in the centre of the city, where a great concourse of people assembled to witness so unprecedented a contest. When the hour came, the man appeared, pulled off his clothes, entered the ring, and threw off his shirt; whilst the butcher, to whom the dog belonged, held the eager animal, on the other side of the ring, by the neck. When the man, without any apparent intimidation, said he was ready, the dog was slipped at him, and advanced in a couchant attitude till within about four feet distance, where he made a spring at the man's throat – the man, at the same instant, dexterously struck him with the edge of his hand across the windpipe, which he seconded with a vigorous kick in the stomach, thus flinging the dog upon his back at some distance. But the dog immediately recovered, and made another spring at the man's throat, which was his invariable object, and which was parried in like manner by his antagonist, hitting him, as before, with his feet. Seven or eight times did the dog renew the attack, whilst the man never once missed his blow, nor received a scratch. At length the dog could rise no more, though not killed, when the man stepped forward, and taking a knife from his breeches pocket, seized the dog, with the intention of cutting his throat; but the butcher, amazed at seeing his dog thus conquered, after having beaten so many bulls, called out that he would give five pounds to save his life – to which the other readily agreed, whilst the surrounding and astonished multitude filled his hat with silver and coppers.

•

The need to avoid contempt and hatred
NICCOLÒ MACHIAVELLI

In this extract, from his classic of *realpolitik*, *The Prince*, Machiavelli argues that, in the interests of state and holding on to power, it is necessary that a prince should avoid being hated. Machiavelli had personal experience of being notably hated. Following the execution of Savonarola in 1498 (another man who received more than his fair share of hate), Florence was ruled by Piero Soderini, who made Machiavelli his chancellor. As well as earning Machiavelli considerable personal enmity among his rivals, the pro-French policy of Soderini won him and those who served him the enmity of the powerful Medici family. Following the return of the Medici to Florence in 1512, Machiavelli found himself out of favour, and he dedicated *The Prince* to Lorenzo de Medici in the vain hope of currying favour with the city-state's new rulers.

Having now spoken of the chief of the qualities above enumerated, the rest I shall dispose of briefly with these general remarks, that a Prince, as has already been said, should consider how he may avoid such courses as tend to make him hated or despised; and that whenever he succeeds in keeping clear of these, he has performed his part, and runs no risk though he incur other infamies. And, as I have said before, a Prince sooner becomes hated by being rapacious and by interfering with the property and with the women of his subjects, than in any other way. From these, therefore, he should abstain. For so long as neither their property nor their honour is touched, the mass of mankind live contentedly, and the Prince has only to cope with the ambition of a few, which can in many ways and easily be kept within bounds.

A Prince is despised when he is seen to be fickle, frivolous, effeminate, pusillanimous or irresolute, against which defects he ought, therefore, most carefully to guard, striving so to bear himself that greatness, courage, wisdom and strength may appear in all his actions. In his private dealings with his subjects his decisions should be irrevocable, and his reputation such that no one would dream of over-reaching or cajoling him.

The Prince who inspires such an opinion of himself is greatly esteemed, and against one who is greatly esteemed conspiracy is difficult; because, when a Prince is understood to be good and to be held in reverence by his subjects, it is not easy to attack him. For a Prince is exposed to two dangers, from within in respect of his subjects, from without in respect of foreign powers. Against the latter he will defend himself with good soldiers and good allies, and if he have good soldiers he will always have good allies; and when things are settled abroad, they will always be settled at home, unless disturbed by conspiracies; and even if there should be hostility from without, if he has taken those measures, and has lived in the way I have recommended, and if he never abandons hope, he will resist every attack, as I have related of Nabis the Spartan.

But as to his own subjects, when affairs are quiet abroad, he has to fear that they may engage in secret plots; against which a Prince best secures himself when he escapes being hated or despised, and keeps on good terms with his people, and this, as I have already shown at length, it is essential that he should do. Not to be hated or despised by the body of his subjects, is one of the strongest safeguards which a Prince can have against conspiracy; for he who conspires always reckons on pleasing the people by putting the Prince to death; but when he sees that instead of pleasing he will offend them, he cannot summon courage to carry out his design. For the difficulties which attend conspirators are infinite, and we know from experience that

while there have been many conspiracies, few of them have succeeded.

He who conspires cannot do so alone, nor can he assume as
his companions any save those whom he believes to be
discontented; but so soon as you impart your design to a
discontented man, you furnish him with the means of removing
his discontent, since by betraying you he can procure for
himself every advantage; so that seeing on the one hand certain
gain, and on the other a doubtful and dangerous risk, he must
either be a rare friend to you, or an inveterate enemy of his
Prince, if he keep your secret.

To bring the matter into narrow compass, I say that on the
side of the conspirator there is distrust, jealousy, and dread of
punishment to deter him, while on the side of the Prince there
is the majesty of the Throne, the laws, the protection of friends
and of the government to defend him; to which if the general
good-will of the people be added, it is hardly possible that any
one should be rash enough to conspire. For while, in ordinary
cases, the conspirator has ground for fear only before the
execution of his villany, in this case he has also cause to fear
after the crime has been committed, since he has the people for
his enemy, and is thus cut off from every hope of shelter.

Of this many instances might be given, but I shall content
myself with one which happened within the recollection of our
fathers. Messer Annibale Bentivoglio, Lord of Bologna and
grandfather of the present Messer Annibale, was conspired
against and murdered by the Canneschi, leaving behind none
belonging to him save Messer Giovanni, then an infant in arms.
Immediately upon the murder the people rose and put all the
Canneschi to death. This resulted from the general esteem in
which the House of the Bentivogli were then held in Bologna;
which feeling was so strong, that when upon the death of
Messer Annibale, no one was left who could govern the State,
there being reason to believe that an illegitimate descendant of
the family was living in Florence, who up to that time had been
thought to be the son of a smith, the citizens of Bologna came

for him to Florence, and entrusted him with the government of their city, which he retained until Messer Giovanni was old enough to govern.

To be brief, a Prince has little to fear from conspiracies when his subjects are well disposed towards him; but when they are hostile and hold him in detestation, he has then reason to fear everything and every one. And well ordered States and wise Princes have provided with extreme care that the nobility shall not be driven to desperation, and that the commons shall be kept satisfied and contented; for this is one of the most important matters that a Prince has to look to.

Among the well ordered and governed Kingdoms of our day is that of France, wherein we find an infinite number of wise institutions, upon which depend the liberty and security of the King, and of which the most important are the Parliament and its authority. For he who gave its constitution to this Realm, knowing the ambition and turbulence of the nobles, and judging it necessary to bridle and restrain them, and on the other hand knowing the hatred, originating in fear, entertained against the nobles by the people, and desiring that these last should be safe, was unwilling that the responsibility for this should rest on the King; and to relieve him of the ill-will which he might incur with the nobles by favouring the people, or with the people by favouring the nobles, appointed a third party to be arbitrator, who without committing the King, might depress the nobles and uphold the people. Nor could there be any better, wiser, or surer safeguard for the King and the Kingdom. And from this we may draw another notable lesson, namely, that Princes should throw on others those offices which entail responsibility, and reserve to themselves those which gain them favour. And I say again that a Prince should esteem the great, but must not make himself odious to the people.

To some it may perhaps appear, that if the lives and deaths of many of the Roman Emperors be considered, they offer examples opposed to the views expressed by me; since we find that some among them who had always lived good lives, and shewn themselves possessed of great qualities, were nevertheless deposed and even put to death by their subjects who had conspired against them.

In answer to such objections, I shall examine the characters of several Emperors, and show that the causes of their downfall have been in no way different from those which I have already noticed. In doing this I shall submit for consideration such matters only as must strike every one who reads the history of these times; and it will be enough for my purpose to take those Emperors who reigned from the time of Marcus the Philosopher to the time of Maximinus, who were, inclusively, Marcus, Commodus his son, Pertinax, Julian, Severus, Antoninus Caracalla his son, Macrinus, Heliogabalus, Alexander and Maximinus.

In the first place, then, we have to note that while in other Princedoms the Prince has only to contend with the ambition of the nobles and the insubordination of the people, the Roman Emperors had a further difficulty to encounter in the cruelty and rapacity of their soldiers, which were so distracting as to cause the ruin of many of these Princes. For it was hardly possible for them to satisfy both the soldiers and the people; since the latter loved peace and therefore preferred temperate Princes, while the former preferred a Prince of a warlike spirit, however harsh, haughty or rapacious, being willing that he should exercise these qualities against the people, as the means of procuring for themselves double pay and indulging their greed and cruelty.

Whence it followed that those Emperors who had not in-herited or made for themselves such influence as enabled them to keep both people and soldiers in check, were always ruined. The most of them, and those especially who came to the Empire new and without experience, seeing the difficulty of dealing with these conflicting interests, set themselves to satisfy the soldiers, and made little account of offending the people. And for them this was a necessary course to take; for as Princes cannot escape being hated by some, they should, in the first instance, endeavour not to be hated by a class; failing in which, they must use every effort to escape the hatred of that class which is the stronger. Wherefore those Emperors who, by reason of their newness, stood in need of extraordinary support, sided with the soldiery rather than with the people, a course which turned out advantageous or otherwise, according as the Prince knew, or did not know, how to maintain his authority over them.

From the causes indicated it resulted that Marcus, Pertinax and Alexander, being Princes of a temperate disposition, lovers of justice, enemies of cruelty, humane, and kindly, had all, save Marcus, an unhappy end. Marcus alone lived and died honoured in the highest degree; and this because he had succeeded to the Empire by right of inheritance, and not through the favour either of the soldiery or the people; and also because, being endowed with many virtues which made him revered, he kept, while he lived, both factions within bounds, and was never either hated or despised.

But Pertinax was chosen Emperor against the will of the soldiery, who being accustomed to a licentious life under Commodus, could not tolerate the decent manner of living to which his successor sought to bring them back. And having thus made himself hated, and being at the same time despised by reason of his advanced age, he was ruined at the very outset of his reign.

And here it is to be noted that hatred is incurred as well on account of good actions as of bad; for which reason, as I have already said, a Prince who is resolved to maintain his authority is often compelled to be other than good. For when the class, be it the people, the soldiers or the nobles, on whom you judge it necessary to rely for your support, is corrupt, you must needs adapt yourself to its humours, and satisfy them, in which case virtuous conduct will only prejudice you.

Let us now come to Alexander, who was so just a ruler that among the praises ascribed to him it is recorded, that during the fourteen years he held the Empire, no man was ever put to death by him without trial. Nevertheless, being accounted effeminate, and thought to be governed by his mother, he fell into contempt, and the army conspiring against him, slew him.

If we next turn to consider the characters of Commodus, Severus and Antoninus Caracalla, we shall find them to have been most cruel and rapacious Princes, who to satisfy the soldiery, scrupled not to inflict every kind of wrong upon the people. And all of them, except Severus, came to a bad end. But in Severus there was such strength of character, that, keeping the soldiers his friends, he was able, although he oppressed the people, to reign on prosperously to the last; because his great qualities rendered him so admirable in the eyes both of the people and the soldiers, that the former remained in a manner awestruck and confounded, while the latter were respectful and contented.

And because his actions, for one who was a new Prince, were thus remarkable, I will point out shortly how well he understood to use both the lion and the fox, each of which natures, as I have observed before, a Prince should know how to assume.

Knowing the slothful nature of the Emperor Julianus, Severus persuaded the army which he commanded in Illyria that it was their duty to go to Rome to avenge the death of Pertinax, who had been slain by the Pretorian guards. Under this pretext, and without disclosing his design on the Empire, he put his army in march, and reached Italy before it was known that he had set out. On his arrival in Rome, the Senate, through fear, elected him Emperor and put Julianus to death. After taking this first step, two obstacles still remained to his becoming sole master of the Empire; one in Asia, where Niger who commanded the armies of the East had caused himself to be proclaimed Emperor; the other in the West, where Albinus, who also had designs on the Empire, was in command. And as Severus judged it dangerous to declare open war against both, he resolved to proceed against Niger by arms, and against Albinus by artifice. To the latter, accordingly, he wrote, that having been chosen Emperor by the Senate, he desired to share the dignity with him; that he therefore sent him the title of

Cæsar, and in accordance with a resolution of the Senate, assumed him as his colleague. All which statements Albinus accepted as true. But so soon as Severus had defeated and slain Niger, and had restored tranquillity in the East, returning to Rome he complained in the Senate that Albinus, wholly unmindful of the favours which he had received from him, had treacherously sought to destroy him; for which cause he was compelled to go and punish his ingratitude. Whereupon he set forth to seek Albinus in Gaul, where he at once deprived him of his dignities and his life.

Whoever, therefore, examines carefully the actions of this Emperor, will find in him all the fierceness of the lion and all the craft of the fox, and will remark how he was feared and respected by the people, and yet not hated by the army, and will not be surprised that, although a new man, he was able to maintain his hold of so great an Empire. For the splendour of his reputation always shielded him from the odium which the people might otherwise have conceived against him by reason of his cruelty and rapacity.

Antoninus Caracalla, his son, was likewise a man of great parts, and endowed with qualities which made him admirable in the sight of the people and endeared him to the army, being of a warlike spirit, most patient of fatigue, an enemy to luxury in food and to every other effeminacy. Nevertheless, his ferocity and cruelty were so extravagant and unheard of, he having put to death a large number of the inhabitants of Rome at different times, and the whole of those of Alexandria at a stroke, that he came to be detested by all the world, and so feared even by those whom he had about him, that at the last he was killed by a centurion in the midst of his army.

And here let it be noted that deaths like this which are the result of a deliberate and fixed resolve, cannot be escaped by Princes, since any one who disregards his own life can effect them. A Prince, however, need the less fear them as they are extremely uncommon. The only precaution he can take is to avoid doing grave wrong to any of those who serve him, or whom he has near him as officers of his Court, a precaution which Antoninus neglected in putting to a shameful death the brother of this centurion, and in using daily threats against the man himself, whom he nevertheless retained as one of his bodyguard. This, as the event showed, was a rash and fatal course.

We come next to Commodus, who, as he took the Empire by hereditary right, ought to have held it with much ease. For being the son of Marcus, he had only to follow in his father's footsteps to content both the people and the soldiery. But being of a cruel and brutal nature, to gratify his rapacity at the expense of the people, he had recourse to the army, and indulged them in every kind of excess. On the other hand, by an utter disregard of his dignity, in frequently appearing in the arena to fight with gladiators, and by other base acts wholly unworthy of the Imperial station, he became despicable in the eyes of the soldiery; and being on the one hand hated, on the other despised, he was at last conspired against and murdered.

The character of Maximinus remains to be described. He was of a very warlike disposition, and on the death of Alexander, of whom we have already spoken, was chosen Emperor by the army who had been displeased with the effeminacy of that Prince. But this dignity he did not long enjoy, since two causes concurred to render him at once odious and contemptible; the one the baseness of his origin, he having at one time herded sheep in Thrace, a fact well known to all, and which led all to look on him with disdain; the other that on being proclaimed Emperor, delaying to repair to Rome and enter on possession of the Imperial throne, he incurred the reputation of excessive cruelty from having, through his prefects in Rome and other parts of the Empire, perpetrated many atrocities. The result was that the whole world, stirred at once with scorn of his mean birth and with the hatred which the dread of his ferocity inspired, combined against him, Africa leading the way, the Senate and people of Rome and the whole of Italy following. In which conspiracy his own army joined. For they, being engaged in the siege of Aquileja and finding difficulty in reducing it, disgusted with his cruelty, and less afraid of him when they saw so many against him, put him to death.

I need say nothing of Heliogabalus, Macrinus, or Julianus, all of whom being utterly despicable, came to a speedy downfall, but shall conclude these remarks by observing, that the Princes of our own days are less troubled with the difficulty of having to make extraordinary efforts to keep their soldiers in good humour. For although they must treat them with some indulgence, it need not be continually shewn, since none of these Princes possess standing armies which, like the armies of the Roman Empire, have strengthened with the growth of their government and the administration of their States. And if it was then necessary to satisfy the soldiers rather than the people, it was because the soldiers were more powerful than the people, whereas now it is more necessary for all Princes, except the Turk and the Soldan, to satisfy the people rather than the soldiery, since the former are more powerful than the latter.

I except the Turk because he has always about him some twelve thousand foot soldiers and fifteen thousand horse, on whom depend the security and strength of his kingdom, and with whom he must needs keep on good terms, all considerations of the people being subordinate. The government of the Soldan is similar, for as he is wholly in their hands, he too must keep well with his soldiers without regard to the people.

And here it may be observed that the State of the Soldan, while it is unlike all other Princedoms, resembles the Christian Pontificate in this, that it can neither be classed as a new, nor as an hereditary Princedom. For the sons of a Soldan who dies do not succeed to the kingdom as his heirs, but he who is elected to the post by those who have authority to make such elections. And this being the ancient and established order of things, the Princedom cannot be accounted new, since none of the difficulties which attend new Princedoms are found in it. For although the Prince be new, the institutions of the State are old, and are so contrived that the elected Prince is accepted as though he were an hereditary Sovereign.

But to return to our subject, I say that whoever reflects on the above reasoning will see, that either hatred or contempt was the ruin of those Emperors whom I have named; and will likewise understand how it happened that some taking one way and some the opposite, one only came to a happy, and all the rest to an unhappy end. For as to Pertinax and Alexander, they being new Princes, it was useless and disadvantageous for them to endeavour to imitate Marcus, who was an hereditary Prince; and similarly for Caracalla, Commodus, and Maximinus it was a fatal error to imitate Severus, since they lacked the qualities which would have enabled them to walk in his footsteps.

In short, a Prince new to the Princedom cannot imitate the actions of Marcus, nor is it necessary for him to imitate those of Severus; but he should borrow from Severus those parts of his conduct which are needed to serve as a foundation for his government, and from Marcus those which are suited to maintain it, and render it glorious when once it has been established.

•

First blast of the trumpet against the monstrous regiment of women

JOHN KNOX

The blast was blown in 1558, against those female rulers – Catherine de Medici, Mary of Guise, Mary Tudor – who were hostile to the Protestant Reformation. Knox revealed a hatred of women in general, however, and thus earned himself the lasting enmity of another female sovereign, albeit a Protestant one, Elizabeth I.

To promote a Woman to beare rule, superioritie, dominion, or empire above any Realme, nation, or Citie, is repugnant to Nature; contumelie to God, a thing most contrarious to his reveled will and approved ordinance; and finallie, it is the subversion of good Order, of all equitie and justice . . . For who can denie but it is repugneth to nature, that the blind shall be appointed to leade and conduct such as do see? That the weake, the sicke, and impotent persons shall norishe and kepe the hole and strong? And finallie, that the foolishe, madde, and phrenetike shal governe the discrete, and give counsel to such as the sober of mind? And such be al women, compared unto man in bearing of authoritie. For their sight in civile regiment is but blindnes; their strength, weaknes; their counsel, foolishnes; and judgment, phrensie, if it be rightlie considered.

. . . Nature, I say, doth paynt them further to be weake, fraile, impacient, feble, and foolishe; and experience hath declared them to be unconstant, variable, cruell, and lacking the spirit of counsel and regiment.

. . . Tertullian in his boke of Women's Apparell, after that he hath shewed many causes why gorgious apparell is abominable and odiouse in a woman, addeth these words, speaking as it were to every woman by name: 'Dost thou not knowe (saith he) that thou art Heva? The sentence of God liveth and is effectuall against this kind; and in this worlde, of necessity it is, that the punishement also live. Thou art the porte and gate of the Devil. Thou art the first transgressor of goddes law. Thou diddest persuade and easely deceive him whome the Devil durst not assault. For thy merit (that is for thy death) it behoved the Sonne of God to suffer the death, and doth it yet abide in thy mind to decke thee above thy skin coates?'

By these and many other grave sentences and quicke interrogations, did this godlie writer labour to bring everie woman in contemplation of herselfe, to the end that everie one depelie weying what sentence God had pronounced against the hole race and doughters of Heva, might not onely learne daily to humble and subject them selves in the presence of God, but also that they shulde avoide and abhorre what soever thing might exalte them or puffe them up in pride, or that might be occasion that they shuld forget the curse and malediction of God. And what, I pray you, is more able to cause woman to forget her oune condition, then if she be lifted up in authoritie above man? It is a thing verie difficile to a man (be he never so constant) promoted to honors, not to be tickled somewhat with pride; (for the winde of vaine glorie doth easilie carie up the drie dust of the earth). But as for woman, it is no more possible that she being set aloft in authoritie above man shall resist the motions of pride, then it is able to the weake reed, or to the turning wethercocke, not to bowe or turne at the vehemencie of the unconstant wind. And therefore the same writer expreslie forbiddeth all women to intermedle with the office of man.

Concluding peroration; addressed to Mary Tudor

CURSED Jesabel of England, with the pestilent and detestable generation of Papistes, make no little bragge and boast, that they have triumphed not only against Wyet, but also against all such as have entreprised any thing against them or their procedinges. But let her and them consider, that yet they have not prevailed against God: his throne is more high than that the length of their hornes be able to reache. And let them further consider, that in the beginning of this their bloodie reigne, the harvest of their iniquitie was not comen to full maturitie and ripenes: No! it was grene, so secret I mean, so covered, and so hid with hypocrisie, that some men (even the servantes of God) thought it not impossible but that wolves might be changed into lambes, and also that the vipere might remove her natural venom. But God, who doth revele in his time apointed the secretes of hartes, and that will have his judgements justified even by the verie wicked, hath now given open testimonie of her and their beastlie crueltie ... so that now, not onlie the blood of Father Latimer, of the milde man of God the Bishop of Cantorburie (Cranmer), of learned and discrete Ridley, of innocent Lady Jane Dudley, and many godly and worthie preachers that cannot be forgotten, such as fier hath consumed, and the sworde of tyrannie most unjustlie hath shed, doth call for vengeance in the eares of the Lord God of hostes; but also the sobbes and teares of the poore oppressed, the groninges of the Angeles, the watchmen of the Lord, yea, and everie earthlie creature abused by their tyrannie, do continuallie crie and call for the hastie execution of the same I feare not to say, that the day of vengeance, whiche shall apprehend that horrible monstre Jesabel of England, and such as maintain her monstruous crueltie, is alredie apointed in the counsel of the Eternall: and I verilie beleve, that it is so nigh, that she shall not reigne so long in tyrannie as hitherto she hath done, when God shall declare him selfe to be her enemie, when he shall poure forth contempt upon her according to her crueltie, and shal kindle the hartes of such as somtimes did favor her with deadly hatred against her, that they may execute his judgements. And therefore let such as assist her, take hede what they do; for assuredlie her empire and reigne is a wall without foundation: I meane the same of the Authoritie of all Women. It hath been underpropped this blind time that is past, with the foolishness of people, and with the wicked lawes of ignorant and tyrannous Princes. But the fier of Goddes Worde is alredie laid to those rotten proppes, (I include the Pope's lawe with the rest,) and presentlie they burn, albeit we espie not the flame. When they are consumed, (as shortlie they will be, for stubble and drie timbre can not long indure the fier,) that rotten wall, the usurped and unjust empire of women, shall fall by itself in despit of all man, to the destruction of so manie as shall labor to uphold it. And therefore let all man be advertised, for THE TRUMPET HATH ONES BLOWEN.

•

A ladies' duel

LEWIS MELVILLE AND REGINALD HARGREAVES

Although the cynic would aver that duels between women are usually conducted with the tongue – an even deadlier weapon than the sword – there are not wanting instances when proficiency with the former instrument has been backed up by not a little skill in the handling of the latter.

Possibly the most famous duel between women adversaries

was that fought between the Comtesse de Polignac and the Marquise de Nesle. Sardonically enough, the cause of their difference was that Richelieu, who exerted such strenuous efforts to discourage duelling in all and every form, but, who, in his day, had been known to fight for the sake of a woman's fair eyes.

The trouble had arisen between the two ladies owing to the rather reprehensible carelessness with which the great man had made his arrangements to rendezvous with them, one being appointed to meet him at two o'clock in the afternoon, and the other at four.

Apart from the lack of gallantry, implied in granting a mere matter of two hours in which to do justice to the first inamorata's charms – not to mention the narrowness of the margin of the recuperative period before charmer the second should eventuate! – Richelieu had committed the additional enormity of leaving the actual arranging of the appointments in the hands of his secretary.

By some catastrophic oversight, this unfortunate creature fixed the same hour for both fair visitants.

They arrived, punctual to the minute (when the attraction is sufficient even the fair sex can be punctual!), and meeting, there was naturally a scene of pyrotechnic exuberance. The *dénouement* was a challenge, the outcome of which was a meeting between the two ladies in the Bois de Boulogne.

As bad luck would have it, the Marquise, as the challenged party, proposed pistols, the very weapon with which the Comtesse was familiar.

At the appointed hour they met, supported by their respective seconds.

Everything in the way of preparation was carried through with the most careful punctilio, until the Comtesse, with the almost pardonable arrogance of the expert, thought fit to break through the strict letter of the regulations, by calling out to her opponent: 'Fire first, and mind you don't miss me; don't you think I'm going to try and miss *you*!'

The reply of the Marquise to this unladylike taunt was to raise her pistol and fire. But – alas! for the principles of markmanship – it was only the branch of a neighbouring tree that fell. Thereupon the Comtesse de Polignac exclaimed, with the *sang-froid* of a tavern bully: 'Your hand trembles too much with passion,' and aiming in her turn, she fired and cut off a small piece of the ear of the Marquise, who fell to the ground as though mortally wounded. Some accounts give it that the ladies were subsequently reconciled, though others, perhaps even more credibly, aver that the little Marquise, although prepared to over-look the stealing of her lover by her rival, could never quite come to forgive the theft of her ear lobe by that rival's shot. In any case, this encounter was one for which, in common decency, Richelieu could not very well exact his usual grim penalties.

•

An Italian family feud
SHOLTO AND REUBEN PERCY

The town of Ostuni is rendered remarkable by an extraordinary duel which took place in it in the year 1664, and in which the principles of honour were grossly violated in the very measures resorted to for their defence. The Count of Conversano, called also Duke of Le Noci, of the family of Aquaviva, and the Prince of Francavilla, of that of Imperiali, were the two most powerful lords in Lower Apulia: the former boasted of his ancient descent, his numerous titles and his great domains, and numbered among his predecessors a succession of nobles whose tyrannical and violent disposition had designated them as a race dreaded by their inferiors, and hated by their equals. The Prince of Francavilla was of Genoese extraction; but his family had been settled in the kingdom from the time of Charles the Fifth, and he emulated the count in pride, while he surpassed him in wealth. Their territories joined, and the constant litigations arising out of their inordinate but ill-timed jurisdictions, were thereby superadded to the long list of mutual injuries recorded by both families. Their animosity broke out at Naples, on some trifling occasion, when they were each in their carriage, and, after a long contest of words, the Count of Conversano challenged the Prince of Francavilla to decide their difference by the sword; the latter declined this mode of combat, as ill suited to his age and infirmities, but consented to the duel if the arms might be exchanged for pistols. His antagonist, who was esteemed the best swordsman in the kingdom, insisted on his first proposal, and excited the prince to accede to it by the application of several blows with the flat side of his weapon. An insult so grossly offered in the public streets, authorized the existing government, carried on through the administration of a viceroy, to suspend or check the consequences likely to arise, by placing the aggressor under arrest for a time, and subsequently ordering them both to retire to their respective estates. But the feelings of unsatisfied hatred, and of insulted pride, were not likely to be allayed by this exclusion from the world; and in a short time the Prince of Francavilla proposed a champion in his cause, in the person of his sister's only son, the Duke of Martina, of the house of Carraccioli. This young man was but just returned from his travels, and his education was not completed, so that although the Count of Conversano admitted, with a brutal anticipation of success, the substitution of this youthful adversary, it was agreed that a year more should elapse previous to the final termination of their differences, and the field of battle was fixed at Ostuni, the jurisdiction of which town had been previously claimed and disputed by both noblemen. The eyes of the whole kingdom were directed with anxious and fearful expectation towards this spot; but the wishes of the majority were entirely on the side of the Duke of Martina, whose youth, accomplishments and amiable disposition, called forth the interest of all ranks. His uncle, actuated more by fear of the shame attendant on defeat, than by feelings of affection for his relative, endeavoured to ensure success by the following stratagem. A gentleman, who had been some time, as was the custom in those days, a retainer in his family, left it abruptly one night, and sought the Count of Conversano's castle, into which he gained admission by a recital of injurious treatment and fictitious wrongs, heaped upon him by the tyrannical and arbitrary temper of the Prince of Francavilla. A complaint of this nature was always the passport to the count's favour and good graces, and he not only admitted this gentleman to the full enjoyment of his princely hospitality, but having found that he was an experienced and dexterous swordsman, passed most of his time in practising with him that art, which he soon hoped would ensure the triumph he most valued on earth.

A few days previous to that fixed for the duel, the guest, under pretence of paying a visit to his relatives, withdrew from the Count of Conversano's territories, and secretly returned to those of his employer; where he lost no time in communicating to his nephew all the peculiarities and advantages repeated experience had enabled him to remark in the count's manner of fencing. The Duke of Martina was thereby taught that the only chance of success which he could look to, was by keeping on the defensive during the early part of the combat; he was instructed that his antagonist, though avowedly the most able manager of the sword in the kingdom, was extremely violent, and that if his first thrusts could be parried, his person, somewhat inclined to corpulency, would speedily become exhausted from the effects of his own impetuosity. The Duke of Martina, furnished with this salutary advice, and strong in the conviction of what he deemed a just cause, waited in calm anxiety the day of battle; and the behaviour of the two combatants on the last morning, strongly characterizes their different dispositions, as well as the manners and habits of the age they lived in. The Duke of Martina made his will, confessed himself, and took an affectionate leave of his mother, who retired to her oratory to pass in prayer the time her son devoted to the conflict; while the Count of Conversano ordered a sumptuous feast to be prepared, and invited his friends and retainers after the fight; he then carelessly bade his wife farewell, and brutally alluding to his adversary's youth and inexperience, remarked, *Vado a far un capretto*. 'I am going to kill a kid.'

The parties met at the place appointed, it was an open space before a monastery of friars at Ostuni; but these good fathers, by their intercessions and prayers, prevailed upon the combatants to remove to another similar spot of ground in front of the Capuchin convent, in the same town; here the bishop and clergy, carrying the Host in solemn procession, attempted in vain to dissuade them from their bloody purpose: they were dismissed with scorn, and the duel began. It was of long duration, and afforded the duke an opportunity of availing himself of the counsels he had received: when he found the count began to be out of breath and off his guard, he assumed the offensive part, and, having wounded him, demanded if he was satisfied, and proposed to desist from any further hostility; but, stung to the soul by this unexpected reverse, the count refused all offers of accommodation, and by blind revenge and redoubled animosity, soon lost all command of himself, and received a second wound, which terminated the contest together with his life. It appears that the Prince of Francavilla, whose principles were as little honourable as those of his adversary, and whose thirst of revenge was no less satiable, had appointed a band of assassins to waylay and murder him on his way home, had he returned victorious from the conflict.

•

Fighting is delicious to an Englishman
MISSON DE VALBOURG

It is tempting to suppose that the English love of violence is a modern phenomenon, occurring most frequently on and around the football terraces. However, as a Frenchman travelling in England in the year 1695 reminds us, the English love of fighting is nothing new.

Anything that looks like fighting is delicious to an Englishman. If two little boys quarrel in the street the passengers stop, make a ring round them in a moment, and set them against one another that they may come to fisticuffs. When 'tis come to a fight, each pulls off his neckcloth and his waistcoat and gives them to hold to some of the standers-by. Then they begin to brandish their fists in the air. The blows are aimed all at the face. They kick one another's shins; they tug one another by the hair. He that has got the other down may give him one blow or two before he rises, but no more; and let the boy get up ever so often, the other is obliged to box him again as often as he requires it. During the fight the ring of bystanders encourage the combatants with great delight of heart, and never part them while they fight according to the rules. And these bystanders are not only boys, porters and rabble, but all sorts of men of fashion, some thrusting by the mob that they may see plain, others getting upon stalls; and all would hire places if scaffolds could be built in a moment. The father and mother of the boys let them fight on as well as the rest, and hearten him that gives ground or has the worst.

These combats are less frequent among men than children, but they are not rare. If a coachman has a dispute about his fare with a gentleman that has hired him, and the gentleman offers to fight him to decide the quarrel, the coachman consents with all his heart. The gentleman pulls off his sword, lays it in some shop, with his cane, gloves and cravat, and boxes in the manner that I have described above. If the coachman is soundly drubbed, which happens almost always, that goes for payment; but if he is the beater, the beatee must pay the money about which they quarrelled. I once saw the late Duke of Grafton at fisticuffs in the open street with such a fellow, whom he lammed most horribly. In France we punish such rascals with our cane, and sometimes with the flat of our sword; but in England this is never practised. They use neither sword nor stick against a man that is unarmed; and if any unfortunate stranger (for an Englishman would never take it into his head) should draw his sword upon one that had none, he'd have a hundred people upon him in a moment.

•

A night at the opera
W. S. ROCKSTRO

The composer George Frederick Handel came to Hamburg in 1703. He was not long in making friends, and the first musician to whom he seriously attached himself was Johann Mattheson, the principal tenor singer at the Opera, and Handel's elder by four years. He was also a composer in his own right. The two friends went to operas, concerts, choirs and even brothels together and were for a while inseparable. And yet Mattheson's ego could not allow him to take second place to Handel, as this account shows.

It seems almost certain that Mattheson was absent from Hamburg, when Handel's 'Passion Music' was performed as part of the ceremonial appertaining to the Lutheran Holy Week. He returned, however, in good time for the forthcoming winter season, for the opening of which he had prepared an opera, entitled *Cleopatra* – his third complete dramatic work – founded upon a *libretto* written for him by Friedrich Christian Feustking, a theological student, whose attempts at dramatic poetry were so contemptible that one can only wonder how he ever came to be engaged at the theatre at all. The work was produced, for the first time, on 20 October 1704; the Composer himself performing the part of Antonius – the principal Tenor – while Handel presided at the Harpsichord. Unfortunately, the death of Antonius, some considerable time before the conclusion of the piece, left Mattheson unemployed during great part of the evening. His insufferable egoism prompted him to fill up this leisure time by supplanting Handel in the Orchestra. Handel, however, refused to vacate his post. Mattheson was furious at his resistance; and, in passing out of the theatre, gave him a violent box on the ear. The natural and no doubt anticipated result of this insult was, an impromptu duel, fought, then and

there, before a crowd of spectators, in front of the Opera-house
– which, it will be remembered, was appropriately situated
upon the Goose-market. Providentially, Mattheson broke his
sword against a broad metal button on his opponent's coat, and
to this circumstance Handel in all probability was indebted for
his life. As the encounter did not take place, according to
Mattheson's account, until 5 December, it is clear, that, at the
first performance of *Cleopatra*, either the Composer did not
demand, or the Conductor did not refuse to give up, the
disputed seat at the Harpsichord. Handel had, quite certainly,
made a like concession to Mattheson's vanity on former occasions, and would probably have done so again, had no deeper
sense of provocation existed; but, a comparison of collateral
dates shows that, at this particular moment, he was excessively
annoyed at Mattheson's interference with his position at the
house of the English Resident . . . The whole history of this
interference is characterized by an exhibition of bad taste, which
would be almost incredible, but for the effrontery with which
Mattheson, blinded by his ineffable self-importance, gibbets
himself for the instruction of an admiring posterity. We cannot
wonder that Handel was offended. However, he was too good a
Christian to bear malice; and . . . the quarrel was speedily
reconciled. Handel dined with Mattheson on 30 December. In
the evening, the pacified combatants assisted together at the
rehearsal of his first dramatic work, *Almira*. And, from that
time forward, the rival Composers became better friends than
ever.

•

Affairs of honour

JOSEPH ADDISON

The club, of which I have often declared myself a member, were
last night engaged in a discourse upon that which passes for the
chief point of honour among men and women; and started a
great many hints upon the subject which I thought were entirely
new. I shall therefore methodise the several reflections that
arose upon this occasion, and present my reader with them for
the speculation of this day . . .*

The great point of honour in men is courage, and in women
chastity. If a man loses his honour in one rencounter, it is not
impossible for him to regain it in another; a slip in a woman's
honour is irrecoverable. I can give no reason for fixing the
point of honour to these two qualities; unless it be that each sex
sets the greatest value on the qualification which renders them
the most amiable in the eyes of the contrary sex. Had men
chosen for themselves, without regard to the opinions of the
fair sex, I should believe the choice would have fallen on
wisdom or virtue; or had women determined their own point of
honour, it is probable that wit or good-nature would have
carried it against chastity.

Nothing recommends a man more to the female sex than
courage; whether it be that they are pleased to see one who is a
terror to others fall like a slave at their feet, or that this quality
supplies their own principal defect, in guarding them from
insults and avenging their quarrels, or that courage is a natural
indication of a strong and sprightly constitution. On the other
side, nothing makes a woman more esteemed by the opposite
sex than chastity; whether it be that we always prize those most

* 23 June 1711.

who are hardest to come at, or that nothing besides chastity, with its collateral attendants, truth, fidelity, and constancy, gives the man a property in the person he loves, and consequently endears her to him above all things.

I am very much pleased with a passage in the inscription on a monument erected in Westminster Abbey to the late Duke and Duchess of Newcastle: 'Her name was Margaret Lucas, youngest sister to the Lord Lucas of Colchester; a noble family, for all the brothers were valiant, and all the sisters virtuous.'

In books of chivalry, where the point of honour is strained to madness, the whole story runs on chastity and courage. The damsel is mounted on a white palfrey, as an emblem of her innocence; and, to avoid scandal, must have a dwarf for her page. She is not to think of a man, till some misfortune has brought a knight-errant to her relief. The knight falls in love, and did not gratitude restrain her from murdering her deliverer, would die at her feet by her disdain. However, he must waste many years in the desert, before her virgin heart can think of a surrender. The knight goes off, attacks everything he meets that is bigger and stronger than himself; seeks all opportunities of being knocked on the head; and after seven years' rambling returns to his mistress, whose chastity has been attacked in the meantime by giants and tyrants, and undergone as many trials as her lover's valour.

In Spain, where there are still great remains of this romantic humour, it is a transporting favour for a lady to cast an accidental glance on her lover from a window, though it be two or three storeys high; as it is usual for the lover to assert his passion for his mistress, in single combat with a mad bull.

The great violation of the point of honour from man to man, is giving the lie. One may tell another he whores, drinks, blasphemes, and it may pass unresented; but to say he lies, though but in jest, is an affront that nothing but blood can expiate. The reason perhaps may be, because no other vice implies a want of courage so much as the making of a lie; and therefore telling a man he lies, is touching him in the most sensible part of honour, and indirectly calling him a coward. I cannot omit under this head what Herodotus tells us of the ancient Persians, that from the age of five years to twenty, they instruct their sons only in three things, to manage the horse, to make use of the bow and to speak truth.

The placing the point of honour in this false kind of courage, has given occasion to the very refuse of mankind, who have neither virtue nor common sense, to set up for men of honour. An English peer, who has not been long dead, used to tell a pleasant story of a French gentleman that visited him early one morning at Paris, and after great professions of respect, let him know that he had it in his power to oblige him: which, in short, amounted to this, that he believed he could tell his lordship the person's name who jostled him as he came out from the opera; but before he would proceed, he begged his lordship that he would not deny him the honour of making him his second. The English lord, to avoid being drawn into a very foolish affair, told him that he was under engagements for his two next duels to a couple of particular friends. Upon which the gentleman immediately withdrew; hoping his lordship would not take it ill, if he meddled no further in an affair from whence he himself was to receive no advantage.

The beating down this false notion of honour, in so vain and lively a people as those of France, is deservedly looked upon as one of the most glorious parts of their present king's reign. It is pity but the punishment of these mischievous notions should have in it some particular circumstances of shame and infamy; that those who are slaves to them may see, that instead of advancing their reputations they lead them to ignominy and dishonour.

Death is not sufficient to deter men, who make it their glory to despise it; but if every one that fought a duel were to stand in the pillory, it would quickly lessen the number of these imaginary men of honour, and put an end to so absurd a practice.

When honour is a support to virtuous principles, and runs

parallel with the laws of God and our country, it cannot be too much cherished and encouraged: but when the dictates of honour are contrary to those of religion and equity, they are the greatest depravations of human nature, by giving wrong ambitions and false ideas of what is good and laudable; and should therefore be exploded by all governments, and driven out as the bane and plague of human society.

•

This great foundation of misanthropy
JONATHAN SWIFT

In this letter to Pope written in 1725, Dean Swift describes the sort of people he hates most in the world.

29 *September* 1725

I am now returning to the noble scene of Dublin, into the *grande monde*, for fear of burying my parts, to signalize myself among curates and vicars, and correct all corruptions crept in, relating to the weight of bread and butter, through those dominions where I govern [St Patrick's Cathedral]. I have employed my time (beside ditching) in finishing, correcting, amending and transcribing my travels, in four parts complete, newly augmented, and intended for the press, when the world shall deserve them, or rather when a printer shall be found brave enough to venture his ears. I like the scheme of our meeting after distresses and dispersions, but the chief end I propose to myself in all my labours is, to vex the world rather than divert it; and if I could compass that design, without hurting my own person or fortune, I would be the most indefatigable writer you have ever seen, without reading. I am exceedingly pleased that you have done with translations: Lord-treasurer Oxford often lamented that a rascally world should lay you under a necessity of misemploying your genius for so long a time. But since you

will now be so much better employed, when you think of the
world, give it one lash the more, at my request. I have ever
hated all nations, professions and communities; and all my love
is toward individuals; for instance, I hate the tribe of lawyers,
but I love counsellor such a one, and judge such a one: It is so
with physicians, (I will not speak of my own trade,) soldiers,
English, Scotch, French and the rest. But principally I hate and
detest that animal called man; although I heartily love John,
Peter, Thomas and so forth. This is the system upon which I
have governed myself many years, (but do not tell;) and so I
shall go on till I have done with them. I have got materials
toward a treatise, proving the falsity of that definition *animal
rationale*, and to shew it should be only *rationis capax*. Upon this
great foundation of misanthropy, (though not in Timon's
manner,) the whole building of my travels is erected; and I
never will have peace of mind till all honest men are of my
opinion: by consequence you are to embrace it immediately, and
procure that all who deserve my esteem may do so too. The
matter is so clear that it will admit of no dispute; nay, I will
hold a hundred pounds that you and I agree in the point.

•

John Wilkes and the perils of journalism
LEWIS MELVILLE AND REGINALD HARGREAVES

John Wilkes was an English politician and journalist who distinguished himself among his parliamentary colleagues by attacking
George III in his periodical, the *North Briton*, for which he was
expelled from the House in 1764, and imprisoned. Although repeatedly re-elected, he was not permitted to resume his seat until 1774.
Other public figures attacked in the pages of the *North Briton* had
resort to more direct methods of complaint, and Wilkes was obliged
to fight duels with two of them, Earl Talbot, in 1762, and Samuel
Martin, in 1763. The following extracts describe these encounters.

In 1762 was fought the celebrated duel between Earl Talbot and John Wilkes. The dispute had originated in words used in the twelfth number of the *North Briton*, on 21 August, which conveyed reflections injurious to Earl Talbot, when Wilkes wrote the following letter to Colonel Berkeley:

'Winchester, 30 *September* 1762

Sir,

Lord Talbot, by your message, has at last brought this most important question to the precise point where my first answer to his Lordship fixed it, if he preferred that. As you have only seen the two last letters, I must entreat you to cast an eye over those preceding; because I apprehend they will justify an observation or two I made this morning, when I had the honour of paying my respects to you at camp. Be assured, that, if I am between heaven and earth, I will be on Tuesday evening at Telbury's, the Red Lion, at Bagshot, and on Wednesday morning will play this duel with his Lordship.

It is a real satisfaction to me that his Lordship is to be accompanied by a gentleman of Colonel Berkeley's worth and honour.

This will be delivered to you by an Adjutant, who attends me at Bagshot. I shall not bring any servant with me, from the fear of any of the parties being known. My pistols only, or his Lordship's, at his option, shall decide this point.

I beg the favour of you to return me the letters, as I mean to leave Winchester this evening. I have Lord Bruce's leave of absence for ten days.

I am, etc.,

John Wilkes.

I hope we may make a *partie quarrée* for supper on Tuesday, at Bagshot.'

To this lively letter the following reply was sent:

'Camp, near Winchester, 30 *September* 1762

Sir,

I have sent all the letters, and shall depend upon the pleasure of supping with you at Telbury's, the Red Lion, at Bagshot, Tuesday evening. My servant will attend me, as the going alone would give room for suspicion; but you may depend upon his following your directions at Bagshot, and that he shall not be seen where you would not have him. I am much obliged by your favourable opinion, and am, etc.,

H. Berkeley.'

In a letter to Earl Temple, Wilkes gives the following account of this singular meeting:

'Red Lion, at Bagshot,
Tuesday, 10 *at night,* 5 *October* 1762

My Lord,

I had the honour of transmitting to your Lordship copies of seven letters which passed between Lord Talbot and me. As the affair is now over, I inclose an original letter of Colonel Berkeley's, with a copy of mine previous to it, which fixed the particulars of our meeting, and therefore remained a secret, very sacredly kept by the four persons concerned.

I came here at three this afternoon, and about five was told that Lord Talbot and Colonel Berkeley were in the house. Lord Talbot had been here at one, and was gone again, leaving a message, however, that he would soon return. I had continued in my room where I was at my first coming for fear of raising any suspicion. I sent a compliment to Colonel Berkeley, and that I wished to see him; he was so obliging as to come to me directly. I told him that I supposed we were to sup together with Lord Talbot, whom I was ready to attend as became a private gentleman, and that he and Mr Harris (my Adjutant), as our seconds, would settle the business of the next morning, according to my letter to him from Winchester, and his answer. Berkeley said that his Lordship wished to finish the business immediately. I replied, that the appointment was to sup together that evening and to fight in the morning; that in consequence of such an arrangement, I had, like an idle man of pleasure, put off some business of real importance, which I meant to settle before I went to bed. I added, that I came from Medmenham Abbey, where the jovial monks of St Francis had kept me up till four in the morning; that the world would therefore conclude that I was drunk, and form no favourable opinion of his Lordship from a duel at such a time; that it more became us both to take a cool hour of the next morning, and as early as was agreeable to his Lordship. Berkeley said that he had undertaken to bring us together, and as we were both now at Bagshot, he would leave us to settle our own business. He then asked me if I would go with him to his Lordship. I said I would any moment he pleased. We went directly with my Adjutant.

I found his Lordship in an agony of passion. He said I had injured him, that he was not used to be injured or insulted. What did I mean? Did I, or did I not, write the *North Briton* of August the 21st, which affronted his honour? He would know; he insisted on a direct answer; here were his pistols. I replied, that he would soon use them; that I desired to know by what right his Lordship catechised me about a paper that did not bear my name; that I should never resolve the question to him till he made out the right of putting it; and that if I could have entertained any other idea, I was too well bred to have given his Lordship and Colonel the trouble of coming to Bagshot. I observed that I was a private English gentleman, perfectly free and independent, which I held to be a character of the highest dignity; that I obeyed with pleasure a gracious Sovereign, but would never submit to the arbitrary dictates of a fellow-subject, a Lord Steward of his Household, my superior indeed in rank, fortune and abilities, but my equal only in honour, courage and liberty. His Lordship then asked me if I would fight him that evening. I said that I preferred the next morning, as it had been settled before, and gave my reasons. His Lordship replied that he insisted on finishing the affair immediately. I told him that I should very soon be ready; that I did not mean to quit him, but would absolutely first settle some important business relative to the education of my only daughter, whom I tenderly loved, that it would take but very little time; and that I would immediately decide the affair in any way he chose, for I had brought both sword and pistols. I rang the bell for pen and ink, and paper, desiring his Lordship to conceal his pistols, that they might not be seen by the waiters. He soon after became half frantic, and used a thousand indecent expressions, that I should be *hanged, damned*, etc., etc. I said that I was not to be frightened, nor in the least affected by such violence; that God had given me a firmness and spirit equal to his Lordship's, or any man's; that cool courage should always mark me; and that it would be seen how well bottomed he was.

After the waiter had brought pen, ink and paper, I proposed that the door of the room should be locked, and not opened till our business was decided. His Lordship, on this proposition, became quite outrageous; declared that this was mere *butchery*, and that I was a wretch who sought his life. I reminded him that I came there on a point of honour to give his Lordship satisfaction; that I mentioned the circumstance of shutting the door only to prevent all possibility of interruption; and that I would in every circumstance be governed, not by the turbulence of the most violent temper I had ever seen, but by the calm determination of our two seconds, to whom I implicitly submitted. His Lordship then asked me if I would deny the paper. I answered that I would neither own nor deny it; if I survived, I would afterwards declare, but not before.

Soon after he grew a little cooler, and in a soothing tone of voice, said: "I have never, I believe, offended Mr Wilkes, why has he attacked me? He must be sorry to see me unhappy." I asked upon what grounds his Lordship imputed the paper to me? That Mr Wilkes would justify any paper to which he had put his name, and would equally assert the privilege of not giving any answer whatever about a paper to which he had not; that that was my undoubted right, which I was ready to seal with my blood.

He then said he admired me exceedingly, really loved me, but I was an unaccountable animal – such parts! But would I kill him who had never offended me? etc., etc. We had after this a good deal of conversation about the Bucks Militia and the day his Lordship came to see me on Wycombe Heath before I was colonel. He soon after flamed out again, and said to me, "You are a murderer, you want to kill me, but I am sure I shall kill you, I know I shall, by G–d! If you will fight, if you will kill me, I hope you will be *hanged*. I know you will." I asked if I was first to be *killed* and afterwards to be *hanged*? That I knew his Lordship fought me with the King's pardon in his pocket, and I fought him with a halter about my neck. That I would fight him for all that, and if he fell I should not tarry here a moment for the tender mercies of such a Ministry; but would directly proceed to the next stage where my valet waited for me, from thence I would make the best of my way to France, as men of honour were sure of protection in that country. He then told me that I was an *unbeliever*, and wished to be killed. I could not help smiling at this, and observed that we did not meet at Bagshot to settle articles of faith, but points of honour; that, indeed, I had no fear of dying, but I enjoyed life as much as any man; that I am as little subject to be gloomy or even peevish, as any Englishman whatever; that I valued life and the fair enjoyments of it so much I would never quit it with my own consent, except on a call of honour.

I then wrote a letter to your Lordship, respecting the education of Miss Wilkes, and gave you my poor thanks for the steady friendship with which you have so many years honoured me. Colonel Berkeley took the care of the letter, and I have since desired him to send it to Stowe; for the sentiments of the head at such a moment are beyond all politics, and indeed everything else, except such virtue as Lord Temple's.

When I had sealed my letter, I told his Lordship I was entirely at his service, and I again desired that we might decide the affair in the room, because there could not be a possibility of interruption; but he was quite inexorable. I had brought a flask of powder and a bag of bullets. Our seconds then charged the pistols which my Adjutant had brought. They were large horse-pistols. It was agreed that we should fire at the word of command, to be given by one of our seconds. They tossed up, and it fell to my Adjutant to give the word.

We then left the room, and walked to a garden at some distance from the house. It was near seven, and the moon shone brightly. We stood about eight yards distant, and agreed not to turn round before we fired, but to continue facing each other. Harris gave the word. Both our fires were in very exact time, but neither took effect.

I walked up immediately to his Lordship, and told him, that now I avowed the paper. His Lordship paid me the highest encomiums on my courage, and said, he would declare everywhere that I am the noblest fellow God ever made. He then desired that we might now be good friends, and retire to the inn to drink a bottle of claret together, which we did with great good humour and much laughter.

His Lordship afterwards went to Windsor, Colonel and my Adjutant to Winchester, and I continue here until tomorrow morning, waiting the return of my valet, to whom I have sent a messenger. Berkeley told he was grieved at his Lordship's passion, and admired my coolness and courage beyond his farthest idea – that was his expression.

   I am, my Lord, etc.,

     John Wilkes.'

In 1763 Wilkes got involved in another duel, with Mr Martin, Secretary to the Treasury. The *North Briton*, of which he was the editor, with its usual acrimony against the members of the Administration, had introduced some characteristic sketches, supposed to allude to Samuel Martin, Member of Parliament for Camelford, and Secretary to the Treasury, and afterwards the hero in Churchill's poem, 'The Duellist'. The following was the offensive paragraph:

'The Secretary of a certain board, and a very apt tool of Ministerial persecution, who, with a snout worthy of a Portuguese inquisitor, is hourly looking out for carrion in office, to feed the maw of the insatible vulture, *imo, etiam in senatum venit, notat et deseignat unumquemque nostrûm*, he marks us, and all our innocent families, for beggary and ruin. Neither the tenderness of age, nor the sacredness of sex, is spared by the cruel Scot.'

In a further number notice is again taken 'of the most treacherous, base, selfish, mean, abject, low-lived, and dirty fellow, that ever wriggled himself into a secretaryship'.

In consequence of that paragraph, which Martin applied to himself, he made use of very insulting language in the House of Commons, when speaking of the *North Briton*, upon which Wilkes sent him the following letter:

           'Great George Street, 16 *November*, 1763

Sir,

You complained yesterday before five hundred gentlemen, that you had been *stabbed in the dark* by the *North Briton*. But I believe you were not so much in the *dark* as you affected and chose to be. Was the complaint made before so many gentlemen on purpose that they might interpose? To cut off every pretence of this kind, as to the author, I whisper in your ear, that every passage of the *North Briton* in which you have been named or alluded to, was written by

Your humble servant,
John Wilkes.'

'Arlington Street, 16 *November*, 1763

Sir,

As I said in the House of Commons yesterday, that the writer of the *North Briton*, who had stabbed me in the dark, was a cowardly as well as a malignant scoundrel, and your letter of this morning's date acknowledges that every passage of the *North Briton* in which I have been named, or even alluded to, was written by yourself, I must take the liberty to repeat, that you are a malignant and infamous scoundrel, and that I desire to give you an opportunity of showing me whether the epithet *cowardly* was rightly applied or not. I desire that you may meet me in Hyde Park immediately, with a brace of pistols, so concealed that nobody may see them, and I will wait in expectation of you one hour. As I shall call on my way home at your house to deliver this letter, I propose you go from thence directly to the ring in Hyde Park, from whence we may proceed, if it be necessary, to any more private place. And I mention that I shall wait an hour, in order to give you the full time to meet me.

I am, sir, your humble servant,
Samuel Martin.'

When the parties met in Hyde Park, they walked together a little while to avoid some company which seemed coming up to them. They brought each a pair of pistols. When they were alone, the first fire was from Martin's pistol, which missed

Wilkes. The pistol in Wilkes's hand only flashed in the pan. The gentlemen then each took one of the remaining pistols. Wilkes missed, and the ball of Martin's pistol lodged in Wilkes's belly. He bled immediately very much. Martin came up, and desired to give him all the assistance in his power. Wilkes replied that Martin behaved like a man of honour; that he was killed; and insisted on Martin's making his immediate escape, adding, that no person should know from him how the affair happened. Upon this they parted. Wilkes was carried home; but would not tell any circumstance of the case, till he found it was perfectly known. He only said to his surgeon, that it was an affair of honour.

The day following, Wilkes, imagining himself in great danger, returned to Martin his letter, that no evidence might appear against him, and insisted upon it, with his own relatives, that in case of his death, no trouble should be given to Martin, for he had behaved as a man of honour.

The ball was extracted by Mr Graves, a surgeon. It had struck Wilkes's coat-button, entered his belly half an inch below the navel, and sunk obliquely on the right side towards the groin, but it had not penetrated the cavity of the abdomen. It was extracted behind.

When he was able to write, he sent notice by letter to the Speaker of the House of Commons of the condition of his health; and on Friday, the 16th, the House made the following order: 'That Dr Heberden, physician, and Mr Caesar Hawkins, one of His Majesty's serjeant-surgeons, be desired to attend John Wilkes, Esq., to observe the progress of his cure; and that they, together with Dr Brocklesby and Mr Graves, do attend this House to report their opinion thereupon, on the 19th of January next, in case the said John Wilkes, Esq., be not then able to attend in his place.'

The order being sent to Dr Heberden, by order of the Speaker, he sent it to Dr Brocklesby, with a letter, desiring to know when he might attend Dr Brocklesby to Wilkes. Dr Brocklesby sent the order to the House and Dr Heberden's letter to Wilkes, who immediately showed his delicacy of feeling on the subject by sending a polite card to Dr Heberden, saying, that he was well satisfied with the attention and skill of Dr Brocklesby and Mr Graves, that he did not wish to see Dr Heberden for some weeks; he sent a similar card to Mr Hawkins. Martin immediately proceeded to Paris, and on Wilkes's arrival in that city, notes and a friendly visit were exchanged between them.

Martin's conduct in this transaction had been highly honourable; but the public was so much exasperated at the danger to which Wilkes had been exposed, that no credit was given to the spirit which his antagonist had displayed. On the contrary, it was remarked that Martin had taken no notice of the objectionable passage in the *North Briton* until about eight months after the publication, and that in so public and official a manner before the House, as almost to demand an interference. He was also accused of having during that period practised every day at a target, Sundays not excepted, and also with not having returned Wilkes's letter till a month after the duel with a view, as it was suggested, had Wilkes speedily recovered, of making use of it in evidence of his being concerned in the *North Briton*.

•

The follies of duelling
TOBIAS SMOLLETT

The cantankerous Scots-born author of *The Adventures of Roderick Random*, and *The Expedition of Humphrey Clinker*, conducted a long feud with the novelist, Henry Fielding, whom he had accused of plagiarism, in a pamphlet entitled *The Faithful Narrative of Habakkuk Hilding*. Following the death of his daughter in 1763, Smollett travelled extensively in France and Italy and, upon his return in 1765, he published an account of his travels, from which this account of the follies of duelling is taken. The book made him another enemy in the person of Laurence Sterne, who, publishing an account of his own travels in France and Italy, referred to Smollett throughout as Smelfungus.

Nice, January 3, 1764

Madam, – In your favour which I received by Mr M–l, you remind me of my promise, to communicate the remarks I have still to make on the French nation; and, at the same time, you signify your opinion, that I am too severe in my former observations. You even hint a suspicion that this severity is owing to some personal cause of resentment; but, I protest, I have no particular cause of animosity against an individual of that country. I have neither obligation to, nor quarrel with, any subject of France; and when I meet with a Frenchman worthy of my esteem, I can receive him into my friendship with as much cordiality as I could feel for any fellow-citizen of the same merit. I even respect the nation for the number of great men it has produced in all arts and sciences. I respect the French officers in particular, for their gallantry and valour; and especially for that generous humanity which they exercise towards their enemies, even amidst the horrors of war. This liberal spirit is the only circumstance of ancient chivalry, which I think was worth preserving. It had formerly flourished in England, but was almost extinguished in a succession of civil wars, which are always productive of cruelty and rancour. It was Henry IV of France, a real knight-errant, who revived it in Europe. He possessed that greatness of mind which can forgive injuries of the deepest dye. And as he had also the faculty of distinguishing characters, he found his account in favouring with his friendship and confidence some of those who had opposed him in the field with the most inveterate perseverance. I know not whether he did more service to mankind in general, by reviving the practice of treating his prisoners with generosity, than he prejudiced his own country by patronizing the absurd and pernicious custom of duelling, and establishing a *punto*, founded in diametrical opposition to common sense and humanity.

I have often heard it observed, that a French officer is generally an agreeable companion, when he is turned of fifty. Without all doubt, by that time, the fire of his vivacity, which makes him so troublesome in his youth, will be considerably abated; and, in other respects, he must be improved by his experience. But there is a fundamental error in the first principles of his education, which time rather confirms than removes. Early prejudices are for the most part converted into habits of thinking; and, accordingly, you will find the old officers in the French service more bigoted than their juniors to the punctilios of false honour.

A lad of a good family no sooner enters into the service than he thinks it incumbent upon him to show his courage in a rencontre. His natural vivacity prompts him to hazard in company every thing that comes uppermost, without any respect to his seniors or betters; and ten to one but he says something which he finds it necessary to maintain with his sword. The old officer, instead of checking his petulance, either by rebuke or silent disapprobation, seems to be pleased with his impertinence, and encourages every sally of his presumption. Should a quarrel ensue, and the parties go out, he makes no efforts to compromise the dispute; but sits with a pleasing expectation to learn the issue of the rencontre. If the young man is wounded, he kisses him with transport, extols his bravery, puts him into the hands of the surgeon, and visits him with great tenderness every day until he is cured. If he is killed on the spot, he shrugs up his shoulders – says, *Quelle dommage! c'étoit un aimable enfant! ah, patience!* and in three hours the defunct is forgotten. You know, in France, duels are forbid, on pain of death; but this law is easily evaded. The person insulted walks out; the antagonist understands the hint, and follows him into the street, where they justle as if by accident, draw their swords, and one of them is either killed or disabled, before any effectual means can be used to part them. Whatever may be the issue of the combat, the magistrate takes no cognizance of it; at least, it is interpreted into an accidental rencontre, and no penalty is incurred on

either side. Thus, the purpose of the law is entirely defeated, by
a most ridiculous and cruel connivance. The meerest trifles in
conversation, a rash word, a distant hint, even a look or smile
of contempt, is sufficient to produce one of these combats; but
injuries of a deeper dye, such as terms of reproach, the lie
direct, a blow, or even the menace of a blow, must be discussed
with more formality. In any of these cases, the parties agree to
meet in the dominions of another prince, where they can
murder each other without fear of punishment. An officer who
is struck, or even threatened with a blow, must not be quiet,
until he either kills his antagonist, or loses his own life. A friend
of mine, a Nissard, who was in the service of France, told me,
that some years ago, one of their captains, in the heat of
passion, struck his lieutenant. They fought immediately. The
lieutenant was wounded and disarmed. As it was an affront that
could not be made up, he no sooner recovered of his wounds,
than he called out the captain a second time. In a word, they
fought five times before the combat proved decisive; at last, the
lieutenant was left dead on the spot. This was an event that
sufficiently proved the absurdity of the punctilio which gave
rise to it. The poor gentleman who was insulted, and outraged
by the brutality of the aggressor, found himself under the
necessity of giving him a further occasion to take away his life.
Another adventure of the same kind happened a few years ago
in this place. A French officer having threatened to strike
another, a formal challenge ensued; and it being agreed that
they should fight until one of them dropped, each provided
himself with a couple of pioneers to dig his grave on the spot.
They engaged just without one of the gates of Nice, in presence
of a great number of spectators, and fought with surprising
fury, until the ground was drenched with their blood. At length
one of them stumbled, and fell; upon which the other, who
found himself mortally wounded, advancing, and dropping his
point, said, '*Je te donne ce que tu m'as ôté.*' 'I give thee that which
thou hast taken from me.' So saying he dropped dead upon the
field. The other, who had been the person insulted, was so

dangerously wounded, that he could not rise. Some of the spectators carried him forthwith to the beach, and putting him into a boat, conveyed him by sea to Antibes. The body of his antagonist was denied christian burial, as he died without absolution, and every body allowed that his soul went to hell; but the gentlemen of the army declared, that he died like a man of honour. Should a man be never so well inclined to make atonement in a peaceable manner, for an insult given in the heat of passion, or in the fury of intoxication, it cannot be received. Even an involuntary trespass from ignorance or absence of mind must be cleansed with blood. A certain noble lord of our country, when he was yet a commoner, on his travels, involved himself in a dilemma of this sort at the court of Lorrain. He had been riding out, and strolling along a public walk, in a brown study, with his horsewhip in his hand, perceived a caterpillar crawling on the back of a marquis, who chanced to be before him. He never thought of the *petit-maître*; but lifting up his whip, in order to kill the insect, laid it across his shoulders with a crack, that alarmed all the company in the walk. The marquis's sword was produced in a moment, and the aggressor in great hazard of his life, as he had no weapon of defence. He was no sooner waked from his reverie than he begged pardon, and offered to make all proper concessions for what he had done through mere inadvertency. The marquis would have admitted his excuses, had there been any precedent of such an affront washed away without blood. A conclave of honour was immediately assembled; and after long disputes, they agreed, that an involuntary offence, especially from *such a kind of man, d'un tel homme*, might be atoned by concessions. That you may have some idea of the small beginning from which many gigantic quarrels arise, I shall recount one that lately happened at Lyons, as I had it from the mouth of a person who was an ear and eye witness of the transaction. Two Frenchmen, at a public ordinary, stunned the rest of the company with their loquacity. At length one of them, with a supercilious air, asked the other's name. 'I never tell my name,' said he, 'but in a whisper.' 'You may have very good reasons for keeping it secret,' replied the first. 'I will tell you,' resumed the other. With these words, he rose; and going round to him, pronounced, loud enough to be heard by the whole company, '*Je m'appelle Pierre Paysan; et vous êtes un impertinent.*' So saying, he walked out. The interrogator followed him into the street, where they justled, drew their swords, and engaged. He who asked the question was run through the body; but his relations were so powerful, that the victor was obliged to fly his country. He was tried and condemned in his absence; his goods were confiscated; his wife broke her heart; his children were reduced to beggary; and he himself is now starving in exile. In England, we have not yet adopted all the implacability of the punctilio. A gentleman may be insulted even with a blow, and survive, after having once hazarded his life against the aggressor. The laws of honour in our country do not oblige him either to slay the person from whom he received the injury, or even to fight to the last drop of his own blood. One finds no examples of duels among the Romans, who were certainly as brave and as delicate in their notions of honour as the French. Cornelius Nepos tells us, that a famous Athenian general, having a dispute with his colleague, who was of Sparta, a man of a fiery disposition, this last lifted up his cane to strike him. Had this happened to a French *petit-maître*, death must have ensued. But mark what followed: the Athenian, far from resenting the outrage in what is now called a gentlemanlike manner, said, 'Do, strike if you please; but hear me.' He never dreamed of cutting the Lacedemonian's throat; but bore with his passionate temper, as the infirmity of a friend who had a thousand good qualities to overbalance that defect.

I need not expatiate upon the folly and the mischief which are countenanced and promoted by the modern practice of duelling. I need not give examples of friends who have murdered each other, in obedience to this savage custom, even while their hearts were melting with mutual tenderness; nor will I particular-ize the instances which I myself know, of whole families ruined, of women and children made widows and orphans, of parents deprived of only sons, and of valuable lives lost to the community, by duels, which had been produced by one unguarded expression, uttered without intention of offence, in the heat of dispute and altercation. I shall not insist upon the hardship of a worthy man's being obliged to devote himself to death, because it is his misfortune to be insulted by a brute, a bully, a drunkard or a madman. Neither will I enlarge upon this side of the absurdity, which, indeed, amounts to a contradiction in terms; I mean the dilemma to which a gentleman in the army is reduced when he receives an affront. If he does not challenge and fight his antagonist, he is broke with infamy by a court martial; if he fights and kills him, he is tried by the civil power, convicted of murder, and, if the royal mercy does not interpose, he is infallibly hanged: all this, exclusive of the risk of his own life in the duel, and his conscience being burdened with the blood of a man whom, perhaps, he has sacrificed to a false punctilio, even contrary to his own judgment. These are reflections which I know your own good sense will suggest; but I will make bold to propose a remedy for this gigantic evil, which seems to gain ground every day. Let a court be instituted for taking cognizance of all breaches of honour, with power to punish by fine, pillory, sentence of infamy, outlawry, and exile, by virtue of an act of parliament made for this purpose; and all persons insulted shall have recourse to this tribunal. Let every man who seeks personal reparation with sword, pistol or other instrument of death, be declared infamous, and banished the kingdom. Let every man convicted of having used a sword or pistol, or other mortal weapon, against another, either in duel or rencounter, occasioned by any previous quarrel, be subject to the same penalties. If any man is killed in a duel, let his body be hanged upon a public gibbet for a certain time, and then given to the surgeons. Let his antagonist be hanged as a murderer, and dissected also; and some mark of infamy be set on the memory of both. I apprehend such regulations would put an effectual stop to the practice of duelling, which nothing but the fear of infamy can support; for I am persuaded, that no being capable

of reflection would prosecute the trade of assassination at the
risk of his own life, if this hazard was at the same time
reinforced by the certain prospect of infamy and ruin. Every
person of sentiment would, in that case, allow, that an officer,
who in a duel robs a deserving woman of her husband, a
number of children of their father, a family of its support, and
the community of a fellow-citizen, has as little merit to plead
from exposing his own person, as a highwayman or
housebreaker, who every day risks his life to rob or plunder
that which is not of half the importance to society. I think it
was from the Buccaneers of America, that the English have
learned to abolish one solecism in the practice of duelling.
Those adventurers decided their personal quarrels with pistols;
and this improvement has been adopted in Great Britain with
good success: though in France, and other parts of the continent,
it is looked upon as a proof of their barbarity. It is, however,
the only circumstance of duelling which savours of common
sense, as it puts all mankind upon a level, the old with the
young, the weak with the strong, the unwieldy with the nimble,
and the man who knows not how to hold a sword with the
spadassin, who has practised fencing from the cradle. – What
glory is there in a man's vanquishing an adversary over whom
he has a manifest advantage? To abide the issue of a combat in
this case, does not even require that moderate share of resolution
which nature has indulged to her common children. Accordingly, we have seen many instances of a coward's provoking a
man of honour to battle. In the reign of our second Charles,
when duels flourished in all their absurdity, and the seconds
fought while their principals were engaged, Villiers, Duke of
Buckingham, not content with having debauched the Countess
of Shrewsbury, and publishing her shame, took all opportunities
of provoking the Earl to single combat, hoping he should have
an easy conquest, his Lordship being a puny little creature,
quiet, inoffensive, and every way unfit for such personal
contests. He ridiculed him on all occasions; and at last declared
in public company, that there was no glory in cuckolding

Shrewsbury, who had not spirit to resent the injury. This was an insult which could not be overlooked. The Earl sent him a challenge; and they agreed to fight at Barns Elms, in presence of two gentlemen, whom they chose for their seconds. All the four engaged at the same time. The first thrust was fatal to the Earl of Shrewsbury; and his friend killed the Duke's second at the same instant. Buckingham, elated with his exploit, set out immediately for the Earl's seat at Cliefden, where he lay with his wife, after having boasted of the murder of her husband, whose blood he showed her upon his sword, as a trophy of his prowess. But this very Duke of Buckingham was little better than a poltroon at bottom. When the gallant Earl of Ossory challenged him to fight in Chelsea-fields, he crossed the water to Battersea, where he pretended to wait for his Lordship; and then complained to the House of Lords, that Ossory had given him the rendezvous, and did not keep his appointment. He knew the House would interpose in the quarrel, and he was not disappointed. Their lordships obliged them both to give their word of honour, that their quarrel should have no other consequences.

I ought to make an apology for having troubled a lady with so many observations on a subject so unsuitable to the softness of the fair sex; but I know you cannot be indifferent to any thing that so nearly affects the interests of humanity, which I can safely aver have alone suggested every thing which has been said by, madam, your very humble servant.

•

The Rivals: Sheridan applies for redress
ANONYMOUS

The author of plays such as *The Rivals* (1775) and *The School for Scandal* (1777) had a profound dislike of the theatre, and once declared that he never saw a play if he could help it. Early on in his career he fell in love with Eliza Linley, a beautiful singer, on whose behalf he fought two duels with her other admirer, a Captain Matthews. Surviving the second of these farcical affairs of honour, described here, Sheridan subsequently eloped with Eliza to France, where they were married.

When Mr Sheridan became the avowed suitor of Miss Linley, the celebrated vocal performer, her father, the late composer, did not at first encourage his suit, and he had many rivals to overcome in his attempts to gain the lady's affections. His perseverance, however, increased with the difficulties that presented themselves; and his courage and resolution in vindicating Miss Linley's reputation from a calumnious report, which had been basely thrown out against her, obtained for him the fair prize for which he twice exposed his life.

Mr Matthews, a gentleman, then well known in the fashionable circles at Bath, had caused a paragraph to be inserted in a public paper at that place, which tended to prejudice the character of this young lady, and Mr Sheridan immediately applied for redress to the publisher, who gave up the writer's name.

Mr Matthews had, in the mean time, set out for London, and was closely followed by Mr Sheridan. They met, and fought a duel with swords, at a tavern in Henrietta-street, Covent-garden. Mr Sheridan's second on the occasion was his brother, Charles Francis, afterwards Secretary at War in Ireland.

Great courage and skill were displayed on both sides; but Mr Sheridan having succeeded in disarming his adversary, compelled him to sign a formal retractation of the paragraph which had been published.

Sheridan instantly returned to Bath; and thinking, very properly, that as the insult had been publicly given, the apology should have equal notoriety, caused it to be inserted in the same paper. Mr Matthews soon heard of the circumstance; and irritated at his defeat, as well as at the use which his antagonist had made of his apology, determined to call upon Mr Sheridan for satisfaction. A message was accordingly sent, and a meeting agreed upon.

Mr Sheridan would have been fully justified, according to the most delicate punctilios of honour, in declining the call; but he silenced all the objections that were started by his friends, and the parties met on Kingsdown.

The victory was desperately contested, and after a discharge of pistols, they fought with swords. They were both wounded, and closing with each other, fell on the ground, where they continued to fight until they were separated. They received several cuts and contusions in this arduous struggle for life and honour, and a part of Matthews's sword was actually broken off in Sheridan's ear.

Miss Linley did not suffer the prowess of her champion to remain long unrewarded, and accompanied him on a matrimonial trip to the Continent. The ceremony was again performed on their return to England, with the consent of the lady's parents.

•

Whether duelling be contrary to the laws of Christianity

JAMES BOSWELL

On Friday, April 10, I dined with him [Dr Johnson] at General Oglethorpe's, where we found Dr Goldsmith.

Armorial bearings having been mentioned, Johnson said they were as ancient as the siege of Thebes, which he proved by a passage in one of the tragedies of Euripides.

I started the question, whether duelling was consistent with moral duty. The brave old General fired at this, and said, with a lofty air, 'Undoubtedly a man has a right to defend his honour.' GOLDSMITH, (turning to me,) 'I ask you first, Sir, what would you do if you were affronted?' I answered, I should think it necessary to fight. 'Why then, (replied Goldsmith,) that solves the question.' JOHNSON. 'No, Sir, it does not solve the question. It does not follow, that what a man would do is therefore right.' I said, I wished to have it settled, whether duelling was contrary to the laws of Christianity. Johnson immediately entered on the subject, and treated it in a masterly manner; and so far as I have been able to recollect, his thoughts were these: 'Sir, as men become in a high degree refined, various causes of offence arise; which are considered to be of such importance, that life must be staked to atone for them, though in reality they are not so. A body that has received a very fine polish may be easily hurt. Before men arrive at this artificial refinement, if one tells his neighbour – he lies, his neighbour tells him – he lies; if one gives his neighbour a blow, his neighbour gives him a blow: but in a state of highly polished society, an affront is held to be a serious injury. It must, therefore, be resented, or rather a duel must be fought upon it; as men have agreed to banish from their society one who puts up with an affront without fighting a duel. Now, Sir, it is never unlawful to fight in self-defence. He, then, who fights a duel, does not fight from passion against his antagonist, but out of self-defence; to avert the stigma of the world, and to prevent himself from being driven out of society. I could wish there was not that superfluity of refinement; but while such notions prevail, no doubt a man may lawfully fight a duel.'

Let it be remembered, that this justification is applicable only to the person who *receives* an affront. All mankind must condemn the aggressor.

The General told us, that when he was a very young man, I think only fifteen, serving under Prince Eugene of Savoy, he was sitting in a company at table with a Prince of Wirtemberg. The Prince took up a glass of wine, and, by a fillip, made some of it fly in Oglethorpe's face. Here was a nice dilemma. To have challenged him instantly, might have fixed a quarrelsome character upon the young soldier: to have taken no notice of it, might have been considered as cowardice. Oglethorpe, therefore, keeping his eye upon the Prince, and smiling all the time, as if he took what his Highness had done in jest, said '*Mon Prince,* –'

(I forget the French words he used, the purport however was,) 'That's a good joke: but we do it much better in England;' and threw a whole glass of wine in the Prince's face. An old General who sat by, said, '*Il a bien fait, mon Prince, vous l'avez commencé:*' and thus all ended in good humour.

•

Dr Johnson's hatred of Americans
JAMES BOSWELL

From this pleasing subject, he, I know not how or why, made a sudden transition to one upon which he was a violent aggressor; for he said, 'I am willing to love all mankind, *except an American:*' and his inflammable corruption bursting into horrid fire, he 'breathed out threatenings and slaughter'; calling them, 'Rascals – Robbers – Pirates'; and exclaiming, he'd 'burn and destroy them'. Miss Seward, looking to him with mild but steady astonishment, said, 'Sir, this is an instance that we are always most violent against those whom we have injured.' – He was irritated still more by this delicate and keen reproach; and roared out another tremendous volley which one might fancy could be heard across the Atlantick. During this tempest I sat in great uneasiness, lamenting his heat of temper; till, by degrees, I diverted his attention to other topicks.

•

Bad blood: Edmund Burke's hatred of Warren Hastings
LORD MACAULAY

Warren Hastings was the first governor-general of British India (1774–84). He is generally credited with having rebuilt British prestige in India, but his policies drew the violent opposition of Charles James Fox, Philip Francis and Edmund Burke, who was set on reforming the East India Company. Burke took personal insult to Hastings, as Lord Macaulay describes here. It was Burke who brought a charge of corruption against Hastings in 1787, a charge of which Hastings was eventually acquitted.

From the Ministry . . . Hastings had every reason to expect support; and the Ministry was very powerful. The Opposition was loud and vehement against him. But the Opposition, though formidable from the wealth and influence of some of its members, and from the admirable talents and eloquence of others, was outnumbered in parliament, and odious throughout the country. Nor, as far as we can judge, was the Opposition generally desirous to engage in so serious an undertaking as the impeachment of an Indian Governor. Such an impeachment must last for years. It must impose on the chiefs of the party an immense load of labour. Yet it could scarcely, in any manner, affect the event of the great political game. The followers of the coalition were therefore more inclined to revile Hastings than to prosecute him. They lost no opportunity of coupling his name with the names of the most hateful tyrants of whom history makes mention. The wits of Brooks's aimed their keenest sarcasms both at his public and at his domestic life. Some fine diamonds which he had presented, as it was rumoured, to the royal family, and a certain richly carved ivory bed which the Queen had done him the honour to accept from him, were favourite subjects of ridicule. One lively poet proposed, that the great acts of the fair Marian's present husband should be immortalized by the pencil of his predecessor; and that Imhoff should be employed to embellish the House of Commons with paintings of the bleeding Rohillas, of Nuncomar swinging, of Cheyte Sing letting himself down to the Ganges. Another, in an exquisitely humorous parody of Virgil's third eclogue, propounded the question, what that mineral could be of which the rays had power to make the most austere of princesses the friend of a wanton. A third described, with gay malevolence, the gorgeous appearance of Mrs Hastings at St James's, the galaxy of jewels, torn from Indian Begums, which adorned her head dress, her necklace gleaming with future votes, and the depending questions that shone upon her ears. Satirical attacks of this description, and perhaps a motion for a vote of censure, would have satisfied the great body of the Opposition. But there were two men whose indignation was not to be so appeased, Philip Francis and Edmund Burke.

Francis had recently entered the House of Commons, and had already established a character there for industry and ability. He laboured indeed under one most unfortunate defect, want of fluency. But he occasionally expressed himself with a dignity and energy worthy of the greatest orators. Before he had been many days in parliament, he incurred the bitter dislike of Pitt, who constantly treated him with as much asperity as the laws of debate would allow. Neither lapse of years nor change of scene had mitigated the enmities which Francis had brought back from the East. After his usual fashion, he mistook his malevolence for virtue, nursed it, as preachers tell us that we ought to nurse our good dispositions, and paraded it, on all occasions, with Pharisaical ostentation.

The zeal of Burke was still fiercer; but it was far purer. Men unable to understand the elevation of his mind have tried to find out some discreditable motive for the vehemence and pertinacity which he showed on this occasion. But they have altogether failed. The idle story that he had some private slight to revenge has long been given up, even by the advocates of Hastings. Mr Gleig supposes that Burke was actuated by party spirit, that he retained a bitter remembrance of the fall of the coalition, that he attributed that fall to the exertions of the East India interest, and that he considered Hastings as the head and the representative of that interest. This explanation seems to be sufficiently refuted by a reference to dates. The hostility of Burke to Hastings commenced long before the coalition; and lasted long after Burke had become a strenuous supporter of those by whom the coalition had been defeated. It began when Burke and Fox, closely allied together, were attacking the influence of the crown, and calling for peace with the American republic. It continued till Burke, alienated from Fox, and loaded with the favours of the crown, died, preaching a crusade against the French republic. We surely cannot attribute to the events of 1784 an enmity which began in 1781, and which retained undiminished force long after persons far more deeply implicated than Hastings in the events of 1784 had been cordially forgiven. And why should we look for any other explanation of Burke's conduct than that which we find on the surface? The plain truth is that Hastings had committed some great crimes, and that the thought of those crimes made the blood of Burke boil in his veins. For Burke was a man in whom compassion for suffering, and hatred of injustice and tyranny, were as strong as in Las Casas or Clarkson. And although in him, as in Las Casas and in Clarkson, these noble feelings were alloyed with the infirmity which belongs to human nature, he is, like them, entitled to this great praise, that he devoted years of intense labour to the service of a people with whom he had neither blood nor language, neither religion nor manners in common, and from whom no requital, no thanks, no applause could be expected.

His knowledge of India was such as few, even of those Europeans who have passed many years in that country, have attained, and such as certainly was never attained by any public man who had not quitted Europe. He had studied the history, the laws, and the usages of the East with an industry, such as is seldom found united to so much genius and so much sensibility. Others have perhaps been equally laborious, and have collected an equal mass of materials. But the manner in which Burke brought his higher powers of intellect to work on statements of facts, and on tables of figures, was peculiar to himself. In every part of those huge bales of Indian information which repelled almost all other readers, his mind, at once philosophical and poetical, found something to instruct or to delight. His reason analysed and digested those vast and shapeless masses; his imagination animated and coloured them. Out of darkness, and dulness, and confusion, he formed a multitude of ingenious theories and vivid pictures. He had, in the highest degree, that noble faculty whereby man is able to live in the past and in the future, in the distant and in the unreal. India and its inhabitants were not to him, as to most Englishmen, mere names and abstractions, but a real country and a real people. The burning sun, the strange vegetation of the palm and the cocoa tree, the ricefield, the tank, the huge trees, older than the Mogul empire, under which the village crowds assemble, the thatched roof of the peasant's hut, the rich tracery of the mosque where the imaun prays with his face to Mecca, the drums, and banners, and gaudy idols, the devotee swinging in the air, the graceful maiden with the pitcher on her head, descending the steps to the riverside, the black faces, the long beards, the yellow streaks of sect, the turbans and the flowing robes, the spears and the silver maces, the elephants with their canopies of state, the gorgeous palanquin of the prince, and the close litter of the noble lady, all these things were to him as the objects amidst which his own life had been passed, as the objects which lay on the road between Beaconsfield and St James's Street. All India was present to the eye of his mind, from the halls where suitors laid gold and perfumes at the feet of sovereigns to the wild moor where the gipsy camp was pitched, from the bazar, humming like a bee-hive with the crowd of buyers and sellers, to the jungle where the lonely courier shakes his bunch of iron rings to scare away the hyænas. He had just as lively an idea of the insurrection at Benares, as of Lord George Gordon's riots, and of the execution of Nuncomar as of the execution of Dr Dodd. Oppression in Bengal was to him the same thing as oppression in the streets of London.

He saw that Hastings had been guilty of some most unjustifi-able acts. All that followed was natural and necessary in a mind like Burke's. His imagination and his passions, once excited, hurried him beyond the bounds of justice and good sense. His reason, powerful as it was, became the slave of feelings which it should have controlled. His indignation, virtuous in its origin, acquired too much of the character of personal aversion. He could see no mitigating circumstance, no redeeming merit. His temper, which, though generous and affectionate, had always been irritable, had now been made almost savage by bodily infirmities and mental vexations. Conscious of great powers and great virtues, he found himself, in age and poverty, a mark for the hatred of a perfidious court and a deluded people. In Parliament his eloquence was out of date. A young generation, which knew him not, had filled the House. Whenever he rose to speak, his voice was drowned by the unseemly interruption of lads who were in their cradles when his orations on the Stamp Act called forth the applause of the great Earl of Chatham. These things had produced on his proud and sensitive spirit an effect at which we cannot wonder. He could no longer discuss any question with calmness, or make allowance for honest differences of opinion. Those who think that he was more violent and acrimonious in debates about India than on other occasions, are ill informed respecting the last years of his life. In the discussions on the Commercial Treaty with the Court of Versailles, on the Regency, on the French Revolution, he showed even more virulence than in conducting the impeachment. Indeed it may be remarked that the very persons who called him a mischievous maniac, for condemning in burning words the Rohilla war and the spoliation of the Begums, exalted him into a prophet as soon as he began to declaim, with greater vehemence, and not with greater reason, against the taking of the Bastile and the insults offered to Marie Antoinette. To us he appears to have been neither a maniac in the former case, nor a prophet in the latter, but in both cases a great and good man, led into extravagance by a sensibility which domineered over all his faculties.

It may be doubted whether the personal antipathy of Francis, or the nobler indignation of Burke, would have led their party to adopt extreme measures against Hastings, if his own conduct had been judicious. He should have felt that, great as his public services had been, he was not faultless, and should have been content to make his escape, without aspiring to the honours of a triumph. He and his agent took a different view. They were impatient for the rewards which, as they conceived, were deferred only till Burke's attack should be over. They accordingly resolved to force on a decisive action with an enemy for whom, if they had been wise, they would have made a bridge of gold. On the first day of the session of 1786, Major Scott reminded Burke of the notice given in the preceding year, and asked whether it was seriously intended to bring any charge against the late Governor-General. This challenge left no course open to the Opposition, except to come forward as accusers, or to acknowledge themselves calumniators. The administration of Hastings had not been so blameless, nor was the great party of Fox and North so feeble, that it could be prudent to venture on so bold a defiance. The leaders of the Opposition instantly returned the only answer which they could with honour return; and the whole party was irrevocably pledged to a prosecution.

Burke began his operations by applying for Papers. Some of the documents for which he asked were refused by the ministers, who, in the debate, held language such as strongly confirmed the prevailing opinion, that they intended to support Hastings. In April, the charges were laid on the table. They had been drawn by Burke with great ability, though in a form too much resembling that of a pamphlet. Hastings was furnished with a copy of the accusation; and it was intimated to him that he might, if he thought fit, be heard in his own defence at the bar of the Commons.

Here again Hastings was pursued by the same fatality which had attended him ever since the day when he set foot on English ground. It seemed to be decreed that this man, so politic and so successful in the East, should commit nothing but blunders in Europe. Any judicious adviser would have told him that the best thing which he could do would be to make an eloquent, forcible, and affecting oration at the bar of the House; but that, if he could not trust himself to speak, and found it necessary to read, he ought to be as concise as possible. Audiences accustomed to extemporaneous debating of the highest excellence are always impatient of long written compositions. Hastings, however, sat down as he would have done at the Government-house in Bengal, and prepared a paper of immense length. That paper, if recorded on the consultations of an Indian administration, would have been justly praised as a very able minute. But it was now out of place. It fell flat, as the best written defence must have fallen flat, on an assembly accustomed to the animated and strenuous conflicts of Pitt and Fox. The members, as soon as their curiosity about the face and demeanour of so eminent a stranger was satisfied, walked away to dinner, and left Hastings to tell his story till midnight to the clerks and the Serjeant-at-arms.

All preliminary steps having been duly taken, Burke, in the beginning of June, brought forward the charge relating to the Rohilla war. He acted discreetly in placing this accusation in the van; for Dundas had formerly moved, and the House had adopted, a resolution condemning, in the most severe terms, the policy followed by Hastings with regard to Rohilcund. Dundas had little, or rather nothing, to say in defence of his own consistency; but he put a bold face on the matter, and opposed the motion. Among other things, he declared that, though he still thought the Rohilla war unjustifiable, he considered the services which Hastings had subsequently rendered to the state as sufficiently to atone even for so great an offence. Pitt did not speak, but voted with Dundas; and Hastings was absolved by a hundred and nineteen votes against sixty-seven.

•

Aaron Burr is provoked to fight Colonel Hamilton
JAMES PARTON

The senator for New York, Aaron Burr, tied with Thomas Jefferson in the presidential election of 1800. One man helped ensure that the

House of Representatives' nomination went to Jefferson and not Burr. That man was Colonel Alexander Hamilton who, at every step of Burr's political career, without a single exception, by open efforts, by secret intrigue or by both, had utterly opposed and forbidden his advancement. He had injured Burr in the estimation of Washington. He had prevented the president from giving Burr a military appointment. He slandered Burr at the dinner-table.

Burr was not a man to resent promptly a personal injury, but it was clear to all that the two men were on a collision course. Hamilton's role in Burr's defeat for the governorship of New York brought matters to a head, with Burr's discovery of a letter in which Hamilton's many baseless slanders of Burr were made plain. Burr subsequently challenged his implacable enemy to a duel, which was fought on 11 July 1804. It ended the political careers of both the victor and the loser.

During the late election for governor, a letter from Dr Charles D. Cooper to a friend, found its way into the papers, which contained two sentences relating to Colonel Burr. One was this:

'General Hamilton and Judge Kent have declared, in substance, that they looked upon Mr Burr to be a dangerous man, and one who ought not to be trusted with the reins of government.'

This was the other: 'I could detail to you a still more despicable opinion which General Hamilton has expressed of Mr Burr.'

Six weeks after the election, the paper containing this letter was put into Colonel Burr's hands, and his attention called to the allusions to himself.

In the afternoon of June 17th, Mr William P. Van Ness, one of Burr's staunchest friends, the *Aristides* of the pamphlet war of 1802, received a note from Colonel Burr, requesting him to call at Richmond Hill on the following morning. He went. At the request of Burr, he conveyed Dr Cooper's letter to General Hamilton, with the most offensive passage marked, and a note from Colonel Burr, which, as briefly as possible, called attention to the passage, and concluded with the following words: 'You must perceive, sir, the necessity of a prompt and unqualified acknowledgment or denial of the use of any expressions which would warrant the assertions of Mr Cooper.'

Hamilton was taken by surprise. He had not, before that moment, seen Cooper's letter. Having read it, and the note of Colonel Burr, he said that they required consideration, and he would send an answer to Mr Van Ness's office (Van Ness was a lawyer) in the course of the day. Late that evening he called at Mr Van Ness's residence, and told him that a press of business had prevented his preparing a reply, and would prevent him for two days to come; but on the 20th he would give him a communication for Colonel Burr.

In that communication, which was very long, Hamilton declined making the acknowledgment or denial that Burr had demanded. Between gentlemen, he said, *despicable* and *more despicable* was not worth the pains of distinction. He could not consent to be interrogated as to the justice of the *inferences* which others might have drawn from what he had said of an opponent during fifteen years' competition. But he stood ready to avow or disavow explicitly any *definite* opinion which he might be charged with having expressed respecting any gentleman. He trusted that Colonel Burr, upon further reflection, would see the matter in the same light. If not, he could only regret the fact, and abide the consequences.

This letter was oil upon the flames of Burr's indignation. His reply was prompt and decided. Hamilton's letters can generally be condensed one half without the loss of an idea, Burr's compact directness defies abbreviation:

'Your letter of the 20th inst.,' wrote he, 'has been this day received. Having considered it attentively, I regret to find in it nothing of that sincerity and delicacy which you profess to value. Political opposition can never absolve gentlemen from the necessity of a rigid adherence to the laws of honor and the rules of decorum. I neither claim such privilege nor indulge it in others. The common sense of mankind affixes to the epithet adopted by Dr Cooper the idea of dishonor. It has been publicly applied to me under the sanction of your name. The question is not, whether he has understood the meaning of the word, or has used it according to syntax, and with grammatical accuracy; but, whether you have authorized this application, either directly or by uttering expressions or opinions derogatory to my honor. The time "when" is in your own knowledge, but no way material to me, as the calumny has now first been disclosed, so as to become the subject of my notice, and as the effect is present and palpable. Your letter has furnished me with new reasons for requiring a definite reply.'

Hamilton seems to have read his doom in that letter. He said to Mr Van Ness, who brought it, that it was such a letter as he had hoped not to receive; it contained several offensive expressions; and seemed to close the door to reply. He had hoped that Mr Burr would have desired him to state what had fallen from him that might have given rise to the inference of Dr Cooper. He would have done that frankly, and he believed it would not have been found to exceed justifiable limits. And even then, if Mr Burr was disposed to give another turn to the discussion, he was willing to consider his last letter undelivered. But if that were not withdrawn, he could make no reply.

Mr Van Ness detailed these ideas to Colonel Burr, and received from him a paper of instructions to guide him in replying, verbally, to General Hamilton. This paper expresses with force and exactness the view of this affair then taken, and always adhered to, by Colonel Burr. It read as follows:

A. Burr, far from conceiving that rivalship authorizes a latitude not otherwise justifiable, always feels greater delicacy in such cases, and would think it meanness to speak of a rival but in terms of respect; to do justice to his merits; to be silent of his foibles. Such has invariably been his conduct toward Jay, Adams, and Hamilton; the only three who can be supposed to have stood in that relation to him.

That he has too much reason to believe that, in regard to Mr Hamilton, there has been no reciprocity. For several years his name has been lent to the support of base slanders. He has never had the generosity, the magnanimity, or the candor to contradict or disavow. Burr forbears to particularize, as it could only tend to produce new irritations; but, having made great sacrifices for the sake of harmony; having exercised forbearance until it approached to humiliation, he has seen no effect produced by such conduct but a repetition of injury. He is obliged to conclude that there is, on the part of Mr Hamilton, a settled and implacable malevolence; that he will never cease, in his conduct toward Mr Burr, to violate those courtesies of life; and that, hence, he has no alternative but to announce these things to the world; which, consistently with Mr Burr's ideas of propriety, can be done in no way but that which he has adopted. He is incapable of revenge, still less is he capable of imitating the conduct of Mr Hamilton, by committing secret depredations on his fame and character. But these things must have an end.

Upon meeting General Hamilton for the purpose of making the above explanation, Mr Van Ness was informed by him, that he had prepared a written reply to Colonel Burr's last letter, and had left it in the hands of his friend Mr Pendleton. The verbal explanation was therefore withheld, and General Hamilton's letter conveyed to Colonel Burr. It was as follows:

Your first letter, in a style too peremptory, made a demand, in my opinion, unprecedented and unwarrantable. My answer, pointing out the embarrassment, gave you an opportunity to take a less exceptionable course. You have not chosen to do it; but by your last letter received this day, containing expressions *indecorous* and improper, you have increased the difficulties to explanation intrinsically incident to the nature of your application. If by a 'definite reply' you mean the direct avowal or disavowal required in your first letter, I have no other answer to give, than that which has already been given. If you mean any thing different, admitting of greater latitude, it is requisite you should explain.

This letter, as might have been expected, produced no effect; as Mr Van Ness hastened to inform General Hamilton's friend. Van Ness added, that what Colonel Burr demanded was this: a general disavowal of any intention on the part of General Hamilton, in his various conversations, to convey impressions derogatory to the honor of Burr. Pendleton replied, that he believed General Hamilton would have no objection to make such a declaration!

Hamilton, of course, declined making the disavowal. But he gave Van Ness a paper, in his own hand, the purport of which was that if Colonel Burr should think it proper to inquire of General Hamilton the nature of the conversation with Dr Cooper, General Hamilton would be able to reply, with truth, that it turned wholly on political topics, and did not attribute to Colonel Burr any instance of dishonorable conduct, nor relate to his private character. And in relation to any other conversation which Colonel Burr would specify, a frank avowal or denial would be given.

A 'mere evasion', said Burr, when he had read this paper.

Other correspondence followed, but it is too familiar to the public, and too easily accessible, to require repetition here. Throughout the whole of it we see, on the one hand, an exasperated man resolved to bring the affair to a decisive and final issue; on the other, a man striving desperately, but not dishonorably, to escape the consequences of his own too ungarded words. Burr's final recapitulation, drawn up for the guidance of his second, was as follows:

Colonel Burr (in reply to General Hamilton's charge of indefiniteness and inquisition) would only say, that secret whispers traducing his fame, and impeaching his honor, are at least equally injurious with slanders publicly uttered; that General Hamilton had, at no time, and in no place, a right to use any such injurious expressions; and that the partial negative he is disposed to give, with the reservations he wishes to make, are proofs that he has done the injury specified.

Colonel Burr's request was, in the first instance, proposed in a form the most simple, in order that General Hamilton might give to the affair that course to which he might be induced by his temper and his knowledge of facts. Colonel Burr trusted with confidence, that, from the frankness of a soldier and the candor of a gentleman, he might expect an ingenuous declaration. That if, as he had reason to believe, General Hamilton had used expressions derogatory to his honor, he would have had the magnanimity to retract them; and that if, from his language, injurious inferences had been improperly drawn, he would have perceived the propriety of correcting errors, which might thus have been widely diffused. With these impressions, Colonel Burr was greatly surprised at receiving a letter which he considered as evasive, and which in manner he deemed not altogether decorous. In one expectation, however, he was not wholly deceived, for the close of General Hamilton's letter contained an intimation that, if Colonel Burr should dislike his refusal to acknowledge or deny, he was ready to meet the consequences. This Colonel Burr deemed a sort of defiance, and would have felt justified in making it the basis of an immediate message. But as the communication contained something concerning the indefiniteness of the request, as he believed it rather the offspring of false pride than of reflection, and as he felt the utmost reluctance to proceed to extremities, while any other hope remained, his request was repeated in terms more explicit. The replies and propositions on the part of General Hamilton have, in Colonel Burr's opinion, been constantly in substance the same.

Colonel Burr disavows all motives of predetermined hostility, a charge by which he thinks insult added to injury. He feels as a gentleman should feel when his honor is impeached or assailed; and, without sensations of hostility or wishes of revenge, he is determined to vindicate that honor at such hazard as the nature of the case demands.

The letter concluded with the remark that the length and fruitlessness of the correspondence proved it useless 'to offer any proposition, except the simple message which I shall now have the honor to deliver'.

The challenge was then given and accepted . . .

For the very purpose of preventing suspicion, it had been arranged that Colonel Burr's boat should arrive some time before the other. About half-past six, Burr and Van Ness landed, and leaving their boat a few yards down the river, ascended over the rocks to the appointed place. It was a warm, bright, July morning. The sun looks down, directly after rising, upon the Weehawken heights, and it was for that reason that the two men removed their coats before the arrival of the other party. There they stood carelessly breaking away the branches of the underwood, and looking out upon as fair, as various, as animated, as beautiful a scene, as mortal eyes in this beautiful world ever behold. The haze-crowned city; the bright, broad, flashing, tranquil river; the long reach of waters, twelve miles or more, down to the Narrows; the vessels at anchor in the harbor; misty, blue Staten Island, swelling up in superb contour from the lower bay; the verdant flowery heights around; the opposite shore of the river, then dark with forest, or bright with sloping lawn; and, to complete the picture, that remarkably picturesque promontory called Castle Point, that bends out far into the stream, a mile below Weehawken, and adds a peculiar beauty to the foreground; – all these combine to form a view, one glance at which *ought* to have sent shame and horror to the duelist's heart, that so much as the thought of closing a human being's eyes for ever on so much loveliness, had ever lived a moment in his bosom.

Hamilton's boat was seen to approach. A few minutes before seven it touched the rocks, and Hamilton and his second ascended. The principals and seconds exchanged the usual salutations, and the seconds proceeded immediately to make the usual preparations. They measured ten full paces; then cast lots for the choice of position, and to decide who should give the word. The lot, in both cases, fell to General Hamilton's second, who chose the *upper* end of the ledge for his principal, which, at that hour of the day, could not have been the best, for the reason that the morning sun, and the flashing of the river, would both interfere with the sight. The pistols were then loaded, and the principals placed, Hamilton looking over the river toward the city, and Burr turned toward the heights, under which they stood. As Pendleton gave Hamilton his pistol, he asked,

'Will you have the hair-spring set?'

'*Not this time*,' was the quiet reply.

Pendleton then explained to both principals the rules which had been agreed upon with regard to the firing; after the word *present*, they were to fire as soon as they pleased. The seconds then withdrew to the usual distance.

'Are you ready?' said Pendleton.

Both answered in the affirmative. A moment's pause ensued. The word was given. Burr raised his pistol, took aim, and fired. Hamilton sprang upon his toes with a convulsive movement, reeled a little toward the heights, at which moment he involuntarily discharged his pistol, and then fell forward headlong upon his face, and remained motionless on the ground. His ball rustled among the branches, seven feet above the head of his antagonist, and four feet wide of him. Burr heard it, looked up, and saw where it had severed a twig. Looking at Hamilton, he beheld him falling, and sprang toward him with an expression of pain upon his face. But at the report of the pistols, Dr Hosack, Mr Davis, and the boatman, hurried anxiously up the rocks to the scene of the duel; and Van Ness, with presence of mind, seized Burr, shielded him from observation with an umbrella, and urged him down the steep to the boat. It was pushed off immediately, and rowed swiftly back to Richmond Hill, where Swartwout, with feelings that may be imagined, received his unhurt chief – a chief no more!

Mr Pendleton raised his prostrate friend. Dr Hosack found him sitting on the grass, supported in the arms of his second, with the ghastliness of death upon his countenance. 'This is a mortal wound, doctor,' he gasped; and then sunk away into a swoon. The doctor stripped up his clothes, and saw at a glance that the ball, which had entered his right side, must have penetrated a mortal part. Scarcely expecting him to revive, they conveyed him down among the large rocks, to the shore, placed him tenderly in the boat, and set off for the city. The doctor now used the usual restoratives, and the wounded man gradually revived. 'He breathed,' to quote the doctor's words; 'his eyes, hardly opened, wandered without fixing upon any object; to our great joy, he at length spoke. "My vision is indistinct," were his first words. His pulse became more perceptible, his respiration more regular, his sight returned. Soon after recovering his sight, he happened to cast his eye upon the case of pistols, and observing the one that he had had in his hand lying on the outside, he said, "Take care of that pistol; it is undischarged and still cocked; it may go off and do harm. Pendleton knows" (attempting to turn his head toward him) "that I did not intend to fire at him."

'Then he lay tranquil till he saw that the boat was approaching the wharf. He said, "Let Mrs Hamilton be immediately sent for; let the event be gradually broke to her, but give her hopes." Looking up we saw his friend, Mr Bayard, standing on the wharf in great agitation. He had been told by his servant that General Hamilton, Mr Pendleton, and myself had crossed the river in a boat together, and too well he conjectured the fatal errand, and foreboded the dreadful result. Perceiving, as we came nearer, that Mr Pendleton and myself only sat up in the stern sheets, he clasped his hands together in the most violent apprehension; but when I called to him to have a cot prepared, and he at the same moment saw his poor friend lying in the bottom of the boat, he threw up his eyes, and burst into a flood of tears and lamentation. Hamilton alone appeared tranquil and composed. We then conveyed him as tenderly as possible up to the house. The distress of his amiable family were such that, till the first shock had abated, they were scarcely able to summon fortitude enough to yield sufficient assistance to their dying friend." '

By nine in the morning the news began to be noised about in the city. A bulletin soon appeared on the board at the Tontine Coffee House, and the pulse of the town stood still at the shocking intelligence. People started and turned pale as they read the brief announcement:

GENERAL HAMILTON WAS SHOT BY COLONEL BURR THIS MORNING IN A DUEL. THE GENERAL IS SAID TO BE MORTALLY WOUNDED.

Bulletins, hourly changed, kept the city in agitation. All the circumstances of the catastrophe were told, and retold, and exaggerated at every corner. The thrilling scenes that were passing at the bedside of the dying man – the consultations of the physicians – the arrival of the stricken family – Mrs Hamilton's overwhelming sorrow – the resignation and calm dignity of the illustrious sufferer – his broken slumbers during the night – the piteous spectacle of the *seven* children entering together the awful apartment – the single look the dying father gave them before he closed his eyes – were all described with amplifications, and produced an impression that can only be imagined. He lingered thirty-one hours. The duel was fought on Wednesday morning. At two o'clock, on Thursday afternoon, Hamilton died.

•

Castlereagh and Canning
ANONYMOUS

Viscount Castlereagh was secretary of war during the wars with Napoleon Bonaparte. Serving in the same government as the foreign secretary was George Canning. In 1809 Castlereagh alleged Canning's political betrayal, and challenged him to a duel which was fought on 21 September. An account of the duel and its causes is given here. What is not mentioned is that Castlereagh had a button shot off his lapel, and also that the King, George III, wrote a letter to the cabinet on the impropriety of the duel, which led to the resignation of both men. In 1812 Castlereagh was appointed foreign secretary, a position which he held until 1822, when he committed suicide, after which Canning was reappointed to this office.

A duel took place early this morning between Lord Castlereagh and Mr Canning, in which the latter received a wound in the left thigh; but happily it is not dangerous, being merely a flesh wound.

The meeting took place at Putney Heath. Lord Yarmouth seconded Lord Castlereagh, and Mr R. Ellis accompanied Mr Canning. We understand they fired by signal, at the distance of ten yards. The first missed; and no explanation taking place, they fired a second time, when Mr Canning was wounded in the left thigh, on the outer side of the bone; and thus the affair terminated. He was put into a coach, and conveyed to Gloucester Lodge, his newly purchased seat at Brompton, and Lord Castlereagh returned to his house in St James's-square.

The circumstances of this celebrated political duel were the following: It had been long reported that there were divisions in the Duke of Portland's cabinet, and that a change in some of the highest offices of State would take place. These divisions became public in the latter end of September, when Lord

Castlereagh, then Secretary of War, sent a challenge to Mr Canning, who held the seals of the foreign office.

Lord Castlereagh's complaint was, that, they being both members of the cabinet, Mr Canning had applied clandestinely to get him removed from office, for the purpose of bringing in the Marquis Wellesley in his place. Before Easter, it was affirmed, he made this application to the Duke of Portland, and obtained his promise that Lord Castlereagh should be removed from office. 'Notwithstanding this promise,' said Castlereagh in his letter which accompanied the challenge, 'by which I consider you presumed it unfit that I should remain charged with the conduct of the war, and by which my situation as a minister of the Crown was made dependent on your will and pleasure, you continued to sit in the same cabinet with me, and left me not only in the persuasion that I possessed your confidence and support as a colleague, but allowed me, in breach of every principle of good faith, both public and private, to originate and proceed in a new enterprise of the most arduous and important nature (the Walcheren expedition), with your apparent concurrence and ostensible approbation. You are fully aware that, if my situation in the Government had been disclosed to me, I could not have submitted to remain one moment in office, without the entire abandonment of private honour and public duty. You knew I *was* deceived, and you *continued* to deceive me.'

Without presuming to cast any unfavourable imputation on the well-earned fame of Mr Canning, it cannot be denied that, if Lord Castlereagh's statement was correct, Mr Canning's conduct was most unjustifiable, both on public and on private grounds – both as a statesman and a gentleman. If he considered Lord Castlereagh as unfit to manage the important charge with which he was entrusted, and indeed the Walcheren expedition alluded to afforded a convincing proof of the correctness of his opinion, it was his duty not to remain with him in the cabinet one single hour, if he could not overrule his proposals; but to coincide in a project which he condemned, and to continue to act in conjunction with a minister whose removal he had urged on the plea of incapacity, was an act most unaccountable on the part of Mr Canning, and only tends to show, that men placed in a public situation will be guilty of acts which they would scorn, as dishonourable, in the common affairs of life.

•

The duellists

LEWIS MELVILLE AND REGINALD HARGREAVES

This amazing quarrel, which lasted nineteen years, between two soldiers of the Napoleonic period, was the inspiration for a short story by Joseph Conrad and a film directed by Ridley Scott.

This most curious duel was brought to a termination in 1813, and the cause of the protracted fighting was as follows:

A captain of Hussars, named Fournier, who was a desperate duellist, and endowed, as the French say, 'with deplorable skill', had challenged and killed, on a most frivolous pretence, a young man named Blumm, the sole support of a family. At the event the entire town put forth a cry of lamentation – a cry of malediction on the murderer. The young man's funeral was attended by an immense multitude, and sympathy was felt for the bereaved family in every household. There was, however, as it happened, a ball at the quarters of General Moreau. The ball was expressly given to the citizens of Strasbourg, and the General, apprehensive that the presence of Fournier might be offensive to his guests of the evening, charged Captain Dupont, his aide-de-camp, to prevent him from entering the ball-room. He accordingly posted himself at the entrance, and when Fournier made his appearance, he exclaimed: 'Do you dare to show yourself here?' 'The deuce! what does this mean?' asked Fournier. 'It means,' replied Captain Dupont, 'that you ought to have understood that on the day of the funeral of poor

Blumm, it would have been only decent to remain at home, or certainly not to appear at a reunion in which you are likely to meet with the friends of your victim.' 'You mean *enemies*; but I would have you to know that I fear nobody, and that I am in a mood to defy all the world,' said Fournier.

'Ah, bah! You shall not enjoy that fancy tonight; you must go to bed, by order of the General,' rejoined Dupont. 'You are mistaken, Dupont,' said Fournier; 'I cannot call the General to account for insulting me by closing his door upon me, but I look to you and to *them*, and I am resolved to pay you handsomely for your commission as door-keeper which you have accepted.' 'Oh, as for that, my dear fellow, I'll fight you when you like. The fact is, your insolent and blustering behaviour has displeased me for a long time, and my hand itches to chastise you.' 'We shall see who is the chastiser,' said Fournier.

The duel came off, and Fournier was laid on the grass with a vigorous sword-thrust. 'That's the *first* touch,' he exclaimed as he sank. 'Then you wish to have another bout, do you?' asked Dupont.

'Most assuredly, my brave fellow, and before long, I hope,' said Fournier.

In a month Fournier got well; they fought again; this time Dupont was grievously wounded, and in falling he exclaimed: 'That's the *second*. As soon as possible again; and then for the *finish*.' The two adversaries were about equal with the sword; but with the pistol the chances would have been very different. Fournier was an absolute crack shot. According to M. de Pontécoulant, often when the Hussars of his regiment were galloping past smoking, he amused himself with smashing their pipes between their lips!

All have seen some wonderful doings with the pistol. All have known a determination to hit a certain part of the adversary, and it was hit. Some have seen hens held out by the hand of a negro hit by a pistol bullet; but the feat of hitting a pipe in the mouth of a galloping horseman is beyond ordinary comprehension. If Fournier could do that, then Dupont was perfectly justified in refusing to try him at that game, as he proposed. They fought again with swords, but the *finish* was not forthcoming; it was only a slight wound on both sides; but now they resolved to continue the contest until either of them should confess himself beaten or *satisfied*. They drew up formal terms of the warfare as follows:

1. Every time that Dupont and Fournier shall be a hundred miles from each other, they will each approach half the distance to meet sword in hand.

2. Should one of the contracting parties be prevented by the duties of the service, he who is free must go the entire distance, so as to reconcile the duties of the service with the exigencies of the present treaty.

3. No excuse whatever, excepting those resulting from military obligations, will be admitted.

4. The present being a *bona fide* treaty, cannot be altered from the conditions agreed upon by the consenting parties.

The contract was religiously executed in all its rigour. More-over, the contracting parties found no difficulty in keeping their engagements; this state of war became to them a normal condi-tion, a second nature. Their eagerness to meet was like that of two lovers. They never crossed swords without first shaking hands in the most boisterous manner.

Their correspondence during this periodic duel is the essence of burlesque. Take the following:

'I am invited to breakfast with the officers of the regiment of Chasseurs at Suneville. I hope to be able to accept this pleasant invitation. As you are on leave in that town, we will take advantage of the opportunity, if you please, to get a thrust at each other!'

Here is another, less familiar, perhaps, but not less tender:

'My dear friend, I shall be at Strasbourg on the 5th of November proximo, about noon. Wait for me at the Hôtel des Postes. We shall have a thrust or two.'

Such was the style and such the tenor of the entire correspondence.

At intervals the promotion of one of them provisionally interrupted the meeting; this was one of the cases anticipated by Article 3 of the treaty. As soon as they got on equality of rank in the service, the party last promoted never failed to receive a letter couched in the following terms, written by Fournier:

'My dear Dupont, I hear that the Emperor, doing justice to your merit, has just promoted you to the grade of Brigadier-General. Accept my sincere congratulations on a promotion, which by your future and your courage is made natural, a mere matter of course. I have two reasons for exultation in this nomination. First, the satisfaction of a fortunate circumstance for your advancement; and secondly, the facility now vouchsafed to us, to have a thrust at each other on the first opportunity.'

They afterwards became generals. Dupont was ordered to join the army in Switzerland. He arrived, unexpectedly, in a village occupied by the staff, and which had not a single inn or tavern in it. The night was dark. Not a light was seen excepting at the window of a small cottage. Dupont went to the door, entered, and found himself face to face with Fournier.

'What! *You* here?' exclaimed the latter rapturously. 'Now for a thrust!'

They set to at once, conversing as they fought.

'I thought you were promoted to some high administrative function?'

'You were wrong; I am still of the trade. The Minister has sent me to the fourth *corps d'armée*, and here I am.'

'And your first visit is to me? It is very kind of you. *Sacrebleu!*'

Dupont drove his sword through Fournier's neck, and held him spitted to the wall, saying:

'You will admit that you did not expect that thrust!'

Dupont still held him fast, and Fournier muttered:

'I'll give you a thrust quite equal to this.'

'What thrust can you give?'

'Why, as soon as you lower your arm, and before you can parry, I shall lunge into your belly.'

'Thank you for the hint. Then we shall pass the night in this position.'

'That's an agreeable prospect! But, really, I am not very comfortable.'

'Drop your sword, and I set you free.'

'No, I must stick you in the belly.'

Meanwhile, some officers, attracted by the noise they were making, rushed in and separated the two generals.

Thus the contest continued, the contract being faithfully fulfilled on both sides. At length, however, Dupont thought of marrying, and he set his wits to work to find out how to make an end of the engagement. He must either kill Fournier, or muzzle him effectually. He went to him one morning, it was at Paris. 'Ah!' said the latter at seeing him. 'Glad to see you. Let's have a brush together.'

'A word first, my dear fellow,' said Dupont. 'I am on the point of getting married. We must end this quarrel, which is becoming rather rancid. I now come to get rid of you. In order to secure a definitive result, I offer to substitute the *pistol* for the sword – there!'

'Why, man, you are stark mad!' exclaimed the dead-shot Fournier, astounded by the proposal.

'Oh, I know your skill with the pistol, *mon ami* . . . But, let me tell you, I have hit upon a plan which will equalize the conflict. Here it is. Near Neuilly there is an enclosure with a little wood in it. It is at my disposal. My proposal is this. We shall enter the wood, each provided with a pair of horse-pistols, and then, having separated, and being out of sight of each other, we shall track each other as best we can, and fire at our convenience.'

'Capital! Agreed!' exclaimed Fournier, 'but let me give you, *mon vieux*, a little piece of advice.'

'If you please,' said Dupont.

'Well, don't go too far with your marriage project. It will be time and trouble lost; for I warrant you'll die a bachelor.'

On the day appointed Fournier and Dupont set out in their hunt. Having separated, and got out of sight of each other, as agreed, they crept about or advanced like cautious wolves or foxes, striving to catch a glance at each other through the thicket, whenever the motion of the leaves showed their presence. All at once, as though by a common movement, both came in sight together, standing behind two trees. They squatted down, and thus remained for a few minutes. The situation was delicate – critical. To stir was certain death, to one of them, at least. Dupont, however, was the first to make the attempt, or rather to pretend to do so. He raised the flap of his coat, and allowed one end to project out of cover. Bang! came a bullet in the instant, cutting through the cloth.

'That settles *one* shot,' ejaculated Dupont, with a sigh of thanksgiving.

After a short interval Dupont returned to the charge, but this time on the other side of the tree. Holding his pistol with the left hand, he presented the barrel as though about to fire, and at the same instant he held out his hat with the right. Bang! came another bullet, driving the hat into the bushes.

'Now, my brave, it's all up with you!' exclaimed Dupont, stalking out, both pistols in hand and cocked; and marching up to Fournier, he said:

'Your life is at my disposal, but I will not take it.'

'Oh, just as you please about that,' muttered Fournier. Dupont continued:

'Only you must remember that I do not give up my right of property in it. Beware of ever crossing my path again, for if you do, I may probably put my two bullets into your brains, as I might this instant.'

Such was the termination of this long quarrel of nineteen years, ending with the marriage of one of the parties, who contrived at last to beat the unapproachable crack-shot at his own weapon.

•

Daniel O'Connell and the beggarly Corporation of Dublin

LEWIS MELVILLE AND REGINALD HARGREAVES

Daniel O'Connell was the founder of the Catholic Association, whose political agitation culminated in the Catholic Emancipation Act of 1829. He was a member of parliament where he worked for the repeal of the union of Great Britain and Ireland. All his life he attracted controversy. Here is an account of a dispute leading to a fight with pistols, not with those who resisted his work for an independent Ireland, but with a representative of the Dublin City Corporation.

After a meeting at Capel Street, in January, previous to the late Aggregate Meeting, Daniel O'Connell attended; and in illustrating some matter which he was anxious to enforce, he alluded, in a contemptuous manner, to the Corporation of Dublin. 'The beggarly Corporation of Dublin' was, it seems, one of the epithets of scorn used in reprobation of this act. J. N. D'Esterre, a member of the Corporation, having seen this phrase, addressed a letter on the 25th (the day after the Aggregate Meeting) to O'Connell requiring to know whether he was fairly reported. On the day after O'Connell sent an answer, in which he said he would not avow nor disavow what had been reported in the newspapers. But, he added, if D'Esterre wrote to him to know his opinion of the Common Council of Dublin, as a body, he could easily satisfy him by saying that no expression which language could furnish was sufficient to convey the sentiments of contempt he had for that body. O'Connell, besides, requested that D'Esterre should consider his answer as forming the close of the epistolary correspondence on this topic.

On Friday, a letter was left in Merrion Square for O'Connell, during his absence at the Courts. Its direction was different from the former one which came from D'Esterre; and James O'Connell, who had instructions to open any communications that were directed to his brother in his absence, ascertained the quarter from whence it came. He sought merely for the signature, and on perceiving it to be D'Esterre's, he immediately closed the letter, and stated in a note to D'Esterre the circumstances under which he opened it. He said he was ignorant of its contents, not wishing, after the request his brother had made on the day previous, to know anything more of D'Esterre's epistolary messages. He added, that his brother did not expect to hear a second time from D'Esterre through the medium of *a letter*. Things remained in this condition till Sunday. On that day James O'Connell received a note from D'Esterre, containing disrespectful observations on himself and his brother. Immediately after the receipt of it, he sent his friend, Captain O'Mullan, to D'Esterre to say, that after he had adjusted his affair with his brother, he would bring him to account for his conduct to himself peculiarly. Captain O'Mullan at the same time intimated that Counsellor O'Connell was astonished at not hearing, in what he conceived the *proper way*, from D'Esterre.

Nothing farther happened on Sunday; and on Monday morning, Mr Lidwell, who remained several days to be the friend of O'Connell, though some members of his family were seriously indisposed, left town for home, despairing of any issue being put to the controversy. Monday passed; and on Tuesday considerable sensation was created by a rumour that D'Esterre was advised to go to the Four Courts to offer O'Connell personal violence. Neither of the parties came in contact. But it seems D'Esterre was met on one of the quays by Richard O'Gorman, who remonstrated with him, by stating that he conceived he was pursuing a very unusual sort of conduct. This occurred about three o'clock; but no challenge followed. About four it was understood that D'Esterre was in the street; and O'Connell paraded about with one or two friends, but did not come across his antagonist. A multitude soon collected about him, among whom there could not be less than five hundred gentlemen of respectability; and O'Connell then had no other resource left than to take refuge in a house in Exchequer Street. In a short time Judge Day entered, in his magisterial capacity, to put him under arrest. The Hon. Justice said he would be satisfied if he had the guarantee of O'Connell's honour that he would proceed no farther in the business. 'It is not my business, Mr Justice,' said O'Connell, 'to be the aggressor. Further, however, I must tell you, that no human consideration will induce me to go.' The Hon. Justice then retired; and O'Connell shortly after repaired to Merrion Square. No challenge of any kind grew out of Tuesday's proceedings.

On Wednesday morning, however, it was at length intimated to O'Connell that D'Esterre intended to call upon him for a meeting. Twelve o'clock was fixed upon for the nomination of hour and place. There was some overture made to enlarge the time; but O'Connell's friend would not consent. His friend was Major Macnamara, of Doolen, in the county of Clare, a Protestant gentleman attached to no party, and of the highest respectability. The friend of D'Esterre was Sir Edward Stanley.

After some discussion the parties fixed upon Bishop's Court, County Kildare, as the place. It is about twelve miles distant from Dublin, and constituted part of Lord Ponsonby's demesne. The hour appointed was half-past three o'clock. At three precisely, O'Connell, attended by his second, Surgeon Macklin, and a number of friends, was on the ground.

About four, D'Esterre, attended only by Surgeon Peel, Sir Edward Stanley (his second), and a Mr D'Esterre, of Limerick, appeared. There was some conversation between the seconds as to position, mode of fire, etc., which, added to other sources of delay, occupied forty minutes. During this interval D'Esterre took occasion to say that his quarrel with O'Connell was not of a religious nature. To the Catholics, or their leaders, he said he had no animosity whatever.

At forty minutes past four the combatants were on the ground; they both displayed the greatest coolness and courage.

The friends of both parties retired, and the combatants, having a pistol in each hand, with directions to discharge them at their discretion, prepared to fire. They levelled, and before the lapse of a second, both shots were heard. D'Esterre's was first, and missed. O'Connell's followed instantaneously, and took effect in the thigh of his antagonist, about an inch below the hip. D'Esterre fell, and both surgeons hastened to him. They found that the ball had 'traversed the hip', and could not be found. There was an immense effusion of blood. All parties prepared to move towards home, and arrived in town before eight o'clock.

D'Esterre died at five o'clock on February 3rd.

The particulars of this duel were reported as follows:

The Dublin Corporation, at the period, was considered as the stronghold of the Protestant ascendancy, and the hostility to what were called the Catholic claims was carried to great excess. Mr O'Connell, the champion of his party, assumed a tone equally violent and acrimonious; and at a meeting of the Catholics held in Dublin, spoke of the Corporation of that city in the most contemptuous terms, and amongst other abusive epithets, called it 'a beggarly Corporation', an expression which soon became a byword with their opponents.

Mr D'Esterre, a young man of great respectability and high spirit, felt indignant at the reproach cast upon the body of which he was a member; and there is reason to believe that his indignation was fanned by the instigation of his colleagues, who were anxious to rid themselves of such a formidable opponent as O'Connell. D'Esterre, therefore, addressed a letter to O'Connell, to know whether he had used the expression which the public papers attributed to him. O'Connell, in reply, neither admitted nor disclaimed the alleged charge, but stated that no terms, however reproachful, could exceed the contemptuous feelings he entertained for the Corporation as a public body. To this he added, that his letter must close all correspondence on the subject. Mr D'Esterre was advised to address another letter to Mr O'Connell, which was returned unread by that gentleman's brother. Various reports were circulated, and it was stated that D'Esterre intended to offer personal violence, should he meet him in the streets. Thus did a week pass, during which threats and violent language were exchanged between the two hostile parties, and it was generally concluded that a duel could not be avoided. Mr George Lidwell, at Mr O'Connell's request, had waited a few days in Dublin expecting a message from Mr D'Esterre, and at length Sir Edward Stanley, Barrack-master of Dublin, and a friend of Mr D'Esterre, waited on O'Connell with the hostile message so long expected. The challenge was accepted, and the necessary arrangements were made between Major Macnamara and Sir Edward Stanley.

●

On the pleasure of hating
WILLIAM HAZLITT

There is a spider crawling along the matted floor of the room where I sit (not the one which has been so well allegorized in the admirable *Lines to a Spider,* but another of the same edifying breed) – he runs with heedless, hurried haste, he hobbles awkwardly towards me, he stops – he sees the giant shadow before him, and, at a loss whether to retreat or proceed, meditates his huge foe – but as I do not start up and seize upon the struggling caitiff, as he would upon a helpless fly within his toils, he takes heart, and ventures on, with mingled cunning, impudence, and fear. As he passes me, I lift up the matting to assist his escape, am glad to get rid of the unwelcome intruder, and shudder at the recollection after he is gone. A child, a woman, a clown, or a moralist a century ago, would have crushed the little reptile to death – my philosophy has got beyond that − I bear the creature no ill-will, but still I hate the very sight of it. The spirit of malevolence survives the practical exertion of it. We learn to curb our will and keep our overt actions within the bounds of humanity, long before we can subdue our sentiments and imaginations to the same mild tone. We give up the external demonstration, the *brute* violence, but cannot part with the essence or principle of hostility. We do not tread upon the poor little animal in question (that seems barbarous and piti-ful!) but we regard it with a sort of mystic horror and super-stitious loathing. It will ask another hundred years of fine writing and hard thinking to cure us of the prejudice, and make us feel towards this ill-omened tribe with something of 'the milk of human kindness', instead of their own shyness and venom.

Nature seems (the more we look into it) made up of antipathies: without something to hate, we should lose the very spring of thought and action. Life would turn to a stagnant pool, were it not ruffled by the jarring interests, the unruly passions of men. The white streak in our own fortunes is brightened (or just rendered visible) by making all round it as dark as possible, so the rainbow paints its form upon the cloud. Is it pride? Is it envy? Is it the force of contrast? Is it weakness or malice? But so it is, that there is a secret affinity, a *hankering* after evil in the human mind, and that it takes a perverse, but a fortunate delight in mischief, since it is a never-failing source of satisfaction. Pure good soon grows insipid, wants variety and spirit. Pain is a bitter-sweet which never surfeits. Love turns, with a little indulgence, to indifference or disgust: hatred alone is immortal. Do we not see this principle at work everywhere? Animals torment and worry one another without mercy: children kill flies for sport: everyone reads the accidents and offences in a newspaper, as the cream of the jest: a whole town runs to be present at a fire, and the spectator by no means exults to see it extinguished. It is better to have it so, but it diminishes the interest; and our feelings take part with our passions, rather than with our understandings. Men assemble in crowds, with eager enthusiasms, to witness a tragedy: but if there were an execution going forward in the next street, as Mr Burke observes, the theatre would be left empty. A strange cur in a village, an ideot, a crazy woman, are set upon and baited by the whole community. Public nuisances are in the nature of public benefits. How long did the Pope, the Bourbons, and the Inquisition keep the people of England in breath, and supply them with nick-names to vent their spleen upon! Had they done us any harm of late? No: but we have always a quantity of superfluous bile upon the stomach, and we want an object to let it out upon. How loth were we to give up our pious belief in ghosts and witches, because we liked to persecute the one, and frighten ourselves to death with the other! It is not so much the quality as the quantity of excitement that we are anxious about: we cannot bear a state of indifference and *ennui*: the mind seems to abhor a *vacuum* as much as ever matter was supposed to do. Even when the spirit of the age (that is, the progress of intellectual refinement, warring with our natural infirmities) no longer allows us to carry our vindictive and headstrong humours into effect, we try to revive them in description, and keep up the old bugbears, the phantoms of our terror and our hate, in imagination. We burn Guy Faux in effigy, and the hooting and buffeting and maltreating that poor tattered figure of rags and straw makes a festival in every village in England once a year. Protestants and Papists do not now burn one another at the stake: but we subscribe to new editions of *Fox's Book of Martyrs*; and the secret of the success of the *Scotch Novels* is much the same – they carry us back to the feuds, the heart-burnings, the havoc, the dismay, the wrongs and the revenge of a barbarous age and people – to the rooted prejudices and deadly animosities of sects and parties in politics and religion, and of contending chiefs and clans in war and intrigue. We feel the full force of the spirit of hatred with all of them in turn. As we read, we throw aside the trammels of civilization, the flimsy veil of humanity. 'Off, you lendings!' The wild beast resumes its sway within us, we feel like hunting-animals, and as the hound starts in his sleep and rushes on the chase in fancy, the heart rouses itself in its native lair, and utters a wild cry of joy, at being restored once more to freedom and lawless, unrestrained impulses. Every one has his full swing, or goes to the Devil his own way. Here are no Jeremy Bentham Panopticons, none of Mr Owen's impassable Parallelograms, (Rob Roy would have spurned and poured a thousand curses on them), no long calculations of self-interest – the will takes its instant way to its object; as the mountain-torrent flings itself over the precipice, the greatest possible good of each individual consists in doing all the mischief he can to his neighbour: that is charming, and finds a sure and sympathetic chord in every breast! So Mr Irving, the celebrated preacher, has rekindled the old, original, almost exploded hell-fire in the aisles of the Caledonian Chapel, as they introduce the real water of the New River at Sadler's Wells, to the delight and astonishment of his fair audience. *'Tis pretty, though a plague*, to sit and peep into the pit of Tophet, to play at *snap-dragon* with flames and brimstone (it gives a smart electrical shock, a lively fillip to delicate constitutions), and to see Mr Irving, like a huge Titan, looking as grim and swarthy as if he had to forge tortures for all the damned! What a strange being man is! Not content with doing all he can to vex and hurt his fellows here, 'upon this bank and shoal of time,' where one would think there were heartaches, pain, disappointment, anguish, tears, sighs, and groans enough, the bigoted maniac takes him to the top of the high peak of school divinity to hurl him down the yawning gulf of penal fire; his speculative malice asks eternity to wreak its infinite spite and calls on the Almighty to execute its relentless doom! The cannibals burn their enemies and eat them, in good fellowship with one another: meek Christian divines cast those who differ from them but a hair's breadth, body and soul, into hell-fire, for the glory of God and the good of his creatures! It is well that the power of such persons is not co-ordinate with their wills: indeed, it is from the sense of their weakness and inability to control the opinions of others, that they thus 'outdo termagant,' and endeavour to frighten them into conformity by big words and denunciations.

The pleasure of hating, like a poisonous mineral, eats into the heart of religion, and turns it to rankling spleen and bigotry; it makes patriotism an excuse for carrying fire, pestilence, and famine into other lands: it leaves to virtue nothing but the spirit of censoriousness, and a narrow, jealous, inquisitorial watchfulness over the actions and motives of others. What have the different sects, creeds, doctrines in religion been but so many pretexts set up for men to wrangle, to quarrel, to tear one another in pieces about, like a target as a mark to shoot at? Does any one suppose that the love of country in an Englishman implies any friendly feeling or disposition to serve another, bearing the same name? No, it means only hatred to the French, or the inhabitants of any other country that we happen to be at war with for the time. Does the love of any virtue denote the wish to discover or amend our own faults? No, but it atones for an obstinate adherence to our own vices by the most virulent intolerance to human frailties. This principle is of a most universal application. It extends to good as well as evil: if it makes us hate folly, it makes us no less dissatisfied with distinguished merit. If it inclines us to resent the wrongs of others, it impels us to be as impatient of their prosperity. We revenge injuries: we repay benefits with ingratitude. Even our strongest partialities and likings soon take their turn. 'That which was luscious as locusts, anon becomes bitter as colonquintida': and love and friendship melt in their own fires. We hate old friends: we hate old books: we hate old opinions; and at last we come to hate ourselves.

I have observed that few of those, whom I have formerly known most intimate, continue on the same friendly footing, or combine the steadiness with the warmth of attachment. I have been acquainted with two or three knots of inseparable companions who saw each other 'six days in the week', that have broken up and dispersed. I have quarrelled with almost all my old friends, (they might say this is owing to my bad temper, but) they have also quarrelled with one another. What is become of 'that set of whist players', celebrated by Elia in his notable *Epistle To Robert Southey, Esq.* (and now I think of it – that I myself have celebrated in this very volume) 'that for so many years called Admiral Burney friend?' They are scattered, like last year's snow. Some of them are dead – or gone to live at a distance – or pass one another in the street like strangers; or if they stop to speak, do it coolly and try to *cut* one another as soon as possible. Some of us have grown rich – others poor. Some have got places under Government – others a *niche* in the Quarterly Review. Some of us have dearly earned a name in the world; while others remain in their original privacy. We despise the one; and envy and are glad to mortify the other. Times are changed; we cannot revive old feelings; and we avoid the sight and are uneasy in the presence of those, who remind us of our infirmity, and put us upon an effort of seeming cordiality, which embarrasses ourselves and does not impose upon our *quondam* associates. Old friendships are like meats served up repeatedly, cold, comfortless and distasteful. The stomach turns against them. Either constant intercourse and familiarity breed weariness and contempt; or if we meet again after an interval of absence, we appear no longer the same. One is too wise, another too foolish for us; and we wonder we did not find this out before. We are disconcerted and kept in a state of continual alarm by the wit of one, or tired to death of the dullness of the other. The *good things* of the first (besides leaving stings behind them) by repetition grow stale, and lose their startling effect; and the insipidity of the last becomes intolerable. The most amusing or instructive companion is at best like a favourite volume, that we wish after a time to *lay upon the shelf*; but as our friends are not willing to be laid there, this produces a misunderstanding and ill-blood between us. – Or if the zeal and integrity of friendship is not abated, or its career interrupted by any obstacle arising out of its own nature, we look out for other objects of complaint and sources of dissatisfaction. We begin to criticize each other's dress, looks and general character. 'Such a one is a pleasant fellow, but it is a pity he sits so late!' Another fails to keep his appointments, and that is a sore that never heals. We get acquainted with some fashionable young men or with a mistress, and wish to introduce our friend; but he is awkward and sloven, the interview does not answer, and this throws cold water on our intercourse. Or he makes himself obnoxious to opinion – and we shrink from our own convictions on the subject as an excuse for not defending him. All or any of these causes mount up in time to a ground of coolness or irritation – and at last they break out into open violence as the only amends we can make ourselves for suppressing them so long, or the readiest means of banishing recollections of former kindness, so little compatible with our present feelings. We may try to tamper with the wounds or patch up the carcase of departed friendship, but the one will hardly bear the handling, and the other is not worth the trouble of embalming! The only way to be reconciled with old friends is to part with them for good: at a distance we may chance to be thrown back (in a waking dream) upon old times and old feelings: or at any rate, we should not think of renewing our intimacy, till we have fairly *spit our spite*, or said, thought, and felt all the ill we can of each other. Or if we can pick a quarrel with someone else, and make him the scape-goat, this is an excellent contrivance to heal a broken bone. I think I must be friends with Lamb again, since he has written that magnanimous Letter to Southey, and told him a piece of his mind! – I don't know what it is that attaches me to H(aydon) so much, except that he and I, whenever we meet, sit in judgment on another set of old friends, and 'carve them as a dish fit for the Gods'. There was L(eigh) H(unt), John Scott, Mrs (Novello), whose dark raven locks made a picturesque background to our discourse, B(arnes), who is grown fat, and is, they say, married, R(ickman); these had all separated long ago, and their foibles are the common link that holds us together. We do not affect to condole or whine over their follies; we enjoy, we laugh at them until we are ready to burst our sides, '*sans* intermission, for hours by the dial'. We serve up a course of anecdotes, *traits*, master-strokes of character, and cut and hack at them until we are weary. Perhaps some of them are even with us. For my own part, as I once said, I like a friend the better for having faults that I can talk about. 'Then,' said Mrs (Montagu), 'you will never cease to be a philanthropist!' Those in question were some of the choice-spirits of the age, not 'fellows of no mark or likelihood'; and we so far did them justice: but it is well that they did not hear what we sometimes said of them. I care little what anyone says of me, particularly behind my back, and in the way of critical and analytical discussion – it is looks of dislike and scorn, that I answer with the worst venom of my pen. The expression of the face wounds me more than the expression of the tongue. If I have in one instance mistaken this expression, or resorted to this remedy where I ought not, I am sorry for it . . . But the face was too fine over which it mantled, and I am too old to have misunderstood it! . . . I sometimes go up to [Montagu's?]; and as often as I do, resolve never to go again. I do not find the old homely welcome. The ghost of friendship meets me at the door, and sits with me all dinner-time. They have got a set of fine notions and new acquaintance. Allusions to past occurrences are thought trivial, nor is it always safe to touch upon more general subjects. M(ontagu) does not begin as he formerly did every five minutes, 'Fawcett used to say,' &c. That topic is something worn. The girls are grown up, and have a thousand accomplishments. I perceive there is a jealousy on both sides. They think I give myself airs, and I fancy the same of them. Every time I am asked, 'If I do not think Mr Washington Irving a very fine writer?' I shall not go again until I receive an invitation for Christmas-day in company with Mr Liston. The only intimacy I never found to flinch or fade was a purely intellectual one. There was none of the cant of candour in it, none of the whine of mawkish sensibility. Our mutual acquaintance were considered merely as objects of conversation and knowledge, not at all of affection. We regarded them no more in our experiments than 'mice in an air-pump': or like malefactors, they were regularly cut down and given over to the dissecting-knife. We spared neither friend nor foe. We sacrificed human infirmities at the shrine of truth. The skeletons of character might be seen, after the juice was extracted, dangling in the air like flies in cobwebs: or they were kept for future inspection in some refined acid. The demonstration was as beautiful as it was new. There is no surfeiting on gall: nothing keeps so well as a decoction of spleen. We grow tired of everything but turning others into ridicule, and congratulating ourselves on their defects.

We take a dislike to our favourite books, after a time, for the same reason. We cannot read the same works for ever. Our honey-moon, even though we wed the Muse, must come to an end; and is followed by indifference, if not by disgust. There are some works, those indeed that produce the most striking effect at first by novelty and boldness of outline, that will not bear reading twice: others of a less extravagant character, and that excite and repay attention by a greater nicety of details, have hardly interest enough to keep alive our continued enthusiasm. The popularity of the most successful writers operates to wean us from them by the cant and fuss that is made about them, by hearing their names everlastingly repeated, and by the number of ignorant and indiscriminate admirers they draw after them: — we as little like to have to drag others from their unmerited obscurity, lest we should be exposed to the charge of affectation and singularity of taste. There is nothing to be said respecting an author that all the world have made up their minds about: it is a thankless as well as hopeless task to recommend one that nobody has ever heard of. To cry up Shakespear as the God of our idolatory seems like a vulgar, national prejudice: to take down a volume of Chaucer, or Spenser, or Beaumont and Fletcher, or Ford, or Marlowe, has very much the look of pedantry and egotism. I confess it makes me hate the very name of Fame and Genius when works like these are 'gone into the wastes of time', while each successive generation of fools is busily employed in reading the trash of the day, and women of fashion gravely join with their waiting-maids in discussing the preference between Paradise Lost and Mr Moore's Loves of the

Angels. I was pleased the other day on going into a shop to ask, 'If they had any of the *Scotch Novels*?' to be told – 'That they have just sent out the last, Sir Andrew Wylie!' – Mr Galt will also be pleased with this answer! The reputation of some books is raw and *unaired*: that of others is worm-eaten and mouldy. Why fix our affections on that which we cannot bring ourselves to have faith in, or which others have long ceased to trouble themselves about? I am half afraid to look into Tom Jones, lest it should not answer my expectations at this time of day; and if it did not, I should certainly be disposed to fling it into the fire, and never look into another novel while I lived. But surely, it may be said, there are some works, that, like nature, can never grow old; and that must always touch the imagination and passions alike! Or there are passages that seem as if we might brood over them all our lives, and not exhaust the sentiments of love and admiration they excite: they become favourites, and we are fond of them to a sort of dotage. Here is one:

> – Sitting in my window
> Printing my thoughts in lawn, I saw a God,
> I thought (but it was you), enter our gates;
> My blood flew out and back again, as fast
> As I had puffed it forth and sucked it in
> Like breath; then was I called away in haste
> To entertain you: never was a man
> Thrust from a sheepcote to a sceptre, raised
> So high in thoughts as I; you left a kiss
> Upon these lips then, which I mean to keep
> From you for ever. I hear you talk
> Far above singing!

A passage like this indeed leaves a taste on the palate like nectar, and we seem in reading it to sit with the Gods at their golden tables: but if we repeat it often in ordinary moods, it loses its flavour, becomes vapid, 'the wine of *poetry* is drank, and but the lees remain'. Or, on the other hand, if we call in the aid of extraordinary circumstances to set it off to advantage, as the reciting it to a friend, or after having our feelings excited by a long walk in some romantic situation, or while we have

> – play with Amaryllis in the shade,
> Or with the tangle of Neaera's hair –

we afterwards miss the accompanying circumstances, and instead of transferring the recollection of them to the favourable side, regret what we have lost, and strive in vain to bring back 'the irrevocable hour' – wondering in some instances how we survive it, and at the melancholy blank that is left behind! The pleasure rises to its height in some moments of calm solitude or intoxicating sympathy, declines ever after, and from the comparison and a conscious falling-off, leaves rather a sense of satiety and irksomeness behind it . . . 'Is it the same in pictures?' I confess it is, with all but those from Titian's hand. I don't know why, but an air breathes from his landscapes, pure, refreshing as if it came from other years; there is a look in his faces that never passes away. I saw one the other day. Amidst the heartless desolation and finery of Fonthill, there is a portfolio of the Dresden Gallery. It opens, and a young female head looks from it; a child, yet woman grown; with an air of rustic innocence and the graces of a princess, her eyes like those of doves, the lips about to open, a smile of pleasure dimpling the whole face, the jewels sparkling in her crisped hair, her youthful shape compressed in a rich antique dress, as the bursting leaves contain the April buds! Why do I not call up this image of gentle sweetness, and place it as a perpetual barrier between mischance and me? – it is because pleasure asks a greater effort of the mind to support it than pain; and we turn, after a little idle dalliance, from what we love to what we hate!

As to my old opinions, I am heartily sick of them. I have reason, for they deceived me sadly. I was taught to think, and I was willing to believe, that genius was not a bawd – that virtue was not a mask – that liberty was not a name – that love had its seat in the human heart. Now I would care little if these words were struck out of my dictionary, or if I had never heard them.

They are become to my ears a mockery and a dream. Instead of patriots and friends of freedom, I see nothing but the tyrant and the slave, the people linked with kings to rivet on the chains of despotism and superstition. I see folly join with knavery, and together make up public spirit and public opinions. I see the insolent Tory, the blind Reformer, the coward Whig! If mankind had wished for what is right, they might have had it long ago. The theory is plain enough; but they are prone to mischief, 'to every good work reprobate'. I have seen all that had been done by the mighty yearnings of the spirit and intellect of men, 'of whom the world was not worthy', and that promised a proud opening to truth and good through the vista of future years, undone by one man, with just glimmering of understanding enough to feel that he was a king, but not to comprehend how he could be king of a free people! I have seen this triumph celebrated by poets, the friends of my youth and the friends of man, but who were carried away by the infuriate tide that, setting in from a throne, bore down every distinction of right reason before it; and I have seen all those who did not join in applauding this insult and outrage on humanity proscribed, hunted down (they and their friends made a by-word of), so that it has become an understood thing that no one can live by his talents and knowledge who is not ready to prostitute those talents and that knowledge to betray his species, and prey upon his fellow-man. 'This was some time a mystery: but the time gives evidence of it.' The echoes of liberty had awakened once more in Spain, and the morning of human hope dawned again: but that dawn has been overcast by the foul breath of bigotry, and those reviving sounds stifled by fresh cries from the time-rent towers of the Inquisition – man yielding (as it is fit he should) first to brute force, but more to the innate perversity and dastard spirit of his own nature, which leaves no room for farther hope or disappointment. And England, that arch-reformer, that heroic deliverer, that mouther about liberty and tool of power, stands gaping by, not feeling the blight and mildew coming over it, nor its very bones crack and turn to a paste under the grasp and circling folds of this new monster, Legitimacy! In private life do we not see hypocrisy, servility, selfishness, folly and impudence succeed, while modesty shrinks from the encounter, and merit is trodden under foot? How often is 'the rose plucked from the forehead of a virtuous love to plant a blister there'! What chance is there of the success of real passion? What certainty of its continuance? Seeing all this as I do, and unravelling the web of human life into its various threads of meanness, spite, cowardice, want of feeling, and want of understanding, of indifference towards others and ignorance of ourselves – seeing custom prevail over all excellence, itself giving way to infamy – mistaken as I have been in my public and private hopes, calculating others from myself, and calculating wrong; always disappointed where I placed most reliance; the dupe of friendship, and the fool of love; have I not reason to hate and to despise myself? Indeed I do; and chiefly for not having hated and despised the world enough.

•

The Duke of Wellington's hostile meeting in Battersea Park

LEWIS MELVILLE AND REGINALD HARGREAVES

It is proverbially difficult in private life to keep a secret which has been communicated to more than two persons. It seems impossible to prevent in public life the oozing out of matters which are discussed between sovereigns and their ministers, provided the matters themselves are looked at from different points of view. George IV had friends apart from his constitutional advisers, and the inferior members of the Duke's administration were not all as reticent as their superiors. Mr George Dawson, one of the Lords of the Treasury, made a speech at Derry, which cost him his place for the moment, but fell like a thunderbolt upon Ireland. Palace gossip complained that the King was coerced by his too-powerful minister, and England and Scotland were agitated with the fear of coming evils. It was at this juncture, in December 1828, that Dr Curtis, formerly head of one of the colleges in Salamanca, but then the titular Roman Catholic Primate in Ireland, wrote to the Duke, and extracted a reply which, with entire disregard of propriety and honour, he hastened to make public. Then came an imprudent communication from Lord Anglesey to the Catholic Association, then a proposal from Mr Peel – not now for the first time made – to resign; and finally such an appeal to the patriotism of his colleague by the Duke, as Robert Peel found it impossible to resist. The results are well known. The King, after a vain attempt to form an administration hostile to the Roman Catholic claims, placed himself, with undisguised reluctance, in the hands of his Cabinet, and on February 4, 1829, the House of Commons was requested in the Speech from the Throne, first to put down the Catholic Association, and then to consider whether the disabilities under which his Majesty's Roman Catholic subjects laboured could be removed 'consistently with the full and permanent security of our establishment in Church and State, with the maintenance of the reformed religion established by law, of the rights and privileges of the bishops and of the clergy of this nation, and of the churches committed to their charge'.

How this announcement was received, and what consequences followed – how the King made one effort more to keep the laws as they were, and failed – these are points of history which all who desire may investigate for themselves. So are the details of the Duke's duel with Lord Winchelsea, one of the great champions of Protestantism in and out of the House of Lords. Lord Winchelsea had taken an active part in October 1828, at a public meeting on Penenden Heath, to protest against Catholic emancipation and to pledge the English people to resist it to the death. He was a subscriber, also, to King's College, in London, towards the building of which the Duke had been a contributor, for the avowed purpose of strengthening the Established Church in the Metropolis. He now withdrew his name from the list of supporters, accompanying that act with a letter to the *Standard* newspaper, in which he violently assailed the Duke's private character. This was carrying political hostility further than the Duke could allow. He obtained from Lord Winchelsea an acknowledgment that the article had been written by him, and then, in a letter, mildly though firmly expressed, requested that the charge in the newspaper should be withdrawn and apologized for. Lord Winchelsea declined to retract and to apologize, and the matter being referred to friends, a hostile meeting was agreed upon. It is a curious feature in this somewhat unfortunate occurrence that, when the moment for the action arrived, it was found that the Duke did not possess a pair of duelling pistols. Considering the length of time which he had spent in the Army, and the habits of military society towards the close of last century, that fact bore incontestable evidence to the conciliatory temper and great discretion of the Duke. Sir Henry Hardinge, therefore, who acted as the Duke's friend, was forced to look for pistols elsewhere, and borrowed them at last – he himself being as unprovided as his principal – from Dr Hume, the medical man who accompanied them to the ground.

The details of this remarkable duel are well known. The combatants met in Battersea Fields, now converted into Battersea Park – the Duke attended by Sir Henry Hardinge, Lord Winchelsea by the Earl of Falmouth – and Lord Winchelsea, having received the Duke's fire, discharged his pistol in the air. A written explanation was then produced by Lord Winchelsea's second, which the Duke declined to receive unless the term 'apology' were introduced into it, and the point being yielded, they separated as they had met, with cold civility. The Duke's opinion respecting the propriety, indeed the necessity, of the course which he followed on the occasion, had undergone no change. 'You speak as a moralist,' he observed, smiling, 'and I assure you that I am no advocate of duelling under ordinary circumstances; but my difference with Lord Winchelsea, considering the cause in which it originated, and the critical position of affairs at the moment, can scarcely be regarded as a private quarrel. He refused to me, being the King's minister,

what every man in or out of office may fairly claim – the right
to change his views under a change of circumstances on a great
public question. He did his best to establish the principle that a
man in my position must be a traitor unless he adhere through
thick and thin to a policy once advocated. His attack upon me
was part of a plan to render the conduct of public affairs
impossible to the King's servants. I did my best to make him
understand the nature of his mistake, and showed him how he
might escape from it. He rejected my advice, and there remained
for me only one means of extorting from him an acknowledgment that he was wrong.'

'But he behaved well on the ground, at all events, he refused
to fire at you.'

'Certainly he did not fire at me; and seeing that such was his
intention, I turned my pistol aside, and fired wide of him; but
that did not make amends for the outrageous charge brought
against me in his letter. It was only the admission that the
charge was outrageous which at all atoned for that; and it
would have been more creditable to him had he made it when
first requested to do so, than at last. He behaved, however, with
great coolness, and was, I am sure continues to be, very sorry
that he allowed his temper to run away with him.'

•

Real hatred

LEO TOLSTOY

This description of 'real hatred' is taken from Tolstoy's account of his
own schooldays.

Yes, it was real hatred – not the hatred we only read about in
novels, which I do not believe in, hatred that is supposed to
find satisfaction in doing some one harm – but the hatred that
fills you with overpowering aversion for a person who, how-

ever, deserves your respect, yet whose hair, his neck, the way he walks, the sound of his voice, his whole person, his every gesture are repulsive to you, and at the same time some unaccountable force draws you to him and compels you to follow his slightest acts with uneasy attention. Such was the feeling I experienced for St-Jérome.

St-Jérome had been with us for eighteen months now. Today when I consider the man in cold blood I find that he was a good Frenchman, but French to the highest degree. He was not stupid, he was tolerably well informed, and he fulfilled his duties towards us conscientiously: but he possessed the distinctive traits of his fellow countrymen which are so different from the Russian character – he was shallow and selfish, vain, domincering and full of ignorant self-conceit. All this I heartily disliked. Needless to say, grandmamma had explained to him her views on corporal punishment and he dared not beat us; but in spite of this he often threatened us, especially me, with the rod, and pronounced the word *fouetter* [to flog] something like *fouatter* in a detestable manner and with an intonation which suggested that it would afford him the greatest pleasure to flog me.

I was not in the least afraid of the physical pain of the punishment – I had never experienced it – but the bare idea of being struck by St-Jérome threw me into paroxysms of suppressed despair and fury.

It had happened that Karl Ivanych in a moment of irritation had personally brought us to heel with a ruler or his braces, but that I can look back upon without the slightest anger. Even at the time I am speaking of (when I was fourteen), if Karl Ivanych had happened to give me a beating I would have taken it unperturbed. I was fond of Karl Ivanych, I remembered him as long as I remembered myself and was accustomed to regard him as one of the family; but St-Jérome was an arrogant self-satisfied man for whom I felt merely the involuntary respect which all *grown-ups* inspired in me. Karl Ivanych was a comical old 'school-usher' whom I loved from the bottom of my heart but whom in my childish comprehension of social standing ranked below us.

St-Jérome, on the other hand, was an educated handsome young dandy, trying to be anyone's equal. Karl Ivanych always scolded and punished us dispassionately; one saw that he considered it a necessary but disagreeable duty. St-Jérome, on the contrary, liked to play the part of lord and master: when he punished us it was plain that he did so rather for his own pleasure than for our good. He was carried away by his own importance. His florid French phrases, which he pronounced with a strong emphasis on the last syllable of every word, with circumflex accents, I found unspeakably obnoxious. When Karl Ivanych got cross he used to say 'play-acting', 'vicket poy', 'Spanish fly' (which he always called '*Spaniard* fly'). St-Jérome called us '*mauvais sujet, vilain garnement*' [bad lot, knave] and so forth – names which offended my self-respect.

Karl Ivanych used to make us kneel in the corner with our faces to the wall and the punishment lay in the physical pain occasioned by such an uncomfortable position. St-Jérome stuck out his chest, made a grandiose gesture with his hand and exclaimed in a theatrical voice: '*A genoux, mauvais sujet!*' ordering us to kneel in front of him and beg his pardon. The punishment lay in the humiliation.

They did not punish me, and no one so much as mentioned what had happened to me, but I could not forget all that I had suffered during those two days – the despair, the shame, the fear and the hatred. Although after that St-Jérome apparently washed his hands of me, and hardly concerned himself with me at all, I could not get into the way of regarding him with indifference. Every time our eyes happened to meet I felt that my look only too plainly expressed my animosity, and I hastened to assume a nonchalant air; but when I fancied that he saw through my pretence I blushed and had to turn away.

In short, it was a terrible trial to me to have anything to do with him.

•

The altar flame goes out: Pushkin's last duel
ERNEST J. SIMMONS

Pushkin is one of Russia's greatest poets. It was his misfortune to have been married to a most vain and beautiful woman, Natalia Goncharova. Because of her the tsar, who cared little for poetry, made Pushkin a Gentleman of the Bedchamber so that the couple could be generally available for court functions and balls. A proud but poor man, Pushkin could not refuse although the post was something of a humiliation for him. As well as the tsar, a Baron D'Anthès had an eye on his wife. The baron was the adopted son of Heeckeren, the Dutch ambassador. It was no help to Pushkin that he trusted his wife. What mattered at court was what people thought, and people thought that Natalia and the baron were having an affair. Pushkin had challenged the baron before, and bloodshed had only just been avoided by the good offices of Pushkin's friends. Tongues wagged the more when D'Anthès married Natalia's sister, for it was said that he had done so only in order to be nearer Natalia herself. Finally the poet could stand it no longer and he wrote Heeckeren an insulting letter, believing him to be the guiding spirit behind much of the conduct of his son. Pushkin also realized that the father's diplomatic position would make it impossible for him to fight the duel, and thus the obligation would rest on D'Anthès. At any rate, the letter could be answered only by a duel, which was precisely what Pushkin desired. Here is an account of the duel and its tragic aftermath.

After sending this letter to Heeckeren Pushkin felt as though he had been relieved of some unbearable pain. The accumulated black bile of weeks of suffering had suddenly been discharged. He was quiet, happy, and at times even jolly. That same day (January 26) A. I. Turgenev saw him twice, and on each occasion he conversed in lively fashion, joked, and laughed. This bright exterior may have been designed to deceive his old friend concerning the true state of affairs. But the peace of a man who has made an important and irrevocable resolution had entered Pushkin's heart. Fate would take care of the rest.

Heeckeren received the insulting letter the day on which it was sent. He was just about to go to Count Stroganov's to dine. According to his own story, he hesitated over the proper measures to take in answering such a vile offense. His official position made it difficult for him to challenge Pushkin, and if he did, in view of the previous challenge to his son, D'Anthès might be regarded as a coward. If he accepted and were killed, then D'Anthès would feel it necessary to avenge him; and if the duel proved fatal to his son, his wife might be left entirely without support. He proceeded to Stroganov for counsel, and the count advised that D'Anthès should make the challenge. This suited Heeckeren. He at once wrote to Pushkin:

Not recognizing either your handwriting or your signature [an insulting falsification], I have had recourse to Vicomte d'Archiac, who brings this letter to you with the request to make known to him whether or not the letter I am answering actually comes from you. Its contents have gone so completely beyond all possible limits that I refuse to answer to all the details of this epistle. You appear to have forgotten that it was you who retracted the challenge which you addressed to Baron George Heeckeren and which was accepted by him. The proof of what I say exists here, written by your hand, and has reposed in the hands of seconds. There remains only to say that Vicomte d'Archiac visits you in order to agree upon a place of meeting with Baron George Heeckeren, and I add that this encounter permits of no delay. Later I will teach you to respect the dignity with which I am clothed and which no conduct on your side must offend.

The letter was approved and also signed by D'Anthès.

When D'Archiac arrived, Pushkin accepted the challenge without even bothering to read Heeckeren's pompous communication. Later in the day D'Archiac wrote Pushkin a note to the effect that he would remain at home until eleven that evening to receive his second; after that hour he would be at a ball given by Countess Razumovskaya.

On this occasion the matter of a second was a troublesome one for Pushkin. He wanted no repetition of the situation connected with his previous challenge. Everything must be kept a secret. If close friends discovered his intentions, they would surely try to prevent the duel. Pushkin was determined that this duel should take place. Certain of his friends as seconds could not be trusted to keep the affair from the knowledge of Zhukovski, Vyazemski, or even from the tsar. And Pushkin was very successful in keeping his secret. Apart from the active figures in the challenge, perhaps only two other people learned of it from him. Alexandra Goncharova knew of the letter to Heeckeren. In his immediate family this loving, sympathetic Cinderella of the household was probably the only one to share his secret, and in her strange relations with Pushkin she had long since learned the virtue of silence. On the evening of the twenty-sixth he visited Princess Vyazemskaya, and perhaps out of sheer habit – she held his confidence in many intimate matters – he entrusted the news to her. However, as though to forestall any chance of intervention, Pushkin had already determined that the duel should be fought as quickly as possible.

On the night of the twenty-sixth, having as yet failed to obtain a second, Pushkin attended the ball at Razumovskaya's. There he met D'Archiac and conversed with him about the difficulty. The attention of Vyazemski was drawn to the pair, and, no doubt thinking some mischief was up, he approached. They quickly broke off their conversation, and Vyazemski was none the wiser. Destiny showed the way, and Pushkin blindly followed. He caught sight of Arthur C. Magenis, an official of the English embassy, whom he valued as an honorable and discreet Englishman. Pushkin now asked him to act as a second. Without definitely accepting, Magenis agreed to talk the matter over with D'Archiac. But D'Archiac refused to discuss the subject with him, since he had not been formally constituted a second. When Magenis sought out Pushkin to report, he had already left for home. Unwilling to visit him at such a late hour, for fear of arousing the suspicions of his wife, Magenis sent him a note at two o'clock in the morning. He refused to be a second, since the possibility of a peaceful settlement had already been precluded. (By rule, the first duty of a second was to try to effect a reconciliation.) Thus the day of the challenge had passed, and Pushkin had failed to obtain a second.

On the morning of the twenty-seventh Pushkin arose at eight o'clock. He drank tea, wrote a bit, and walked about his study in high spirits, singing to himself. This was to be his day of reckoning. At about ten o'clock a letter arrived from D'Archiac. He demanded that Pushkin send him at once a properly accredited second. A sudden fear seized Pushkin that the negotiations would be prolonged and that the news of the intended duel would leak out over the city. All the burning impatience for vengeance behind his calm exterior bursts forth in his answer:

I have no desire to take the loafers of Petersburg into my confidence concerning my family affairs; consequently, I did not agree to any conversation between seconds. I will appear only at the place of meeting. Since it is Mr Heeckeren who has challenged me and is offended, he can choose one [a second] if he feels this necessary; I accept him in advance, even if he be one of his own cavalrymen. As for the hour and the place, I am entirely at his service. According to Russian custom, this is sufficient. Vicomte, I beg you to believe that this is my final word and that there is nothing more for me to answer concerning this affair, and that I shall move only in order to present myself at the place of meeting.

Pushkin, of course, knew perfectly well that his demand was contrary to the rules of the duel. A second of his own choosing was absolutely necessary for legal reasons and those of honor. The letter was simply an impulsive outburst provoked by the exasperating delay and by his own inability to obtain a second. But get one he must.

Whether he met Konstantin Danzas on the street by sheer chance in his search, as is generally asserted, or deliberately selected him, is not positively known. But for various reasons the latter possibility is the more likely. Pushkin probably sent for him. This is the Danzas of the Lyceum days, the fun-loving schoolmate, the 'typographer' of the *Lyceum Sage*. He was now a lieutenant colonel in the army, something of an epicure, careless of life and ambition, but brave, honest, and loyal. Pushkin had seen little of him since their graduation, yet they had never ceased to be warm friends. He turned to him now in this last emergency.

Danzas arrived about noon, and Pushkin received him cheerfully. Closeted in his study, he explained the business. Danzas agreed to be his friend's second and left to obtain the pistols, promising to meet him at an appointed place. Meanwhile, an answer to his letter came from D'Archiac, in which he insisted that Pushkin must find his own second and that no further negotiations would be undertaken until he had done so.

A strange calm descended upon Pushkin as he prepared himself. Some small business had to be concluded. An authoress, A. O. Ishimova, whom he wished to persuade to do some translations of Barry Cornwall for the *Contemporary*, had invited him to call that day. He wrote her a letter with his regrets and sent his copy of Cornwall, indicating the passages to be rendered. Then he washed himself, put on clean linen, donned his great bearskin coat, and departed at one o'clock. No one in the house knew his destination.

Having taken a sleigh, he met Danzas, and together they drove to the French embassy, where D'Archiac lived. On the way Pushkin chatted about simple, everyday matters. At the embassy he presented Danzas to D'Archiac. Then he clearly recited before both witnesses everything that had taken place between him, D'Anthès, and Heeckeren. The reason for sending the insulting letter, Pushkin explained, was that the diplomat and his son had violated their promise to leave his wife in peace; and he read the fatal letter aloud. 'Now the only thing I have to tell you,' he concluded, 'is that if the affair is not settled this very day, the first time I meet Heeckeren, father or son, I will spit in his face.' Then, turning to Danzas, he officially declared him his second and left both witnesses to decide upon the conditions of the duel.

The conditions were quickly drawn up. The duel was to take place at five o'clock that day at a lonely spot near Black River on the outskirts of the city. Pistols were the weapons. The adversaries were to stand five paces from the barriers, which in turn were to be ten paces apart. At a given signal they were to advance, but under no circumstances might they pass the barriers in order to shoot. If there were misses on both sides, the adversaries would fire again under the same conditions.

There was no retreat now. The duel was a sure thing. With the conditions all carefully written out, Danzas hastened to Volf's well-known confectionery shop on the Nevski Prospekt, where he had promised to rejoin Pushkin . . .

Pushkin cared nothing about the conditions which his second showed him. The duel was the thing. After drinking a glass of water or lemonade, he left the confectioner's shop with Danzas at about four o'clock. The meeting was at five. They hired a sleigh and set out towards the Troitski Bridge. The January weather was cold, and a stiff wind blew. Outwardly Pushkin seemed calm; his mind was clear and his conversation cheerful. Dueling was no new experience for him. His courage had been tried on several fields and not found wanting. But this was no ordinary contest arising out of some fancied slight or harsh words in a drunken spree. Fierce resentment, his own honor and that of his wife, and the good opinion of Petersburg society were mingled in the complexity of reasons that drove him to seek a desperate conclusion. The gravity of the cause seemed to portend grave consequences. Yet any deep thoughts that coursed through his brain or any anxiety for his wife and children never came to the surface on this fateful ride.

As they turned into the Palace Quay, Natasha's carriage suddenly approached from the opposite direction. Perhaps she will see him, thought Danzas hopefully. He might tell her of the duel; she would beg him to return home, and all would be saved! The terrible feeling that the great poet might be going to his death had been preying on the second's mind. But Natasha was nearsighted, and Pushkin deliberately turned his face the other way. The two vehicles passed without any sign of recognition from husband or wife. And the little sleigh continued on its destined way.

Groups of Petersburg high society were returning from an afternoon of tobogganing on the hills outside the city. Many of them knew Pushkin and Danzas, and bows were frequently exchanged. Noticing Count I. M. Borkh and his wife in one carriage, Pushkin remarked: 'There is a model pair for you.' Since Danzas seemed to miss his point, he continued: 'Why, the wife lives with the coachman and the husband with the postillion.'

Prince V. D. Golitsyn yelled as he passed: 'Why are you going so late [to the hills]? Everybody is coming home.'

Many of these revelers were well acquainted with the bitter relations between Pushkin and D'Anthès, but none guessed why he was driving outside the city limits at this late hour in the afternoon. By the frozen Neva loomed the forbidding Peter-Paul fortress which was used as a prison.

Pushkin jokingly asked his comrade: 'You are not taking me to the fortress, are you?'

'The road to Black River by way of the fortress is the shortest,' Danzas solemnly answered.

Both parties arrived at the same time. The two seconds conversed briefly and finally settled upon a spot for the duel. It was a short distance from the road and concealed by thick bushes, which would prevent the coachmen from witnessing the fight. The snow was knee-deep, and the seconds, with the help of D'Anthès, trampled down a long narrow lane. Pushkin, shrouded in his bearskin coat, sat on a mound of snow and watched the preparations with apparent indifference. When they had cleared a sufficient space, Danzas asked him if it was satisfactory.

'It is all the same to me; only hurry it,' he impatiently replied.

Twenty paces were measured off, and the seconds used their capotes to indicate the barriers. They began to load the pistols.

'Well, have you finished?' asked Pushkin, growing more and more impatient to begin.

All was ready. The adversaries took up their positions, weapons in hand. Danzas gave the signal to begin by waving his hat. With firm steps the two enemies advanced towards their respective barriers. Pushkin reached his first and raised his pistol. D'Anthès, who had walked only four paces, fired. Pushkin dropped, exclaiming: 'I'm wounded!'

He had fallen on Danzas' capote, his head in the snow and the barrel of the pistol stuck in the snow. Both seconds ran to him, and D'Anthès approached. After several moments of silence Pushkin raised himself on his left elbow and said:

'Wait; I have enough strength to take my shot.'

D'Anthès returned to his post, stood sideways, and covered his breast with his right arm. Danzas gave Pushkin another pistol for the one which had dropped in the snow. Supporting himself on his left elbow, Pushkin took steady aim with a firm right hand. He was a dead shot. He fired, and D'Anthès fell.

'Bravo!' shouted Pushkin, throwing his pistol aside. The duel was ended.

But Pushkin had been seriously wounded. The bullet hit the upper part of the thigh bone where it joins the pelvis, and was deflected deep into the lower abdomen. After firing he collapsed in a half-faint. He quickly recovered, however, and asked D'Archiac:

'Is he killed?'

'No, but he has been wounded in the arm and the breast,' was the reply.

D'Anthès' arm had received Pushkin's shot. The ball had gone through, striking a button and merely bruising the ribs. His protective gesture had no doubt saved his life.

'It is strange,' said Pushkin. 'I thought it would give me pleasure to kill him, but I do not feel that now.'

D'Archiac tried to mutter words of reconciliation, but Pushkin interrupted him:

'In the end it is all the same; if we both recover, we shall try again.' For him there could never be any peace between them.

Pushkin was losing much blood. The coachmen were called, and with their aid a litter of fence poles was constructed. He was carried to the road and placed in the sleigh. They set out, Danzas and D'Archiac on foot and D'Anthès bringing up the rear in his own sleigh. Pushkin suffered much pain but never breathed a word of complaint. After traveling a short distance they met a carriage which had been sent by Heeckeren for just such an occasion. Without saying who sent it, D'Anthès and his second offered it to Pushkin. Danzas accepted, and at the same time refused their proposal to keep his part in the duel a secret.

Pushkin was placed in the carriage and, with Danzas beside him, began the slow, tortuous route back to Petersburg. Pushkin, however, did not appear to suffer much. He chatted with Danzas, joked a bit, and related several anecdotes. The talk concerned duels in general, and he recalled his fight with Zubov in Kishinev. Then he remembered the duel of his friend, Shcherbachev, who had been fatally wounded in the abdomen. As though suddenly sensing the seriousness of his own hurt, Pushkin remarked: 'I'm afraid my wound is the same as Shcherbachev's.'

Before they reached his house Pushkin gave Danzas detailed instructions about what to say to his wife, for he was afraid of alarming her. When they arrived, at six o'clock, Danzas went into Natasha's room and found her with her sister Alexandra.

His sudden appearance surprised Natasha, and she looked at him in fright, as though she expected some bad news. Danzas told her that Pushkin had been wounded in a duel with D'Anthès but not seriously. She rushed to the entrance. Pushkin attempted to quiet her, saying that he was not dangerously hurt and would call for her as soon as he got into bed. Natasha fell in a faint.

Pushkin's old valet carried him in his arms into the house.

'Does it grieve you to have to carry me?' Pushkin asked him.

He was brought into his study, the room he loved best. Clean linen was ordered, and after being undressed he was placed on the divan. Meanwhile, Danzas had run for a doctor . . .

Doctors were hard to find at that hour. Danzas tried several without success, including Arendt, the tsar's physician. He finally discovered Sholts, an obstetrician, who promised to come at once with another doctor. Danzas returned to Pushkin's house, and by seven o'clock Sholts and Dr Zadler arrived. Pushkin asked his wife, Danzas, and Pletnev, who had just come on a visit, to leave the study.

'I feel badly,' he said, giving his hand to Sholts.

The doctors examined the wound, and Zadler left to get some necessary instruments.

'What do you think of the wound?' Pushkin asked Sholts in a clear voice. 'When I was shot I felt a hard blow in the side and a burning pain in the loins; much blood was lost on the road — tell me frankly, how do you find the wound?'

'I cannot hide from you the fact that your wound is dangerous.'

'Tell me — is it fatal?'

'I imagine that this will not be concealed from you long,' replied Sholts. 'But let us hear the opinions of Arendt and Salomon, who have been sent for.'

'I thank you. You have behaved like an honorable man with me.' Pushkin raised his hand to his forehead. 'I must put my house in order.' Then, after several minutes of silence, he said: 'It seems that I am losing a great deal of blood.'

Sholts looked at the wound again and applied a new compress.

'Do you not wish to see some of your close friends?' asked the doctor.

'Farewell, friends!' said Pushkin, glancing around at the books in his study. 'Really, do you think that I have not an hour to live?'

'Oh, no, not that; but I thought it would be pleasant for you to see some of them. Mr Pletnev is here . . .'

'Yes – but I should like Zhukovski. Give me some water; I am nauseated.'

Sholts felt his pulse and found it very weak. Zhukovski was sent for, and Danzas returned. Finally Arendt and Salomon arrived with Zadler at about eight o'clock. Pushkin asked the tsar's physician to tell him exactly what his chances were. He was not afraid of the truth, he said, and then there were certain matters that had to be taken care of if he must expect the worst.

'If that is the case,' replied Arendt after examining him, 'then I must tell you that your wound is very dangerous, and as for your recovery, I have almost no hope.'

Pushkin thanked him. Ice packs were placed on his abdomen, and he was given a cold drink. Arendt said that he had to return and report to the tsar. Pushkin requested him to ask the sovereign not to prosecute his second. Arendt promised and departed. On the way out he said to Danzas: 'It is a vile joke: he will die.'

In the meantime, Spasski, Pushkin's family doctor, came. Pushkin had little faith in him, but now, thoroughly aware of the seriousness of his condition, he asked Spasski not to give his wife any false hopes.

'She is not a dissembler,' he said. 'You know her well. She must learn all. However, do with me what you wish; I agree to everything and am ready for anything.'

Spasski left the room to attend to Natasha, and on his return he told Pushkin that she was quieter.

'Poor thing, she suffers in innocence, and she may suffer still more in the opinion of people,' said her husband.

Then, with extraordinary clarity of mind, which rarely deserted him in the midst of his suffering, he suddenly remembered that he had received an invitation that day to attend the funeral services of Grech's son, who had died from consumption. He asked Spasski to send his regrets. At this point they prevailed upon him to call a priest. The holy father soon arrived, and the last rites of the Church were administered.

The news of the duel and of Pushkin's critical condition had spread throughout the city like wildfire. Friends began to appear – Zhukovski, the Vyazemskis, M. Vielgorski, P. I. Meshcherski, P. A. Valuev, A. I. Turgenev, and aunt Zagryazhskaya. Every time his wife came into the room or even stood at the door, he seemed to sense her presence and asked if she were there. He did not want her to see him suffer.

At midnight Dr Arendt returned from the tsar. He had nothing to say about Pushkin's request concerning Danzas, but there is a tradition that he brought a personal note from Nicholas to the wounded man which read: 'If God does not permit us to see thee any more in this world, I send thee my farewell and this last advice: die a Christian. About thy wife and children do not worry: I will take care of them.'

Touched by the communication, Pushkin is supposed to have strongly desired to keep this letter, but Arendt had been ordered to return it to the tsar. It is very improbable, however, that Nicholas ever sent such a personal letter. There is no doubt that he did entrust a written statement to Arendt himself, and that this was repeated to Pushkin, but the precise nature of its contents will never be known.

Pushkin called for Danzas and dictated to him from memory a list of all his debts for which he had no written record. Then he took a ring from his finger and gave it to his second as a keepsake, and he told Danzas that he wanted no one to avenge him.

In the long hours of the night Pushkin's suffering grew intense. Gangrene had set in, and the pain became unbearable. He ordered a servant to bring him a box from the writing table.

Danzas entered the room just in time to see him concealing a pistol under the bedclothes. Pushkin surrendered the weapon, confessing that his pain was so great that he wished to shoot himself. This extreme suffering continued unabated until seven o'clock on the morning of the twenty-eighth. Pain convulsed him, and he tried to stifle his cries for fear of arousing his wife, who remained in the living room in a prostrate condition. An attempt was made to drain the wound in order to relieve his agony.

After seven o'clock the pain lessened somewhat. He asked for his wife, for Alexandra Goncharova, and for his children, since he wished to bid them farewell. The children entered, half-asleep, and were led up to him. He raised his eyes to each in turn, placed his hand on their heads, and blessed them. With a cry Natasha threw herself on her husband. All in the room wept. Throughout his suffering Pushkin had been most solicitous for her welfare. He did not wish her to remain in the room, but he summoned her on several occasions. Aware of the moral torture she was undergoing, he tried to lighten her burden.

'Be quiet; you are not to blame for this,' he told her. And again: 'Do not reproach yourself for my death; this is a matter which concerned me alone.'

After his family left the room Pushkin's close friends were summoned. Zhukovski kissed his cold, outstretched hand and could say nothing. He pressed Vyazemski's hand and murmured: 'Farewell; be happy.' He embraced A. I. Turgenev and whispered that he loved him. Then he called for his old friend Mme Karamzina. She came soon, and he asked her to bless him, which she did. He kissed her hand, and she left the room in tears. The ever-faithful Elizaveta Khitrovo stormed the house in a frenzy of grief. They tried to keep her out, but she would not be denied a last visit with the poet whose genius she worshiped.

Crowds of admirers stood outside, on the stairs, and in the anteroom. 'Is he better?' 'Is there any hope?' were questions asked on every side. One old man, who kept a shop next to the house, exclaimed in wonderment: 'The Lord my God! Why I remember once how a field marshal died, but it was not like this!' Many of these onlookers – friends, strangers, and even foreigners – wept. What was it that touched them? Zhukovski gave the answer: In general, genius is good. In the worship of genius all people are akin, and when it leaves this earth forever, all lament with the same brotherly grief. Pushkin, in his genius, was not only the property of Russia but of all Europe.

At midday occurred one of those sudden turns for the better which are so illusory in fatal illnesses. Pushkin's condition seemed to improve, and his spirits rose. Hope gripped those at the bedside. After all, doctors were often wrong. But Pushkin himself was not deceived. About two o'clock his friend V. I. Dal arrived, a physician and writer. Pushkin greeted him with a smile and joked faintly. Dal scarcely left his side thereafter and offered him hope which he refused to accept.

'There is no living for me here; I shall die. That is clear, and it must be so!' he declared.

Toward nightfall the pains began again. His fortitude was extraordinary, his complaints few. Dr Arendt had seen death on many battlefields and admitted that he had never encountered such endurance. Leeches were applied to relieve the fever, and ice packs were placed on his head. His thoughts went back to his old Lyceum comrades and his schooldays. If only Pushchin and Malinovski were present, he said, it would be easier for him to die. Several times that night he asked what hour it was. And when Dal told him, he replied:

'How long must I suffer so! Please hurry!'

On the morning of the twenty-ninth the press of people outside became so great that Danzas, fearing a demonstration, requested the authorities to send guards. Pushkin was rapidly growing weaker. He lay motionless with his eyes closed. At about two o'clock he suddenly demanded raspberries. When they were brought he asked that his wife be sent in to serve them. On her knees she fed him with a spoon. Pushkin stroked the head of his beautiful Natasha, murmuring:

'There, there, it is nothing. Thank God, all will be well!'

A peaceful expression came over his face, and his words deceived Natasha. As she went out she said to Spasski: 'You see, he will live; he will not die!'

Zhukovski and Vielgorski stood at the head of his bed and Turgenev by the side. Dal whispered to Zhukovski:

'He is going.'

Once he gave his hand to Dal, and pressing it, said:

'Raise me; come, higher, higher . . . well, come on!' Then, recovering, he continued: 'I dreamt that I was climbing up on top of those bookcases with you, up high . . . and I got dizzy.'

After a little while he again opened his eyes, and grasping Dal's hand, said:

'Well, let us go now, please, and together.'

On his request Dal raised him a bit higher. Suddenly, as if awakening from a sleep, he opened his eyes wide, and his face brightened.

'Life is ended!' he whispered.

'What is ended?' asked Dal, not hearing him clearly.

'Life is ended!' Pushkin repeated audibly and emphatically. 'It is difficult to breathe; I am choking!' These were his last words.

At the moment of death Natasha entered the room. She threw herself on her knees before the body. All her thick chestnut hair fell in disorder about her shoulders. Sobbing, she stretched out her hands to her husband and cried:

'Pushkin, Pushkin, are you living?'

Thus in death, as in life, he was for her 'Pushkin' – only Pushkin, the poet.

When they had all left the room Zhukovski remained, and in the strange silence that ensued he sat for a long time looking at the face of the dead man. His feelings were memorably recorded:

'I never beheld anything in his face like that which I saw during the first few minutes after death. His head was a little bent; the hands, which a few minutes before had moved so convulsively, were now quietly extended, as though resting after hard work. But what his face expressed I am not able to tell in words. For me it was so new and at the same time so familiar! It was neither sleep nor rest! It was not an intellectual expression, always so natural to this face; nor was it even a poetic expression! No! Some profound, wonderful thought played over it, something like a vision, like some complete, deep, gratifying knowledge. While gazing at his face I wished to ask him: "What do you see, friend?" And what would have been his answer if at that moment he could have risen again? These are the moments in our lives which perfectly deserve being called great. At that precise moment it may be said that I saw death itself, divinely mysterious, death without its veil. What a stamp it placed on his face, and how wonderfully death expressed its own and his secret! I swear to you I have never seen on his face an expression of such profound, sublime, and triumphal thought. Of course, such a look had flashed across it before. But it was revealed in its purity only when, in the meeting with death, everything earthly had vanished from his face. Such was the end of our Pushkin.'

•

Mr and Mrs: Lady Bulwer Lytton
and her husband
HUGH KINGSMILL

Sir Edward Bulwer Lytton, later Lord Lytton, was, as the extracts given below show, unhappy in his marriage. Bulwer modelled himself on Byron, and was therefore precluded from being a satisfactory husband, even if his wife had been less difficult than she unquestionably was. 'Their quarrels were followed by reconciliations and apologies,' Lord Lytton writes, 'but each one left a scar behind.' Lady Bulwer resented the time Bulwer gave to his work, and his friendships with other women. In order to touch her husband, and keep him by her side, she used to

*foretell her early death, but the tenderness thus evoked in Sir Bulwer was
in due course converted into exasperation at the non-fulfilment of the
forecast. In 1836 there was a legal separation, and Lady Bulwer spent
the rest of her long life raging against her husband, writing novels about
him, and, on one occasion, as described below, driving him away from the
platform during an election address.*

LEAVING A SCAR BEHIND

(*Narrated by Lady Bulwer Lytton*)

'Upon his asking me with whom I was going to the christening
of Mr Fonblanque's child that night, and I replying, "with Lady
Stepney", he then repeated as fast as he could, a dozen times
running, "My mother calls her that ugly old woman!" He then
called out, "Do you hear me, Madam?" "Of course, I hear
you!" "Then why the—in—don't you answer me?" "I did not
think it required an answer." "D—your soul, Madam!" he
exclaimed, seizing a carving-knife (for we were at dinner, and
he had told the servants to leave the room till he rang), and
rushing at me, cried, "I'll have you to know that whenever I do
you the honour of addressing you, it requires an answer." I
said, "For God's sake, take care what you are about, Edward!"
He then dropped the knife and, springing on me, made his great
teeth meet in my cheek, and the blood spurted over me. The
agony was so great that my screams brought the servants back,
and presently Cresson, the cook, seized him by the collar, but he
broke from him, and seizing one of the footman's hats in the
hall, rushed down Piccadilly.'

'SIR LIAR'

(*From a letter of Lady Bulwer's to A. E. Chalon*)

'Remember that whatever I write to you or to anybody else
about that Infernal Clique and its Triton of the Humbugs, Sir
Liar, is *not* private and confidential but *public* and *diffusive*. In
one of his letters to Messalina Blessington, where he so

paternally and amiably alludes to having been to Brighton while his son was at school there, you must know that his son was *then* with me in Ireland and was not at school for three years after that. How much better his threatening letter to me will read in print, written before I published my first book, in which the following honourable and manly passage occurs: "If you publish that or any other book, Madam, *I will ruin you.* I'll say that you were my mistress, that you drink, you forge. Beware! I have not hitherto crossed your path – woe be to you whenever I do!" Don't you think Messalina Blessington had reason to talk of his noble mind and his deep feeling! . . . When I showed this noble letter to everyone – the only notice I took of it – the monster denied it upon *oath* (so he did being the author of *The New Timon*), and said it was a forgery of mine! but I have got the letter, postmark, frank and all, with all his other abominations of love (? !) and hate, and they shall not be printed but facsimiled.'

FROM LADY BULWER LYTTON'S APPEAL TO THE JUSTICE AND CHARITY OF THE ENGLISH PUBLIC

(1857)

'The ruinous climax of this conspiracy to suppress my only means of subsistence (her novels) necessitates my making ONE more appeal to the candour and conscience of the public . . . Oh! women of England, in your happy homes – wives, mothers, and daughters – how would *you* feel, how would *you* act under similar outrages, if such should befall you? which God forbid! How would *you* like to have had your first child turned out of the house the moment it was born, with the summary announcement from your lord and master that "he would not have your time and attention taken up with any d—d child"? And though in after-years a whole page in a stilted novel (vide *Zanoni*) might be devoted to blowing prismatic bubbles about the "depth and purity of a father's love for his first-born" – as a few natural feelings on *paper* entail neither trouble nor expense, but are, on the contrary, extremely lucrative – I doubt whether this public tribute would not in your hearts, as well as in mine, instead of atoning for have still further lacerated the wound caused by this brutal private fact ... Sir Edward Bulwer Lytton has circled my life with a snare, and crowned it with a curse; my miserable, lonely, laborious, and disinherited existence *he* has made ONE GREAT AGONY, composed of innumerable exquisite infinitesimal tortures ... "But forgiveness?" I hear the word; I acknowledge the strong claim the Redeemer of the world has given it upon *every* erring heart. BUT DOES GOD HIMSELF FORGIVE TILL HIS FORGIVENESS IS ASKED? OR CAN EVEN HE BE APPEASED WITHOUT REPENTANCE AND CESSATION FROM SIN?'

LADY BULWER APPEALS TO THE ELECTORS OF HERTFORD

June 8, 1858

'The moment I drove into the field the mob began to cheer; and even Sir Liar's two powdered flunkeys, and both his postilions, took off their hats and caps, and joined. I instantly alighted, and walked over calmly and deliberately to the hustings, just putting the crowd aside with my fan, and saying, "My good people, make way for your member's wife." They then began to cheer, and cry "Silence for Lady Lytton!" Sir Liar's head fell *literally* as if he had been shot; Mrs Clarke said she *never* saw such a thing in her life; he staggered against the post, and seemed not to have strength to move. I then said, in a loud, calm, and stern voice, "Sir Edward George Earle Bulwer Lytton, as I am not in the habit of stabbing in the back, it is to *you* in the first instance, that I address myself. In the step your cruelty and your meanness have driven me into taking this day, I wish you to hear every word I have to say; refute them if you can; deny them if you dare." Then, turning to the crowd, I said, "Men of Herts! if you have the hearts of men, hear me!" "We will. God bless you! Speak out." Here Sir Liar, with his hands before his face, made a rush from the hustings. The mob began to hiss, and cry "Ah, coward! he's guilty; he dare not face her," which *he* must have had the *pleasure* of hearing, for instead of attending the public breakfast in the Corn Exchange, he bolted from the town, and left them all in the lurch . . . And when I described the manner in which my poor child's young heart had been broken, how she had been slaved to death over her quack of a father's German translations (he not knowing one word of German!), her scanty wardrobe, the wretched house in which she died, the poor boors gave me their tears, which I was more grateful to them for than for all their cheers. After a pause I rewhetted my razor. (Details of her financial distress follow.) "Nevertheless, my good people, don't suppose that I have lightly or without first trying everything made a show of myself here today. Friends and foes have for the last year warned Sir Edward Bulwer Lytton not to drive me to this public exposure, but he preferred parting with his character to his money. Everyone knows that he has plenty of money, and scarcely a shred of character; so that it was all the more generous of him to part today unreservedly with so small a supply." (Roars of laughter.)'

•

An Indian fight

WILLIAM F. 'BUFFALO BILL' CODY

As it was getting very late in the fall, we were compelled to winter at Fort Bridger; and a long, tedious winter it was. There were a great many troops there, and about four hundred of Russell, Majors & Waddell's employees. These men were all organized into militia companies, which were officered by the wagon-masters. Some lived in tents, others in cabins. It was known that our supplies would run short during the winter, and so all the men at the post were put on three-quarter rations to begin with; before long they were reduced to one-half rations, and finally to one-quarter rations. We were forced to kill our poor worn-out cattle for beef. They were actually so poor that we had to prop them up to shoot them down. At last we fell back on the mules, which were killed and served up in good style. Many a poor, unsuspecting government mule passed in his chips that winter in order to keep the soldiers and bull-whackers from starvation.

It was really a serious state of affairs. The wood for the post was obtained from the mountains, but having no longer any cattle or mules to transport it, the men were obliged to haul it themselves. Long lariats were tied to the wagons, and twenty men manning each, they were pulled to and from the mountains. Notwithstanding all these hardships, the men seemed to be contented and to enjoy themselves.

The winter finally passed away, and early in the spring, as soon as we could travel, the civil employeés of the government, with the teamsters and freighters, started for the Missouri river; the Johnson expedition having been abandoned.

On the way down we stopped at Fort Laramie, and there met a supply train bound westward. Of course we all had a square meal once more, consisting of hard tack, bacon, coffee and beans. I can honestly say that I thought it was the best meal I had ever eaten; at least I realized it more than any other, and I think the rest of the party did the same.

On leaving Fort Laramie, Simpson was made brigade wagon-master, and was put in charge of two large trains, with about four hundred extra men, who were bound for Fort Leavenworth. When we came to Ash Hollow, instead of taking the usual trail over to the South Platte, Simpson concluded to follow the North Platte down to its junction with the South Platte. The two trains were travelling about fifteen miles apart, when one morning while Simpson was with the rear train, he told his assistant wagon-master, George Woods and myself to saddle up our mules, as he wanted us to go with him and overtake the head train.

We started off at about eleven o'clock, and had ridden about seven miles when – while we were on a big plateau, back of Cedar Bluffs – we suddenly discovered a band of Indians coming out of the head of a ravine, half a mile distant, and charging down upon us at full speed. I thought that our end had come this time, sure. Simpson, however, took in the situation in a moment, and knowing that it would be impossible to escape by running our played-out mules, he adopted a bolder and much better plan. He jumped from his own mule, and told us to dismount also. He then shot the three animals, and as they fell to the ground he cut their throats to stop their kicking. He then jerked them into the shape of a triangle, and ordered us inside of the barricade.

All this was but the work of a few moments, yet it was not done any too soon, for the Indians had got within three hundred yards of us, and were still advancing, and uttering their demoniacal yells or war-whoops. There were forty of the redskins and only three of us. We were each armed with a Mississippi yager and two Colt's revolvers.

'Get ready for them with your guns, and when they come within fifty yards, aim low, blaze away and bring down your man!'

Such was the quick command of Simpson. The words had hardly escaped from his mouth, when the three yagers almost simultaneously belched forth their contents. We then seized our revolvers and opened a lively fire on the enemy, at short range, which checked their advance. Then we looked over our little barricade to ascertain what effect our fire had produced, and were much gratified at seeing three dead Indians and one horse lying on the ground. Only two or three of the Indians, it seemed, had fire-arms. It must be remembered that in those days every Indian did not own a needle gun or a Winchester rifle, as they now do. Their principal weapons were their bows and arrows.

Seeing that they could not take our little fortification, or drive us from it, they circled around us several times, shooting their arrows at us. One of the arrows struck George Wood in the left shoulder, inflicting only a slight wound, however, and several lodged in the bodies of the dead mules; otherwise they did us no harm.

The Indians finally galloped off to a safe distance, where our bullets could not reach them, and seemed to be holding a council. This was a lucky move for us, for it gave us an opportunity to reload our guns and pistols, and prepare for the next charge of the enemy. During the brief cessation of hostilities, Simpson extracted the arrow from Wood's shoulder, and put an immense quid of tobacco on the wound. Wood was then ready for business again.

The Indians did not give us a very long rest, for with another desperate charge, as if to ride over us, they came dashing towards the mule barricade. We gave them a hot reception from our yagers and revolvers. They could not stand, or understand, the rapidly repeating fire of the revolvers, and we again checked them. They circled around us once more and gave us a few parting shots as they rode off, leaving behind them another dead Indian and a horse.

For two hours afterwards they did not seem to be doing anything but holding a council. We made good use of this time by digging up the ground inside the barricade with our knives and throwing the loose earth around and over the mules, and we soon had a very respectable fortification. We were not troubled any more that day, but during the night the cunning rascals tried to burn us out by setting fire to the prairie. The buffalo grass was so short that the fire did not trouble us much, but the smoke concealed the Indians from our view, and they thought that they could approach close to us without being seen. We were aware of this, and kept a sharp look-out, being prepared all the time to receive them. They finally abandoned the idea of surprising us.

Next morning, bright and early, they gave us one more grand charge, and again we 'stood them off'. They then rode away half a mile or so, and formed a circle around us. Each man dismounted and sat down, as if to wait and starve us out. They had evidently seen the advance train pass on the morning of the previous day, and believed that we belonged to that outfit and were trying to overtake it; they had no idea that another train was on its way after us.

Our hopes of escape from this unpleasant and perilous situation now depended upon the arrival of the rear train, and when we saw that the Indians were going to besiege us instead of renewing their attacks, we felt rather confident of receiving timely assistance. We had expected that the train would be along late in the afternoon of the previous day, and as the morning wore away we were somewhat anxious and uneasy, at its non-arrival.

At last, about ten o'clock, we began to hear in the distance the loud and sharp reports of the big bull-whips, which were handled with great dexterity by the teamsters, and cracked like rifle shots. These were as welcome sounds to us as were the notes of the bag-pipes to the besieged garrison at Lucknow, when the reinforcements were coming up and the pipers were heard playing, 'The Campbells are Coming'. In a few moments we saw the lead or head wagon coming slowly over the ridge, which had concealed the train from our view, and soon the whole outfit made its appearance. The Indians observed the approaching train, and assembling in a group they held a short consultation. They then charged upon us once more, for the last time, and as they turned and dashed away over the prairie, we sent our farewell shots rattling after them. The teamsters, seeing the Indians and hearing the shots, came rushing forward to our assistance, but by the time they reached us the red-skins had almost disappeared from view. The teamsters eagerly asked us a hundred questions concerning our fight, admired our fort and praised our pluck. Simpson's remarkable presence of mind in planning the defense was the general topic of conversation among all the men.

When the teams came up we obtained some water and bandages with which to dress Wood's wound, which had become quite inflamed and painful, and we then put him into one of the wagons. Simpson and myself obtained a remount, bade good-bye to our dead mules which had served us so well, and after collecting the ornaments and other plunder from the dead Indians, we left their bodies and bones to bleach on the prairie. The train moved on again and we had no other adventures, except several exciting buffalo hunts on the South Platte, near Plum Creek.

•

Famous sport: Charles Kingsley and CardinalNewman

SUSAN CHITTY

Book reviewing often inspires accusations of literary 'log-rolling' – writing a favourable review of a book written by a friend or relation regardless of the book's merit. Here Charles Kingsley, author of *Hereward the Wake* and *Westward Ho!*, had sought to do a good turn for his brother-in-law's book. In the course of so doing, however, he made an enemy of none other than Cardinal Newman, as this extract explains.

In January 1864 Kingsley reviewed Volumes VII and VIII of Froude's *History of England* for *Macmillan's Magazine*, no doubt with a view to giving his brother-in-law a 'puff'. The volumes dealt with the Elizabethan period and must have revived in his breast the anti-Popish feelings to which he had given such free rein in *Westward Ho!* for he allowed the following paragraph to slip into his article: 'Truth for its own sake has never been a virtue of the Roman clergy. Father Newman informs us that it need not, and on the whole ought not, to be; that cunning is the weapon which Heaven has given the saints wherewith to withstand the brute male force of the wicked world which marries and is given in marriage.'

The statement to which Kingsley referred was supposed to have been made by Newman in a sermon entitled 'Wisdom and Innocence', published in 1844. What the sermon actually said was that the weapons with which the Church defends herself, prayer, holiness, and innocence, are to the world of physical strength so incomprehensible that it must believe that the Church conquers by craft and hypocrisy. 'The words "craft" and "hypocrisy" are but the versions of "wisdom" and "harmlessness", in the language of the world.'

Newman was not a subscriber to *Macmillan's Magazine*. He was at that time leading a life of seclusion with the Oratorians at Birmingham and, like Kingsley, was far from well. An anonymous well-wisher, however, saw to it that he received a copy of the magazine with the offending passage marked. He wrote a letter of gentle protest to *Macmillan's*, denying that he sought either reparation or even an answer to his letter: 'I do but wish to draw the attention of yourselves, as gentlemen, to a grave and gratuitous slander, with which I feel you will be sorry to find associated a name so eminent as yours.' There followed a lengthy exchange of private letters between the two clergymen and Kingsley printed an apology in the February issue of *Macmillan's*:

> In your last number I made certain allegations against the teaching of Dr John Henry Newman which I thought were justified by a Sermon of his, entitled 'Wisdom and Innocence'. Dr Newman has by letter expressed, in the strongest terms, his denial of the meaning which I have put upon his words. It only remains therefore for me to express my hearty regret at having so seriously mistaken him.

At this point the matter might have rested had not Newman suddenly decided to publish his correspondence with Kingsley with a final section entitled 'Reflections on the Above'. The most significant passage of the 'Reflections', which took the form of a mock-dialogue between the two contenders, ran as follows:

Mr Kingsley exclaims: 'Oh, the chicanery, the wholesale fraud, the vile hypocrisy, the conscience-killing tyranny of Rome! We have not far to seek evidence of it! There's Father Newman to wit; − one living specimen is worth a hundred dead ones. He, a Priest, writing of Priests, tells me that lying is never any harm.'

I interpose: 'You are taking an extraordinary liberty with my name. If I have said this tell me when and where.'

Mr Kingsley replies: 'You said it, Reverend Sir, in a Sermon which you preached when a Protestant, as vicar of St Mary's, and published in 1844, and I could read you a very salutary lecture on the effects which that Sermon had at the time on my opinion of you.'

I make an answer: 'Oh not it seems as a Priest, speaking to Priests, but let us have the passage.'

Mr Kingsley relaxes: 'Do you know, I like your *tone*. From your *tone* I rejoice, greatly rejoice − to be able to believe you did not mean what you said.'

I rejoin: '*Mean* it! I maintain I never *said* it, whether as a Protestant or a Catholic!'

Mr Kingsley replies: 'I waive that point.'

Newman's dialogue was considered 'famous sport' by the periodicals of the day. 'How briskly', wrote the editor of the *Athenaeum*, 'do we gather round a brace of reverend gentlemen when the prize for which they contend is which of the two shall be considered the father of lies.' Even R. H. Hutton of the *Spectator*, a friend and admirer of Kingsley, applauded Newman's wit:

A more opportune Protestant ram for Father Newman's sacrificial knife could scarcely have been found; and the thicket in which he caught himself was, as it were, of his

own choosing, he having rushed headlong into it quite
without malice, but also without proper consideration of
the force and significance of his own word. Mr Kingsley
made a random charge against Father Newman in *Macmillan's Magazine*. The sermon in question certainly contains
no proposition of the kind to which Mr Kingsley alludes.
My Kingsley ought to have said, what is obviously true,
that on examining the sermon no passage will bear any
colourable meaning at all like that he had put upon it.

Thus provoked, Kingsley all too hastily snatched up his pen
and dashed off the pamphlet 'What Then Does Dr Newman
Mean?' 'I am answering Newman now,' Kingsley told a friend,
'and though I give up the charge of conscious dishonesty, I
trust to make him and his admirers sorry that they did not leave
me alone. I have a score of more than twenty years to pay, and
this is an instalment of it.' The person who was made to feel
sorry, however, was not Newman, for the pamphlet was a
disastrous failure. Having already accepted Newman's explanation of the meaning of 'Wisdom and Innocence', Kingsley could
now only appeal to the lowest prejudices of his readers by
showing that no man could be honest who believed in such
things as monks, nuns, miracles, stigmata, the virginity of
Christ's mother and, of course, celibacy.

Kingsley did not wait for Newman's reply to his pamphlet.
One of his periodic 'brain storms' was upon him which, added
to an ulcerated bowel was a cause for real alarm. There is a
panicky little note in Fanny's hand among the Macmillan papers
which runs: 'Sir James Clarke insists that he leaves at once for
Spain. Nothing less will renovate his mind and body.' Froude
was planning to go to Madrid to consult manuscripts for his
History and had invited Kingsley at the last minute to accompany him. Kingsley had accepted with alacrity and even
suggested prolonging the voyage as far as Gibraltar and returning by sea; 'I have always felt that one good sea voyage would
add ten years to my life,' he told Froude. 'Remember that I can

amuse myself in any hedge, with plants and insects and a cigar and that you may leave me anywhere, any long, certain that I shall be busy and happy. I cannot say how the thought of going has put fresh life into me.'

Kingsley left in such a hurry that he did not even stay to conduct the Easter services at Eversley that were so dear to him, but was in Paris to witness strange 'idolatrous' rites in Notre Dame by Good Friday. Apart from these, he declared, 'These Frenchmen are a civilized people. The splendour of this city is beyond all I could have conceived, and the beautiful neatness and completeness of everything delights my eyes.' Nevertheless he did not at first abandon himself to France with quite the enthusiasm with which he had given himself to Germany in 1851. In the intervening thirteen years he had grown more insular, and was inclined to make remarks like, 'The Landes are not unlike Hartford Bridge Flat,' 'Pau is a mixture of Bath and Edinburgh,' and 'Biarritz is just a cross between Bude and Scarborough.' Biarritz took its revenge on him for this last calumny, for he fell ill there and was unable to accompany Froude into Spain. (One wonders whether some embarrassment at his treatment of Spain and the Spaniards in *Westward Ho!* did not also have an inhibiting effect.) He was content instead to gaze at 'the awful Pyranees' from his bedroom window.

In other respects too this Charles Kingsley on holiday was not the one who had humped a knapsack twenty miles a day over the Eifel, but an altogether gentler character who

lounged about on the rocks, watching the grey lizards (I haven't seen any green ones yet) smoking penny Government cigars, which are very good ... and luxuriating in the blessed, blessed feeling of having nothing to do! I start sometimes and turn round guiltily, with the thought surely I ought to be doing something, I have forgotten something, and then feel there is nothing to do even if I wanted.

Sometimes he fell asleep for two hours at a time on the sand.

He was enchanted by the little long-woolled sheep of the Basque peasants and 'the cows you could put under your arm'. Their owners, he told Fanny, 'put brown holland pinafores on their backs, and persuade them, as a great favour to do a little work. But they seem to get so fond of them that the oxen have much the best of the bargain.' He spent much time with the six-year-old daughter of a chemist living opposite and wrote to tell Mary (now twelve years old) 'She knits all her own woollen stockings and we have given her *Mlle. Lili*, and she has learnt it all by heart, and we have great fun making her say it.'

At last he tore himself away from the seashore and made for Pau, 'that beats all cities seen for beauty'. In spite of an internal upset which he put down to the water, 'which is horrible, I suppose from the great age of the town', he now felt strong enough to tackle the Pyrenees and surprise the 'Mossoos, who can't walk you see, and think it an awful thing' by strolling up in an hour to a plateau from which the magnificent Pic du Midi could be viewed. Evidently the locals regarded this as an expedition that required horses and guides. (It did not occur to Kingsley that they might hold this view for economic reasons.) 'A Wellington College boy,' he declared in a letter to Grenville, 'could trot there in three-quarters of an hour.' Nevertheless he did not linger amid the eternal snows, but succumbed quickly to the lure of the warm, lazy, pleasure-loving south.

Near Béziers he had his first glimpse of the Mediterranean.

There it is, – the sacred sea. The sea of all civilization, and almost all history, girdled by the fairest countries in the world; set there that human beings from all its shores might mingle with each other and become humane – the sea of Egypt, of Palestine, of Greece, of Italy, of Byzant; the sea, too, of Algeria, and Carthage, and Cyrene, and fair lands now desolate. Not only to the Christian, nor to the classic scholar, but to every man to whom the progress of his race from barbarism toward humanity is dear, should the Mediterranean Sea be one of the most august and precious objects on this globe; and the first sight of it should inspire reverence and delight as of coming home – home to a rich inheritance in which he has long believed by hearsay, but which he sees at last with his own mortal corporal eyes.

Kingsley's immediate reaction, on seeing the sea, was to get into it. 'We ran literally through it for miles between Agde and Cette.'

At Arles he admitted to admiring the beauty of 'those Arlesiennes whose dark Greek beauty shines, like diamonds set in jet, in the doorways of the quaint old city'. At Nîmes he basked in

the mere pleasure of existence in this sunny South. I am sitting, after a café-au-lait at 8.30 at an open window. Gardens, trees, flowers, fountains, outside, with people sitting out on the benches already, doing nothing but simply live; and more and more will sit there, till late tonight; from 7 to 10 the whole population of this great city will be in the streets, not sunning but mooning themselves, quite orderly and happy, listening to music, and cutting their little jokes, along the boulevards, under the beautiful trees these French have the sense to plant. I understand them now. They are not Visigoths, these fellows. They are the descendants of the old Roman Gauls, the lovers of the town, and therefore they make their towns livable and lovable with trees and fountains, and bring the country into the town, while the Teutons take the town out into the country, and love each man his own garden and park.

Once more he allowed himself a delicious *frisson* at the massive monuments that the 'giant iniquity' had left behind, in this case the Pont du Gard, 'that *thing*, hanging between earth and heaven, the blue sky and green woods showing through its bright yellow arches, and all to carry a cubic yard of water to Nîmes, twenty miles off, for public baths and sham sea-fights in the amphitheatre'. In true Kingsley fashion he could not resist the urge to walk across it: 'one false step and one was one hundred feet below, but that is not my line.' Once more he admired the Roman baths, repeating that with all their sins their creators were the cleanest people the world has ever known. 'The remarkable thing was the Roman ladies' baths in a fountain bursting up out of the rock, where, under colonnades, they walked about, in or out of the water as they chose. All is standing, and could be used tomorrow, if the prudery of the priests allowed it.'

An ecstatic day was spent roaming the countryside round Nîmes. Kingsley wrote home to Fanny,

> I was in a new world; *Genista Anglica*, the prickly needle furze of our commons (rare with us) is in great golden bushes; and box, shrubby thyme, a wonderful blue lily, bee orchis and asters, white, yellow, purple (which don't dry, for the leaves fall off). Then wild rosemary, and twenty more plants I never saw. We went . . . into a natural park of ilex and poplar (two or three sorts,) and watched such butterflies till Case said, 'This is too perfect to last', which frightened me and made me pray; and there was reason; for such a day I never had in all my life of beauty and wonder.

Strangely enough Newman had fallen under the spell of the Mediterranean in just the same way some years earlier. But whereas in Kingsley the voluptuousness of the South induced a sense of guilt that now decided him to turn his steps for home, instead of joining Froude in Barcelona, Newman had stayed on in Sicily after his companion returned to England.

Kingsley now started on the long journey back to Eversley, wearing a beard ('If I am laughed at, I shall cut it off') and carrying striped Basque stockings for the girls and red Basque berets for the boys. As he travelled north he wondered idly 'if Newman is answering again', and whether he was 'returning to fresh trouble and battle'. Fanny in her letters had not announced the appearance of the *Apologia*, but when her husband returned it was to find the completed work on his table, waiting for an answer.

The *Apologia pro Vita sua* was originally published in weekly instalments by Longman. It consisted of three sections, the first two of which were entitled 'Mr Kingsley's Method of Disputation' and 'True Mode of meeting Mr Kingsley'. It was only the third section, the autobiography, that was eventually published in book form. In it Newman explained, with deep and moving sincerity, the whole course of his religious life, and explained, step by step, how he came to the brink of the abyss from which the next logical step must be Rome.

Kingsley could not bring himself to open the *Apologia* for some days after his return. 'I shall not read him yet,' he told Macmillan, 'till I have recovered my temper about Priests – which is not improved by the abominable idolatry which I have seen in France.' This idolatry had undoubtedly banked the fires of battle while he was abroad. From Paris he had written to his curate Frederick Stapleton, 'When I get back, I will tell further volumes as to what I have seen of the Mari-idolatry of France. I could not have conceived such things possible in the 19th Century. But I have seen enough to enable me to give Newman such a *revanche* as will make him wince, if any English common sense is left in him, which I doubt.'

In the end Kingsley decided not to reply to the *Apologia* at all. This could have been because he had at last recognized that theological controversy was not his strong point. He had once explained to a Wesleyan opponent, 'My business is attack, and not defence. If I cannot make myself understood the first time of speaking, I am not likely to do it by any subsequent word splitting explanations.' More likely, it was because he was not well enough to write. As he explained to F. D. Maurice, 'I am come back from France better not but well, and unable to take any mental exertion.' Instead he wrote Macmillan a letter 'which you may show to anyone including Mr Hutton'.

I have determined to take no notice whatever of Dr Newman's apology.

1) I have nothing to retract, apologize for, explain. Deliberately, after 20 years of thought, I struck as hard as I could. Deliberately I shall strike again, if it so pleases me, though not one literary man in England approved. I know too well of what I am talking.

2) I cannot trust – I can only smile at – the autobiography of a man who (beginning with Newman's light, learning, and genius) ends in believing that he believes in the Infallibility of the Church and the Immaculate Conception. If I am to bandy words, it must be with sane persons.

3) I cannot be weak enough, to put myself a second time, by a fresh act of courtesy, into the power of one who, like a treacherous ape, lifts to you meek and suppliant eyes, till he thinks he has you within his reach, and then springs, gibbering and biting, at your face. Newman's conduct in this line has so much disgusted Catholics themselves that I have no wish to remove their just condemnation of his doings.

In the opinion of his contemporaries, Newman undoubtedly emerged victorious from the contest. Few men have had the misfortune to be so utterly and publicly confounded as was Kingsley in 1864. Even the faithful Fanny admitted that 'he had crossed swords with one who was too strong for him'. From that day to this, however, there have been people who have insisted that Kingsley was, after all, not so completely wrong. As recently as 1969 Mr Egner published a book entitled *Apologia Pro Charles Kingsley* in which he pointed out that 'Kingsley courted disaster by gratuitously insulting Newman in the first place, but his accusations themselves were far more substantial than Newman allowed.'

It only remains to inquire why Kingsley permitted himself the 'gratuitous insults' that provoked the *Apologia*. The answer lies, of course, in his strong personal antipathy to Newman, whom he had never met. Newman stood for the things that Kingsley most disliked and feared in himself. He was a Catholic and he was effeminate. We have already seen how close to Roman Catholicism Kingsley had come himself as an undergraduate, a fact that he admitted in the first letter he wrote to Newman in the course of the controversy: 'It was in consequence of that Sermon that I finally shook off the strong influence which your writing exerted on me.' That Kingsley regarded the cat-like Cardinal as effeminate he had freely admitted in a letter written twelve years earlier: 'In him and all that school, there is an element of foppery – even in dress and manner; a fastidious, maundering die-away effeminacy, which is mistaken for purity and refinement; and I confess myself unable to cope with it.' In the same letter he told his correspondent, 'I have been through that terrible question of "Celibacy versus Marriage" once already in my life. And from what I have felt about it myself, and seen others feel, I am convinced that it is the cardinal point.'

In his muddled way Kingsley connected the honouring of the Virgin with this effeminacy. In another letter, written about the same time, he poured scorn on the advice of a Roman Catholic priest who had said to one of his female correspondents, 'Go to the Blessed Virgin. She is a woman, and can understand all a woman's feelings.' 'Ah! thought I. If your head had once rested on a lover's bosom, and your heart known the mighty stay of a *man's* affection, you would have learnt to go now in your sore need, not to the mother, but to the Son – not to the indulgent virgin, but to the strong man, Jesus Christ.'

Looking back one feels that little purpose was served by the spectacle of two such eminent men sparring in public. Certainly the cause of truth did not benefit, though that hardly concerned those at the ringside, as Monckton Milnes admitted at the time of Kingsley's death. 'How preferable was Newman's gentlemanlike falsehood to his [Kingsley's] strepitose fidgety truth.' Newman's career undoubtedly benefited from the contest. As a result of it his star, which had grown increasingly dim since his exile from Oxford, was once more in the ascendant, and indeed one suspects that he may have prolonged the controversy for this purpose. At the Provincial Synod of the Birmingham clergy that summer he was publicly thanked, although he still had many years to wait before he received his cardinal's hat. The one unquestionably good result of the row was that it produced the *Apologia*, one of the major works of nineteenth-century literature. It was Kingsley's misfortune to be the fly embedded in the clear amber of his antagonist's apology.

•

Natural antipathy: Huxley and the parsons
ADRIAN DESMOND AND JAMES MOORE

Following the publication of Darwin's *On the Origin of Species*, one of the great champions of natural selection was T. H. Huxley, a biologist and agnostic who doubted all things that were not immediately open to scientific verification. Chief among the opponents of Darwin's new thinking was the Church of England and its own self-appointed champion, the anatomist Richard Owen. Huxley saw the church and Owen as the irreconcilable enemies of science, and treated them both with equal contempt.

The future protagonists over apes and ancestry were striking up their positions. In March Huxley attacked Owen's human sub-class. Owen could be crucified on the question; Huxley knew it, and he relished a propaganda victory.

Owen had already delivered his stock talk on man and apes at the Royal Institution. Spencer had heard the lecture here in 1855 and called it 'anything but logical'. Now Huxley took a diametrically opposing line on the very same platform. In his own Royal Institution lecture in March 1858 on 'The Special Peculiarities of Man', he compared the baboon, gorilla and man, and emphasized their complete continuity. Man was no further from the gorilla, structurally speaking, than the gorilla was from a baboon. 'It is true that we are in possession of the links between the [baboon] & the Gorilla which we have not between the latter & man – but that does not affect the question. No one will pretend that, of two roads, one is shorter than the other because it has milestones along it.' Huxley was prepared to go even further, wondering just how much he could get away with: 'Nay more I believe that the mental & moral faculties are essentially & fundamentally the same in kind in animals & ourselves.' 'I can,' he continued, 'draw no line of demarcation between an instinctive and a reasonable action.' It left only one conclusion: 'to the very root & foundation of his nature man is one with the rest of the organic world'.

Of course, in another sense, there was an 'infinite' gap. Man had speech, and thus tradition, which made him the 'only organic being in whose very nature is implanted the necessary condition for unlimited progress'. But while Huxley admitted this, there was no disguising his iconoclastic intent; he was rushing towards a collision with Owen. Man was finding his own polemical way into the picture of progress and evolution.

This tit-for-tat antagonism did not augur well for *Natural Selection* being considered dispassionately. But it did ensure the gorilla's central role in the coming debate. With Huxley and Owen at one another's throats, apes and morality were to become explosively intertwined. And Huxley's heterodoxy, fired by hatred for Owen, was easing him towards evolution. Indeed, in his next Royal Institution lecture he tackled the species problem in a more open way than ever before. He still believed that 'the question is at present insoluble'. But if a solution *is* possible, it 'must come from the side of indefinite modifiability'. He had never admitted that much before.

Huxley knew virtually nothing of natural selection, but he did know that Darwin was well into his big book. And he was beginning to realize that he had been wrong-footed. The more he argued that 'Theology & Parsondom' are the 'irreconcilable enemies of Science', the more he sensed that a certain type of evolution could serve his purpose well. Indeed, having squared up to Owen and seen him slip on a pickled brain, he sensed the pay-off in adopting an antagonistic theory of mind and morals. His gladiatorial attitude was at last pushing him Darwin's way.

The young bloods were manoeuvring fast. Fresh from hammering Owen, Huxley now seized on transmutation as a solid wedge to split science from theology. It fitted his campaign for a decently salaried scientific civil service, a new professional authority at the call of an imperial nation. Authority came with a single voice, and any clerical dilution of the message was abhorred.

His parson-hating was at its height. The 'origin of man' question allowed him to skewer 'whatever dares to stand in the way' of a secular biology, and whoever doubts that 'it is as respectable to be modified monkey as modified dirt'. This militance moved him further into Darwin's camp. He did not *want* reconciliation with the clergy. It defeated his object: hence his desire to push the debate in more inflammatory directions. If the orthodox were allowed to prove that Genesis was compatible with geology, then 'I for my part,' he announced that January, 'will undulate to prove that rape, murder & arson are positively enjoined in Exodus . . . Depend upon it there is no safety in trying to put new wine into old bottles.' He wanted to make the old curates uncomfortable and vacate their chairs for his new specialists. A 'new Reformation' was dawning, a fresh revolt against ecclesiastical privilege. 'If I have a wish to live thirty years, it is that I may see the foot of Science on the necks of her enemies.' There spoke a man who had scrimped and struggled, trying to make ends meet, only to see the Cambridge clergy on a thousand pounds a year.

Huxley was swinging into line with Spencer, Chapman and

the *Westminster* crew, most of whom believed in evolution. On other points they were aligning too. Spencer was castigating Richard Owen's rival science of ideal archetypes, of divine thoughts made incarnate, words made flesh in the stately procession of animal life through the ages. 'Terrible bosh', Spencer called this, a sop to the priests, and he set out to make a 'tremendous smash of it'. Simpler, material explanations were called for. Animals had developed gradually, by the piling '*of adaptations upon adaptations*'.

For years Huxley had been lampooning Owen's philosophy, using comparative anatomy. The previous June (1858), at the prestigious Royal Society, he had pulled off a coup, smashing Owen's majestic etherial archetype while Owen himself was in the chair. On the morning Darwin received Wallace's paper, Huxley was regaling Hooker: 'I wonder how Richardus, "Rex anatomicorum" feels this morning. I am deuced seedy but that is just punishment for us "democrats."' Owen was being alienated, squeezed out – the future Darwinian generals were making any accommodation with Darwin's old friend impossible. Hatreds were already festering, a public fight over evolution was assured.

•

Christian hatreds

LEO TOLSTOY

Men of the Christian world, having accepted under the guise of Christian teaching a perversion of it compiled by the Church, which replaced paganism and at first partially satisfied people by its new forms, have ceased with time to believe in this perverted Church Christianity, and have finally reached the point where they are left without any kind of religious understanding of life, or guidance for conduct resulting from it. And since, without this understanding of life and behavioural guidance common, if not to all, then to the majority of people, human life is bound to be irrational and wretched, the longer such an existence continues among the peoples of the Christian world, the more irrational and wretched their life becomes. And today life has reached such a level of irrationality and wretchedness that it cannot continue in its previous forms.

The majority of the working people, deprived of land and consequently of the possibility of enjoying the fruits of their labour, hate the landowners and capitalists who hold them in servitude. The landowners and capitalists, knowing how the workers feel about them, fear and detest them and hold them in servitude with the help of organized governmental force. And as the situation of the workers continues to deteriorate, their dependence on the rich increases; and as the rich grow richer their power, fear and loathing of the working populace increases in equal proportion. And there is the same steady increase in the arming of nation against nation, and the expenditure of more and more of the servile worker's labour on land, water, submarine and air forces, with the sole purpose of preparing for international wholesale slaughter. And this slaughter has been, and is, committed, and cannot but be committed, since all the Christian peoples (not individually, but as nations) are united in States that hate both one another and the other non-Christian States, and are prepared to attack one another at any moment. Moreover, there is not one large Christian State which, following some unnecessary patriotic tradition, does not hold one or several smaller nations in its power against their will, compelling them to participate in the life of the larger State they hate: Austria, Prussia, England, Russia, France, with their subject nations: Poland, Ireland, India, Finland, Caucasus, Algeria, etc. Thus, apart from the growing hatred between poor and rich and between the large nations, there is an ever-increasing hatred between the oppressed nations and their subjugators. What is worst of all is that all this hatred, which is so contrary to human nature (as for instance between the larger nations and between the subjected and the subjugators), is not only not condemned like all other malicious sentiments between people, but, quite the opposite, it is praised and elevated as laudable service and virtue. The hatred of the oppressed workers for the rich and powerful is extolled as love of liberty, brotherhood and equality. The hatred of the Germans for the French and the English, and of the English for the Yankees, and of the Russians for the Japanese, etc., and vice versa, is considered the virtue of patriotism. Likewise, and even more highly valued, is the patriotic hatred the Poles have for the Russians and Prussians, and the Prussians for the Poles and Finns, and vice versa.

That is not all. All these expressions of malice do not even demonstrate that the life of the Christian nations cannot continue in this direction. These evil sentiments could be incidental, temporary phenomena if among these nations there were some kind of religious guiding principle shared by all. But there is not; there is nothing even resembling a common religious guiding principle among the Christian nations of the world. There is the lie of Church religion, and not just one but various different ones contending with one another: the Catholic, Orthodox, Lutheran and so forth; there is the lie of science, again, several different ones contending with one another; there is the lie of politics on both an international and a party level: there are the lies of art, of traditions and customs. There are a great many widely differing lies, but there is no guidance, no moral guidance, stemming from a religious outlook on the world. And the people of the Christian world live like animals, guided in life by nothing other than personal interests and mutual strife; and they are only differentiated from animals by the fact that since time immemorial animals have kept the same stomachs, claws, and fangs, while humanity moves, ever more rapidly, from dirt roads to railroads, from horses to steam, from spoken sermons and letters to the printing press, telegraphs, and telephone; from sailing boats to ocean liners; from side arms to gunpowder, cannons, machine guns, bombs and bomber planes. And life with telegraphs, telephones, electricity, bombs and aeroplanes, and with enmity between all peoples, who are guided not by some unifying spiritual principle but by alienating animal instincts, and who use intellectual faculties for their own pleasure, is becoming more and more futile and calamitous.

•

A pugilistic encounter
ANDRÉ GIDE

I have given up attempting to fathom for what reason my mother sent me to board at school when I was moved into the eighth class. The École Alsacienne objected in principle to the *lycée* sleeping-in system and had no dormitories; but the masters were each of them encouraged to take in a small number of boarders. I was put into Monsieur Vedel's house, though I was no longer in his class. Monsieur Vedel lived in a house that had belonged to Sainte-Beuve, whose bust stood at the end of a passage and filled me with amazement. This peculiar lady saint was presented to my astonished gaze under the aspect of a paternal old gentleman, wearing a tasselled cap on his head. Monsieur Vedel had indeed told us Sainte-Beuve was 'a great critic', but there are limits to a child's credulity.

There were five or six of us boarders, sleeping in two or three rooms. I shared a room on the second floor with a great, apathetic, anaemic creature, incapable of mischief, who was called Roseau. I have no recollection of my other companions. Yes, though; there was the American Barnett, who had filled me with admiration, when he made himself ink moustaches on his first day in class. He wore a loose jersey and wide knickerbockers; his face was pock-marked but extraordinarily open and merry; he looked bursting with joy and health, and a kind of inward turbulence set him constantly inventing such perilous eccentricities that he wore a halo of prestige in my eyes, and positively transported me with enthusiasm. He always wiped his pen in his tangled locks. The first day that he arrived at Vedel's, when we were all at recreation in the little garden behind the house, he planted himself right in the middle, and flinging his shoulders proudly back, there, under all our eyes, he peed upwards into the air. We were thunderstruck by his effrontery.

This little garden was the scene of a pugilistic encounter. As a rule I was placid enough, rather too gentle if anything, and I detested scraps, being convinced no doubt that I should always get the worst of it. And here I must recount an adventure, the recollection of which still rankles in me bitterly. One day as I was going home from school through the Luxembourg, I chanced to take the path that skirts the railings opposite the little garden – not my usual way but hardly any longer. As I went, I crossed a group of boys, belonging, no doubt, to the Communal school, in whose eyes, I suppose, the boys of the École Alsacienne were hateful little aristocrats. I caught their jeers as I passed them, their mocking, spiteful glances, and went on my way looking as dignified as I could; but suddenly the biggest boy of the group left his companions and came up to me. My heart sank into my boots. He planted himself in front of me.

'Wh – wh – at do you want?' I stammered out.

He did not answer but fell into step beside me on my left hand. I kept my eyes fixed on the ground as I walked, but I felt him staring at me, and felt the others staring at me too from behind. I should have liked to sit down.

'There! That's what I want!' he said suddenly and fetched me a great blow in the eye with his fist.

I saw stars and pitched headlong into a horse-chestnut tree, where I fell into the little trench left at its foot for the purpose of watering. I rose covered with mud and confusion. My black eye was very painful, and as I had not yet learnt the wonderful elasticity of the eye, I was convinced it had been put out. As the tears gushed from it, 'That's it,' thought I, 'it's all running away.' But what was still more painful to me was to hear the other boys' laughter and jokes and the congratulations they showered on my aggressor.

For that matter, I no more liked giving blows than receiving them. All the same, at Vedel's there was a great big, carroty-haired boy with a low forehead (his name has fortunately escaped me) who really took too great advantage of my pacifism. Twice, three times, I bore with his sarcasms; but suddenly I was seized with a holy rage; I rushed up and fell upon him while the other boys made a circle round us. He was considerably bigger and stronger than I; but I had the advantage of taking him by surprise; and then, to my own astonishment, my fury multiplied my strength tenfold; I punched him, I shoved him, and in a moment I had him down. Then, when he was on the ground, intoxicated by my triumph, I dragged him after the manner of the ancients, or what I thought was such – I dragged him by the hair of his head until a handful of it came off in my hand. I was even slightly disgusted by my victory on account of all the greasy hair he left in my hand, but I was above all amazed at having been victorious; beforehand it had appeared so utterly impossible, that I must really have lost my head to have attempted it. My success secured me my schoolfellows' respect and allowed me to live in peace for a long time to come. It convinced me too that there are many things that seem impossible only as long as one does not attempt them.

•

A vendetta

MARK TWAIN

During my three days' stay in the town, I woke up every morning with the impression that I was a boy – for in my dreams the faces were all young again, and looked as they had looked in the old times – but I went to bed a hundred years old, every night – for meantime I had been seeing those faces as they are now.

Of course I suffered some surprises, along at first, before I had become adjusted to the changed state of things. I met young ladies who did not seem to have changed at all; but they turned out to be the daughters of the young ladies I had in mind – sometimes their granddaughters. When you are told that a stranger of fifty is a grandmother, there is nothing surprising about it; but if, on the contrary, she is a person whom you knew as a little girl, it seems impossible. You say to yourself, 'How can a little girl be a grandmother?' It takes some little time to accept and realize the fact that while you have been growing old, your friends have not been standing still, in that matter.

I noticed that the greatest changes observable were with the women, not the men. I saw men whom thirty years had changed but slightly; but their wives had grown old. These were good women; it is very wearing to be good.

There was a saddler whom I wished to see; but he was gone. Dead, these many years, they said. Once or twice a day, the saddler used to go tearing down the street, putting on his coat as he went; and then everybody knew a steamboat was coming. Everybody knew, also, that John Stavely was not expecting anybody by the boat – or any freight, either; and Stavely must have known that everybody knew this, still it made no difference to him; he liked to seem to himself to be expecting a hundred thousand tons of saddles by this boat, and so he went on all his life, enjoying being faithfully on hand to receive and receipt for those saddles, in case by any miracle they should come. A malicious Quincy paper used always to refer to this town, in derision as 'Stavely's Landing'. Stavely was one of my earliest admirations; I envied him his rush of imaginary business, and the display he was able to make of it, before strangers, as he went flying down the street struggling with his fluttering coat.

But there was a carpenter who was my chiefest hero. He was a mighty liar, but I did not know that; I believed everything he said. He was a romantic, sentimental, melodramatic fraud, and his bearing impressed me with awe. I vividly remember the first time he took me into his confidence. He was planing a board, and every now and then he would pause and heave a deep sigh; and occasionally mutter broken sentences – confused and not intelligible – but out of their midst an ejaculation sometimes escaped which made me shiver and did me good: one was, 'O God, it is his blood!' I sat on the tool-chest and humbly and shudderingly admired him; for I judged he was full of crime. At last he said in a low voice:

'My little friend, can you keep a secret?'

I eagerly said I could.

'A dark and dreadful one?'

I satisfied him on that point.

'Then I will tell you some passages in my history; for oh, I *must* relieve my burdened soul, or I shall die!'

He cautioned me once more to be 'as silent as the grave', then he told me he was a 'red-handed murderer'. He put down his plane, held his hands out before him, contemplated them sadly, and said:

'Look – with these hands I have taken the lives of thirty human beings!'

The effect which this had upon me was an inspiration to him, and he turned himself loose upon his subject with interest and energy. He left generalizing, and went into details – began with his first murder; described it, told what measures he had taken to avert suspicion; then passed to his second homicide, his third, his fourth and so on. He had always done his murders with a bowie-knife, and he made all my hairs rise by suddenly snatching it out and showing it to me.

At the end of this first *séance* I went home with six of his fearful secrets among my freightage, and found them a great help to my dreams, which had been sluggish for a while back. I sought him again and again, on my Saturday holidays; in fact I spent the summer with him – all of it which was valuable to me. His fascinations never diminished, for he threw something fresh and stirring, in the way of horror, into each successive murder. He always gave names, dates, places – everything. This by and by enabled me to note two things: that he had killed his victims in every quarter of the globe, and that these victims were always named Lynch. The destruction of the Lynches went serenely on, Saturday after Saturday, until the original thirty had multiplied to sixty – and more to be heard from yet; then my curiosity got the better of my timidity, and I asked how it happened that these justly punished persons all bore the same name.

My hero said he had never divulged that dark secret to any living being; but felt that he could trust me, and therefore he would lay bare before me the story of his sad and blighted life. He had loved one 'too fair for earth', and she had reciprocated 'with all the sweet affection of her pure and noble nature'. But he had a rival, a 'base hireling' named Archibald Lynch, who said the girl should be his, or he would 'dye his hands in her heart's best blood'. The carpenter, 'innocent and happy in love's young dream', gave no weight to the threat, but led his 'golden-haired darling to the altar', and there, the two were made one; there also, just as the minister's hands were stretched in blessing over their heads, the fell deed was done – with a knife – and the bride fell a corpse at her husband's feet. And what did the husband do? He plucked forth that knife, and kneeling by the body of his lost one, swore to 'consecrate his life to the extermination of all the human scum that bear the hated name of Lynch'.

That was it. He had been hunting down the Lynches and slaughtering them, from that day to this – twenty years. He had always used that same consecrated knife; with it he had murdered his long array of Lynches, and with it he had left upon the forehead of each victim a peculiar mark – a cross, deeply incised. Said he:

'The cross of the Mysterious Avenger is known in Europe, in America, in China, in Siam, in the Tropics, in the Polar Seas, in the deserts of Asia, in all the earth. Wherever in the uttermost parts of the globe, a Lynch has penetrated, there has the Mysterious Cross been seen, and those who have seen it have shuddered and said, "It is his mark, he has been here." You

have heard of the Mysterious Avenger – look upon him, for
before you stands no less a person! But beware – breathe not a
word to any soul. Be silent, and wait. Some morning this town
will flock aghast to view a gory corpse; on its brow will be seen
the awful sign, and men will tremble and whisper, "He has been
here – it is the Mysterious Avenger's mark!" You will come
here, but I shall have vanished; you will see me no more.'

This ass has been reading the 'Jibbenainosay', no doubt, and
had had his poor romantic head turned by it; but as I had not
yet seen the book then, I took his inventions for truth, and did
not suspect that he was a plagiarist.

However, we had a Lynch living in the town; and the more I
reflected upon his impending doom, the more I could not sleep.
It seemed my plain duty to save him, and a still plainer and
more important duty to get some sleep for myself, so at last I
ventured to go to Mr Lynch and tell him what was about to
happen to him – under strict secrecy. I advised him to 'fly', and
certainly expected him to do it. But he laughed at me; and he
did not stop there; he led me down to the carpenter's shop,
gave the carpenter a jeering and scornful lecture upon his silly
pretensions, slapped his face, made him get down on his knees
and beg – then went off and left me to contemplate the cheap
and pitiful ruin of what, in my eyes, had so lately been a
majestic and incomparable hero. The carpenter blustered,
flourished his knife, and doomed this Lynch in his usual volcanic
style, the size of his fateful words undiminished; but it was all
wasted upon me; he was a hero to me no longer but only a
poor, foolish, exposed humbug. I was ashamed of him, and
ashamed of myself; I took no further interest in him, and never
went to his shop any more. He was a heavy loss to me, for he
was the greatest hero I had ever known. The fellow must have
had some talent; for some of his imaginary murders were so
vividly and dramatically described that I remember all their
details yet.

●

The gentle art of making enemies:
Whistler versus Ruskin

JAMES WHISTLER

James Abbott McNeill Whistler was an American painter who was at the centre of the Aesthetic Movement, and he became as famous for his many feuds as for his ideas of art. Not the least of his feuds – he also 'sparred' with Oscar Wilde – was with John Ruskin, the art critic. In 1877 Ruskin accused him of 'flinging a pot of paint into the public's face', and Whistler sued. The following account of the trial is taken from Whistler's own book, *The Gentle Art of Making Enemies*, in which he also collected a series of his polemical pieces and vituperative letters to the press and other 'friends'.

The Action

In the Court of Exchequer Division on Monday, before Baron Huddleston and a special jury, the case of Whistler *v.* Ruskin came on for hearing. In this action the plaintiff claimed £1,000 damages.

Mr Serjeant Parry and Mr Petheram appeared for the plaintiff; and the Attorney-General and Mr Bowen represented the defendant.

Mr SERJEANT PARRY, in opening the case on behalf of the plaintiff, said that Mr Whistler had followed the profession of an artist for many years, both in this and other countries. Mr Ruskin, as would be probably known to the gentlemen of the jury, held perhaps the highest position in Europe and America as an art critic, and some of his works were, he might say, destined to immortality. He was, in fact, a gentleman of the highest reputation. In the July number of *Fors Clavigera* there appeared passages in which Mr Ruskin criticized what he called 'the modern school', and then followed the paragraph of which

Mr Whistler now complained, and which was. 'For Mr Whistler's own sake, no less than for the protection of the purchaser, Sir Coutts Lindsay ought not to have admitted works into the gallery in which the ill-educated conceit of the artist so nearly approached the aspect of wilful imposture. I have seen, and heard, much of cockney impudence before now; but never expected to hear a coxcomb ask two hundred guineas for flinging a pot of paint in the public's face.' That passage, no doubt, had been read by thousands, and so it had gone forth to the world that Mr Whistler was an ill-educated man, an impostor, a cockney pretender, and an impudent coxcomb.

Mr WHISTLER, cross-examined by the ATTORNEY-GENERAL, said: 'I have sent pictures to the Academy which have not been received. I believe that is the experience of all artists ... The nocturne in black and gold is a night piece, and represents the fireworks at Cremorne.'

'Not a view of Cremorne?'

'If it were called a view of Cremorne, it would certainly bring about nothing but disappointment on the part of the beholders. (*Laughter.*) It is an artistic arrangement. It was marked two hundred guineas.'

'Is not that what we, who are not artists, would call a stiffish price?'

'I think it very likely that that may be so.'

'But artists always give good value for their money, don't they?'

'I am glad to hear that so well established. (*A laugh.*) I do not know Mr Ruskin, or that he holds the view that a picture should only be exhibited when it is finished, when nothing can be done to improve it, but that is a correct view; the arrangement in black and gold was a finished picture, I did not intend to do anything more to it.'

'Now, Mr Whistler. Can you tell me how long it took you to knock off that nocturne?'

... 'I beg your pardon?' (*Laughter.*)

'Oh! I am afraid that I am using a term that applies rather

perhaps to my own work. I should have said, "How long did you take to paint that picture?"'

'Oh, no! permit me, I am too greatly flattered to think that you apply, to work of mine, any term that you are in the habit of using with reference to your own. Let us say then how long did I take to – 'knock off', I think that is it – to knock off that nocturne; well, as well as I remember, about a day.'

'Only a day?'

'Well, I won't be quite positive; I may have still put a few more touches to it the next day if the painting were not dry. I had better say then, that I was two days at work on it.'

'Oh, two days! The labour of two days, then, is that for which you ask two hundred guineas!'

'No; – I ask it for the knowledge of a lifetime.' (*Applause.*)

'You have been told that your pictures exhibit some eccentricities?'

'Yes; often.' (*Laughter.*)

'You send them to the galleries to incite the admiration of the public?'

'That would be such vast absurdity on my part, that I don't think I could.' (*Laughter.*)

'You know that many critics entirely disagree with your views as to these pictures?'

'It would be beyond me to agree with the critics.'

'You don't approve of criticism then?'

'I should not disapprove in any way of technical criticism by a man whose whole life is passed in the practice of the science which he criticizes; but for the opinion of a man whose life is not so passed I would have as little regard as you would, if he expressed an opinion on law.'

'You expect to be criticized?'

'Yes; certainly. And I do not expect to be affected by it, until it becomes a case of this kind. It is not only when criticism is inimical that I object to it, but also when it is incompetent. I hold that none but an artist can be a competent critic.'

'You put your pictures upon the garden wall, Mr Whistler, or hang them on the clothes-line, don't you – to mellow?'

'I do not understand.'

'Do you not put your paintings out into the garden?'

'Oh! I understand now. I thought, at first, that you were perhaps again using a term that you are accustomed to yourself. Yes; I certainly do put the canvases into the garden that they may dry in the open air while I am painting, but I should be sorry to see them "mellowed."'

'Why do you call Mr Irving "an arrangement in black"?' (*Laughter.*)

Mr Baron Huddleston: 'It is the picture, and not Mr Irving, that is the arrangement.'

A discussion ensued as to the inspection of the pictures, and incidentally Baron Huddleston remarked that a critic must be competent to form an opinion, and bold enough to express that opinion in strong terms if necessary.

The Attorney-General complained that no answer was given to a written application by the defendant's solicitors for leave to inspect the pictures which the plaintiff had been called upon to produce at the trial. The Witness replied that Mr Arthur Severn had been to his studio to inspect the paintings, on behalf of the defendant, for the purpose of passing his final judgment upon them and settling that question for ever.

Cross-examination continued: 'What was the subject of the nocturne in blue and silver belonging to Mr Grahame?'

'A moonlight effect on the river near old Battersea Bridge.'

'What has become of the nocturne in black and gold?'

'I believe it is before you.' (*Laughter.*)

The picture called the nocturne in blue and silver was now produced in Court.

'That is Mr Grahame's picture. It represents Battersea Bridge by moonlight.'

Baron Huddleston: 'Which part of the picture is the bridge?' (*Laughter.*)

His Lordship earnestly rebuked those who laughed. And

witness explained to his Lordship the composition of the picture.

'Do you say that this is a correct representation of Battersea Bridge?'

'I did not intend it to be a "correct" portrait of the bridge. It is only a moonlight scene, and the pier in the centre of the picture may not be like the piers at Battersea Bridge as you know them in broad daylight. As to what the picture represents, that depends upon who looks at it. To some persons it may represent all that is intended; to others it may represent nothing.'

'The prevailing colour is blue?'

'Perhaps.'

'Are those figures on the top of the bridge intended for people?'

'They are just what you like.'

'Is that a barge beneath?'

'Yes. I am very much encouraged at your perceiving that. My whole scheme was only to bring about a certain harmony of colour.'

'What is that gold-coloured mark on the right of the picture like a cascade?'

'The "cascade of gold" is a firework.'

A second nocturne in blue and silver was then produced.

WITNESS: 'That represents another moonlight scene on the Thames looking up Battersea Reach. I completed the mass of the picture in one day.'

The Court then adjourned. During the interval the jury visited the Probate Court to view the pictures which had been collected in the Westminster Palace Hotel.

After the Court had re-assembled the 'Nocturne in Black and Gold' was again produced, and Mr WHISTLER was further cross-examined by the ATTORNEY-GENERAL: 'The picture represents a distant view of Cremorne with a falling rocket and other fireworks. It occupied two days, and is a finished picture. The black monogram on the frame was placed in its position with reference to the proper decorative balance of the whole.'

'You have made the study of Art your study of a lifetime. Now, do you think that anybody looking at that picture might fairly come to the conclusion that it had no peculiar beauty?'

'I have strong evidence that Mr Ruskin did come to that conclusion.'

'Do you think it fair that Mr Ruskin should come to that conclusion?'

'What might be fair to Mr Ruskin I cannot answer.'

'Then you mean, Mr Whistler, that the initiated in technical matters might have no difficulty in understanding your work. But do you think now that you could make *me* see the beauty of that picture?'

The witness then paused, and examining attentively the Attorney-General's face and looking at the picture alternately, said, after apparently giving the subject much thought, while the Court waited in silence for his answer:

'No! Do you know I fear it would be as hopeless as for the musician to pour his notes into the ear of a deaf man. (*Laughter*.)

'I offer the picture, which I have conscientiously painted, as being worth two hundred guineas. I have known unbiased people express the opinion that it represents fireworks in a night-scene. I would not complain of any person who might simply take a different view.'

The Court then adjourned.

The ATTORNEY-GENERAL, in resuming his address on behalf of the defendant on Tuesday, said he hoped to convince the jury, before his case closed, that Mr Ruskin's criticism upon the plaintiff's pictures was perfectly fair and *bonâ fide*; and that, however severe it might be, there was nothing that could reasonably be complained of . . . Let them examine the nocturne in blue and silver, said to represent Battersea Bridge. What was that structure in the middle? Was it a telescope or a fire-escape? Was it like Battersea Bridge? What were the figures at the top of the bridge? And if they were horses and carts, how in the name of fortune were they to get off? Now, about these pictures, if the plaintiff's argument was to avail, they must not venture publicly to express an opinion, or they would have brought against them an action for damages.

After all, Critics had their uses. He should like to know what would become of Poetry, of Politics, of Painting, if Critics were to be extinguished? Every Painter struggled to obtain fame.

No artist could obtain fame, except through criticism.

. . . As to these pictures, they could only come to the conclusion that they were strange fantastical conceits not worthy to be called works of Art.

. . . Coming to the libel, the Attorney-General said it had been contended that Mr Ruskin was not justified in interfering with a man's livelihood. But why not? Then it was said, 'Oh! you have ridiculed Mr Whistler's pictures.' If Mr Whistler disliked ridicule, he should not have subjected himself to it by exhibiting publicly such productions. If a man thought a picture was a daub he had a right to say so, without subjecting himself to a risk of an action.

He would not be able to call Mr Ruskin, as he was far too ill to attend: but, if he had been able to appear, he would have given his opinion of Mr Whistler's work in the witness-box.

He had the highest appreciation for *completed pictures*; and he required from an artist that he should possess something more than a few flashes of genius!

Mr Ruskin entertaining those views, it was not wonderful that his attention should be attracted to Mr Whistler's pictures. He subjected the pictures, if they chose, to ridicule and contempt. Then Mr Ruskin spoke of 'the ill-educated conceit of the artist, so nearly approaching the action of imposture'. If his pictures were mere extravagances, how could it redound to the credit of Mr Whistler to send them to the Grosvenor Gallery to be exhibited? Some artistic gentleman from Manchester, Leeds, or Sheffield might perhaps be induced to buy one of the pictures because it was a Whistler, and what Mr Ruskin meant was that he might better have remained in Manchester, Sheffield, or Leeds, with his money in his pocket. It was said that the term 'ill-educated conceit' ought never to have been applied to Mr Whistler, who had devoted the whole of his life to educating himself in Art; but Mr Ruskin's views as to his success did not accord with those of Mr Whistler. The libel complained of said also, 'I never expected to hear a coxcomb ask two hundred guineas for flinging a pot of paint in the public's face.' What was a coxcomb? He had looked the word up, and found that it came from the old idea of the licensed jester who wore a cap and bells with a cock's comb in it, who went about making jests for the amusement of his master and family. If that were the true definition, then Mr Whistler should not complain, because his pictures had afforded a most amusing jest! *He did not know when so much amusement had been afforded to the British Public as by Mr Whistler's pictures.* He had now finished. Mr Ruskin had lived a long life without being attacked, and no one had attempted to control his pen through the medium of a jury. Mr Ruskin said, through him, as his counsel, that he did not retract one syllable of his criticism, believing it was right. Of course, if they found a verdict against Mr Ruskin, he would have to cease writing, but it would be an evil day for Art, in this country, when Mr Ruskin would be prevented from indulging in legitimate and proper criticism, by pointing out what was beautiful and what was not.

Evidence was then called on behalf of the defendant. Witnesses for the defendant, Messrs Edward Burne-Jones, Frith, and Tom Taylor.

Mr EDWARD BURNE-JONES called.

Mr BOWEN, by way of presenting him properly to the consideration of the Court, proceeded to read extracts of eulogistic appreciation of this artist from the defendant's own writings.

The examination of witness then commenced; and in answer to Mr BOWEN, Mr JONES said: 'I am a painter, and have devoted about twenty years to the study. I have painted various works, including the "Days of Creation" and "Venus's Mirror", both of which were exhibited at the Grosvenor Gallery in 1877.

I have also exhibited "Deferentia", "Fides", "St George", and "Sybil". I have one work, "Merlin and Vivian", now being exhibited in Paris. In my opinion complete finish ought to be the object of all artists. A picture ought not to fall short of what has been for ages considered complete finish.'

Mr BOWEN: 'Do you see any art quality in that nocturne, Mr Jones?'

Mr JONES: 'Yes ... I must speak the truth, you know' ... (*Emotion.*)

Mr BOWEN: ... 'Yes. Well, Mr Jones, what quality do you see in it?'

Mr JONES: 'Colour. It has fine colour, and atmosphere.'

Mr BOWEN: 'Ah. Well, do you consider detail and composition essential to a work of Art?'

Mr JONES: 'Most certainly I do.'

Mr BOWEN: 'Then what detail and composition do you find in this nocturne?'

Mr JONES: 'Absolutely none.'

Mr BOWEN: 'Do you think two hundred guineas a large price for that picture?'

Mr JONES: 'Yes. When you think of the amount of earnest work done for a smaller sum.'

Examination continued: 'Does it show the finish of a complete work of art?'

'Not in any sense whatever. The picture representing a night scene on Battersea Bridge is good in colour, but bewildering in form; and it has no composition and detail. A day or a day and a half seems a reasonable time within which to paint it. It shows no finish – it is simply a sketch. The nocturne in black and gold has not the merit of the other two pictures, and it would be impossible to call it a serious work of art. Mr Whistler's picture is only one of the thousand failures to paint night. The picture is not worth two hundred guineas.'

Mr BOWEN here proposed to ask the witness to look at a picture of Titian, in order to show what finish was.

Mr SERJEANT PARRY objected.

Mr BARON HUDDLESTON: 'You will have to prove that it is a Titian.'

Mr BOWEN: 'I shall be able to do that.'

Mr BARON HUDDLESTON: 'That can only be by repute. I do not want to raise a laugh, but there is a well-known case of "an undoubted" Titian being purchased with a view to enabling students and others to find out how to produce his wonderful colours. With that object the picture was rubbed down, and they found a red surface, beneath which they thought was the secret, but on continuing the rubbing they discovered a full-length portrait of George III in uniform!'

The witness was then asked to look at the picture, and he said: 'It is a portrait of Doge Andrea Gritti, and I believe it is a real Titian. It shows finish. It is a very perfect sample of the highest finish of ancient art. The flesh is perfect, the modelling of the face is round and good. That is an "arrangement in flesh and blood"!'

The witness having pointed out the excellences of that portrait, said: 'I think Mr Whistler had great powers at first, which he has not since justified. He has evaded the difficulties of his art, because the difficulty of an artist increases every day of his professional life.'

Cross-examined: 'What is the value of this picture of Titian?' – 'That is a mere accident of the saleroom.'

'Is it worth one thousand guineas?' – 'It would be worth many thousands to me.'

Mr FRITH was then examined: 'I am an R.A.; and have devoted my life to painting. I am a member of the Academies of various countries. I am the author of the "Railway Station", "Derby Day", and "Rake's Progress". I have seen Mr Whistler's pictures, and in my opinion they are not serious works of art. The nocturne in black and gold is not a serious work to me. I cannot see anything of the true representation of water and atmosphere in the painting of "Battersea Bridge". There is a pretty colour which pleases the eye, but there is nothing more. To my thinking, the description of moonlight is not true. The picture is not worth two hundred guineas. Composition and detail are most important matters in a picture. In our profession men of equal merit differ as to the character of a picture. One may blame, while another praises, a work. I have not exhibited at the Grosvenor Gallery. I have read Mr Ruskin's works.'

Mr Frith here got down.

Mr TOM TAYLOR – Poor Law Commissioner, Editor of *Punch*, and so forth – and so forth: 'I am an art critic of long standing. I have been engaged in this capacity by the *Times*, and other journals, for the last twenty years. I edited the "Life of Reynolds", and "Haydon". I have *always* studied art. I have seen these pictures of Mr Whistler's when they were exhibited at the Dudley and the Grosvenor Galleries. The "Nocturne" in black and gold I do not think a serious work of art.' The witness here took from the pockets of his overcoat copies of the *Times*, and, with the permission of the Court, read again with unction his own criticism, to every word of which he said he still adhered. 'All Mr Whistler's work is unfinished. It is sketchy. He, no doubt, possesses artistic qualities, and he has got appreciation of qualities of tone, but he is not complete, and all his works are in the nature of sketching. I have expressed, and still adhere to the opinion, that these pictures only come "one step nearer pictures than a delicately tinted wall-paper".'

This ended the case for the defendant.

Verdict for plaintiff.   Damages one farthing.

•

Fathers and sons: Lord Alfred Douglas and the Marquess of Queensberry
RICHARD ELLMANN

Oscar Wilde's foremost biographer, Richard Ellmann, describes the feud that existed between aristocratic father and son, and which had as its most tragic victim Wilde himself.

He [Lord Alfred] thrived on quarrels, but the others did not. He had an inexhaustible stock of combative energy, but when this had run its course, he was as shiftless as he had been before mistranslating *Salome*. His father was furious over his failure to take his degree, and having no one else to blame, blamed Wilde. Queensberry had other problems as well. His oldest son, Drumlanrig, was private secretary to Lord Rosebery, then Foreign Minister under Gladstone but to be Prime Minister the next year (1894). Queensberry had begun to see homosexuals everywhere, and suspected that Rosebery was influencing Drumlanrig in this direction. Quick to go on the rampage, and hearing that Rosebery was at Bad Homburg, Queensberry followed him there in August 1893 with a dogwhip. The Prince of Wales intervened, and the police asked the Marquess to leave. The next month, on 11 September, Queensberry's second son Percy married the daughter of a Cornish clergyman, an alliance opposed by the atheist Queensberry because he considered the family both too paltry and too pious. To the author of *The Spirit of the Matterhorn* the prospective descendants of such a match could hardly have been less promising. His personal life was also agitating. On 1 November 1893 Queensberry married for the second time. His wife was Ethel Weedon, a young woman of a respectable Eastbourne family, none of whom came to the wedding. She left him immediately, and started proceedings for annulment, alleging 'malformation of the parts of generation' as well as 'frigidity and impotency'. To be called impotent seven years after having been judicially declared adulterous, and after having begotten four children, was a heavy load for this active man of fifty. He contested the suit, claimed the marriage had been consummated, and hired George Lewis to defend him.

Queensberry repeatedly demanded that Douglas stop seeing Wilde. On 8 November 1893, Wilde wrote a long letter to Lady Queensberry about Douglas's disturbed state, which suggests some trepidation in the writer too:

16 Tite Street

Dear Lady Queensberry, You have on more than one occasion consulted me about Bosie. Let me write to you now about him.

Bosie seems to me to be in a very bad state of health. He is sleepless, nervous, and rather hysterical. He seems to me quite altered.

He is doing nothing in town. He translated my French play last August. Since then he has really done nothing intellectual. He seems to me to have lost, for the moment only I trust, his interest even in literature. He does absolutely nothing, and is quite astray in life, and may, unless you or Drumlanrig do something, come to grief of some kind. His life seems to me aimless, unhappy and absurd.

All this is a great grief and disappointment to me, but he is very young, and terribly young in temperament. Why not try and make arrangements of some kind for him to go abroad for four or five months, to the Cromers in Egypt if that could be managed, where he would have new surroundings, proper friends, and a different atmosphere? I think that if he stays in London he will not come to any good, and may spoil his young life irretrievably, quite irretrievably. Of course it will cost money no doubt, but here is the life of one of your sons – a life that should be brilliant and distinguished and charming – going quite astray, being quite ruined.

I like to think myself his greatest friend – he, at any rate, makes me think so – so I write to you quite frankly to ask you to send him abroad to better surroundings. It would save him, I feel sure. At present his life seems to be tragic and pathetic in its foolish aimlessness.

You will not, I know, let him know *anything about my letter*. I can rely on you, I feel sure. Sincerely yours

OSCAR WILDE

In spite of the request for secrecy, Wilde's *De Profundis* makes clear that the idea of Douglas's going to Lord Cromer in Cairo was a stratagem they had hit upon together. Douglas had reason enough to leave the country. There had been a scandal in which he was involved. A letter from Beerbohm to Turner offers a mystifying account:

> Robbie Ross has returned to this country for a few days and of him there have been very great and intimate scandals and almost, if not quite, warrants: slowly he is recovering but has to remain at Davos during his convalescence for fear of a social relapse. I must not disclose anything (nor must you) but I may tell you that a schoolboy with wonderful eyes, Bosie, Bobbie, a furious father, George Lewis, a headmaster (who is now blackmailing Bobbie), St John Wontner [a police solicitor], Calais, Dover, Oscar Browning, Oscar, Dover, Calais, and returned cigarette-cases were some of the ingredients of the dreadful episode . . . The *garçon entretenu*, the schoolboy Helen 'for whom those horned ships were launched, those beautiful mailed men laid low', was the same as him of whom I told you that he had been stolen from Bobbie by Bosie and kept at the Albemarle Hotel: how well I remember passing this place one night with Bobbie and his looking up sadly at the lighted windows and wondering to me behind which of the red curtains lay the desire of his soul.

This highspirited jumble has to be supplemented by a letter from Oscar Browning to Frank Harris. Browning's brother-in-law, the Reverend Biscale Hale Wortham, kept a boys' school, St Laurence, in Bruges. Robert Ross went to visit the Worthams during the holidays. A sixteen-year-old boy named Philip Danney, son of an army colonel, was staying there, and Ross, who had known the boy since he was fourteen, invited him to visit him in London.

While Danney was staying with him, Ross mentioned the fact casually in a letter to Douglas, then at Goring with Wilde.

Douglas responded by rushing to London and bringing the boy back to Goring. 'On Saturday,' says Browning, 'the boy slept with Douglas, on Sunday he slept with Oscar. On Monday he returned to London and slept with a woman at Douglas's expense. On Tuesday he returned to Bruges three days late. His master inquired into the facts and told them to me as I have related them.' Colonel Danney, an officer in the Guards, got wind of the matter, and the police solicitors were consulted. Ross and Douglas had to hotfoot it to Bruges on 15 October 1893 and meet with Wortham. Ross gave back Danney's letters. Wilde's name was kept out of it. 'It is an absolute fabrication,' said Ross. Colonel Danney, according to Browning, 'wished to prosecute the offenders, but the lawyer said, "They will doubtless get two years but your son will get six months."' So the father, unlike Queensberry after him, decided to let the matter drop. Ross's relations heard of the affair, and called him – as he later admitted in open court – 'the disgrace of the family, a social outcast, a son and brother unfit for society of any kind.' It was decided that he should leave the country, and he went to Davos partly for reasons of health but mostly as Beerbohm said to avoid 'a social relapse.' He ventured back to London in the first days of the next year, but life could never be so free and easy again. The tiger had flexed its paws; Wilde would not be warned.

DOUGLAS RETURNED

Children begin by loving their parents. After a time they judge them. Rarely, if ever, do they forgive them.

On their second day back in London, 1 April 1894, Wilde and Douglas were lunching at the Café Royal when the Marquess of Queensberry caught sight of them. He regarded their lunching together as an open defiance of him, a sign that his son had lapsed back into the old vile habits. They invited him to their table, however, and he was momentarily overborne by Wilde's charm. 'I don't wonder you are so fond of him,' he said to Douglas, 'he is a wonderful man.' Then, returning home, he had second thoughts. Taking his paternal duties seriously, he wrote a long letter to his son the same afternoon:

1 April 1894

Alfred, – It is extremely painful for me to have to write to you in the strain I must, but please understand that I decline to receive any answers from you in writing in return. After your recent hysterical impertinent ones I refuse to be annoyed with such, and I decline to read any more letters. If you have anything to say do come here and say it in person. Firstly, am I to understand that, having left Oxford as you did, with discredit to yourself, the reasons of which were fully explained to me by your tutor, you now intend to loaf and loll about and do nothing? All the time you were wasting at Oxford I was put off with an assurance that you were eventually to go into the Civil Service or to the Foreign Office, and then I was put off with an assurance that you were going to the Bar. It appears to me that you intend to do nothing. I utterly decline, however, to just supply you with sufficient funds to enable you to loaf about. You are preparing a wretched future for yourself, and it would be most cruel and wrong for me to encourage you in this. Secondly, I come to the more painful part of this letter – your intimacy with this man Wilde. It must either cease or I will disown you and stop all money supplies. I am not going to try and analyse this intimacy, and I make no charge; but to my mind to pose as a thing is as bad as to be it. With my own eyes I saw you both in the most loathsome and disgusting relationship as expressed by your manner and expression. Never in my experience have I ever seen such a sight as that in your horrible features. No wonder people are talking as they are. Also I now hear on good authority, but this may be false, that his wife is petitioning to divorce him for sodomy and other crimes. Is this true, or do you not know of it? If I thought the actual thing was true, and it became public property, I should be quite justified in shooting him at sight. These christian English cowards and men, as they call themselves, want waking up.

Your disgusted so-called father,
QUEENSBERRY

Douglas's reaction to even mild criticism was ferocious. He had mentioned in a letter to his mother how once, when he had replied to some of her recriminations by a savage letter, he showed it to Wilde, who had torn it up with the words, 'After all, nobody has a right to be unkind to his mother.' But he did not give Wilde a chance to see the telegram which he sent off to his father on 2 April: 'WHAT A FUNNY LITTLE MAN YOU ARE.' Queensberry was in fact an inch shorter than Douglas, being five feet eight inches. He matched his son in *amour propre* and ferocity. When Wilde heard about the telegram, he was dismayed. As he said later, but probably forbore to say at the time, 'it was a telegram of which the commonest street-boy would have been ashamed.' Bosie could not stop doing things Wilde thought unworthy of him. Queensberry's reply on 3 April was vehement, but even in his rage he somewhat mollified his threat to cut Bosie off entirely. Still, it was hardly a letter to bring about better relations:

You impertinent young jackanapes. I request that you will not send such messages to me by telegraph. If you send me any more such telegrams, or come with any impertinence, I will give you the thrashing you deserve. Your only excuse is that you must be crazy. I hear from a man at Oxford that you were thought crazy there, and that accounts for a good deal that has happened. If I catch you again with that man I will make a public scandal in a way you little dream of; it is already a suppressed one. I prefer an open one, and at any rate I shall not be blamed for allowing such a state of

things to go on. Unless this acquaintance ceases I shall
carry out my threat and stop all supplies, and if you are not
going to make any attempt to do something I shall certainly
cut you down to a mere pittance, so you know what to
expect.

It was perhaps now that Wilde protested that he could not be a
catspaw between father and son. Douglas insisted that he had
nothing to do with the quarrel, but seems to have thought it
advisable none the less to take a month's trip to Florence,
arranging for Wilde to follow him there, but surreptitiously.
Wilde left for Paris on 27 April and stayed till 6 May before
going on to Florence. His attempt to keep his presence in
Florence a secret was perhaps doomed to fail, since his height
and dress and theatrical nature made him conspicuous wherever
he went.* One person known to have recognized them was
André Gide, who met them in a café, and felt at first unwelcome.
He was queasy about being seen with them. The relationship of
Wilde and Douglas was notorious, and, in letters to Paul
Valéry, Gide at first did not mention the encounter at all, and
only after some weeks allowed that he had run into Wilde,
accompanied by *'un autre poète d'une génération plus nouvelle'*, as if
Douglas's name would give too much away. If Wilde was
disconcerted, he recovered quickly; he offered Gide two drinks,
four stories and their flat, which they had hired for a month but
used only for two weeks. Gide agreed, then decided to leave it
for a *pensione*.

   Wilde had probably run out of money, and had to return
early in June to London, probably to borrow. He had also
decided to consult a solicitor, and did so in late May.

---

* Wilde seems to have gone alone, at the invitation of Mary Smith Costelloe,
to visit the brother of the novelist Vernon Lee on 19 May: 'It was a great
success. Oscar talked like an angel, and they all fell in love with him, even
Vernon Lee, who had hated him almost as much as he had hated her. He, for
his part, was charmed with her.'

Unfortunately, as he probably heard, George Lewis's services had been pre-empted by Queensberry, so he accepted a suggestion that came from Robert Ross and went to see another solicitor named C. O. Humphreys, a choice that turned out to be a bad one, since homosexuality was quite outside Humphreys' field of knowledge. What advice Wilde got from Humphreys on this occasion is unrecorded, but for the moment he did not try to bind the Marquess over to keep the peace. As for the Marquess, he had seen and heard enough, and made an unannounced visit to Wilde in Tite Street on 30 June. The confrontation was described twice by Wilde, and once by Queensberry, who said in a letter that Wilde had shown him the white feather. The version Wilde gave was quite different. He said he denied all charges and made Queensberry leave the house. This was not quite the whole story. In *De Profundis* Wilde described the scene with more anguish: 'in my library at Tite Street, waving his small hands in the air in epileptic fury, your father, with his bully, or his friend, between us, had stood uttering every foul word his foul mind could think of, and screaming the loathsome threats he afterwards with such cunning carried out.'

Wilde evidently more or less outfaced the Marquess on this occasion, though it does not seem possible that he, as he later said, 'drove him out'; he quailed at the thought of such a scene being played in public. Chance appears to have protected him, for, as he said in *De Profundis*, 'He [went] from restaurant to restaurant looking for me, in order to insult me before the whole world, and in such a manner that if I retaliated I would be ruined, and if I did not retaliate I would be ruined also.' Douglas continued to taunt his father, claiming to be altogether unmoved by the threats which had obviously shaken Wilde. He wrote in early June 1894:

As you return my letters unopened I am obliged to write on a postcard. I write to inform you that I treat your absurd threats with absolute indifference. Ever since your exhibition at O.W.'s house, I have made a point of appearing with him at many public restaurants such as The Berkeley, Willis's Rooms, the Café Royal, etc., and I shall continue to go to any of these places whenever I choose and with whom I choose. I am of age and my own master. You have disowned me at least a dozen times, and have meanly deprived me of money. You have therefore no right over me, either legal or moral. If O.W. was to prosecute you in the Central Criminal Court for libel, you would get seven years' penal servitude for your outrageous libels. Much as I detest you, I am anxious to avoid this for the sake of the family; but if you try to assault me, I shall defend myself with a loaded revolver, which I always carry; and if I shoot you or he shoots you, we shall be completely justified, as we shall be acting in self-defence against a violent and dangerous rough, and I think if you were dead not many people would miss you.

A.D.

The 'ridiculous pistol' that Douglas carried went off in the Berkeley later, according to Wilde, and created further scandal. There was no doubt that Frank Harris was right in warning Wilde about this time that he was putting himself between the bark and the tree. He had become the instrument of Douglas's ancient battle with his father. The dangerous quarrel somehow exhilarated Douglas. In cruel summary Wilde said later, 'The prospect of a battle in which you would be safe delighted you. I never remember you in higher spirits than you were for the rest of that season. Your only disappointment seemed to be that nothing actually happened, and that no further meeting or fracas had taken place between us.' Although it has often been said that Wilde aspired to misfortune, he had no such conscious aim. As for Douglas, he demanded misfortune as the final token of Wilde's love.

Wilde's increasing anxiety is plain. At the beginning of July he approached George Lewis (now Sir George), perhaps within a few days of Queensberry's visit to Tite Street. Lewis's answer was polite but distant, considering how long and intimately Wilde had known him and his family.

7 July 1894

Dear Mr Wilde,

I am in receipt of your note. The information that you have received that I am acting for Lord Queensberry is perfectly correct, and under these circumstances you will see at once that it is impossible for me to offer any opinion about any proceedings you intend to take against him.

Although I cannot act against him, I should not act against you.

Believe me

Yours faithfully

GEORGE M. LEWIS

Wilde now went again to Humphreys, who wrote to Queensberry asking him to retract his libels or risk litigation. The Marquess replied that he had nothing to retract, having made no direct accusation against Wilde, but that he wanted the association with his son to end. There the matter was allowed to rest for the moment.

•

Pistol-packing Marcel Proust

RONALD HAYMAN

It is hard to imagine the author of *Remembrance of Things Past* as given to duelling, but as the biographer and playwright Ronald Hayman explains, Marcel Proust fought at least one duel during his life, and narrowly avoided a second.

It was good to have an excuse for seeing less of the eccentric and irascible Montesquiou, who enjoyed upsetting people with provocative and unpredictable behaviour. Proust was always scrupulously polite when they were together, but once, invited to dinner, he was warned the meal would be served by bats, and once, after sending Montesquiou a pot of hydrangeas, he was told they'd been presented to a grave which thanked him and sent him greetings. This meant they'd been thrown out of the window. Other gestures were less unfriendly. By the end of 1896, Montesquiou, who was preparing an anthology, *Roseaux pensants* (*Thinking Reeds*), had decided to include a story from *Les Plaisirs et les jours*. He sent Proust a four-page letter, and after promising to provide better proof than the length of the letter that he was taking an interest in him, Montesquiou again complained about the mimicry. Proust's conciliatory reply was returned with angry jottings in the margin, like a school essay which had infuriated a teacher. 'Impertinent', 'inadmissible direct criticism', 'bitterness at not having received a written appreciation of his book', 'frivolous', 'insolent and untrue – friendship can descend, not rise'. Montesquiou even awarded a mark: 'The top mark being 20, this bit of epistolary homework does not deserve more than minus fifteen.'

Montesquiou's provocations he always ignored, but he couldn't ignore a public insult thrown at him when *Le Journal* published a belated review of *Les Plaisirs et les jours*, which had been on sale for eight months. The review was signed Raitif de la Bretonne, which was the *nom de plume* of Jean Lorrain, who seldom missed an opportunity to attack Montesquiou, and assumed Proust was one of his lovers. Seven months previously, reviewing Montesquiou's *Les Hortensias bleues*, Lorrain launched his first attack on Proust, who was mentioned in the preface, calling him 'one of those pretty little society boys who have succeeded in becoming pregnant with literature'. The second attack came in the review of 3 February 1897. Not content with denouncing Proust's prose as elegiacally sentimental, precious and pretentious, Lorrain sneered at Proust for extracting a preface from Anatole France. 'For his next book, you can be sure, M. Proust will extricate a preface from the redoubtable

Alphonse Daudet, who will be unable to disoblige either Mme Lemaire or his son Lucien.' The only possible response was a challenge to a duel, and Proust gained prestige by securing as one of his seconds the painter Jean Béraud, a regular at the salons of the comtesse Potocka and Mme Lemaire, and, as the other, Gustave de Borda, who'd won a reputation as a formidable swordsman and was in great demand as a second in society duels.

Through their seconds Proust and Lorrain arranged to fight with pistols on the afternoon of Saturday 6 February at the Tour de Villebon in the Bois de Meudon. Reynaldo and Robert de Flers both came along with their friend. Had the duellists been fighting with swords, they'd have been obliged to go on fighting until one of them was wounded, but the etiquette with pistols was to miss unless the grievance was exceptionally serious. Though he felt nervous, Proust behaved impeccably; he'd have shaken hands with his opponent if his seconds hadn't stopped him. Two shots were fired, but, as Sunday's *Figaro* reported, 'nobody was hurt, and the seconds declared that this meeting ended the dispute'. 'Marcel was brave, frail and charming,' reported de Flers, and Hahn wrote in his diary: 'During these three days Marcel's coolness and firmness, though they seemed incompatible with his nervousness, did not surprise me.'

Of the young men Proust met in Cabourg, his favourite was the nineteen-year-old Marcel Plantevignes, who was introduced to him in the casino by the vicomtesse d'Alton. Marcel Plantevignes was holidaying with his parents; his father was a rich manufacturer of neckties. The young Marcel was soon visiting the older one every evening at the hotel, where he read to the boy from his work in progress, but one day on the promenade, meeting a lady who often teased Proust about his indifference to women, Marcel was warned that Proust was a homosexual. Cutting the woman short, he made his escape, but next time she met Proust she made a joke about his young friend, and soon afterwards he wrote to accuse Marcel

Plantevignes of stabbing him in the back and 'clumsily spoiling a friendship which could have been very beautiful'. The boy couldn't understand how he'd offended Proust, and when his father called at the hotel, wanting to find out, Proust not only refused to explain but challenged him to a duel. When the uncomprehending Camille Plantevignes paid him a second visit, Proust merely told him to find seconds as soon as possible. Reluctantly he approached the vicomte d'Alton, only to be told he'd already agreed to act as Proust's second, but he and the marquis de Pontcharra, who was to be Proust's other second, promised to see whether the dispute could be settled amicably. Though Proust was adamant, his intention was to fire into the air if they fought with pistols, and several days passed before he hinted to d'Alton that his grievance stemmed from a conversation between Marcel and a woman. By paying a third visit to Proust at the hotel, Camille Plantevignes persuaded him to meet Marcel and listen to the boy's explanation.

In cutting the woman short, Marcel had used the words 'I know, I know,' which Proust took to mean Marcel knew he was a homosexual, when all the boy had meant was 'I know what you're going to tell me.' 'But how did you know?' Proust demanded, and Marcel had to answer: 'Because that's what they all say on the promenade.' 'Proust's face, already ivory-coloured, seemed to become even paler, taking on the tint of polished marble.' Sorrowfully and sarcastically he said: 'How charming to arrive somewhere preceded by one's reputation!' He then asked the boy what he believed and what his parents believed. Told none of them believed a word of it, he was conciliatory, but warned Marcel to be more discreet: 'Our friendships, our loves, are made in order to be mocked and vilified. Don't tell anyone you come to see me. Better still, say you aren't seeing me any more.'

•

Rudyard Kipling's Vermont feud

FREDERIC F. VAN DE WATER

In 1892 the author Rudyard Kipling married Caroline Balestier, the sister of his recently deceased American agent, Wolcott Balestier, with whom he had written a novel, *The Naulahka*. For the next four years they lived in her hometown of Brattleboro, Vermont, in a house they built called 'Naulakha' (*sic*). Soon after his arrival in the United States, Kipling fell out with his near neighbour, land-agent and brother-in-law, Beatty Balestier.

'We had a fight over property,' Beatty told me. 'And by God, I still think I was right about it. You know that mowing right across the road from Naulakha? I owned it then. Rud and Caroline wanted it. They were afraid that sometime it would get into other hands and someone would build a house there that would block their view. I told Rud I'd sell it to him for a dollar. I said to him, "Hell, I don't care about the property as a building-site. All I want off it is the hay for my stock. You agree to let me keep on mowing it, and you can have it."'

He stirred in his chair and the rasp of long-cherished grievance came into his voice.

'And then, by God, I heard that Caroline had had a landscape architect up and was going to turn that mowing into a formal garden. I didn't believe it but when they came one night to dinner at my house, I asked about it and Caroline said it was true. I told her, "You're in my house; you're my guest but by Christ, once you've left it, I'll never speak to you again as long as I live."

'We had a quarrel then, Caroline and I. Rud didn't say anything. He just sat there.'

For a full year thereafter, there was grim and boding silence between the households, and Beatty was no longer bailiff to the

Kipling establishment. Thus, his own fortunes sank steadily lower while his brother-in-law's soared. This did not tend to soothe him, but if Kipling had held his tongue, if he had adhered more stoutly to British reticence and had not gossiped about Beatty, he might have lived and died in Dummerston and his heirs might still be occupying the grey-green house above the Connecticut. But he did talk and, since all rural regions are whispering galleries, his opinion of Beatty, not diminished by repetition, found its way back to his kinsman's ears.

Anger, born thirty-nine years earlier, heated and sharpened Beatty's voice as he repeated that disastrous, faintly comic insult.

'Rud stopped in the Brooks House for a drink. Colonel Goodhue was there and they got to talking about me. Rud said, "Oh, Beatty is his own worst enemy. I've been obliged to carry him for the last year; to hold him up by the seat of his breeches."'

Someone snickered and Beatty broke off his recital to glare.

'By God, that's what he said. "By the seat of his breeches."'

That was the precipitating affront, the fulminate that set Balestier on fire when he met Kipling, riding his bicycle on the Pine Hill road.

Beatty's harsh, hooked features had been younger then but the rage that had fired him thirty-nine years before when he had shouted defamation at his brother-in-law still glowed in his voice as he told me the tale.

Kipling had stood and endured it, sucking the cut on his wrist. When Beatty paused for breath, the other had asked, 'Let's get this straight. Do you mean personal violence?'

For a genius, he seemed at that moment to be singularly dense. He testified that Beatty replied, 'Yes, by God. I'll give you one week to retract the lies you've been telling and if you don't, I'll blow out your Goddamned brains.'

So Kipling testified. So it may have been, though those who knew Beatty best doubt it. A gun would have been too impersonal, too chill a weapon for so ardent a lover of physical strife. Beatty insisted in court; he swore to me, that all he ever promised his brother-in-law was the licking of his life.

Mulvaney, or Learoyd of the mighty fists, or Crook O'Neill of the Black Tyrone or any of the many valiant men whom Kipling sired would have dragged his traducer from the buckboard and have done his earnest best to beat his head off. Beatty would have understood and respected such a retort but Kipling answered, 'You will have only yourself to blame for the consequences,' nor could Beatty's further insults drive him beyond that mild counter-attack. It may be that authors of the most virile prose or verse are at heart the meekest of men.

'In the course of the conversation,' Kipling testified, 'he also called me a liar, a coward and a cheat.'

Beatty at last ran out of invective. He turned his team and drove home. Kipling mounted his bicycle and pedalled back to Naulakha to consult his wife.

On the following Sunday, while Beatty was in Brattleboro with his own wife and little daughter, Sheriff Starkey arrested him on a warrant charging 'assault with indecent and opprobrious names and epithets and threatening to kill' against Rudyard Kipling.

These were 'the consequences' to which Kipling had referred darkly. This was a law-revering Britisher's reprisal. It is possible that he hoped merely to frighten his brother-in-law into contrition. It was, as Kipling shortly learned, dangerous to try to frighten Beatty.

The man's insurgent mind ever worked most brilliantly under the drive of strong stimulant – anger, danger, alcohol. In the fell clutch of the 200-pound sheriff, he did not weep or cry aloud. Kipling may have been encouraged by the meekness with which Beatty submitted to arrest. Presently, as the drama that rocked the Balestier family and thrilled the neighbourhood and amused the English-speaking world unfolded, Kipling felt anything but heartened. He had joined battle with an antagonist too crafty, too heavily armoured. Beatty did not mind scandal. He liked publicity. He doted on battle and he had no morbid craving for privacy. In these and in many other matters he was the direct opposite of his brother-in-law. Gradually Beatty's purpose grew plain, even to those less astute than Rudyard Kipling.

There is a saying in this region: 'Give a calf enough rope and he'll hang himself.' Beatty supplied plenty of rope.

Defendant and plaintiff faced each other before William S. Newton, justice of the peace and Brattleboro's town clerk, who had issued the warrant. Kipling was ill at ease. He got no comfort at all from his brother-in-law's calm. Beatty's answer to 'Uncle Billy' Newton's questions were quiet and malign.

Had he threatened the distinguished author, Mr Rudyard Kipling? He had indeed. With a licking.

Had he called Mr Kipling this and that and the other? Beatty admitted this, too, and supplied several epithets Mr Kipling seemed to have forgotten.

Then, Justice Newton would be obliged to hold Mr Balestier, pending further hearing. Mr Balestier, no doubt, was ready to furnish bond. Mr Balestier grinned and shook his head. He was not ready to furnish any such thing.

Did Mr Balestier understand that if bail were not forthcoming, he could be committed to jail? Mr Balestier replied that he understood that entirely. He was ready – he looked even eager – to go to jail. Might he first have a single hour's stay to take his wife and baby home?

The plaintiff was beginning to suffer now. He, too, had a quick and vivid mind. He could see where the apparently safe course he had taken now was leading. He, the rich and famous man, was about to cast his poor, obscure brother-in-law into prison. Kipling had been a newspaperman. He remembered too the animosity he had sown among men of his own former calling. He could imagine the witches' sabbath reporters would delight to hold over such a plight as this into which he had thrust himself. He saw in all its ghastly splendour what Beatty had discerned from the first. Kipling had a bear by the tail.

The plaintiff flourished a cheque-book. He babbled to Justice Newton, 'I shall be glad to supply the defendant's bail myself.'

Uncle Billy did not have to weigh the legal merit of this Gilbert and Sullivan proposal. Beatty promptly refused to accept his brother-in-law's aid. He seemed poisonously willing to go to jail. At length, he was released on his own recognizance to appear in court again the following Tuesday.

The hearing was adjourned. Kipling fled. Beatty drove home in triumph. Local correspondents of the metropolitan newspapers sprinted for the telegraph office.

When the hearing was reopened on Tuesday, Beatty's cup was full and Kipling's misery complete. Reporters had arrived by the dozens. Most of the region, likewise, had declared an impromptu holiday. The whole world was to be audience to the quarrel two men had begun on a hill road and Kipling, who loathed newspaper intrusion upon his affairs, who detested the invasion of his privacy by any save a few sanctified, had brought this down upon his own head. The crowd overwhelmed Uncle Billy's office. The hearing was adjourned to the town hall where it played to a capacity audience.

Meanwhile, between Sunday and Tuesday, there had been turmoil and anguish in the Balestier clan. Beatty alone had remained direly calm. He was having a fine time. He was deaf to all attempts at compromise. Other members of the family were summoned from New York and elsewhere when the feverish efforts of local relatives had failed to get the lid back on the scandal.

Joseph Balestier, Beatty's favourite uncle, came post-haste. He sought out his recalcitrant nephew and pled with him. If he would only apologize to Kipling, even at this late date, the whole ghastly affair might blow over, unpublicized. The warrant could be withdrawn, the thing could be hushed up.

'He said,' Beatty told me, "Beatty, you can't go on with this. You mustn't. Think of your family."

'I told him: "Go on with it? What the hell can I do? Goddamn it, who's arrested, anyway?"'

The hearing was all that Beatty had hoped and Kipling had

feared. C. C. Fitts, state's attorney, conducted the prosecution. Colonel Kittredge Haskins appeared for the plaintiff and Beatty was represented by George B. Hitt. The town hall was packed and in the forefront of the crowd were the maliciously gleeful representatives of the Press.

They enjoyed themselves. So did Beatty. So, too, did the rest of the audience that for four years had endured thwarted curiosity concerning the celebrated and reticent owner of the mansion on the Dummerston hillside. It was a good show and it lasted all day. Justice Newton, contemporary press reports say, 'allowed wide latitude in examination and cross-examination'. He had a good time, too. Everyone had a good time save the wretched plaintiff who sweated and twisted and suffered.

The audience saw reticence ripped from Kipling by Hitt's ironical cross-examination. They were thrilled by the intimate details of the family row that questions dragged forth. They enjoyed the sufferer's occasionally savage retorts.

The direct examination of Kipling by Fitts went smoothly and glibly enough. Kipling gave his version of the hill-road encounter with Beatty. He admitted that Beatty had made no attempt to get out of his buckboard but had waved his arms and shouted a good deal.

The witness also testified that he and Beatty had not spoken for a year before the preceding Wednesday. He insisted that he believed himself in danger of his life at Beatty's hands.

'I honestly think he will kill me sometime,' he told the court, 'if he loses his head again.'

He added that, at the time of the encounter, he thought Beatty insane. He 'was shaking all over, raving mad'.

Hitt's cross-examination lasted the rest of the morning and part of the afternoon. It was caustic, intrusive and excessively painful to a man who wished all of his life, save his published works, to remain inviolably private.

Kipling admitted that his trouble with Beatty had begun in May the year before at a visit to Beatty's home. Thereafter, he testified, he had gone twice to Beatty's farm to see him but had failed both times. He confirmed in substance the 'seat of his breeches' conversation with Colonel Goodhue, but insisted that he had not talked to many persons of his relations with his brother-in-law.

'I suppose,' Hitt sneered, 'that you haven't discussed it with reporters,' and Kipling snapped, 'The assumption is correct.'

Hitt pounced on the allegation that Kipling was supporting Beatty and shook it like a terrier. He forced the witness to admit that for the last year he had not been carrying his brother-in-law. Kipling also testified that the many loans he had made Balestier always had been paid in full. He professed to have held, until the recent assault, only the kindliest feelings for his kinsman. Was it, Hitt asked, out of his kindliness that he had sworn out this warrant? 'No. I have a distinct aversion to being shot at.'

Hitt delved into the more distant past. Under his goading questions, the suffering witness was prodded into an implausibly great-hearted pose. He testified that he had promised the late Wolcott Balestier to watch over and guide his friend's younger brother. He spoke of Beatty, who was four years his junior, as 'this poor boy' and hinted that the prime reason that had moved him to settle in Vermont was concern for Beatty's welfare.

'Then,' Hitt asked, 'taking care of Mr Balestier has been your chief occupation?'

'I have also,' the witness answered, 'written a thing or two.'

Attorney for the defendant then took up the actual encounter of the preceding Wednesday. Kipling reiterated his belief that Beatty had been crazy. He said his kinsman had been 'blue with fury'.

'Not red?' Hitt asked, 'Not white?'

'No,' Kipling replied. 'Blue,' and Justice Newton rapped to check the courtroom titter.

'If you think that Mr Balestier was crazy, why don't you have him examined and adjudged insane?'

'That,' Kipling retorted, 'would probably keep my brains in my head.'

Further grilling brought out that Kipling had seen no gun on Wednesday and that he had never known Beatty to go about armed, but the witness clung to his earlier statement that he had felt himself, during the quarrel, in danger of being shot.

'You shared that quarrel with Mr Balestier, didn't you? You made no attempt to smooth it out?'

The harried witness retorted, 'This was the first time I had had my life threatened. I did not know the precise etiquette in such cases.'

'But you made no acknowledgement that you might just possibly be in the wrong?'

Kipling raised his voice: 'I would not retract a word under threat of death from any living man.'

At last the ordeal was over. The hearing ended. Beatty was held in $400 bail for the September Grand Jury. He was bound over in $400 more to keep the peace. Technically, the victory was Kipling's. He found small ground for satisfaction. The worst was not yet.

The comic feud brightened the pages of the American Press. It was featured, twisted into all manner of shapes, served up with a variety of sauces. The newspapermen were not merciful. One reported the hearing under a by-line 'By Terrence Mulvaney'. Even the Brattleboro *Reformer* published inept parody, beginning,

> 'What's that a-loping down the lane?' said the copper-
>   ready-made.
> 'It's Rudyard, running for his life,' the first selectman said.
> 'Who's pawing up the dust behind?' said the copper-
>   ready-made.
> 'It's Beatty, seeking Brother-in-Law,' the first selectman
>   said.

Heretofore, Kipling had been pestered. The seclusion he longed for had been marred, but most of the earlier intruders had been pilgrims, approaching with awe and worship the threshold of the Master. Now all was changed. The spotlight was on him and the world was laughing. It was no comfort to feel that he had turned that bitter radiance on himself.

Even in his study at Naulakha, more fiercely guarded than ever before, he could hear that enduring, distant, galling mirth. Where once an occasional reporter had tried to see him, a dozen now haunted his gates. A group of Brattleboro worthies came as a deputation to assure him he had the sympathy and the support of all the best people in the region, but he thought they stifled mirth while they said it.

Beatty and the newspapermen liked each other. He drank and yarned and roistered with them. He took some of them fishing. He and they enjoyed themselves. He knew that, despite the outcome of the hearing, he actually had won.

His diabolical mind, once the sheriff had arrested him, had laid hold upon a plan of vengeance more blighting, more comically scathing than any physical assault. And the end of his triumph was yet a long way off. The case would come before the Grand Jury. Perhaps Beatty would be indicted. He hoped most earnestly that he would be, for if he were, Kipling still raw and bleeding from his last ordeal would have to appear as a witness not once but twice more. Beatty had solid ground for his vindictive glee.

The Grand Jury was to meet in September. In August the Kiplings left Vermont for ever. Theirs was the haste of headlong flight. They took only their most personal belongings with them. They sailed from Hoboken, 2 September, on the liner *Lahn*.

'I expect to come back,' Kipling told reporters coldly, 'when I get ready. I haven't the least idea when that will be.'

'He never has come back to Vermont. He never will while I'm alive,' Beatty told me almost forty years later.

The Kiplings returned to New York in February 1899. Newspapers said they planned to reopen their Vermont home in the spring. The eminent and reputable of Brattleboro and Dummerston hailed the news with solemn joy. They set about preparing a round robin to Kipling, urging him to come and live among them once more. This promised, among other things, a reception and a dinner of state upon his arrival. It is questionable whether the recluse author or his vengeful brother-in-law regarded this proposal with the greatest horror.

'By God,' Beatty told me, 'I wasn't going to let him come back into my country again. It would have blackened my face. I'd have had to get out myself.'

He chuckled. The fiendish expedient still had a pleasant flavour.

'He didn't come back, because I scared him off again. I knew Rud's weakness. He'd had a hell of a time on the witness-stand. I knew he'd run if he thought he'd have to appear in court again.'

New York papers for 12 February 1899 announced that Beatty Balestier was bringing action for $50,000 damages against Rudyard Kipling for 'malicious persecution, false arrest and defamation of character'.

The World said Beatty had come to New York to institute the suit. *The Times* said he would arrive in Manhattan in a few days. Actually no suit ever was brought at all. There was scant ground on which such an action might stand. It was the hollowest of bluffs, but it worked. The Kiplings stayed away from Vermont. After the author's own grave illness in New York and the death of his elder daughter, Josephine, they went back to England never to set foot on American soil again. Matthew Howard, their coachman, who had been left as caretaker at Naulakha, made a special trip across the Atlantic to take his employers some cherished keepsakes from their Vermont home, among them an oil-portrait of the dead daughter.

Kipling visited Canada in 1906. That was his nearest subsequent approach to his first home. He found in the dominion, so his autobiography says, 'Safety, Law, Honour, Obedience', and on the other side of the line 'frank, brutal decivilization'. In the framing of this judgement, Beatty no doubt had his share. By then Naulakha had been sold to Miss Mary Cabot.

Indian draperies that Caroline Kipling first hung still adorn the mansion's windows. The stranded ark watches Wantastiquet and Brattleboro's far roofs and the long vista of the Connecticut valley down which its builder and first owner fled.

In the once carefully guarded study still stands the desk on which Kipling wrote much of his best work, and on which he carved the legend his Greek galley slave scratched on his oar: 'Oft was I weary as I toiled at thee.' Caroline Kipling sent back orders from England that this carving should be erased before the place was sold. No one knows why.

Over the mantel is the text that Lockwood Kipling carved for his son: 'For the night cometh when no man can work.' That night has come for both the principals in a childish, serio-comic feud. Only a few months after Rudyard Kipling's ashes were laid in Westminster Abbey, Beatty Balestier followed his kinsman and enduring enemy up a straighter and steeper way than the Pine Hill road.

●

An even better hater
JAMES AGATE

I am a good lover, but an even better hater. I have an unparalleled zest for the most moderate of dislikes. I mislike – to put it no more strongly – a great many women and nearly all men, with a special aversion for the type of man adored by women, mincing-mouthed, luxuriant-polled *genre coiffeur*. I mislike the purist who claims that one language should be enough for any writer and secretly begrudges Caesar his dying Latinism; and I mislike all those honest folk who insist upon taking you at the foot of the letter instead of at the top, or at least half-way down. I dislike all aldermen, mayors, beadles, janitors, pew-openers, the whole bag of officialdom; all sham repentances and most sincere ones; all those to whom the night brings counsel, the *oncle à succession*, and the pliant inheritor; the little ninny who

insists that the *Moonlight Sonata* is by Mendelssohn. I have a
contempt for the Christian who looks down upon the Jew, the
white man who animadverts against the black. I have a horror
of the Freemason in his cups; of the players of solo-whist; of the
actor with pretensions towards edification claiming to raddle his
face that ultimately fewer women may raddle theirs, who 'asks a
blessing' on his Hamlet. I hate the commonplaces of the train,
the street, and the market. I abhor the belly of the successful
man and the swelling paunch of the Justice. But my particular
loathing is reserved for the unknowledgeable fool who says in
his heart: 'These things are not within my experience; therefore
they cannot be true.'

What a plague is *ennui*! To have been everywhere, seen
everything, done everything, to have used up the senses and let
slip the supreme boon, is of all moral diseases the last incurable.
To be tired of oneself and one's proficiencies, of the feel of a
cue, the whip of a club, the way the racquet comes up in the
hand, the touch of reins, the 'handle' of your favourite book, all
this is indeed to find the world flat and unprofitable. Nothing
remains, says your quack, but to take his pills. Nothing remains
but to follow my system of exercises, declares some frock-
coated Hercules.

There is, we have often been told, valour and to spare in the
spirit's triumph over the flesh. But there is ignominy, I take it,
in a romantic spleen giving way to massage, in a fine frenzy of
melancholy yielding before a system of exercises. I know nothing
more humiliating than this o'ercrowing of the spirit by the
body. Hamlet himself had done less girding at the world if he
had not been, as Gertrude remarks, in poor condition. That the
world is out of joint is an old cry. It belongs to our day to
advertise all that loss of figure and excess of flesh, baldness and
superfluous hair, tuberculosis, which are our inheritance. I have
never been able to fathom the delicate arts' survival of these
natural shocks. Greatly in their favour has been the lateness of
the world's discovery of electricity, X-rays, Swedish drills, and
physical exercises. A Musset the picture of rude health, a

Chopin who should dedicate a nocturne to Mr Sandow, a Shelley *père de famille*, a Baudelaire who should be an inside right to be reckoned with – these were unthinkable. But it is no part of the story-teller's business to argue, especially when he is not too sure of his case, and you could shatter mine by citing the admirable boxer who is responsible for *Pelléas and Mélisande*.

•

How I became an anti-Semite
ADOLF HITLER

Once, as I was strolling through the Inner City, I suddenly encountered an apparition in a black caftan and black hair locks. Is this a Jew? was my first thought.

For, to be sure, they had not looked like that in Linz. I observed the man furtively and cautiously, but the longer I stared at this foreign face, scrutinizing feature for feature, the more my first question assumed a new form:

Is this a German?

As always in such cases, I now began to try to relieve my doubts by books. For a few hellers I bought the first anti-Semitic pamphlets of my life. Unfortunately, they all proceeded from the supposition that in principle the reader knew or even understood the Jewish question to a certain degree. Besides, the tone for the most part was such that doubts again arose in me, due in part to the dull and amazingly unscientific arguments favouring the thesis.

I relapsed for weeks at a time, once even for months.

The whole thing seemed to me so monstrous, the accusations so boundless, that, tormented by the fear of doing injustice, I again became anxious and uncertain.

Yet I could no longer very well doubt that the objects of my study were not Germans of a special religion, but a people in themselves; for since I had begun to concern myself with this question and to take cognisance of the Jews, Vienna appeared to me in a different light than before. Wherever I went, I began to see Jews, and the more I saw, the more sharply they became distinguished in my eyes from the rest of humanity. Particularly the Inner City and the districts north of the Danube Canal swarmed with a people which even outwardly had lost all resemblance to Germans.

And whatever doubts I may still have nourished were finally dispelled by the attitude of a portion of the Jews themselves.

Among them there was a great movement, quite extensive in Vienna, which came out sharply in confirmation of the national character of the Jews: this was the *Zionists*.

It looked, to be sure, as though only a part of the Jews approved this viewpoint, while the great majority condemned and inwardly rejected such a formulation. But when examined more closely, this appearance dissolved itself into an unsavoury vapour of pretexts advanced for mere reasons of expedience, not to say lies. For the so-called liberal Jews did not reject the Zionists as non-Jews, but only as Jews with an impractical, perhaps even dangerous, way of publicly avowing their Jewishness.

Intrinsically they remained unalterably of one piece.

In a short time this apparent struggle between Zionistic and liberal Jews disgusted me; for it was false through and through, founded on lies and scarcely in keeping with the moral elevation and purity always claimed by this people.

The cleanliness of this people, moral and otherwise, I must say, is a point in itself. By their very exterior you could tell that these were no lovers of water, and, to your distress, you often knew it with your eyes closed. Later I often grew sick to my stomach from the smell of these caftan-wearers. Added to this, there was their unclean dress and their generally unheroic appearance.

All this could scarcely be called very attractive; but it became positively repulsive when, in addition to their physical uncleanliness, you discovered the moral stains on this 'chosen people'.

In a short time I was made more thoughtful than ever by my

slowly rising insight into the type of activity carried on by the Jews in certain fields.

Was there any form of filth or profligacy, particularly in cultural life, without at least one Jew involved in it?

If you cut even cautiously into such an abscess, you found, like a maggot in a rotting body, often dazzled by the sudden light – a kike!

What had to be reckoned heavily against the Jews in my eyes was when I became acquainted with their activity in the press, art, literature, and the theatre. All the unctuous reassurances helped little or nothing. It sufficed to look at a billboard, to study the names of the men behind the horrible trash they advertised, to make you hard for a long time to come. This was pestilence, spiritual pestilence, worse than the Black Death of olden times, and the people was being infected with it! It goes without saying that the lower the intellectual level of one of these art manufacturers, the more unlimited his fertility will be, and the scoundrel ends up like a garbage separator, splashing his filth in the face of humanity. And bear in mind that there is no limit to their number; bear in mind that for one Goethe Nature easily can foist on the world ten thousand of these scribblers who poison men's souls like germ-carriers of the worst sort, on their fellow men.

It was terrible, but not to be overlooked, that precisely the Jew, in tremendous numbers, seemed chosen by Nature for this shameful calling.

Is this why the Jews are called the 'chosen people'?

I now began to examine carefully the names of all the creators of unclean products in public artistic life. The result was less and less favourable for my previous attitude towards the Jews. Regardless how my sentiment might resist, my reason was forced to draw its conclusions.

The fact that nine tenths of all literary filth, artistic trash, and theatrical idiocy can be set to the account of a people, constituting hardly one hundredth of all the country's inhabitants, could simply not be talked away; it was the plain truth.

And I now began to examine my beloved 'world press' from this point of view.

And the deeper I probed, the more the object of my former admiration shrivelled. The style became more and more unbearable; I could not help rejecting the content as inwardly shallow and banal; the objectivity of exposition now seemed to me more akin to lies than honest truth; and the writers were – Jews.

A thousand things which I had hardly seen before now struck my notice, and others, which had previously given me food for thought, I now learned to grasp and understand.

I now saw the liberal attitude of this press in a different light; the lofty tone in which it answered attacks and its method of killing them with silence now revealed itself to me as a trick as clever as it was treacherous; the transfigured raptures of their theatrical critics were always directed at Jewish writers, and their disapproval never struck anyone but Germans. The gentle pin-pricks against Wilhelm II revealed its methods by their persistency, and so did its commendation of French culture and civilization. The trashy content of the short story now appeared to me as outright indecency, and in the language I detected the accents of a foreign people; the sense of the whole thing was so obviously hostile to Germanism that this could only have been intentional.

But who had an interest in this?

Was all this a mere accident?

Gradually I became uncertain.

The development was accelerated by insights which I gained into a number of other matters. I am referring to the general view of ethics and morals which was quite openly exhibited by a large part of the Jews, and the practical application of which could be seen.

Here again the streets proved an object lesson of a sort which was sometimes positively evil.

The relation of the Jews to prostitution and, even more, to the white-slave traffic, could be studied in Vienna as perhaps in no other city of Western Europe, with the possible exception of the southern French ports. If you walked at night through the streets and alleys of Leopoldstadt, at every step you witnessed proceedings which remained concealed from the majority of the German people until the War gave the soldiers on the eastern front occasion to see similar things, or, better expressed, forced them to see them.

When thus for the first time I recognized the Jew as the cold-hearted, shameless, and calculating director of this revolting vice traffic in the scum of the big city, a cold shudder ran down my back.

But then a flame flared up within me. I no longer avoided discussion of the Jewish question; no, now I sought it. And when I learned to look for the Jew in all branches of cultural and artistic life and its various manifestations, I suddenly encountered him in a place where I would least have expected to find him.

When I recognized the Jew as the leader of the Social Democracy, the scales dropped from my eyes. A long soul struggle had reached its conclusion.

Even in my daily relations with my fellow workers, I observed the amazing adaptability with which they adopted different positions on the same question, sometimes within an interval of a few days, sometimes in only a few hours. It was hard for me to understand how people who, when spoken to alone, possessed some sensible opinions, suddenly lost them as soon as they came under the influence of the masses. It was often enough to make one despair. When, after hours of argument, I was convinced that now at last I had broken the ice or cleared up some absurdity, and was beginning to rejoice at my success, on the next day to my disgust I had to begin all over again; it had all been in vain. Like an eternal pendulum their opinions seemed to swing back again and again to the old madness.

All this I could understand: that they were dissatisfied with their lot and cursed the Fate which often struck them so harshly; that they hated the employers who seemed to them the heartless bailiffs of Fate; that they cursed the authorities who in their eyes were without feeling for their situation; that they demonstrated against food prices and carried their demands into the streets: this much could be understood without recourse to reason. But what inevitably remained incomprehensible was the boundless hatred they heaped upon their own nationality, despising its greatness, besmirching its history, and dragging its great men into the gutter.

This struggle against their own species, their own clan, their own homeland, was as senseless as it was incomprehensible. It was unnatural.

It was possible to cure them temporarily of this vice, but only for days or at most weeks. If later you met the man you thought you had converted, he was just the same as before.

His old unnatural state had regained full possession of him.

I gradually became aware that the Social Democratic press was directed predominantly by Jews; yet I did not attribute any special significance to this circumstance, since conditions were exactly the same in the other papers. Yet one fact seemed conspicuous: there was not one paper with Jews working on it which could have been regarded as truly national, according to my education and way of thinking.

I swallowed my disgust and tried to read this type of Marxist press production, but my revulsion became so unlimited in so doing that I endeavoured to become more closely acquainted with the men who manufactured these compendiums of knavery.

From the publisher down, they were all Jews.

I took all the Social Democratic pamphlets I could lay hands on and sought the names of their authors; Jews. I noted the names of the leaders; by far the greatest part were likewise members of the 'chosen people', whether they were representatives in the Reichsrat or trade-union secretaries, the heads of organizations or street agitators. It was always the same gruesome picture. The names of the Austerlitzes, Davids, Adlers, Ellenbogens, etc., will remain forever graven in my memory.

One thing had grown clear to me: the party with whose petty representatives I had been carrying on the most violent struggle for months was, as to leadership, almost exclusively in the hands of a foreign people; for, to my deep and joyful satisfaction, I had at last come to the conclusion that the Jew was no German.

Only now did I become thoroughly acquainted with the seducer of our people.

A single year of my sojourn in Vienna had sufficed to imbue me with the conviction that no worker could be so stubborn that he would not in the end succumb to better knowledge and better explanations. Slowly I had become an expert in their own doctrine and used it as a weapon in the struggle for my own profound conviction.

Success almost always favoured my side.

The great masses could be saved, if only with the gravest sacrifice in time and patience.

But a Jew could never be parted from his opinions.

At that time I was still childish enough to try to make the madness of their doctrine clear to them; in my little circle I talked my tongue sore and my throat hoarse, thinking I would inevitably succeed in convincing them how ruinous their Marxist madness was; but what I accomplished was often the opposite. It seemed as though their increased understanding of the destructive effects of Social Democratic theories and their results only reinforced their determination.

The more I argued with them, the better I came to know their dialectic. First they counted on the stupidity of their adversary, and then, when there was no other way out, they themselves simply played stupid. If all this didn't help, they pretended not to understand, or, if challenged, they changed the subject in a hurry, quoted platitudes which, if you accepted them, they immediately related to entirely different matters, and then, if again attacked, gave ground and pretended not to know exactly what you were talking about. Whenever you tried to attack one of these apostles, your hand closed on a jelly-like slime which divided up and poured through your fingers, but in the next moment collected again. But if you really struck one of these fellows so telling a blow that, observed by the audience, he couldn't help but agree, and if you believed that this had taken you at least one step forward, your amazement was great the next day. The Jew had not the slightest recollection of the day before, he rattled off his same old nonsense as though nothing at all had happened, and, if indignantly challenged, affected amazement; he couldn't remember a thing, except that he had proved the correctness of his assertions the previous day.

Sometimes I stood there thunderstruck.

I didn't know what to be more amazed at: the agility of their tongues or their virtuosity at lying.

Gradually I began to hate them.

All this had but one good side: that in proportion as the real leaders or at least the disseminators of Social Democracy came within my vision, my love for my people inevitably grew. For who, in view of the diabolical craftiness of these seducers, could damn the luckless victims? How hard it was, even for me, to get the better of this race of dialectical liars! And how futile was such success in dealing with people who twist the truth in your mouth, who without so much as a blush disavow the word they have just spoken, and in the very next minute take credit for it after all.

No. The better acquainted I became with the Jew, the more forgiving I inevitably became towards the worker.

In my eyes the gravest fault was no longer with him, but with all those who did not regard it as worth the trouble to have mercy on him, with iron righteousness giving the son of the people his just deserts, and standing the seducer and corrupter up against the wall.

Inspired by the experience of daily life, I now began to track down the sources of the Marxist doctrine. Its effects had become clear to me in individual cases; each day its success was apparent to my attentive eyes, and, with some exercise of my imagination, I was able to picture the consequences. The only remaining question was whether the result of their action in its ultimate form had existed in the mind's eye of the creators, or whether they themselves were the victims of an error.

I felt that both were possible.

In the one case it was the duty of every thinking man to force himself to the forefront of the ill-starred movement, thus perhaps averting catastrophe; in the other, however, the original founders of this plague of the nations must have been veritable devils; for only in the brain of a monster – not that of a man – could the plan of an organization assume form and meaning, whose activity must ultimately result in the collapse of human civilization and the consequent devastation of the world.

In this case the only remaining hope was struggle, struggle with all the weapons which the human spirit, reason, and will can devise, regardless on which side of the scale Fate should lay its blessing.

Thus I began to make myself familiar with the founders of this doctrine, in order to study the foundations of the movement. If I reached my goal more quickly than at first I had perhaps ventured to believe, it was thanks to my newly acquired, though at that time not very profound, knowledge of the Jewish question. This alone enabled me to draw a practical comparison between the reality and the theoretical flim-flam of the founding fathers of Social Democracy, since it taught me to understand the language of the Jewish people, who speak in order to conceal or at least to veil their thoughts; their real aim is not therefore to be found in the lines themselves, but slumbers well concealed between them.

For me this was the time of the greatest spiritual upheaval I have ever had to go through.

I had ceased to be a weak-kneed cosmopolitan and become an anti-Semite.

Just once more – and this was the last time – fearful, oppressive thoughts came to me in profound anguish.

When over long periods of human history I scrutinized the activity of the Jewish people, suddenly there rose up in me the fearful question whether inscrutable Destiny, perhaps for reasons unknown to us poor mortals, did not with eternal and immutable resolve, desire the final victory of this little nation.

Was it possible that the earth had been promised as a reward to this people which lives only for this earth?

Have we an objective right to struggle for our self-preservation, or is this justified only subjectively within ourselves?

As I delved more deeply into the teachings of Marxism and thus in tranquil clarity submitted the deeds of the Jewish people to contemplation, Fate itself gave me its answer.

The Jewish doctrine of Marxism rejects the aristocratic principle of Nature and replaces the eternal privilege of power and strength by the mass of numbers and their dead weight. Thus it denies the value of personality in man, contests the significance of nationality and race, and thereby withdraws from humanity the premise of its existence and its culture. As a foundation of the universe, this doctrine would bring about the end of any order intellectually conceivable to man. And as, in this greatest of all recognizable organisms, the result of an application of such a law could only be chaos, on earth it could only be destruction for the inhabitants of this planet.

If, with the help of his Marxist creed, the Jew is victorious over the other peoples of the world, his crown will be the funeral wreath of humanity and this planet will, as it did thousands of years ago, move through the ether devoid of men.

Eternal Nature inexorably avenges the infringement of her commands.

Hence today I believe that I am acting in accordance with the will of the Almighty Creator: *by defending myself against the Jew, I am fighting for the work of the Lord.*

●

Why we hate insects

ROBERT LYND

It has been said that the characteristic sound of summer is the hum of insects, as the characteristic sound of spring is the singing of birds. It is all the more curious that the word 'insect' conveys to us an implication of ugliness. We think of spiders, of which many people are more afraid than of Germans. We think of bugs and fleas, which seem so indecent in their lives that they are made a jest by the vulgar, and the nice people do their best to avoid mentioning them. We think of blackbeetles scurrying into safety as the kitchen light is suddenly turned on — blackbeetles which (so we are told) in the first place are not beetles, and in the second place are not black. There are women who will make a face at the mere name of any of these creatures. Those of us who have never felt this repulsion — at least, against spiders and blackbeetles — cannot but wonder how far it is natural. Is it born in certain people, or is it acquired like the old-fashioned habit of swooning and the fear of mice? The nearest I have come to it is a feeling of disgust when I have seen a cat retrieving a blackbeetle just about to escape under a wall and making a dish of it. There are also certain crawling creatures which are so notoriously the children of filth and so threatening in their touch that we naturally shrink from them. Burns may make merry over a louse crawling in a lady's hair, but few of us can regard its kind with equanimity even on the backs of swine. Men of science deny that the louse is actually engendered by dirt, but it undoubtedly thrives on it. Our anger against the flea also arises from the fact that we associate it with dirt. Donne once wrote a poem to a lady who had been bitten by the same flea as himself, arguing that this was a good reason why she should allow him to make love to her. It is, and was bound to be, a dirty poem. Love, even of the wandering and polygynous kind, does not express itself in such images. Only while under the dominion of the youthful heresy of ugliness could a poet pretend that it did. The flea, according to the authorities, is 'remarkable for its powers of leaping, and nearly cosmopolitan'. Even so, it has found no place in the heart or fancy of man. There have been men who were indifferent to fleas, but there have been none who loved them, though if my memory does not betray me, there was a famous French prisoner some years ago who beguiled the tedium of his cell by making a pet and a performer of a flea. For the world at large, the flea represents merely hateful irritation. Mr W. B. Yeats has introduced it into poetry in this sense in an epigram addressed 'to a poet who would have me praise certain bad poets, imitators of his and of mine':

> You say as I have often given tongue
> In praise of what another's said or sung,
> 'Twere politic to do the like by these,
> But where's the wild dog that has praised his fleas?

When we think of the sufferings of human beings and animals at the hands – if that is the right word – of insects, we feel that it is pardonable enough to make faces at creatures so inconsiderate. But what strikes one as remarkable is that the insects that do man most harm are not those that horrify him most. A lady who will sit bravely while a wasp hangs in the air and inspects first her right and then her left temple will run a mile from a harmless spider. Another will remain collected (though murderous) in presence of a horse-fly, but will shudder at sight of a moth that is innocent of blood. Our fears, it is evident, do not march in all respects with our sense of physical danger. There are insects that make us feel that we are in the presence of the uncanny. Many of us have this feeling about moths. Moths are the ghosts of the insect world. It may be the manner in which they flutter in unheralded out of the night that terrifies us. They seem to tap against our lighted windows as though the outer darkness had a message for us. And their persistence helps to terrify. They are more troublesome than a subject nation. They are more importunate than the importunate widow. But they are most terrifying of all if one suddenly sees their eyes blazing crimson as they catch the light. One thinks of nocturnal rites in an African forest temple and of terrible jewels blazing in the head of an evil goddess – jewels to be stolen, we realize, by a foolish white man, thereafter to be the object of a vendetta in a sensational novel. One feels that one's hair would be justified in standing on end, only that hair does not do such things. The sight of a moth's eye is, I fancy, a rare one for most people. It is a sight one can no more forget than a house on fire. Our feelings towards moths being what they are, it is all the more surprising that superstition should connect the moth so much less than the butterfly with the world of the dead. Who says a cabbage-grower has any feeling against butterflies? And yet in folk-lore it is to the butterfly rather than to the moth that is assigned the ghostly part. In Ireland they have a legend about a priest who had not believed that men had souls, but, on being converted, announced that a living thing would be seen soaring up from his body when he died – in proof that his earlier scepticism had been wrong. Sure enough, when he lay dead, a beautiful creature 'with four snow-white wings' rose from his body and fluttered round his head. 'And this', we are told, 'was the first butterfly that was ever seen in Ireland; and now all men know that the butterflies are the souls of the dead waiting for the moment when they may enter Purgatory.' In the Solomon Islands, they say, it used to be the custom, when a man was about to die, for him to announce that he was about to transmigrate into a butterfly or some other creature. The members of his family, on meeting a butterfly afterwards, would explain: 'This is papa', and offer him a coconut. The members of an English family in like circumstance would probably say: 'Have a banana'. In certain tribes of Assam the dead are believed to return in the shape of butterflies or house-flies, and for this reason no one will kill them. On the other hand, in Westphalia the butterfly plays the part given to the scapegoat in other countries, and on St Peter's Day, in February, it is publicly expelled with rhyme and ritual. Elsewhere, as in Samoa – I do not know where I found all these facts – probably in *The Golden Bough* – the butterfly has been feared as a god, and to catch a butterfly was to run the risk of being struck dead. The moth, for all I know, may be the centre of as many legends, but I have not met them. It may be, however, that in many of the legends the moth and the butterfly are not very clearly distinguished. To most of us it seems easy enough to distinguish between them; the English butterfly can always be known, for instance, by his clubbed horns. But this distinction does not hold with regard to the entire world of butterflies – a world so populous and varied that thirteen thousand species have already been discovered, and entomologists hope one day to classify twice as many more. Even in these islands, indeed, most of us do not judge a moth chiefly by its lack of clubbed horns. It is for us the thing that flies by night and eats holes in our clothes. We are not even afraid of it in all circumstances. Our terror is an indoor terror. We are on good terms with it in poetry, and play with the thought of

> The desire of the moth for the star.

We remember that it is for the moths that the pallid jasmine smells so sweetly by night. There is no shudder in our minds when we read:

> And when white moths were on the wing,
> And moth-like stars were flickering out,
> I dropped the berry in a stream,
> And caught a little silver trout.

No man has ever sung of spiders or earwigs or any other of our pet antipathies among the insects like that. The moth is the

only one of the insects that fascinates us with both its beauty
and its terror.

I doubt if there have ever been greater hordes of insects in
this country than during the past spring. It is the only complaint
one has to make against the sun. He is a desperate breeder of
insects. And he breeds them not in families like a Christian but
in plagues. The thought of the insects alone keeps us from
envying the tropics their blue skies and hot suns. Better the
North Pole than a plague of locusts. We fear the tarantula and
have no love for the tse-tse fly. The insects of our own climate
are bad enough in all conscience. The grasshopper, they say, is a
murderer, and, though the earwig is a perfect mother, other
insects such as the burying-beetle have the reputation of parri-
cides. But, dangerous or not, the insects are for the most part
teasers and destroyers. The greenfly makes its colonies in the
rose, a purple fellow swarms under the leaves of the apple, and
another scoundrel, black as the night, swarms over the beans.
There are scarcely more diseases in the human body than there
are kinds of insects in a single fruit tree. The apple that is rotten
before it is ripe is an insect's victim, and, if the plums fall green
and untimely in scores upon the ground, once more it is an
insect that has been at work among them. Talk about German
spies! Had German spies gone to the insect world for a lesson,
they might not have been the inefficient bunglers they showed
themselves to be. At the same time, most of us hate spies and
insects for the same reason. We regard them as noxious creatures
intruding where they have no right to be, preying upon us and
giving us nothing but evil in return. Hence our ruthlessness.
We say: 'Vermin', and destroy them. To regard a human being
as an insect is always the first step in treating him without
remorse. It is a perilous attitude and in general is more likely to
beget crime than justice. There has never, I believe, been an
empire built in which, at some stage or other, a massacre of
children among a revolting population has not been excused on
the ground that 'nits make lice'. 'Swot that Bolshevik' no
doubt, seems to many reactionaries as sanitary a counsel as

'Swot that fly'. Even in regard to flies, however, most of us can only swot with scruple. Hate flies we may, and wish them in perdition as we may, we could not slowly pull them to pieces, wing after wing, and leg after leg, as thoughtless children are said to do. Many of us cannot endure to see them slowly done to death on those long strips of sticky paper on which the flies drag their legs and their lives out – as it seems to me, a vile cruelty. A distinguished novelist has said that to watch flies trying to tug their legs off the paper one after another till they are twice their natural length is one of his favourite amusements. I have never found any difficulty in believing it of him. It is an odd fact that considerateness, if not actually kindness, to flies has been made one of the tests of gentleness in popular speech. How often has one heard it said in praise of a dead man: 'He wouldn't have hurt a fly!' As for those who do hurt flies, we pillory them in history. We have never forgotten the cruelty of Domitian. 'At the beginning of his reign,' Suetonius tells us, 'he used to spend hours in seclusion every day, doing nothing but catch flies and stab them with a keenly sharpened stylus. Consequently, when someone once asked whether anyone was in there with Caesar, Vibius Crispus made the witty reply: "Not even a fly."' And just as most of us are on the side of the fly against Domitian, so are most of us on the side of the fly against the spider. We pity the fly as (if the image is permissible) the underdog. One of the most agonizing of the minor dilemmas in which a too sensitive humanitarian ever finds himself is whether he should destroy a spider's web, and so, perhaps, starve the spider to death, or whether he should leave the web, and so connive at the death of a multitude of flies. I have long been content to leave Nature to her own ways in such matters. I cannot say that I like her in all her processes, but I am content to believe that this may be owing to my ignorance of some of the facts of the case. There are, on the other hand, two acts of destruction in Nature which leave me unprotesting and pleased. One of these occurs when a thrush eats a snail, banging the shell repeatedly against a stone. I have never thought of the incident from the snail's point of view. I find myself listening to the tap-tap of the shell on the stone as though it were music. I felt the same sort of mild thrill of pleasure the other day when I found a beautiful spotted ladybird squeezing itself between two apples and settling down to feed on some kind of aphides that were eating into the fruit. The ladybird, the butterfly, and the bee – who would put chains upon such creatures? These are insects which must have been in Eden before the snake. Beelzebub, the god of the other insects, had not yet any endangering power on the earth in those days, when all the flowers were as strange as insects and all the insects were as beautiful as flowers.

•

On being hateful to one's own father
QUENTIN CRISP

This celebrated homosexual exhibitionist describes, in his book, *The Naked Civil Servant*, how he was hated by his own father.

My father hated me chiefly because I was revolting but also because I was expensive. Sometimes he would turn on me at the dinner table and hiss, 'Don't eat so much butter on your bread.' To such injunctions I paid even less heed than usual for our life now seemed to be luxurious. I have since decided that with the move out of London my father had abandoned common sense altogether and plunged into a financial gamble that in his own way he was shortly to win.

We occupied what I would now call a very ordinary four-bedroom house and employed a housemaid and a gardener. This last feature of opulence was due not so much to the size of the garden as to the fact that nothing would have induced me to till or even to scratch the soil. I don't hold with flowers even when they are as good as artificial ones.

We also had a car but this could hardly be looked upon as a status symbol. Every car that my father bought was broken-down. He chose them like this deliberately so that he could spend almost all the weekend in the garage repairing them. This was a way of avoiding being with his family. Man goes and buys a car and lies beneath. When he was not tinkering with it, he was making the car the subject of one of our recurring Strindberg dramas. Every Sunday afternoon he asked my mother if she would like to go for a drive. She, who had learned her lines perfectly, said that she would.

'Where would you like to go?'

My mother then ploughed her way conscientiously through the list of places that were within driving distance. She was told that they were too far away or at the top or bottom of hills that were bad for the car. Then she was allowed to say, 'Well, anywhere. I don't mind.'

'If you don't care where we go,' my father would conclude, 'we might as well stay at home.'

But we didn't and the whole afternoon was hell.

About eighteen months after we moved to High Wycombe, the dreary ritual of our lives was interrupted by my mother going away for a few days. What caused this to happen, I can't remember. Perhaps she left in self-defence. This was a very rare occurrence as neither my father nor I could boil a kettle unless conditions were favourable. This was further evidence of the rigid sexual structure of the world at this time. Men fetched coal from cellars and hammered nails; women boiled kettles. You knew where you were even though you hated it.

My father and I got on shakily but, to my amazement, not badly. We spoke to each other. He asked me what I intended to do with my life and at last I understood that the future was now. Neither of my parents ever said to me, 'You're mad but, when you go out into the world, you will doubtless meet people as mad as you and I can only hope that you get on all right with them.' Such words as these would have been a great help. Instead, my mother protected me from the world and my father threatened me with it. My feeling of inadequacy increased steadily. I remember a day when my mother and I stood beside the road at Loudwater station and waited for my father to emerge from the London train. As we stood there, a stream of men in dark suits and bowler hats went by us. I thought, 'I'll never be able to get into step with them.' I felt as I had in childhood when two other children turned a skipping-rope and urged me to run under it and start jumping. I couldn't do it.

Hateful was the dark-blue serge ... O, why should life all labour be? Perhaps I was a born lotus-eater suffering from permanent symptoms of withdrawal.

At the end of one of the ominous but not hostile conversations with my father that took place during my mother's absence, he said, 'The trouble is you look like a male whore.'

This cheered me up a little as I had not then taken my final vows. I was in a twilit state between sin and virtue. The remark was the first acknowledgment that he had ever made of any part of my problem. In gratitude I promised that when I went up to London at Christmas, I would try not to come back.

•

The Communist–Anarchist feud
GEORGE ORWELL

At the end of 1936 George Orwell went to Spain to fight for the Republicans, as a POUM Trotskyite militiaman, and was wounded. The Republicans were supported by the Soviet Union and, in return for the supplies they sent to Spain, they exercised a total control of the Republican government through the small Spanish Communist Party and its foreign commissars. This led to the brutal suppression of any internal Republican opposition. Here Orwell describes the internecine hatred between the Stalinist PSUC and UGT; the Trotskyist POUM; and the Anarchist CNT. Reading it you almost have to remind yourself that the Republicans were supposed to be fighting the Facists, not each other. Small wonder then, that the Fascists won.

I had told everyone for a long time past that I was going to leave the POUM. As far as my purely personal preferences went I would have liked to join the Anarchists. If one became a member of the CNT it was possible to enter the FAI militia, but I was told that the FAI were likelier to send me to Teruel than to Madrid. If I wanted to go to Madrid I must join the International Column, which meant getting a recommendation from a member of the Communist Party. I sought out a Communist friend, attached to the Spanish Medical Aid, and explained my case to him. He seemed very anxious to recruit me and asked me, if possible, to persuade some of the other ILP Englishmen to come with me. If I had been in better health I should probably have agreed there and then. It is hard to say now what difference this would have made. Quite possibly I should have been sent to Albacete before the Barcelona fighting started; in which case, not having seen the fighting at close quarters, I might have accepted the official version of it as truthful. On the other hand, if I had been in Barcelona during the fighting, under Communist orders but still with a sense of personal loyalty to my comrades in the POUM, my position would have been impossible. But I had another week's leave due to me and I was very anxious to get my health back before returning to the line. Also – the kind of detail that is always deciding one's destiny – I had to wait while the bootmakers made me a new pair of marching boots. (The entire Spanish army had failed to produce a pair of boots big enough to fit me.) I told my Communist friend that I would make definite arrangements later. Meanwhile I wanted a rest. I even had a notion that we – my wife and I – might go to the seaside for two or three days. What an idea! The political atmosphere ought to have warned me that that was not the kind of thing one could do nowadays.

For under the surface-aspect of the town, under the luxury and growing poverty, under the seeming gaiety of the streets, with their flower-stalls, their many-coloured flags, their propaganda-posters, and thronging crowds, there was an unmistakable and horrible feeling of political rivalry and hatred. People of all shades of opinion were saying forebodingly: 'There's going to be trouble before long.' The danger was quite simple and intelligible. It was the antagonism between those who wished the revolution to go forward and those who wished to check or prevent it – ultimately, between Anarchists and Communists. Politically there was now no power in Catalonia except the PSUC and their Liberal allies. But over against this there was the uncertain strength of the CNT, less well-armed and less sure of what they wanted than their adversaries, but powerful because of their numbers and their predominance in various key industries. Given this alignment of forces there was bound to be trouble. From the point of view of the PSUC-controlled Generalidad, the first necessity, to make their position secure, was to get the weapons out of the CNT workers' hands. As I have pointed out earlier, the move to break up the party militias was at bottom a manoeuvre towards this end. At the same time the pre-war armed police forces, Civil Guards, and so forth, had been brought back into use and were being heavily reinforced and armed. This could mean only one thing. The Civil Guards, in particular, were a gendarmerie of the ordinary continental type, who for nearly a century past had acted as the bodyguards of the possessing class. Meanwhile a decree had been issued that all arms held by private persons were to be surrendered. Naturally this order had not been obeyed; it was clear that the Anarchists' weapons could only be taken from them by force. Throughout this time there were rumours, always vague and contradictory owing to newspaper censorship, of minor clashes that were occurring all over Catalonia. In various places the armed police forces had made attacks on Anarchist strongholds. At Puigcerd, on the French frontier, a band of Carabineros were sent to seize the Customs Office, previously controlled by Anarchists, and Antonio Martín, a well-known Anarchist, was killed. Similar incidents had occurred at Figueras and, I think, at Tarragona. In Barcelona there had been a series of more or less unofficial brawls in the working-class suburbs. CNT and UGT members had been murdering one another for some time past; on several occasions the murders were followed by huge, provocative funerals which were quite deliberately intended to stir up political hatred. A short time earlier a CNT member had been murdered, and the CNT had turned out in hundreds of thousands to follow the cortège. At the end of April, just after I got to Barcelona, Roldán Cortada, a prominent member of the UGT, was murdered, presumably by someone in the CNT. The Government ordered all shops to close and staged an enormous funeral procession, largely of Popular Army troops, which took two hours to pass a given point. From the hotel window I watched it without enthusiasm. It was obvious that the so-called funeral was merely a display of strength; a little more of this kind of thing and there might be bloodshed. The same night my wife and I were woken by a fusillade of shots from the Plaza de Cataluña, a hundred or two hundred yards away. We learned next day that it was a CNT man being bumped off, presumably by someone in the UGT. It was of course distinctly possible that all these murders were committed by *agents provocateurs*. One can gauge the attitude of the foreign capitalist Press towards the Communist–Anarchist feud by the fact that Roldán Cortada's murder was given wide publicity, while the answering murder was carefully unmentioned.

The 1st of May was approaching, and there was talk of a monster demonstration in which both the CNT and the UGT were to take part. The CNT leaders, more moderate than many of their followers, had long been working for a reconciliation with the UGT; indeed the keynote of their policy was to try and form the two blocks of unions into one huge coalition. The idea was that the CNT and the UGT should march together and display their solidarity. But at the last moment the demonstration was called off. It was perfectly clear that it would only lead to rioting. So nothing happened on 1 May. It was a queer state of affairs. Barcelona, the so-called revolutionary city, was probably the only city in non-Fascist Europe that had no celebrations that day. But I admit I was rather relieved. The ILP contingent was expected to march in the POUM section of the procession, and everyone expected trouble. The last thing I wished for was to be mixed up in some meaningless street-fight. To be marching up the street behind red flags inscribed with elevating slogans, and then to be bumped off from an upper window by some total stranger with a sub-machine-gun – that is not my idea of a useful way to die.

•

Hemingway slaps Eastman in the face
THE NEW YORK TIMES

Ernest Hemingway says he slapped Max Eastman's face with a book in the offices of Charles Scribner's Sons, publishers, and Max Eastman says he then threw Hemingway over a desk and stood him on his head in a corner.

They both tell of the face-slapping, but Mr Hemingway denies Mr Eastman threw him anywhere or stood him on his head in any place, and says that he will donate $1,000 to any charity Mr Eastman may name – or even to Mr Eastman himself – for the pleasure of Mr Eastman's company in a locked room with all legal rights waived.

Mr Eastman's most recent book was *The Enjoyment of Laughter*, published by Simon & Schuster.

He was sitting in Max Perkins's office at Scribner's Wednesday – Mr Perkins is editor for that firm – discussing a new book called *The Enjoyment of Poetry*, when Mr Hemingway walked in, he said yesterday.

Using a few *Death in the Afternoon* phrases in what he describes as a 'kidding manner', Mr Hemingway commented on an essay by Mr Eastman that had been entitled 'Bull in the Afternoon'.

Mr Eastman had written:

'Come out from behind that false hair on your chest, Ernest. We all know you.'

The volume containing this essay happened to be on Mr Perkins's crowded desk, 'and when I saw that', says Mr Hemingway, 'I began to get sore'.

In what he hoped was a playful manner, he said, he bared his chest to Mr Eastman and asked him to look at the hair and say whether it was false.

He persuaded Mr Eastman to bare his chest and commented on its comparatively hairless condition.

'We were just fooling around, in a way,' Mr Hemingway said yesterday. 'But when I looked at him and I thought about the book, I got sore. I tried to get him to read to me, in person, some of the stuff he had written about me. He wouldn't do it. So that's when I socked him with the book.'

'Was he in a chair or standing up?'

'He was standing over there,' pointing to a window with a window seat in Mr Perkins's office. 'I didn't really sock him. If I had I might have knocked him through that window and out into Fifth Avenue. That would be fine, wouldn't it? That would have got me in wrong with my boss, and he might have had me arrested. So, though I was sore, I just slapped him. That knocked him down. He fell back there on the window seat.'

'But how about throwing you over the desk?' Mr Hemingway was asked, 'and standing you on your head in a corner?'

'He didn't throw anybody anywhere. He jumped at me like a woman – clawing, you know, with his open hands. I just held him off. I didn't want to hurt him. He's ten years older than I am.'

Mr Perkins's office retains the somewhat Old World atmosphere that it had in the days – not long past – when it was the rule that gentlemen should not smoke in Scribner's because women were employed in the offices.

'How about books and papers being knocked off the desk?' Mr Hemingway was asked. 'Mr Eastman says –'

'Sure, some books were knocked off. He jumped at me, I held him off, there was a little, a little wrestle.'

According to the Eastman version, after Mr Hemingway was knocked down he patted Mr Eastman's shoulder in an embarrassed fashion and smiled.

Mr Hemingway explained that he had felt sorry for Mr Eastman, for he knew that he had seriously embarrassed him by slapping his face.

'The man didn't have a bit of fight. He just croaked, you know, at Max Perkins. "Who's calling on you? Ernest or me?" So I got out. But he didn't do any throwing around. He just sat and took it.

'I felt sorry for him. Max Perkins told me, he said "no one has any right to humiliate a man the way you have." And I guess he's right. I feel kind of sorry, but he shouldn't go around telling these lies.'

Mr Hemingway had a large swelling over his left eye, high up on his forehead. Asked if this was a result of the battle of Thursday he grinned and shook his head.

He pulled off his coat and showed a deep scar in the biceps of his right arm.

'Max Eastman didn't do that to me, either,' he said. He showed another scar. 'Or that.'

Mr Hemingway gave his present weight at a little under 200 pounds, said that Mr Eastman was narrower at the shoulders, just as big around the waist.

'Here's a statement,' he offered, as the interview closed. 'If Mr Eastman takes his prowess seriously – if he has not, as it seems, gone in for fiction – then let him waive all medical rights and legal claims to damages, and I'll put up $1,000 for any charity he favors or for himself. Then we'll go into a room and he can read his book to me – the part of his book about me. Well, the best man unlocks the door.'

Mr Hemingway is sailing for Spain today. It is understood that Mr Eastman left yesterday to spend a weekend at Martha's Vineyard.

Mr Perkins and other members of the Scribner staff refused to do more than verify the fact that the affair had taken place, taking the stand that 'this is a personal matter between the two gentlemen in question'.

•

A royal adversary

MICKEY HERSKOWITZ

Following his abdication from the throne of England, the Duke of Windsor took his duchess to the Bahamas, where he had been appointed royal governor.

Most men – and women – would have been elated to find themselves in proximity to David Windsor and the former Wallis Warfield Spencer Simpson, perhaps eventually to claim a friendship. But [Alfred] de Marigny was not most men.

To begin with, he had an enduring contempt for royalty, one of the products of a childhood that was cold and lonely and scarred by a family secret. He was born Marie Alfred de Fouquereaux, the son of a sugar planter. He had rejected a family title, avoided using it, and was embarrassed when society hostesses – and his ex-wives – enjoyed doing so.

He had believed his mother was dead until he met her by chance when he was eighteen. He adopted her name, de Marigny, as a deliberate affront to his father, who he believed had neglected and deceived him.

These circumstances would be soon used against him, by a prosecution bent on painting his past as shady, his character as questionable, his way in society as having been eased by a dubious title.

In light of his own difficulties and the Duke's contribution to them, de Marigny was never inclined to view with charity the misadventures of Windsor, neither then nor in retrospect.

History may judge the former King less narrowly than does de Marigny. Certainly, to the generations that came along before and after the war, he was not a venal man but a lovesick one: weak, too easily used, trained to rule a kingdom but not to hold a job. If at one time his ideas and his words coincided with what the Nazis wanted to hear, his defenders would argue that the Duke thought he was on the side of peace. In his heart, the choice was never between England and Germany. He was for England and a negotiated peace, against war and Communism.

Even as late as his duties in the Bahamas, the Duke had not caught on to the diplomatic nuance: 'negotiated peace' was a euphemism for capitulation to Hitler and the Third Reich.

But it would be misleading to suggest that the differences between the Duke and de Marigny were political.

In his determination to show that he was not in awe of the Royal Governor, de Marigny ignored the royal protocol, and his attitude ranged from rudeness to open disrespect. At the least, his behavior was unwise, and reinforced among Nassau's white establishment a sense that de Marigny was arrogant, stubborn, and altogether too foreign.

The feud that simmered between the ex-King and the ex-Count was in part fueled by pettiness, but one or two cases turned on basic issues of fairness and compassion.

They had met twice before, the first time briefly, socially, when de Marigny was twenty-two, studying economics in London and beginning to play the stock market. Windsor was then the Prince of Wales, and ten years his elder. De Marigny was introduced to the Prince at Ascot by a Lord Ronald Graham, who had befriended him. His first impression was quite favorable. The Prince was polite, attentive enough to chat a minute about Mauritius, de Marigny's birthplace.

He was surprised by His Royal Highness's stature – five-foot-seven, of average build, neither slight nor sturdy. It was easy to see why women were so easily smitten. They found him boyish, almost 'pretty', with a face unwrinkled and untroubled by thought.

It was not until later, when he accepted an invitation to the château of a man named Charles Bedeaux, that de Marigny

understood the attention he had been paid. Lord Ronald was a
Nazi sympathizer, or more, and hoped to recruit Alfred and
others like him. The dinner was attended by people of similar
persuasion, and their star exhibit that night was the Prince of
Wales.

Their host, Bedeaux, would later commit suicide in prison
after being arrested by the Allies as a collaborator. To the end,
the Windsors defended him.

Initially, in the Bahamas, the Windsors' contacts were pleasant, and they welcomed de Marigny as an interesting presence at
their official and social activities. His stock soared with the
island's discriminating hostesses.

He met the Duchess for the first time at a formal, white-tie
reception given in honor of the royal couple aboard Wenner-
Gren's yacht, the *Southern Cross*. He recorded his impression:
'She was a remarkable-looking woman, not a hair out of place,
the makeup perfect, the dress exquisite, from one of the great
couturiers. She wore little jewelry, and then simple but elegant
pieces . . .

'I was surprised at how tall she looked next to the Duke, who
seemed overshadowed by his wife. She looked the part of the
aristocrat, and he the attendant. When she spoke, only her lips
moved. Her face was wrinkle-free. Everything about her had
been studied meticulously. I watched her in admiration. She had
tumbled a king from his throne and she played her role with
poise and dignity.'

To his surprise, the Duchess thanked de Marigny for opening
the island's first beauty parlor, now located in the rooms above
his grocery. She informed him that she had flown in a hairdresser
from New York to instruct his manager, Mrs Bethel, on how to
do her hair.

Unsure that the Duke would remember him, or acknowledge
it if he did, de Marigny kept his silence as the Duchess
introduced him as 'the gentleman who had the beauty salon
installed for my benefit'. The Duke studied him for a moment
and said, 'We met in England, did we not?'

'Once at Ascot,' he replied, 'through Lord Ronald Graham, and again at a château in Scotland.'

The Duchess moved away to greet her guests. A waiter passed by, carrying a silver tray of champagne glasses. The two men lifted their glasses, and the Duke recited in perfect French, in a low voice: 'Man is a strange animal . . . *il brûle ce qu'il a adoré et adore ce qu'il a brûlé.*' ('He burns what he adored and adores what he burned.')

The meaning of those words escaped him, but de Marigny passed off the toast as a sample of the Duke's taste for the theatrical gesture.

Shortly after the evening on the *Southern Cross*, he was invited to a reception at Government House, the first since the Duke and Duchess had returned to the official residence. The Duchess greeted him as an old friend. Her pride was evident as she pointed out the improvements in the old pink stucco mansion, which stood high on a hill, amid a grove of tall palms. De Marigny thought he was seeing a glimpse of her real self, the usually unrevealed Duchess. 'I could understand,' he wrote in a diary he kept at the time, 'how a frail and effeminate little man like the Duke could have lost his heart and his throne over her. She had the charm of a femme fatale, and a serene control that made her irresistible. I had a glimpse through her eyes of the warmth and passion that she disguised so well under her cool appearance.'

De Marigny considered himself a serious observer of the female species. He was prepared to add the Duchess to his list of women who by their beauty or cunning rearranged the future, along with Helen of Troy, Cleopatra, and Madame du Barry – women who have always attracted man's imagination and sexual desire. He admired the Duchess and what she represented: an élite sorority of women, not necessarily beautiful, whose well-disguised talents gave them power.

From then on, de Marigny became part of the accepted group to invite whenever His Highness and the Duchess were in attendance. He dined with them at the home of Frederick

Sigrist, who, with Tommy Sopwith, designed the Hurricane fighter plane; again at the Wenner-Grens', on Hog Island; and twice as the guest of the William Taylors. He thought it odd that he never met Sir Harry and Lady Oakes at these more intimate functions. They had lent their estate to the royal couple, and yet had once again failed to step across society's threshold.

The excitement that greeted the surprise arrival of the Windsors soon paled. Beyond the stately pink house on the hill, the island's blacks lived in squalor in a ghetto called Grant's Town. Many of the houses had dirt floors, and water was scarce. Some Nassau businessmen had begun to regard the Duke as an expensive luxury to a colony where eighty percent of the people lived in poverty. It had been the custom for previous governors to return their yearly salary of six thousand pounds to the island's treasury. His Royal Highness kept his. Breaking tradition was to be his way of life. To add to the colony's debt, the Executive Council had to pay ten thousand pounds to repair and redecorate Government House to the satisfaction of the new occupants.

Finally, there were four or five episodes that caused the bad blood between the Duke of Windsor and Alfred de Marigny, one consequence of which may have been the trial of an innocent man for murder.

The first, most personal, and most damaging of these bouts involved the water rights to property de Marigny had acquired on Eleuthera, one of the cays (pronounced 'keys') sprinkled around Nassau like pebbles in an aquarium.

He was building a home there, and had taken on as another project a system that would supply fresh water from his well to the black villagers, who had none. They boiled sea water or captured rain in buckets, when it rained, and in the thin, barren soil nothing flourished except disease and hardship.

So de Marigny provided the pipes, the windmill, and a reservoir, and the House of Assembly approved the project. All he needed was the signature of the governor to begin.

One day de Marigny was visited by a new neighbor, a well-known British writer who had built a lavish home east of his.

Her name was Rosita Forbes, and she was an old friend of the Duke of Windsor.

She arrived on horseback, looking very sporty and very British. During tea she lamented the fact that she had no source of fresh water on her property. Missing the hint, de Marigny suggested that she install gutters and a water tank.

He was still waiting for a permit to be signed, when he heard from a source in the colonial office that the delay had to do with Rosita Forbes. She had asked the Duke to intervene, and divert the water lines intended for the natives to her exclusive use instead.

A confrontation with the Royal Governor was inevitable. De Marigny drove to Government House, where an aide-de-camp, Captain George Wood, led him into the library used by the Duke as an office.

He explained the reason for his visit. Windsor tapped tobacco into his pipe and seemed pensive. 'As a matter of fact,' he said, 'I was about to write you on that matter. I'd hope you would be reasonable. Mrs Forbes has spent a tremendous amount of money to build that house of hers. Not only did she provide work for dozens of needy people, she will spend more money and employ more people to develop the gardens. This is a factor one should not overlook.'

He took a pull on his pipe and added, 'Between us, my friend, the Negroes on the Cay have been living without running water from the time they arrived here. They have managed.'

De Marigny was startled by the shallowness of the argument. 'I am afraid that the governor does not see the picture as I see it,' he replied. 'Here is an Englishwoman who spent a fortune on a place before first determining whether fresh water was available. I humbly remind the governor that the water in question is mine. I would have never thought that the governor would place the whim of Mrs Forbes against the vital necessity of native Bahamians, who need water for their survival.'

The Duke left his desk, walked to a bookcase at the other end of the office, and began flipping the pages of a book. He watched de Marigny out of the corner of his eye. The captain tried to explain that one rose when His Royal Highness rose, and that the interview was now closed.

'Captain Wood,' said de Marigny, stretching his long legs, 'we are not in Buckingham Palace. We are here on a glorified reef. The welfare of the majority should be his one and foremost objective.'

'His Royal Highness, sir. You are talking about His Royal Highness.'

'Captain,' said de Marigny, 'if the British government felt that the Duke was someone of importance, he would not have been sent to rot on this miserable reef. Like them, I sometimes feel that our Prince is nothing more than a pimple on the ass of the British Empire.'

The Duke of Windsor slammed shut his book and left the room, ending, with the same finality, any chance of a civil relationship between de Marigny and himself. De Marigny rose deliberately and made his way out of the building. In the weeks and years ahead, de Marigny's closing line would be widely repeated and quoted, and it would not endear him to those who would soon hold his fate in their hands.

Three days later, the permit was signed by the governor, and the blacks of Eleuthera were at last to receive free, fresh water.

If those words were meant to wound the Duke – 'a pimple on the ass of the British Empire' – de Marigny surely succeeded, for he had said openly what Windsor knew to be true. Decades of British neglect had made the Bahamas almost impossible to govern. He had no real power; the House of Assembly passed the laws, and the Bay Street Merchants controlled the rest.

The white power structure in the Bahamas opposed many things, change foremost among them. There was a mentality very close to what existed in the American South in the 1940s. In his approach to relations with the black race, the Duke regarded the segregation of the South as a fine model. He pictured a kind of paternalism that kept blacks in their place: no voting rights; separate housing and schools and health care, as good as could be afforded on the wages their bosses believed in keeping low to make the economy work.

The Duke of Windsor made nice speeches about improving their wages and eliminating their hunger. But during his tenure, no black entered Government House through the front door.

Nor did the Bahamas want or seek financial support from London, or the influence that might go with it. That was an echo of the South's long opposition to federal aid as a threat to states' rights and a way of life that has now vanished from the American scene, along with the American scene itself.

... Even in such remote ports as Nassau, profiteering in wartime was not considered good form. He was not proud of those rare occasions when he did so, but de Marigny took satisfaction at least once in outbidding the Duke of Windsor.

He made a splendid buy on an insurance auction of wines saved from a warehouse fire. The insurers were obligated to advertise the sale in the newspaper, but a friend arranged to have the ad buried on a back page, in the smallest possible type, giving only the time and date. In those days a box of cigars was a worthy bribe. On the day of the auction, only a handful of people came to bid.

The booty included five cases of Hennessy Five-Star cognac, a find worth a small fortune, especially at a time when cognac country was occupied by the Germans.

Several days after the auction, de Marigny received a visit from Captain Wood, on behalf of His Royal Highness. The captain was a typical officer of the period, infused with the attitude that colonials are lesser breeds whose only function is to serve the desires of the English overlord.

His Royal Highness had been distressed to learn that the auction of the warehouse inventory had already taken place. His Royal Highness had had his eye on the Hennessy's. Now he was in the awkward position of asking a favor of a man he disliked. Would he be kind enough to spare a couple of cases?

De Marigny replied that the bottles were not for sale.

Wood was amused. 'You did not expect that His Royal Highness would *buy* them, did you, old chap?'

De Marigny ignored him. 'I will make an exception for the governor. I could let him have two cases for five hundred pounds, and a bargain at that.'

Captain Wood brushed his mustache. 'That is absurd. I have never heard such rubbish.' He took his leave.

A week later, two of the bottles of cognac were delivered to Government House with de Marigny's card. The Duke sent back a personal note of thanks.

It was not true that Alfred never missed an opportunity to taunt or annoy the Royal Governor, but most of the episodes clearly ended in his favor.

In spite of the war, and the local politics, the parade of distinctive visitors to Nassau continued uninterrupted. The actress Madeleine Carroll arrived with her leading man, Sterling Hayden, to make a film called *Bahamas Passage*. Most of it had already been filmed in a studio in Hollywood; exterior shots of Nassau would give the picture an air of authenticity.

At a party given by Christie, Miss Carroll met de Marigny, with whom she chatted in fluent French ... She disliked the cocktail parties and the crowds that pestered her with silly remarks and requests for autographs.

They formed a fast friendship. The film stars liked de Marigny's idea of entertainment: a flying visit to Eleuthera and a day on the pink sandy beach; a bicycle ride around Nassau; picnics with fresh lobsters caught and prepared before their eyes.

Months later the cast returned to Nassau for the film's premiere. Madeleine asked de Marigny to host a small party at his home after the showing ... As it happened, the Duke and Duchess had planned a larger, formal affair at Government House in the actress's honor. Someone – Harold Christie or Captain Wood – had remembered to invite everyone but Miss Carroll. She was unaware that a reception had been scheduled.

The theater was packed, and when the film ended, the crowd

rushed out to watch as the lovely actress departed. The Windsors dawdled long enough to see her emerge to cheers – she curtsied to the Duke and bowed to the Duchess – then grab the arm of de Marigny and hurry to his car.

The Duke looked on, astonished. He canceled his party on the spot.

•

John Reith and that horrid fellow Churchill
CHARLES STUART

The BBC's first Director General was Sir John (later Lord) Reith. Reith knew how attractive the power of the airwaves was to politicians, and fought to establish for radio a degree of political independence. The first real test of strength between the BBC and the Government came during the General Strike of 1926. This set the pattern for future relations between the two sides. During the General Strike, Winston Churchill was in charge of Government propaganda. But to Churchill's anger Reith insisted that the BBC could not be used as a propaganda tool. For this and other frustrations of Churchill's will, Reith earned the great man's lasting enmity, as Charles Stuart describes in his introduction to Lord Reith's published diaries.

[Reith's] public life in this decade covered a variety of tasks. First, there was his period at Imperial Airways in 1938–9 when, though far from contented with his situation, he had solid grounds for thinking that a greater opportunity would soon appear. Then, between 1940 and 1950, he was successively a cabinet minister, a naval officer working in the Admiralty and, after 1945, part-time chairman of three public concerns, the Commonwealth Telecommunications Board, the Hemel Hempstead New Town Corporation, and the National Film Finance Corporation, all important and useful post-war tasks but none requiring the application of the whole of his formidable energies.

The sensation that he was adrift did not stem, therefore, from unemployment in the strict sense of that word. Except for three months in 1942 he was never without a job. It arose because he was constantly hoping, and was constantly disappointed in his hopes, for positions of greater responsibility and status. He sought these, not for their own sake nor for the public recognition that they would bring, but so that, in his father's words, he could do 'as much good to his fellow men as he possibly could and so serve God in his generation'. That he did not have such opportunities he ascribed to the ill-will of Winston Churchill. His feelings towards Churchill are the key to his sense of frustration and failure during the second war. There is no doubt that by 1940 Churchill had built up a strong dislike of him. He associated him with his opponents within the Conservative party, particularly Baldwin and Chamberlain, and he blamed him, unjustly, for having prevented him from broadcasting his views on India in the early 1930s, which he later described with typical exaggeration as keeping him off the wireless for eight years. On the other hand there is equally no doubt that John Reith disapproved of Churchill long before he became prime minister. This is plain from his diary during the General Strike and, ten years later, during the Abdication crisis, and it is confirmed by his references to Churchill in the brief period at the beginning of 1940 when they were Cabinet colleagues under Chamberlain. It was then, and not only when Churchill became prime minister, that his diary contained references to him as 'a horrid fellow' and that he exclaimed in fury, 'how I dislike him'. They were plainly incompatible, being at once too alike in their domineering egotism and too widely separated in their attitudes to life, the one cheerful and hedonist, the other pessimistic and suspicious of pleasure. The fierce patriotism and determination to win the war which they shared were not enough to overcome their wider differences of temperament.

It was, therefore, unlikely that when Churchill became prime minister he would spare much thought for Reith, nor did he. John Reith's reaction was an intensification of his dislike which he made no effort to conceal. Such conduct was exceptionally unwise in one who craved for political advancement. Some of those in Churchill's confidence, particularly Beaverbrook and Brendan Bracken, to their great credit, were aware of the loss to the government in this failure fully to use Reith's talents at a time of national emergency. Although he disapproved of them fully as much as of Churchill, they tried hard to coax him into greater cooperation. John Reith refused to be coaxed. Throughout the summer of 1940 when he attended the regular meetings of ministers outside the War Cabinet to hear the prime minister's reports on the progress of the war, he went in a mood of resentment and irritation. He regarded these meetings as 'farcical affairs and damned insulting' having 'nothing to them' and he deplored the sycophantic remarks made at them by the majority of his colleagues. Even when the business of his department forced his attendance at a genuine Cabinet meeting, as at Christmas 1940, his comments in his diary were no less critical:

> The PM called a meeting about [air-raid] shelters which had nothing to do with me. For an hour and a half I sat opposite him, watching him and his tricks.

For his last year in the government he would not even attend what he termed 'the below the second salt kind of ministerial meetings'. By November 1941 he noted in the context of the opening of Parliament:

> The sight of Churchill naturally bothered me. I absolutely hate him.

And in January 1942 when informed that some ministers were going to welcome the prime minister on his return from Washington he replied that he 'certainly wasn't going'.

John Reith's dismissal from the government in February 1942 must, then, be seen against the background of his conduct as a minister. For nearly two years he had done nothing to help himself with Churchill and a good deal to harm himself. Once dismissed, he quickly made things worse, rejecting the offerings of goodwill made to him and concentrating his bitterness against Churchill personally. It is true that he refused to give vent to his ill-will in the Press or in Parliament, but he did not stop himself talking. So, in October 1942, he recorded that he had expressed himself 'with some freedom about Churchill and his rotten gang'. It was natural, in these circumstances, that Churchill should turn a deaf ear to the pleas of John Reith's friends for his reinstatement in some ministerial or quasi-ministerial position. He was left to make his way in the Admiralty as best he could. As it turned out, his work there was of outstanding importance while he was in charge of the department responsible for the supply of all materials needed for the invasion of Europe. The achievement of this department still awaits its official history. When D-Day came it had attained almost one hundred per cent efficiency; of the landing ships asked for, ninety-nine per cent had been available, of the landing craft, ninety-eight per cent, involving in absolute numbers, 126 ships, 777 major craft and 1570 minor. Even Churchill recognized the magnitude of this work when he made special arrangements for John Reith to receive the CB (Military). Reith was genuinely pleased by this award but it did not long moderate his hatred of Churchill. When the general election of 1945 led to the catastrophic defeat of the Conservatives and of their leader there was 'no question about his jubilation'.

John Reith was to remain adrift for another five years but Churchill had no part in this. Reith's hopes of being appointed to the management of one of the newly established state monopolies, such as Transport or Steel, or even to the chairman-ship of the BBC were frustrated by the decisions of Attlee and his government. None of this was the work of 'Churchill and his rotten gang'. Nevertheless his hatred remained as strong as ever it had been and was sustained by the publication of the early volumes of Churchill's memoirs, each one of which aggravated and irritated him more. When Churchill returned as prime minister he wrote in his diary, 'I suppose I do positively hate that man ... he is an unprincipled and unscrupulous megalomaniac.' And when, in April 1955, Churchill finally retired he noted:

Good Friday, 8 April 1955 I wrote to the wretched Churchill thus:

'Here is someone who worked faithfully and well for you, but whom you broke and whose life you ruined. You were kind enough, some years later, to agree that you had misjudged; you wrote that you were very sorry and that the State was in my debt. I couldn't remind you of this while you had opportunity to put things right; but I can now, and say that I am sorry to feel as I do.'

Of course people would say it was awful to have written such a letter, undignified and all the rest of it. But if I hadn't done it I should be much more bothered than I am likely to be having done it.

Yet he had not worked faithfully in any political sense nor had his life been ruined by his dismissal in 1942. When he wrote this letter he was chairman of the Colonial Development Corporation and had just signed its annual report in which it was stated that the 'really significant development' for that body was that its emphasis had 'now swung to looking forward instead of backwards'. Within six months he was to accept renewal as CDC chairman. So this continued harping on the evil consequences for him of Churchill's hostility was no longer rational. Indeed, his hatred of Churchill had by this time lost any foundation in reason. It sprang, to use Sir William Haley's words in another context, 'from an unhappiness really based elsewhere' – in himself.

•

Simply Sinatra

KITTY KELLEY

A few days after Frank had flown to Mexico City to meet his wife, newspaper columnist Robert Ruark, who was in Havana, discovered the presence of [Mafioso 'Lucky'] Luciano and denounced Frank for consorting with a deported drug peddler, procurer, and thug. Ruark wrote:

> If Mr Sinatra wants to mob up with the likes of Lucky Luciano, the chastened panderer and permanent deportee from the United States, that seems to be a matter for Mr Sinatra to thrash out with the millions of kids who live by his every bleat . . . This curious desire to cavort among the scum is possibly permissible among citizens who are not peddling sermons to the nation's youth and may even be allowed to a mealy-mouthed celebrity if he is smart enough to confine his social tolerance to a hotel room. But Mr Sinatra, the self-confessed savior of the country's small fry, by virtue of his lectures on clean living and love-my-neighbor, his movie shorts on tolerance, and his frequent dabbling into the do-good department of politics, seems to be setting a most peculiar example for his hordes of pimply, shrieking slaves, who are alleged to regard him with the same awe as a practicing Mohammedan for the Prophet.

The effect of the column was astonishing. The United States immediately cut off all shipments of narcotic drugs to Cuba, and Harry J. Anslinger, Federal Narcotics Commissioner, said the ban would continue as long as the vice czar remained on the island. The next day, Cuban police arrested Luciano and threw him into a prison before sending him back to Italy. The episode became national news, and Frank was depicted as a friend of mobsters.

'Any report that I fraternized with goons and racketeers is a vicious lie,' he said. 'I was brought up to shake a man's hand when I am introduced to him without first investigating his past.'

But Sinatra . . . later visited Luciano in Naples, where Frank gave the Mafia boss a solid gold cigarette case inscribed 'To my dear pal, Charlie, from his friend Frank Sinatra.'

Sinatra's response did not satisfy anyone, least of all Metro-Goldwyn-Mayer executives, who dispatched a representative to talk to Robert Ruark to 'see if we can't straighten this whole thing out'. In an effort to contain the damage, Frank's agents also sent a man to see the Scripps-Howard columnist to find out how many more columns he was going to do on Sinatra.

[Sinatra's Press agent] George Evans tried to salvage what he could of Frank's besmirched image by announcing that in his next film, *The Miracle of the Bells*, the singer was going to be cast as a Catholic priest and that he would donate his $100,000 wages to the church.

Ruark wrote another column, saying that he was not mollified.

> I was told a week earlier that some such effort would be made to remove the muck that Sinatra's association with hoodlums had left on his sinewy frame. As I say, it is elegant press relations – the best, because Sinatra, the mock clergyman, hurriedly wipes out the picture of Sinatra, the thug's chum.

Lee Mortimer, the entertainment editor of the *New York Daily Mirror*, berated Frank for befriending 'cheap hoodlums', adding that his fans were morons to worship a man who wanted to socialize with gangsters.

A few weeks later, *It Happened in Brooklyn* was released to generally good reviews for Frank, except from Lee Mortimer.

'This excellent and well-produced picture ... bogs down under the miscast Frank (Lucky) Sinatra, smirking and trying to play a leading man,' wrote the columnist.

Frank had seethed over Mortimer's assaults in the past and more than once had threatened to get even. He told Joe Candullo, a friend who was a musician, to give the columnist a message: 'If you don't quit knockin' me and my fans, I'm gonna knock your brains out.'

'Every time Frank read one of Mortimer's columns, he went into a towering rage,' said Jack Keller, 'and threatened that the next time he saw this guy he was going to wallop him.'

On April 8, 1947, Frank and Jack Keller [partner to George Evans] were in Palm Springs relaxing with friends. Jack returned to Los Angeles in the afternoon and asked Frank to come with him, but Sinatra said he wanted to stay for the afternoon sun.

That night, Frank went to Ciro's, a Hollywood nightclub, and sat with several friends, including Sam Weiss, a two-hundred-pound music publisher, and his date, Luanne Hogan, a nightclub singer.

Around midnight, Frank saw Lee Mortimer leave with singer Kay Kino. With Sam Weiss behind him and three other men at his side, Frank jumped up and followed the couple to the front door. While Frank's men moved forward to hold Mortimer, who weighed barely one hundred twenty pounds, Frank lunged at the columnist. He called him a 'fucking homosexual' – a 'degenerate' – and slugged him behind the left ear. Mortimer fell, and Sinatra's friends pinned him to the ground while Frank continued slugging at him and screamed in his face, 'I'll kill you the next time I see you. I'll kill you.'

Nat Dallinger, a photographer for King Features Syndicate, who had been standing at the bar, saw the fight and ran to the columnist's rescue. 'I rushed out and saw Mortimer go down and several men grab hold of him. I tried to pull them off, and somebody said, "Are you going to get tough too?" I said, "No, but four men against one are too many."'

Frank and his friends finally backed off while Dallinger called the press and took the columnist to West Hollywood Emergency Hospital.

Before leaving, Frank told a reporter: 'For two years he has been needling me. He has referred to my bobby-soxer fans as morons. I don't care if they do try to tear your clothes off. They are not morons. They are only kids, fourteen and fifteen years old. I think I have had more experience with their tactics than any other star in the country, but I have never beefed. Honestly, I intended to say hello to Mortimer. But when I glanced in his direction, he gave me a look. I can't describe it. It was one of those contemptuous who-do-you-amount-to looks. I followed him outside and I saw red. I hit him. I'm all mixed up. I'm sorry that it happened, but I was raised in a tough neighborhood, where you had to fight at the drop of a hat, and I couldn't help myself.'

At two a.m., Jack Keller's phone rang. It was an Association Press reporter asking where Frank was.

'He's in Palm Springs,' replied Keller, who had left him there hours before.

'No, you're wrong,' said the reporter. 'He's in town, and he just hit a guy on Sunset Boulevard who's still rolling down the street.'

'I just left him in Palm Springs,' insisted Keller.

'Well, I know it was him,' said the reporter. 'He just hit a guy by the name of Lee Mortimer.'

Before Keller died in 1975, he left tape-recorded reminiscences in which he told his version about what happened that night.

'After the AP guy called, the UP called and so did the downtown papers. Finally I just turned the phone off. Just about that time, a timid little knock comes on my door, and who's standing there but Frank.

'"Jeez, I think we're in trouble," he said.

'"You bet your ass we're in trouble and we better get out of here before the reporters start showing up," I said.'

Both of them jumped into Frank's car and headed for

[Sinatra's personal manager] Bobby Burns's house to decide what to do. At three a.m., Keller came up with the solution.

'There's only one thing to do,' he said. 'It's the only way to get out of this thing. Otherwise, you're going to have every newspaper in America against you, because regardless of what *they* think of this guy Mortimer, they resent anyone of their number being manhandled by an actor. So, Frank, you've got to pick up the phone and call all the papers and say, "This is Frank Sinatra" and listen to their questions. Then you've got to tell each one of them that when you walked out of Ciro's, Mortimer and this Chinese dame were standing there and you heard him say to her, "There's that little dago bastard now!"

'This is a slur on your nationality, and no one in their right mind would expect you to take this in good grace. Knowing your temper, the press will go along with you and be more or less on your side. It's the only thing you can do to come out of this looking good.'

Frank seized on the suggestion and started making calls, the first of them to Hollywood columnist Hedda Hopper.

'Hedda, this is Frank Sinatra,' he said. 'I hate to wake you up. But I've been in a little fracas, and I wanted you to know the truth of what happened. Lee Mortimer has been poking at me in print for two and a half years. I saw him tonight at Ciro's, and he called me a name reflecting both on my race and my ancestry. I had no way of hitting back at him except with my fist. So this time I let him have it.'

The next day the papers reported that Frank had floored Mortimer with one punch because he had called him a dago. Outraged by the reports, Mortimer denied the charge. 'I was standing on the steps outside the restaurant when I was hit without warning,' he said. He promptly swore out a warrant for Frank's arrest, charging him with assault and battery. Conviction carried a maximum fine of one thousand dollars or six months in jail, or both. He also sued Frank for twenty-five thousand dollars in damages.

Arrested the next day during a radio rehearsal, Frank sailed into the courtroom smiling and proclaiming his innocence. 'I plead not guilty and wish a jury trial sometime late next month,' he said. The sheriff revoked his gun permit, and the judge set bail at five hundred dollars.

The next day Mortimer reported that he had received two anonymous phone calls threatening him unless he dropped his charges.

'The first voice was guttural,' he said. 'After asking my name, the voice said, "Get out of town. Get out of town immediately, and don't prosecute Sinatra." The next call, the voice was lighter and smoother. I was told to get out of town right away and the person added, "If you don't, we're going to take you over and take care of you."'

The Hearst organization moved into action behind its columnist and gave the story headlines for five days in a row. *Time* magazine said that the space devoted to the episode was 'almost fit for an attempted political assassination'.

MGM attorneys investigated the case and found that there was no basis to Frank's assertions that Mortimer had called him 'a dago', or 'a dirty dago' or 'a dago son of a bitch', as he had alleged on various occasions. Furthermore, MGM boss Louis B. Mayer was not about to tangle with the powerful Hearst organization, whose newspaper chain reached one out of every four readers in America. He demanded that the matter be settled at once. He told Frank to pay Lee Mortimer nine thousand dollars in damages, apologize publicly, and admit the truth. Jack Keller fought the decision.

'The MGM attorneys insisted that Hearst had gotten to the courts and that Frank was going to have to do thirty days in jail,' he said. 'I pleaded with him not to settle. I told him to do the time in jail because he'd get so much more publicity, but MGM prevailed on him and he paid the nine thousand.'

Frank retained Pacht, Ross, Wamer, and Bernhard, the law firm that represented Bugsy Siegel. Isaac Pacht and Siegel's lawyer, N. Joseph Ross, drafted a statement: 'Frank stated that the whole episode arose when acquaintances stopped at his table and claimed to have overheard Mortimer make a remark which aroused Frank's anger and resentment. On further inquiry, Sinatra ascertained that Mortimer had made no remark and had not even known Sinatra was in the café and therefore that no provocation really existed for the subsequent occurrence.'

A few nights later, Frank attended a party at Charles Feldman's house, where William Randolph Hearst, Jr., was a guest. 'Young Bill', as the newspaper heir was known, looked askance as Frank walked into the room with his bodyguards. An argument ensued, and Frank left the party. Years later Hearst said, 'I resented Sinatra surrounding himself with hood types rather than becoming a gentleman.'

After the Mortimer fight, Frank received only negative press coverage from the Hearst papers. Since no star – not even Frank Sinatra – could survive a broadside from this behemoth chain and syndicate, George Evans flew to Hollywood to work on Louella Parsons, the Hearst columnist with forty million readers. He begged her to have lunch with Frank, but she refused. George kept calling. After five more invitations, she finally relented on condition that George pick her up at home and deliver her to the Beverly Hills Club, where Frank was to be sitting in a booth awaiting her arrival. Frank did as he was told and was there smiling as she walked in. He groveled.

'I know I did many things I shouldn't have, things I'm now sorry for,' he said. He offered to escort the columnist to the Walter Winchell Tribute Dinner at the Mocambo a few weeks later.

Through the good offices of Marion Davies, Hearst's mistress for thirty years, Frank got an appointment with the press lord, who was eighty-four years old and in failing health. John Hearst, Jr., was visiting his grandfather in Marion Davies's pink stucco house at 1007 North Beverly Drive on the day that Frank arrived for his audience with William Randolph Hearst.

'He drove up by himself – no limousines, no bodyguards, no hangers-on. He was very contrite,' recalled John Hearst.

Miss Davies smoothed the way for Frank. Like him, she had

always admired Eleanor Roosevelt, hated Westbrook Pegler, and didn't have much use for Lee Mortimer. She had wanted to intercede for Frank, and so she had suggested that he come for tea with Hearst, knowing that he would be a charming visitor for the old man, who was too ill to see many people. Frank stayed at the Davies mansion for an hour; he got his pardon . . .

Frank wanted the role of Terry Malloy in *On the Waterfront* so that he could return to Hoboken as a conquering hero. The producer, Sam Spiegel, wanted Marlon Brando to play the part. 'I wanted Frank to play the priest, but he wanted to play the Marlon Brando role,' said Spiegel.

Smarting over losing the lead to Brando, an actor he despised – Sinatra called Brando 'Mumbles' and 'the most overrated actor in the world' – Frank sued Sam Spiegel for $500,000, claiming breach of contract. He and Spiegel later settled the lawsuit amicably, without any exchange of money.

In 1954 and 1955 Frank made more movies than any other star in Hollywood. He played a psychopathic assassin in *Suddenly*; a saloon pianist in *Young at Heart*; a physician in *Not as a Stranger*; a theatrical agent in *The Tender Trap*; the proprietor of 'the oldest established permanent floating crap game in New York' in *Guys and Dolls*; and a drug-addicted card dealer, Frankie Machine, in *The Man with the Golden Arm*, which was his favorite movie and the one that earned him an Oscar nomination for best actor.

'I'm in demand – fortunately, yes,' he said in 1955. 'All these wonderful roles came together – *Guys and Dolls, The Tender Trap, Golden Arm* – and I have got five (*Johnny Concho, High Society, The Pride and the Passion, The Joker Is Wild*, and *Pal Joey*) planned ahead, including two for my own company – a pretty even split between straight parts and musicals, but I don't call it a comeback. I wasn't away anywhere.'

Frank resented the press for writing up his current success as a 'comeback', thereby implying that he had returned after a long period of failure. At the *Guys and Dolls* premiere in Hollywood, he opened the program prepared by the studio advertising department and found his show business career described 'with ups and downs matching the steepness of a Himalayan mountain peak. After soaring to what was almost national adulation a dozen years ago, a combination of poor roles, a bad press, and other things sent his career zooming downward. He was reputedly washed up. Today his "second career" is in high gear.' Frank was furious.

The next day, he screamed about the program's summary of his career. 'Where do they get that stuff – "He was reputedly washed up." "My career zoomed downward." "My second career." Maybe I didn't make movies for a couple of years, but I bet I made more money on TV, in nightclubs, and making records than half the stars in Hollywood.'

Still, Frank couldn't ignore his meager record sales in the bad years, and he was embarrassed by some of the recordings he had made at Columbia Records. 'Nowadays I hear records I made three or four years ago and I wish I could destroy the master records,' he said. 'It was all because of emotion. No doubt about it.'

When Columbia reissued those records to cash in on his new success, Frank retaliated by denouncing the company, saying that he had been forced to record music licensed by Broadcast Music Inc. (BMI), in which Columbia's parent company, CBS, had an interest. He gave scathing interviews to the press and sent telegrams to senators and congressmen, demanding antitrust action against Columbia to bar broadcasters from owning music publishing and recording firms.

The focus of his anger was Mitch Miller, director of artists and repertoire, whom he accused of ruining his career by selecting inferior songs with cheap musical gimmicks such as barking dogs and washboards for accompaniment.

'Before Mr Miller's advent on the scene, I had a successful recording career which quickly went into decline,' said Frank. 'It is now a matter of record that since I have associated myself with Capitol Records, a company free of broadcasting affiliations, my career is again financially, creatively, and artistically healthy.'

Mitch Miller was outraged by Frank's attack. 'His career went down the drain because of his emotional turmoil over Ava Gardner,' he said. 'I had nothing to do with him losing his movie contract, losing his television show, losing his radio show. I had nothing to do with him losing his voice. He should look to himself as the cause of his own failure and stop trying to blame others. Besides, his contract gave him total control over all his material. He didn't have to do anything he didn't want to do. And as far as gimmicks go, let me tell you that the microphone is the greatest gimmick of all. Take away the microphone and Sinatra and most other pop singers would be slicing salami in a delicatessen.'

Despite the angry telegrams, no congressional action was taken against Columbia Records or Mitch Miller, but Frank became obsessed with hating Miller and refused all entreaties by friends to make up. When Erroll Garner recorded 'On the Street Where You Live', he called Frank in Las Vegas and played the recording for him.

'Wonderful, wonderful,' said Frank. 'Whose orchestra is that with you?'

'Mitch Miller,' said Garner.

Frank hung up the phone.

Years later, Miller was in Las Vegas staying at the Sands, and Jack Entratter dragged him over to Frank to shake hands. 'It's time you two became friends again,' he said. Miller very agreeably extended his hand and said, 'Hi, Frank, how are you.' Frank, who was sitting with a large table of friends, looked up and said, 'Fuck off.'

'It was very embarrassing,' recalled Miller, 'and it's kind of crazy because I never really did anything to him except record some great records.'

Columnist Dorothy Kilgallen experienced the same kind of rage after her 1956 newspaper series entitled 'The Real Frank Sinatra Story' appeared in the *New York Journal-American*, detailing, among other things, Frank's romances with Anita Ekberg, Gloria Vanderbilt, Kim Novak, Jill Corey, Jo Ann Tolley, Melissa Weston, and Lisa Ferraday.

'A few of the women, like Ava and Lana, were public idols themselves and priceless examples of feminine beauty,' she wrote. 'Many more, of course, have been the fluffy little struggling dolls of show business, pretty and small-waisted and similar under the standard layer of peach-colored Pan-Cake makeup – starlets who never got past first base in Hollywood, assorted models and vocalists, and chorus girls now lost in the ghosts of floor shows past. Others belonged to the classification most gently described as tawdry.'

Frank sent Miss Kilgallen a tombstone carved with her name. Then he incorporated her into his nightclub act, ridiculing her as 'the chinless wonder'. At the Copa he said, 'Dorothy Kilgallen isn't here tonight. I guess she's out shopping for a new chin.' At the Sands, he held up one of his car keys and said, 'Doesn't that look like Dorothy Kilgallen's profile?' He continued his unstinting vitriol for the next nine years, refusing to relent until the day she died. Informed of her death in November 1965, he said, 'Well, guess I got to change my whole act now.'

•

Chronology of a feud: Truman Capote and Gore Vidal

GERALD CLARKE

Of all the friendships he made no other was quite so unusual as the one with Gore Vidal. Younger than he was by almost exactly a year, Vidal had worked even more furiously for early success and had already finished two novels when they met in December, 1945, at the apartment of Anaïs Nin, who was to become famous for her diaries. 'When the bell rang I went to the door,' she wrote, describing Truman's entrance. 'I saw a small, slender young man, with hair over his eyes, extending the softest and most boneless hand I had ever held, like a baby's nestling in mine.' A few minutes later that baby's hand was also extended to Vidal for the first time. 'Well, how does it feel to be an *enfant terrible?*' Truman asked him, giving that French phrase a mangled pronunciation all his own. However he pronounced it, he was aware what it meant and that there could be but one *enfant terrible* at a time. Even as he shook that little hand, Vidal knew the same, and from the beginning theirs was more a rivalry, a bloodthirsty match of wits, than an alliance of affection.

Aside from youth and promise, they appeared totally dissimilar. Vidal was tall, fair, and good-looking, with a pencil-sharp profile that was appropriate for his pugnacious personality; unlike Truman, he was masculine in appearance, dress and manner. Unlike Truman too, he had enjoyed a conventional, if highly privileged, boyhood. His grandfather was a senator from Oklahoma; his father had held a sub-Cabinet office in the Roosevelt Administration. His mother, after their divorce, had married an Auchincloss and provided Gore with an entrée into society; before entering the Army in 1943, he had graduated from one of the country's best and oldest prep schools, Phillips Exeter Academy in New Hampshire.

In other, perhaps more profound ways, they were surprisingly alike, however: both felt that they had been emotionally abandoned by their mothers, both were attracted to members of their own sex, and both were possessed by the desire to achieve immortality through the written word. Gore later declared that he wanted to be remembered 'as the person who wrote the best sentences in his time', and that was Truman's wish too. If Truman thought of himself as a condor waiting to pounce on literary fame, Gore believed that he was a golden eagle who, if he could not find fame first, would quickly snatch it away. 'Gore was terribly anxious to be the number one young American writer,' said Truman, 'and he was afraid that maybe I was going to do him out of it.' For a year or more, they were content none the less to soar together in relative harmony over the fields and canyons of Manhattan. Gore took Truman to the Everard Baths, a well-known homosexual bathhouse. Truman took Gore to Phil Black's Celebrity Club, a vast, mostly homosexual dance hall in Harlem. Almost every week they met for lunch in the Oak Room of the Plaza, where they nibbled at their friends during the first course, devoured their enemies during the second, and savored their own glorious futures over coffee and dessert. 'It was deadly to get caught in the crossfire of their conversation,' recalled someone who once joined them. 'They were a pair of gilded youths on top of the world.'

'I rather liked Gore,' Truman said. 'He was amusing, bright, and always very vinegary, and we had a lot of things in common. His mother was an alcoholic, and my mother was an alcoholic. His mother's name was Nina, and my mother's name was Nina. Those things sound superficial, but they're not. And we were both terribly young and at the same time very knowledgeable about what we were doing. We used to sit at those little lunches at the Plaza, and he would explain to me exactly, in the greatest detail – he was very methodical about it – how he was going to manage his life. He planned to become the grand old man of American letters, the American Somerset Maugham. He wanted to write popular books, make lots of money, and have a house on the Riviera, just as Maugham did. He always used to say, "Longevity's the answer. If you live long enough, everything will turn your way." I would say, "Gore, you will do it all if you really want to." And he did, too. He got it all except for one thing: he will never be as popular as Maugham was, and none of his books will ever be as good or readable as the best of Maugham. He has no talent, except for writing essays. He has no interior sensitivity – he can't put himself into someone else's place – and, except for *Myra Breckinridge*, he never really found his voice. Anybody could have written *Julian* or *Burr*.'

An eventual collision was all but ordained, and it finally came, perhaps as early as 1948, in the apartment of Tennessee Williams. 'They began to criticize each other's work,' said Williams. 'Gore told Truman he got all of his plots out of Carson McCullers and Eudora Welty. Truman said: "Well, maybe you get all of yours from the *Daily News*." And so the fight was on. They never got over it.' Truman himself could not recall the origin of the dispute, but did remember that 'it was very, very, very unpleasant, whatever it was about, and after that Gore and I were never friends. Tennessee just sat back and giggled.'

From then on it was open war, and their friends were soon entertaining one another with the latest reports from the battlefield. When one of them was praised for having achieved so much so early, the other (his identity varies according to who is telling the story) angrily exploded: 'Why, he's twenty-two if he's a day!' − a comment so delightfully daffy that it soon acquired a small fame of its own. 'The first time I ever saw Gore, I remarked how extremely talented Truman was,' said Glenway Wescott, an older writer who claimed neutrality. 'Gore, who was lunatic competitive, blew up and said, "How can you call anybody talented who's written only one book at twenty-three? I've written three books, and I'm only twenty-two!"' In like manner, Truman became furious whenever Gore's name was mentioned, stamping his feet like Rumpelstiltskin. 'He has no talent!' he would exclaim. 'None, none, none!'

Much as he carried on about it − 'Have you heard what Gore's done now?' he would indignantly ask Phoebe Pierce − their feud was more of a game than a real war for Truman, and it seemed clear to those who knew them both that Truman was less concerned about Gore than Gore was about him. The reason was obvious to everyone but Gore: Truman had won; the title of reigning literary prodigy was his. Young as he was, he was a mature writer with a distinct and confident voice. Prolific as he was, Gore was still floundering for both a style and a subject, and few took his work very seriously. Williams privately complained that Gore's third novel, *The City and the Pillar*, which gained a certain notoriety because of its homosexual theme, contained not one 'really distinguished line', and Anaïs Nin, to whom Gore was closely attached, found his work lifeless. 'Action, no feeling,' she wrote in her diary. Truman's stories, on the other hand, 'entranced' her, and she admired 'his power to dream, his subtlety of style, his imagination. Above all, his sensitivity.' Such sentiments, echoed nearly everywhere he went, were bitterly galling to Gore, who could not accept the image of that tiny figure standing on a pedestal he believed to be rightfully his. Traveling through Europe with Tennessee in 1948, he spent much of his time talking about Truman. 'He's infected with that awful competitive spirit and seems to be continually haunted over the successes or achievements of other writers, such as Truman Capote,' Tennessee wrote a friend. 'He is positively obsessed with poor little Truman Capote. You would think they were running neck-and-neck for some fabulous gold prize' . . .

A curious pair from Tangier, a countess of undetermined nationality and her American boyfriend, had passed through Ischia one day. They traveled in an exuberant and expansive style – along with a Great Dane, an Afghan, two dachshunds, two Chihuahuas, and a tiny mutt called Mr Brown – and to Truman, who by then was becoming bored with the island's familiar faces, they seemed to carry with them the glamour and mystery of the Casbah. Tangier, which happened to be on the itinerary of several of his friends, including Paul and Jane Bowles, suddenly presented itself as an ideal successor to Ischia, an inexpensive place to relax and work through the summer and fall. Thus it was that after a quick visit to Paris and a long, dusty train ride through Spain, he and Jack crossed the Straits of Gibraltar and landed in Tangier on July 2.

Yet even before they set foot there, that 'ragamuffin city', as Truman was to call it, was a disappointment. Knowing how galling his own presence would be to Truman, Gore, who was not one of the friends Truman had expected to see, had flown from Paris and prepared a small surprise. 'Come to the dock with me,' he told Paul Bowles. 'Watch his face when he catches sight of me.' As the boat from Spain nudged the pier, Truman first spotted Bowles, who was tall and stood out from the crowd. He leaned over the railing, grinning broadly and waving the inevitable Bronzini scarf. Then he saw Gore, who was smugly grinning back at him, and, in a kind of slapstick routine, both he and his smile abruptly vanished. 'His face fell like a soufflé placed in the ice compartment,' said Bowles, 'and he disappeared entirely below the level of the railing for several seconds. When he had assumed a standing position again, he was no longer grinning or waving.' His comical expression of dismay was all that Gore could have hoped for, and after staying only long enough to make Truman think that his entire summer would be ruined, Gore triumphantly departed.

... At the end of 1975 Truman finished work on *Murder by Death*. He returned briefly to New York, then in the middle of January began a speaking tour that was to take him to thirty colleges and universities. Almost immediately he recognized his mistake. Although he had given readings in the past, they were usually isolated, separated by many months. Never before had he undertaken such a rigorous schedule, which kept him constantly on the road, like a politician running for office.

John Knowles saw him at the University of Florida, where, to accommodate a large and eager crowd, his hosts had arranged for him to speak outdoors. His reading was a singular success, as was the question period that followed. 'Are you a homosexual?' asked one truculent young man. With perfect timing, Truman paused, then brought down shouts on the young man's head with a sly question of his own. 'Is that a proposition?' he inquired. But when Knowles visited his hotel room afterward, he discovered that once off stage, Truman had retreated into a numbed daze. 'With the jet lag and endless motels, he hardly knew where he was. He had a couple of vodkas to revive himself, and he was on the moon. He just dwindled away. His energy was gone; his coherence was gone.'

Some writers thrive on public readings. Others do not. That Truman ever agreed to undertake such a series was yet another sign that he was out of touch, even with his own body and soul. Perhaps he thought, quite erroneously, as his accountant, Arnold Bernstein, could have told him, that he needed the money (fifty thousand dollars, after expenses and agents' fees) to help pay for the house in Malibu. Perhaps he hoped to draw attention to the next chapter of *Answered Prayers*, which was to appear in the May *Esquire*. Perhaps, after all the screaming over 'La Côte Basque', he merely needed assurance that he was still loved and admired. Whatever he expected, it was insufficient reward for a tour that he soon confessed was 'the stupidest thing I've ever done. It's like going from one torture pit into another.'

Adding to his despondency was an unexpected assault from another quarter: Gore Vidal. In a boozy interview he had given some months before, Truman had inadvertently handed Gore the weapon he seemed to have been waiting for. Gore, he had asserted, had once become so inebriated and obnoxious that he had been ejected from a party at the Kennedy White House – literally thrown out, like a drunk at a rowdy bar. 'It was the only time he had ever been invited to the White House and he got drunk,' Truman had said. '*Annnnd* . . . he insulted Jackie's mother, whom he had never met before in his *life*! But I mean insulted her. He said something to the effect that he had always hated her. But he'd never even met the woman. And she just went into something like total shock. And Bobby [Kennedy] and Arthur Schlesinger, I believe it was, and one of the guards just picked Gore up and carried him to the door and threw him out into Pennsylvania Avenue.'

Not untypically, Truman had embroidered events. Gore had indeed said or done something to alienate the Kennedys during a White House party in November, 1961. He admitted, in fact, to a sharp exchange of words with Bobby Kennedy, in which, sounding more like New York City taxi-drivers than the Attorney General of the United States and a writer famous for his wit, they had snarled, one after the other: 'Why don't you go fuck yourself!' But Gore had not been thrown bodily out the door, and Truman's comments, which were printed in *Playgirl*, were, at the very least, injudicious. Gore intended not only to brand him a liar – 'I'm looking forward to getting that little toad!' he announced – but also to wound him financially. To those ends, he filed suit in a New York State court, charging that Truman had libeled him and caused him 'great mental anxiety and suffering' and demanding both an apology and one million dollars in damages. The Capote–Vidal feud, which had seemed to amuse the participants as much as it did most of the rest of the world, had suddenly turned extremely nasty.

The depositions provided the only comedy in an otherwise ugly confrontation. When had he last seen Truman? Gore was asked. At a party in the late sixties, Gore replied.

'Q: What occurred on that occasion?

'A: I sat on him.

'Q: What do you mean?

'A: I didn't have my glasses on and I sat down on what I thought was a stool and it was Capote.

'Q: Where was Capote sitting at the time you sat on him?

'A: On a smaller stool.'

For his part, Truman managed to mangle the title of Gore's first novel, *Williwaw*; *Willie Wonka*, Truman called it, thereby indicating how little he had thought of it. He also suggested that in bringing suit, Gore was behaving like a child. Although he considered some of Gore's printed remarks about him to be libelous, he said, he would never lower himself by suing. 'I just don't believe in that. I especially don't believe in writers or artists suing each other. I think that is very childish, but that is my own point of view' . . .

Froth and brouhaha were as necessary to Truman as his art, however, and it was only to be expected that after several months of hard and steady work he began looking for some mischievous diversion. He found it, all too easily, in a collision with a once-treasured friend, Lee Radziwill.

Gore's libel suit against him ... had been dragging on for more than three years, and there was no end in sight. From the outset Truman had expected Lee to come to his rescue and say that she had been the source for his story. But now, in the spring of 1979, he was startled to learn that without giving him so much as a hint, Lee – his love, his Galatea – had done just the opposite. She had become a witness for the prosecution. 'I do not recall ever discussing with Truman Capote the incident or the evening which I understand is the subject of this lawsuit,' she had told Gore's lawyer.

Stunned, Truman indulged himself in another of his retaliation fantasies. Convinced that if the facts were ever made public, Gore would be so embarrassed that he would immediately raise the white flag of surrender, he secretly gave his copies of their depositions to *New York* magazine, which in early June obediently printed long excerpts.

'It's all I can do to contain myself,' Truman said, so excited that his words tumbled over one another into a long and almost manic monologue. 'Until the magazine was actually on the press I could hardly breathe, but right now it is rolling down the chutes along with Gore's career. All along I knew that if people read these depositions, they would know that he was like Captain Queeg in *The Caine Mutiny*. Now they are about to explode and destroy his career. I will have the greatest single revenge in literary history. Nothing equals it. For the rest of his life he'll wake up in the morning and be happy for ten minutes – and then he'll remember what happened on that day in June. The humiliation for him! I love it! I love it! I love it! When he dies, they'll write on his tombstone, "Here Lies Gore Vidal: He Messed Around with T.C."'

Why had Lee turned against him? he wondered. Why had she testified in behalf of Gore, whom she disliked? 'Why she betrayed me is one of the world's great mysteries, like those statues on Easter Island,' he said. When his own call to her was not returned, he nagged Liz Smith into calling her and requesting an explanation. Liz did as she was bidden, and she gave him Lee's answer. 'I'm tired of Truman riding on my coattails to fame,' Lee had told her. 'And Liz, what difference does it make? They're just a couple of fags.'

●

Vermin: Nye Bevan's hatred of Tories
MICHAEL FOOT

The son of a Welsh miner, Aneurin Bevan became a member of Parliament in 1929, and was made Minister of Health and Housing under the Labour Government of 1945. It was Bevan who was responsible for introducing the National Health Service. Here another leading Labour politician, Michael Foot, describes Bevan's abiding hatred of Tories.

> If the Tories give a man a bad name, must the Whigs hang him?
>
> William Hazlitt

'The day is here', proclaimed the *Daily Mirror* in its best stentorian manner on the Monday morning of 5 July 1948, and on that day the Labour Government's great social security measures, headed by the National Health Service, came into operation. Amid so much other bleak news, here was certainly a theme for celebration, and on the night of 4 July the Prime Minister delivered a national broadcast which included a few words of graceful tribute to all political parties for the contributions made to the development of Britain's social services. On that same Sunday Aneurin Bevan spoke at the great rally held every year by the Labour Party in the north at Belle Vue, Manchester. He felt that Attlee's generosity to the other political parties was excessive and drew attention to the point when the statement was shown to him. Still, he had his own special reasons for a sense of release. He could set the achievement of the National Health Service in an historical context somewhat different from Attlee's and at the same time bend more of his mind to the topic which Attlee appeared to neglect altogether – the Government's general political strategy.

'The eyes of the world are turning to Great Britain. We now have the moral leadership of the world and before many years we shall have people coming here as to a modern Mecca, learning from us in the twentieth century as they learned from us in the seventeenth century.' These were the words from Bevan's Belle Vue peroration selected by the *Manchester Guardian* as the keynote of the speech, and they may sound far removed from party recriminations about ration cuts, the balance of payments and disinflationary budgets. But Bevan, as usual, had led to his climax by credible, imperceptible degrees. He had presented an elaborate moral defence of the Health Service, paying his tribute to those who had served the voluntary hospitals in the past, but insisting, 'private charity can never be a substitute for organized justice'. This led naturally to more spacious applications of the doctrine. Every choice between awkward alternatives in the allocation of scarce resources posed moral questions. Labour demanded that the weak should be succoured first, but Churchill preferred a free-for-all; so 'what is Toryism but organized spivvery?' But before the end he struck a practical and topical note about the Government's next steps: 'In 1950 we shall face you again with all our programme carried out. And when I say all, I mean all. I mean *steel* is going to be added.' The challenge would involve a great struggle; every obstacle would be put across the Government's path, including 'the old battered carcass' of the House of Lords.

Undoubtedly it was these last references which Bevan considered political dynamite. For the rest, he mixed his moral philosophy and his lash for the Tories in a way which the audience at least found inoffensive. At one point, contrasting Labour's social programme with the memories of his own youth on the Means Test, he added: 'That is why no amount of cajolery can eradicate from my heart a deep burning hatred for the Tory Party that inflicted those experiences on me. So far as I am concerned they are lower than vermin. They condemned millions of first-class people to semi-starvation. I warn young men and women: don't listen to the seduction of Lord Woolton. He is a very good salesman. If you are selling shoddy stuff, you have to have a good salesman. The Tories are pouring out money in propaganda of all sorts and are hoping by this organized, sustained mass suggestion to eradicate all memory of what we went through. But I warn you, they have not changed – if they have, they are slightly worse than they were.'

That night he had quite an argument with Hugh Delargy, at the time M.P. for one of the Manchester constituencies (later M.P. for Thurrock), who had become one of his closest friends and most fervent admirers but who often undertook the risky assignment of telling his hero what he preferred not to hear. A word of criticism could on occasion unloose cascades of raillery and abuse. Bevan was astonished to be told that the Belle Vue reference to vermin might get him into trouble. 'Nonsense, boy', he said. (All his friends were 'boy,' according to the Welsh mannerism, no matter how old they were.) 'People will only have to read the report to know what I was referring to.' In Wales, Tories were something to be stamped out, politically speaking, of course; like snakes or, yes, vermin; what term could be more appropriate? No one could complain of that. And next morning, 5 July, the newspapers seemed to bear out his judgment. 'MR BEVAN'S BITTER ATTACK ON CONSERVATIVES. No "Free for all" Policy under Labour,' ran the headlines over the longest report in the *Manchester Guardian*. 'BEVAN: my burning hatred for the Tories', was the headline in an early edition of the *Daily Express*, changed in a later edition to 'BEVAN: I HATE THE TORIES': not, it might be thought, a sensational confession. Only one newspaper picked on the fatal word. *The Times* headline read: 'Mr Bevan's "Burning Hatred". Attack on Tory "vermin"'. And possibly it was this nose for news of a *Times* sub-editor, so much more discriminating than that of his yellower rivals, which unloosed the storm. Bevan himself was quite oblivious: why was Delargy always discovering bogys under the bed? He spent that Monday visiting hospitals in Lancashire and nothing marred the geniality of the occasion. No one, he said, could accuse him of political bias in selecting those to run the new service; the 'universal measure of disagreement' he had achieved was proof of his complete impartiality. That night he stayed in Manchester to see the first showing of a Theatre Workshop production – Ewan MacColl's *The Other Animals*. Next day he returned to London to attend the annual meeting of the National Institute of the Deaf, where the new hearing aid provided and produced by the new National Health Service was on display. Nothing made him prouder than the entirely fresh departure in care for the deaf made while he was Minister of Health. Hearing specialists and aural technicians were brought together to devise an instrument for mass production and they invented one costing a tenth of the commercial product. In the next few months and years, assistance was provided for tens of thousands of deaf people who had never been able to afford any hearing aid before.

But the deaf were not news; 'vermin' were – even if the newspapers were not the first to pounce. On the Monday night, Capt. Gammans, Tory M.P. for Hornsey, called Bevan 'the Conservatives' best propagandist; even in a moment of crisis Socialism will still only appeal to class hatred and inferiority complex'. Lord Reading in the House of Lords said he had never read a more deplorable speech. By Thursday the *Daily Express* claimed to be inundated with protests. On Friday an exchange of letters between Mr Lionel Heald K.C. and Bevan was made public. Mr Heald protested that he had recently agreed to continue service as governor of the Middlesex Hospital; but since he was also a Conservative, did the Minister want his services? Bevan replied as quietly as he could; regretting that remarks made upon a political platform had been taken so much amiss, but insisting that of course the Health Service required the assistance of all, irrespective of party. That night other hands went to work. Someone daubed across the outside of Bevan's house at 23 Cliveden Place the inscription in huge black letters: 'VERMIN VILLA – HOME OF A LOUD-MOUTHED RAT'. At last, one week after the notorious speech had been delivered, the newspapers began to extract the full measure of political profit from it.

Under the title 'Vermin', Lord Kemsley's *Sunday Times* wrote: 'Tories are "lower than vermin" said Mr Aneurin Bevan . . . nothing said at a political meeting for a long time has been more talked about or will be longer remembered'. 'We do not ask,' wrote the *Observer*, 'that democratic argument should lack vigour or even invective; but to attack policy is not to insult persons. Free and frank speaking is quite different from the irresponsible falsehoods and disgusting abuse recently flung by various members of the Cabinet at Mr Churchill, the middle class, and now at every member of the Conservative Party . . . These dirty missiles may not harm the actual target but they foul the whole air through which they pass. They cause the ordinary citizen to despise politics, and to make politics contemptible is not just a trifling breach of manners. It is a crime against a democratic society.' The *Sunday Dispatch* epitomized the case in one mammoth headline: 'THE MAN WHO HATES 8,093,858 PEOPLE' – that being the total who had voted Conservative at the 1945 election. Useless to argue that the phrase could bear other interpretations; that the demons Bevan might have had in mind were the Means Test inquisitors of his youth or their lineal political descendants who greeted, with such niggardly applause and such miserly care for the cost, the prospective human triumphs of the National Health Service; the meaning had now become fixed for ever in British political mythology.

During that awkward week Bevan received from 10 Downing Street an envelope marked 'Strictly Personal' within another envelope sealed thus: 'To be opened by the Minister only. No action till he calls for his secret papers'. Inside Attlee scrawled in a barely decipherable hand:

My dear Aneurin,

I have received a great deal of criticism of the passage in your speech in which you describe the Conservatives as vermin, including a good deal from our own Party.

It was, I think, singularly ill-timed. It had been agreed that we wished to give the new Social Security Scheme as good a send-off as possible and to this end I made a *non-*polemical broadcast. Your speech cut right across this. I have myself done as much as I could to point out the injustice of the attacks made upon you for your handling of the doctors, pointing out the difficulties experienced by your predecessors of various political colours in dealing with the profession. You had won a victory in obtaining their tardy co-operation, but these unfortunate remarks enable the doctors to stage a comeback and have given the general public the impression that there was more in their case than they had supposed.

This is, I think, a great pity because without doing any good it has drawn attention away from the excellent work you have done over the Health Bill. Please, be a bit more careful in your own interest.

Yours ever,
Clem

The rebuke, if rebuke there had to be, could hardly have been framed more delicately, and after his first irritation that Attlee had accepted the criticism of his Belle Vue utterances without asking him about them first, Bevan bore no grudge. His general relations with his leader at this time were growing more affectionate. But he never ceased to be amazed at Attlee's apparent belief that the war with the Tories could be fought without battles, without wounds, or even without bruises. It was not merely that the leader's trumpet gave an uncertain sound. Months would pass without the waiting army of Labour being roused by so much as a squeak.

Another leader had different views on the requirements and

opportunities of political warfare – Winston Churchill. He brooded for a few days while Bevan seemed to be successfully dismissing the incident with a few playful asides – at Holyhead, for example, boasting that Welshmen rather than 'the bovine and phlegmatic Anglo Saxons' were needed to push through great reforms. At a dinner given in his honour by the Monmouthshire County Council (which Lord Raglan, Lord Lieutenant of the County, refused in his verminian capacity to attend), he said that he had never regarded himself as a politician but more as 'a projectile discharged from the Welsh valleys'. In a full-dress Commons debate on housing, the word was muttered, but never daringly thrown down like a gauntlet. The Cabinet, said Lord Woolton in a speech in the country, were 'frightened of Mr Aneurin Bevan', and maybe some others were too. But not Churchill. Having held his fire for a few days, he launched his counter-attack, not in a casual outburst but in a speech in the country in which every sentence was sharpened and polished. The National Health Service, he said, had been 'marred and prejudiced in its initiation by the clumsy and ill-natured hands of the Minister of Health to whom it was confided. Needless antagonisms have been raised largely by bad manners . . . with the medical profession, and the whole process of imposing this new contribution has been rendered more painful by the spirit of spite and class hatred of which Aneurin Bevan has made himself the expression . . . He has chosen this very moment to speak of at least half the British nation as lower than vermin . . . We speak of the Minister of Health but ought we not rather to say the Minister of Disease, for is not morbid hatred a form of mental disease . . . and indeed a highly infectious form? Indeed I can think of no better step to signalize the inauguration of the National Health Service than that a person who so obviously needs psychiatric attention should be among the first of its patients . . .'

The thrusts struck hard as they were intended to: 'Minister of Disease' was no gentle piece of mockery; its purpose was to kill. But Bevan replied in terms which somehow dissuaded Churchill from pursuing this theme in their continuing vendetta. The reply was delivered at 'the big meeting' of the Durham Miners' Gala, the great carnival of the working class where the names of the previous speakers, dating back to 1880, tell of a tradition of the English people which Churchill never knew: Peter Lee, Prince Kropotkin, Charles Bradlaugh, Michael Davitt, Keir Hardie, Bob Smillie, Tom Mann, A. J. Cook; a splendid array. No one speaking at Durham can banish from his consciousness the records of the class struggle recited on the banners carried proudly through the streets. Here was a good arena for replying to Tory Britain.

'When I speak of Tories,' Bevan began, 'I mean the small bodies of people who, whenever they have the chance, have manipulated the political influence of the country for the benefit of the privileged few.' So much for the 'vermin' label; everyone ought to have known what he meant. Then he turned to the main charge: 'I want to spend a little time comparing what Churchill did when he had the power in peacetime with what we have done . . . In 1926 when Churchill was Chancellor of the Exchequer – one of the most disastrous Chancellors of the Exchequer in British history – the infant mortality rate was seventy in a thousand. In 1946 it was forty-three, last year it was better than that again, and the first half of this year is better still. In 1926, 2,092 mothers died in childbirth. In 1946, 1,205 died. Now who ought to be called the Minister of Disease? I am keeping the mothers and children alive but he half-starved them to death. He has the impudence to call me Minister of Disease when every vital statistic by which the health and progress of the population can be measured is infinitely better now under the provision of a common miner than it was then under the supervision of an aristocrat. I know if you took the vital statistics of the aristocrats they were as well off then as now. He looked after them all right. I am not concerned about that. I am concerned about our own people.' And that indeed was the drumbeat in Bevan's oratory. He could not and would not expunge from his memory 'the story of 1926 and of the Tory barbarism of that time'. Churchill did so readily and even boasted of it. 'It is,' continued Bevan, 'a queer definition of a gentleman, one who is able to forgive and forget the wrongs done to other people. I am prepared to forget and forgive the wrongs that were done to me. I am not prepared to forget and forgive the wrongs done to my people. We need twenty years of power to transfer the citadels of capitalism from the hands of a few people to the control of the nation. Only after twenty years can we afford to be polite. Then maybe I won't have enough energy to be rude, but while we have the energy, let us be rude to the right people.' These last words may have stirred fresh tremors of loathing in respectable middle-class homes. But at Durham they were delivered with the sweetest of smiles in the softest of accents, once the fifty-thousand-odd audience had been reduced to the required anticipatory hush. Being rude to the right people was a highly honoured tradition among miners. Having been scorched by the invective, they now basked in the raillery. Those picnic dinners had never been tastier on as perfect a day as Durham had ever known.

•

The man who came to dinner
SAMUEL HOPKINS ADAMS

Alexander Woollcott was an American columnist and critic whose reputation for irascibility and antipathy inspired the play (and later the film) *The Man who Came to Dinner*, in which the monstrous Woollcott became the monstrous Sheridan Whiteside and was played to the hilt by Monty Woolley. Woollcott's biographer describes the great man's capacity for picking a fight.

One proof of Woollcott's innate vigour is that he never abated his zeal for a fight. In his mood he was the modern replica of the medieval ruffler, swaggering abroad with hat cocked and thumb in girdle, seeking the *casus belli* and, if it came not, baiting it with choice provocations. Like Sir Nigel, he loved a good bicker. Too often it was his friends whom he galled. Towards his enemies he was calmly indifferent after the first clash.

Something incurably cantankerous in his make-up incited him to these impartial affronts. At times it would seem that he had a grudge against the world, partly suppressed through his years of struggle but seething up in reasonless irritability as soon as he felt able to afford that luxury. '. . . His arrogance and venom,' thought Edmund Wilson, 'arose from the vulnerability of an excessively sensitive man rather badly favoured by nature and afflicted by glandular disorders.'

Though he engendered, he did not secrete, personal rancour. In twenty years of association Booth Tarkington heard him speak of only three persons with actual dislike. Shortly before his death he told me that in all his life he had genuinely hated but two people. He spat his venom; he planted his dart; he forgot or ignored consequences.

The rumours of his wars were wafted abroad on gusts of publicity. What started as a private feud was presently in national circulation. Partly this was Woollcott luck (for he enjoyed it); partly that design for living in the limelight which he early worked out. Many of his insults, rooted in this principle, were strictly ersatz. Without warning, he would greet a guest with 'Good evening, Mrs Emptyhead,' or 'What! You here again, Brainless?' For no ascertainable reason except possibly an ill-digested breakfast, his welcome to a friend whom he had not seen for a year might be, 'Your face revolts me, Repulsive. What about getting the hell out of here?' Such sallies were usually perpetrated before a crowd and were timed for effect upon the audience. Mr Woollcott presents Mr Woollcott as the Fabulous Monster.

That he attacked with peculiar vivacity and made enemies with singular facility is explicable, if not excusable, on the ground of his inability to measure the virulence of his own poison. I have known him to express honest surprise when a grossly offensive letter was resented.

'What did I say to stir *him* up?' he asked wonderingly.

I pointed out that he had merely accused the recipient of bad faith, favour-currying, and abandonment of principle.

'That's your own lack of intelligence,' said he witheringly. 'I didn't mean it that way at all.'

Nevertheless, he wrote a frank and honourable explanation. His pen had, in the first instance, run away with him. It often did. He was as prone to overwrite in private communications as in print: in fact, more so.

His rare apologies were apt to be irritant rather than emollient. As an example of what he considered the *amende honorable*, the following letter has its envenomed points:

> Dear —:
>
> I've tried by tender and conscientious nursing to keep my grudge against you alive, but I find it has died on me. In the matter of —, I still think that you were incredibly cruel in intention and a liar after the event; but it dawns on me a little late that, like most people I know, I, too, have been both cruel and dishonest at one time or another in my life. Anyway, what of it?

There follow a brace of gross insults, a hint of personal violence, a solicitous inquiry for the recipient's health which had been poor, and the signature,

> Your former companion-in-arms,
>   A. Woollcott

He had suffered so much from the jeers of his fellows in college, as he told Howard Dietz, that he made it a principle always to hit before the other fellow. Encountering Edmund Wilson he growled, 'You're getting very fat,' obviously, comments Wilson, to forestall a comment upon his own corpulence. Gene Fowler's welcome to Bomoseen was the oft-used 'Hello,

Repulsive,' followed by the commentary that 'a low police reporter' was hardly the happiest choice for John Barrymore's biographer. Nevertheless, the future author of *Good-night, Sweet Prince* spotted it as a bluff, covering 'as warm a heart as I ever encountered'. In this diagnosis James M. Cain concurred, though with qualifications. Introduced to Will Woollcott, he said, 'Your brother has a heart of gold'; then, swallowing hard, conscientiously added, 'and how I hate the son-of-a-bitch!'

Total strangers, innocent of intentional offence, could rasp the thin-skinned author to snarling churlishness. An old lady in a Cleveland bookstore where Woollcott was on exhibit with other authors, asked him to autograph her copy of *While Rome Burns*, saying courteously:

'My daughter, to whom I am sending this, will appreciate it so much, Mr Woollcott.'

Aleck seized the book and inscribed it, 'To an old bore', whereupon the recipient slammed it on the floor and stalked away.

At the close of the show a clerk brought around a book for signature.

'No,' snorted Aleck. 'It's bad enough having to pander to the customers without being held up by the hired help.'

A week after the tour a publisher, making the rounds of the trade, 'found the entire book departments of Halle Brothers in Cleveland and Marshall Field in Chicago seething with rage against him'.

Yet this same bristling, offensive curmudgeon could interrupt a busy day to hunt (and find) an opening for a stagestruck young girl on no more valid a claim than that she was the niece of an Army nurse who had served with him at Savenay in the old, fondly remembered days of glamour and stench.

Business considerations never inhibited Aleck's rancour. Book reviewers are supposed to treat all publishers, even their own, alike. At least once Alexander Woollcott, L.H.D., then touching occasionally upon books in his *New Yorker* department, 'Shouts and Murmurs', blackballed a prominent publisher. He had taken Random House sharply to task for what he declared an inept and unscholarly translation of Marcel Proust. Having met and talked with Proust in Paris, at the time of the World War, he felt a special interest in him, and a personal resentment against any maltreatment of his prose. In rebuttal, Frederick A. Blossom, the translator, published a letter in the New Yorker, pointing out that the critic's difficulties were not with his, Blossom's, English, but with Proust's French. Incensed, Woollcott indicated that, to him, Random House was as good as dead thenceforth.

Instead of remaining obligingly inert, the concern brought out a novel which Woollcott liked. He wrote to Bennett Cerf, head of the firm:

> Dear Cerf:
> By some miracle you have published a book which is not second rate. Please send me twelve copies at once.
>   Yours sincerely,
>   A. Woollcott

The reply was in the same spirit.

> Dear Woollcott:
> By some miracle you can buy those twelve copies at Brentano's.
>   Yours very truly,
>   Bennett Cerf

Random House publications were thereafter permanently out so far as Woollcott the reviewer was concerned.

To one basic principle of journalistic ethics Woollcott was steadfast. He would not use the printed page as a weapon of personal spite. His tongue sufficed him in that department. While a guest at the Coffee House, he addressed Charles Hanson Towne, one of the club patriarchs, in terms so gross that that gentleman invited him to repeat them outside on the sidewalk. It would have been truly global warfare, since the clubman's rotundity was almost equal to his insulter's. Moreover, he was giving the other more than ten years' handicap.

Peaceable-minded members intervened. Nothing in the line

of overt violence came of it. Some weeks later at The Players, a fellow member of Mr Towne said: 'Have you seen this week's *New Yorker*?'

'No.'

'Alexander Woollcott pays his respects to you.'

'Does he? I wonder where the skin comes off,' said Towne, not much concerned one way or the other.

When he looked up the article he found the mention of him an anecdote not only inoffensive, but pleasant. Subsequently, Woollcott had occasion to refer to his challenger again. There was not a trace of venom. One may infer that, while the Sage of Bomoseen did not cherish any tenderer emotions towards Towne than before, he either respected him or the standards of honourable journalism or, what is probable, both.

Though a Woollcott editorial liaison typically began in close harmony and ended in Billingsgate, only once did open warfare result, and then with the one magazine towards which he felt a personified loyalty and affection, the *New Yorker*, '. . . the best editorial accomplishment that has taken place in this country in my lifetime', in his opinion.

His success in its pages had been built largely upon brief biographies of his friends. What little return in kind there had been was sketchy and laudatory. When, after the close of the 'Shouts and Murmurs' series, the *New Yorker* decided to do a Profile series on him, he was more than ready to collaborate by supplying all data at his command. The magazine's decision was not reached without considering its probable effect upon the subject. The project originated with Wolcott Gibbs who, since his trying experience as editorial go-between with Aleck, had been pressing Ross to let him do a character sketch of the office Gila monster. Ross [editor of the *New Yorker*] thought it likely that the write-up would make trouble, but maybe it was worth risking. Gibbs produced a three-part opus and turned over to its subject for correction and suggestions. Aleck okayed it.

'With certain reservations,' he telegraphed Gibbs, 'you have made me very happy.'

There is some reason for believing that these reservations applied to an old and close friend of Aleck's whose identity was cloaked (in part, at least) under the pseudonym of Sergeant Quirt. This odd character in real life had graduated *summa cum fraude*, as one of his several victims put it, from a career of temporarily successful low finance, into a Federal penitentiary, as duly set forth in the *New Yorker* article; from there into Chicago journalism. Aleck pointed out the unfairness of imperilling 'Quirt's' efforts to go straight, through publication of the article.

There is still current in Chicago newspaperdom a semi-apocryphal legend about it, with a flavour of that ruffianly classic, *The Front Page*, to the effect that the *New Yorker* wired the managing editor of the Chicago paper, asking whether knowledge of the fact that one of their reporters was an ex-convict would result in his discharge. The reply came back, 'No: but which of the five do you mean?'

'Sergeant Quirt' remained in the sketch. There was a practical reason why the magazine did not wish to alienate Woollcott: he was planning to renew his editorial connection with it. A second letter to Gibbs resolved any misgivings:

> Your qualms about my reception of what you describe as the unamiable part of it were baseless . . . I beg of you to believe that you can print this Profile just as it stands without making me feel bitter towards the *New Yorker* or any less tender towards Ross than I already feel.

He assured Thornton Wilder, who had read the first article and was concerned, that the Profile had not 'afflicted' him in any degree.

He did, however, assert his opinion that the treatment accorded to the pseudonymous Quirt was 'despicable,' while disclaiming any special interest in him and asserting that there were eight hundred people who took precedence over him in his (Woollcott's) esteem.

The Profile, as published, seemed to many of Aleck's friends, including the present writer, to have emphasized his more grotesque and displeasing qualities, with too little recognition of his underlying character. This is the trend of the thumbnail-school biography. Woollcott had done far worse to others, as in his astringent article on Owen Wister. For what followed I attempt no explanation, since the magazine staff differ over the cause of wrath; I simply record the fact that Aleck was hurt and angered as never before in his life. Indignant protests from his friends may well have contributed to his abrupt change of attitude . . . He wrote to Harold Ross:

> To me you are no longer a faithless friend. To me you are dead. Hoping and believing I will soon be the same, I remain
> Your quondam crony,
>   A. Woollcott

The plan for his return to the staff was abandoned. That productive coordination was ended for ever.

When it seemed probable to him, in 1941, that he had not long to live, Aleck wrote to Ross, making overtures for reconciliation. Ross was more than willing: he was both regretful and puzzled over the whole affair. A visit to Bomoseen was projected. The invalid's health took a turn for the better. It seemed he wasn't going to die, after all. Not for a time, anyway. The invitation was withdrawn. The two former comrades never saw one another again.

There is a faintly ludicrous corollary to the split. Loyalty to their friend impelled Alfred Lunt and his wife, Lynn Fontanne, to cancel their subscription to the weekly and ban it from their home. What was their shock, upon a visit to Bomoseen, to find the current issue on the table! Aleck was at first nonplussed by their perturbation. Then he grinned.

'Why not?' he said airily. 'I've never stopped having it sent. I'm making some suggestions now about articles.'

The rupture with Ross left scars. At that time Woollcott was fighting on another front an action which was pure, unadulterated joy of battle to his soul, if only because a national magazine spread the gory details before its millions of readers. In one of Philadelphia's suburbs there lives a millionaire patent-medicine man named Barnes, whose collection of Renoirs, Cézannes, Picassos, Matisses, and other modern painters is without parallel west of the Atlantic. Though inhospitable to the general public, Dr Barnes welcomes art students to his gallery, and maintains a ten-million-dollar fund for their training. He is a vigorous, humorous man in his sixties with a taste for polemics of the rough-and-tumble sort. If he has a weakness, it is that he is just a shade ostentatious in his contempt for Philadelphia's society and club folk, as well as of celebrities of any sort who might conceivably and erroneously feel themselves superior to a self-made specimen like himself. Carl W. McArdle, writing in the *Saturday Evening Post*, thinks him a frustrated artist and dual personality, 'Scientist, art connoisseur, and educator, who in his dealings with the public is a combination of Peck's Bad Boy and Donald Duck'. Locally he is regarded as a holy terror and has never taken any pains to ameliorate that impression. He and Woollcott had one point in common: neither shrank from publicity.

In the winter of 1939 Woollcott took a house in Philadelphia's Rittenhouse Square, where he entertained lavishly for three weeks. He knew all about Barnes, as Barnes knew all about him. Hence it was presumably with some motive other than expectation that he wrote the drug magnate, inviting himself to view the famous art collection. Barnes says that the communication was in the form of a telegram, collect; but that is merely his rampant sense of humour breaking out. His reply, through a supposititious secretary, was that Dr Barnes was out on the lawn, singing to the birds, and must not be disturbed. So witty was the letter, in its writer's own informed opinion, that he could not resist telling the *Philadelphia Record* all about it, with the gratifying result of an editorial, 'All Woollcott and a Yard

Wider', exulting over the fact that the author had 'been served a metaphorical bellyful'.

This was the gage of battle, indeed. Woollcott's weapon was to hand. He knew Benedict Gimbel, Jr., President of the Pennsylvania Broadcasting Company, and sent word to ask him for the courtesies of the studios to make some recordings and also a broadcast. Mr Gimbel put every facility at his disposal. Thus armed, the Town Crier wrote a carefully courteous letter to Barnes, explaining that his limit of visual endurance was six pictures a day, and that 'whereas I quite understand the pardonable pride in your collection which has led you to besiege me with invitations to examine it', he regretfully found that time was lacking. Further, he hoped that the patron of art would not object to having the whole matter brought out in a radio interview next day.

This threw the thrasonical doctor off balance: he could do no better than challenge his opponent to produce any proof of having been invited to the gallery, through which opening he received another thrust:

'I am afraid it will be impossible for me to continue this correspondence ... but I promise to come out and see the pictures the next time I pass this way.' Assuming prematurely that he had the best of the bout, Barnes congratulated himself upon 'trimming the fringe of your intellectual trousers, carried so high that your mental bottom was exposed to the public at large'.

Nevertheless, an uneasy dissatisfaction with the outcome possessed his mind, for when Leonard Lyons devoted an item to the epistolary exchange in his syndicated column, 'The Lyon's Den', Barnes poured out his soul in a letter denouncing Woollcott and enclosing a batch of clippings to support his cause. The subject of the clippings was mildly amused. He wrote to Lyons:

Dr Albert Barnes is so easy to tease that it may seem hardly sporting to do it. All I had to do in Philadelphia was to keep promising that I would come out to see his pictures.

The last promise elicited nine letters from him. To test him for your own amusement, drop him a line saying that, although you received his communication, it was mistakenly carried off by the cleaning woman and you did not have time to read it. You could then assume that it included an invitation to visit his picture gallery and protest that your duties in New York would not allow you to avail yourself of the opportunity. You will thereupon get eighteen letters from him.

One important point of strategy in the toy warfare escaped the usually discerning Dr Barnes. During the progress of the controversy, Woollcott was making a stage appearance in Philadelphia. The Barnes publicity advertised it by columns of invaluable and unpurchasable space. The doughty doctor had been taken for a ride by one of the most expert and resourceful press agents in the theatrical world.

The vanquished warrior's services to the victor's play did not end there. They were transferred from the local to the national field when Barnes, still smarting, imparted his woes to McArdle for use in the latter's *Saturday Evening Post* character sketch, where the whole campaign was duly set forth. As the pseudo-Woollcott play was now running with three companies from coast to coast, authors and actors were appreciative of the stimulus to general interest afforded by publicity in a national magazine.

The McArdle–*Post* version of the set-to gave Dr Barnes all the best of it. Did that satisfy the subject? Far from it. He took vehement exception to the Fontaine Fox-styled headline, 'The Terrible-Tempered Dr Barnes'.

Having a subject of special local interest to exploit, the *Post* naturally plastered the fashionable Main Line, where Barnes lived, with advertising matter.

'Barnes got himself into his chauffeur-driven car,' a member of the magazine staff describes the ensuing battle, 'and went steaming from drugstore to drugstore, tearing down and taking

away the display posters. Hot on his heels was another car filled
with Curtis promotion men who would tear into the drugstore
and put up new cards.'

The doctor also issued a hastily prepared and highly spiced
pamphlet in terms which might have been interpreted as provocative of libel action. If such was his hope, it was disappointed.
The editors ignored his aspersions upon their product, but
offered Woollcott space to reply in a pen portrait of the art-
collecting medicine man. Aleck evinced no interest. Barnes,
having served his purpose, was now squeezed dry. No more
value in him.

'He isn't worth my time or your space,' he told the *Post*.

Aleck's enduring friends – I use the term in its double sense –
bore with him out of tolerance, compromise, or kindly understanding of a character that had its elements of tragedy. They
realized that there was a deep-seated reason for these outbreaks;
that he suffered from an inner exasperation, constantly if secretly
inflamed by the ineluctable sense of his inadequacy. A relative
reproached him for one of these lapses:

'What's wrong with you, Aleck, that you put people's backs
up that way? You've got everything in life that you want.'

'How in hell do you know what I want, when I don't know
myself?' was the savage retort.

One of his oldest and fondest associates offers this theory to
account for his sudden, unreasoning violations of the social
amenities, amounting, at the worst, to breaches of decency and
fairness.

Take the case of a person who suffers from, say, incurable
and recurrent neuralgia. He goes along equably enough
most of the time. Then comes a seizure of atrocious pain,
and he lashes out at whatever object is nearest. Something
of that condition existed in Aleck's psychological make-up.
What it was, I would not undertake to say. But when it
came upon him, he would struggle for self-control as long
as he could. Then some petty occasion would set him off.

It might be a contradiction to something he had said, or a distasteful political opinion, or nothing more than an inane remark that set off the explosion. All restraint was dissolved. For a time he would be a maniac, at large with a deadly weapon. When the paroxysm was over, he would return to normal. I doubt whether he was ever really remorseful for these outbreaks since he could find self-exculpation for them. The rupture of old friendships saddened him, though his pride would not let him admit it.

The wonder is that his facility in the gentle art of making enemies did not strew his path with more wreckage of friendships than actually marked it. On the credit side must be set the fact that those who knew him best held him in indestructible affection; yet the number of these to whom he had not given just cause for offence could be reckoned on the fingers of one hand.

Alice Duer Miller, between whom and Aleck there existed a mutual affection, uninterrupted in a quarter-century of intimate association, suggested a radio discussion between them on the topic of quarrels, 'You advocating them as a means of clearing up inherent disagreements between friends, I disapproving of them on the ground that nothing worth quarrelling about could ever really be forgiven.'

The design was never carried out. It might well have been a classic of the air.

•

Artistic temperament

STEPHEN NAIFEH AND GREGORY WHITE SMITH

Jackson Pollock was one of the principal exponents of American Abstract Expressionism, for my money one of the most hateful movements in the history of art. Pollock would roll out a large canvas on the floor and drip and splatter paint on it, arguing that the expression of the artist's whole content was directed by mystic forces. By the account of Naifeh and White Smith, Pollock was not an easy person to get along with and frequently picked fights with fellow artists and critics. The critic Harold Rosenberg hated the drunken boorish Pollock and wrote an article on the American action painters in the December 1952 issue of *Art News* just days after one of Pollock's shows had closed. The article ridiculed Pollock's avowed mysticism and accused him of megalomania and of being 'a commodity with a trademark'. Pollock's wife, Lee Krasner, was of uncertain temperament herself and, as Pollock's biographers explain, reacted violently to Rosenberg's article.

Lee Krasner's fury mounted as she listened to Bradley Walker Tomlin read the article out loud. Tomlin, a genteel man with an intellectual bent, undoubtedly helped her through Rosenberg's dense, elliptical, allusive argument, but Lee didn't need an interpreter to know that Jackson was being savaged. To her, the implication of lines like 'the new painting has broken down every distinction between art and life', were all too clear: just as Jackson's life was going to hell, so was his art. Who else could Rosenberg be talking about when he referred to 'private Dark Nights', 'daily annihilation', 'megalomania', and 'easy painting'? After years of what Lee considered humiliations and slights from both Rosenberg and his wife, the article amounted to nothing less than a declaration of war – the opening salvo in a collision of epic dimensions.

If Harold Rosenberg wanted a fight, she would give him the fight of his life.

When Lee tried to rally her troops, however, she found the ranks distressingly thin. Tomlin, sympathetic but too sweet-tempered for combat, offered moral support but little else. Clyfford Still, who came by the house soon after the dispute erupted, wrote Rosenberg the usual blistering letter calling the article 'an attack on painting', but successfully resisted a long-term enlistment in any cause other than his own. Clement Greenberg [the critic], Lee's most logical ally, was curiously silent at first. When she urged him to launch a quick counter-attack, he balked, dismissing the whole notion of 'action paint-ing' as 'a purely rhetorical fabrication'. Besides, he explained, 'You get in a fight only if you respect someone, and I don't respect Harold. He doesn't tell the truth.' There were, of course, other reasons for Greenberg's uncharacteristic reticence. He had already begun to feel a rumble of discontent at the *Partisan Review* over his strident, dogmatic advocacy of a certain brand of abstract art. James Johnson Sweeney had recently been added to the *Review*'s editorial board in the full knowledge that he was no admirer of Greenberg's criticism. With his own power base threatened, Greenberg must have decided that it was hardly the time to engage Rosenberg, a well-respected and well-connected member of the same circle, in public combat. Especially over an article that, in Greenberg's opinion, was an attack not on him but on Jackson, an artist whose work he no longer respected at a time when he was increasingly preoccupied with his talented and attractive young protégée Helen Frankenthaler, who was proving far more receptive than Jackson to his formalist prescriptions. Besides, hadn't Jackson called him 'a fool'?

At first, even Jackson proved a reluctant ally. According to Conrad Marca-Relli, who saw him soon after the article ap-peared, his initial reaction was more annoyance than anger. Like Lee, he never doubted that Rosenberg had used him as a model – he later referred to the article routinely as 'Rosenberg's piece on me' – and he remembered his trainboard conversation with Rosenberg about 'the act of painting'. But to Jackson's unsubtle intellect, it appeared that Rosenberg had merely mangled his ideas. 'How stupid,' he remarked to Marca-Relli. 'I talked about the act of painting, exposing the act of painting, not action painting. Harold got it all wrong.' 'It sounded to him completely absurd,' says Marca-Relli. But at a time when the world seemed set against him, with money short and interest in his paintings flagging, Jackson readily accepted Lee's more paranoid view that he had, in fact, been deeply maligned, that 'getting it wrong' was tantamount to being wronged. Soon his official reaction, as reported by Lee, changed from 'annoyed' to 'appalled', and the article became the focus of his antagonism toward an increasingly hostile world.

It wasn't long before the war escalated. Several days after the article appeared, Willem de Kooning and Philip Pavia stopped by Jackson's house and found Lee still venting her rage. Unthinkingly, de Kooning 'announced his liking for the article' and proceeded to defend it and Rosenberg from Lee's withering assaults. The discussion 'reached new heights' of rancor and vituperation, according to one account, until de Kooning and Pavia beat a hasty retreat under heavy fire. It might have been just another of the hundreds of arguments that Rosenberg's article sparked, but Lee refused to let it rest. In a hail of telephone calls, she accused de Kooning of 'betraying her, betraying Jackson, betraying art'.

In fact, Lee's list of grievances against de Kooning, both real and imagined, went back more than a decade, to the late thirties. She had 'adored' him then. Strikingly handsome, Continental, gifted, the young Dutchman was everything Lena Krasner wanted in a man. Before meeting Jackson, she had considered *de Kooning* 'the greatest painter in the world'. Love – or at least infatuation – had followed inevitably. At a New Year's Eve party in the late thirties, she had thrown herself at him, sitting on his lap, playing the coquette. At the climactic moment, however, just as she was about to kiss him, he opened his knees and let her drop comically to the floor, humiliating her in front of friends and fellow artists. After drowning her shame in booze, she began to rail at him, calling him 'a phony' and 'a shit', until Fritz Bultman dragged her away and forced her into the shower with all her clothes on.

That night still ranked as one of the worst of Lee's life. In the years since, her scorned infatuation had turned to bile. She accused de Kooning of suborning Jackson's drinking, sabotaging his reputation, and, worst of all, 'refusing to acknowledge that [Jackson] was number one'. For the same reasons, compounded by jealousy, Lee hated the woman de Kooning had married, Elaine Fried, a smart, sociable, witty, vital, unpretentious, and – most galling – attractive young artist. Over the years, the two women had successfully gilded their rivalry with a chilly cordiality that fooled no one except their husbands. Lee suspected that Elaine, a close friend of Tom Hess, had been behind the second-class treatment Jackson received in Hess's book, *Abstract Painting: Background and American Phase*. She had forgiven Hess (she and Jackson asked him to write a book on the black-and-white paintings), but both de Koonings had remained high on her long list of enemies. De Kooning's defense of Rosenberg catapulted him to the top of that list.

Lee had even more trouble recruiting Jackson for this new front in her widening war. Jackson and Bill de Kooning had enjoyed a friendly, if not warm, mutual respect since Lee introduced them in the early forties. When Lionel Abel visited Springs in 1948, Jackson told him, 'We've just had a painter here who's better than me,' Abel remembers. 'He was talking about Bill de Kooning. They were competitive, but there was a lot of generosity lurking in that competitiveness.' The same summer, Jackson 'bragged' to Harry Jackson and Grace Hartigan about de Kooning and sent both young artists to see him at his studio in New York. Reuben Kadish recalls that Jackson always considered de Kooning 'one of the top guys', a sentiment he shared with Dorothy Seiberling when she interviewed him for the *Life* article in the summer of 1949. 'Pollock's taste in contemporary art,' she wrote in her notes, 'runs to similarly obscure painters [like] de Kooning.' The Club, Jackson's celebrity, and the rising tide of resentment it engendered among other artists had tested but not undermined the 'lurking generosity' between the two men. To Lee's great mortification, they continued to drink together occasionally – more by coincidence than planning – to enjoy each other's company, and to admire each other's art, even as the battle lines were being drawn around them.

Unlike her allies, Lee's enemies coalesced against her with dreadnought efficiency. Rosenberg and de Kooning had enjoyed a casual friendship since the Project days. During the summer of 1952, when de Kooning set up a studio in the big house that Leo Castelli rented in East Hampton, the two men saw more of each other than they had in the previous decade. Both enjoyed the gamesmanship of intellectual discourse around the dinner table; both were used to being the center of attention: Rosenberg for his towering size and intellect, de Kooning for his looks. In conversation, both liked to play agent provocateur: Rosenberg by 'saying things just to be contrary', de Kooning by dropping an incendiary remark then stepping back to watch others battle over it. They also shared a thoughtful, if not deep, philosophical streak. (When asked if he would rather be 'a half-assed philosopher or a great painter', de Kooning replied, 'Let me think about that.') To the subject of art, both brought what Leslie Fiedler called 'a European eye' and an interest in ideas. If they differed, it was on the question of how those ideas related to painting: Rosenberg the radical ideologue; de Kooning the pragmatic, workmanlike Lowlander.

Ironically, the catalyst that transformed this casual friendship into a formidable alliance was Lee Krasner. Over the years, her dogged, single-minded promotion of Jackson had left deep reservoirs of ill will among those she had 'elbowed out of Jackson's path'. 'She built this Chinese Wall around him,' recalls Philip Pavia, 'and everyone resented it.' Both de Kooning and Rosenberg had felt Lee's protective coldness and her blazing temper. Not surprisingly, Rosenberg cast his antagonism in a political light: 'Some people have been around Stalinists so long,' he quipped, 'they start acting like Stalin.' Behind the enmity of both men, urging them on, lay the deeper, more bitter, and perhaps more manipulative anger of their wives, May Rosenberg and Elaine de Kooning, both of whom felt, for different reasons, that Jackson (and Lee) had monopolized the limelight for too long. At dinner parties, the two couples and their friends joked bitterly about Lee and the 'life-and-death' passion she brought to her role as Jackson's shield and right arm. They took a certain furtive pleasure in her desperate, and increasingly unsuccessful, struggle to contain his self-destructive impulses and to conceal his peccadilloes from the world. To them, she was sometimes 'Lady Macbeth', who would 'gladly stab to make a king or get a lover', sometimes Medea, ready to 'stab or choke *Jackson*' rather than see him delivered into the hands of his detractors. Whatever their other differences may have been, they were united in their hatred of Lee.

In this crossfire of personal antagonisms, ideas were the first casualty. Rosenberg liked de Kooning's paintings well enough – although not as much as those of Hofmann, Baziotes, and Gorky – but they bore little relationship to the theory of 'action painting'. Nor was de Kooning anything like the revolutionary hero portrayed in 'The American Action Painters'. In addition to being neither American nor, after 1952, nonfigurative, he was a thoughtful, controlled artist whose bravura brushwork belied the hours of preparation, execution, and evaluation that went into it. According to his wife, he 'would sit and look for two hours for every five minutes of painting'. Far from liberating himself from all aesthetic 'Value', he openly carried on a dialogue with the European Beaux Arts tradition in which he was trained, and admired such unrevolutionary artists as Frederic Remington.

Fortunately, de Kooning considered Rosenberg's ideas as irrelevant as Rosenberg considered de Kooning's paintings. Herbert Ferber, who worked in a neighboring studio on Broadway, recalls that de Kooning dismissed Rosenberg's theories as 'a lot of nonsense'. One day he walked into de Kooning's studio and saw why. 'There were fifty or seventy-five pounds of paint on the floor that he had just scraped off,' recalls Ferber. 'I said, "What's that expensive stuff doing on the floor?" and he said, "Well, you know, you have to think about what you do. I didn't like it, so I try this, and I scrape it off and try that." That,' says Ferber, 'is not "action painting".'

But ideological consistency no longer mattered – if it ever

did. At cocktail parties and openings, in artists' studios and East Hampton living rooms, at the Club and over the phone lines, the battle was joined.

Lee spread the story that Rosenberg had stolen the idea and the phrase 'action painting' from Jackson. While acknowledging their conversation, Rosenberg indignantly denied the plagiarism charge. (To Lionel Abel, he admitted that Jackson had used the term 'action painting' first but only because he, Rosenberg, 'had put the idea in Jackson's mouth'. Later, under fire, Rosenberg vehemently denied that he owed the idea *or* the phrase to anyone, least of all Jackson.) Rosenberg not only denied the charge, he denied that the article was even *about* Jackson. He accused Jackson of 'painting like a monkey', invoking the stories that had been published in the wake of the *Life* article about a zookeeper and her precocious chimp. The comment quickly made the rounds. Lee and Jackson's partisans accused de Kooning of 'craving recognition at Jackson's expense', and Rosenberg of 'pushing Jackson out of the way to get de Kooning in'. May Rosenberg accused Lee of 'wanting to destroy everybody except for Jackson'. Lee called May 'paranoid', 'psychotic', and 'a madwoman', implying that only a madwoman could put up with Harold's cheating. May fired back accusations that Lee had 'an aggravated case of dementia', implying that only a madwoman could put up with Jackson's drinking. May also charged that Lee only wanted to make money and had curried favor among rich collectors for years and greedily kept other artists away.

The dispute spread quickly. Lee launched counteroffensives not just against the Rosenbergs and the de Koonings but against anyone who defended them. She attacked the Club, as a hotbed of resistance to Jackson's reputation. The list of maligned artists grew longer and longer and soon included even old friends like Wilfrid Zogbaum. For whatever reason – perhaps because, having conquered Jackson, she craved new, more titanic collisions – Lee was determined to turn her attack on Rosenberg into a test of faith: a referendum on Jackson

Pollock. Everyone in the art world would be forced to declare loyalties, to choose sides: either you were for Jackson or against him.

It was a disastrous miscalculation.

In the battle for hearts and minds, Rosenberg proved a formidable adversary. At the Club and the Cedar Tavern (an unofficial annex of the Club), his towering figure, fierce visage, and glib wit 'made him an instant object of adoration'. To many artists, he played the intellectual mentor who, like Breton, was among them if not of them. (At a concert of works by John Cage, Rosenberg stood up and announced to the overcrowded room: 'This is for artists only. Everyone else can go home.') The artists liked the intellectuals he gathered around him: men like Tom Hess and Edwin Denby; and the nonstop intellectual conversation they generated. It made them feel good about themselves and the importance of what they were doing. When the article on 'action painting' appeared, they didn't stop to ponder the details. As with so many of Rosenberg's other ideas, they knew they liked the *sound* of it. According to Leslie Fiedler, they reveled in the sheer masculinity of it. To the generation that had come through the Project, it justified the years of barroom antics, hard drinking, misogyny, and competitive cocksmanship. To the new generation of younger artists, it exploded the stereotype of the artist as foppish, worthless, and — worst of all in the can-do, postwar culture — ineffectual. At a time when anxiety about 'making it' was just beginning to be felt, they took comfort in its defiant anticommercialism. They warmed to its antihistorical and pro-American prejudices. Although they made fun of it, they even liked Rosenberg's dense, indecipherable style. It made them feel that art was indeed a higher calling that touched on issues so profound and philosophical that it was impossible, even for an intellect as great as Rosenberg's, to communicate them clearly to ordinary minds.

But mostly they liked it because it wasn't Greenberg. Finally, someone had challenged Pope Clement; a gate-crasher had confronted the 'bloody concierge' of avant-garde art. Finally, someone had found a different way of looking at abstract paintings; finally, someone was offering artists an escape from what they perceived as the yoke of Greenberg's caprice. They had had enough of his visiting their studios and 'telling them what to paint' (a charge Greenberg would later vigorously deny); of his summarily dismissing young painters like Larry Rivers; of his deciding what was good, what was bad, who was great and who wasn't. In the Cedar Tavern, Milton Resnick heard Greenberg bragging 'that he juried a show and gave somebody a prize on the condition that he turn the picture upside down because it looked better that way'. 'You son of a bitch', Resnick hissed as he got up from the table. 'I'm never going to sit with you again.' The other artists at the table followed him out the door. Everyone who heard the story applauded.

Neither Rosenberg's popularity nor Greenberg's disrepute, however, proved fatal to Lee's cause. If she had limited her attacks to Rosenberg, both she and Jackson might have emerged relatively unscathed from the usual round of name-calling and social trench warfare. It was by attacking Willem de Kooning that Lee doomed Jackson's cause to certain failure.

No artist was more respected or better liked. Far more convincingly than Rosenberg, de Kooning was 'one of the boys'. At the Club, he volunteered to wash glasses and sweep up after meetings. Unlike Jackson, he lived in the heart of the artists' community, a relatively small patch of New York City described by Irving Sandler as 'centered in the studios on and around East Tenth Street, the Cedar Street Tavern, and the Club'. At a time when Robert Motherwell was 'living his haute bourgeois life' uptown and Clyfford Still maintained a monastic isolation, de Kooning was always available to younger artists. Sensitive and self-effacing, he brought to all his conversations enormous intensity, unpretentious intelligence and a dry, almost inadvertent sense of humor. (At a reception, he told Mrs John D. Rockefeller, 'You look like a million bucks.')

Unlike Jackson's celebrity, which many artists considered an invention of Clement Greenberg's, de Kooning's reputation derived from the only legitimate source: his fellow artists. He had worked his way up 'through the ranks', earning their respect and support long before winning gallery recognition or media attention. Young artists especially, like Grace Hartigan, found him 'a devastating experience because of his brilliant articulateness'. They admired his thoughtful, persuasive art. Unlike Jackson's work – about which even his admirers often complained, 'What the hell can you do with it?' – de Kooning's embraced them. 'People could hook into the traditional in his paintings,' says Nicholas Carone. 'You know, a beautiful line, a nice passage.' 'De Kooning provided a language you could write your own sentences with,' said Al Held. 'Pollock didn't do that.' Jackson may have been a force of nature, but de Kooning was the embodiment of culture. In fact, despite Rosenberg's requirement that vanguard artists break with the past, most artists stood behind de Kooning (and, by association, Rosenberg) precisely *because* he, in turn, stood squarely in the *artiste peintre* tradition. He was 'in the line': Cézanne, Matisse, Picasso, Hofmann, Matta, Gorky, de Kooning. 'If you had a choice and you wanted to pick up on the whole grand tradition of Western art,' recalls Irving Sandler, 'you were against Jackson and with Bill.' At the Club, a painter named Ari Stillman stood up and announced: 'The young artists think de Kooning is Number One because he's interested in "good" painting.' Pollock he dismissed as a 'primitive Breakthrough Boy', a 'freak'. 'Jackson may have been the genius,' says Sandler, 'but the *painter* was Bill.'

Finally, and perhaps most important, de Kooning reciprocated the respect his colleagues lavished on him. 'When he came over for dinner,' recalls Eleanor Hempstead, 'it didn't matter if you had an El Greco or a Rubens or a Rembrandt on the wall, he went right for *your* work. Even if it was just some little watercolor, he would go and look at it and make a nice remark like "Did you do this?" in an admiring way. He always commented.'

For all Lee's efforts, for all the rising talk of 'civil war' and the art world dividing into opposing camps, there was, as John Myers pointed out with a touch of sadness, 'only one camp, really, and that was de Kooning's . . . It was Jackson against the world.'

•

Papa Hemingway tries to pick a fight
GEORGE PLIMPTON

Ernest Hemingway was interested in what had gone on in Stillman's Gym with Archie Moore. George Brown had told him about what had happened, and I was surprised to hear from Hemingway, because he and I had had a falling-out over a *Paris Review* interview I had done with him on the craft of writing. He had sent me a savage letter saying that I had wasted his time and diverted his attention from more important things. I had felt rotten about it, as much for the disappointment of realizing how much venom he could let loose as for having monopolized his time.

Hemingway was famous at the art of making enemies, especially of people who were close to him. Archibald MacLeish once told me about the time Hemingway had been badly injured in an automobile accident in Montana. MacLeish had set out across the country to comfort his friend (an arduous enough trip to take in the late twenties when this happened), and had arrived only to be lambasted by the patient. 'He somehow got the idea in his head that I had come to gloat over his impending death. He looked like anything but a dying man to me. He was growing a black beard, and Pauline, his wife, had to fight to keep the nurses off him.' Increasingly, this bitterness seemed to become a part of his character. During his latter days in Cuba, when he would get cranky, he would go up to the tower of the *finca* to shoot at the vultures coming over the trees in the air

currents, pretending that they were people he did not like . . .
the critic Bernard de Voto, William Faulkner . . . the latter an
ironic choice in that Faulkner had said (indeed, in a *Paris Review*
interview) that he wanted to come back in his next life as a
buzzard. It occurred to me, of course, to wonder if *I* had ever
been responsible for the end of a vulture, one just tilting across
the big ficus by the front of the house, idly musing how nicely
he was digesting a long-gone mouse he'd found, when *puff!* he
was hit and dropped like a black feather duster onto the little
baseball diamond below the hill.

What made it especially taxing to be acquainted with
Hemingway was not only the unpredictable nature of the sort
MacLeish (and a great many others) experienced but also
Hemingway's constant testing of his friends to see if they
measured up to expectations. And it did not take much to fall
swiftly from grace. Peter Viertel, a dashing novelist–sportsman
very much in the Hemingway mold, was disgraced one
afternoon simply because he got seasick aboard the *Pilar*,
Hemingway's boat, out in the Gulf Stream. Although Viertel's
distress was thought to have been brought on by a turtle soup
Hemingway insisted on his sampling, Hemingway's feelings
about him changed abruptly. Viertel was required to leave the
finca, where he had been staying as a houseguest, and to move
to a hotel in town. Although he was working on the screenplay
of *The Old Man and the Sea*, Hemingway would not talk to him.
No one could patch it up. 'He gets sick,' Hemingway would
say.

'But you really must speak to him.'

'What for? He gets *sick*.'

In my own experience with him I had been tested a few
times. Once he asked me to come with him and shoot live
pigeons in competition at a gun club outside Havana – 'You're
good with a gun, huh?' – and before I could tell him that I knew
almost nothing of the art he said that he was going to get some
good bets down on me. In the predawn hours of the day of the
shoot the phone rang in the room of the Ambos Mundos Hotel,

where I was tossing nervously, and I can remember the relief with which I heard his voice, scratchy and weak over the connection, telling me that the gun club had been closed for a period of mourning: the president of the place had committed suicide just the evening before.

'Oh God!' I cried, as if the president were a blood relative and it was the first I had heard of the news. 'Oh God!'

Then the falling-out had come along, none the less, over the *Paris Review* interview, and I doubted I would ever hear from him again. But one day in New York he rang up, and I heard his tentative voice at the other end – I always had the sense that he disliked phones, or that he was uneasy with them – and he said he had heard about the Archie Moore fight; he wanted me to come around to the Sherry-Netherland Hotel.

I went around and told him about my experience in the ring. He was glad to see me and he was good company. He was very pleased about the notion of the fight, and told me he wished I had come out and trained with him in Ketcham, Idaho. 'You'd have done better,' he said. Sometimes I think he got the priorities mixed up, thinking that it wasn't to provide material for notebooks that I was fighting as much as to undergo a physical test – truly as if what I was after was Archie Moore's championship. When I said things had been difficult, he said, 'If you'd have come out to Ketcham, we'd have made a strong fighter out of you.' He urged me to get into the ring again as soon as possible. 'The elephant hunter,' he said, 'can't begin to call himself one until his fiftieth elephant.'

'Good God,' I said.

'Truly, and even then he's only just beginning to understand the character of his game.'

He himself had started boxing when he was fourteen. Big for his age, he had been invited to spar in a Chicago gym with Young A'Hearn, who was a fair middleweight. He got laid out with a smashed-in nose, but it didn't seem to discourage him. He went back to the gym for more lessons.

'I knew he was going to give me the works the minute I saw his eyes . . .'

'Were you scared?'

'Sure. He could hit like hell.'

'Why'd you go in there with him?'

'I wasn't that scared.'

That was the start of it, and since then Hemingway had turned the tables and pummeled a lot of people.

George Brown told me Papa was a dirty fighter who took every advantage that he could, and on a number of occasions when the two of them had sparred he had tried to knee George. Once, he brought his fist down on the top of George's head during a clinch, and George had to 'cool' him. He wouldn't explain quite how he had done it; he smiled and looked away.

'Don't even fool with him,' he told me.

'Well, I don't mean to.'

'It may happen.'

'Well, you won't tell me what to do.'

'Well, I lean on him,' he finally told me. 'I joke with him, and tell him how *strong* he is, and all the time I'm hanging over those big shoulders of his, digging him a few shots in the kidney region, always talking to him, though, to keep him calm, like talking to a duck whose throat has been cut, and soon enough the strength drains out of him and he feels more like sitting down than fighting. That's how to handle him.'

'Oh, yes,' I said.

'You have to be careful. He's not predictable.'

George was right. That spring, I flew over from Florida to see the Hemingways in Cuba. He seemed so gracious and friendly. I remember standing with him on a fisherman's wharf where he had docked the *Pilar* – we'd had a first-rate day fishing out on the Gulf Stream – he was in such a good mood as we stepped off the boat and proceeded up the dock that I thought I would press him with a question about a literary device that had always puzzled me.

'Papa,' I asked, 'what is the significance of those white birds that sometimes turn up in your, um ... sex scenes? I've always ...'

I mentioned this in a high, cheery voice, as if it were a natural enough matter to come up in conversation; actually it always *had* puzzled me, especially the white bird that flies out of the gondola in the love scene between the young princess and Colonel Cantwell in *Across the River and Into the Trees*.

He stopped and whipped around toward me and I could see that I had made a mistake. His whiskers seemed to bristle like an alarmed cat's. 'I suppose you think you can do better,' he shouted at me.

'No, no, Papa,' I said. 'Certainly not.'

I noticed how small his eyes had become, suddenly, and bloodshot, as if affected by the flush of rage that showed on his cheekbones, and if I had not been carrying a very excellent picnic hamper of his with some wine left over in it and some cheese, he might well have bulled me off the dock into the bay.

I hoped he would calm down. The next day at lunch at the *finca* there were three of us, the Hemingways and myself, not counting Christobal, who was Hemingway's favorite cat, and who lolled next to his plate – a sort of Roman emperor of a cat who from his supine position occasionally dropped his head back, his jaws agape, and accepted a morsel of food from his master's fingers as if a grape were being dropped down a pipe. He was absolutely inert; his tail never moved – a calico-marked receptacle.

I was remarking on this to myself when suddenly the Hemingways began to have an argument – a sort of Mr-and-Mrs dispute, except that they were arguing not about who was going to set out the garbage the next morning but about how many lions they had seen on a particular day during their latest safari in Africa. As soon as the argument started, the cat snapped its jaws shut and began to look edgy. I've forgotten exactly what the discrepancy of the numbers was; Hemingway said that they had seen eight lions, and Miss Mary said eleven, something like that, and she could prove it by looking it all up in her diary. Hemingway said her diary wasn't reliable; it took someone who was truly experienced to count lions milling around a waterhole, and she was probably counting the same lion twice. Miss Mary had something sharp to say in reply to that, and while this niggling was going on, Hemingway suddenly looked across the table and saw me sitting there.

He looked at me almost as if he had noticed me for the first time. Since lions were the nub of their dispute, that was the first quick impression – the big-cat character of the large grizzled head turning, the intense curiosity of that first formidable look, all of this compounded by the evident testiness, so that one had the forboding sense of what a gazelle must feel when he looks up to find a lion staring at him over a bush.

Hemingway pushed back his chair. Its legs shrilled on the tile floor and Christobal jumped off the table.

'Let's see how good you are,' Hemingway said.

I had no idea what he was talking about. But then, as he came around the end of the refectory table, I could see that he was assuming a semicrouch, his hands bunched at his waist, and I realized he wanted to spar – he wanted to take a look at George Brown's pupil.

But of course it was something else, too; he was belligerent now, and he wanted to lash out at someone. Perhaps he remembered my impertinent question about the white bird the day before. I pushed back my chair and stood up to face him – my hands up in front of my chin – and I put on a tremendous smile to indicate that I hoped he'd calm down and all of this was going to be in good fun. I put out my left hand, flicking it an inch or so off his whiskers, to keep him away, and he stepped past quickly. His hands were rolled at belt level, and one of them came up in a left hook and I was banged hard alongside the head, past my guard, and I staggered backward and my chair went over. I felt the sympathetic response at work, the tears beginning to spring out; my smile wobbled; I moved around behind the fallen chair, keeping it between us, and I leaned over it and kept my left out. I noticed once again how small the eyes were in his face, and furious like a pig's, and yet how surprising and utterly unnatural it would have been actually to hit out at those whiskers.

In the corner Christobal was playing with a ping-pong ball, quite oblivious of the shuffling of feet, of the chair's going over, as if he had his own workout to conduct, and I remember the sharp *toc* sound of the ball as he slapped it round the tile floor: A side glance: I could see Miss Mary sitting, head down, picking at her salad. No relief there.

I thought of George Brown's instructions – to drape myself over his shoulders and talk to him like a farmer's wife to a dying duck. But under the circumstances that seemed quite illogical: it meant getting close to him, and to the fists beginning to roll once again in tight quick circles at his waist.

But then suddenly I was inspired – perhaps not even consciously; could it have been simple resignation? – to stop and drop my hands by my side.

'How do you do that?' I asked, trying to keep my voice contained, as if a question which I could not understand had come up in a math class.

'Huh?'

'I mean, I don't understand how you did that,' I went on. 'That punch.'

He looked pleased. 'Pretty good, huh?'

'I mean, to be able to do that with your hands hung so low.'

'Yes.' Across the chair his hands stopped their rolling movement; he flexed his fingers as if tired of bunching them. 'Counterpunch,' he announced. 'Look here,' he said. He was as pleased as an inventor showing off a machine. 'The principle . . .' He came around the chair to show me. He said, 'No, no, no, not that way,' and he pushed my hands around until I was doing it properly. I was cuffed around a little bit more, but it was to illustrate a point in the art of the counterpunch and not as a target of his frustration. I kept asking him questions. How come his knuckles were so flat? Was that from fighting? He stopped and rubbed them. No, they had flattened out over the years, he said, a couple of them when he was trying to punch out a dent in a German helmet. He looked pleased to have been asked.

'Oh, yes,' I said.

Miss Mary looked up from her salad and smiled at us. I remember hoping she wasn't going to butt into the nice time we were having and insist on the number of lions she'd seen on that day long past . . .

•

The hate that hate produced
MALCOLM X

In 1946 Malcolm Little was sentenced to prison on burglary charges. While in prison he became acquainted with Elijah Muhammad's Black Muslim sect and was converted to its Utopian and highly racist point of view. Paroled in 1952 he became an outspoken defender of Muslim doctrines. In 1963 the now self-styled Malcolm X was expelled from the Black Muslim movement and he formed his own group, the Organization of Afro-American Unity. By the time of his murder in 1965, Malcolm X was world-famous as 'the angriest black man in America'.

In this extract from his autobiography, Malcolm X describes the hostile press reception of a television programme about the Black Muslims, *The Hate that Hate Produced*.

In late 1959, the television program was aired. 'The Hate That Hate Produced' – the title – was edited tightly into a kaleido-scope of 'shocker' images . . . Mr Muhammad, me, and others speaking . . . strong-looking, set-faced black men, our Fruit of Islam . . . white-scarved, white gowned Muslim sisters of all ages . . . Muslims in our restaurants, and other businesses . . . Muslims and other black people entering and leaving our mosques . . .

Every phrase was edited to increase the shock mood. As the producers intended, I think people sat just about limp when the program went off.

In a way, the public reaction was like what happened back in the 1930s when Orson Welles frightened America with a radio program describing, as though it was actually happening, an invasion by 'men from Mars'.

No one now jumped from any windows, but in New York City there was an instant avalanche of public reaction. It's my personal opinion that the 'Hate . . . Hate . . .' title was primarily responsible for the reaction. Hundreds of thousands of New Yorkers, black and white, were exclaiming 'Did you hear it? Did you see it? Preaching *hate* of white people!'

Here was one of the white man's most characteristic behavior patterns – where black men are concerned. He loves himself so much that he is startled if he discovers that his victims don't share his vainglorious self-opinion. In America for centuries it had been just fine as long as the victimized, brutalized and exploited black people had been grinning and begging and 'Yessa, Massa' and Uncle Tomming. But now, things were different. First came the white newspapers – feature writers and columnists: 'Alarming' . . . 'hate-messengers' . . . 'threat to the good relations between the races' . . . 'black segregationists' . . . 'black supremacists', and the like.

And the newspapers' ink wasn't dry before the big national weekly news magazines started: 'Hate-teachers' . . . 'violence-seekers' . . . 'black racists' . . . 'black fascists' . . . 'anti-Christian' . . . 'possibly Communist-inspired . . .'

It rolled out of the presses of the biggest devil in the history of mankind. And then the aroused white man made his next move.

Since slavery, the American white man has always kept some handpicked Negroes who fared much better than the black masses suffering and slaving out in the hot fields. The white man had these 'house' and 'yard' Negroes for his special serv-ants. He threw them more crumbs from his rich table, he even let them eat in his kitchen. He knew that he could always count on them to keep 'good massa' happy in his self-image of being so 'good' and 'righteous'. 'Good massa' always heard just what he wanted to hear from these 'house' and 'yard' blacks. 'You're such a good, *fine* massa!' Or, 'Oh, massa, those old black nigger fieldhands out there, they're happy just like they are; why, massa, they're not intelligent enough for you to try and do any better for them, massa —'

Well, slavery time's 'house' and 'yard' Negroes had become more sophisticated, that was all. When now the white man picked up his telephone and dialed his 'house' and 'yard' Negroes — why, he didn't even need to instruct the trained black puppets. They had seen the television program; had read the newspapers. They were already composing their lines. They knew what to do.

I'm not going to call any names. But if you make a list of the biggest Negro 'leaders', so-called, in 1960, then you've named the ones who began to attack us 'field' Negroes who were sounding *insane*, talking that way about 'good massa'.

'By no means do these Muslims represent the Negro masses —' That was the first worry, to reassure 'good massa' that he had no reason to be concerned about his fieldhands in the ghettoes. 'An irresponsible hate cult' . . . 'an unfortunate Negro image, just when the racial picture is improving —'

They were stumbling over each other to get quoted. 'A deplorable reverse-racism' . . . 'Ridiculous pretenders to the ancient Islamic doctrine' . . . 'Heretic anti-Christianity —'

The telephone in our then small Temple Seven restaurant nearly jumped off the wall. I had a receiver against my ear five hours a day. I was listening, and jotting in my notebook, as press, radio and television people called, all of them wanting the Muslim reaction to the quoted attacks of these black 'leaders'. Or I was on long-distance to Mr Muhammad in Chicago, reading from my notebook and asking for Mr Muhammad's instructions.

I couldn't understand how Mr Muhammad could maintain his calm and patience, hearing the things I told him. I could scarcely contain myself.

My unlisted home telephone number somehow got out. My

wife Betty put down the phone after taking one message, and it was ringing again. It seemed that wherever I went, telephones were ringing.

The calls naturally were directed to me, New York City being the major news-media headquarters, and I was the New York minister of Mr Muhammad. Calls came, long-distance from San Francisco to Maine . . . from even London, Stockholm, Paris. I would see a Muslim brother at our restaurant, or Betty at home, trying to keep cool; they'd hand me the receiver, and I couldn't believe it, either. One funny thing – in all that hectic period, something quickly struck my notice: the Europeans never pressed the 'hate' question. Only the American white man was so plagued and obsessed with being 'hated'. He was so guilty, it was clear to me, of hating Negroes.

'Mr Malcolm X, why do you teach black supremacy, and hate?' A red flag waved for me, something chemical happened inside me, every time I heard that. When we Muslims had talked about 'the devil white man' he had been relatively abstract, someone we Muslims rarely actually came into contact with, but now here was that devil-in-the-flesh on the phone – with all of his calculating, cold-eyed, self-righteous tricks and nerve and gall. The voices questioning me became to me as breathing, living devils.

And I tried to pour on pure fire in return. 'The white man so guilty of white supremacy can't hide *his* guilt by trying to accuse The Honorable Elijah Muhammad of teaching black supremacy and hate! All Mr Muhammad is doing is trying to uplift the black man's mentality and the black man's social and economic condition in this country.

'The guilty, two-faced white man can't decide *what* he wants. Our slave foreparents would have been put to death for advocating so-called "integration" with the white man. Now when Mr Muhammad speaks of "separation", the white man calls us "hate-teachers" and "fascists"!

'The white man doesn't *want* the blacks! He doesn't *want* the blacks that are a parasite upon him! He doesn't *want* this black man whose presence and condition in this country expose the white man to the world for what he is! So why do you attack Mr Muhammad?'

I'd have *scathing* in my voice; I *felt* it.

'For the white man to ask the black man if he hates him is just like the rapist asking the *raped*, or the wolf asking the *sheep*, "Do you hate me?" The white man is in no moral *position* to accuse anyone else of hate!

'Why, when all of my ancestors are snake-bitten, and I'm snake-bitten, and I warn my children to avoid snakes, what does that *snake* sound like accusing *me* of hate-teaching?'

'Mr Malcolm X,' those devils would ask, 'why is your Fruit of Islam being trained in judo and karate?' An image of black men learning anything suggesting self-defense seemed to terrify the white man. I'd turn their question around: 'Why does judo or karate suddenly get so ominous because black men study it? Across America, the Boy Scouts, the YMCA, even the YWCA, the CYP, PAL – they *all* teach judo! It's all right, it's fine – until *black men* teach it! Even little grammar school classes, little girls, are taught to defend themselves –'

'How many of you are in your organization, Mr Malcolm X? Right Reverend Bishop T. Chickenwing says you have only a handful of members –'

'Whoever tells you how many Muslims there are doesn't know, and whoever does know will never tell you –'

The Bishop Chickenwings were also often quoted about our 'anti-Christianity'. I'd fire right back on that:

'Christianity is the white man's religion. The Holy Bible in the white man's hands and his interpretations of it have been the greatest single ideological weapon for enslaving millions of non-white human beings. Every country the white man has conquered with his guns, he has always paved the way, and salved his conscience, by carrying the Bible and interpreting it to call the people "heathens" and "pagans"; then he sends his guns, then his missionaries behind the guns to mop up –'

White reporters, anger in their voices, would call us

'demagogues', and I would try to be ready after I had been asked the same question two or three times.

'Well, let's go back to the Greek, and maybe you will learn the first thing you need to know about the word "demagogue". "Demagogue" means, actually, "teacher of the people". And let's examine some demagogues. The greatest of all Greeks, Socrates, was killed as a "demagogue". Jesus Christ died on the cross because the Pharisees of His day were upholding their law, not the spirit. The modern Pharisees are trying to heap destruction upon Mr Muhammad, calling him a demagogue, a crackpot and fanatic. What about Gandhi? The man that Churchill called "a naked little fakir", refusing food in a British jail? But then a quarter of a billion people, a whole subcontinent, rallied behind Gandhi – and they twisted the British Lion's tail! What about Galileo, standing before his inquisitors, saying "The earth *does* move!" What about Martin Luther, nailing on a door his thesis against the all-powerful Catholic church which called him "heretic"? We, the followers of The Honorable Elijah Muhammad, are today in the ghettoes as once the sect of Christianity's followers were like termites in the catacombs and the grottoes – and they were preparing the grave of the mighty Roman Empire!'

I can remember those hot telephone sessions with those reporters as if it were yesterday. The reporters were angry. I was angry. When I'd reach into history, they'd try to pull me back to the present. They would quit interviewing, quit their work, trying to defend their personal white devil selves. They would unearth Lincoln and his freeing of the slaves. I'd tell them things Lincoln said in speeches, *against* the blacks. They would drag up the 1954 Supreme Court decision on school integration.

'That was one of the greatest magical feats ever performed in America,' I'd tell them. 'Do you mean to tell me that nine Supreme Court judges, who are past masters of legal phraseology, couldn't have worked their decision to make it stick as *law*? No! It was trickery and magic that told Negroes they were desegregated – Hooray! Hooray! – and at the same time it told whites "Here are your loopholes."'

The reporters would try their utmost to raise some 'good' white man whom I couldn't refute as such. I'll never forget how one practically lost his voice. He asked me did I feel *any* white man had ever done anything for the black man in America. I told him, 'Yes, I can think of two. Hitler, and Stalin. The black man in America couldn't get a decent factory job until Hitler put so much pressure on the white man. And then Stalin kept up the pressure –'

But I don't care what points I made in the interviews, it practically never got printed the way I said it. I was learning under fire how the press, when it wants to, can twist, and slant. If I had said 'Mary had a little lamb', what probably would have appeared was 'Malcolm X Lampoons Mary'.

Even so, my bitterness was less against the white press than it was against those Negro 'leaders' who kept attacking us. Mr Muhammad said he wanted us to try our best not to publicly counterattack the black 'leaders' because one of the white man's tricks was keeping the black race divided and fighting against each other. Mr Muhammad said that this had traditionally kept the black people from achieving the unity which was the worst need of the black race in America.

But instead of abating, the black puppets continued ripping and tearing at Mr Muhammad and the Nation of Islam – until it began to appear as though we were afraid to speak out against these 'important' Negroes. That's when Mr Muhammad's patience wore thin. And with his nod, I began returning their fire.

'Today's Uncle Tom doesn't wear a handkerchief on his head. This modern, twentieth-century Uncle Thomas now often wears a top hat. He's usually well-dressed and well-educated. He's often the personification of culture and refinement. The twentieth-century Uncle Thomas sometimes speaks with a Yale or Harvard accent. Sometimes he is known as Professor, Doctor, Judge, and Reverend, even Right Reverend Doctor. This twentieth-century Uncle Thomas is a *professional* Negro . . . by that I mean his profession is being a Negro for the white man.'

Never before in America had these handpicked so-called 'leaders' been publicly blasted in this way. They reacted to the truth about themselves even more hotly than the devilish white man. Now their 'institutional' indictments of us began. Instead of 'leaders' speaking as themselves, for themselves, now their weighty-name organizations attacked Mr Muhammad.

'Black bodies with white heads!' I called them what they were. Every one of those 'Negro progress' organizations had the same composition. Black 'leaders' were out in the public eye – to be seen by the Negroes for whom they were supposed to be fighting the white man. But obscurely, behind the scenes, was a white boss – a president, or board chairman, or a some other title, pulling the real strings.

It was hot, hot copy, both in the white and the black press. *Life*, *Look*, *Newsweek* and *Time* reported us. Some newspaper chains began to run not one story, but a series of three, four, or five 'exposures' of the Nation of Islam. The *Reader's Digest* with its worldwide circulation of twenty-four million copies in thirteen languages carried an article titled 'Mr Muhammad Speaks', by the writer to whom I am telling this book; and that led off other major monthly magazines' coverage of us.

•

An intensely personal duel: Jimmy Hoffa and Bobby Kennedy

ARTHUR SCHLESINGER JR

As counsel for the United States Senate Permanent Subcommittee on Investigations, Robert Kennedy led the committee's attention to labour racketeering. Gangsters, attracted by the spectacular growth of trade union welfare and pension funds, and by the convenience of unions as a cover for exercises in bribery and extortion, were engaged in the systematic invasion of the American labour movement. Of these, the Teamsters Union was worst affected. Kennedy loathed the labour racketeers and most of all, he loathed the Teamsters' leader, Jimmy Hoffa. Kennedy's pursuit of the corrupt union official was relentless. The two men's hatred of each other is explained by Kennedy's biographer. It is often suggested that Hoffa may have had something to do with the murders of the Kennedy brothers. Hoffa himself disappeared, presumed murdered by the mob, in 1975.

For all the impassable differences in values and objectives, the two men were not without superficial similarities. Both were blunt, candid and commanding. Both drove themselves and their staffs relentlessly. Both, in separate ways, had an instinct for the underdog; both had the instinct of underdogs themselves. Both had devoted friends and deadly enemies. Both had strong veins of sardonic humor. Both prided themselves on physical fitness. Neither smoked. Kennedy drank sparingly; Hoffa never. Neither wore hats. Both loved their wives. Both were risk-takers: 'Hoffa,' said Edward Bennett Williams, 'is the kind of man who will jump out of a sixth floor window one day. If he survives, he will jump out of an eighth floor window the next day.' There was that aspect to Kennedy.

The same image recurred when journalists wrote about them: 'the coiled spring of a man constitutionally unrelaxed ... like the impatient discipline of the hungry fighter, completely confident but truly relaxed only in the action he craves'. This was Hal Clancy of Boston writing about Kennedy; but John Bartlow Martin, writing about Hoffa, said, 'It is as though the core of Hoffa's personality were all a tightly-wound steel spring ... He is always stripped for a fight, for action'. Martin summarized the resemblances in the *Saturday Evening Post* in 1959. They were both, he wrote, 'aggressive, competitive, hard-driving, authoritarian, suspicious, temperate, at times congenial and at others curt'. Nothing bothered Kennedy more in Martin's manuscript than this passage. 'He was amazed and simply could not understand; it had never occurred to him; he had thought of himself as good and Hoffa as evil.' Martin retained the passage; his relations with Kennedy were not impaired.

It was an intensely personal duel. Going home, Kennedy had to drive past the Teamsters' marble palace. One night, smiling wryly, he said to Martin, 'My first love is Jimmy Hoffa.' Another night Kennedy and Salinger left the office at one in the morning. As they drove along, Kennedy noticed a light burning in Hoffa's office. 'If he's still at work, we ought to be,' Kennedy said, and they went back for two more hours. Hoffa often did indeed work late, but he also, according to Williams, heard of Kennedy's reaction and thereafter, when his day's work was done, took special pleasure in leaving his office lights blazing away.

Hoffa knew what respectable people thought of him and did not care. 'I'm no damn angel,' he told John Martin. '. . . I don't apologize. You take any industry and look at the problems they ran into while they were building up – how they did it, who they associated with, how they cut corners. The best example is Kennedy's old man.' As for the son, 'Hell, I hated the bastard,' said Hoffa at the end of his life. '. . . He was a vicious bastard and he had developed a psychotic mania to "get" me at any cost.'

During the hearing Hoffa used to fix Kennedy with, as Kennedy perceived it, 'a deep, strange, penetrating expression of intense hatred . . . the look of a man obsessed by his enmity, and it came particularly from his eyes. There were times when his face seemed completely transfixed with this stare of absolute evilness.' The look sometimes went on for five minutes or so, as if he thought that by staring long and hard enough he could destroy his adversary. 'Now and then, after a protracted, particularly evil glower, he did a most peculiar thing: he would wink at me.' Hoffa told Victor Lasky years later, 'I used to love to bug the little bastard. Whenever Bobby would get tangled up in one of his involved questions, I would wink at him. That invariably got him.' Hoffa laughed and laughed.

Kennedy vacillated between thinking Hoffa evil and thinking him mad. It was widely supposed he hated Hoffa; but some who worked most closely with him did not think so. Angie Novello said later, 'Deep down he had great respect for Hoffa.' Carmine Bellino and LaVern Duffy both said that he 'liked' Hoffa. In some obscure personal sense he did, though liking was far overborne by moral disapproval. In later times, when his self-awareness and sense of the complexity of life increased, Kennedy might have seen Hoffa in another context, appreciated his vitality, his impudence, his struggle and the material benefits he had won for the Teamsters. But, just as Hoffa never forgave Kennedy for having been born rich and for believing in the possibility of justice under capitalism, so Kennedy could never forgive Hoffa for his vindictiveness toward dissenting members of his own union, for his ties with the underworld, for his conviction that American society was irremediably corrupt. 'We were like flint and steel,' said Hoffa. 'Every time we came to grips the sparks flew.' Hoffa thought that Kennedy 'got his jollies playing God'. Kennedy, Murray Kempton said, perceived 'the devil' in Hoffa, 'something absolutely insatiable and wildly vindictive . . . He recognized in Hoffa a general fanaticism for evil that could be thought of as the opposite side of his own fanaticism for good.'

●

Cries and whispers

INGMAR BERGMAN

Childhood in the grace and favour parsonage of Sophiahemmet, the everyday rhythm, birthdays, church festivals, Sundays. Duties, games, freedom, conformity and security. The long dark way to school in winter, the games of marbles and bicycle rides in spring, and reading aloud by the fire on autumn Sunday evenings.

We didn't know Mother had gone through a passionate love affair or that Father suffered from severe depression. Mother was preparing to break out of her marriage, Father threatening to take his own life. They were reconciled and decided to continue together 'for the sake of the children', as was said at the time. We noticed nothing, or very little.

One autumn evening, I was busy with my film apparatus in the nursery. My sister was asleep in Mother's room and my brother was out practising shooting. I suddenly heard a violent argument going on downstairs, Mother crying and Father talking angrily, frightening sounds I had never heard before. I crept out on to the stairs and saw Mother and Father in violent altercation in the hall, Mother trying to pull her coat towards her, but Father holding firmly on to it. Then, she let go of the coat and rushed towards the porch. Father got there before her and, pushing her aside, stood in front of the door. Mother went for him and they struggled. She struck him in the face; he threw her against the wall and she lost her balance and fell. My sister woke in the tumult, came out onto the landing and began to cry. Mother and Father stopped.

I can't remember clearly what happened next. Mother was sitting on the sofa in her room, her nose bleeding. She was trying to calm my sister. I was in the nursery looking at my cinematograph. I fell pathetically to my knees and promised God he could have my films and all my apparatus as long as Mother and Father became friends again.

My prayers were heard. The Pastor of Hedvig Eleonora parish (Father's superior) intervened, my parents were reconciled, and the immensely rich Aunt Anna took them off on a long holiday trip through Italy. Grandmother stepped in, and order and the illusion of security were restored.

•

Victims of the John Wayne complex: The Hell's Angels

HUNTER S. THOMPSON

Of all their habits and predilections that society finds alarming, the outlaws' disregard for the time-honoured concept of an eye for an eye is the one that frightens people most. The Hell's Angels try not to do anything halfway, and outcasts who deal in extremes are bound to cause trouble, whether they mean to or not. This, along with a belief in total retaliation for any offence or insult, is what makes the Angels such a problem for police and so morbidly fascinating to the general public. Their claims that they don't start trouble is probably true more often than not, but their idea of provocation is dangerously broad, and one of their main difficulties is that almost nobody else seems to understand it. Yet they have a very simple rule of thumb: in any argument a fellow Angel is *always right*. To disagree with a Hell's Angel is to be *wrong* – and to persist in being wrong is an open challenge.

Despite everything psychiatrists and Freudian castrators have to say about the Angels, they are tough, mean and potentially dangerous as packs of wild boar. The moment a fight begins, any leather fetishes or inadequacy feelings are entirely beside the point, as anyone who has ever tangled with them will sadly testify. When you get in an argument with a group of outlaw motorcyclists, your chances of emerging unmaimed depend on the number of heavy-handed allies you can muster in the time it takes to smash a beer bottle. In this league, sportsmanship is for old liberals and young fools.

Many of their 'assault victims' are people who have seen too many Western movies; they are victims of the John Wayne complex, which causes them to start swinging the moment they sense any insult. This is relatively safe in some areas of society, but in saloons frequented by outlaw motorcyclists it is the worst kind of folly. 'They're always looking for somebody to challenge them,' said a San Francisco policeman. 'And once you're involved with them, it's all or nothing. A stranger who doesn't want anything to do with them, if one of the bums says something to his woman, he can't take offence or he'll have to fight four or five Angels, not just the one. People should understand this.'

One of the Frisco Angels explained it without any frills: 'Our motto, man, is "All on One and One on All". You mess with an Angel and you've got twenty-five of them on your neck. I mean, they'll break you but good, baby.'

The outlaws take the 'all on one' concept so seriously that it is written into the club charter as Bylaw Number 10: 'When an Angel punches a non-Angel, all other Angels will participate.'

The outlaws never know, from one moment to the next, when they might have to grapple with some foe bent on humiliating the colours. Here is a hazy, yet fairly instructive account of a clash with an ex-Angel named Phil and his XKE Jaguar. For several hours prior to the incident, Phil had been drinking and arguing in a roadhouse with a half-dozen members of the Oakland chapter. Finally they told him to leave or be stomped. Phil went outside, backed his car off about fifty yards from the row of bikes at the curb, then ploughed into them like a bulldozer, breaking the leg of one Angel who tried to get his bike out of the way. This is how the Lynch report told it:

> On November 4, 1961, a San Francisco resident driving through Rodeo, possibly under the influence of alcohol, struck a motorcycle belonging to a Hell's Angel parked outside a bar. A group of Angels pursued the vehicle, pulled the driver from the car and attempted to demolish the rather expensive vehicle. The bartender claimed he had seen nothing, but a cocktail waitress in the bar furnished identification to the officers concerning some of those

responsible for the assault. The next day it was reported to the officers that a member of the Hell's Angels gang had threatened the life of this waitress as well as another woman waitress. A male witness who definitely identified five participants in the assault, including the president of the Vallejo Hell's Angels and the Vallejo 'Road Rats' [since absorbed by Angels], advised officers that because of his fear of retaliation by club members he would refuse to testify to the facts he had previously furnished.

Motorcycles are knocked over by cars every day all over the nation, but when the incident involves outlaw motorcyclists it's something else again. Instead of settling the thing with an exchange of insurance information or, at the very worse, an argument with a few blows, the Hell's Angels stomped the driver (a former member) and 'attempted to demolish the vehicle'. I asked one of them whether the police exaggerated this aspect, and he said no, they had done the natural thing: smashed headlights, kicked in doors, broken windows and torn various components off the engine.

Another instructive clash occurred soon after the Monterey incident, when the outlaws were still feeling tough. It began as an everyday act of revenge, but it didn't come off. Perhaps for this reason, the police report was unusually restrained:

On September 19, 1964, a large group of Hell's Angels and Satan's Slaves converged on a bar in South Gate (Los Angeles County), parking their motorcycles and cars in the street in such a fashion as to block one half of the roadway. They told officers that three members of the club had recently been asked to stay out of the bar and that they had come to tear it down. Upon their approach the bar owner locked the doors and turned off the lights and no entrance was made, but the group did demolish a cement block fence. On arrival of the police, members of the clubs were lying on the sidewalk and in the street. They were asked to leave the city, which they did reluctantly. As they left, several were heard to say that they would be back and tear down the bar.

In all, it was a pretty quiet outrage, and except for the demolition of a fence, it went into the books as a routine victory for law and order. It was also a good example of the total-retaliation ethic: when you're asked to stay out of a bar you don't just punch the owner – you come back with your army and tear the place down, destroy the whole edifice and everything it stands for. No compromise. If a man gets wise, mash his face. If a woman snubs you, rape her. This is the thinking, if not the reality, behind the whole Hell's Angels act. It is also the aspect of the story that gets to the editors of news magazines. The combined testimony of 104 police departments is proof enough that the outlaws are unable to enforce their savage codes on any level of society but their own . . . and yet the white-collar, button-down world is obviously alarmed to hear that these codes exist at all. Which they do, and they are also adhered to, as noted in the concluding paragraphs of the California Attorney-General's report:

The group seeks to exploit the so-called 'gangsters' code' of group loyalty and threats to persons who might appear in court against them. There have been instances of Hell's Angels punishing witnesses by physical assault. In the event the witness or victim is female, the women associates of the Angels seem willing to participate in threats to discourage testimony. A practical problem seen in various cases is that both victims and witnesses generally exist in the same environment as do the Hell's Angels. While gang rapes and forced sex perversions may have occurred, the victims and witnesses frequently are not of the higher social strata and thus are vulnerable to the mores of 'saloon society'. It is believed that the only feasible approach to the solution of this problem is for investigating officers to recognize it and take all steps possible to protect witnesses both before and after trial.

Not many members of saloon society will find consolation in these words. The Angels and their allies bear grudges much longer than police feel it's necessary to protect witnesses, and cops have a tendency to lose interest in a prosecution witness about five minutes after the jury comes in with a verdict. No bartender who has caused the arrest of an Angel will ever feel anything but panic at the sound of motorcycle engines in the street and the clumping of leather boot heels coming towards his door. The Angels don't wilfully trace their enemies from one place to another, but they spend so much of their time in bars that they are likely to turn up thirsty almost anywhere. And once an enemy is located, the word goes out fast on the network. It takes only two or three Angels, and no more than five minutes, to wreck a bar and put a man in the hospital. Chances are they won't be arrested . . . but even if they are, the damage is already done.

An intended victim – such as the bar owner in South Gate, who suffered only the loss of a fence in the first attack – will always know that his place has a certain distinction: it is marked, and as long as the Hell's Angels or Satan's Slaves exist, there is a chance that some of them will come back to finish the job.

●

The divine feud: Bette Davis and
Joan Crawford
SHAUN CONSIDINE

The filming of *Whatever Happened to Baby Jane?* brought together two of Hollywood's most implacable enemies: Bette Davis and Joan Crawford. Theirs must rank as the greatest feud in movie history.

> Hollywood expected an eruption when Joan Crawford
> and Bette Davis got together for *Whatever Happened to
> Baby Jane?* But it turned out to be love in bloom.
>
> Hedda Hopper

> Yes, I know. Everybody believed we would kill each
> other. But we fooled them. We were tempted to hang
> a sign on the set, saying, 'Sorry folks, we're getting
> along beautifully.'
>
> Bette Davis

'There is *no* feud,' Bette told Mike Connolly of the Hollywood *Reporter* after the first week of filming. 'We wouldn't have one. A man and a woman yes, and I can give you a list, but never two women – they'd be too clever for that.'

There was an implied test of strength between the two women, but 'they had to play that game of denying there was any competition between them,' said Bette's daughter B.D. 'Mother's favorite line at the beginning of the picture was, "We're just two professional dames doing our jobs." It was beneath them to compete with each other. Both felt so superior that they couldn't acknowledge their hatred let alone express it.'

On their first free Saturday evening, Bette and Joan had dinner with columnist Hedda Hopper at her home. 'The three of us were dressed in black,' said Hedda. 'As we sat down to dinner, I said we looked like three black-widow spiders.' For cocktails Bette made do with Hedda's scotch on the rocks, but Joan produced her own flask of hundred-proof vodka from her handbag. 'I say if you're going to have a drink, have what you want,' she declared.

The filming was going beautifully, they chorused.

'Joan is wonderful, she's going to win all the awards,' said Bette.

'No, no,' said Joan, 'Bette has Oscar written all over her performance.'

She had to concentrate very hard on getting into character every day, Bette admitted.

'I'm aware of that,' said Joan. 'You didn't say good morning to me for a full five minutes today.'

'I get absent-minded,' said Bette. 'And sometimes that can be mistaken for something else.'

Then there was the problem of the name-calling, said Joan.

'*Oh?*' said Hedda, alert and ready for some good old-fashioned nasty dish.

'Yes,' said Joan to Davis, 'you flip when they call you Bet, just as I do when they call me Jo-ann. I was amused today when you told someone: "If you called me Bette, I'd like you much better." '

'Yes,' said Bette, 'it can be tedious.'

Caught in the middle of this Girl-Scout debate, Hedda tried to liven up the proceedings by asking which star had top billing in the picture.

'We tossed a coin and I won,' said Bette proudly.

'She comes first,' said a smiling Joan. 'She plays the title role.'

A few cocktails later, after the trio had discussed Hollywood today ('A ghost town,' said Joan; 'It's been taken over by the agents,' said Bette), the two stars freshened up for the journey home. 'When Joan reached into her purse and began to apply lipstick, Bette immediately followed suit, applying lipstick to *her* mouth,' wrote Hedda. 'Then Joan exited first, in her chauffeur-driven car, while Bette called her secretary.'

AP reporter Bob Thomas was also treated to an act of sweetness and compatibility between the two. 'A convincing performance,' he called it. 'The display of felicity persuaded everyone, perhaps even themselves. But it couldn't last. Inevitably, the spirit of competition entered into everything. They competed in their interviews, in their performances, in their relationships with the cast and the crew.'

By week number two, although the two stars were still pros in front of the camera during the day, at night their fangs began to show.

'My dad had to spend an awful lot of time trying to keep

them happy,' said Bill Aldrich. 'But he never took sides. Luckily he had worked with some very tough guys in his time, so he played it right down the middle with the two ladies. He was just as tough as they were. Otherwise I don't think he would have survived.'

When the director arrived home at night, Crawford would call. 'Did you see what that (bleep) did to me today?' Joan would say. As soon as he hung up, the phone would ring again. This time it was Bette calling. 'What did that (bleep) call you about?' she would ask.

'Mother was on the phone to Aldrich for at least an hour every night,' said B.D. 'She would come home, take off her makeup, then, with hair flying all over the place, she would sit in her giant bed, in her master bedroom, with her papers all around her, and the phone. We would have to bring her dinner to her on a tray, then she would call Aldrich. She'd rehash everything that happened on the set that day that Aldrich had to apologize for – all the slights she suffered that were unfair – and the terrible things Joan had done to her, which he would have to prevent her from doing the following day. Then she'd go into discussing the next day's scenes and how they were really going to fix Joan tomorrow. And I always had this funny image of Joan Crawford calling Aldrich and saying the exact same things.'

'First one, then the other,' said Aldrich. 'I could rely on it every night. They were like two Sherman tanks, openly despising each other.'

Bette felt that Joan was deliberately trying to upstage her by not adapting to the pace of her performances. While she barked out such character lines as 'You *miserable* bitch!' Joan would respond with an air of heavenly grace, as if she were performing in a sweet Noël Coward drawing-room play.

'Bette had a certain tempo to her lines,' said Bob Aldrich, 'which Joan wouldn't respond to. She had her own, softer rhythm, which meant that when she came off her lines and Bette came in, Bette would have to slow down.'

'This is not a fairy tale, for chrissake,' Davis said to Aldrich at one point. 'Can't she at least snap back at me?'

'I will try, dear Bette, I will try,' said Joan the movie star.

'Oh, brother!' said Bette the actress.

'Crawford never reacted to anything,' said Lukas Heller. 'She sat in her wheelchair or in bed and waited for her close-ups. As the camera got closer, she would widen those enormous eyes of hers. She considered that acting.'

According to Aldrich, there were also some problems over the makeup the two stars wore for their roles in the film. Bette went to extremes with her cosmetic application. 'I wanted to look outrageous, like Mary Pickford in decay,' she said. 'It was my idea to wear the ghastly white base, scads of black eye shadow, a cupid's bow mouth and the beauty mark.' It was Crawford's hairdresser, Peggy Shannon, who suggested that Bette add more layers each day. 'I had worked with the extras in those Technicolored musicals at MGM,' said Shannon. 'We would give them these gorgeous faces. They were so in love with the way they looked, they never washed their faces. You would see them days later walking down La Brea Avenue with the original makeup still on. Each day they just added more. I told Bette that. She loved the idea. "Yes," she said, "that's it! I'll put it on with a shovel every day."'

As Bette became more hideous, Crawford insisted on improving her looks. When her original makeup tests were done, she fought with Bob Aldrich. 'She loathed the makeup he suggested she wear,' said Joan's makeup artist, Monte Westmore. 'He wanted Joan to be horrendously ugly, like Bette. For the test, I had to put huge lines under her eyes and the shadows on her face made her look like she had jowls. She looked rotten, like she had been on dope. Having been a glamour queen all her life, it upset her enormously to look like that. That was his concept, and we tested that way, but Joan would not approve the tests. So a compromise was reached; they met each other halfway.'

'Miss Crawford was a *fool*,' said Bette Davis. 'A good actress looks the part. Why she insisted on making Blanche look glamorous, I just don't know.'

'I am aware of how Miss Davis felt about my makeup in *Baby Jane*,' Crawford said in 1973. 'But my reasons for appearing somewhat glamorous were just as valid as hers, with all those layers of rice powder she wore and that ghastly lipstick. But Miss Davis was always partial to covering up her face in motion pictures. She called it "Art". Others might call it camouflage – a cover-up for the absence of any real beauty. My character in *Jane* was a bigger star, and more beautiful than her sister. Once you've been as famous as Blanche Hudson was, you don't slip back and become a freak like Miss Davis preferred to see her character. Blanche also had class. Blanche had glamour. Blanche was a *legend*.'

'Blanche was a *cripple*,' Bette Davis argued. 'A recluse. She never left the house or saw anybody, yet Miss Crawford made her appear as if she lived in Elizabeth Arden's beauty salon.'

Ernest Haller, the cinematographer, had photographed Bette in *Jezebel* and *Mr Skeffington*; and Joan in *Mildred Pierce* and *Humoresque*. On *Whatever Happened to Baby Jane?* he was told to forget the past: to photograph the characters, not the stars. 'If I lit either of them this way ten years ago they'd have my head,' he said. When asked on the set to choose his favorite star, the cinematographer diplomatically replied, 'In terms of sheer beauty, the most lovely face I ever photographed was Hope Hampton.'

According to the movie's editor Michael Luciano, both stars saw the rushes for the first few days, then stayed away.

'Why do I have to look so damn old?' Crawford said after viewing the early dailies. 'It's like I have a grandmother playing my part.'

'She started crying and crying that first week,' said Vik Greenfield. 'And Bette in exasperation finally said, "Joan, if you're so unhappy with this film, I'll play your part and you'll play mine." With that, Crawford broke down again and wept: "I can't play *her*. She's twice as ugly."'

Bette also sobbed when she first saw herself as Jane. Then she complained there were too many flattering close-ups of Joan.

'There were far more close-ups than the script called for,' Ernest Haller agreed.

'Mother had a tendency to find many things wrong,' said B.D. Hyman. 'She became so hysterical at the rushes she stopped going. But she never stopped complaining about Joan and her tricks.'

B.D., who had a small role in the film, had her own memorable encounter with her mother's rival. On the first day she was introduced to Joan Crawford, the star pulled back her hand 'as if I were diseased'.

Pointing to her twin daughters, Cindy and Cathy, who were sitting quietly on the sidelines wearing matching outfits and knitting, Crawford asked B.D. not to talk to the girls, ever. 'They have been carefully brought up and shielded from the wicked side of the world,' said Joan, 'and you obviously have not. I don't want your influence to corrupt them.'

B.D.'s mouth 'fell open'. When she repeated the tale to Bette, the star raged. 'How dare she pull that crap with me. I'll kill her. That bitch is loaded half the time.'

Joan spiked her Pepsi with vodka, Davis claimed. 'She had that bottle by her elbow every *minute*. When one was finished her secretary would bring her another. Everyone *knew* what was in it.'

'She used to drink "white water" on *Autumn Leaves*,' said Bob Sherman. 'It was a paper cup filled with vodka. She'd start drinking it after noon and continue throughout the day and night.'

'Bob Aldrich liked to drink Coke out of a paper cup,' said Phil Stern. 'When he had a case of the stuff brought in, Joan had a Pepsi vending machine set up. Every time his back was turned, she used to throw out his Coke and replace it with Pepsi. One day when they were casually going over the script, out of nowhere he said, "Furthermore Joan, I'd appreciate it if you'd stop filling my goddamn paper cup with Pepsi."'

But Pepsi was good for you, Joan told everyone. 'It helped indigestion and irregularity, and it was good for tired feet.' Taking her slippers off she would demonstrate, rolling the Pepsi bottle under each foot twenty times. 'It relaxes the tootsies and keeps your ankles thin,' she claimed.

'You hang around that woman long enough,' said Bette, 'and you'll pick up all *kinds* of useless shit.'

> I hate this fucking picture, but I need the money, and
> if it goes over I'll get a nice percentage of the profits.
> Joan Crawford to writer Roy Newquist

As filming of *Baby Jane* continued, embellishments to the characters and plot were added by both stars. While Blanche was being starved to death by her evil sister, Joan lost weight in some areas of her body. As the hollows in her cheeks grew deeper and her waist grew smaller, her breasts became larger. 'Christ!' said Bette. 'You never know what size boobs that broad has strapped on! She must have a different set for each day of the week! She's supposed to be shriveling away, but her tits keep growing. I keep running into them, like the Hollywood Hills.'

Famished from hunger, in one scene Joan was to wheel herself to Bette's bedroom where she finds some chocolates hidden in a drawer and proceeds to gorge herself. Averse to chocolate, Joan, prior to the filming of the scene, had her maid wrap 'tiny chunks of chopped meat' in the candy box. Unaware of the substitute, Bette Davis, during a break in filming, reached for one of the fake bonbons, popped it into her mouth, began to chew, then gagged.

'Christ!' said Bette.

'Protein, Bette, protein,' said Joan. 'It's good for you.'

'Balls!' said Bette.

In the script another unsavory item was added to the invalid's menu. 'By the way, Blanche,' said Bette in the setup, 'I was cleaning the bird's cage when it escaped and flew away.'

That day, for lunch, Joan was served the dead bird, laid out on a bed of pineapple rings.

Columnist Sidney Skolsky said it was Bette who suggested the next *entrée*, and contributed the teaser line, 'By the way, Blanche, there are rats in the cellar.'

'I am not sure if it was in the original script,' said writer Lukas Heller.

'Bette proposed that, instead of a dead parakeet, they substitute a dead rat,' said Skolsky. 'Aldrich called the prop man, and a rat was found.'

Crawford, unaware of the switch, lifted the silver serving cover and 'screamed loud and clear, then fainted', while Bette cackled loudly in the background.

'When I was at the Plaza Hotel in New York some months later, I gave a big cocktail party,' Bette told this writer, 'and I asked them to serve the pâté in the shape of a rat. When my guests lifted the serving cover, they were *horrified*. I laughed myself silly. It was a *wonderful* idea.'

During the third week of filming, Bette and Joan's respective autobiographies were released. 'Sisters under the celluloid . . . Hollywood's most bona-fide dazzlers', was how Bob Downing of *Variety* described them. The books were accurate reflections of the two stars' personas, the reviewer believed. Crawford's sleek and shimmering 'with scarcely a jarring note', while Bette's had 'flashes of venom . . . It is the truer reflection of a human being'.

Joan had the makings of a good book in her, said Bette, 'but this *isn't* it'; and Crawford observed that her rival's memoirs were depressing – due largely to the lack of men in her life. 'Poor Bette,' said Joan, 'it appears she's never had a happy day – or night – in her life.'

'*Whaaaatt!*' said Bette on hearing that. 'I've had affairs; not as many as her, but outside of a cathouse, who has?'

*

During a joint interview with reporter Joe Hyams, when Joan appeared with her book under her arm and placed it on the table in front of her, Bette excused herself, went to her dressing room, and returned with her book. When the Hyams piece appeared, he was obliged to feature both books, on either side of his column. Joan then proceeded to get herself booked, solo, on a local TV show. The afternoon it was scheduled to be shown, she asked Bob Aldrich if she could watch it at work. 'Bob Aldrich had a portable TV brought to the soundstage,' said Bob Gary. 'We all sat around this big oval table to watch the show. There was a chair for Joan, and one for Bette, and in between them Bette placed a chair for her *Baby Jane* doll. When the show began, Bette got up and went to a corner of the room where a phonograph was set up. As soon as Joan appeared on the TV, Bette turned on the phonograph and began to play her *Baby Jane* song ("I've Written a Letter to Daddy"). While Joan was trying to watch herself on TV, Bette was dancing and singing in the corner, as loud as she could. I've never seen her be that far-out rude to Joan before. Bob Aldrich is sitting there, being quiet. He is walking on eggs the whole time. And Joan is a model of control. Anyone else would haul off and belt Bette.'

'Mother would have *loved* a confrontation with Joan. But Crawford was too smart for her games,' said B.D. Hyman.

'You could never lay a glove on Joan Crawford,' Bob Sherman believed. 'She came from MGM and Louis B. Mayer. When she didn't like someone on a picture she would go to Uncle Louis and say, "Cut his balls off, Uncle Louis. Or else I'm going to be unhappy." And he would do her dirty work.'

By the fourth week of shooting, Bette had had it up to her famous eyeballs with Joan's ladylike posturing and her pretense of infinite patience. 'Bette came from Warner Brothers,' Bob Sherman continued. 'Unlike Joan she was a very straight-on lady who wouldn't go behind your back. She'd kill you right upfront. Once during the movie she took off on me and hit me real hard.'

This was the day Bette filmed the sequence standing in front of the rehearsal mirror. 'She sees herself for the first time as Baby Jane and realizes what a hideous mess she is and screams,' said Sherman. 'When it was over, she seemed upset, a little uptight. We were standing outside her dressing room and, to comfort her, I decided to remind her that the next day she was going to work on the scene where she grabs a hold of Joan and batters her in the music-room. I threw my arm around her and said, "Oh, don't worry about it, Bette, tomorrow you'll get the chance to kick the brains out of Joan." Suddenly she pulled back and said to me: "Oh you think I'm *pretending* to be upset? You think that I'm being a phony like *that* cunt?" And she proceeded to call me every dirty name she could think of.'

The door to Crawford's trailer was open during Bette's tirade. 'Joan was in there listening,' said Sherman. 'And then I realized what Bette was doing. She was yelling at me but tearing off in a tangential way at Crawford. She couldn't do it directly to Joan because Joan never gave her a chance. So I got it with both barrels blasting, and while she was screaming at me, out of the corner of my eye I could see Crawford's door slowly closing. Joan heard everything. Eventually, to stop Bette, I said, "I'm sorry you feel this way, because I like you." If I said, "I respect you," she would have cut my head off. But like was a better word because how can you yell at someone who likes you? She said, "Oh, come on in," and we went into her trailer and had a drink.'

At home, as in previous times of vocational stress, Bette unleashed her repressed fury on her nearest and dearest. But, lacking a husband to fly at, and with daughter B.D. already grown to five feet ten inches ('I towered over Mother; she wouldn't touch me'), Bette had to aim her punches at her real-life sister, Bobby.

Recovered from two nervous breakdowns, Bobby was apparently still a source of irritation to Bette. 'She's *jealous* of me,' said the star. 'She's always *tried* to drag me down. But she's never won. Ha! Even her bouts in the loony bin were kept from the press and didn't hurt me. But they sure cost me a pretty penny, she was in the rubber room at Payne Whitney more than once . . . and what I went through visiting her I can't describe.'

Parallel to Blanche in *Baby Jane*, Bobby was dependent on her sister, Bette, for sustenance and survival. During the making of the film, she lived in a room above the garage at Bette's estate, and for her keep she worked as her sister's cook and house-keeper. But apparently she spoiled the children and spent too much money on food. One night, at dinner, she ruined the roast beef. Knocking the serving plate out of her sister's hand, Bette was 'actually about to kick her' when B.D. intervened. The brawl continued in the kitchen. 'Mother let go with one hand and hit her in the face. In an instant they were pulling each other's hair, kicking at each other, and screeching like a pair of alley cats.'

Banished to her room over the garage, Bobby told B.D. she forgave Bette. She was scared to be on her own, she said, and she understood Bette. 'She has pressures that she has to vent sometimes, and I'm a convenient target . . . but underneath it all I know she loves me.'

'I *do*,' said Bette. 'She's a tough customer, but she knows how to behave in my house, or I'll kick her out on her ass.'

> In the scene where I was supposed to imitate Joan over the phone, I wasn't able to do it. Joan had to dub in her voice for me. She was very pleased about that.
>
> Bette Davis
>
> Nobody can imitate me. You can always see imper-sonations of Katharine Hepburn and Marilyn Monroe. But not me. Because I've always drawn on myself only.
>
> Joan Crawford

To save time and money, while one unit was filming the exteriors of the Hudson house on McCadden Drive, a second cameraman, strapped to the front of the car, was filming Bette, driving her beat-up Mercedes along Wilcox Avenue and at Sunset and La Brea. At the McCadden Drive house that evening, Bette arrived in time to witness Joan being photographed through the iron bars of her upstairs bedroom window. Set up on a huge crane outside the window, the camera was supposed to zoom in on the imprisoned Blanche, clinging to her iron bars, feebly calling out for help. As Aldrich yelled for action, Joan wheeled herself to the window and lifted herself to the bars; as the lens moved in for its horrifying close-up, the director, looking through the viewfinder, saw a frightened but *fabulous*-looking Crawford. 'Joan was wearing *lipstick* and ludicrously long *eyelashes*,' said Bette. 'It was *sooo* funny. In her cry for help, my terrified costar insisted on looking like she was posing for the cover of *Vogue*.'

When *Life* magazine visited the *Baby Jane* set, Bette, in the name of vanity, got to compete with Joan. A team had been assigned to photograph various Hollywood stars, when Crawford and Davis were added to the list. Assisting on the shoot was New York illustrator, Joe Eula.

'We needed an old-time but classy background for Bette and Joan,' said Eula, 'so we decided to photograph them sitting on the front of a vintage Rolls-Royce. I set it up. We rented the car in Hollywood and drove it right up to the studio gates. Those doors swung up like an airplane hangar, and we rolled that mother onto a section of the soundstage. We had the lights set, and we were ready for the two dames. It was fairly early in the day, and they arrived wearing formal gowns, furs, and diamonds, behaving like they always dressed like this for breakfast. Bette arrived first, and Miss Crawford was late. So we sat and waited, and Davis was a little miffed. But once Crawford arrived, the two pros got in there and did their stuff. They arched their backs, threw their heads back, and we were back in the golden days when these two superstars ruled the town.'

There were no pleasantries or dialogue exchanged between the two, Eula recalled. 'Not a word. That's why we had them sitting on the headlights, one on each side of the Rolls. We couldn't put them within arm's reach or the fur would really fly. It was over in twenty minutes. Then one went off with her Pepsi bottle full of vodka, and the other one muttered, "She's so fucking unprofessional." But somehow you could sense that deep down they respected one another.'

When filming ran behind schedule, the stars agreed to come in on a Sunday to rehearse the physically difficult scene where Baby Jane brutalizes her sister, Blanche. In rehearsals, Crawford agreed that there would be no stand-in involved. When the time came to shoot, she changed her mind. 'She amused *me*,' said Bette. 'Joan was really *not* my kind of actress. In one simple scene where I was supposed to slap her, I knew how to do it without hurting her. It's an old theatrical trick. All you do is cup your hand as you touch someone; the one being hit throws her head back, and the sound is added later. But she had her double play the scene, which made it very tense and awkward for me.'

The prelude to the terror – where Joan as the crippled Blanche lifts herself downstairs by the banister, then crawls to the phone to call the doctor – had been shot previously, and edited by Michael Luciano. 'We used a close-up of Joan on the phone, then cut to a long shot of Bette standing in the doorway behind her, watching. The next frame was of Joan. She senses she is being watched. She turns her head slowly, sees Bette and begins to babble incoherently. Then the violence begins.'

Crossing the hallway, Bette hangs up the phone, raises her foot, and viciously kicks Joan in the head with her shoe. She keeps on kicking her, savagely, across the hallway and into the living room.

'When it came to the actual filming of that scene, Crawford became afraid again. She said, "I'm not doing it. I don't trust Miss Davis. She's going to kick my teeth in." And she may have been right,' said Bill Aldrich.

A dummy was used for the close shots. While the hand-held

camera stayed on Bette's face and upper body, her flying feet were kicking a mannequin, not Joan, across the room. 'She was kicking so hard and so viciously, we were all afraid she would break her foot,' said a cast member. 'And all the while, Joan Crawford is watching this from the side of the soundstage, not with fear or revulsion, but with fascination, pleasure almost, as if she enjoyed the thought of being abused by Bette.'

For the long range two-shots, Joan had to lie on the floor and keep rolling over, as if propelled by the kicking from Bette. As staged, Bette's right foot, encased in the familiar ankle-strapped shoe, was supposed to whizz past Joan without touching her. On one take, however, it was reported that she did indeed manage to make contact with the royal Crawford noggin.

Crawford screamed.

'I barely touched her,' Bette said without apology.

'She raised a fair-sized lump on Joan's head,' said Hedda Hopper.

'Her scalp was cut and required three stitches,' another writer reported.

'I don't believe that Bette ever hurt her,' said Bob Sherman. 'If she did, it was an accident. She was too much of a pro for that kind of behavior.'

'To my credit I have never indulged in physical punches, only verbal ones,' Bette claimed.

'There are those with the scars who would claim otherwise,' said Bob Downing of *Variety*.

Joan would of course be avenged. On Friday morning, August 24, the last scene in Blanche's bedroom was shot. Bound and gagged and strung up underneath a spotlighted portrait of herself, Joan was to be untied, then carried from the room by Bette. Because of the camera setup, Crawford knew no double could be used. She was determined that Davis experience her full star weight, and more.

'There is a way of making it easy on the actor who is doing the carrying,' said Bob Aldrich, 'but Crawford wanted Bette to suffer every inch of the way.'

To add to the burden, it was said that Joan had weights strapped on underneath her long gown.

'I was told it was a special weightlifter's belt, lined with lead,' said author Hector Arce.

'I'm not sure just what she had on, but you could clearly see that when Bette lifted Joan off the bed, she was straining herself,' Bob Gary recalled.

'It was a long, difficult scene,' said Lukas Heller. 'Bette had to lift her from the bed, carry her across the room and into the hallway.'

In the first try, halfway across the room, Joan, who was supposed to be unconscious, began to cough and opened her eyes, which meant that the scene had to be done over.

'There was no break in the shot,' said Heller. 'It was one continuous take. Bette carried her from the bed across the room and out the door. Then, as soon as she got in the hallway, out of the camera's range, she dropped Joan and let out this bloodcurdling scream.'

'It was the most terrible scream I have ever heard,' said Bob Gary. 'My back! Oh, God! My back!' she screamed as Joan got to her feet and strolled contentedly back to her dressing room.'

'And Still No Feud'

> With one more week to go on the filming of *Whatever Happened to Baby Jane?*, the film is on schedule and there is still no feud between the stars. Bette feeds her lines off-camera to Joan for her close-ups.
>
> A press release from Warner Brothers

•

Reasons to kill a president: The hatred of Jack Kennedy

HENRY HURT

President John F. Kennedy was assassinated on 22 November 1963 as his presidential motorcade crossed Dallas's Dealey Plaza. Henry Hurt has written one of the most detailed and persuasive books about what happened on that November day, and here he examines those people who hated Kennedy, perhaps even enough to have killed him.

The dawn of the sixties was accompanied by two powerful forces that surged through America, pulling and grinding at each other with a passion that can be seen much more clearly a quarter century later. One force was highly visible, the other not so clearly perceived but every bit as potent.

On the one hand, there was the palpable exuberance of that slim majority of American voters who had elected John F. Kennedy. They applauded his promise of a bold and unprecedented new direction for the country and the world. They believed that President Kennedy's vibrant espousal of new ideas would make the world community a better place for everyone – including multitudes of the hungry, ignorant, and sick. His election was seen as a signal that compassion and the sharing of material wealth with those less fortunate, both here and abroad, would be high priorities. There was the fervent belief that this new dimension would foster peace, justice, and equality around the world.

In his inaugural speech, President Kennedy exhorted Americans to 'ask not what your country can do for you – ask what you can do for your country'. Such ringing phrases evoked wild enthusiasm from Kennedy's constituency, so many of whom were young, charmingly articulate, and wealthy. The men and women in the new Kennedy White House were described at the time as 'the richest, prettiest, most interesting young people in the country'.

The tone was clearly set for what would come to be called Camelot. But not everyone across the land was pleased. Surging through America with equal intensity was a second force, one overshadowed by the glitter and self-adulation of the highly visible Kennedy supporters. This constituency represented a virtually total dissent from the frenzied loyalty of the Kennedy people. The dissent by some elements of this constituency was far more sinister than the traditional give-and-take in politics. Inevitably, the voices and tones of this dissent were viewed against the vibrant enthusiasm surrounding the new President. The very eagerness of Kennedy's supporters nourished the feeling that his accomplishments would take a terrible toll from those certain constituencies that were in fundamental opposition to all he stood for. To these opponents, there was a threatening ring in the privileged young President's exhortation that people should ask what they could do for their country. Many of them believed that they already did the maximum for their country, since it unhesitatingly helped itself and others to their wealth.

In an odd way, the enthusiasm for the new President was so ostentatious that it dominated the news here and abroad, as if he had won a mandate, ignoring completely the fact that he had barely squeaked in. Thus, the depth and breadth of his opposition was largely overlooked. So was its intensity, fed by the outrage of powerful adversaries who viewed the young President as having used them to get himself elected, then made political capital by turning against them. The feral intensity of the violent opposition to Kennedy blazed clear at Dealey Plaza. If Kennedy partisans saw in their President the dawn of a new age for America, so did the violent opposition. The question is whether the opponents determined that it was not to be.

In addition to the unsuspected virulence of Kennedy's domestic opposition, he faced opposition around the globe from Communist governments. The most immediate and explosive of these challenges was Fidel Castro, who had taken control of Cuba on January 1, 1959. When Kennedy took office in January 1961, he inherited the heated commitment of US military and intelligence officials to rid the Western Hemisphere of Castro, whom they viewed as a Soviet puppet on the doorstep of the US mainland. There were, of course, no more ardent allies of this official commitment than the thousands of fiery exiles who had sought refuge from Castro in the United States.

The first major effort against Castro was launched in April 1961 with the US-backed invasion by exiles at Cuba's Bay of Pigs. Coming only three months after President Kennedy took office, the invasion was a disaster that humiliated practically everyone connected with it. When the facts began to surface, President Kennedy faced the nearly hysterical wrath of the exiles, who accused him of betrayal by shortchanging them on military support, thus dooming their cause. Many of Kennedy's military and intelligence advisors were also angry at their commander-in-chief for the same reason. On the other side of the coin, Castro directly blamed the President for sponsoring the aborted invasion designed to topple him from power.

Castro's anger toward Kennedy was menacingly intensified by his sure knowledge that official elements of the US government – presumably with the sanction of President Kennedy – were repeatedly trying to assassinate him. Castro ultimately claimed that there were twenty-four US attempts to murder him. In subsequent years a Congressional committee confirmed at least eight US attempts to assassinate the Cuban premier.

In its persistent efforts to murder Castro, the United States reached beyond its routine arsenal of military and intelligence resources. It is now officially conceded that the CIA recruited certain high-level figures from organized crime to carry out murder plots against Castro. As freakish as this collusion appears, both sides had important reasons for wanting to murder the Cuban leader. Not only had he established a hostile Communist government at the edge of the United States, but he had also closed down the narcotics, gambling, and prostitution operations run so lucratively by the US mob. Perhaps it should not be too surprising that these unlikely conspirators had joined forces.

There was an added reason for the mob's willingness to participate in the assassination plots – their desire to turn down the heat from the Justice Department. From the earliest days of the Kennedy administration, the Justice Department, under the direction of Attorney General Robert Kennedy, had exhibited an unparalleled commitment to fight organized crime in the United States. This commitment, taken with the full blessing of the President, particularly puzzled mob bosses, who felt they had virtually delivered the presidency to Kennedy when they brought in the state of Illinois by a whisker – giving him the twenty-seven electoral votes that guaranteed him his razor-thin margin of victory over Richard Nixon in the 1960 presidential election.

In addition to his domestic opposition and that of the pro-Castro and anti-Castro forces, the oil industry had turned savagely against President Kennedy by 1963 because of his support for tax reform that threatened the oil-depletion allowance. This struck at one of the most lucrative tax loopholes ever enjoyed by the fabled oil millionaires of Texas, Louisiana, and other states with substantial oil interests.

Added to this stew of Kennedy opposition were the right-wing extremists and racists, angry over the Kennedy brothers' promise to bring full desegregation to the South. Many feared that desegregation would virtually destroy hallowed traditions involving families, politics, and economics.

All things considered, it is probable that a greater diversity of elements wanted President Kennedy out of office than had been at work during any previous presidency in American history. In simple terms, the most threatening forces boiled down to several darkly potent groups:

Anti-Castro exiles
Pro-Castro elements, including perhaps Castro himself

Organized crime

Powerful oil interests

Right-wing and racist domestic factions

Elements of US military and intelligence, enraged over Kennedy's denunciation of their efforts following the Bay of Pigs disaster

Such forces possessed in abundance the classic ingredients for murder – motive, means, and opportunity. In fact, with such a rare confluence of threatening elements, a great range of shifting opportunities for assassination presented itself, as the President, with increasing frequency during 1963, moved about the country on political trips.

In retrospect, the possibility of a successful political assassination seems immense.

●

J. Edgar Hoover's war against Martin Luther King

ATHAN G. THEOHARIS AND JOHN STUART COX

J. Edgar Hoover ran the FBI for forty-eight years. As early as 1925 he opened 'obscene' files to record damaging personal information on a host of prominent American figures, from the Roosevelts to the Kennedys. He used these files ruthlessly, transforming the Bureau from a small government agency into one of America's most powerful institutions and, in the process, he undermined the very principles of American democracy. Of all the personalities Hoover sought to manipulate or destroy, it was the black American civil rights leader, Martin Luther King, whom he hated most.

Hoover's intelligence service to [Lyndon B.] Johnson was performed, of course, covertly – and, of course, illegally. But while willingly compromising the integrity of the FBI in order to curry favor with the president, Hoover had compromised Johnson too, as the president could no longer afford to challenge Hoover: the Director might retaliate by leaking the records of the Bureau's assistance. The leverage Hoover acquired thereby ensured his continued tenure as Director throughout Johnson's presidency. And this was starkly put to the test before the end of that year.

During a rare press conference with selected Washington newspaper-women on 18 November 1964, Hoover gave vent to his strongly felt and decidedly controversial prejudices. First, he denounced the recently released report of the Warren Commission on President Kennedy's assassination for its criticism of the FBI's failure to fully brief the Secret Service on alleged presidential assassin Lee Harvey Oswald. (Hoover's remarks dramatized his overreaction to any criticism of the FBI and his tendency to assume that, unlike other federal agencies, the FBI should be shielded from critical scrutiny.) He then savagely attacked Martin Luther King, Jr., on the same score. Dismissing King's charge that the FBI had failed to prosecute civil rights cases because most FBI agents stationed in the South were southerners, Hoover branded King 'the most notorious liar in the country'.

Responding the next day to Hoover's attack, King reiterated his interest in meeting with the Director to discuss civil rights matters and, in a carefully considered comment, attributed Hoover's uncalled-for personal attack to the fact that he 'has apparently faltered under the awesome burden, complexities and responsibilities of his office'. At the same time, leaders of the major civil rights organizations met with Johnson to express their support for King. (The president listened quietly to their protest, but gave no indication of his position.) And, in an editorial entitled 'Time to Retire', the *New York Times* questioned the wisdom of President Johnson's 8 May executive order. Expressing concern over Hoover's inability to accept legitimate criticism and citing his recent intemperate comments, the *Times* concluded, 'Under the circumstances, it would be wise to let the mandatory provisions of the federal retirement law take effect on Mr Hoover's 70th birthday.'

Then, in a 24 November speech in Chicago, the embattled Director exacerbated his problems with the civil rights and liberal communities. Defending the FBI's civil rights record, he denounced the criticism of 'zealots or pressure groups' as having been 'spearheaded at times by Communists and moral degenerates'. Hoover's crude attempt to discredit his critics unleashed a storm of protest from civil rights leaders, who called for his resignation.

At this juncture, with Hoover's seventieth birthday five weeks away and his continued tenure as FBI Director resting only on Johnson's executive order, inevitably the question arose whether the president had reconsidered his decision of the previous May.

The issue surfaced during a 28 November press conference in connection with a remark by Hoover that he continued to command the president's support and had been assured that he could remain as Director for the remainder of Johnson's presidency. Johnson was intentionally vague when answering repeated inquiries. On the one hand, he characterized the public disagreement between Hoover and King as a difference between strong-minded individuals and defended their right to freedom of expression. On the other, he refused to confirm that Hoover had his assurance of indefinite tenure, urging reporters to consult the record surrounding the 8 May executive order.

Because that order had extended Hoover's tenure only for 'an indefinite period of time', Johnson's press conference neither silenced the protests nor resolved the question of Hoover's continuing in office. Forced to respond to a *Newsweek* story, based on reliable White House sources, that the president did in fact plan to replace the Director, White House press secretary George Reedy denied that the president ever 'entertained any such idea' and had 'never heard of such a plan'. Reedy, however, did not substantiate Hoover's claim that he had an assurance of indefinite tenure.

A decidedly insecure Director resolved to take the offensive. First, on Hoover's behalf, Tolson wrote to *Newsweek*, branding its story 'a new low in reporting'. (The story had claimed not only that Johnson intended to replace Hoover, but also that Hoover had placed five agents on the staff of House Appropriations Subcommittee Chairman John Rooney.) *Newsweek* in turn insisted that it had based its story on a 'most responsible White House source' and had learned from Justice Department officials about the agents on Rooney's staff. Second, on 4 December Hoover granted a rare interview to proclaim that he felt 'fine' and was in 'better physical condition than I have been in years. I intend to remain active because I don't like the rocking-chair life. If I retired, I wouldn't enjoy life very much.' Hoover also defended his earlier comments about King and reiterated his determination to respond to any criticism of the FBI, as it was essential to retain public trust in the Bureau.

In the event, Hoover weathered the storm of November – December 1964 simply because he could continue to command Johnson's support. So long as Johnson failed to rescind his executive order, in part because he had come to rely on the intelligence services Hoover provided and in part because (in his own description) he preferred having 'Hoover inside the tent pissing out rather than outside pissing in', Hoover's position was secure. And thus it remained throughout Johnson's tenure.

The stage had been set thereby for a new, more brutal attack on King. The assault began in November 1964 when DeLoach offered to Ben Bradlee of *Newsweek* copies of a purported FBI microphone surveillance transcript recording Dr King's illicit sexual activities. The same information was offered to *Los Angeles Times* Washington bureau chief David Kraslow, with a further titillating description placing King in the midst of a sex orgy. *Chicago Daily News* reporter James McCartney was shown FBI photographs of King leaving a motel with a white woman, the implication being that King had had sexual relations with her. Others who were offered copies of transcripts, photographs, or recordings allegedly detailing King's illicit sexual activities included *New York Times* reporter John Herbers, *Chicago Daily News* columnist Mike Royko, *Atlanta Constitution* editors Ralph McGill and Eugene Patterson, and *Augusta* (Georgia) *Chronicle* reporter Lou Harris.

Hoover's war against King extended far beyond disseminating derogatory personal information, however. Having learned of King's planned meeting with Teamsters' president Jimmy Hoffa and interest in avoiding publicity about this meeting, Hoover ordered an aide 'to alert friendly news media of the meeting once the meeting date is learned so that arrangements can be made for appropriate press coverage of the planned meeting to expose and disrupt it'. Hoover was subsequently advised that the FBI had successfully alerted a *New York Daily News* reporter and a national columnist to the scheduled meeting and that 'in view of publicity in the New York Daily News regarding this proposed meeting, King and his aides had decided that it would be unwise to meet with Hoffa'. Friendly reporters were thereupon alerted to King's imminent trip to Washington so that they could quiz him about the canceled meeting. Advised that this 'counterintelligence aim to thwart King from receiving money from the Teamsters has been quite successful to date', Hoover proclaimed this 'excellent'.

Like Hoover's office folder on John F. Kennedy, the Martin Luther King, Jr., folder was massive, numbering between 500 and 600 pages. An unspecified number of pages of King's files were withheld in their entirety under court order of 31 January 1977, requiring the purging of FBI files of 'all known copies of the recorded tapes, and transcripts thereof, resulting from the FBI's microphone surveillance, between 1963 and 1968, of . . . Martin Luther King, Jr.; and all known copies of the tapes, transcripts and logs resulting from the FBI's wiretapping, between 1963 and 1968, of the [Southern Christian Leadership Conference's] offices in Atlanta, Georgia, and New York, New York, the home of Martin Luther King, Jr., and places of public accommodation occupied by Martin Luther King, Jr.' In effect, then, this withholding notice confirms that Hoover maintained in his office the tapes and transcripts produced by the FBI's tapping and bugging of King.

But even purged, Hoover's office file on King records the intensity of the Director's commitment to use the vast resources of the FBI to discredit King and 'remove King from the national picture'. On Hoover's order, for instance, DeLoach met with NAACP leader Roy Wilkins and attempted to persuade Wilkins to convene a meeting of prominent civil rights leaders for the stated purpose of briefing them on the FBI's civil rights activities. DeLoach could then brief them as well, 'on a highly confidential basis', on the 'security background of King and [phrase deleted, but a reference to King's alleged illicit sexual activities]. The use of a tape, such as contemplated in [Assistant Director William Sullivan's] memorandum, together with a transcript for convenience in following the tape, should be most convincing.'

The tape in question was to be a composite made from the FBI's bugging of King's hotel rooms. Such a tape had been mailed to King's wife, Coretta, the previous month with an accompanying anonymous letter to King. The letter, a copy of which Hoover maintained in his office file, called King 'a colossal fraud and an evil vicious one at that' and added that 'like all frauds your end is approaching'. Its crude but threatening conclusion warned:

> The American public, the church organizations that have been helping – Protestant, Catholic and Jews will know you for what you are – an evil, abnormal beast. So will others who have backed you. You are done. King, there is only one thing left for you to do. You know what it is. You have just 34 days [a reference to the date when King was to be awarded the Nobel Peace Prize] in which to do [*sic*] (this exact number has been selected for a specific reason, it has definite practical significant [*sic*]). You are done. There is but one way out for you. You better take it

before your filthy, abnormal, fraudulent self is bared to the nation.

Another containment effort had involved a December 1963 news story reporting *Time* magazine's selection of King as 'Man of the Year'. Hoover's specific strategy cannot be ascertained because of heavy deletions in the released FBI documents. But part of this effort involved working with sympathetic news media, as one of Hoover's aides queried whether Assistant Director Sullivan had 'decided yet if we can tell [name deleted], [title deleted] of Radio Free Europe, about the "script"? Marrie and I are ready to go.'

Finally, Hoover's handwritten comment on a 27 January 1964 memo from Sullivan pertaining to a proposed installation of a bug in King's hotel room in Milwaukee sums up the personal and political motives behind Hoover's campaign against King. The Milwaukee police, Sullivan had advised Hoover, had rented the room next to King's suite in order to provide security. In view of this, he said, the Milwaukee SAC felt that 'the likelihood of King's going ahead with any [phrase deleted but sexual] plans is greatly minimized.' Hoover, contemptuous of his aide's defeatism, wrote: 'I don't share the conjecture. King is a "tom cat" with obsessive degenerate sexual urges.'

Hoover's obsession with discrediting King continued even after the civil rights leader's murder. Thus, when the Director learned that Senate Republican minority leader Hugh Scott proposed to introduce a bill to strike a commemorative medal in honor of King, he directed that the senator (who was described as having 'always been very friendly' and having a 'cooperative attitude' toward the FBI 'over the years') be briefed 'on a most confidential basis as to the background of Martin Luther King. Obviously, Scott has been "hoodwinked" as to King's true background.'

Hoover's hatred of King, like his hatred of Dillinger thirty years earlier, seems to have grown beyond all reason and to have been deeply involved with the civil rights leader's supposed sexual prowess. According to several accounts, the Director had become obsessed with both men, in his later years constantly alluding to them in conversations in a kind of involuntary incantation, as if all of the world's evil had been reposed in their two vile bodies. The irrationality of his behavior by this time, in fact, recalls the description of the paranoid in *The Authoritarian Personality*, who, although he 'is beset by an overall hatred, . . . nevertheless tends to "pick" his enemy, to molest certain individuals who draw his attention upon themselves: he falls, as it were, negatively in love'.

•

The key to the Krays

JOHN PEARSON

The Kray twins were London's most powerful underworld figures during the sixties, until, on 8 March 1969, they were each sentenced to life imprisonment. In his remarkable book John Pearson explains how successful fighting was the key to the rise of the Krays.

People were becoming slightly wary of the twins. One of their oldest friends, who knew them long before the army, noticed a change in them. 'I began to see that I could only go so far with them, and however friendly they were being, they seemed to keep themselves that little bit apart. Neither of them liked being touched. Put your hand on Reggie's shoulder and you'd feel him wince. You wouldn't do it twice.'

But it was Ronnie people really feared: 'We was all scared of him to tell the truth – not just because of what he knew. He had a funny way of looking at you and yet not looking at you that always made you think he was reading your mind.'

Sometimes he spent the evening brooding in his chair and left early. At other times he decided that he was drinking and picked a dozen hangers-on to go with him. 'It was always a bit of an event going to a pub with the twins. They used to like a crowded pub with a good singer and a lot of talent and perhaps the chance of trouble. When you went in with them people would stop talking and make room for you at the bar. We used to like that.' And sometimes at the billiard hall Ronnie would make his favourite announcement – 'Well, we've decided on a little row with so-and-so tonight. Who's for and who's against?'

It would be like a raiding-party with everyone bringing out his favourite weapon and piling into ancient battered cars outside the hall. The twins were always in the lead and would usually keep the destination secret. 'It was really all a bit of a lark. Sort of an outing. But it was a funny thing – wherever we went, to a pub or dance hall or another club, there was always trouble.' As for the fighting, friends of the twins insist that this was always deadly serious. 'They were a wicked couple really. They were frightened of no one and loved every minute of it. Something got into them once a fight started, and you could see that they enjoyed their bit of violence, really enjoyed it. If I was cutting somebody or putting the boot in, I'd usually hold back a bit – never the twins though. If you watched their faces while they did it, you'd see real hate. They always went the limit.'

At this stage there was no clear purpose to those nightly gatherings. But gradually, behind the fooling, boozing and aimless brawling of this one small cockney gang the outlines of something bigger started to appear. The gang began to change.

The key to this change lay in the twins and in their power as fighters. They were not particularly big men. Ronnie was 5 feet 10 inches, Reggie half an inch shorter. Reggie tipped the scales at eleven stone, Ronnie at twelve and a half. Many of their fights were with much larger men, yet in the several hundred bar brawls, woundings, shootings, punch-ups they were involved in, they never once appear to have come off second best. Neither was shot or cut or damaged seriously.

Both were abnormally tough; their teenage boxing training had left them strong in the arms and shoulders, and taught them both the precise use of their fists. They needed little sleep.

Ronnie is reputed to have drunk fifty-five brown ales in one night at the billiard hall and carried on next day as usual. But from the start they made it clear that they intended to become professionals of violence. They had their jokes, but behind the fooling there was one thing they took seriously – fighting. Here they knew their job, took no unnecessary risks and carefully refused to hamper themselves by effete conventions of fair play. These were for amateurs. If it was necessary to hit someone, they hit first and hardest and put the boot in afterwards. If they were cutting someone's face or backside, they used a knife or sharpened cutlass. 'Razors,' Ronnie used to say, 'are old-fashioned and strike us as babyish. You can't put no power behind a razor.'

Reggie developed what was known as his 'cigarette punch'. With his right hand he would offer somebody a cigarette and as the man opened his mouth to take it, would hit him on the side of the jaw with a swift left. It required timing and you needed to know the exact spot to hit. Reggie practised it for hours on a punch-bag and the cigarette punch broke many jaws. An open jaw will fracture easily.

Similarly, the 'little wars' that everyone enjoyed against the neighbouring gangs were organized in deadly earnest by the twins. For most of their followers 'they were just a lark, an outing, a sort of club activity'. But for the twins there was too much at stake to leave anything to chance. They quickly learned the elements of leadership and imposed strict discipline. They began using many of the military principles they had avoided in the army; Ronnie Kray's fantasies of Lawrence of Arabia started to make sense . . .

The twins had enemies. One was 'Mad' Frankie Fraser. It was a good nine years since this aggressive little man had taken sides with Billy Hill against the twins and gone to prison for his attack on Jack Spot. Now he was out, and Ronnie had heard rumours that he was friendly with another of the twins' old enemies – a fair-haired tearaway from Watney Street called Myers. There was resentment over a long firm of his that the twins had destroyed. Since meeting Fraser he had changed his name to Cornell and moved south of the river, where they had both joined the Richardsons. By October Cornell, Fraser and both the Richardsons were down on Ronnie's list.

Even today there are criminals in London who puzzle over why the Krays and Richardsons ever had to clash: the criminal activities of the Richardsons seemed to begin at the opposite pole from those of the Krays. The twins were traditional cockney villains, dangerous men who soon became the most powerful criminals in London. Charlie and Eddie Richardson were different. They were not cockney villains, violent outsiders like the Krays. They were straightforward, middle-class businessmen. Charlie Richardson ran scrap-metal yards and long firms south of the river, dabbled in government surplus, floated dubious companies. Eddie Richardson had a legitimate wholesale chemist's business bringing in at least £4,000 a year; Charlie had his office in Park Lane and his family house at Bromley. A year before the twins would have dismissed the Richardsons as straight men. There is a tendency for large-scale fraud to need the threat of violence in the background. By 1964 the Richardsons had started to enjoy it. After their arrest it was the details of their gang brutality that caught the headlines – the mock courts in the Park Lane offices before the Richardsons, the pliers on the teeth and fingernails and the electrode treatment for those who let them down.

This did not worry Ronnie too much. What did disturb him was the threat of competition. He also heard that Cornell – himself one of the Richardson torturers – had called him 'that fat poof'. Reggie urged caution. Ronnie wanted blood and was soon finding reasons to shed it. Fraser had taken over a chain of fruit machines that the twins had owned. Cornell had moved in on the West End pornography business. Just before Christmas 1965 Ronnie and the Richardsons met late one night at the Astor Club, off Berkeley Square. Both sides were armed. Insults were uttered and at one point it looked as if the shooting was about to start.

A few weeks later the twins were summoned to a meeting with two important visitors from the American Mafia. They spent two days together, talking as equals, and reached an understanding. The Americans were anxious to increase their stake in London gambling. 'Junkets' – big organized gambling parties – would soon be flying in on a regular basis from California and New York. This meant big money, on which the Americans were anxious to take their cut. In readiness they were investing heavily in several new London gambling clubs and hotels. Millions of dollars were at stake; nothing must go wrong. Provided the twins were ready to guarantee the new clubs freedom from trouble they would have their percentage.

It was a nice nest-egg to look forward to, but not if the Richardsons began throwing their weight about.

From then on all that counted was war against the Richardsons. No further business was accepted, no risks were taken. The Firm was mobilized and the information service stepped up. Fresh arms were purchased; caches of arms and ammunition were established in different parts of London. Everybody on the Firm was issued with an automatic. Ronnie wanted something more impressive for himself and Reggie; through Alan Cooper he bought two brand new Browning machine-guns for £75 each. He also asked for Mills bombs and limpet mines; Cooper said these were not available.

Ronnie enjoyed the Brownings, spending hours oiling them and studying the instruction manual. But weapons didn't make a war; he wanted allies, too, and in January held a meeting at Fort Vallance with the two other gangs who had most to lose from the rise of the Richardsons. From Clapham came two brothers who led a gang of thieves who had been closely involved in the Great Train Robbery and had clashed with the Richardsons. From North London came three more brothers whose gang had long operated by courtesy of the twins.

Ronnie was eloquent about the menace of the Richardsons; after they had drunk a lot he began talking of his old dream of a federation of gangs. They should form a defensive alliance, a firm treaty that if one gang were attacked the others would come to its aid.

'And if someone's killed?'

'It'd be up to the rest of us to do something about it.'

This seemed a good idea and they shook hands on it.

The war began in February after a shouting match in the Stork Club between Ronnie and Fraser; the twins left Cedra Court, the Colonel took command. The following few weeks were probably the happiest of his life. He was the guerrilla leader, armed to the teeth and ready for anything. Messages passed back and forth in code, meetings were summoned beneath forgotten bridges and in the backs of lorries, spies brought in a flow of tidings of the enemy. Obscure East End pubs became the Colonel's headquarters. Raids were planned and ambushes prepared; Reggie was with him, as he always was in time of trouble, the worries about Frances now forgotten, the humdrum business of the Firm irrelevant.

For once the twins appeared to have an enemy worth fighting. One night a raiding-party shot up The Widow's Pub in Tapp Street from a car, five minutes after the twins had left. A few days later a car mounted the pavement in Vallance Road, knocking down a man who looked like Ronnie. The twins put on bullet-proof vests and started making preparations to use the machine-guns against the Richardsons. Fate robbed them of the pleasure.

An early morning fight broke out on 8 March 1966 between two rival gangs at Mr Smith's Club on the London–Eastbourne Road at Catford; a thirty-year-old gangster called Richard Hart was killed. For once the twins were uninvolved: this was a Richardson job. For some time they had been infiltrating this drab segment of South London suburb; the night Hart was shot, Eddie Richardson and Frankie Fraser had arrived at the club soon after midnight, armed and ready for a showdown with the local gang protecting the place.

It should have been a routine takeover. For once the local gang fought back, shooting it out over the blackjack tables. When the police arrived Hart was already dead, Fraser was badly wounded and Eddie Richardson was having his gunshot wounds treated at Lewisham Hospital. Most of the top Richardson gangsters were involved; the police could move in now and it was clear that the Richardsons were finished. In one night at the 'Battle of Mr Smith's Club' the only gang that had tried to challenge the twins for control of London seemed to have destroyed itself.

The twins had had their war won for them. This was the moment when they could have made themselves the richest criminals in Britain. Instead Ronnie slipped a 9-mm Mauser automatic into his shoulder holster and asked Scotch Jack Dickson to drive him to The Blind Beggar.

It was a very casual death. Cornell was perched on a stool at the far end of the bar, drinking light ales with a couple of friends that night after Hart was killed. The pub was almost empty; it was 8.30 pm and the evening trade had barely started – a couple in the saloon bar near the door, an old man sipping Guinness in the public bar on the far side of the partition. The barmaid had just put a record on the juke-box to liven things up when Ronnie's arrival made this superfluous. Ian Barrie was with him. Both had guns.

'Well, just look who's here,' said Cornell, and smiled. He had an unattractive smile. Instead of a reply Barrie fired two warning shots into the ceiling to send the barmaid scurrying for safety in the cellar. Then Ronnie shot Cornell through the head and walked back to the street where his car was waiting. When he had gone, the barmaid went to the wounded man, but there was little she could do. By the time Cornell reached hospital he was already dead. When the police arrived at The Blind Beggar nobody had seen a thing.

'I never like hurting anybody unless I feel it personally,' Ronnie had always said; when he shot George Cornell he was repaying him for several ancient insults as well as for calling him a 'fat poof' behind his back. But there was more to it than that. Ronnie believed his honour as a leader was involved, for Hart was an ally. As one of the Firm put it, 'One of ours had gone so it was up to Ronnie to do one of theirs.'

It had to be Cornell: there was no one else left from the Richardsons' gang worth killing. Fraser was in hospital with a police guard by his bed. The Richardson brothers were in custody, along with everyone who had been at Mr Smith's. Cornell was the one important member of their gang who was not involved and so was the ideal victim. Thanks to his information service, Ronnie had known exactly where to find him; he had been trailing him for weeks.

•

How Glasgow gangs fight it out
JIMMY BOYLE

Jimmy Boyle grew up in Glasgow's Gorbals. To survive he had to fight and steal, and soon Jimmy was on his way to a career in crime. These extracts reveal the transformation of a youthful thug into a hardened villain. Thanks to the Special Unit at Barlinnie Prison, Boyle is now a reformed character.

By this time we were drinking wine in the toilets and smoking. Another gang had sprouted up in the school and we would fight with each other and one time I sat in class with a bayonet down the side of my trouser leg as a fight was looming with the other gang. I ended up fighting with the leader of the gang and he pulled a flick knife on me during the fight – which was supposed to be a fair one. A 'Square-Go' is one where the fists, head and feet are used, but no weapons. When this guy pulled out the flick knife it was one of my pals who saw it and shouted to me and I got it off him and kicked it to my pal but the Headmaster came in and caught us, taking both of us to stand outside the door of his room. While there, we never spoke but the other guy's face was in a mess and mine was OK. All the girls had to walk past the Headmaster's room to get to their classes and it was good to watch them seeing his face and asking if I had done it, with their teachers shouting at them for speaking to us. The other guy was looked on as the best fighter in the school so this was a big victory for me and I loved it. We stood there for some time until the police came, which surprised me as it had been a fair fight. They let the other guy go and the two uniformed cops took me between them and walked me all the way to Lawmoor Street Police Station. I walked past neighbours who asked me what was wrong and I shouted that it was OK and that nothing was wrong. The cops said I was to be sent away and they left me in a small room for a couple of hours but then they let me go and nothing further happened.

By this time Johnny Boris was sentenced to an Approved School, and a new kid, Johnnie Crosby, who had just come out of one, joined our class. Johnnie's uncle had been sentenced to death and reprieved so this was a big talking point for us and he joined our gang. There was a lot of coming and going in the school at this time due to the new housing development. Some of my pals who used to come down to our district at nights after moving house started making new pals up there and from this there grew more gangs, some of which became rivals of ours.

Meanwhile my reputation was expanding amongst the kids of my age, and with the police who were keeping a close eye on me. Our group took up street fighting more seriously though we still did the odd bit of stealing. This meant that we would meet and go to other parts of the district and fight rival gangs. At nights we would all be standing around the corner when someone would say that members of a rival gang were nearby and we would go for them, just like that and they did the same with us. There would be frequent meets to have a full gang fight but these took place very seldom as by the time we had made arrangements the cops would usually be on the spot though there were times when we would be fully into it before they arrived. All sorts of weapons were used: knives, hatchets, bayonets, and swords, but they were for show rather than for use. The main rival gang to us in the Gorbals was 'The Stud' and we fought continually and went for each other individually when we met on the street. Eventually there was an arrangement made for me and the leader of the 'Stud' to fight each other on a one-to-one basis. The fight was to be on the 'Stud' territory, in a place called 'The Raw', a piece of waste ground that had once held houses which had since been knocked down. It was a 'Square Go' and by the time we had got there the place was filled with people from all over the district. The area was in complete darkness with everyone squeezing around us to see what was going on, so there was little space left to fight. Anyway we went ahead and flew at each other but the minute both of us rolled on the ground everyone started booting the two of us. The boots were from each of our supporters trying to help us, but thank Christ someone called that the cops were coming and this scattered everybody and we made off. If they hadn't called out, the chances are that the two of us would have been kicked to death. I spent days looking for guys who had kicked me but it was hard trying to find out as they had all been at it.

Not long after this the 'Stud' began to fall away and we went looking for greener pastures. By now it was all a case of getting a reputation and this was only gained through fighting other gangs. We started fighting the gangs in Castlemilk, some of whom had been our pals and part of our old gang, but they became as much against us as we them. We beat them without any bother. All during these fights no one was badly hurt as they were only boys' fights, till one hot summer's night in a desolate part of the district we had a fight with a gang in Govanhill, which is a fringe district of the Gorbals. Most of the guys in the gang there came from the Gorbals and we all knew each other pretty well. All of us were armed to the teeth and I had a butcher's knife, the others had their own weapons. As the two gangs came into sight of each other they broke into a run throwing bottles as they came. This usually broke the groups up and we met and fought the individual who was nearest. I was fighting this guy who had a hammer that kept bouncing off my head and during the struggle we ended up in the closemouth with me on top of him. I hacked the butcher's knife into his face and slashed him, the skin parted and the blood started pouring over both of us. Between the blood coming from him and from my head, we were covered in it. On seeing us most of the others took fright and bolted but we were each helped by our pals.

This was the first time I had slashed anyone and really I didn't feel any remorse or pity for the guy as my head was sore and cut and I was cursing that I didn't give him worse, with my pals telling me not to worry as we would get him again. Certainly I had hit Owny with the knuckleduster but that was different as this time I had gone out to fight with a weapon intending to use it. The reason that I didn't feel any sorrow was that all the other fights had prepared me for this and I was actually looking forward to using the weapon as were the others. In the other fights I hadn't slashed or hurt anyone seriously although we boasted amongst ourselves as though we had. So when it did happen it wasn't just an idle boast and in fact it lent credibility to the earlier boasts and fantasy tales that we had been spreading. Another aspect that, for me, made slashing all the more a proper action was the injuries I suffered myself, a couple of gashes and bumps on the head from the hammer blows. They were a great prize in a strange sort of way because they let the others see that the victory was all the more deserved. It didn't take that incident long to circulate the district and other gangs outside. Within days I was a force to be reckoned with and some kids were saying that I was as 'mad as a brush'. There was a sort of hero worship about all of this and I was placed on a higher pedestal by all my own gang, but like reputations in other fields, you've got to deliver the goods otherwise you're in trouble . . .

The 'criminal code' isn't a thing that has been written up by top gangsters. It is an unwritten code of ethics. There are done things and things that are not done. It isn't the done thing to 'grass' or inform on anyone. It isn't the done thing to 'bump' or cheat someone from a robbery that you have all taken part in.

There are lots of these unwritten rules that could fill another book but these are just two examples that exist between guys in crime and on the whole they abide by them.

In Glasgow three guys were causing quite a stir in the criminal world around this time and were becoming pretty big. They were Willie Smith and Malky and Willie Bennett, all from the Govan area. Willie Smith and I were firm friends and we would go down to Govan to see them all the while building a stronger friendship. All of us were young and not really established yet.

Meanwhile back in the Gorbals, Artie and I were moving around and picking up money here and there. We were in 'The Wheatsheaf Bar' one night when two brothers, part of a large family of brothers who were very much a mob on their own, came in and tried to hassle the chargehand for booze or cash, so he called to us. We spoke to the brothers in a nice way because we didn't really want trouble with them. We walked outside the pub and along Rutherglen Road. I had a knife in my coat pocket, the brothers had bottles of beer and one had a tumbler. But while we walked the atmosphere began to get very hot and it ended up in a fight with the older brother jumping on my back. I pulled the knife and stuck it into his face while Artie grappled with the other then they ran off. We knew they were going for the rest of the family so we made for a street corner in Cumberland Street where we got together a group of friends and we all went looking for them, but they were not to be seen. However, on the way back we came across another group that we had had trouble with, and a running fight took place in Crown Street. There was quite a bit of stabbing and cutting going on and with the pubs just coming out the streets were crowded. To make matters worse there was a large crowd round a car accident blocking a part of Crown Street so there was panic when the fighting took place amongst them. When the police finally came the whole thing broke up but as a result lots of innocent people were injured.

I found Artie in a close covered in blood, he had a slash

wound running the length of his face but when the blood was wiped off it was only a superficial cut and though it would leave a fine mark it wouldn't leave a bad scar. We were walking along Cumberland Street and I threw away my knife as police cars were all over the place. When they saw us they grabbed us into the squad car and took us to the police station. By now the political criminal code was very much ingrained in me and I said nothing to them. Any questions they had to put were met by a wall of silence. We were charged with seven serious assaults and locked up. Other guys had been injured in the fight but they wouldn't dare come forward for fear of being charged. Later we were taken to the Police Headquarters, charged again then locked up in the cells. While we were lying there the brothers we fought with had been to Artie's house, kicked the door off its hinges and raided the place, hoping to get him as he lay in bed. But only his old mother was there.

While lying in the cells awaiting these charges, I wasn't too upset as there had been a good fight and I wasn't thinking of it in terms of society but simply from the gang-fight point of view. At no time did I express concern for any of the people who were injured or give them any thought at all. The only feeling of any kind was my own misfortune at being caught. All through the night, a long line of detectives from the junior ranks to the most senior came in to see us, looking through the square judas hole and shouting names to me as they did to most prisoners. It didn't really affect us and I would laugh at them when they said it in the hope of showing them that it didn't matter what they said as they were the enemy and all bastards anyway. Both of us were given a series of Identification Parades the following day which was a Sunday and we were allowed to see our lawyers. On the Monday morning we were taken for fingerprinting and photographing, but by now I was familiar with the whole procedure. There was no more fear of the unknown.

Both of us were remanded to Barlinnie Prison and taken there. By this time all the guys in the place had heard we were coming and had the usual odds and ends like toothpaste, soap or sweets and reading material ready for us. There had been a lot of publicity about the assaults describing innocent people being injured and though the Press made a big thing out of it, the guys in the prison saw it in another way and they were immediately sympathetic to our getting caught. They asked what our chances were of getting off and how the I.D. parades went, and there they were assessing and judging the whole thing, as we did with each other's cases. From any point of view the situation was bad but there was this unfeeling thing about it. Both of us were held till after the Christmas and New Year periods and I was given bail in January 1963. As I walked out of the prison gate I was met by Frank and we went home. We went back up to visit Artie and took him the things that he was allowed while waiting trial and we brought him up to date with the news.

About this time the gang of brothers were looking out for me and rumour had it that they were intent on crippling me. I was walking the streets with a revolver and a knife, ready for anything. Not long after being released on bail, I was buying the morning papers which come out the night before and I had a knife wrapped up in the newspaper, folding it very neatly, and in my waistband was a Walther automatic pistol. I was approached by two beat cops who asked what I was doing out, and I told them that I was on bail awaiting trial. They followed me part way along the road little knowing what I was carrying. I had decided to leave for London as that was where Frank had been for a good few months and I felt I would be better off down there for the moment. But needing some cash, I managed to do a job stealing a load of whisky and was in a pub one night waiting to see a guy about selling it. The pub was near the Clyde waterfront and there were two exits, one into the main road and the other into a dark side street and I chose the latter. It was extremely dark and the snow was lying pretty thick on the ground when I walked out. Without any warning I was hit on the side of the head, a mighty blow, and my immediate reflex was to go for the weapon I had on me, but I was hit from the other side and dragged towards a small van. I began to struggle as the blows were systematically landed on my head and spreadeagled body. There was quite a group around hitting me with hammers and hatchets on the head, but paying particular attention to my kneecaps and my hands. I lay there feeling every blow land but shock seemed to wash away pain and all I could think of was would I live and all the while sickening blows were landing all over my body for what seemed an eternity. I was left lying unconscious in the snow in the middle of the street.

When I came to I saw people passing by in the main street and cars and buses flashing past. It all seemed very normal and I crawled over to a nearby dark close that had a faint gas light glowing and lay there trying to feel the extent of my damage. I knew that I was pretty bad and the pain was crippling whenever I moved. When I finally managed to get onto my feet I saw that gut was hanging out of my trouser bottom, and the blood was running down my face from head wounds. Every move was an effort as I crawled to get a taxi but I found it hard as they took me for a drunk man. I finally managed to get home to my Ma's and it was just like a 'B' movie as I crawled into the house in a terrible state seeing the horror reflected on her face at my condition. I lost consciousness as I sat into the chair. Ma had two aunts in the house and they all came to the decision to call an ambulance which was a mistake because calling an ambulance meant the police would automatically arrive. I kept coming and going and remember the cops trying to get out of me what had happened and me saying that I had fallen.

I woke up in hospital. While the doctors were patching me up they told me that I would be in for some time, but I had other ideas. My problem was being unable to move, but this was resolved by the presence of Frank who had heard that I was in hospital and had come up. I signed myself out and he got transport and we left. No sooner had we arrived in my Ma's house when the cops were at the door – detectives. They were told that I was still in hospital but they went downstairs and waited in the car probably thinking that I hadn't arrived home yet. I was helped down to a neighbour's house to stay the night, every movement an agony. My legs at the knees had stiffened up and my back was a mass of bruises from the hammer blows. A large, deep wound was below my left knee-cap and my head was cut in several places all of which had stitches in them. What was worrying me was that the cops, knowing what was happening, were intent on arresting me on a holding charge as they anticipated all sorts of gang wars break-ing out. Sleep was slow in coming that night as the pain was excruciating but I had time to think over the night's events. There was no fear now, unlike before when I had been grabbed by the mob; that was real fear. All my thoughts were on means of revenge, as a 'come back' was important. This was a sign of strength in any group, as it would make others think twice about coming after me, if they knew I would come back for revenge. The following morning I was taken to a safe house to lie and rest.

The brothers who had done the damage were dropping it around the district that I was lying in the hospital crippled and that anyone else looking for trouble would know to expect the same. Within a few hours the rumour was going round that I was in a bad way and would never walk again. I discussed this with two friends and we decided that there was no way for an immediate retaliation but that we should blow these myths going round. I was half carried to a car and driven to a pub in the Gorbals. All my injuries were hidden by my hair and clothes, only the hand ones showed. The point was to blow the cripple thing and just to be there would discredit the rumours and the other mob. We managed to get some of the big mouths into the pub and when they saw me they immediately started talking about the rumour going round. We had a good laugh at them, though it was hurting me, but it was important for us to show a good front. We knew that when this reached the other mob they would be puzzled as they knew only too well that they had given me a thorough going over. The fact that I was sitting in a pub was the last thing they would be expecting. It was a small consolation but it was all worth it.

•

The bloodiest literary brawl
BRIAN BOYD

Vladimir Nabokov arrived in the United States in 1940, to take up an academic career. One of the Russian's earliest friends was the American writer and critic Edmund Wilson. Here, Brian Boyd, Nabokov's biographer, explains how, over a period of some twenty years, a satisfying friendship turned sour, and became a bitter literary feud.

On the way back to New York at the end of March [1941], Nabokov stopped in Ridgefield, Connecticut, to see Mikhail Chekhov. Their ideas for adapting *Don Quixote* no longer coincided (Chekhov wanted a Christian or rather an anthroposophical apotheosis at the end), and the project was called off. From Ridgefield, Nabokov traveled on a little further to Stamford to spend a night with Edmund Wilson and Wilson's third wife, Mary McCarthy.

Wilson and Nabokov had seen each other several times over the past few months, but it was in Stamford that their keen interest in each other turned into warm friendship. The lean, intense Nabokov, with his full-voweled Russian version of a Cambridge accent, and short, plump, puffy-faced Wilson, with his loud, curiously high-pitched voice, went line by line through the proofs of Nabokov's translation of 'Mozart and Salieri'. In the glow of their collaboration, Nabokov for once was amenable to emendations, even grateful for them. The two men could not agree on the subject of Russian prosody, a difference that would gradually become tiresome and vexing to them both when repeated on and off for the next twenty-five years, but for the moment they overwhelmed and exhilarated each other with their energy.

Mary McCarthy, then a twenty-eight-year-old former *Partisan Review* editor just starting to write her first fiction, watched them with delight. In her words, 'they had an absolute ball together. Edmund was always in a state of *joy* when Vladimir appeared; he *loved* him.' As Clarence Brown would remark in a review of *The Nabokov–Wilson Letters*, 'both of them well past the midpoint of life, formed the sort of friendship that is normally possible only in youth'. Wilson's young son Reuel heard the name 'Volodya', but could say it only as 'Gardenia'. Nabokov thought the name enchanting; Wilson declared with mock grandeur, 'you're the gardenia in the buttonhole of Russian literature'. Out on a long stroll together, Wilson asked Nabokov whether or not he believed in God. 'Do you?' countered Nabokov. 'What a strange question!' muttered Wilson, and fell silent . . .

Now that they were established in Cambridge the Nabokovs saw more of Edmund Wilson and Mary McCarthy. McCarthy was shocked at the Nabokovs' plain fare and their indifference to their surroundings, to things like the hideous lampshades and the brass ashtrays in their sitting room. On the other hand, when Nabokov visited the Wilsons he made friendly fun of McCarthy's fussing over culinary delicacies by concocting for her fancy treats his own even fancier names. He also disclosed as a grim family secret that at home they might have a carp served up with boiled potatoes and carrots and live off the dish for a week. McCarthy believed him.

Often in Cambridge the Nabokovs would meet the Wilsons in the Levins' much more spacious home. Elena Levin saw the two friends as 'such opposite kinds of human: Volodya subtle, reclusive, familial; Edmund blunt, commonsensical, and after three drinks he "collapsed like a bag of potatoes", in Volodya's words'. Even early on, Harry Levin noticed, the two men, for all the richness of their relationship and their admiration for each other, also grated against each other – and this in the peak years of their friendship. Wilson disliked Nabokov's unrufflable self-confidence and frank self-delight and his dismissiveness of other writers. Nabokov admired Wilson's range of interests but also found it rather amusingly forced. Once Wilson asked him to invite entomologists to a party he was giving at Craigie Circle. None turned up, but, not realizing this, Wilson cornered the two or three guests – actually Nabokov's literature colleagues from Wellesley – assuming they were M.C.Z. scientists, and tried to talk shop. As Nabokov recalled with a smile, his guests 'were indeed taken aback by the famous Edmund Wilson's sudden interest in insect lore'.

Judging art at its highest and most impersonal, Nabokov had implacable standards, and as a critic he hugely enjoyed hurling writers he deemed interlopers down the slopes of Olympus. At a personal level, on the other hand, he would look for what he could find to like in other people's work. He respected the vulnerability of others and was as sensitive to his friends as he was undemanding of his students. Wilson, on the other hand, had a compulsive competitiveness that meant he had to counterbalance praise with reproach, either providing a list of corrections, no matter how captious, or implying that at the midpoint of a story he had seen a rather better way to finish it than its author had chosen. Wilson seemed to expect the recipient to be charmed by his behavior, by the special Wilsonian tartness of judgment and independence of imagination. Even at an early stage in their relationship, Nabokov detected this irrationality in his friend. Nevertheless he was deeply fond of Wilson, and almost from the start wrote to him with a warmth that Wilson seldom matched. To their common friend Roman Grynberg, Nabokov confided that with Wilson the 'lyrical plaint' that adorns Russian friendship seemed to be lacking – as it generally was, he felt, among Anglo-Saxons: 'I love a violin in personal relationships, but in this case there is no way one can let out a heartfelt sigh or casually unburden a soft fresh bit of oneself. Still, there's a good deal else to make up for it' . . .

At this point it may be worth commenting on Nabokov's

penchant for literary deception. As he explained in his mimicry article and elsewhere, he detected in nature a playful deceptiveness and found nothing more exhilarating than the surprise of seeing through the deception to a new level of truth. He liked to offer the same surprises in literature, feigning falsehood when he was telling the truth or vice versa, for the sake of the reader's pleasure in penetrating the illusion.

He behaved the same way in person. As Elena Levin recalled, 'when he tells you the truth he winks at you to confuse you'. He would often concoct highly plausible impromptu inventions and pay his listeners the compliment of assuming that they could see through the trompe l'oeil. Those not so well attuned to him often missed the point.

Edmund Wilson was such a person. He became convinced that Nabokov was a malicious practical joker and decided, especially as their relationship deteriorated, that schadenfreude was a key to Nabokov's personality. The worst recorded instance of a hoax Nabokov played on Wilson is no more than this: once 'in a convertible, with Mary McCarthy at the wheel and her husband beside her, Nabokov, who was sitting with his wife in the back, leaned forward and nimbly removed Wilson's awful brown hat – impersonating, as it were, a roguish breeze'. Wilson ignored Nabokov and turned to Véra: 'Your husband has a rather strange sense of humor.'

With his prickly competitiveness, Wilson attempted to ensure he would never be caught out by Nabokov, and as a result imagined hoaxes that had never existed. He telephoned Nabokov shortly after reading *The Real Life of Sebastian Knight* to tell him he had discovered that the whole novel was built as a chess game. Nabokov told him, quite truthfully, that this was not the case. Wilson wrote back to say: 'I don't believe a word you say about your book and am furious at having been hoaxed by it (though my opinion of it has rather gone up than otherwise).' A year later, after reading a book of new verse Wilson had sent him, Nabokov complimented him that the opening lines of one of his poems, 'After reading, / writing late' were 'in tone, rhythm and atmosphere ... most beautifully like Pushkin's mumble: *mne ne spitsya, | net ognya'* ('I can't sleep, there is no light'). A month later Wilson wrote back:

> You know that you played on me unintentionally a more successful hoax than any that you premeditated. I was sure that you had invented the Pushkin poem about lying awake at night which sounded so much like mine. I told Mary and other people so and cited it as an example of the lengths to which you would go in the concoction of literary frauds, and swore that I would not for anything in the world give you the satisfaction of looking it up and of not being able to find it. Then I did look it up one night and found that it did actually exist. I was furious.

Wilson seemed fated to misinterpret Nabokov, but that did not yet impair their friendship or Wilson's generosity ...

The one thing that did help Nabokov was a new relationship with the *New Yorker*. Over the last two years the *New Yorker* had accepted a handful of his poems, but he had continued to publish his stories in the *Atlantic* for much less than the *New Yorker* could pay. Katharine White, one of the creators of the *New Yorker*, came back from Maine at the beginning of 1944 to work there again. As Wilson told Nabokov, 'one of the ideas she came back with was to get you to do stories for them. She had torn out all your things in the *Atlantic*.' Wilson encouraged her in her design, and it would be her and the *New Yorker*'s interest in his work that would lead to Nabokov's most satisfying relationship with any American publisher until *Lolita*'s success turned every publisher into an eager suitor. Wilson, knowing of his friend's financial troubles, and for once having money to spare, offered Nabokov a loan that he would not accept. On Wilson's prompting, Katharine White in June 1944 offered Nabokov an advance of five hundred dollars against future contributions to the *New Yorker*, in return for giving the magazine the rights to a first consideration of his new work. He would maintain a first-reading contract with the *New Yorker*, generously increased as his English reputation grew, for another three decades . . .

After an uncomfortable squeeze into Anna Feigin's apartment on West 104th Street, the Nabokovs were able to move back to Ithaca on September 1 [1954], two weeks ahead of schedule, into number 30, Belleayre Apartments ('sic!' notes Nabokov), at 700 Stewart Avenue, right on the edge of the campus. Nabokov now asked Doussia Ergaz to hold off her search for a European publisher for *Lolita*, as James Laughlin of New Directions had asked to see the novel. Laughlin had published *The Real Life of Sebastian Knight* when no one else would take on something so strange, and although Nabokov had been disappointed by the meager financial rewards of publishing with New Directions, it seemed worth a try. Always ready to launch the original and the challenging, Laughlin nevertheless found *Lolita* too great a risk: it would be unthinkable, he wrote, to publish the book without destroying Nabokov's reputation and his own.

As soon as he reached Ithaca, Nabokov resumed work on his masses of notes and drafts for *Eugene Onegin*, fearing that if he did not bring the project to a reasonable stage of completion he might tire of it all. He returned to New York for an English Institute conference at Columbia University, where on September 14 he presented a paper called 'Problems of Translation: *Onegin* in English', a brilliant, impassioned attack on rhymed translations, a convincing demonstration of the impossibility of conveying the explicit sense and the implicit associations behind Pushkin's lines to an English reader by any means except absolute literal fidelity. The conference organizer, Reuben Brower, reported to Nabokov that his paper had a succès fou.

Lectures at Cornell resumed in the last week of September. By now Nabokov was much happier than he had been in his first years at Cornell. His salary had risen to $6,500, his largest course was extremely popular, he was engaged in scholarly projects of note (*Eugene Onegin, The Song of Igor's Campaign*, the

Anna Karenin edition, and the planned book on masterpieces of European fiction), he had already managed to write two creative masterpieces since arriving in Ithaca (*Conclusive Evidence* and *Lolita*), and now that he had no new material to prepare for class he had much more time free during the college year for his own work as a Russian scholar or an English writer.

He spent the fall term working feverishly to finish *Eugene Onegin*, only to realize it would still take him many more months. Meanwhile Edmund Wilson had suggested that Nabokov show *Lolita* to his current publisher, Farrar, Straus. Roger Straus turned the book down and counseled Nabokov against publishing it pseudonymously, for although that might at first safeguard Cornell, it would weaken the book's chances in court. There, the only possible defense would be that it was a first-rate work of art by a reputable man of letters who had handled a repellent subject with perfect literary tact.

Edmund Wilson himself was next to receive the manuscript. He recoiled at once. One night in a typically Wilsonian gesture he called Nabokov up at 11:00 p.m., asked him to identify a moth he had caught, and did not say a word about the novel, although his friend had been eagerly awaiting his response. Despite his immediate personal dislike of the book, Wilson nevertheless remained determined to help it find a publisher. When Jason Epstein of Doubleday visited him at Wellfleet, he took the two black binders down from a shelf: 'Here's a manuscript by my friend Volodya Nabokov. It's repulsive, but you should read it.' Elena Wilson [Wilson's wife] and Mary McCarthy, however, were still ahead of Epstein in the queue. According to the version Nabokov learned some time later, Wilson read only half of the manuscript: in order to have it seen by as many as might be able to help with publication, he had reserved one of the binders for himself and passed the other on to Mary McCarthy. Only at the end of November did Nabokov receive Wilson's report of Elena Wilson's judgment (very positive), McCarthy's (negative and perplexed), and Wilson's own: 'I like it less than anything else of yours I have read.'

Nabokov took some months to reply: 'Belatedly but with perfectly preserved warmth,' he began, 'I now want to thank you for your letters.' His reply *was* a warm one, but over the next year, after hearing how cursorily Wilson had scanned the book, he could not conceal a different kind of warmth as he tried to prod his friend into reading *Lolita* properly: 'I would like you to read it some day'; 'When you do read *Lolita*, please mark that it is a highly moral affair' . . .

Late in May [1957], Edmund Wilson came to visit the Nabokovs for the weekend. Once again the two men revived their dispute about English and Russian versification, a conflict that had already simmered for a decade and a half and that in 1965 would erupt into the literary explosion of the year.

Summing up for his guest the notes on prosody he had recently added to his *Eugene Onegin*, Nabokov indicated that he still followed the assumption he had once set before Wilson: 'I am quite, quite sure that Russian versification can be explained better to an English poet by the vague similarities between it and English versification than by the blatant differences between the two languages.' Wilson noted in his diary: 'Volodya's insistent idea that Russian and English verse are basically the same is, actually, I have become convinced, a part of his inheritance from his father, a leader of the Kadets in the Duma and a champion of constitutional monarchy for Russia after the British model, a belief that these two so dissimilar countries are, or ought to be, closely associated.' Wilson's reaction here seems typical of his behavior toward Nabokov in this phase of their friendship. Rather than listen to Nabokov, he constructed an absurd biographical explanation of what he supposed his friend to be saying. In fact, Nabokov was fully aware of the 'blatant differences' between the two prosodic systems, and a few months earlier had written that even if by some miracle an English version of *Eugene Onegin* could render Pushkin's exact sense *and* the whole constellation of his rhymes, the miracle would be pointless, since the English conception of rhyme does not correspond at all to the Russian.

When Nabokov announced that Pushkin's knowledge of English and other languages was rudimentary, Wilson once again dismissed Nabokov's discovery and resorted to jaundiced psychology: 'These false ideas, of course,' he declared in his diary, 'are prompted by his compulsion to think of himself as the only writer in history who has been equally proficient in Russian, English and French.' But Nabokov had at first assumed like many others that Pushkin knew English, German, Greek, and Italian, and only on examining the detailed evidence did he find Pushkin continually starting and restarting to learn these languages and never reaching the point where he could easily read foreign poets other than the French in the original.

Wilson kept his most critical thoughts to himself, and even in the matters where they constantly disagreed he and Nabokov could still enjoy each other's company. Nabokov challenged his guest to read *Eugene Onegin* aloud. Wilson started to perform with disastrous gusto, putting the wrong syllabic stress on the first word that had more than one syllable: 'Moy dyaDYA', which means, and matches, 'My unCLE'. He garbled every second word, Nabokov reported, 'turning Pushkin's iambic line into a kind of spastic anapest with a lot of jaw-twisting haws and rather endearing little barks that utterly jumbled the rhythm and soon had us both in stitches'.

The author of *Memoirs of Hecate County* and the author of *Lolita* shared an amused taste for sexual spice in their literary dishes. As Wilson later reported, he brought his friend '*Histoire d'O*, that highly sophisticated and amusing pornographic work, and in return he sent me in my quarters a collection of French and Italian poems of a more or less licentious character, which I think he had been consulting in connection with his translation of Pushkin.' The morning Wilson left, Nabokov came out to see him off. Wilson, sitting propped up in the back of the car with his gouty foot on the seat, congratulated Nabokov on looking fresh after his bath. Nabokov leaned into the car and murmured, in parodic homage to *Histoire d'O*, 'Je mettais du rouge sur les lèvres de mon ventre' . . .

On July 7 [1965], a week after arriving at Suvretta House, St Moritz, Nabokov read Edmund Wilson's review of his *Eugene Onegin* and at once cabled Barbara Epstein at the *New York Review of Books*: 'Please reserve space in next issue for my thunder.'

Reviews of *Eugene Onegin* had been appearing for almost a year. All praised the sheer quantity of information in the commentary, though some reproached Nabokov for capricious selections, digressiveness, or captiousness of tone. All praised the literal accuracy of the translation, but most wished that Nabokov had tried to match both the music and the naturalness of Pushkin's language, to make the poem seem *not* a mere translation. A brief exchange of letters with a previous translator, Babette Deutsch, early in 1965, had served as a preliminary skirmish for the battle that was now about to commence.

Wilson began his review by referring to his friendship with Nabokov, then launched into a fierce personal attack:

> Since Mr Nabokov is in the habit of introducing any job of this kind which he undertakes by an announcement that he is unique and incomparable and that everybody else who has attempted it is an oaf and an ignoramus, incompetent as a linguist and a scholar, usually with the implication that he is also a low-class person and a ridiculous personality, Nabokov ought not to complain if the reviewer, though trying not to imitate his bad literary manners, does not hesitate to underline his weaknesses.

Of course Nabokov had made no such announcement, and in fact commended and drew on translators like the Ivan Turgenev – Louis Viardot team and André Lirondelle, and commentators like Lerner, Shchyogolev, Khodasevich, Tomashevski, Tynyanov, and others. And as Clarence Brown comments, Wilson seems to have overlooked the modesty of Nabokov's aims: to translate only the exact sense without presuming, as verse translators did, that he could offer a fair approximation of Pushkin's music and grace.

Wilson's principal charge was that the 'bald and awkward language' of Nabokov's translation had nothing in common with Pushkin, and he sought to explain it thus:

> One knows also the perversity of [Nabokov's] tricks to startle or stick pins in the reader, and one suspects that his perversity here has been exercised in curbing his brilliance; that – with his sado-masochistic Dostoevskian tendencies so acutely noted by Sartre – he seeks to torture both the reader and himself by flattening Pushkin out and denying to his own powers the scope for their full play.
>
> Aside from this desire both to suffer and make suffer – so important an element in his fiction – the only characteristic Nabokov trait that one recognizes is the addiction to rare and unfamiliar words.

Throughout his work Nabokov stresses that a world as rich as ours cannot be easily understood. On the other hand, for that very reason it proves a delight to discover, if one makes the effort. In writing fiction, he constructs his invented worlds to match, so that at first they resist the mind in certain ways in order to offer us more in the long run. But this central aspect of Nabokov's work Wilson had for many years misconstrued as a desire to humiliate and torment the reader. Nabokov's *Onegin* operates on the same principle as his fiction: like the world itself, Pushkin's masterpiece is a complex marvel, and there can be no easy substitute for mastering its priceless particulars. Far from desiring to vex his readers, Nabokov hoped to offer them the full flavor of Pushkin: by choosing, for instance, an unusual word like 'rememorating', he could convey both the archaism and the vocalic resonance of Pushkin's choosing *vospomnya* instead of the more usual *vspomnya*. Wilson instead read that generosity of intent as a penchant for willful cruelty.

Wilson criticized some of Nabokov's rare words as nonexistent, only because he had not deigned to look them up in Webster's. He ignored Nabokov's choice of method, his attempt to provide a humble pony, his deliberate decision not to offer smooth English so that he could direct readers to the irreplaceable Russian. To quote Clarence Brown once more, Wilson spent most of his time in the review complaining that the translation

> did not read smoothly, contained unusual words, and was even downright wrong. In making the latter point, Wilson committed the almost unbelievable hubris of reading Nabokov several petulant little lessons about Russian grammar and vocabulary, himself blundering all the while. (Where were the Russian friends to whom he constantly alludes?) He also disliked the tone of everything, found the manners of his 'personal friend' to be characteristically unsupportable, dismissed the commentary not so much for any faults he found as for its conveying more than anyone wished to know, and ended with an insulting compliment on the physical appearance of the books.

Why did Wilson aim such a willfully peevish attack at someone who had long been a close friend? Wilson's great talent had always been for turning up stones with the queerest crabs underneath, for discovering literary interest where others had not yet looked – in, say, the Civil War writers he incorporated into *Patriotic Gore*. Nabokov, on the other hand, maintained that literature mattered not at the level of the tolerable but only at that of the supreme masterpiece, where a work of art seems to extend the limits of the humanly possible, and he had long irritated Wilson by his readiness to dismiss writers with reputations as high as those of Balzac, Stendhal, Dostoevsky, or Mann. But in his relations with friends he always tried to signal the strengths of their books, whereas Wilson regarded it as a virtue, a rather endearing trait – proof of his frank and unbiased judgment – to criticize friends harshly to their faces. 'Disagreement truly interested him,' writes Edith Oliver. ' "Embarrassing!" he said. "What does that mean? I have never known what that meant." He felt that anything in print . . . was discussable.'

But even that attitude cannot explain the seething animosity of his attack on Nabokov. We must return to the beginnings of their relationship.

Nabokov, who always liked a sparring partner, welcomed the boldly combative spirit in Wilson. At the same time, he never felt Wilson was any competition. When Andrew Field later wrote of their relationship that there was 'hardly a moment when the tension of being competitors is dropped', Nabokov asked him to replace it with '"when the tension between two highly dissimilar minds, attitudes and educations is slackened". We were never competitors. In what, good gracious?' On their common ground, Russian language and literature and history, Nabokov knew he was incomparably better informed than Wilson. Nor did he have any doubts that as a writer he was in a different class from his friend or for that matter any other contemporary he had read.

Wilson came to resent Nabokov's dismissal of other writers and his unshakable self-assurance, and as early as 1945 he wrote to him of 'your insatiable and narcissistic vanity'. Nabokov played up to that image, deliberately teasing his friend. When Wilson wrote that he had begun to learn chess, for instance, Nabokov had replied: 'I hope you will soon be playing well enough for me to beat you.'

Nabokov's confidence that Wilson was no competitor only intensified his friend's drive to prove that he could challenge and even outdo Nabokov. Wilson wrote fiction himself, and in the years when he first knew Nabokov he was composing his favorite among his books, the stories of *Memoirs of Hecate County*. As he read Nabokov's works, he regularly imposed alternative continuations that he implied would be better than Nabokov's own versions. He liked *Laughter in the Dark* 'better before it got rather implausible toward the end. I thought that the unfortunate hero was going to develop color audition and detect the whereabouts of the girl by hearing her red dress, or something.' He read *Pale Fire* with amusement, 'but it seems to me rather silly . . . I expected that the professor would turn out to be the real King and that the commentator would be the assassin.' He subjected *The Real Life of Sebastian Knight*, 'Rusalka', and *Bend Sinister* to the same strange treatment.

In these rewritings of Nabokov, Wilson's rivalry operated at an instinctive level. Criticism offered him a more conscious and more potent weapon. He was, after all, often considered the best American critic of his time. As early as 1947 he had proposed an article on Nabokov's works as a whole. In 1952 he proudly announced to Véra Nabokov that he would soon set to reading all her husband's works and would write an essay on them 'that will somewhat annoy him'. Throughout the next ten years he would repeat the promise and the threat again and again. He had come to the conclusion that he had discovered the secret source of Nabokov's art in schadenfreude, and that he had a psychological explanation for this in line with his thesis in *The Wound and the Bow* that artistic creativity springs from trauma. In Nabokov's works 'everybody is always being humiliated' because 'he himself, since he left Russia and as a result of the assassination of his father, must have suffered a good deal of humiliation'. Nabokov later responded to this: 'the "miseries, horrors and handicaps" that he assumes I was subjected to . . . are mostly figments of his warped fancy . . . He has not even bothered to read *Speak, Memory*, the records and recollections of a happy expatriation that began practically on the day of my birth.'

If the charge of schadenfreude could be leveled at anyone, it would not be at Nabokov, who detested bullfighting and hunting and all cruelty to animals, but at Wilson. As Nabokov noted in his diary in 1967 on reading one of Wilson's *New Yorker* pieces, 'Only a scoundrel could write that he could understand "the sexual satisfaction" of seeing a woman stepping on a milk-glutted kitten and causing it to explode.'

The eroticism of Wilson's *Memoirs of Hecate County* had ensured only that the book was banned from sale and forgotten. When *Lolita*, on the other hand, brought Nabokov fortune, fame, and ringing acclaim, it sharply intensified Wilson's irritation that he could not quite compete and that Nabokov knew it. In the year of *Lolita*'s American appearance, Wilson failed to reply to one of Nabokov's letters, and when Nabokov wrote again, suspecting the cause of Wilson's silence, he took care not to mention *Lolita* by name. But he still tried to keep the friendship alive: 'You have quite forgotten me,' he wrote late in 1960, after Wilson again failed to reply to another letter. After seeing Wilson in 1962, their closest common friend, Roman Grynberg, wrote to Nabokov asking what had made Wilson so angry with him. 'Envy? But you are so different!'

Pushkin had always been their meeting-ground, and would now become their battlefield. In 1962, William McGuire wrote that Dwight MacDonald and Wilson wanted to see the *Onegin* proofs. Nabokov replied: 'Sorry – I definitely do not wish them to be shown to anybody, least of all to Wilson.' A year later, however, when the proofs were finalized, he gave McGuire permission to send them to Wilson, 'but if he starts questioning things, please don't inform me of his questions'.

When the first favourable review of *Eugene Onegin* appeared in the summer of 1964, the Bollingen Press was delighted. Nabokov set little store by the acclaim: 'The only good of it is that some of its banal compliments might be useful for . . . a full-page advertisement . . . Otherwise, I have no illusions about these articles. None of the reviewers is really competent.' The Bollingen Foundation kept looking forward to Wilson's article, but Nabokov warned that he did not expect much from it: 'As I have mentioned before, his Russian is primitive, and his knowledge of Russian literature gappy and grotesque. He is a very old friend of mine, and I do hope our quarter-of-a-century correspondence . . . will be published someday.'

Nabokov had not anticipated he would learn from Wilson's review, but he was shocked to find the degree to which 'a dear friend' could be 'transformed into an envious ass'. After reading the article, Nabokov wrongly supposed that Wilson had already read the *Onegin* proofs and written his article before visiting him in Montreux early in 1964, but meanly said nothing of the impending attack. In fact, although Nabokov had given McGuire permission to send Wilson proofs in September 1963, Wilson had begun to read the translation only in its published version and in the summer of 1964.

In his commentary to *Eugene Onegin*, Nabokov wonders why on one occasion 'Pushkin, vindictive Pushkin, with his acute sense of honor and *amour-propre*' did not call out to a duel a famous rake who had challenged him with an insulting epigram. Endowed with a Pushkinian sense of amour propre himself, Nabokov never thought for a moment of not defending himself. Yet his first riposte was a surprisingly gentle letter to the *New York Review of Books*. After alluding to his long friendship with Wilson and his gratitude for Wilson's past kindnesses, he went on to list and explain eight blunders in Wilson's Russian and his English and let these facts speak for themselves. He concluded: 'I suggest that Mr Wilson's didactic purpose is defeated by the presence of such errors (and there are many more to be listed later), as it is also by the strange tone of his article. Its mixture of pompous aplomb and peevish ignorance is certainly not conducive to a sensible discussion of Pushkin's language and mine.'

In the same issue appeared Wilson's reply. He had consulted with Max Hayward, whose translation of *Doctor Zhivago* he had harshly criticized in 1958, only to disclose even then how patchy his own Russian was. Since that date the two men had become drinking buddies, and Hayward now formulated a riposte for Wilson. Nabokov had written: 'I do not think Mr Wilson should try to teach me how to pronounce this or any other Russian vowel.' Now Hayward prompted Wilson to take issue with Nabokov's description of one Russian consonant and to declare that the sound as Nabokov explained it was 'a feature of ByeloRussian. Now, I have heard Mr Nabokov insist on the superiority of the Petersburg pronunciation to that of Moscow, and I am rather surprised to find him recommending the pronunciation of Minsk.'

Anthony Burgess, who earlier in the year had reviewed the *Onegin* translation, would later recall modestly that after reading Wilson's attack and Nabokov's reply, 'small reviewers like me scuttled out of the crossfire and left it to the giants'. In fact, in the letters columns, review pages, and editorials of the *New York Review of Books*, the *New Republic, Poetry*, and elsewhere, others continued to join the fray, and Nabokov was vexed that many who knew no Russian or missed the point of his translating the way he did took Wilson's side and hissed at the hideousness of a translation he had never tried to prettify.

In late October and early November he wrote a long article on the whole furor destined for the *New York Review of Books* but ultimately published in *Encounter*. He began by saying he never responded to criticism of his creative work, but that scholarship 'possesses an ethical side, moral and human elements. It reflects the compiler's honesty or dishonesty, skill or sloppiness. If told I am a bad poet, I smile; but if told I am a poor scholar, I reach for my heaviest dictionary.' He defended literality, disposed quickly of a few criticisms made in other reviews, then turned to the Wilson article, no longer with restraint in his voice but gloating over 'the unusual, unbelievable, and highly entertaining opportunity . . . of refuting practically every item of criticism in his enormous piece . . . It is a polemicist's dream come true.'

Discussing every example of his own seemingly bizarre renderings that Wilson had tried to fault, he showed that 'all have pedigrees of agony and rejection and reinstatement, and should be treated as convalescents and ancient orphans, and not hooted at as impostors by a critic who says he admires some of my books.' His precision and erudition were devastating, his irony unsparing:

In translating *slushat' shum morskoy* (Eight:IV:11) I chose the archaic and poetic transitive turn 'to listen the sound of the sea' because the relevant passage has in Pushkin a stylized archaic tone. Mr Wilson may not care for this turn

– I do not much care for it either – but it is silly of him to assume that I lapsed into a naïve Russianism not being really aware that, as he tells me, 'in English you have to listen *to* something'. First, it is Mr Wilson who is not aware that there exists an analogous construction in Russian, *prislushivat'sya k zvuku*, 'to listen closely to the sound' – which, of course, makes nonsense of the exclusive Russianism imagined by him, and secondly, had he happened to leaf through a certain canto of *Don Juan*, written in the year Pushkin was beginning his poem, or a certain *Ode to Memory*, written when Pushkin's poem was being finished, my learned friend would have concluded that Byron ('Listening debates not very wise or witty') and Tennyson ('Listening the lordly music') must have had quite as much Russian blood as Pushkin and I.

After the publication of 'Nabokov's Reply' in Britain, the *Observer* described the affair as the bloodiest literary brawl since F. R. Leavis went for C. P. Snow's jugular vein, and in its honor the Royal Shakespeare Company performed a highly successful reading of Nabokov's translation at the Aldwych. There was something unintentionally apt about comparing the Nabokov–Wilson broil to Snow's and Leavis's arguments for and against uniting the 'two cultures' of science and art. Nabokov was a scientist, and in preparing his *Butterflies of Europe* he had told Weidenfeld he would prefer if necessary to feature a slightly damaged specimen from a species' type locality rather than a fresher specimen from elsewhere: 'We shall always sacrifice "beauty" to science with the result that genuine beauty will be achieved.' In *Eugene Onegin* he followed the same principles: he sacrificed the facile 'beauty' of imitating Pushkin's verse form at the expense of his sense and opted instead for the ruthless fidelity that could achieve a deeper truth and therefore a more genuine beauty.

There were a number of aftershocks of the controversy: a couple of brief blasts and counterblasts in print from Wilson and Nabokov early in 1966 and again in 1968, and a rather more curious private exchange. Wilson seemed to feel that his criticism had been simply robust frankness rather than vicious hostility, and sent a copy of the article to his and Nabokov's friend Roman Grynberg. Grynberg wrote to Nabokov that, ever since, Wilson had been waiting for his reply: 'He doesn't see how pathetic he is.' Then Wilson surprised Nabokov by sending him a Christmas card at the end of 1965 that would have been 'charming and even witty in other circumstances'. The next year he sent another card: 'I'm sorry our controversy has come to an end. I have rarely enjoyed anything so much.' With stiff politeness Nabokov replied: 'Although I did not relish quite as much as you tell me you did our "controversy". I would like to thank you for your Christmas greetings.' Two years later he noted in his diary: 'Odd dream: somebody on the stairs behind me takes me by the elbows. E. W. Jocular reconciliation.' It was not to be.

•

Harold Wilson and the BBC

MICHAEL COCKERELL

Almost every modern British Prime Minister has come to hate the BBC. One who made his feelings quite plain on this score was Harold Wilson.

Harold Wilson's quarrels with the BBC were to flare into open conflict during the general election of March 1966. He had decided he wanted to conduct a quiet campaign. The image would be of a Prime Minister and his Government resolutely tackling the problems they had been bequeathed – with calm confidence and efficiency. In two of Labour's five election broadcasts, the Prime Minister spoke reassuringly to the camera from behind an imposing desk. 'Harold Wilson expressed to me the opinion that a political leader should try to look, particularly on television, like a family doctor,' said Sean Lemass, the Irish Prime Minister, who met Wilson immediately after the election campaign. 'The family doctor image Mr Wilson wanted to project was of the kind of man who inspires trust by his appearance as well as by his soothing words and whose advice is welcome.' But while the Prime Minister wanted a quiet campaign, Ted Heath believed his only chance lay in raising the temperature. Wilson became convinced that the BBC was aiding and abetting the Opposition leader in his efforts.

The Prime Minister's plan was to say little that was new or newsworthy at his daily press conferences, while Heath's was constantly to raise fresh issues. Wilson complained that the BBC's nightly *Campaign Report* either followed the Tories' lead or attempted itself to set the agenda for the election. When Labour's campaign was concentrating on housing or prescription charges, the BBC mounted discussions about two of the issues that Wilson specifically wanted to avoid – the Common Market and the trade unions. The Prime Minister angrily rejected a BBC invitation to be interviewed on the so-called 'noose trial'. Some car workers in Cowley had revealed that they had been 'tried' by their Union for not joining an unofficial strike; in the mock courtroom a hangman's noose had swung down from the rafters. 'No noose is good noose', was the private slogan of Wilson's campaign committee, which wanted the story buried. During the election, Wilson turned down frequent requests for interviews from *Campaign Report* – while he accepted all three from the ITN equivalent, *Election '66*. He claimed that the BBC only wanted him to discuss issues raised by Heath; in fact, three of the BBC invitations had come with no strings attached.

The root of the problem was that – as with its coverage of party conferences – the BBC was developing its political journalism in a way which did not suit the Prime Minister. While only eleven years earlier the Corporation had been too timid even to carry a single word about the general election, now it wanted to cover the campaign fully – like a newspaper. But sharp reporting and studio 'punch-ups' on topical issues clashed with the Prime Minister's desire to conduct a low-key campaign. In his diary, Richard Crossman, who was Wilson's chief campaign adviser, noted that Labour had decided on a 'deliberately boring approach' and he objected to television's treatment of the election, which he claimed 'concentrates so on personalities and leadership and gimmicks that the viewer gets a picture of bickering politicians and no real understanding of the issues involved'. The BBC now replaced the capitalist press as Wilson's whipping boy in his election speeches. Privately he complained about two other matters. One was that the BBC often referred to him in its election reports as the 'Leader of the Labour Party' rather than the Prime Minister. The BBC replied that it was following precisely the same procedure as in the previous election with Sir Alec Douglas-Home.

Wilson's other major complaint was over the BBC's handling of a possible televised confrontation between himself and Heath. The Prime Minister had publicly come out in favour of a confrontation, though privately he was totally opposed to the idea. 'We felt that a confrontation would have given Heath an advantage,' says Lady Falkender, 'he was trying to make his leadership stick, while Harold was by then a very well-known figure and by definition lots of people would have tuned into him. It would have given Heath a lot of exposure in a setting that he wanted and needed – exposure as a potential Prime Minister. Harold's office would have rubbed off on Heath. He decided that Heath was not going to appear on equal terms with him.' Wilson's complaint was that the BBC had gone on pushing proposals for a confrontation, against his will, whereas in 1964 it had immediately accepted Sir Alec's refusal. The problem was that tactically Wilson wanted neither to appear with Heath, nor for it to look publicly as if he was refusing to do so. As Nigel Lawson remarked sardonically in the *Spectator*: 'Wilson had already declared himself – on BBC television no less – in favour of a confrontation with Heath. The BBC naturally took this up. Wilson is in effect accusing the BBC of taking him at his own word. This is admittedly somewhat eccentric, but hardly evidence of Tory bias.'

Throughout the campaign Wilson's resentment at the BBC mounted and he determined to take retributive action once the polls had closed. To journalists following his campaign, it had all the makings of a Sicilian vendetta. The irony was that despite the BBC's attempts at independent coverage, Wilson had largely succeeded in running the low-key campaign he planned. 'The Tories can't find a way to break through the complacent acceptance by the electorate of Super Harold,' Richard Crossman noted. Ted Heath was having the greatest difficulty in projecting himself to the electorate. In speeches and on television he had come up with the slogan '9–5–1' to prove how disastrous the Labour Government's record was. Wages were rising by 9 per cent a year, prices by 5 and production by only 1 per cent, he claimed. It may have been bad for the economy, but it was an ideal formula for winning an election. Heath's best joke of the campaign also backfired. A fortnight before polling day, he made a speech deriding the way the Prime Minister latched on to successful show business personalities. Referring to the news that London Zoo had just sent a panda over to mate in Moscow, Heath said: 'No doubt in a month's time we shall see Mr Wilson having tea at Number 10 with a pregnant panda.' It seemed the Leader of the Opposition was publicly conceding that he did not expect to find himself in Downing Street after the election. As the campaign reached its end, Heath looked an increasingly forlorn figure on television, while Wilson appeared ever more confident.

The TV highlight of the campaign for the Prime Minister was his meeting at the Bull Ring in Birmingham. In the previous election eighteen months earlier, Sir Alec Douglas-Home had so suffered from the hecklers there that he felt the election slipping away from him. This time local Tories planned to avenge their fallen leader. Wilson had timed his speech so that it would coincide with ITN's main bulletin of the night, then at nine o'clock. Geoffrey Cox, the Editor of ITN, decided to take a live extract into the bulletin. Wilson had arranged that he would be given a cue when ITN was on the air by his new press secretary, Gerald Kaufman. 'Harold felt that this appearance on the news was very important because we knew that Labour voters watch ITV and he needed to know exactly when ITN was piping him in live. He had prepared a passage – he knew precisely how many words he spoke to the minute – 140 – and he needed a signal when he was going on the air.'

Geoffrey Cox was in ITN's London control room watching Wilson's speech coming down the line from Birmingham for the twenty minutes before the news bulletin began. The audience was packed with Conservative barrackers – many of them students. 'Wilson began slowly, lingering over the sentences of his written speech and this leisurely approach stimulated the hecklers,' says Cox. 'For the next twenty minutes we in the control room were treated to a virtuoso performance by a remarkable television performer, as Harold Wilson varied his replies from scorn to wisecracks, from derision to apparent indignation, seeming deliberately to tease the audience. He was certainly in no hurry to get on to the main parts of his speech. The reason was not hard to guess. He was playing the audience along, warming them up as the compère of an entertainment show warms up his audience until he was ready to come in.'

Gerald Kaufman remembers that he stood waiting in the hall, just below the Prime Minister's lectern. 'Harold obviously couldn't get the signal direct that he was on the air, as he was speaking in this enormous barn-like auditorium. What happened was that ITN gave the signal to another member of Harold's staff, who then passed it down the hall to me. I was in Harold's eyeline and I gave it to him. He immediately stopped what he was saying and turned to his prepared passage.' According to Geoffrey Cox there was a dramatic transformation: 'Harold Wilson dropped the attitude of the jesting debater. And, almost as if he had changed his very garb, became in a flash the serious statesman. Gravity now marked his features as he set out the core of his argument swiftly and vigorously. The crowd which had by then passed from heckling to uproar, were taken by surprise and for a moment silenced. But within a minute or so they were back on the attack. At home the audience saw the Prime Minister seeking to expound his policy to the country, being shouted and yelled at, but battling on in the face of uproar – steadily putting his message across and pausing only to deliver an occasional riposte. It provided some of the most remarkable television seen in a news programme. I let it run for four and half minutes.'

The BBC did not carry live coverage of the Birmingham meeting or of any other speech in the 1966 campaign. It felt Harold Wilson had been so skilled at exploiting his live coverage in 1964 that he effectively took over editorial control of the news bulletin. The Corporation wanted itself – and not the Prime Minister – to decide what to transmit from his speeches. Harold Wilson saw this reversal of policy as a further instance of how he received better treatment at the hands of ITV than he did from the BBC. He also found that Sir Hugh Greene was less amenable to changing TV schedules on polling day than he had been eighteen months earlier. The Prime Minister pressed him to postpone showing its popular spy series, *The Man from UNCLE*, until the polls had closed: but Auntie said *UNCLE* must stay. For Wilson this was yet another slight in what he saw as a consistent campaign against him. When he arrived at Lime Grove to make his final election broadcast he was in a state of fury with the Corporation.

To the viewers he projected his family doctor image. His appeal for stability and patriotism made an ironic contrast to Ted Heath's final broadcast the previous night calling for radical change. In the Lime Grove hospitality room after the broadcast, Wilson vehemently attacked Paul Fox – the Head of Current Affairs, who had taken over from Grace Wyndham Goldie on her retirement – and other senior BBC officials. The Prime Minister claimed he had been fighting the election against two enemies – the Conservatives and the BBC. He wanted the

Corporation to pay dearly and publicly: he had devised an exemplary punishment. It would take the form of robbing the BBC of the expensive scoop it had planned for the day after the election. On that morning, Wilson was due to travel back to London by train from Liverpool. The BBC had equipped a whole carriage with electronic gear and proposed to transmit the first ever live interview from a train. Wilson would by then be either the victorious Prime Minister or the shock loser of the election. The BBC equipment could only transmit on a certain stretch of line in Buckinghamshire, where a receiving dish had been set up on a hill overlooking the track: the interview was planned to take place as the train came out of the tunnel near Bletchley. But Wilson now declared that he would refuse to do the interview.

He stormed out of Lime Grove and set off for his Merseyside constituency. The next day Paul Fox sent Wilson's favourite producer, Stanley Hyland, to try to change the Prime Minister's mind. Although Hyland had a friendly dinner with Wilson in the Adelphi Hotel in Liverpool on election night, he failed. 'It's nothing personal against you, Stanley,' said Wilson, 'but I'm going to teach your masters a lesson they won't forget in a hurry.' The next morning, Labour had won by a landslide. Hyland and his reporter, John Morgan, joined the train hoping that in the euphoria of victory the Prime Minister would relent. He did not. They found themselves locked out of Wilson's carriage, with men guarding the door. Hyland and Morgan sat disconsolately together in their specially equipped electronic studio, alternately stamping their feet with rage and sucking their teeth in depression. As the equipment trundled unused to London, the Prime Minister twisted the knife in the BBC's wounds. He agreed to give an exclusive interview to John Whale, the ITN reporter on the train. Whale did not have the advantage of an electronic studio, but arranged to put his recording off the train at Crewe and half an hour later it was on the air. Whale ended the interview pointedly: 'So from what I believe is the first electronically recorded interview in a train, back to the studio in London.'

It was a very public snub for the BBC, which had heavily trailed its railway scoop in advance. Wilson subsequently claimed he had refused the interview because the BBC had taken him for granted: that he had only learned of the proposed interview from reading about it in the press two days before the election. 'They announced they were going to the interview before they invited me to do it,' says Wilson. In fact his office had accepted the BBC's invitation three weeks earlier, on the dissolution of Parliament. Morgan was reduced to interviewing three other political journalists in his expensively equipped carriage. The BBC managed to salvage something from the mess when Wilson arrived at Euston. Waiting to meet him at the station was Desmond Wilcox, who had just joined the BBC after five years with ITV's main current affairs programme, *This Week*. Paul Fox, in overall charge of the BBC's election coverage, correctly calculated that the Prime Minister would not realize that Wilcox had changed sides. Fox instructed Wilcox to take off his BBC identity badge and stand as far from the BBC cameras as he could. Wilcox succeeded in buttonholing the Prime Minister for a five-minute interview on the platform. It had been an ingenious comeback, but did not further endear the BBC to Harold Wilson.

He was back at Number 10 in seemingly unchallenged control. But like Margaret Thatcher nearly twenty years later, Wilson was to learn that a large majority spelt trouble. As his Government stumbled from one crisis to another, the Prime Minister was to become convinced that the BBC was part of a conspiracy to remove him from Number 10.

•

The fighting Windsors: Mrs Simpson and the Queen Mother

MICHAEL THORNTON

Perhaps the most celebrated feud of the century was that which existed between the Queen Mother and the Duchess of Windsor. Michael Thornton explores the history of this royal antipathy.

Wednesday, June 7, 1967, was Derby Day in Britain, and for once, in spite of the vagaries of the English summer, it had dawned with perfect racing weather. Under almost cloudless blue skies, Epsom Downs lay bathed in brilliant sunshine. It flooded the grandstand and the parade ring, highlighted Tattenham Corner, and dappled the course along which the Queen and her family would drive that afternoon in the traditional royal motorcade to the winning post.

In terms of atmosphere, the Derby is hard to upstage, but this year some of its thunder had been unexpectedly stolen. Three hours before the great classic of the turf was due to start, fifteen miles away in the centre of London, another royal occasion was taking place which had captured the public imagination with its dramatic possibilities.

In the shade of the tall spreading plane trees in the Mall, a crowd of more than five thousand, only one hundred of them officially invited, had assembled to watch Queen Elizabeth II unveil a plaque on the wall of Marlborough House to mark the centenary of the birth of her grandmother.

Queen Mary, that magnificent matriarch of the British monarchy, dimly remembered in the public mind for her inimitable toques and superbly upright deportment, had been dead for fourteen years, and it is doubtful that the occasion would have generated such intense interest but for one factor.

Her errant eldest son, the Duke of Windsor, who had abdicated as King Edward VIII in 1936, was attending the unveiling, his first official public appearance in Britain with other members of the Royal Family since his mother's funeral. And – of still greater interest to the jostling onlookers – his twice-divorced American wife, the former Mrs Wallis Simpson, for the first time in their thirty years of marriage, had been formally invited by Buckingham Palace to accompany him.

To many this development seemed the final irony in the long saga of the Windsors. In life, Queen Mary had regarded her eldest son's wife with undisguised horror. A reserved woman, never given to overstatement, she had once written the name of Mrs Simpson in her diary and followed it with a salvo of five exclamation marks. She had consistently refused to receive her, and, when asked by her son to explain the reason, she had replied uncompromisingly, 'because she is an adventuress'. Now, in death, the old queen had become the catalyst for an Establishment olive branch to the daughter-in-law she herself had never known.

It had been widely stated that the unveiling would mark the first official recognition of the Duchess of Windsor by the British sovereign. But Elizabeth II had already met her American aunt-in-law privately two years earlier when she had made a much-publicized visit to the London Clinic following the Duke of Windsor's eye operation.

To royalty watchers, courtiers, and friends of the Royal Family, the real piquancy of this occasion lay not in the reaction of the Queen – a mere child of ten at the time of the Abdication – but in the attitude of her influential and immensely popular mother. The point had been accurately caught the day before by one of the London gossip columns: 'The poignancy of the Duchess's meeting with the members of her husband's family will be heightened by her encounter, for the first time since 1936, with her sister-in-law, the Queen Mother.'

Even Queen Mary, although she had never consented to receive the Duchess of Windsor, had relented sufficiently six years after the Abdication to write, in a letter to her eldest son, 'I send a kind message to your wife.' And in 1951, when Wallis was taken ill in New York, the old lady had actually gone so far as to inquire solicitously after her health.

But the attitude of Queen Elizabeth the Queen Mother towards her American sister-in-law had remained consistent for a third of a century. It was one of icy and unwavering hostility. Enmity had flared between the two women at their earliest encounter in 1934, two years before the Abdication. The Duchess of York, as she then was, took an instant dislike to the sleek, chic, epigrammatic Mrs Simpson. And Wallis, quickly aware of the coolness of this influential member of the Royal Family, unwisely took to mimicking Elizabeth's mannerisms and to deriding her ultra-feminine, sometimes *baroque* style in fashion. 'The Dowdy Duchess' was how Wallis liked to describe her.

During the 326-day reign of King Edward VIII, the Duchess of York, as wife of the heir to the throne, had found herself obliged to meet her brother-in-law's favourite on several occasions. Unexpectedly forced into the position of having to receive Wallis Simpson in her own home, Elizabeth succeeded, without overt discourtesy, in conveying 'a distinct impression' to the intruder that she was 'not sold' on the King's American friend.

Later, at one of Edward VIII's dinner parties in London, the Yorks were again confronted by Mrs Simpson, minus Mr Simpson, and Elizabeth was noticeably remote, royally squashing Winston Churchill's mischievous attempt to raise the matter of George IV's clandestine marriage with Mrs Fitzherbert.

But it was at Balmoral two months later that the Duchess of York openly showed her antipathy towards 'the lady with two husbands living'. Invited to the castle to dine with the King, Elizabeth was visibly angered when Wallis Simpson, casting herself in the role of official hostess, walked forward to receive her. The public snub that was delivered by Elizabeth to Wallis on that September evening in 1936 reverberated throughout international society. It also marked the last meeting between the two women for more than thirty years.

In less than three months, the Duchess of York was to become the new Queen–Empress, and shortly after that Wallis Simpson would become her sister-in-law, but the relationship signified nothing to Elizabeth.

One week before the Windsor wedding, George VI had exercised his prerogative as the fountain of honour and deprived Wallis of royal status. The ex-King was to be His Royal Highness for his lifetime. Wallis was to be merely Her Grace the Duchess of Windsor. As such, she was not entitled to be addressed as 'Ma'am', like the other ladies of the Royal Family. Officially speaking, women would not curtsey to her, and men would not bow, although in the event many did. For the sister-in-law of a reigning sovereign, it was an unparalleled public insult, and for the rest of their lives both the Windsors believed that Queen Elizabeth's personal influence had been responsible for the King's action.

Time did nothing to heal the intense mutual antagonism. Two years after the Abdication, one of the new Queen's ladies-in-waiting was shaken by the uncharacteristic sharpness and implacable anger with which Elizabeth announced that, even if the Duchess of Windsor were to return to Britain, she would not receive her.

The acrimony between the two women haunted the corridors of power. British prime ministers, American presidents, cabinet ministers, ambassadors and even foreign dictators found themselves caught up in it.

'A feud' was how the Duchess of Windsor herself described it, and the motive she attributed to Elizabeth's opposition was jealousy – 'a woman's jealousy'. Some took this to mean jealousy of the Duke of Windsor, whose looks, charm and personality might eclipse the hesitant, stammering figure of Elizabeth's husband, the new King. But later the Windsors would confide to friends that they believed Queen Elizabeth's hostility to be of a more personal kind; that it was not so much jealousy of the Duke, as of the Duchess, for having married him.

The ending of a World War in no way curtailed the smaller

war between the sisters-in-law. And when, in 1952, George VI died suddenly at the early age of fifty-six, his health broken by the burden of kingship his brother had bequeathed him, the widowed Queen's bitterness intensified. Thereafter, on the few occasions when anyone had the temerity to mention the Duchess of Windsor in her presence, Elizabeth would refer to her sister-in-law as 'the woman who killed my husband'.

The early widowhood of her antagonist did nothing to soften Wallis's fierce resentment of the long years of ostracism. Queen Mary's official biographer, visiting the Windsors in France as late as January 1958, considered that the Duchess's 'facial contortion', when speaking of the Queen Mother, seemed 'akin to frenzy'.

And now, eight years later, in the warm June sunshine filtering through the spreading plane trees in the Mall, the stage was set at last for an historic reunion between two charismatic and remarkable women who had detested each other for more than three decades. The band of the Coldstream Guards was playing 'The Skye Boat Song', which struck some onlookers as a strangely appropriate prelude to the return of the man whom a handful of diehard romantics had continued to toast, after his abdication, as 'the King over the Water'.

As on all their joint visits to Britain in the previous thirty years, the Windsors were not accommodated at any of the royal residences and were staying, as usual, at Claridge's. But on this occasion, for the first and last time during their marriage, they drove together in a royal limousine as part of the official procession travelling the short distance, a mere one hundred yards, from St James's Palace to Marlborough House.

The moment their car came into view, they were clapped and cheered by the waiting crowds, and one woman shouted 'Edward' – 'as if she had waited thirty years to do so'. The Windsors took their places at the end of the front line of guests, and closest to the plaque soon to be unveiled. They were followed by the Duke's younger brother, Prince Henry, Duke of Gloucester – now using a walking stick after suffering a slight stroke – and his quiet, self-effacing Duchess, Alice.

Wallis Windsor, dressed in a deep blue shantung coat, with a knee-length hemline noticeably higher than any other woman present, a tiny matching blue straw pillbox hat crowning her elaborately upswept dark hair, and a white mink muffler elegantly draped over each shoulder, at once presented an image startlingly different from the other royal ladies – 'like the denizen of another planet', as one observer described it. Beside her, the Duke of Windsor, in morning dress, fiddled with his tie, looking strained and somewhat nervous.

There was a momentary pause and an atmosphere of intense anticipation before the cheers rang out again as a maroon Rolls Royce drove slowly into view, its occupant instantly recognized and gesturing in inimitable style to the applauding onlookers. The door was held open, and with a vivid flash of colour, out stepped Queen Elizabeth the Queen Mother, dressed in a pale lilac coat, the familiar three strands of pearls, and one of her characteristically ornate hats in a deeper lilac. She was accompanied by her Woman of the Bedchamber, the Hon. Mrs John Mulholland, and by the Comptroller of her Household, Lord Adam Gordon.

Only six months earlier, ironically on the thirtieth anniversary of the Abdication that made her Queen, Elizabeth had undergone a major abdominal operation that was regarded as serious – cancer had been widely rumoured at the time. She had then had a lengthy period of convalescence away from public view, and the unveiling was her first official public appearance since her illness.

In the previous year, Leonard M. Harris had produced a public opinion survey on the leading members of the British Royal Family. From questions to the public about the Queen Mother, Mr Harris had completed 'a picture whose only negative touches are a suggestion of artificiality ("too much smiling") and a hint of dominance ("she tells them where they get off", "I've heard she's a tartar in her own household") . . . In the main,' he concluded, 'the aura is positive and favourable, with only occasional hints that public and private face may not be identical.'

But if Elizabeth on this occasion privately felt any sense of ordeal or distaste over her obligatory encounter with her brother-in-law and his wife, she gave no public indication of it. Smiling and composed as always, and moving gracefully on peeptoe high-heeled shoes, she walked slowly but confidently towards where the Windsors stood.

She greeted the Duke first. Windsor, in exile, had had harsh words to say about the sister-in-law who had so long ignored and ostracized his wife. But as the Queen Mother stretched out a pale-gloved hand towards him, a certain innate chivalry came to the fore, and he bowed his head with courtly grace to kiss her hand. As if in response to this courtesy, Elizabeth averted her head slightly in order that the Duke might also kiss her cheek, a feat which he accomplished with a certain difficulty on account of her veil.

The Queen Mother then turned towards the Duchess of Windsor, who had meantime been watching her with a pleasant, smiling but neutral expression on her face.

'How nice to see you again,' Elizabeth could be heard saying, in the clear, bell-like tones so characteristic of members of her family, the Bowes-Lyons. Again she stretched out her hand, and the Duchess took it. There would be no kisses between these two. The handshake seemed to be maintained for several seconds while the cameras recorded what was clearly an historic moment.

A crowned and anointed queen, and the last Empress of India, the Queen Mother is entitled to a bow or a curtsey from every member of the Royal Family with the exception of the reigning Queen and her husband. Even Prince Philip invariably bows his head to kiss his mother-in-law's hand. But the Duchess of Windsor did not curtsey to her sister-in-law.

Elizabeth gave no sign of having noticed the omission. Appearing to be entirely at ease, she continued to talk to the Duchess for several minutes, moving her head in an animated way from one side to another, recalling the acid sentence which Wallis Windsor had used in her memoirs about a meeting with the Duchess of York in 1936. 'Her justly famous charm was highly evident.'

None of the Queen Mother's subsequent remarks was overheard, but the Duchess was seen to answer what her sister-in-law was saying, although newsreel coverage of the occasion shows her replies to have been somewhat monosyllabic.

Wallis's failure to curtsey to the Queen Mother was re-emphasized a few moments later when the Queen and Prince Philip arrived on the scene. As the reigning monarch walked past her uncle and aunt-in-law, giving them both a somewhat perfunctory nod, the Duchess of Windsor was seen to bob a brief but unmistakable curtsey.

The Duke bowed his head deeply as his niece, the Queen, passed him. In that moment, the Queen Mother looked across the Gloucesters to the Windsors and Wallis returned her glance. It was as if there was awareness between the two adversaries that Wallis had been prepared to curtsey to the daughter but not to the mother.

There followed a short and solemn service, conducted by Dr Robert Stopford, Bishop of London, in thanksgiving for 'the life and example of Thy servant Queen Mary'. Then the Queen walked over and parted the blue curtains covering the plaque – a head of Queen Mary in bronze.

Once the service was over, the Queen and her mother moved around chatting with guests. The Queen Mother went up to the Windsors and was seen to say something which caused them both to smile broadly. For a brief moment, the tension of the occasion was broken.

Then, ahead of her daughter, the Queen Mother said goodbye to the Windsors. The Duke once more went through the process of kissing her hand and cheek. The Duchess shook hands but once again did not curtsey. A moment later, the Queen reached the Duchess and this time Wallis did curtsey.

The Queen, Prince Philip, the Queen Mother and the Duchess of Gloucester departed to Epsom for the Derby. The Windsors had not been invited to join them there in the Royal Box.

Instead they drove off to Kensington Palace for a small private luncheon given for them by the Duke's widowed sister-in-law, Princess Marina, Duchess of Kent. The entire ceremony had lasted a mere quarter of an hour – 'fifteen emotionally charged minutes', as one observer described it the following day.

In that brief space of time, what had once seemed unthinkable in royal circles had finally come to pass. Wallis Warfield Spencer Simpson Windsor had at last taken her place publicly among her husband's family. And for the first time in more than thirty years she had come face to face with the sister-in-law whose animosity had frozen her out of British life and society.

The bitterness between the two women had lasted too long, and gone too deep, to be ended by the mere shaking of hands and a display of superficial politeness. Their feud – certainly the longest and the strangest in the history of Britain's royal house – was to smoulder on for another nine years until time and circumstances dictated an honourable truce.

•

Cold blood: Truman Capote and Kenneth Tynan

GEORGE PLIMPTON

Plimpton describes how an incident involving Kenneth Tynan and Truman Capote on the island of Cuba led to Capote's lifetime hatred of the *Observer*'s drama critic.

One afternoon Tennessee Williams opened the door and stood there blinking with the sunlight blazing around him like St Elmo's fire. He was wearing white flannels, a blue blazer, and a yachting cap, a machismo outfit he had apparently decided would be appropriate for his first meeting with Ernest Hemingway. He groped toward us uncertainly. There were three of us waiting – myself, Ken Tynan, and Hemingway. I had asked Hemingway at the *finca* the day before if he would enjoy meeting the playwright. 'Sure,' he had said. He had seen one of Tennessee's plays – I think it was *Cat on a Hot Tin Roof* – which he admired.

We had waited in the Floridita for Tennessee for almost an hour. I have always imagined that he was back in his hotel room desperately trying on various combinations he thought would be appropriate for meeting Hemingway – cowboy, guerrilla, retired military, rude fisherfolk, or whatever – and having a drink or two to fortify himself. I don't think the meeting went very well for him. Tennessee began by saying that when he lived in Key West he had known Hemingway's former wife Pauline.

'How did she die?' Tennessee suddenly asked.

Hemingway peered at him in the gloom. After a while he offered an explanation that seemed lifted from a freshman Hemingway parody: 'She died and then she was dead.'

A silence ensued. Quite an awkward one, and it served to remind Tennessee – (and he went on to describe it) of the first time he had met William Faulkner. This had occurred in a small restaurant in Rome where Faulkner had sat, overcome with shyness, staring down at a red-checked tablecloth; finally he raised his eyes and looked at Tennessee, who was so affected by the sadness he discovered there, some sense of the martyred, that he burst into tears.

Hemingway leaned forward again. 'Good effort,' he said.

I think Hemingway was slightly puzzled by the encounter. Afterward the two of us drove out to the *finca* in a big canary-yellow convertible with the top down, Hemingway sitting beside the driver with a drink held between his knees. He was thinking about Tennessee. 'Not a predictable sort of man,' he said. 'Is he the commodore of something . . . that yachting cap?'

I said I didn't know. I doubted it.

'Goddamn good playwright,' Hemingway said.

The Floridita was the scene of the exercise in commitment that I came to admire so in Tynan. It began in the annex to the bar — a pleasant patio-like dining area off the back; it blazed with light out there like a summer meadow compared to the dark corridor of the bar. A group of us were sitting around a table eating club sandwiches: Tynan and his wife, Elaine; Tennessee and a United Fruit Company heiress he was traveling with who was referred to as the Banana Queen. Hemingway had thought about joining us, but he had decided to spend his day out at the *finca*.

An American joined our circle. He announced himself as Captain Marks, a soldier of fortune who had been fighting in the hills with Castro and who had marched in the triumphant entry into the city. He looked like a tourist. He wore a linen shirt, but he had on a wide military belt, and after a while he said that Castro had given him an interesting job over in the Morro Castle, on the other side of the harbor — he was in charge of the execution squads. He was being kept very busy, especially in the evenings, and sometimes his squads didn't get through with their work until one or two in the morning. We all stared at him. In fact, Captain Marks went on, that very evening there was going to be quite a lot of activity over in the fortress and he'd be just delighted if we would consider joining him as his guests at what he referred to as 'the festivities'. He made the invitation as easily as he might have offered a round of cocktails at his home. He counted us: 'Let's see . . . five of you . . . quite easy . . . we'll drive over by car . . . tight squeeze . . . I'll pick you up at eight . . .'

At this point there was a sudden eruption from Tynan. He had been sitting, rocking back and forth, in his chair; he came out of it almost as if propelled. He began to shout at Captain Marks. Tynan stutters slightly, and on words which are difficult for him his lips pucker, and his eyes squint shut in his effort to make what he wishes to say emerge.

At first, I don't think Captain Marks was aware that these curious honked explosions of indignation from this gaunt arm-flapping man in a seersucker suit were directed at him, but then Tynan got his voice under control, and Captain Marks could see his opened eyes now, pale and furious, staring at him, and the words became discernible – shouts that it was sickening to stay in the same room with such a frightful specimen as an executioner of men ('l-l-l-loathsome!'), and as for the invitation, yes, he was going to turn up all right, but in order to throw himself in front of the guns of the firing squad! He was going to stop the 'festivities' – the word sprayed from him in rage – and with this he pulled his wife up out of her chair, and as she flailed in his wake like a miscreant child, he rushed for the exit. We heard from him once again, out beyond the heads turned to watch him go past, some indistinguishable cry of dismay.

'What the hell was that?' Captain Marks asked. He shook his head and rolled his eyes; he smiled at us; surely we would all agree that the poor man was looney in the head; wasn't it a shame?

He sighed and went on with his plans with us for the evening as if the tumult caused by Tynan had been as idle a distraction as a police siren going by on the street outside. He would meet us at the such-and-such hotel, in the lobby, at eight o'clock . . . plenty of time to drive through the tunnel to the fortress on the far side of the harbor. He would take whoever turned up.

I was ashamed that I wanted to go. I mentioned it to Hemingway that afternoon out at the *finca*. He was sitting by his swimming pool with the week's mail and journals bound up in rubber bands beside him on the flagstones. The graves of his pets, cats mostly, were there by the side of the pool – small headstones of cement. Black Dog's grave was there; Hemingway told me that when he went swimming, Black Dog would wait with his head resting on his sandals at poolside. Batista's soldiers had killed him just a few months before in the final flurries of the revolution; they came to the *finca* looking for arms when Hemingway was abroad and Black Dog had barked and wouldn't let them in until finally they dispatched him with a rifle butt. In the pool, leaves as big as plates floated on a surface as opaque as a disused cistern's. Down the hill, out of sight, a baseball game was going on; the thin cries drifted up through the thick hillside foliage. It was hot, but with a cool wind blowing. The evening seemed a long way off. I told him about the executions scheduled, and that I was not at all sure about my own attitudes. The idea appalled me – that anyone (always in the newsreels the victims seemed to be wearing freshly laundered white shirts outside their belts) should be stood up and shot. But I was curious, admittedly so, along with being outraged at myself for not having the same attitude of disgust and the commitment to stopping it as did Tynan. I described Tynan's behavior admiringly. 'Damn, you should have seen it, Papa. The face on that man Marks, just stunned, with Ken flapping at him with those long arms, just *steaming* with rage, saying he was going to throw himself in front of the guns. Just grand, with everyone turned around in his chair in the Floridita to see what was going on.'

Hemingway allowed that it was too bad; it had been a mistake to ask Tynan. Seeing such a thing might shift his perception of the revolution since his emotional makeup, while OK, just was not suited to accept such things. He'd give the revolution a bad name.

But he felt I should go. He said it was important that a writer get around to see just about anything, especially the excesses of human behavior, as long as he could keep his emotional reactions in check.

So I went that night to the hotel down by the esplanade to wait for Captain Marks. Tennessee was there with the Banana Queen. No sign of Tynan, of course. No one seemed to know what he was doing. Perhaps he was already in the fortress across the harbor entrance, crouched upon some wall, looking down on the floodlit courtyard with the stake in the sand pit and the men standing around in their stiff parade-ground military hats which turned as they occasionally looked toward the door through which the principals of the 'festivities' would come.

We had all arrived at the hotel early. The conversation was desultory. We were ashamed of one another, and of ourselves. We talked about our reasons for being there. I was armed with what Hemingway had told me. Tennessee had discovered from Captain Marks that a young German mercenary was scheduled to be shot that evening, and he felt that if he had the chance to do so, he'd get close enough to give him a small encouraging smile. He said that there was a tradition of ministers in his family and so it was quite appropriate for him to offer this little service. I wasn't sure that a 'small encouraging smile' from Tennessee was what one hoped for as one's last view on earth, but it seemed as reasonable an excuse as any.

Captain Marks arrived. We all stood up and looked at him, horrified.

'It's been called off,' he said. We hardly listened to him. 'Circumstances ... difficulties ... postponement.' He said all this perfunctorily. He did not seem especially anxious to keep in touch with us about the matter – no jotting down of hotels and room numbers. He had doubtless concluded that we were an odd lot: our own doubts so obviously seethed; we didn't seem grateful; we kept staring at him with our mouths ajar.

Frankly, I have no idea whether Tynan was actually responsible for the evening's 'festivities' being canceled. I like to think that he was; that the officials had got wind of his outraged reaction to Captain Marks in the Floridita, especially his statement that he was going to throw himself in front of the guns. No, it was best to let things cool down; to let this weird fanatic clear off the island. At least they would not have to worry that just as everything was going along smoothly, the blindfolds nicely in place, not too tight, just right, Tynan's roar of rage would peal out of the darkness ('St-st-stop this in-in-infamous be-be-behavior!') and he would flap out at them across the courtyard, puffs of dirt issuing from his footfalls as he came at them like a berserk crane.

Some time after this, Tynan got into a tremendous set-to with Truman Capote which began with a review of *In Cold Blood* in the *Observer* in which Tynan criticized the author at great length for doing less than he might have, despite his being opposed to capital punishment, to save the two murderers in the book, Perry Smith and Dick Hickock, from the Kansas hang-man.

I had always thought that Tynan had been fortified in his stance by his show of commitment in Havana. I once mentioned this to Elaine Dundy, his ex-wife, and she was quite scornful. 'Oh my goodness, no. His pique at Truman was just jealousy. He wanted to write that book *In Cold Blood* himself. What was *he* doing – *Oh Calcutta!* Oh, no, it was just jealousy.'

Whatever, with the appearance of Tynan's review, a predict-ably violent reaction erupted from Capote, who replied to the *Observer* and spoke of Tynan's allegation as coming from one 'with the morals of a baboon and the guts of a butterfly'.

The feud went on for years, and every time I thought of it, or ran into either of the principals, I thought of Tynan and the 'festivities' in Cuba. I never told Capote about it. I would not have dared; his rage was deep seated. Once, I was sitting in a restaurant having dinner with Capote and suddenly, for no apparent reason, he began describing a fantasy to me he had about Tynan. I had the feeling he had turned it delectably around in his mind for years, like rolling a never-melting candy drop against the back of his teeth.

It started with a kidnapping, an abduction on a quiet city side street, with Tynan bundled into the back of a Rolls-Royce – the appurtenances of Truman's story were all very grand – in which he was taken off to a smart clinic in the country, with a long gravel drive up past the stone gateposts, lawns stretching out on either side, where he was deposited in a very well appointed hospital room with a comfortable bed, a bell pull for the nurse, and a pleasant view over the grounds. The meals were excellent. The members of the hospital staff were polite and sympathetic to his every need, almost unctuously so, and well they might have been, because on occasion Tynan was wheeled off to surgery somewhere in the clinic and a limb or an organ would be removed.

Truman announced this chilling detail quite cheerily, as if describing a hat-check girl helping someone off with his coat.

We were sitting in an Eastside Italian restaurant which Truman went to less for the food than for its supposed Mafia connections. At that time the criminal world absorbed Capote, his only reading, according to friends, being detective pulp magazines – they lay throughout his country home in Long Island in thick heaps. He waved for a drink. He told me our waiter was a Mafia hit man. 'He's killed just barrels of people,' Capote said. He leaned comfortably back in his chair and went on about Tynan, describing how carefully the operations in the clinic were done: with every consideration for the patient; the very best teams of doctors involved; extensive post-operative procedures thought of; flowers set along the windowsill with notes of sympathy pegged to them; careful diets, and therapeutic exercises to get what was left in good shape; then, as soon as the patient was beginning to feel sprightly, why, in they would come to cart him off, the nighthawks wheeling outside in the evening, to remove something else, either a limb or an external organ, until finally, after months of surgery and recuperation, everything possible had been removed except one eye and his genitalia. 'Everything else goes!' Truman cried gaily.

'Then what happens *is*' – he leaned far back in his chair for effect – 'that the door to his hospital room opens and in is wheeled a motion-picture projector, a screen, along with an attendant in a white smock who sets everything up and shows *pornographic films*, very high grade, enticing ones, absolutely *nonstop*.'

Capote rocked back and forth, relishing his hospital-room scene. 'Can you think of anything more frustrating?' he called out. He went on to say that eventually what was left of Tynan was taken off and dumped somewhere – Times Square, I think he said – but it was an untidy and uninspired ending; he wasn't putting his mind to it; he yawned.

Graphic as Truman can be at his best – which is in a Mafia restaurant, late in the evening, with a hit man to point out and a carafe of wine at hand, along with some attentive listeners – I had always found myself less taken with his one-eyed torso (thank the Lord!) than with my own mental dramatization: Tynan in the battlements of that dark fortress in Havana, sputtering with rage as he crept toward the courtyard; then his cry pealing out of the darkness ('St-st-stop this in-in-infamous be-be-behavior!'), and the image of him dropping down to the ground and setting out for the group of men, the peaks of their military hats turned toward him, to do something about what outraged him . . .

•

A rotten apple: Lennon and McCartney
RAY COLEMAN

Following the break-up of the Beatles in 1970, animosity flared between John Lennon and Paul McCartney. The ensuing feud, described here, lasted for four years.

Relations between John and Paul began to decline swiftly after John left the group. And although it had been John who made the break, it was a public relations tactic by Paul that broke the news to the world. With his first solo album, called *McCartney*, he issued a press release with forty-one questions and answers which left the world's media in no doubt that Paul was out of the group. It contained barbed references to his non-association with the Beatles. Issued in question-and-answer form, part of the text ran:

> *Did you enjoy working as a solo?*
> Very much. I only had me to ask for a decision and I agreed with me.
> *Is this album a rest away from the Beatles or the start of a solo career?*
> Time will tell . . .
> *Is your break with the Beatles, temporary or permanent, due to personal differences or musical ones?*

Personal differences. Business differences. Musical differences. But most of all because I have a better time with my family. Temporary or permanent? I don't know.

Is it true that neither Allen Klein nor ABCKO (his company) have been or will be in any way involved in the production, manufacturing, distribution or promotion of this new album?

Not if I can help it.

Lennon was furious at what appeared a pre-emptive strike by McCartney to gain the momentum and wrest the decision-making role from him. Paul's dislike of Yoko was one thing: to upstage him by causing the world to surmise that Paul was the one taking the initiative was another. John reacted with a beautifully laconic piece of venom: by telephone he told me for an article I wrote: 'I received a phone call from Paul last Thursday afternoon. He said: "I'm going to leave the Beatles as well." I was happy to hear from Paul. It was nice to find that he was still alive.

'Anyway, Paul hasn't left. I sacked him.'

The sour relationship with Paul continued right up until John and Yoko left to settle in America in 1971. John and Yoko and their newly named Plastic Ono Band had taken flight in a surge of activity that camouflaged the McCartney situation, from the public at least. But when Paul usurped him by releasing the press statement, John was livid. The two men had little contact but newspaper conjecture carried on. McCartney again ended the world's speculation with a letter to the *Melody Maker* on 29 August 1970:

In order to put out of its misery the limping dog of a news story which has been dragging itself across your pages for the past year, my answer to the question: 'Will the Beatles get together again?' is no.

Paul McCartney

By the end of 1970 Paul McCartney began proceedings in the

High Court to wind up the Beatles partnership. Even against the background of bickering it was a difficult decision: he made it during a sojourn with Linda at his farm in Campbeltown, Argyllshire. 'It's not easy being in a top job one second and the next someone says: "Well, we're breaking the group up." And you haven't got a job. It screwed my head for years,' he says. As for the questions that persisted about a reunion: 'It's like asking a divorced couple: Are you getting back together? . . . when you can't stand to look at each other.' It was agony, 'suing my best mates and being *seen* to sue my best mates. That was the worst.' The Beatles were formally ended as a performing group in the High Court on 12 March 1971 and a receiver appointed to look after their business interests. The Beatles continued only as a business name.

On a personal level the wrangles continued and began to manifest themselves in Paul and John's music. Four months before John left for America in September 1971 Paul released a solo album made with Linda McCartney, *Ram*. Two songs in particular, 'Too Many People (Going Underground)' and 'Back Seat Of My Car' (ending with the chant, 'We believe we can't be wrong') were unsubtle jibes at John and Yoko. Quite why Paul, well known for his anodyne tendencies, chose to pick a fight on record, and in public, with such a master of invective as John, will always be a mystery. Lennon's reply was the vitriolic 'How Do You Sleep?', on his classic *Imagine* album. Unlike Paul's songs, John's tactics were not cloak-and-dagger but a full frontal assault:

> So Sgt Pepper took you by surprise
> You better see right through that mother's eyes
> Those freaks was right when they said you was dead
> The one mistake you made was in your head . . .
> You live with straights who tell you you was king
> Jump when your mama tell you anything
> The only thing you done was Yesterday
> And since you've gone you're just Another Day

How do you sleep? . . .
A pretty face may last a year or two
But pretty soon they'll see what you can do
The sound you make is Muzak to my ears
You must have learned something in all those years

The rancour over Yoko, over Klein and Eastman and how best to end the Beatles had now turned bitterly personal. At the root of it lay the fundamental truth which millions of Beatles fans still find unpalatable: John and Paul never had much in common. They had different aspirations: Paul, with his gift for melody and musicianship, and love of popularity, headed securely for the world of entertainment where he will always be a giant figure. John was on a perpetual adventure, picking up and adopting, then quickly rejecting ideas and causes, writing poetry, and writing from within himself. He was an artist with a distinct anti-Establishment backbone. McCartney greatly admired John's mercurial, often whimsical, style, his originality, his arrogance, his wit. To a lesser extent Lennon acknowledged Paul's strengths as a songwriter. But John had little time for craftsmen, dismissing them as 'people who could write little ditties to order'. He sweated over his own work. His post-Beatles writing was inspired by personal relationships, observations and events. John could recognize Paul's commercial power but it was all too often vapid, mawkish, and sentimental in contrast with his hard edge. They were right for each other at a certain period of their lives. But put simply, where McCartney had great talent, Lennon was a genius. By 1971 they had irrevocably parted company, both personally and artistically, and John's feelings were further inflamed by Paul's digs at Yoko, whom John regarded as part of him.

The fight continued in public. Paul gave an interview to *Melody Maker* in November 1971, emphasizing that although the music had ended, business problems still faced them: 'I just want the four of us to get together somewhere and sign a piece of paper saying it's all over and we want to divide the money four ways.

'No one else would be there, not even Linda or Yoko or Allen Klein. We'd just sign the paper and hand it to the business people and let them sort it all out. That's all I want now. But John won't do it. Everybody thinks I am the aggressor. But I'm not, you know. I just want out.

'John and Yoko are not cool in what they are doing. I saw them on television the other night and thought that what they are saying about what they wanted to do together was basically the same as what Linda and I want to do.

'John's whole image now is very honest and open. He's all right, is John. I like his *Imagine* album but I didn't like the others. *Imagine* is what John is really like but there was too much political stuff on the other albums. You know, I only really listen to them to see if there is something I can pinch.' (He laughed.)

What did Paul think of 'How Do You Sleep?'? 'I think it's silly, so what if I live with straights? I like straights. I have straight babies. It doesn't affect *him*. He says the only thing I did was "Yesterday". He knows that's wrong. He knows and I know it's not true.'

Referring to the Beatles' album, *Let It Be*, Paul said: 'There was a little bit of hype on the back of the sleeve for the first time ever on a Beatles album. At the time the Beatles were very strained with each other and it wasn't a happy time. It said it was a new-phase Beatles album and there was nothing further from the truth. That was the last Beatles album and everybody knew it . . . Klein had it re-produced because he said it didn't sound commercial enough.'

Talking of John's Toronto concert with Eric Clapton, Yoko, and Klaus Voormann, Paul said: 'John wanted to do a big thing in Toronto but I didn't dig that at all. I hear that before he went on stage he was sick and that's just what I didn't want. Like anybody else I have been nervous because of the Beatles thing.

'I wanted to get in a van and do an unadvertised concert at a Saturday night hop at Slough Town Hall or somewhere like that. We'd call ourselves Rikki and the Red Streaks or something and just get up and play. There'd be no Press and we'd tell nobody about it. John thought it was a daft idea.

'Before John said he was leaving the Beatles I was lying in bed at home one night and I thought I would like to get a band together like his Plastic Ono Band. I felt the urge because we had never played live for four years. We all wanted to appear on a stage but not with the Beatles. We couldn't do it as the Beatles because it would be so big. We'd have to find a million-seater hall or something.' And in a remark which made John smile, Paul said what he thought of New York: 'I went for a walk in Central Park and there was a layer of dirt on the grass everywhere.' The grass on his farm in Scotland, where he had 100 sheep on sixty acres of land, was so much better than American grass.

John's letter of reply which was published in the *Melody Maker* two weeks later, was accompanied by a request that it be published in full to give 'equal time' to his side of the story. Part of the letter referred to McCartney's claim that if he (Paul) had appeared at George Harrison's summer 1971 Bangladesh concert in New York, Allen Klein would have taken the credit for pulling the Beatles back together again. John's classic letter, positively dripping with invective, ran as follows:

Dear Paul, Linda *et all* the wee McCartneys,
    Thanks for your letter.
    1. We give *you money* for your bits of Apple.
    2. We give *you more money* in the form of royalties which legally belong to Apple (I know we're Apple, but on the other hand we're *not*).
    Maybe there's an answer there somewhere . . . but for the millionth time in these past few years I repeat, *What about the TAX*? It's all very well, playing 'simple, honest ole Paul' in the *Melody Maker* but you know damn well we can't just sign a bit of paper.
    You say, 'John won't do it.' I will if you'll *indemnify* us

against the tax man! Anyway, you know that after we have *our* meeting, the fucking lawyers will have to implement whatever we agree on – right?

If they have some form of agreement between *them* before *we* met, it might make it even easier. It's up to you; as we've said many times, we'll meet you whenever you like. Just make up your mind! E.g. two weeks ago I asked you on the phone, 'Please let's meet without advisers, etc. and decide what we want', and I emphasized especially Maclen [John and Paul's songwriting partnership company within Northern Songs] which is mainly our concern, but you refused – right?

You said under *no condition* would you sell to us and if we didn't do what you wanted, you'd sue us again and that Ringo and George are going to break you John, etc. etc.

Now I was quite straight with you that day, and you tried to shoot me down with your emotional 'logic'. If *you're not* the aggressor (as you claim) who the hell took us to court and shat all over us in public?

As I've said before – have you ever thought that you might *possibly* be wrong about something? Your conceit about us and Klein is incredible – you say you 'made the mistake of trying to advise them against him [Klein] and that pissed them off' and we secretly feel that you're right! Good God! You must *know we're right about Eastman* . . .

One other little lie in your 'It's only Paulie' *MM* bit: *Let It Be* was not the 'first bit of hype' on a Beatle album. Remember Tony Barrow? And his wonderful writing on 'Please Please Me' etc. etc. the early Beatle Xmas records!

And you gotta admit it was a 'new-phase Beatle album', incidentally written in the style of the great Barrow himself! By the way what happened to my idea of putting the parody of our first album cover on the *Let It Be* cover?

Also, we were intending to parody Barrow originally, so it was hype. But what was your *Life* article? Tony Barrow couldn't have done it better. (And your writing inside of the *Wings* album isn't exactly the realist is it?) Anyway, enough of this petty bourgeois fun.

You were right about New York! I do love it; it's the ONLY PLACE TO BE. (Apart from anything else, they leave you alone too!) I see you prefer Scotland . . . I'll bet you YOUR piece of Apple you'll be living in New York by 1974 (two years is the usual time it takes you – right?).

Another thing, whadya mean *big thing* in Toronto? It was completely spontaneous, they rang on the *Friday* – we flew there and we played on the *Saturday*. I was sick because I was stone pissed. Listen to the album, with no rehearsal too. Come on Macka! Own up! (We'd never played together before!) Half a dozen live shows – with no big fuss – in fact we've been *doing* what you've said the Beatles should do, Yoko and I have been doing it for three years! (I said it was daft for the Beatles to do it. I still think it's daft.) So go on and do it! Do it! Do it! E.g. *Cambridge*, 1969, completely unadvertised! (A *very* small hall.) *Lyceum* Ballroom, (1969, no fuss, great show – thirty-piece rock band! 'Live Jam' out soon!) *Fillmore East* (1971 unannounced. Another good time had by all – out soon!!) We even played in the streets here in the Village (our spiritual home!?) with the great David Peel!! We were moved on by the cops even!! It's best just to DO IT.

I know you'll dig it, and they don't even expect the Beatles now anyway!

So *you* think *Imagine* ain't political, it's 'Working Class Hero' with sugar on it for conservatives like yourself!! You obviously didn't *dig the words*. Imagine! You took 'How Do You Sleep?' so literally (read my own review of the album in *Crawdaddy*). *Your* politics are very similar to Mary Whitehouse's – saying *nothing* is as loud as saying *something*.

Listen, my obsessive old pal, it was George's press conference not dat old debbil Klein! *He* said what *you* said – 'I'd love to come but . . .' Anyway, we did it for basically the same reasons – the Beatles bit. They still called it a Beatle show – with just two of them! [Ringo played drums in the superstar band George Harrison formed for the spectacular Bangladesh concert in New York.]

Join the Rock Liberation Front before it gets *you*.

Wanna put your photo on the label like uncool John and Yoko do ya? (Ain't ya got no shame!) If we're *not* cool, WHAT DOES THAT MAKE YOU?

No hard feelings to you either. I know basically we want the same, and as I said on the phone and in this letter, whenever you want to meet, all you have to do is call.

All you need is love
Power to the people
Free all prisoners
Jail the judges
Love and peace
Get it on and rip 'em off

John Lennon

PS The bit that really puzzled us was asking to meet WITHOUT LINDA AND YOKO. I thought you'd have understood BY NOW that I'm JOHNANDYOKO.
PPS Even *your own* lawyers know you can't 'just sign a bit of paper' (or don't they tell you?).

The wounds were deep and lasting. Relations between John and Paul never fully recovered from the encounter. When John wrote that letter, two months after arriving in New York, he scarcely realized that he would never visit Britain again. And it would be four years before Paul finally visited him in New York, the Beatles dead and the business hatchet still not properly buried. At the time of their friction, George Martin said: 'I don't think Linda is a substitute for John Lennon any more than Yoko is a substitute for Paul McCartney.' The producer of the Beatles' records was judging each artist's new direction in music. He was also, unknowingly, echoing their desires. John had shed the Beatles, Paul, and Britain. And he was opening his mind.

•

Killing a Taig: Protestant hatred of Catholics
MARTIN DILLON

Northern Ireland has been scarred by a history of sectarian violence and hatred. Tit-for-tat killings among Protestants and Catholics now occur almost every week. But of all the hatreds that have affected that troubled province, none has been described with more chilling intensity than Martin Dillon's history of the Shankill Butchers. The Butchers were members of the Protestant Ulster Volunteer Force, led by Lenny Murphy, a cut-throat and sadist whose loathing of Catholics knew no bounds. Between 1972 and 1977, Murphy led his gang to kill more people than any other mass murderers in British criminal history.

The question being asked in the summer of 1972 and in the years leading to 1975 was whether the situation would reach new heights of barbarism. The UVF, UDA, Provisional IRA and Red Hand Commandos had in the past demonstrated again and again their potential for taking human life in a most ruthless fashion, but in 1972 both sides indulged themselves in the most grisly sectarian war of attrition against society yet. Few people stood back and examined the reasons for it but merely expressed sympathy with the condemnations made by politicians and clergy. No one sought to make the point that prejudice in a community invariably leads to anything ranging from ridicule to extermination. Northern Ireland has a society where prejudice is so deeply rooted that extermination rather than derision is the likely outcome when nothing is done to erode it. In most instances the victims of prejudice are not the combatants but the innocent. It is difficult, of course, to eradicate prejudice but serious and concerted attempts should have been made to replace it with tolerance and more positive attitudes within the churches and the educational system. Few people took the trouble to analyse the factors that contributed to the growing prejudice of the seventies, such as intolerance stemming from the patriotism underlying the two conflicting ideologies, and the literature which supported them. The classic work, *The Nature of Prejudice* by Gordon W. Allport, defines prejudice in a manner which is relevant to the situation in Northern Ireland: 'An avertive or hostile attitude towards a person who belongs to a group, simply because he belongs to that group, and is therefore presumed to have the objectionable qualities ascribed to that group.' He goes on to make the point that this represents an antipathy based on faulty and inflexible generalization.

A renowned sociologist, Michael MacGreil sj, made the same point in 1970 when considering this issue. He said that in prejudice there is a double assumption in that, first, the group is presumed to possess the negative qualities ascribed to it without examination and without taking the positive qualities into account. Secondly, the person is presumed to possess these qualities without the slightest effort being made to verify the presumption. In other words, the person and the group are denied a fair chance. According to MacGreil, prejudice is unfair, and is likely to be based on false generalizations.

In Northern Ireland Catholics often saw the whole Protestant and Unionist community as the oppressors and, obversely, Protestants believed that all Catholics were subversives and therefore Republicans. As a result, when the IRA began to destroy the fabric of Unionism, Catholics were seen by the Loyalist paramilitaries as the root cause of the evil.

In respect of the Shankill Butchers, there was another element, which was sadism. Many studies have indicated that sadists need aggression and I believe that in Northern Ireland the conflict provides the trigger for this aggression. It also allows misfits to find social acceptance by expressing the prejudice which is not just endemic but socially acceptable. It has been argued that a large percentage of the violence in Northern Ireland has not been political or religious. This is a simplification, for the political and religious background has made the violence possible, has often allowed it to be glamorized and has given it the status of being part of an ideological struggle. It has enabled many people who cannot escape prejudice to find a security within it and to accept its manifestations as a badge of patriotism. There are those who will scoff at the description of much of the conflict in Northern Ireland as politico-religious in character and yet much of the paramilitary literature ... was available to Lenny Murphy and his associates in late 1975 and its content supports my thesis, as the following extract from *Combat* magazine in the autumn of 1975 shows:

> The following areas have been marked down by the enemy for takeover: Cliftonville Road and Antrim Road. Soon, the whole of the Antrim Road from Carlisle Circus to Fortwilliam will be dominated. Stem the tide of Popery's penetration policies. The policy of the Papist Church is to buy as much property as it can in so-called residential areas and let it out at fixed rents to Papists. The idea is to replace the Protestant population with Papists and Republicans.

It was against this background in late 1975 that Lenny Murphy began a new campaign of terror. In spite of the fact that a new Brigade Staff of the UVF had taken over, Murphy was determined to go it alone and to vent his hatred as he thought best. It is an indication of his single-mindedness, his sense of omnipotence and invincibility, that he ignored a plea from within Long Kesh to accept the orders of the new Brigade and not to wage war on any group except armed Republicans. Murphy had only one formula in his mind, which was that all Catholics were potential targets.

This instruction from Long Kesh was issued within days of the overthrow of the young leadership:

> The UVF, Red Hand Commandos and YCV [Young Citizen Volunteers] prisoners of war in Long Kesh fully support and applaud the actions of those senior officers who recently replaced the former Brigade Staff for the sake of the Loyalist people in general and the UVF in particular. For some time the name of the UVF has been abused. Rumours have been allowed to circulate to the effect that funds have been misappropriated and that gangsterism is rife in our ranks. All this has served to damage our relationship with the people and we hope that the new Brigade Staff will soon set about the painstaking task of renewing our lost confidence. The new Brigade Staff are true Ulster Volunteers of long standing who have held responsible posts in the past, and who are completely competent. These men have our trust and our blessing to restructure the UVF. The sole aim of our organisation is to defend the Loyalist people against their enemies, at the same time stating that it is not our wish to wage war on anyone except armed Republicans determined to overthrow Ulster in order to force us into an Irish Republic.

The attempt in the statement to define the enemy and therefore the targets more clearly was in keeping with the Gusty Spence ethos but it did not appeal to Murphy. He decided that his operation would be kept secret, that he would neither seek orders from the Brigade Staff, nor inform them of his planned actions. There were those in the Brigade who knew of Murphy's freelance operation, though not in any detail. They were frightened to interfere.

On 23 and 24 November four young soldiers were murdered in South Armagh. The *Newsletter*, a Belfast-based daily paper, on 24 November dealt graphically with the killing of the soldiers and reported the tough talk of politicians on the need for increased security and stricter measures to deal with the IRA. On the same day Murphy called a meeting with Moore, Edwards and another member of the unit who had become a close ally, Archie Waller. Murphy demanded a response to the weekend violence of the IRA and stated it was time to hit a *Taig*. He called a meeting for that evening and requested that Moore bring along his taxi and his butchery knives. Murphy spent the rest of the day at his home in Brookmount Street where he was now living with his wife and where, in the same street, his parents shared a home with his brothers William and John. Lenny's wife, the nineteen-year-old Margaret Gillespie, had married him in Crumlin Road Prison on 5 May 1973 and she was a new dimension to his life on the outside. The ceremony was conducted before Lenny began his stint in Long Kesh and the officiating minister was the then Moderator of the Presbyterian Church in Ireland.

When Murphy met Moore and the others that evening he knew exactly where to seek a victim and it was of no importance that he would not know the identity of the target. A tour of the Antrim Road, he told the others, would undoubtedly lead to finding a *Taig*. Murphy drank with Moore, Waller and Edwards until after midnight before he resolved finally to make his move. He instructed that no guns would be carried on the job. Instead he chose the knives presented to him by Moore, on the grounds that if they were stopped and searched they could argue that Moore had used them in his previous job at the Woodvale meat plant. Murphy's criminal mind covered every eventuality, including the possibility that the taxi might be stopped by the police or the Army, in which case Moore would also say he was carrying passengers. A short ten-minute route was chosen on the grounds that the shorter the route the less likelihood there would be of them being caught once they had captured their target. The route Murphy mapped out took the team down the Shankill Road, across to the Crumlin Road and down the Antrim Road into Clifton Street with a shorter return journey. The importance of the route was that anyone walking after midnight would be easily identified at a distance and few people would be walking the streets at such a time. More importantly, any person in the vicinity of the lower Antrim Road and Clifton Street was likely to be a Catholic because the sectarian geography of the city determined that Protestants would not use those roads after dark. Murphy proved by this calculation his familiarity with the sectarian dividing lines.

The taxi with Murphy and the others aboard took the planned route with one or two slight variations devised by Murphy. They avoided Clifton Street's main thoroughfare and entered an adjacent area of narrow and darkened streets such as Library Street and Union Street. Both streets were 150 yards from the bottom of the Shankill and less than one mile from Murphy's home.

Elsewhere in Belfast that night thirty-four-year-old Francis Crossan was travelling across the city from a club near his home in the Suffolk area of South Belfast to North Belfast, where his family had been intimidated out of their home one year earlier. On his way to the Holy Cross Bowling Club in the Ardoyne district he passed the spot where his brother Patrick, a bus driver, had been the victim of a sectarian shooting several years earlier. Crossan intended spending a few hours with friends at the Holy Cross and enjoying a few drinks. Sarah Ellen Murphy, no relation of Lenny's, remembers Crossan drinking quietly in a corner of the club. Another member of the club, John Greene, later told police that he chatted with Crossan who was not drinking heavily, just bottles of Guinness. Crossan left the club at ten minutes past midnight. There was no transport available to him so he made his way on foot towards Belfast city centre. It was a foolhardy thing to do but he seems to have been unaware of the danger.

Some time after 12.30 a.m. Moore spotted a man walking down Library Street towards the city's main thoroughfare, Royal Avenue. It was Francis Crossan. Murphy told Moore to stop the taxi alongside the solitary figure, then Murphy, Edwards and Waller rushed out of the vehicle and Murphy hit Crossan over the head with a wheel brace. As Crossan fell to the ground his assailants dragged him into the taxi and drove off.

Within minutes they were on the Shankill Road. Moore later revealed that Murphy kept hitting Crossan with his fists and the wheel brace and kept repeating: 'I'm gonna kill you, you bastard.' Edwards' recollection was that Crossan 'kept squealing the whole time'.

Murphy directed William Moore to drive to an alleyway off Wimbledon Street in the Shankill district. By the time they reached their destination Crossan was quiet and Moore stopped the taxi to allow Murphy and the others to carry Crossan's blood-spattered body out of the vehicle. With Moore's assistance the four men carried him deep into the alleyway and dragged him along the ground until they were out of sight of the roadway. Murphy then took out a large butcher's knife and stood over Crossan who was lying on the ground breathing heavily, his eyes closed. Murphy set about hacking at Crossan's throat until the head was almost severed from the trunk. Finally, and triumphantly, he held the knife aloft. It was a demonstration by Murphy of the 'ultimate way to kill a man'. Murphy's clothes and hands were covered in blood and the interior of the taxi was also blood-smeared. Murphy ordered the others to accompany him to his home, where they washed out the taxi and removed their bloodstained clothing, which was later burned. The knife was carefully wiped clean and returned to Moore for safekeeping. Edwards and Waller remained in Murphy's house that night and Moore drove home.

·

Bitter legacy: Picasso's millions
GERALD McKNIGHT

Gerald McKnight describes the background to the feud between Picasso's widow and his mistress.

Olga Koklova was a member of the fashionable Diaghilev ballet, a great beauty and a member of the displaced Russian upper middle class of Tsar Nicholas. At a time when Picasso was finding in the ballet a rich seam of inspiration, she became his favourite model – with predictable results. What had been lacking in Fernande excited him in Olga, a dark, soulful and voluptuous lady. She also offered a convenient path to the social milieu which he privately despised but which increasingly provided customers for his works. Olga and her set introduced him to a circle of moneyed Parisians and artists who regarded him as 'a coming young man'.

After five years of this, he should have known better. Instead, he made the mistake of marrying this reduced-in-circumstances lady from the Russian *haute bourgeoisie* when she was about to have his child. Paulo's imminent arrival painted a false gloss of hope and fulfilment over their widely different characters. The uncharacteristically pretty paintings Picasso achieved of his son gave way to grotesque studies in which Olga was portrayed as a monster. When they parted in 1935, their marriage had been dissolved though not ended. Olga refused divorce on the grounds that they had married under Spanish law, which forbade it. Picasso turned his back on her social aspirations and took refuge in the soft arms of his next lover.

Marie-Thérèse Walter's love for Picasso is lost in obscurity but it lasted until the end of her life. Their affair originated under Olga's sharp nose, causing great unpleasantness, but Picasso was never disturbed by these womanly tirades. He saw them as inevitable in a world of 'goddesses or doormats'. It is questionable which of these he found more psychologically satisfying.

Olga was certainly no doormat. She continued to haunt his life, demanding recognition as his wife until her death in 1955. Marie-Thérèse came closer to the warm cosiness of a hearthrug, if not quite a doormat. As a model she had the flowing, aqueous lines he was using increasingly in both his paintings and his sculpture. Though blonde, in contrast to his other women, and lacking the capacity to match his sharp, quaint wit, Marie-Thérèse gave refuge to his soul as well as to his body.

They first became lovers in 1927 during one of Olga's irrepressible campaigns to engage Picasso's failing interest in her endless round of parties and socially acceptable *divertissements*. In an act of rebellion, he made Marie-Thérèse pregnant, and the birth of her daughter was the final cause of the dissolution of his marriage.

Maya was born in 1935, the year Picasso left his wife to preside in solitary state over her tea table. He then moved in with Marie-Thérèse, but remained living with her for a bare year before their baby was born, though revisiting them on and off for years afterwards. Why he did not stay longer is partly explained by the advent of another, very different, woman, Dora Maar. Here was a dynamic and beautiful individual whose attractions did not begin and end in bed, or on the modelling couch. Dora was an artist and photographer from Yugoslavia, dark, passionate, witty and intelligent. Their affair lasted from 1936 until 1943 and she is to be seen in Picasso's vast black and white masterpiece, *Guernica*, painted in passionate reaction to German bombing during the Spanish Civil War. Prophetically, Dora Maar is portrayed as a woman weeping for a lost lover.

Marie-Thérèse left Picasso on the day she discovered that Dora Maar's interest in him, ostensibly photographic, was better developed than any film. She and Picasso remained occasional lovers, pride preventing her from admitting to the encroachment of a rival, but the loss of Picasso as a constant companion may have affected Marie-Thérèse's mind. For several of her earliest years, Maya's mother kept up the fiction that he was still living with them, telling the child to be quiet 'as your father is working upstairs'. A room which he used as a studio at the top of Maya's grandmother's house, where they lived, was kept permanently locked, though Picasso was only an infrequent visitor. In the family it is generally believed that Marie-Thérèse fostered this illusion for her daughter's sake, but Maya loyally refuses to accept this. 'My father was always coming to visit us and stay with us, all his life,' she maintains. 'He and my mother shared a love nothing could destroy.'

She would visit her father in his studio in the rue des Grands Augustins and they would speak to each other in Spanish, which few of the visitors understood. 'We'd chat about his women friends without them knowing, which was crazy,' she says. At a time when her mother and Dora Maar were competing for Picasso's affection, it must also have been very revealing. Maya claims to have shared this privileged insight into Picasso's intimate world until she reached the age of twenty, when she felt that she had to break free. 'As a young girl, I'd sit on the stairs in my grandmother's house in Paris, where he occasionally worked, and listen to him talking to women. When I got too old for that sort of thing, it was time to go.' Earlier she had complained to her father about his relations with Dora Maar, and how upsetting they were to her mother. She claims that as a result he never asked Dora to his studio again.

Certainly the gap between the two women, Marie-Thérèse and Dora Maar, was wide in terms of both intellect and sophistication. Dora was travelled, entertaining and amusing. Marie-Thérèse was thought to possess a vague and uncertain personality which bordered on the neurotic. Picasso's tenderness for her was largely physical and aesthetic, the warm curves and loops of his many studies of her expressing more clearly than words the nature of the attraction she held for him. And with Dora, whom Picasso regarded as a charming plaything, there were no children. She was a free spirit, caring for no such ties. Françoise Gilot, who was to succeed both Dora and Marie-Thérèse, noted a rigidity in her which reminded her of an ancient French expression: 'She carried herself like the holy sacrament.' No doubt Picasso's interest in her was more earthy.

The long affair with Françoise Gilot, whom he first met in Paris when she was a young art student in the early days of the Second World War, was Picasso's most mature match. She and the woman who succeeded her, Jacqueline Roque, filled his latter days from the start of his sixties until his death at the age of ninety-one. Without Françoise's children, and Jacqueline's unfortunate lack of them, there would have been no dispute, no bitter wrangling, over the succession to his great wealth. The jealousy and rivalry between the two women, each in her own way strong and influential in affecting the framework of Picasso's life, were the foundation of the feud that followed his death.

Françoise had been Picasso's constant companion for seven years, in Paris and latterly in the South of France where he had bought the villa La Californie in Cannes, when one day they were approached on the beach by a couple called Ramié, middle-aged and commercially minded. Georges and Suzanne Ramié ran a gallery in Vallauris, the Madoura, where they made and sold pottery. Seizing her moment, Madame Ramié immediately tried to lure Picasso into paying them a visit, urging him to try his hand at designing and making ceramics. The craft offered an exciting new medium for an artist of his calibre, she explained, one equally as creative as drawing, painting or sculpture. Any ceramic designs he produced would be true 'Picassos'. Françoise took an immediate dislike to Madame Ramié, but Picasso listened to her attentively. He agreed to drive over one afternoon to the gallery, if only to satisfy his curiosity. Maybe there would be something new for him in ceramics. In his restless frame of mind at the time, it seemed worth a try.

Françoise, already aware of the threat posed by Picasso's growing boredom, could only encourage and support his enthusiastic impulse. They were driven over – Picasso never learnt how to drive – and the Ramiés soon had Picasso drawing fish, eels and sea urchins on fired clay. The results in their unglazed state were disappointing, and Picasso was eager to see the final effect. As it was impossible to arrange this immediately, he left the gallery and might well have forgotten the experiment altogether had not he and Françoise again bumped into the Ramiés in the following summer of 1947. They asked if he would like to see his completed work. He was delighted to find it transformed, the colours warm, rich and glowing. The first 'Picasso pots' entranced him and opened up an entire new avenue of shape and form.

Françoise felt pleased when her lover steeped himself in this new activity. Quite soon he was producing at the gallery a range of original works of astonishing variety and beauty. Françoise should perhaps have guessed that this activity would bring a new woman into his life but as the mother of his babies . . . she may have felt secure against newcomers.

Every summer for five years Picasso continued developing this new art form, mastering every known technique and continually inventing fresh and fascinating forms. Then, in 1952, the Ramiés announced that, needing someone to help in the gallery, they had invited their young cousin, Jacqueline Roque, recently divorced from an engineer called Hutin, to take on the job. She and her daughter Catherine were living in a small villa between Golfe-Juan and Juan-les-Pins called Le Ziquet – in Provençal dialect 'the little goat', as Françoise sharply pointed out. Picasso was introduced to Jacqueline and found her young, beautiful and sympathetic. He became a regular visitor to her home.

That winter the gallery was unusually quiet. Jacqueline found plenty of time to cultivate Picasso, to learn his often demanding ways. Contact with him when he was on an artistic 'high' was an inflammable situation for a young and beautiful girl, as Françoise herself should have remembered. The relationship nevertheless ripened while, surprisingly, his mistress seemed scarcely to have given it a thought. Perhaps it was because she had known so many 'other women' in his life; too many to worry her head over one young girl at a gallery. A year or so before, Picasso had begun a passing affair with a seventeen-year-old Parisian girl, Geneviève Laporte. His loyalty to Françoise wavered occasionally, she knew, but she felt no serious qualms about him now that she had his children.

Even when his irritability and irrational changes of mood led to friction and rows between them, she saw no threat from the dark-haired Jacqueline. The younger woman was welcomed by her whenever Picasso, as he often did, brought her home with him. Jacqueline slowly became part of his working life, as other women always had been and always would be. Jealousy was not an emotion Françoise allowed herself to feel, and anyway there seemed no cause for it. But her own relationship with him was no longer what it had been. Her 'sacred monster' had become a brute who did his best to savage her with words. When she could stand no more of his vindictive attacks, she fled to Paris, seeking at least a respite. She took the children with her. Only when she returned did Françoise realize the extent of her mistake.

Jacqueline Roque was installed in her place. Françoise's clothes were still in the wardrobes; Jacqueline had been wearing them. Picasso, most plainly, was no longer Françoise's lover and protector, merely the father of their children. Her life with him was over, and she could blame nobody but Jacqueline. Françoise stayed on a while, putting up with her conqueror's daily visits for the sake of the children, but now she must endure a secondary role in what she had called Picasso's 'kingdom'. She was no longer its queen.

When she eventually surrendered the keys, her successor had already taken full possession of the house. All that was left to the mistress who had given Picasso the two children he professed to love so dearly, and whom he had painted in their infancy so touchingly, was her memories. 'Whatever you do from now on, your life will be lived before a mirror that will throw back at you everything you have lived through with me, because each of us carries around with him the weight of his past experiences,' Picasso told her sententiously. It was that sentence which prompted her to begin her chronicle of life with him, the book she called *Life with Picasso*. In doing so, had she realized it, she was handing Jacqueline the ultimate weapon.

The book, written in collaboration with a distinguished American art critic, Carlton Lake, was unreservedly frank. Françoise wrote: 'Until now I had seen him, through his inner life, as a unique phenomenon. But now in his seventies I saw him spending his energies in the most frivolous and irresponsible ways. I saw him for the first time from outside . . . And all the standards he had set up and so carefully observed were thrown aside . . .

'"You won't last as long as I will," he told me. He couldn't seem to bear the idea that anyone who had been part of his life should survive him. I recalled how he told me at the beginning, "Every time I change wives I should burn the last one. That way I'd be rid of them. They wouldn't be around now to complicate my existence. Maybe that would bring back my youth, too. You kill the woman and you wipe out the past she represents."'

The book was scrupulously fair to her successor. Françoise managed to make Jacqueline sound like the nurse of fiction who steals the heart of the wounded warrior. In the few passages showing the three of them together, Jacqueline is described weeping with frustration when Picasso refuses to accept her views on the bullfight, tears streaming down her face while she pathetically wipes them and her hair out of her eyes. Françoise stands aloof, refusing to begin a fight she knows she cannot win. Picasso's classification of women as 'goddesses or doormats' was never more vividly portrayed.

The book won almost universal praise except for reviews like that in *The Times*, which obviously considered anything so frank to be irredeemably 'vulgar'. In the *Observer*, Arthur Koestler noted sympathetically that the book demonstrated 'a mathematical proof: so much goodwill on both sides, and all in vain'. Koestler recalled the passage where, having come into Picasso's life as 'a rather prim virgin of twenty-one', Françoise showed how her self-control – 'all my life I had been warned away from public displays or emotions' – could tantalize Picasso. 'When I shout at you and say disagreeable things, it's to toughen you up,' she reported her lover as shouting at her in fury. 'I'd like you to get angry, shout and carry on, but you don't. I'd like just once to see you spill your guts out on the table, laugh, cry – play *my* game.'

A dangerous game indeed, but no more so than the effect of publishing the book. Those outside her circle of friends believe it enabled Jacqueline to create, in Emilienne's [Picasso's daughter-in-law] words, 'a vacuum around Picasso'. Under

Jacqueline's protection, it was impossible to gauge how many of his subsequent actions were his alone, and how many were prompted by her.

Marie-Thérèse maintained at the time that Jacqueline had 'wrought a fundamental change' in her old lover. In the admiring view of her friends Jacqueline was 'a saint' who loved and watched over Picasso like a guardian angel, but others in the family were less charitable. 'She kept him as though in prison,' Emilienne has said. 'That was her whole existence, she thought of nothing else.' Emilienne's daughter, Marina, echoes this more forcefully. 'After the marriage, my grandfather seemed to lose his humanity. We saw absolutely nothing of him, we received absolutely nothing from him. My feeling is that most of that must have originated with Jacqueline; it could have come from no one else.'

To Françoise, the attack Picasso subsequently made on the book, whether or not it was inspired by Jacqueline, was astounding. 'I had been careful never to make any statement in it which I could not substantiate with absolute proof, even with letters which I had at the time. Yet he attacked it, saying it was full of lies!' When Picasso brought a legal action against Calman Levy, her publishers, in 1964, Françoise was forced to provide documentation to substantiate her claims. Picasso lost the case in the lower court, then took it to appeal and lost again.

As Françoise says: 'It had already been proved that what I said was true. The appeal judge now had to decide on an altogether different aspect of the case. His point was: "Yes, it is true, but is it indiscreet?" Our lawyers argued that the ten years we had spent together constituted a *community of fact*. If Pablo could sue me for writing the book, then for all the portraits that he had painted of me with my nose on the wrong side and so on, I would be able to sue him. If he was entitled to his version of the facts, then so was I.' Again, and this time finally, Picasso lost the case. Françoise's evidence had ridiculed his claim. As she says: 'The book was *not* indiscreet, because Pablo had made a habit of living his entire life in a glasshouse. He wasn't the slightest bit averse to publicity, and this applied equally to his so-called private life.'

So Picasso and Jacqueline could go no further. If their intention had been to reduce the impact of the book, to play down the public's conception of Françoise's role in Picasso's life, they had achieved the exact opposite. The publicity surrounding Picasso's action against Françoise ensured that she was now a famous woman, the cast-off mistress of a celebrated artist.

When Picasso congratulated her on her successful defence, Françoise could have accused him of using the whole costly court action to make a stupid and vindictive attack on her, but she knew very well who was responsible. '[Jacqueline] had a Lady Macbeth complex,' Françoise declares. 'Even though Lady Macbeth did not do those things herself, she introduced them into Macbeth's soul.' The manipulative genius which Shakespeare's heroine shows was echoed, Françoise believes, in Jacqueline. 'Shakespeare was a good psychologist. He had knowledge of the human soul. In Jacqueline's psychological make-up, if you look at it closely, you will see that there is a parallel to the Macbeth situation. To me, she is slightly megalomaniac.'

Jacqueline now faced the unenviable task of comforting the loser, a man who could not abide defeat despite his cheery words of congratulation to Françoise. However much or little she had encouraged Picasso to mount this futile attack, however much she would continue to denounce the book as 'discredited' and 'vulgar', her rivalry had ensured its success. Jacqueline had misjudged the strength of the opposition. Blinded perhaps by the adulation she felt for Picasso's genius, she had prompted him in all good faith to fight the losing battle. Forty-five years in age separated her from him, but there was another, perhaps greater, gulf between them, that of understanding. Françoise had a definite advantage there.

Nevertheless, in his old age – he was by now in his eighties – the 'doormat' was more in demand than the goddess.

Jacqueline's subservience to his every need and whim was a constant stimulation to Picasso's waning energies. And perhaps, when all is said and done, her natural reluctance to share him with his previous mistress, despite the cost of two unsuccessful actions, was flattering.

Jacqueline has always declared that it was the book that turned Picasso against the children, causing what French journalist Nicolas Adam called 'the final break in the family'. She voiced her own disgusted reaction to it and talked openly of her husband's distress over it. Friends like David Duncan and his wife, their American neighbours, listened sympathetically when she complained of the 'invasion of Pablo's privacy'. The general opinion of both friends and family, however, was that whether or not Picasso had read the enjoyable, well-written story Jacqueline had poisoned his mind against both it and its author.

Following the failure of Picasso's action on appeal, it seemed the most that he and Jacqueline could do to thwart Françoise and her children in their fight to be duly recognized was to foster the belief that *Life with Picasso* was a vulgar and catchpenny intrusion into the life of a great man which had caused him distress. Then in the spring of 1964 both children were told, abruptly and without explanation, that they were no longer welcome at their father's home. For ten years until then, recognized as his children and bearing his name, they had spent holidays at Christmas and in summer with him and Jacqueline. Now, apparently, their father wished for no further contact with them. Only once, on his own admission, did Claude Picasso encounter his father in the flesh after the barriers went up. 'We happened to pass each other in the street in Cannes one day,' he told Peter Lewis of the *Daily Mail*. 'We spoke for about a minute before he passed on. He was with my stepmother, of course.' One is left to wonder what can have been said.

Jacqueline and others blamed the book for his estrangement, but Françoise knew that the rift had started well before it was published. It could not possibly have been the cause of Picasso's animosity towards his children. In her considered opinion, that could only have been produced and encouraged by Jacqueline. 'She confused people. She said it was "on account of my abominable book". All nonsense! It is not abominable at all. It is very nice to Pablo. Anyway, she made it appear that the children had been rejected *because* of it. Whereas, they were rejected after they had acquired their father's name, which is quite a different story. And that's the truth.'

The legal victory gave Françoise the right to publish her story anywhere in the world. *Life with Picasso* became a bestseller, a Book of the Month selection in the United States, and a widely discussed work. It left on record the intimate story of Picasso's life as both lover and father. More important still, the tried and tested status of the book's statements about her children's parentage provided a keynote in Françoise's campaign to ensure Claude and Paloma's rights of succession. 'I had set up a trust, the *conseil de famille*, on the children's behalf, with Picasso as a trustee. That and the maintenance payments he was making for them kept a sort of distant relationship going between us. It at least showed that Picasso had acknowledged the children were his, which was most important.'

But when she filed a suit to establish their rights to inherit, he opposed it. Picasso had allowed them the use of his name, now Maître Dumas was instructed to fight against any right of inheritance. Late in 1970 he succeeded in having the case thrown out of the small provincial court of Grasse. As Picasso said to a somewhat baffled court reporter after the hearing: 'They have my name. Isn't that enough?' Françoise Gilot did not think it was.

After his death, she made an urgent reassessment of her departed lover's motives. She was still uncertain to what extent he had planned the imbroglio her children were involved in, but it was clear to her that she was the root cause of Picasso's mischief. 'I saw that it was *our* fight, the tug-of-war between us, which had set the scene. Pablo was determined to do this to me after his death, since he had failed to do it while he was alive. In that context it became clear to me that the struggle between us had been more important than our love affair.' She also recognized that Jacqueline, the usurper of her place in Picasso's life, had influenced Picasso in ways which materially affected her children. The refusal to let them share in their father's funeral, or even enter his house after he died, was a stinging insult, but it was the recollection of all the years until now when they had been turned away from his door without explanation that really burned. In Françoise's eyes, Jacqueline had played a leading part in this for no other reason than her desire to expunge all reminders of his former mistress.

Françoise's first act upon hearing of Picasso's death was therefore to urge Claude and Paloma to continue to press their rightful claims against the estate as determinedly as she had pressed them against Picasso during his lifetime while they were minors. From her home in California she kept in close touch with the unfolding drama, furious at Picasso's dismissal of his own children and saddened by Pablito's senseless suicide, but increasingly seeing Jacqueline as the biggest obstacle in her children's path. The widow's refusal to let them share in their father's funeral was the last straw, strengthening Françoise's determination to see that Jacqueline did not trample over everything she had gained for her children. In doing this, she appears not to have worried that her actions might be construed as petty spite, or the jealousy of a deposed mistress. She sought only to complete a task she had set herself when life with Picasso became unbearable. Then he seemed to have betrayed all the trust she had put in his assurances. She substituted Jacqueline for Picasso now because she believed the widow had, as she put it to her children, 'used undue influence' over him.

Françoise's supreme coolness in fighting for her children's rights impressed both of them, especially Paloma. It made her confident. And later, when she was more mature, she adopted the attitude: 'well, as I have all the convenience of being Picasso's daughter, I may as well use that as a tool.' If that was the weapon which had been used against her, let it also be the strength on which she would build her career. Claude, on the other hand, took a somewhat different view of their destiny. He had been born with a genetic heart defect, a narrowing of the pulmonary artery, which made it necessary for him to take extra care in everything he did. As a child he had not been allowed to join in normal games, the rough-and-tumble of school and adolescent life. His mother believes that this enhanced the disparity between her two children, augmenting the existing difference in looks and character between them. 'Paloma has a lot of her father's characteristics: the strength, the taste for power. She looks like Picasso's sister, Lola; whereas Claude, who looks more like his father physically than she does, is much more like me inside. Though he is now thirty-nine, he is still not so assured as Paloma who is nearly three years younger.'

Françoise had now divorced Luc Simon and had remarried. Her second husband was the distinguished, Nobel Prize-winning discoverer of anti-polio vaccine, Dr Jonas Salk. His support helped her to continue the fight. He maintained that the children's 'sacred monster' of a father had done terrible things to their wellbeing and self-esteem. Perhaps everyone had forgotten, the great scientist said, that Picasso had named his daughter Paloma after the celebrated 'dove of peace'. The irony of his later behaviour towards her was, in Dr Salk's eyes, 'simply incomprehensible'. As he said with feeling: 'The refusal to permit his own children to see their father or to bid him farewell was shocking, an indignity to the dead as well as to the living.'

Françoise had, besides, found a 'friendly and wise counsellor in Gaston Bouthoul, a lawyer who, though old [he died in 1980], was completely trustworthy. He advised that there was a loophole in Picasso's case to deny Claude and Paloma rights of succession, he said we must not be too Utopian, but it was worth pressing on. This was good to hear at a time when it seemed everything was against us and Pablo was at his most hostile.' After Picasso's death, Françoise no longer waged the battle herself but referred the children to Bouthoul's loophole, which seemed to be valid.

They had fought to establish their right to a place in Picasso's succession at a time when their ages would have enabled them to qualify under the terms of the subsequent 1972 Act. As has been said, this Act establishes the legal rights of inheritance of *enfants adulterins* if descent is proven within two years of the illegitimate child's twenty-first birthday. Since the Act had been passing through the legislature while the case to establish the children's rights of succession was being unsuccessfully fought the first time, and since Bouthoul had craftily registered a request for exemption from the new Act's age-rule once it was passed, he felt sure that, had Picasso's death not forced them to postpone their action, Claude and Paloma would by now have overturned the judge's earlier decision on appeal.

Since Jacqueline now exercised control over everything, the danger as Françoise saw it was that the widow would override all the advantages which the mistress had won for Claude and Paloma, and latterly for Maya also, during their minority. It was no longer possible for her to act for them directly as they were of age, but she was determined that her legal experience and competence would still guide them. 'They hadn't been very hot on what I was doing, but I thought I could see further ahead than they could. When Claude reached the age of twenty-one I had filed a suit giving him the right to claim exclusion from the age barrier affecting claimants under the new Act. This was well before the Act was passed but it stood him in stead later. The same thing was true for Paloma. But I knew if they didn't handle things in the right way now that their father was dead, it might come to nothing.'

Françoise had always believed the illegitimacy label was most unjust. 'Under French law at that time, even if Picasso had been free to marry me and had done so, the children would not have been legitimized, because Olga, his ex-wife, would still have been alive.' This unfairness was the crux of her campaign to have a change made in the law. In January 1972, when the new Act came into force, giving far greater rights to children born out of wedlock, she had the satisfaction of knowing that her efforts had been successful. Picasso's death had forced her children to postpone their legal attempts to establish their rights, but as soon as they re-entered their cases, claiming absolute rights under the new law to a place in the succession, Jacqueline opposed them. The battle between the widow and the mistress was on.

•

Big Brother hates everyone
CHRISTOPHER BOOKER

Following the death of Mao Tse Tung in 1976, the Chinese government pursued a vicious campaign of hate against Mao's widow, Chiang Ching, and the three men who had done most to support her during the Cultural Revolution of 1966–7. Here, Christopher Booker looks at the hostility that permeated Chinese society and describes how hate is one of the basic psychic patterns in the life of any society.

> The city's loudspeaker system took up the refrain, 'Down with Chiang Ching, Wang Hung-Wen, Chang Chun-Chiao and Yao Wen-Yuan' – the four chief targets. Fireworks went off as tens of thousands of people raised their voices in a deafening chorus of slogans above the sound of the horns and drums.
>
> (News report from Peking, 1976)

> The horrible thing about the Two Minutes Hate was not that one was obliged to act a part, but on the contrary that it was impossible to avoid joining in. Within thirty seconds any pretence was always unnecessary. A hideous ecstasy of fear and vindictiveness, a desire to kill . . . seemed to flow through the whole group . . . and yet the rage that one felt was an abstract, undirected emotion which could be switched

from one object to another like the flame of a blow-lamp.

(George Orwell, *1984*)

In recent years the image of Chinese life most frequently presented in the West, particularly on television, has been that of a teeming anthill, of 700 million industrious citizens, all toiling happily under the inspiration of Big Brother Mao to build a new nation, after centuries of oppression, division and misery.

Many Westerners, as with Russia in the 1930s, have been disposed to take China at this face valuation, as a society showing an almost miraculous degree of unity and harmony.

There has, however, been one gigantic contradiction in the picture: namely, the enormous part obviously played in everyday Chinese life (which not even the most sycophantic admirers of Mao's China could disguise) by public expressions of aggression and hostility.

Not only have we been aware in the past decade of the remarkable persistence in such a 'happy and harmonious' society of an apparently endless succession of subversives, 'capitalist roaders' and 'Confucian deviationists', from the enemies of the Cultural Revolution, through Liu Shao-chi and Lin Piao, to the presently hated 'Gang of Four', but few things have been so conspicuous in the television films as the degree to which China's social unity seemed to be expressed not in smiling harmony but in expressions of hatred – even on the faces of the little children in the schools, acting out their playlets against American imperialist aggression and 'goulash deviationism'.

Rarely has the world seen a more vivid example of that phenomenon of mass-psychology which, although it was brilliantly portrayed by Orwell in *1984*, has astonishingly never received proper analysis – viz. the absolutely unchanging requirement of Utopian, totalitarian movements for a constant supply of 'enemies', however imaginary, upon whom they can lavish a continual stream of aggression.

Whether we think of Hitler's Germany, Mao's China or Stalin's Russia, we are aware that any such great collective movement requires three things.

The first is a Utopian vision or fantasy of the idealized future (however vaguely drawn) to which the whole forward thrust of the society can be directed – whether it be the perfect Communist state, or the thousand-year Reich.

The second is the semi-deification of the superhuman leaders, or 'dream heroes', who will lead and inspire the struggle – the Fuehrer under the searchlights of Nuremburg, the icons of Lenin, Stalin, Marx or Mao.

The third, to provide psychic personification of something to struggle against, is the constant invocation of 'enemies', both external and internal, whose very existence gives both justification to the battle, and a ready explanation for everything that goes wrong in pursuit of the dream – Jews, capitalist roaders, Wall Street imperialists, or whatever.

But even though all extremist political movements, whether of the Left or the Right, conform to this psychological pattern, we should not of course only be ready to perceive it in its extreme forms.

It is in fact one of the most basic psychic patterns in the political and social life of any society, particularly ones which are threatened by any degree of violent change or disintegration, which inevitably leads to the desire by various groups in that society for simple, instantly compelling and largely fantasy-based 'solutions'.

We see it, for instance, wherever a conflict arises which tempts each side to exaggerate the other into a monstrous caricature. In British politics, we saw a particularly striking example in 1963/4 in the considerable psychic energy which was generated around Harold Wilson's vision of a 'New Britain', which would somehow be dynamic, classless, efficient and forged in 'the white heat of the technological revolution' – as opposed to the bumbling stagnant, 'old-school tie' and 'grouse moor' complacency of 'thirteen years of Tory rule'.

We saw it in the late 1950s and 1960s in the great imaginary struggle of those who wanted to be thought 'young' and 'swinging' and 'with it' (with their 'dream heroes' from the world of pop culture), against the 'squares' and 'blue meanies', later translated only too readily by some into 'Fascists'.

In the end, however, all these expressions of the same psychic phenomenon are perversions of the same, fundamentally religious archetype. The 'promised land' to which we aspire (like the 'lost Eden' of the past) are symbols of a sense of wholeness and unity from which we obscurely feel that we have been exiled.

To admit that any of those detestable qualities which are standing between us and the perfect world might actually lie in ourselves is obviously impossible. It is so much more comforting to project them on to other people, and other groups, because it makes our view of the world so much simpler. All that is wrong is the fault of 'the others' – the Fascists, the Jews, the 'squares', the 'reds under the bed'. If only these villains can somehow be got out of the way, the paradise we deserve will be ours.

The great religions (in their highest expressions) tell us that these things can only be achieved by each individual, in his struggle to recognize his own 'darker' side and thus to work towards a 'whole' view.

But as soon as the battle for salvation becomes collective rather than individual (whether it takes on religious, political or social expression) then the enemies are always outside us. Thus, in the comfort of knowing that we are the elect, do we launch on the world persecution, war, collective hatred and all the other hideous consequences of our own psychic disintegration.

●

Pistols at dawn: Malcolm McLaren and Richard Branson

MICK BROWN

The Sex Pistols, managed by Malcolm McLaren, were the most notorious rock band of the seventies. After EMI rid themselves of the Pistols, they signed with Virgin Records, in spite of McLaren's antipathy for Virgin boss Richard Branson. Mick Brown chronicles McLaren's hatred.

Malcolm McLaren did not arrive at the Virgin offices that December afternoon, as arranged. Nor had he ever intended to. It was not until January that EMI at last rid themselves of The Sex Pistols – 'in view of the adverse publicity generated over the last two months', as an official statement put it – and at a cost of £50,000 in settlement. McLaren then began shopping around for another label, pointedly ignoring Virgin. On 9 March the Pistols finally signed with A & M records, in a ceremony staged, for the benefit of press photographers, outside Buckingham Palace. The managing director of A & M, Derek Green, was sanguine about his controversial new signing. 'Every band is a risk,' he said, 'but in my opinion The Sex Pistols are less of a risk than most.' On 16 March Green issued another, somewhat terser statement, saying that the contract between A & M and The Sex Pistols had been terminated. Complaints from staff about the behaviour of the group at a party at A & M's office to celebrate the signing and protests from other A & M artists about the company's judgement were the reasons cited for the *volte face*. The Sex Pistols received £75,000 in compensation.

To Richard Branson, the worse The Sex Pistols' public image became, the more he wanted them . . . Branson could spend ten times as much money signing half a dozen acts and never achieve the same effect. The Pistols, he believed, were 'The Rolling Stones of their generation. I was going all out to turn them into the seventies' strongest band.' This was not, as it turned out, an accurate thesis. The Pistols' strength lay not in their future potential but in their immediate shock value. They were a highly volatile entity that would need to be properly channelled, if not contained. And Branson knew that Virgin stood a better chance of achieving that than either EMI or A & M had done. He was not answerable to shareholders. There were no major artists on Virgin whose sensibilities were likely to be offended as there had been at the Pistols' previous stop-overs; no American parent company to interfere. The only reputation which worried Richard Branson was that of being the head of a record company which looked increasingly out of touch, out of time. Being spurned by Malcolm McLaren only made him want the group more. McLaren and The Sex Pistols would be a challenge. And it would be fun . . .

From the moment The Sex Pistols contract with A & M was rescinded, Branson was on the phone to McLaren, sometimes three times a day, with the same question. 'When are you going to sign with us, Malcolm?' To Branson's irritation, McLaren prevaricated as long as possible, affecting the disinterest of an ingénue being courted by a philanderer.

McLaren too was in a quandary. While he subsequently made it appear like a carefully premeditated act of cunning, being sacked from EMI and A & M was, in fact, a disaster. Of course, it had made a bloody marvellous spectacle – not to mention £125,000 for doing absolutely nothing – but 'the boys' were growing increasingly restive at having their records, and themselves, banned. And as the Silver Jubilee drew near, the need to find a company to release the Pistols' 'commemorative' recording was becoming acute.

But Virgin was the very last label to which McLaren and Jamie Reid had wanted to sign. As the more doggedly political of the two, Reid in particular despised Richard Branson as an 'entrepreneur hippie' who had sold out everything that was exciting and subversive about the sixties and turned it into big business. Reid found Virgin's 'hippie façade' disconcerting. With EMI or CBS you knew exactly where you stood, whether you liked it or not. It was fat-cats doing business. But with Virgin, he complained, the laid-back sixties seediness and everybody wanting to be on first-name terms, all seemed like a ploy to lull an honest Situationist into a false sense of security. Whenever he met Branson, Reid insisted perversely on addressing him as 'Mr Branson'. In the offices of The Sex Pistols' company, Glitterbest, Branson became known as 'Mr Pickles'.

Malcolm McLaren too believed that groups and management should always be on the worst possible terms with the record company, to avoid co-option and defeat. Never believe Virgin are 'nice people', he would tell the Pistols; they're only after your money.

But for McLaren the enmity was more than ideological. Richard Branson symbolized everything he despised; the world of upper-middle-class, public-school, breadroll-throwing, cultural philistinism. It fostered in McLaren what Jamie Reid identified as 'nigh on complete hatred'. From the outset, McLaren was convinced that Branson wanted only to take The Sex Pistols away from him, 'and grind me into the ground'. But Branson too was instantly on his guard. He knew nothing about Situationism, and cared even less; but he suspected that what McLaren wanted to do was force Virgin, just as he had forced EMI and A&M to drop them – and pay the appropriate price.

One bright May morning in 1977, Malcolm McLaren came to Branson's house in Denbigh Terrace to finalize the signing of The Sex Pistols to Virgin. The mood was cordial, almost jokey. 'You do realize what you're getting into, Richard?' asked McLaren. 'We don't want to go through that business we had with A&M. We want somebody who's going to run with us. It'll be hair-raising, but it'll be fun.'

Branson joked back. 'The question is, Malcolm, do *you* realize what you're getting into?'

That settled, the two men began to discuss plans to rush-release The Sex Pistols' first record for Virgin, a special composition to mark the Queen's Silver Jubilee. Officially entitled 'No Future', it became more popularly known as 'God Save the Queen'.

Virgin's first promotional act on signing The Sex Pistols was to organize a boat trip on the River Thames in the week of the official Jubilee celebrations, to mark the release of 'God Save the Queen'; an idea which seemed to meet everybody's requirements by being both a revolutionary gesture and a wizard prank. John Varnom booked the pleasure cruiser, fittingly named *The Elizabethan* (and which Virgin would actually buy some years later), reassuring the owner that the party was for 'some boring German synthesizer band'. In the mood of schoolboys off on an expedition to plant stinkbombs on speechday, the party set off from Westminster Pier, shadowed by two police launches. Branson and McLaren stood side by side on the upper deck, incongruous partners in crime, the contrast almost comical – McLaren in drainpipes, Branson with shoulder-length hair tumbling over a multicoloured sweater of Hobbit-like cosiness. As the boat bobbed outside the Houses of Parliament, a cacophonous version of 'God Save the Queen' echoed across the Thames to bemused sightseers. It was at that point that the police came on board, and the pleasure cruiser was ordered to return to the shore. As the boat docked, police swarmed on board. 'Fascist pigs', yelled McLaren, at last creating an 'incident' worthy of The Sex Pistols' reputation. In the ensuing mêlée, McLaren, Reid and others of the Pistols camp were dragged up the gangplank and into the waiting police vans. Branson, who had been attempting to play the role of diplomat with the police, was not arrested. The incident showed the basic difference in measure of commitment to the Pistols' ideology of subversion. While McLaren was happy, not to say eager, to be arrested, Branson was equally eager not to be. The next morning he presented himself in court to give evidence, and a character reference, on McLaren's behalf.

The release of 'God Save the Queen' caused an immediate furore. 'No pop song has ever had lyrics like these,' the *Sunday Mirror* raged sanctimoniously, helpfully reproducing them in full on its front page: 'God save the Queen/A fascist régime/Made you a moron/A potential H-bomb/God save the Queen/She ain't no human being/There ain't no future in/England's dream.' Packing ladies at the CBS factory where the record was being manufactured refused to handle it, until threatened with the sack. Television and radio advertising was banned; the BBC refused to play it, and some major retailers to stock it. On what grounds it was hard to discern. By no legal definition was the record 'obscene'; it was hardly even objectionable. But in a week in which Britain was in the self-hypnotized thrall of royalty and its traditions, any criticism carried the odium of high treason. 'But such is the new-found and disturbing power of punk that nothing can stop the disc's runaway success,' ranted the *Sunday Mirror*. Throughout Britain, thousands of teenagers, offered a rude purgative to royal overkill, chorused a noisy amen.

Yet despite selling more than 100,000 copies in its first week of release, 'God Save the Queen' reached only number two in the pop charts – Rod Stewart being at number one. Branson's suspicion that the chart had been 'fixed' to prevent the embarrassing spectacle of an anti-royalist song reaching number one during Jubilee week was lent weight by an anonymous telephone call, alleging that the British Phonographic Industry (the record companies' professional body) and the BBC had colluded to keep the record off the top of the charts. Branson was told that in the week in which The Sex Pistols might have been expected to reach number one the BPI had issued an extraordinary secret directive to the British Market Research Bureau, who compiled the charts, that all chart-return shops connected with record companies should be dropped from the weekly census of best-selling records. Virgin, the stores where most Sex Pistols records were being sold, was therefore struck off the list. One week later, the decision was reversed. But by then Virgin and The Sex Pistols had been denied their first ever number one single.

*

The recording contract which had been agreed between Richard Branson and Malcolm McLaren, after much protracted discussion, was, in lawyers' parlance, unusually 'live' – that is to say, open to constant reappraisal, argument and haggling. McLaren's 'plunder' of EMI and A&M was not repeated. The agreement signed on 12 May 1977 between Glitterbest and Virgin Records gave McLaren and the Pistols an initial payment of just £15,000 for the British rights for material sufficient for one Sex Pistols album, to be paid in twelve instalments. This rather meagre figure was increased by a further £50,000 one month later, when Virgin negotiated the rights to release the Pistols in all other world territories, excluding America, France and Japan.

McLaren insisted that, rather than being paid the advance in one single lump sum, an amount should be paid on the delivery of each track. The staff at Vernon Yard grew accustomed to the spectacle of Malcolm McLaren seated outside Branson's office, clutching a package of tapes under his arm. Almost from day one, the arguments over royalty rates, promotional budgets and artwork waged unceasingly. Making ever more provocative demands and outrageous gestures became an integral part of McLaren's tactics.

The initial air of reasonableness and cordiality had quickly given way to a more chameleon-like personality, shifting and dodging behind a variety of masks; one minute the crafty haberdasher, the next the erudite political activist, the next the polite, smiling business associate. Fred Vermorel, an art-college friend of McLaren's, who later wrote a book about The Sex Pistols, described him as having 'the vision of an artist, the heart of an anarchist, and the imagination of a spiv'. Sometimes Branson's phone would ring at two in the morning. It would be McLaren, intoxicated by an evening of drink and conspiracy with his lawyer, Steven Fisher, with a shopping list of demands. 'I was hoping Branson would be so tired I could beat him down, nag him into submission,' says McLaren. 'What I didn't know was that the man was an insomniac. I would go round and round on the same point, he would commiserate, pretend to understand, but never move an inch. To Richard, it was always the deal; that's what got him excited. Everything else was just water off a duck's back.'

At other times, playing back the office answering-machine first thing in the morning, Branson's secretary would be greeted by a stream of McLaren's comical invective and abuse.

One of McLaren's favourite ploys was to deliberately fly in the face of convention and logic. Coming into the Virgin offices he would make exaggeratedly friendly overtures to the post boy and the receptionist and be sullen and truculent with Branson or Simon Draper. 'It's nothing to do with business, you just don't *feel* right emotionally, Richard,' he would say, in the manner of a schoolmaster lecturing a particularly dull and inattentive pupil.

Curiously, Branson did not dislike McLaren – Malcolm's transparently roguish charm made him hard to *dislike* – but he had never trusted him from the day they had first shaken hands in Leslie Hill's office and McLaren had failed to arrive at the Virgin offices; failed to keep his promise. McLaren would be charming, interesting and warm-hearted; Branson would momentarily drop his guard, and McLaren would immediately try to exploit it. Branson came to realize that 'fair compromise was not really in Malcolm's language'. McLaren, he was convinced, was determined to get the better of him, 'and I was determined not to let him'. Malcolm liked to rattle you, catch you off-guard by making demands nobody could possibly meet. The trick was not to be rattled, but to ride along with them, at least some of the way.

McLaren's stance required an enemy to define it. It was disconcerting to his whole thesis that Branson did not behave like the enemy enough. Even when, in 1978, McLaren returned from Brazil with the news that Great Train Robber Ronnie Biggs was now 'lead singer' of The Sex Pistols and someone McLaren earnestly claimed to be the missing Nazi war criminal Martin Bormann was the new bass-guitarist, Branson took it with disarming enthusiasm. A singing Ronnie Biggs was 'a good idea'. It was McLaren's pleasure always to up the ante . . . 'And we'll call the record "Cosh the Driver"', Richard'. Branson demurred at that. After yet more haggling, the title of the song was changed to 'The Biggest Blow'.

Artwork and advertisements for the Pistols records became a perennial source of conflict, a challenge to Virgin's commitment to Situationist spectacle. Jamie Reid's graphic designs – cut-ups, like a kidnapper's ransom notes – mocked the ethos of the record industry, and The Sex Pistols' relationship with it, with a wickedly funny disrespect for politesse or law. For one single sleeve, Reid adapted the design of the American Express credit card, to depict the 'real relationships within the music industry; the record company as nothing more than a huge pimp – and the band as prostitutes'. American Express won an injunction against the sleeve; copies of the record were recalled for resleeving and Virgin were ordered to pay £30,000 in legal costs. It was an ironic prelude to Richard Branson's association with American Express, some years later, advertising the credit card.

Reid reserved his most venomous attacks for Virgin and Branson. He peppered his designs with slogans which ridiculed Virgin, and then challenged the company to use them. He designed a series of posters including one of Branson himself under the caption 'No One is Innocent', and another bearing a swastika made of cannabis leaves, the Virgin logo and what had become a Sex Pistols' slogan, 'Never trust a hippie'. Branson refused to let them be used on any Virgin-owned material. There were boundaries as to how far he would go, but in his own way Branson was as much committed to creating a spectacle as McLaren and Reid, if for very different reasons. Branson was no insurrectionary. He readily acknowledged that the Pistols felt more strongly about the 'difficulties' in England than he did. Branson's views about England were more platitudinous than revolutionary; England, he would say, is 'a great place to live in, but as a great place it should carry on standing totally for democracy and people should have the absolute freedom to say what they think'.

As to offending royalty, or a significant swathe of popular opinion in releasing 'God Save the Queen', Virgin were strictly neutral – 'Like publishers. What our artists were saying was, in effect, nothing to do with us. We could have books criticising royalty, and books praising royalty. It makes no difference. To have one lone voice attacking royalty in Jubilee week seemed perfectly fair. It also happened to sell a lot of records, and was great for the company.'

•

The rumbling point: Lee Iacocca and Henry Ford II

ROBERT LACEY

As president of the Ford Motor Company from 1970 to 1978, Lee Iaccoca often found himself in conflict with his chairman, Henry Ford II. With so much at stake theirs became one of the most bitter feuds in business history.

The months of May, June, and July 1978, in which Roy Cohn's attack on Henry Ford II reached its climax, were the very months in which Lee Iacocca and Henry Ford II came down to what Henry II would later describe as 'the rumbling point'. Ford World Headquarters was a battlefield. Iacocca's men and Caldwell's men were sniping at each other ceaselessly. Caldwell [Ford's European CEO] and Iacocca could hardly be constrained to address a civil word to each other, and as for Iacocca and Henry II himself, there was now no pretence.

'Things were enormously tense around here,' remembers Franklin Murphy [Ford board director]. 'In fact, I used to hate to come back to the meetings.'

Murphy found Lee Iacocca was getting more and more on edge. 'Lee was not sleeping well. It was just a bad scene. It was a very bad scene . . . I would go in and talk to him, and he would pour it out. It would be like to a priest.'

The headlines being generated by Roy Cohn's recurrent and proliferating attacks upon the reputation of Henry II might be helping Lee Iacocca in his week-by-week battle with the Ford chairman, but the publicity generated by the Pinto affair was not. Three months earlier, the record-setting award of $127.8 million to Richard Grimshaw had provoked a flood of other suits against Ford. The National Highway Safety Administration had started pushing for the recall of all 1971–76 model Pintos, and finally, on June 15, 1978, right on the eve of a public hearing that seemed certain to force Ford to recall the car in any case, the company announced the 'voluntary' recall of 1.37 million Pintos and 30,000 Bobcats (the Mercury version of the subcompact). The cost of this recall was $40 million, and what it amounted to was a modification of the gas-tank filler neck and cap, together with the insertion, between the tank and the rear axle, of a high-density plastic shield, protection at last against the tank splitting open on the nuts of the transmission housing.

The Pinto had been Lee's baby. He had said so himself. He had taken all the credit for the car when the subcompact had sold so well in its early, successful years. But now the car was a public-relations disaster, and it was prompting serious questions about the quality of all the Ford cars built under Iacocca's stewardship.

In 1977 Ford had had to offer an extended warranty on 2.7 million cars with four- and six-cylinder engines which had suffered from excessive wear in cold weather. The problem had been caused by the removal of two small oil holes from the cylinder blocks – part of a cost-cutting exercise. An additional 1.3 million cars had been called back for faulty fans, though this was a problem of design rather than of 'thrifting'. Ford led the industry in recalls. By midsummer 1978, no less than 18.163 million Ford vehicles were the subject of recalls or official probes for safety, mechanical, or emissions defects, and even in a city self-protectively tolerant of transgressions in this area, eyebrows were being raised.

'Our quality was so bad,' said one Ford executive, 'it was getting embarrassing to go to cocktail parties and tell them where you worked.'

This sort of thing worries outside directors very much. Quality and safety are just two among the wide range of concerns that keep a car executive busy – but they are quite predominant anxieties for the men and women whose names are on the letterhead. Outside directors only come into the hothouse atmosphere of headquarters one day a month, and for the other twenty-nine they have to live out in the ordinary world, going to cocktail parties, reading newspapers, and receiving angry letters from shareholders whose six-cylinder Mercury has just given up the ghost.

After more than two years of fairly consistent resistance to Henry Ford's wish to be rid of Lee Iacocca – proof, in itself, that the directors were not in the chairman's pocket – some of the outside board members were beginning to wonder whether Henry II might not be right. Perhaps Lee was not such a great automobile man after all.

'He was the man, who, they said, had gasoline in his veins,' recalls Murphy, 'who'd done the Mustang. And yet here was the company losing money in great amounts and not able to penetrate, to do anything about the small car market, a company in which morals seemed to be rather bad and in which, among everything else, in the most humiliating way, product quality had gone to hell.'

Lee Iacocca has boasted of the record profits that were being enjoyed by Ford in 1977 and 1978, after the bad years following the 1973 oil crisis. But, as is the pattern in Detroit, the prosperity was spread. General Motors was also enjoying record sales in 1978 – 70 percent more than Ford's – and when the Ford figures were analysed, it was clear that much of Ford's profits were not actually coming from the divisions under Iacocca's most direct control. It was Ford of Europe, Henry II's creation and Philip Caldwell's recent fiefdom, which was making the most substantial contribution to the Ford treasury in 1978: no less than 40 percent of total company profits. Ford's US cars – Iacocca's special area of expertise – had been a disaster. Between 1972 and 1977, General Motors had managed to increase its profits from its North American automotive operations by 46.5 percent. But in this same period, Ford's equivalent earnings had actually fallen by 4 percent.

'The fact that we were sinking,' remembers Franklin Murphy, 'that Ford of North America was getting less profitable all the time, was something that was sort of camouflaged by how well we were doing overseas . . . There was great confusion in the management as to what should happen to Ford of North America.'

Lee Iacocca has blamed Henry Ford for this, citing, in particular, Henry II's opposition to small cars, and Henry Ford, for his part, has acknowledged his own failure to see the way things were going. But, at the time, Lee Iacocca does not seem to have argued that strongly for the course that now seems so obvious. In 1976 the Ford president had proudly unveiled his range of new cars with the boast that Ford was still the home of the 'whopper', as if the energy crisis had never been. General Motors was downsizing its model range that year, but Iacocca made fun of GM with a relish which did not suggest that Henry II was twisting his arm very much. WRONG MOVE? ran a headline in the *Detroit News* in February 1976. 'Ford's Iacocca believes GM erred in deciding to downsize big cars.'

Nor were Lee Iacocca's more recent ventures in carmaking that impressive. He seemed to be losing his touch. In 1974 he had brought out a successor to the car that had made him famous, the Mustang II, based on a prototype by Alejandro de Tomaso. Over-sculpted and toylike, as though lifted off a fairground carousel, the Mustang II was a travesty of its famous forebear. In 1977 the Mustang II had sold only 170,700 units, less than 14 percent of the sporty market sector which had come to be dominated by GM's Firebird and Trans Am – the very sector in which the Mustang I had once proudly controlled as much as 78 percent of the market.

[Ford board director] Marian Heiskell remembers discussing cars with Lee Iacocca, and, in particular, the practice of 'thrifting' – the shaving of pennies from the cost of components in order to save millions of dollars overall . . . Having ordered the removal of some trim from around a window, the Ford president had run into the untrimmed glass door because he did not see it while getting into the production version of the car.

'You see, it really doesn't pay to save nickels' was the moral that Iacocca drew from the incident. But this item of wisdom did not appear to have been very deeply assimilated by the carmaking divisions under Iacocca's command, and as the company's US and Canadian operations continued to perform poorly, concern mounted on the topmost floor.

'There was no question,' recalls Marian Heiskell, 'about the fact that we had to build up North America.'

A wider question was of Iacocca's mastery of Ford's international dimension, and of Ford of Europe, in particular. One specific objection that Henry Ford II had to Lee Iacocca was that Lee did not know enough about Europe – and, on this point, he had been able to secure the fairly general agreement of his directors. Many of them had travelled to Europe with both Henry and Lee, and they had observed the two men operate.

Lee Iacocca made much of his Italian origins, but his was an Allentown interpretation of what being Italian was all about, as authentically European as pizza pie – spicy, but definitely made in America. Bill Fugazy had a photo of his friend in his office inscribed, '*Al mio carissimo amico Bill con i migliori augori, Lido,*' but when Walter Hayes travelled in Italy with Iacocca in the late 1960s, he noticed that Lee never ventured once into the local tongue.

Henry II the Europe lover had always seen his family empire as an international one. It was part of its Ford-ness, and he was very conscious that the company he must now hand on was, outside North America, the largest car company in the world. In 1978 Ford produced almost 20 percent of the new cars, trucks, and tractors sold anywhere on the face of the earth. Its

chief executive had to have many of the qualities of an international statesman – and Henry Ford II felt that these qualities
were lacking in Lee Iacocca.

'Why,' remembers one European Ford executive, 'Iacocca
actually came to see me once wearing velvet shoes.'

The shoes did not worry Henry II. The profanities did.
Henry Ford II could swear with the best of them, and he did so
quite unpleasantly when in his cups. But he had never made
four-letter words the habitual currency of his business conversation, as Lee Iacocca did.

Franklin Murphy tried to give Iacocca some friendly advice
on one foreign trip.

'Lee,' he would say, 'you must, you don't understand how
your use of profanity, your nonuse of proper English, really
reflects discredit on you as a person.'

Henry Ford would wince visibly, remembers Murphy, at
some of the obscenities Iacocca would let drop at board meetings.

'Some of our other directors would wince,' says Murphy.
'There are very few boardrooms in which this kind of talk goes
forward . . . Henry knows as many four-letter words as the next
fellow, but never in those board meetings. To him a Ford board
meeting is a holy experience . . . a very important, serious,
consequential thing.'

Perhaps it was just a question of style. But style counted for
much in an equation which was, ultimately, to be all rolled up
in terms of whether one powerful man liked another.

Late on the afternoon of June 26, 1978, a messenger set off
from the East 68th Street offices of Saxe Bacon and Bolan on
what had become quite a routine errand: the delivery of yet
another legal missive to the Wall Street offices of Ford's lawyers,
Hughes Hubbard and Reed. It contained still further allegations
of corruption in the Ford Motor Company, this time that Henry
Ford had accepted no less than $65 million from 'the highest
officials of the Philippine's [*sic*] Government', and that in return

for this payment, Henry II had directed Ford to build a stamping plant in the Philippines at a cost to the company of $50 million.

The accusation was as wild as Cohn's previous ones. For the Philippines' government to lay out $65 million to secure an investment of $50 million did not make sense by anyone's system of accounting, and, having reduced the amount of the alleged bribe to $2 million by a subsequent filing, Roy Cohn was, in due course, to abandon the charge altogether, along with all his others. His friend William Safire wrote a column based on the accusation in the *New York Times*, which he was also, later, totally to withdraw.

'*Henry Ford II*:' Safire wrote on April 14, 1983. 'I took a sneaky, oblique pop at him based on unproven charges, am ashamed of myself, and take this occasion to apologize. That was my worst column.'

Safire's apology appeared in a retrospective column in which he either withdrew or reaffirmed a potpourri of insults he had flung, in the course of the previous decade, at such public figures as Henry Kissinger, Edward Kennedy, and Frank Sinatra, and Safire's two sentences are remarkable for being the only retraction ever printed by any of the journalists who had so gleefully propagated Cohn's charges against Henry Ford II without bothering to check their factual basis.

In June 1978, the significance of Cohn's accusation about the Philippines was that it enabled Henry Ford II to exclude one possible candidate who might have been behind the campaign which he had already publicly identified as a 'personal vendetta'. Until this point it had been plausible to imagine that all the poison could be coming from his estranged wife Cristina. She was just the person to have supplied Roy Cohn with details like the $82,000 price tag on the tulip-wood desk in the Carlyle apartment – and she was certainly angry enough. Only a few months earlier, in February 1978, Cristina Ford had forced her separated husband into court to give four hours' testimony in defence of his wish to sell off some antique furniture and a valuable collection of snuff boxes to which, she said, she had come to feel a deep 'emotional attachment'.

'I was under Librium, what they give crazy people,' she testified, describing the nervous breakdown she had suffered after her husband's departure, and she was clearly very bitter.

Early in 1978 Cristina Ford had been seen in a New York restaurant talking to Roy Cohn, and there were even rumours that he was going to represent her in her divorce – double scourge for Henry. But Cristina could hardly have been the source of Cohn's allegation about the Philippines. The last thing she would have wanted was to embarrass her friend Imelda Marcos with talk of kickbacks. On May 5, 1978, Cristina had issued a statement through her lawyer, Carl Tunick, stating that whatever her domestic quarrels with her husband, she was 'completely out of sympathy' with Roy Cohn's lawsuit. So far as she knew, she said, Henry II's business conduct was 'beyond reproach'. While this did not totally rule her out as one possible source of all the details that were getting to Cohn, it strengthened the argument that other sources must be involved.

When questioned as to where all their detailed inside information was coming from, members of Roy Cohn's law firm had referred to 'disgruntled former employees' of the Ford Motor Company who had been 'fired and humiliated' by Henry II, and Roy Cohn himself, when pushed, gave *Esquire* magazine the name of Paul Bergmoser, the Ford executive who, as chief of purchasing, had handled the details of contracts with Bill Fugazy, and also with Pat de Cicco. Bergmoser, said Cohn, had 'absolute proof of the kickback' – and Bergmoser himself confirmed that he had talked to Cohn, though only in general terms.

Bergmoser was a close associate of Lee Iacocca. So long as he had been on the Ford payroll, 'Bergy' had operated as one of the campaign managers for the Iacocca forces in the Glasshouse. He was Iacocca's contact man with Bill Fugazy, and Fugazy was the logical person to have put Bergmoser in touch with Cohn. That was what Fugazy was so good at, putting people in touch with one another, and as the Cohn assault on Henry II's honesty mounted to a crescendo in June 1978, the obvious question was whether Bill Fugazy was acting as the channel between his old friends Roy Cohn and Lee Iacocca.

The question has several times been put to Fugazy, and he has always, categorically, denied it. But Henry Ford II thought otherwise. He was convinced that Bill Fugazy was deeply implicated in Roy Cohn's attacks upon him, and he also felt sure that the network stretched further than that. By the end of June 1978, in fact, Henry Ford II had come to believe that his own president, Lee Iacocca, a serving officer in the Ford Motor Company, was at least one of the sources – and was certainly the overall inspiration – of the public campaign dedicated to Henry Ford II's humiliation and removal.

Carter L. Burgess, Chief Executive Officer of the American Machine and Foundry Company, onetime US Ambassador to Argentina, and a director of the Ford Motor Company since 1962, worked on the staff of General Eisenhower for a period during the Second World War. In his desk drawer Burgess used to carry a stock of colonel's eagles, and whenever Eisenhower decided that one of his generals was not commanding right, he would send the general along to Burgess's office to pick up the insignia of his new, lower, rank.

'So, you see,' says Carter Burgess, 'I've been raised with total understanding that I'm an expendable quantity in the business world ... and I think we all have to enter life with some understanding that if our superior, for good and sufficient reason, doesn't think that there's a compatible forward relationship, we pay the price.'

Carter Burgess, who, along with Arjay Miller, had been one of Henry II's most stalwart supporters in the two years of boardroom arguments over the future of Lee Iacocca, believes that the Ford president had had a very simple choice in April 1977, when Henry Ford's elevation of Philip Caldwell had, effectively, handed Iacocca his colonel's eagles.

'He should have quit at that point,' says Burgess, 'or laid down his pistol and gone to work.'

That apparently simple and logical choice might have been appropriate in the Army, or for almost any other executive in the Ford Motor Company, but Lee Iacocca was one person to whom it could not apply. The man did not know how to be anything other than number one – and he did not know how to quit either. He did not want to quit. There was nowhere else but Ford for the only son of Nicola Iacocca, the U-Drive-It Ford man, for it was one of the more poignant ironies in the unfolding drama that Lee Iacocca identified with the Ford Motor Company only slightly less than did Henry Ford himself. Lee had had his heart set on that corner office on the twelfth floor for so long that he found it difficult to think of anything else.

He was never going to get it though, not while Henry Ford had breath in his body, and in June 1978, a month after the Cohn-haunted shareholders' meeting, Henry II made another, determined attempt to bring the question to a head. After just over a month of Roy Cohn's mysteriously well informed attacks, Henry had had enough. When his outside directors arrived in Detroit on June 7, 1978, he was waiting for them with two surprise items of news. The company was about to recall the Pinto – the recall notice went out three days later – and Lee Iacocca was definitely going to be fired.

On Iacocca the outside directors' reaction was unanimous.

'We said, "Don't do it!"' remembers Franklin Murphy. 'It was at a committee meeting before dinner. "Don't do it! Let's try to patch this up. Let's see if we can't build a bridge." I realize now we were naïve. But we were so desperately wanting to prevent an explosive episode.'

Later Murphy went downstairs on one of his peacemaking missions to Iacocca's office. 'I said, "Lee, now look, things are quieting down . . . You're not going to be fired."'

According to Lee Iacocca's memory of the conversation, Franklin Murphy reported Henry II as having declared, 'I lost my board today.'

'But that's Lee's interpretation,' says Murphy. 'I can't imagine my saying that he "lost his board", because Henry never lost his board ... We didn't say, "We're going to vote you down." We simply said, "Postpone it," as it were.'

As some sort of compromise, the oddly assorted Office of the Chief Executive was now stretched from three members to four by the inclusion of William Clay Ford – proof, if there had ever been any doubt of it, that the OCE was a political device, not a serious management mechanism, since Bill Ford had not managed anything at the Ford Motor Company for at least twenty years.

At the end of June 1978, Henry Ford II departed with a number of senior executives on a trip to the Far East, together with Kathy DuRoss, who was now being treated as Mrs Henry Ford in everything but name. The journey had been planned for some time, a visit to suppliers in Taiwan, an inspection of Australia – and putting his brother Bill into the OCE had reflected an anxiety on Henry's part as to what Iacocca might get up to in his absence.

His anxiety proved fully justified. Within days of the chairman leaving the country, Iacocca was also on a company plane, heading to Boston and New York to see the two outside directors who had, he thought, over the months, proved most sympathetic to his cause: George F. Bennett, an investment banker from Boston, and Joseph F. Cullman III, chairman of the board of Philip Morris, the tobacco company.

Neither Bennett or Cullman will discuss what actually happened at those meetings in any detail. 'He wanted to point out his position,' says Joseph Cullman. 'He wanted to seek the support he was entitled to.' Cullman had been at the core of the directors who were supporting Iacocca. 'I admired him then,' he says, 'and I admire him now.'

But when Henry Ford II got to hear of his president's travels, he had no doubt at all what was going on. Lee was evidently not intending to go quietly. He was building up support. Both men knew that the battle would be decided in the boardroom, and Lee, as usual, was aiming to be the one who finished up on top. In 1969 Iacocca had managed to bring down Bunkie Knudsen, and now he was planning to do the same to Henry Ford.

You could compare him to the young David, vaulting in his ambition. You could compare him to Icarus, daring to brush his wings against the sun. Or you could just say that Lee Iacocca had taken leave of his senses – and that was the conclusion that the outside directors of the Ford Motor Company came to when they gathered together on July 12, 1978.

'It was an act of insanity,' says Franklin Murphy. 'He just didn't have the cards.'

After thirty years of superbly proficient politicking and climbing, Lee Iacocca had lost sight of the basic rule by which he had always played the game. The Ford Motor Company simply was not a public company which worked the way the business schools say things work. Forty percent of its votes were controlled by the Ford family, and there was nothing that Iacocca, or any other non-Ford, could do about that.

'Lee had a lot of loyal chums out in the system,' says Franklin Murphy, 'and anybody other than Henry Ford, Lee could have castrated – absolutely, quickly. But you don't castrate the man who represents the family who owns the company. And this is something that he didn't understand.'

Henry Ford II went to meet his directors on the afternoon of July 12, 1978, with an ultimatum. He had listened to them last month, and then he had bowed to their will. But this was the end. They would have to choose – and the choice was a simple one.

'Henry said, "It's me or Iacocca,"' remembers Franklin Murphy. 'There was not one negative vote.'

And so the stage was set for the encounter that is already a legend in the Motor City and far beyond – the OK Corral of recent American corporate history. On the evening of July 12, after the Ford directors had met, Lee Iacocca received a phone call from Keith Crain, the publisher of *Automotive News*.

'Say it isn't so,' said Crain.

Iacocca jumped to the conclusion that Crain, a friend of Edsel Ford, had got inside information from the family. But Edsel was working in Australia at the time. Crain had picked up the talk around town and he wanted to finalize his story before his magazine went to bed next day. In the event, Crain had to hold the presses.

At three o'clock on the afternoon of Thursday, July 13, 1978, Lee Iacocca received the phone call summoning him to the office of Henry Ford II, and when he arrived, he was surprised to discover that Henry was not alone. He was waiting for him with his brother William Clay Ford.

In his memoirs, Lee Iacocca interprets the presence of brother Bill at the final showdown as a matter of Henry II wanting a witness. But it was more complicated than that, for William Clay Ford, the company's largest single shareholder, had been one of the people to whom Iacocca had been talking in his last desperate weeks of lobbying, and Bill Ford had given Iacocca a sympathetic ear.

'I thought he was a good person for the job,' says William Clay today.

Over the months Bill Ford had talked quite frequently with his brother, and with Iacocca as well, acting as a sort of family go-between.

'You're a better friend of Lee than I am,' Henry said to him accusingly on one occasion – a comment that Bill recalls today with his oddly leftward-twisting smile.

'Cripes! They had offices ten feet apart! I mean, doors. I mean, great! They've been working together, I don't know for how many years, and supposedly I'm closer to him than he is! So I guess that's why I was present.'

Henry Ford wanted to make sure that Lee Iacocca got the message in no uncertain terms. The board was behind him, and so was the family. There was no court of appeal. When Henry had fired Bunkie Knudsen nine years earlier, he had brought Bill in to make the same thing quite clear – that was how one ordinary mortal now came to be present at this final, skull-jarring encounter between two bull males, each so potent, so talented, and so raging mad.

Bill wept at the sheer power of it. He had 'tears running down his face', Lee Iacocca remembers, and William Clay Ford does not deny that today. It was the dismissal by a father of his son, the final, bitter disinheritance by a king of his erstwhile crown prince – and also, quite simply, the tragic parting of the ways between two men who were so much alike they could not possibly get along.

Lee Iacocca dealt with it in his customary fashion, jabbing, weaving, attacking – a ferocious onslaught of words and insults and anger. He was good when he was calm, and when he was moved, he was very good indeed.

Henry Ford II had comparatively little to say. A better smoulderer than talker, he was most verbose when it came to the incidentals, Lee's 'resignation' date and the pension details.

'There comes a time when I have to do things my way . . .' he said. 'It's personal, and I can't tell you any more. It's just one of those things.'

It was not really a very impressive performance. If it had been the Academy Awards, Lee Iacocca would have won the Oscar – and Bill Ford told him as much as they left, congratulating the ex-president on how well he had argued his case.

Lee Iacocca considered the compliment. 'Thanks, Bill,' he replied. 'But I'm dead, and you and he are still alive.'

The warehouse was the epilogue. Under the terms of his departure, Lee Iacocca was to stay on at the Ford Motor Company for another three months, until October 15, 1978, his fifty-fourth birthday. Staying until then would entitle him to receive his full retirement benefits, a cash and stock package worth over $1.1 million, so long as he did not work for a competitor.

Lee Iacocca tried very hard indeed to remove the standard Ford 'no compete' clause from his severance contract, so that he could still get paid by Ford if he went to work for Chrysler. He hired Edward Bennett Williams, America's premier trial attorney – Roy Cohn not excepted – to negotiate with a Ford committee headed by Bill Ford and Carter Burgess, chairman of the Compensation Committee, and in his memoirs he describes these two men as 'bastards to the bitter end'.

Carter Burgess regards this charge with equanimity.

'I've never said any unfortunate things about his mother,' he says, 'and I don't know why he says those unfortunate things about mine. Mr Iacocca wanted me to overrule "no compete" policy statements that he himself had signed as president, and I wasn't about to overrule his own policy decisions.'

Iacocca stayed in his presidential office on the twelfth floor of the Glasshouse until his birthday and 'retirement' in October. It had been agreed that he would, after that, have the use of another office, which he could keep until he found another job, and on October 16, 1978, he drove to this office in the Ford Parts Distribution Center, on Telegraph Road. What he found there horrified him.

'My new office,' he was later to write, 'was little more than a cubicle with a small desk and a telephone. My secretary . . . was already there, with tears in her eyes. Without saying a word, she pointed to the cracked linoleum floor and the two plastic coffee cups on the desk . . . For me, this was Siberia.'

Lee Iacocca was to describe his exile to this 'obscure warehouse on Telegraph Road' as his 'final humiliation' at the hands of Henry Ford. 'It was enough to make me want to kill,' he said. When Iacocca came to write his memoirs, he told his ghostwriter that he wanted to start with this episode, because, he said, it had been for him the great moment of truth.

You might not guess from reading the dramatic opening to Lee Iacocca's autobiography that any other human being had ever occupied the miserable few feet of warehouse space to which he was consigned in October 1978. But this office had, in fact, had a previous occupant: Ernest R. Breech, chairman of the Ford Motor Company until July 1960. Driving home in that month from World Headquarters in Dearborn, where he was negotiating his own, and rather more amicable, departure from the Ford Motor Company, Ernie Breech happened to see the blue oval outside the Ford Parts Distribution Center on Telegraph Road, and he pulled in to ask if he could see the manager.

'Do you have any spare office space in here?' he inquired, and the manager showed him to a very pleasant office, the best office in the building, a good twenty-one feet long by fourteen feet wide, clean and modern, well lit by windows right along one wall. It had fitted carpet, wall to wall.

Breech decided that this was the retirement office he had been looking for, and he negotiated a modest commercial rent for it with Ford. He made it his headquarters for the best part of twenty-eight years – and he did not spend his time there drawing up membership lists for the country club. In March 1961, Ernest R. Breech was made a director of Trans World Airlines, and in April that year he was elected chairman of the TWA board, charged with the job of disentangling the airline from the clutches of Howard Hughes – the second time that Breech had been called on to save a major privately held company from a shambles.

Ernie Breech remained chairman of TWA for the rest of the decade, finally retiring in 1969, and throughout these years he maintained his office on Telegraph Road.

This office was the one to which Lee Iacocca was consigned in October 1978 – a full 300 square feet of floor space, not counting the outer office of his secretary. There was some cracked linoleum in the secretary's office, and the occupants of the suite were expected to drink their coffee out of plastic cups from the vending machine. Ernie Breech did not, in fact, drink coffee, but for over twenty years the great postwar saviour of the Ford Motor Company was happy to take his lunch in the cafeteria whenever he was at the office, sitting unpretentiously alongside the several hundred blue- and white-collar workers in the building.

The office actually contained better furniture when Lee Iacocca went there than it did in Ernest Breech's day – a large, wide, modern teak desk, a three-cushioned sofa and chair, a stylish brass table lamp with cream shade, and a long, low occasional table. Not too uncomfortable really, as St Helenas go.

Ernie Breech died early in July 1978, just a few days before the sacking of Lee Iacocca, and that suggested a practical solution to Lee's request for a retirement office. He could be given the premises that Ernie had rented for over twenty years on Telegraph Road. Henry Ford II, who knew about the office but had never seen it, gave orders for the arrangements to be made, and one of the functionaries versed in the caste rankings of Monet reproductions, potted palms, and teak-covered filing cabinets made up the package he considered appropriate for an exiled president.

A few days later, the new furniture arrived – the sofa, the brass lamp, the wooden desk wide enough for a testing game of ping-pong – and it is there to this day, unused, in Lee Iacocca's Siberia. The manager of the building considers it all too grand for his own use. He makes do with a slightly smaller office, and quite a narrow, metal and formica-topped desk.

●

The enemies of Private Eye

PETER McKAY

The *Evening Standard* journalist Peter McKay once wrote for the *Eye*, but now is very much in opposition. His antipathy for the editor, Ian Hislop, is well known. Here the great journalist devotes all his skills to describing a few of *Private Eye*'s more famous enemies.

The critic Clive James, himself an *Eye* target, coined a neat description of the *Eye* as the magazine 'that sends children home crying from school'. Ingrams, and Waugh, have little truck with this view, holding that it is the behaviour of the parents which causes the distress in the first place. Waugh adds that, in any case, what is so terrible about the kiddies crying? Kiddies cry all the time. Was he to be impeded by the blubbing of brats whose parents had had rude things said about them? Besides which, an appearance in *Private Eye*, though usually derogatory, is not always considered such a bad thing. A not inconsiderable group of people wear their scars with pride, heeding the consolation of friends who point out that to be attacked in the *Eye* is to have finally arrived on the vaudeville stage that it has created out of British life.

Anthony Haden-Guest is an amusing example of this reaction. An excitable, noisy author of occasional articles for colour supplement magazines, and by no means a major figure even in the shallows of Fleet Street, his possibilities as a *Private Eye* stock character were first identified by Nigel Dempster. There followed a stream of 'Grovel' stories about Haden-Guest's extravagant behaviour at London social events, and he was nicknamed 'The Beast'.

Ingrams loved the image of Haden-Guest as a man who, according to Dempster's flights of fancy, had merely to appear in an upper-class drawing room for a social occasion to degenerate into chaos. Ingrams saw in Haden-Guest elements of Captain Foulenough, a character from the satirical writings of H. B. Morton, who wrote the 'Beachcomber' column in the *Daily Express* for nearly fifty years.

The notoriety Haden-Guest achieved through the 'Grovel' column was envied by many of his friends. Far from being debarred from social events, he became, if anything, more sought after. It is also fair to suggest that, like Denis Thatcher, to an extent he grew into the caricature of himself so lovingly created by Dempster.

But he liked to complain that he was sick and tired of being the butt of *Private Eye* jokes, and on one memorable occasion he was provided with an excellent opportunity for doing so. A team from BBC TV were filming a *Private Eye* luncheon to which Haden-Guest had been invited. At the top of his considerable voice, Haden-Guest announced: '*Private Eye* has ruined my life.' His declaration was greeted by one and all, and eventually even by himself, with loud and prolonged laughter.

In time he moved to New York, where he also developed a lively reputation on the social scene. But he always kept in touch with Dempster, his old tormentor. One night he joined Dempster, myself and the then *Daily Express* New York correspondent Brian Vine at a smart Manhattan restaurant, where he symbolically punished 'Grovel' for the past indiscretions.

Before the aghast eyes of American diners, he threw Dempster over his knee and spanked Nigel to the accompaniment of Brian Vine cracking a spoon on the neck of a champagne bottle. Later they danced together. Few *Private Eye* victims have been able to exact their revenge in so direct a fashion, far less bury their enmity on the dance floor immediately afterwards.

Ingrams is insulated from most of his enemies because he is not a social man. He returns each evening of the on week to Aldworth. On the rare occasions when he stays up in town – at his mother's home in Chelsea – it is usually to go to a concert with Paul Foot. He has never been part of any London dinner-party circuit. Nor is he usually invited to society occasions where he might meet those he attacks.

But in 1986 he was photographed at a Foyle's literary luncheon with the Archbishop of Canterbury, Robert Runcie, a frequent *Eye* target whom Ingrams considers 'useless' because 'he never says what he means'. The Archbishop's wife, Rosalind Runcie, says of *Private Eye*:

> I used to be amused by *Private Eye* and laughed and laughed at one particular picture, and then laughed again when I thought about it. But the magazine has stopped being funny now. It hasn't damaged us because we don't really take any notice of it – though I was intrigued by the fact that Auberon Waugh kept writing about me, about

coming to see me, inviting me out to meals and so on. To be fair he always said I'd refused his invitations. But I have never spoken to him in my life, and I thought: 'Why does he keep writing this about me?' That puzzled me.

One annual event at which he is always exposed to enemies is the *Spectator* magazine's summer party. Here, Ingrams deploys a kind of reverse snobbery, and boasts about the prominent men and women who have cut him dead. Of course, he is a star at such occasions. Ingrams has what an aristocratic Scottish friend of mine defines as a 'difficult-to-know' charisma. He makes no effort to approach anyone. If someone he has not been introduced to approaches him he is bleak to the point of rudeness, especially if it is evident that they have been drinking.

Feuds with *Private Eye*, and Ingrams, are usually for all time; in Fleet Street that is rarely the case. Jocelyn Stevens feuded with the *Eye* and Ingrams for years. At one time we were colleagues on the *Daily Express*, and some tactful soul asked Jocelyn if it was right and proper that we should be seen together. Stevens replied that it was fine by him. He made so many new enemies that from time to time he had to make room for them in his demonology by reprieving old ones.

Ingrams has reached an enviable position as editor of *Private Eye*. Malcolm Muggeridge has cited it as the chief reason for being a journalist: 'You don't have to like any one.' Ingrams also delighted in an old Enoch Powell maxim: 'If you are against everything, sooner or later you will be proved right.'

An indication of how little some people mind about being teased in *Private Eye* is given by the fact that many of them are eager to meet Ingrams and the *Eye* staff. Erin Pizzey (the 'Chiswick Lard Mountain' who gave her first husband such a mauling in the divorce courts that he might have qualified for a place in a battered husbands' hostel, had such a place existed) was once invited by Auberon Waugh to an *Eye* lunch with her second husband. Clearly the memory of the *Eye* reports on the case had faded. There was only one problem: Ingrams had not been consulted, and he did not approve. Before the lunch began he changed around the placement cards so that Bron had to sit at one end of the long table with the Pizzeys, while Ingrams sat at the other end and ignored the guests throughout the meal. He chuckled afterwards about Waugh's fury.

Some *Eye* enemies come in pairs. The Shrimsley brothers are one example. The journalist Alan Brien had been an *Eye* stalwart in the 1960s, but when in 1973 he became the third husband of feminist writer Jill Tweedie, and wrote a book about women's breasts, he was teased regularly. In time, Brien and Tweedie faded from the *Eye* gallery of stock joke characters. Ms Tweedie says now: 'I think I regard *Private Eye* really as a species of spider. You know, it's very interesting and one looks at it, but with a certain repulsion. At the beginning I used to be a bit hurt by it. Later on I found I was rather hurt when they left me out.'

Desmond Wilcox and Esther Rantzen effortlessly became the *Eye*'s most hated couple. Rantzen began her TV career as an assistant to Bernard Braden, an original shareholder in the *Eye*. Soon, Braden was sacked by the BBC and replaced by Rantzen. Wilcox left his wife Patsy to move in with Rantzen, and later he married her. *Private Eye* drew attention to their activities, in particular the perks Miss Rantzen enjoyed in her new job, and the royalties Wilcox earned from books taken in part from transcripts of programmes he worked on.

There were good reasons for highlighting the careers of Rantzen and Wilcox inside a public corporation. But there was also a puritanical element in Ingrams' campaign against them. As far as he was concerned, Esther Rantzen had broken up a marriage, and Wilcox was a pathetic middle-aged man who had ditched his wife for a young floozie.

But Ingrams was no more consistent in this respect than he is in many others. His best friend Paul Foot had married twice, although he got around this in *Who's Who* by stating simply that he was married and had three sons. Booker has married three times, and was equally coy when it came to filling in the *Who's*

Who forms. Ingrams noted the omissions and saw them as hypocrisy, but it did not affect his friendship with them.

Another sure way onto the Ingrams hit list is to call *Private Eye* names. *Daily Mail* editor Sir David English confirmed his permanent position in this select group by referring to an *Eye* article about his paper as 'a festering lie'. Years later, long after even the most devout readers would have forgotten the original row, he was referred to as 'Sir David Fester'.

English has never sued *Private Eye* for any of its attacks, but he has used his newspaper, when appropriate, to hit back. In 1986, after Tory backbencher Sir Frederic Bennett had won £25,000 in damages from the *Eye*, the *Daily Mail* ran a prominent story next day headlined 'Tory knight named as *Private Eye's* "mole" in MP's libel action'. The article was effusively flattering about Sir Frederic and his travails with the 'scurrilous' magazine. The information on Sir Frederic had been supplied to the *Eye* anonymously by Sir Richard Body, a fellow Tory MP and formerly 'Old Muckspreader'. The *Mail* commented: 'The magazine has a dubious reputation for "shopping" its contacts and contributors when the legal going has got rough.' This was seen by Ingrams as a reference to the case of Cecil Parkinson and Nigel Dempster, and he angrily wrote an account of that case in the next issue, putting the blame firmly on Dempster.

But the *Private Eye*–English feud dated back to a far more intriguing skirmish which involved the Queen. During the Yorkshire Ripper case the *Eye* reported that *Mail* executives were entertaining members of the Ripper's family in the north while preparing a background report on the case; the *Eye* suggested that the *Mail* men had promised to pay large sums of money for the exclusive cooperation of the Ripper's family. The mother of one of the girls murdered by the Ripper then wrote to the Queen drawing attention to the *Eye* story, and received a sympathetic reply. This made the front page of several newspapers. The *Mail* responded with a huge article, masterminded by Sir David English, entitled 'Anatomy of a

Festering Lie'. The *Eye* story, supplied by a local freelance journalist who had witnessed the *Mail* men in action, was partly true. The *Mail* did not pay out a huge sum, but it did entertain relatives, and had paid money for exclusive information.

Sir David English and Ingrams could never have been friends, but their attitudes and methods often seemed similar: both enjoyed a kind of tyranny over their employees; both delighted in gossip and mischief; both were puritanical – in his middle age English joined Ingrams in disapproving strongly of adultery, and he too became religious. Both were also obsessional, and their papers often reflected their obsessions. Ingrams battered away at enemies long after they had sunk over the horizon; so did English whose *bête noir* was the 'rival' (the *Mail* always put quote marks around the word) *Daily Express*. I was often reminded of Captain Ahab and his pursuit of Moby Dick by English's eternal quest to harpoon the great, ageing beast which lay on the other side of *Fleet Street*. No matter what depths it plumbed to evade his spear, the *Mail*, with English on the bridge, would follow. Executives who left or were pitched overboard by the *Express* were picked up by English and grilled about their knowledge of the beast's workings.

But English was a canny realist as far as the *Eye* was concerned. He could live with it, and even profit by it. For years he turned a blind eye to Dempster's activities as 'Grovel' because the 'rival' *Daily Express* management was often a prime target of the column. He chortled at the *Eye*'s *Express* nicknames – the *Getsworse*, the *Getsmuchworse* and, for a short time, the *Daily Tits-by-Christmas*.

English is certainly a doughty opponent, especially when one considers the vast gulf that separates a newspaper like the *Mail* from *Private Eye*. Ingrams has never cared much about reader reaction, and certainly he has never refrained from publishing repeated attacks and endless jokes about public figures for fear of producing the counter-productive effect of enlisting sympathy for the victim. A joke only becomes boring when he decides it is – though to be fair he has usually been content to allow readers to express their tedium in the letters pages. English cannot allow himself the luxury of this point of view, and would be hard put to maintain a permanent campaign against the *Eye* in the pages of the *Daily Mail*.

•

A special loathing: Mary McCarthy and Lillian Hellman

WILLIAM WRIGHT

The American novelist and critic Mary McCarthy was a contemporary of the playwright Lillian Hellman. Hellman's biographer William Wright explains how a long and bitter feud between the two foremost women of American letters reached the stage of litigation.

Hellman was alone in her apartment watching 'The Dick Cavett Show' in January 1980 when she heard Mary McCarthy proclaim her a liar to the American public. When the show was over, she telephoned John Hersey whom Hellman felt McCarthy had also slandered ('He trivialized Hiroshima'). 'Well, John,' Hellman said, 'are we going to sue?' The idea had not occurred to Hersey and he urged Hellman to forget about it. She refused.

Of all the writers who accused Hellman of dishonesty, curiously the only such attacker she chose to battle with legal action was Mary McCarthy. McCarthy was important enough, but she had delivered so many such roundhouse slams throughout her career, particularly as the theater critic for *Partisan Review*, that her invective was often taken as hyperbole. A typical example, which happened to contain a left-handed compliment to Hellman, was in a 1946 review of Eugene O'Neill's *The Iceman Cometh*. McCarthy wrote: 'After the oily virtuosity of George S. Kaufman, Lillian Hellman, Odets, Saroyan, the return of a playwright who – to be frank – cannot write is a solemn and sentimental occasion.' Oily or not, by opposing her to the disabled O'Neill, McCarthy implied that Hellman *could* write.

Dick Cavett was undoubtedly aware of McCarthy's history as a giant-killer, and was surely prodding her to do her stuff when he asked her if there were American writers who she felt were overrated. It was akin to asking J. Edgar Hoover if he felt America had any subversives. Cavett was ensuring that the next quarter hour of air time would be filled, and in all likelihood with the sort of literary gore that was McCarthy's specialty. She snapped at the bait and started her catalogue of the undeserving. When she came to Hellman's name, Cavett expressed surprise. And here again he may have been exercising his interviewer's right to incite a guest to mayhem, although he later said he had questioned the Hellman inclusion only because of his admiration for her.

McCarthy was ready with amplification. Hellman, she said, was 'a bad writer, overrated, a dishonest writer'.

Cavett asked what was dishonest about her. 'Everything,' McCarthy replied. 'I once said in an interview that every word she writes is a lie, including "and" and "the."'

When Cavett, who knew Hellman and had had her on his show in the past, got wind of her rage and her plans to sue, he phoned and invited her to come on his show to answer McCarthy's charges. Hellman angrily declined; she would look foolish, she said, going on national television to claim she was not a liar. Instead she proceeded with a defamation suit against Mary McCarthy for $2,225,000, naming Cavett and Channel Thirteen, the PBS affiliate, as co-defendants. McCarthy's statement, according to the complaint, was 'false, made with ill-will, with malice, with knowledge of its falsity, with careless disregard of its truth, and with the intent to injure the plaintiff personally and professionally'. McCarthy was staying in a London hotel when she received a phone call from Herbert Mitgang in New York informing her that Hellman was suing her. McCarthy started laughing. When Mitgang told her the amount, McCarthy, who was not rich, laughed even harder.

The lawsuit was widely covered in the press and immediately became a *cause célèbre* in the literary world. Many of the reports cited animosity between the two women that stemmed from political differences during the Spanish civil war. Hellman expressed surprise that McCarthy would attack her so vehemently since she 'hadn't seen her in ten years and . . . never wrote anything about her'. McCarthy concurred that they hardly knew each other; her judgment, she said, was based primarily on reading Miss Hellman's memoirs.

The careers of the two writers, which paralleled each other chronologically, illustrated the different levels of literary success in America. McCarthy, while six years younger than Hellman, emerged in the late thirties as a bright ornament of the *Partisan Review* crowd, the most formidable of New York's intellectual street gangs. She was brilliant, good-looking and the lover of the magazine's co-editor, the legendary Philip Rahv. Like all in those circles, McCarthy was fiercely political and militantly radical, but was one of the first wave of that group to lose faith in communism.

In a short story of McCarthy's called *The Perfect Host*, published in a book of her short stories called *The Company She Keeps*, she described a run-in with a group of Stalinists at a New York dinner party. The woman at her semifictional table, McCarthy dimly recalls, was based on Hellman. The party was destroyed when McCarthy denounced 'Hellman' and the others for being unpaid agents of the Soviet spy network. The impression was created that this was just another 1930s New York brainy set dinner party, but forty-five years later the denunciations still flew – including the suggestion, made by McCarthy in 1985, that Hellman had been an operative for the KGB.

While McCarthy came to have misgivings about the Loyalist leadership during the Spanish civil war, as did George Orwell and a number of other liberals, that position was neither far enough from Hellman's, nor indeed so unusual, as to launch a lifelong blood feud. Their political enmity became more pronounced at the time of the 1949 Waldorf Conference, which

Hellman so prominently supported and which Mary McCarthy so vigorously denounced as a communist propaganda extravaganza.

McCarthy, however, had many such political enemies for whom she did not bear the special loathing she had for Hellman. There was undoubtedly some jealousy. Despite a number of highly praised novels, McCarthy had never enjoyed Hellman's broad commercial success, nor had she received so many honors and awards or received a standing ovation in Hollywood. Her one best-selling novel, *The Group*, was thought by many (including McCarthy) to represent a lapse of standards. Although she was in many people's eyes a better writer than Hellman – and certainly prettier – she had not approached Hellman's level of fame or popularity. The basic difference seemed to be that McCarthy was a highbrow who had unsuccessfully flirted with middlebrow culture, while Hellman was a middlebrow who had made inroads into the highbrow world.

McCarthy, naturally, denied any personal animus toward Hellman and claimed she simply disapproved strongly of her writing and her character as viewed from an impersonal distance. But she admitted to some disagreeable encounters. In 1948, when Stephen Spender was conducting a seminar at Sarah Lawrence, he asked his students to name two female writers they would like to meet. They named Hellman and McCarthy. McCarthy arrived while Hellman was addressing the class and stood in the rear; she thinks Hellman mistook her for a student. When she heard Hellman tell the young women that John Dos Passos had abandoned the Spanish Loyalists because he didn't like the food in Spain, she became incensed. Dos Passos, by most accounts, had complex reasons for losing faith in the Loyalists and had struggled with his decision. 'She was just brainwashing those girls,' McCarthy said. 'It was really vicious. So finally I spoke up and said, "I'll tell you why he broke with the Loyalists, you'll find it in his novel, *The Adventures of a Young Man*, and it wasn't such a clean break." [Hellman] started to tremble . . . it was a very dramatic moment of somebody being caught red-handed.'

Stephen Spender also recalled the encounter but added an interesting footnote on Hellman: 'Of course, being Lillian, she imagined we had invited her worst enemy, Mary McCarthy, as her fellow guest, out of malice.' If Spender's recollection was correct, it would appear that Hellman was on record as detesting McCarthy thirty years before hostilities erupted on national television. And McCarthy had more than impersonal reasons for her dislike for Hellman.

McCarthy's plan for her defense against Hellman's suit was to take the position that any statements she had made on the television show were presented as opinions, not facts. She was asked by Hellman's lawyers to list every example of Hellman's dishonesty. McCarthy declined on the grounds that such a search would be too difficult and her files were at her house in Paris. Instead she offered some examples of what she called Hellman's 'intellectual dishonesty.'

1. Her representation of herself as the first to refuse to name names before HUAC.

2. Presenting James Wechsler as a friendly HUAC witness when, in McCarthy's view, he had been hostile.

3. Hellman's claim to have been unaware of the purge trials during her visit to Russia in 1937, when the trials had been going on for two years.

4. The impression she creates in *Scoundrel Time* that the only fault in her Stalinism was a passive failure of understanding of the Soviet regime, never giving readers a hint of how actively she supported it.

5. The unbelievability of 'Julia'.

McCarthy also presented a list of people to whom she felt Hellman had been deliberately unfair and who were no longer alive to answer her 'intemperate charges': Henry Wallace, Ernest Hemingway, Errol Flynn, Clifford Odets, Morris Ernst, Lucile Watson, Tallulah Bankhead and Alan Campbell. Whatever the merit of McCarthy's sampler, both in terms of the suit and in terms of Hellman's overall honesty, Hellman seemed to think she was on firm ground in denying she was a liar. About this time she telephoned Joe Rauh on another matter, and in the course of the conversation she brought up her libel action.

'Did you hear about my suit?'

Rauh said that he had.

'What do you think?'

'Lillian, I think it's a big mistake.'

A pause – then, in a deeper tone, 'Why?'

Rauh recognized the fighting mode, but took a deep breath and forged ahead. 'Lillian, every one of us has told a fib now and then. If this ever got to court, they could bring up every word you ever wrote or said and examine it for its truthfulness. Do you really want that?'

Hellman became furious; after a number of heated words, she ended the conversation in anger. Perhaps in Hellman's mind she *was* a totally truthful person who had nothing to fear by pursuing the suit. That does not rule out the possibility that she lied as a matter of course; such self-deception has occurred in others as intelligent as she, and who placed as much importance on personal probity. But she may also have had another motive in pursuing the litigations. McCarthy's lawyer, Ben O'Sullivan, heard that Hellman intended to push the case to trial – it would possibly take a matter of years because of numerous complexities – then drop it. Hellman was now rich, McCarthy was not. Defending a legal action is expensive. Others began to suspect that Hellman was extracting her revenge by the mere act of draining McCarthy's assets with prolonged lawyers' costs.

The literary world at first welcomed the dispute between the two women as a refreshing change from the outworn political and artistic arguments that no one much cared about anymore. And while the putative origin of the scrap was a most worked over and venerable issue – pro- and anti-Stalinism – the public slugfest of two such distinguished ladies had an exhilaratingly rowdy air about it. In their world, the traditional method of settling old scores – the one Hellman had adopted – was to sprinkle cutting asides throughout a memoir. McCarthy had done what she censured Hellman for not doing: making her accusation while the accused, Hellman, was still around to refute it.

Bystanders watching the battle soon began to speak up. Many people saw serious questions of free speech in the lawsuit and felt Hellman had sacrificed any claim to being a civil libertarian. Robert Kraus, writing on the subject for *Harper's*, subtitled his article: 'If you can't call Lillian Hellman a liar on TV, what's the First Amendment all about?' A number of articles appeared on the controversy, and papers like the *Washington Post* and the *Boston Globe* wrote editorials about it. Some were angry, others compassionate, but almost without exception the commentators felt Hellman was wrong to have initiated legal action. Some suggested that she was trying to use her money and the law to clobber a critic into silence, others felt that McCarthy's statement was a literary judgment which the courts were not competent to adjudicate, and still others saw the whole thing as a no-win situation for Hellman and an undeserved hardship for Mc-Carthy.

The New York Times ran an article that presented a collection of brief opinions of the litigation from a number of writers. It mentioned that Norman Mailer had declined comment. A month later, he leaped in with an open appeal in *The Sunday Times Magazine* addressed to both women, for whom he claimed admiration and affection. Heroically, Mailer tried to haul the argument to the mountaintop with the grandiose claim that 'no writer worthy of serious consideration is ever honest except for those rare moments – for which we keep writing – when we become, bless us, not dishonest for an instant.'

While many writers rubbed their eyes, others saw it as a gallant effort to declare both women right. But even if one could accept Mailer's shift of the issue from truth as opposed to falsehood to the loftier matter of artistic truth, he was still missing, perhaps choosing to miss, a glaring difference between not writing the truth, which suggests a failed effort at the truth, and writing lies, which means a deliberate effort to deceive. McCarthy's response to the lawyers' interrogatory had made it clear she was not talking about shooting for the truth and missing – she was talking about a conscious attempt to deceive.

For his pains, Mailer suffered the fate of many peacemakers. Hellman's literary hit man, Richard Poirier, wrote a letter to the *Times* editors denouncing Mailer's stand. Mailer wrote a letter denouncing Poirier that went to Hellman and a few other people. In return he received a letter from Hellman calling off their friendship . . .

•

Bad times

HAROLD EVANS

Harold Evans was editor of *The Sunday Times* for fourteen years and established the 'Insight' style of journalism, which uncovered the Kim Philby scandal diaries and focused worldwide attention on the plight of the Thalidomide victims. Evans described himself as an old-fashioned director, hating the thought that an editor should have to reflect the personal whims and ambitions of a newspaper's proprietor. This had worked well when Times Newspapers had been owned by the Thomson Organization. But in 1981 Australian media tycoon Rupert Murdoch, a more 'hands-on' proprietor than Lord Thomson, bought Times Newspapers and appointed Evans as editor of *The Times*. Evans insisted on guarantees of editorial freedom, but after one turbulent year, Evans resigned and Charles Douglas-Home, Evans's own deputy, was appointed editor in his place. Here he describes how a feud with Murdoch came to a head.

Douglas-Home's behaviour was disturbing because it was in such contrast to the first nine months. It was as if in amateur dramatics he had grown tired of playing the loyal adjutant and was now backstage trying on the insurrectionary's wardrobe. 'I have countermanded your instruction,' he announced on the telephone one evening, when all he meant was that he had changed a photograph I had chosen. He baffled subordinates with remarks meant to be vaguely critical, such as that the editor was too receptive to ideas. It was all done with such lethargic charm that I did not take it seriously. Still, I invited him home to see if there was any misunderstanding between us. He was as affable as ever. He had no grievances or comments on the paper; I would have been surprised if he had, since he had been back in the office only a few days after his sabbatical. We chatted for a while and, lying on the sofa, he suddenly volunteered: 'I don't want your job, you know, Harry. I couldn't do it.'

It had never occurred to me that he could; nor had I envisaged any vacancy in the editorship. 'I would never work for that monster Murdoch,' he added.

I had not mentioned Murdoch or asked Douglas-Home for any such assurances. I knew that my resistances to Murdoch were hazardous as well as disagreeable, but I told myself I was protected by my record at *The Times* as well as by the national directors. When I returned the following day to an office gripped by fear as the days of the closure ultimatum ticked away, Adrian Hamilton told me of Murdoch's newsroom backbiting. 'Well, at least,' he said, 'you're safe from being sacked. He can't do that because he has no grounds.'

Douglas-Home, who was always curious about Murdoch, was meanwhile volunteering the unsolicited advice that I should forget about him. Then four days after my return he told the economics editor, David Blake, who had an editorial suggestion for me: 'Don't bother with him. He's finished.'

I heard of this at home, so I telephoned Douglas-Home and invited him to elaborate. 'Yes, let's face it, you *are* finished,' he said equably. 'You are not getting on with the proprietor.'

When I put it to him face to face that the proprietor was the man we had both agreed to hold to his guarantees, he repeated that he did not wish to be editor: 'Murdoch is a monster.' I told him, furthermore, that I had myself protected him from Murdoch's criticism of his skill as a journalist. Donoughue, one of the wariest of men, came to see me later: 'Charlie's all right. I've just been talking to him. He says that Murdoch is a monster.'

Over a depressed evening meal with Tina, I explained grandly to her that it was a very stressful time for us all and Murdoch made people jumpy. I called on Rees-Mogg at his home in Smith Square: 'Can I trust Charlie?' I asked him. 'Of course,' he replied. 'Charlie won't let you down.'

It was, of course, true that I was not getting on with the proprietor. I was not a petty barrack-room lawyer looking up every sub-clause of the guarantees. There had to be a rough flexibility. However, the freedom of the staff from direct political pressure, the independence of the foreign service, the freedom within a budget and the allocation of space were all vital rights. Douglas-Home took a more relaxed view. 'It doesn't amount to a *casus belli*,' he said, shrugging his shoulders. I could not then understand how on the one hand he seemed genuinely to regard Murdoch as a wrecker of institutions and yet on the other could not grasp the nature of the threat. I could not 'rub along', as he suggested, on essential freedoms. I did not enjoy offending Murdoch. It was a personal strain and it also carried the risk of alienating him altogether from *The Times*. It was unrealistic to think I could cut him out of the paper altogether. 'If I am to be treated like an outsider, I'll start behaving like one,' he had said over that holiday fracas. I felt that the only sensible course was to make him feel part of the paper, while politely and firmly fending him off from editorial decisions. Surely, when the union confrontation was over, we would begin a new chapter. But one had already opened that second week of February. It was a campaign and it was against me.

The first intimation I had had of it was a telephone call from William Hickey, the *Daily Express* diarist, while I was ill. Was I leaving *The Times*? I said, 'No.' I presumed they had heard something of an offer I had received to go into television; such was my naïvety, it did not occur to me they were exploring the possibility of my ejection from *The Times*. That happy complacency was broken on Wednesday 10 February when *The Guardian* carried a report that the Holdings board had inconclusively discussed my dismissal, and there was something similar in *Private Eye*. I called Eric Roll [national director, Times Newspapers] at once. He was about to leave on a European trip. The *Guardian* report, he said, was not correct, but he needed more time than he had to explain the background. (I learned later that this was a leak to Hugh Stephenson on the *New Statesman* from Dacre.) Could we talk, he asked, when he was back at the end of the following week? I called Peter Roberts of *The Sunday Times*, the only staff man on the Holdings board, since Murdoch had not filled the vacancy created by Heren's [*Times* deputy editor] departure. Roberts was as surprised by the *Guardian* story as I was. There had been no board discussion at all. I called Murdoch at the New York *Post*. I was told, after some delay, that he was not around, but, when I went upstairs to have it out with Long [managing editor, Times Newspapers], his secretary delayed me at his door: 'Mr Long is engaged; he's speaking to the chairman.' I waited. Long seemed to be purring with pleasure in the fifteen minutes of our interview which followed.

'I must have an explanation of this *Guardian* story,' I said. 'Were you present at that meeting?'

'It's not correct. It was just a lunch. You know how Rupert is, always probing. He only raised the question whether he had the right editor for *The Times*.'

'But what's the criticism?'

'Oh, Rupert wants you to put your thumbprint on the paper.' He stroked his moustache. 'Hasn't he told you that, Harry? He's always saying he wants to see an editor's thumbprint on a news-paper.'

'And the others?'

'Well, Pickering wondered if there was a featureish element in the news columns, that's all. Rupert's a remarkable man, you know. Not many people can stand up to the force of his personality.'

I insisted on a statement that day. I said I was prepared to fly to New York to get it. Twenty minutes later Long called me back to his office and asked if I would be happy with the following statement he and Murdoch had drafted which would be issued immediately: 'Reports in competitive newspapers that Harold Evans is about to be replaced as editor of *The Times* are malicious, self-serving and wrong. Mr Evans's outstanding qualities and journalistic skills are recognized throughout the world, as are his improvements to *The Times* over the past twelve months.'

The statement went out, but the rumours were another turn of the screw in the tensions of the office. Two days later they exploded when it was discovered that Murdoch, who was threatening to put the company in the hands of the official receiver, had removed the titles from Times Newspapers and into his News International company. It plunged me into a new distracting confrontation with Murdoch and Long, and it completed the process of demoralization of the staff. More than forty of them were threatened with redundancy, all of them were working under the threat that in seven days there might be a closure, and now there was the prospect that, if this happened, the titles would not be available for a new ownership. *The Times* would go into a commercial coma. There would be no compensation for anyone. We had been so recently back at work after the year's suspension it was all too much. This was the background against which I continued to fight my private battle; and also to explore new ownership for *The Times* should Murdoch shut down.

There was, despite the statement, no relief from harassment. Reports came back to me of Murdoch unflinchingly exposing his right-wing views of the paper to journalists like Colin Welch (a writer I admire) and Andrew Alexander, the entertaining Poujadist of the *Daily Mail*, who was invited to see Murdoch after an interview for an article whose suffocating sycophancy finally broke surface in a New York magazine. Murdoch was pointedly not talking to me in mid-February. Then, in the third week, on his return to London for the final show-down with the unions, he became, for him, a prolific writer of memos. I received a 'Dear Harry – Yours sincerely, Rupert' letter pressing me again on political policy. He wrapped it up, but Brian Horton made it clear it was the message of the autumn and New Year about party politics. He had been in New York with my agreement, seeing what he could do for Murdoch's News bureau, and, when he came back, he was pleased to reveal his closeness to Murdoch.

'I had some chats with Rupert. He's getting in a mess fighting on all fronts at once. I said, "Look, Rupert, one battle at a time. Don't go banging on about Harry and the SDP. Leave that until you've beaten the print unions."'

I asked Horton later to expound a bit on Rupert and the SDP. He thought better of it. He could not remember talking about the SDP.

Murdoch's way of putting it was in a memo: 'My chief area of concern about the paper is one I have raised with you several times: the paper's stand on major issues. Of course it takes attitudes, but I fail to find any consistency in them, anything that indicates the clear position of conscience that a great newspaper must be seen to hold. Just what that position is, it is your duty to define, and it cannot be defined. But it must be defined with clarity and authority and even repetition.'

I replied formally:

Dear Chairman,

    I note what you say about clear policies for *The Times*. I am not accustomed to being accused of lacking a conscience, rather the contrary. You have not, as it happens, made this criticism on several occasions to me but only once (7 January 1982), though I have been made aware of what you have said to other members of the staff when I have not been present.

I would contend that *The Times* has given consistently clear leadership on a number of central if contentious issues.

Allied unity in the *defence* area (Trident being a particular); Western cooperation in the economic area, especially to stabilise *currencies* and prepare the way for new economic growth, an original view on which we have led opinion internationally.

Consistent support for the Government's approach to *pay*, especially in the public sector, which the Chancellor has acknowledged was crucial in winning the civil service pay battle.

Campaigning to improve the *banking* and financial support for industry and for competition in banking as in industry. (We gave the clearest lead of all the British press over the Royal Bank of Scotland and we did get the legislation against foreign banking stopped.)

Specific reform on the *trade unions*.

Campaigning for *free trade* against protection.

Consistent opposition to *Marxist infiltration* of British politics and industry.

Support for President Reagan in his ultimately strong response to *the Polish crisis*, and a concerted effort to revitalise Allied unity.

Running through these and other editorials is a continuous concern for the individual and for the values of free societies, independent of party and vested interest. Interestingly, you will recall that the *New York Times* feature on the new *Times* particularly picked out the improved strength and clarity of the editorials. Would it not be better to discuss such matters?

But of course, while being consistent in our editorial position, we have deliberately opened the paper to a diversity of views in the belief that truth will triumph and that our readers, especially, want a fully informed debate rather than a monolithic line of propaganda.

He was not looking for debate. He was looking for weapons. His next complaint was that the 22 February report by the *Times* labour reporter, David Felton, on the Times Newspapers crisis 'contained at least eleven errors of fact'. I asked Arthur Brittenden, the publicity officer luxuriating under the title director of corporate relations, to identify the eleven errors. He could not. It came down to one denial of a statement by a trade union leader that Murdoch had told them his companies would be in trouble with the banks if he did not get the 600 job cuts he wanted in the five days left of his ultimatum. Even this was repeated by Owen O'Brien, the NATSOPA leader, on 2 March, when he said on *Panorama*: 'He told us that he was bleeding to death; that he was under pressure from his bankers to put matters right.'

Murdoch had better luck with another line. The fact that *The Times* was on the brink of closing again meant it was a subject for journalism of sorts. Louis Heren, asked to comment on BBC's *Newsnight*, chose not to discuss the crisis but to suggest he had been elbowed out of *The Times* and the paper was going downhill. I allowed myself to be irritated by Heren and an article in the *Spectator* by an old *Private Eye* adversary, Patrick Marnham, which lamented the departure of three journalists, Roger Berthoud, Marcel Berlins and Peter Hennessy. (The first two of them were among the eight who had taken the opportunity for redundancy money.) I should have kept on ignoring the harassment. I did publicly, but in my second six-monthly private report to Murdoch I let off steam, describing it all as a manifestation of old-guard reaction, and he saw the chink of vulnerability for which he is always alert. His note of 22 February said: 'You know that I have been concerned about the fluctuations in the *Times* staff of journalists that had so much attention recently. I am frankly disturbed by the decision of Messrs Hennessy, Berthoud and Berlins to leave you.'

This came at the time Murdoch and Long were harrying me for a cut of no fewer than forty-three in the number of journalists. It was a close question whether it could be done without grave damage to the paper. (Douglas-Home, finally agreeing with me that Grant was not up to the task, was reviewing staff in every department for me.) I had only just shot down Long for raising with the journalists' chapel the question of *The Times* maintaining its own staff to report parliament, instead of using the Press Association, which did not maintain full cover. I replied to Murdoch: 'Your main message to me on staff was originally to hire talent to renew the paper. Lately it has been to get staff numbers down urgently. All the new recruits have settled down well. I cannot understand, therefore, why you should say you are concerned about the fluctuations in the staff. They are an inevitable consequence of what you encouraged and what indeed was required.'

Murdoch had no personal knowledge of the three men or their work, any more than he would have of the forty other *Times* journalists he wanted me to lose, though he successfully pumped the sale-room correspondent, Geraldine Norman . . . I wondered where the next attack was coming from. There was a whispering campaign about Evans profligately exceeding his budget, taking on too many journalists, losing too much advertising revenue, having no policies, and morale being bad at *The Times*, etc. A man with the art of second sight, as Swift wrote, might have admirably entertained himself round town by observing the different shapes, sizes and colours of the swarm of lies which buzzed about the heads of some people like flies about a horse's ears in summer. I ignored them and immersed myself in the paper: a meeting I had with Oriana Fallaci on the night Reagan was shot bore fruit in two interviews with Poland's Deputy Premier, Mieczyslaw Rakowski, which Douglas-Home declared the best thing the paper had ever published. I sorted out the legal and editorial problems of a multimillion banking fraud which I had first heard about when prone on a physiotherapist's couch and had asked Stewart Tendler to investigate. I superintended the new sports pages. But I was not to be left alone. One of the larger lies of the period came at me from BBC Television.

It was incubated in an otherwise excellent *Panorama* report on Times Newspapers. The programme was triggered by Murdoch's ultimatum to the print unions, but extended to editorial matters. Elwyn Parry-Jones said that in more than ten years' reporting the affairs of Fleet Street for the BBC he had never before come across such an atmosphere of suspicion and fear. 'Among those who work here are some of Britain's most eminent journalists, dedicated seekers after truth, protagonists of the public's right to know, yet none will reveal in public the accusations they make to me in private. Off the record they talk about editorial interference by Rupert Murdoch, of managerial incompetence and rock-bottom morale among the journalists.' *Panorama* did have critical interviews with three *Sunday Times* journalists – Phil Jacobson, Peter Lennon and Tony Dawe – all of them at or past the point of departure from the paper. Then he went on to *The Times*. 'Harold Evans has been Rupert Murdoch's first editor of *The Times* and clearly he has his fans ... but he has been in conflict with his management and there's evidence of direct interference by Rupert Murdoch in his editorial control of *The Times*.'

Pictures of two pages of an earlier *Times* were shown. They featured artist's sketches of the faces of Libyan terrorists supposedly sent to shoot President Reagan. I remembered the pages well. Jones commented: 'On 11 December *The Times* carried this story about a Libyan hit squad on an inside page. But after a phone call from Rupert Murdoch in America the story was promoted to the front page. It's this sort of interference that people feared.'

The lying insect itself was trivial and contemptible, but the sting was poisonous. It damaged my credibility and my authority, and it was bound further to depress the staff. Somebody else was watching the programme and had the same reaction as I did. It was Brian MacArthur, the new deputy editor of *The Sunday Times*, who sent me a copy of a letter he wrote the next day to Elwyn Parry-Jones to say they had it wrong:

At that time I was executive editor of *The Times* and on
that night I was running the back bench. Earlier that
evening I had chosen the identikit pictures of the suspected
Libyan hit squad for a foreign page. When Harold Evans
saw the page at about 9.15 p.m., he immediately suggested,
in his usual style, that this was (a) a marvellous story and
(b) a marvellous picture, and that it should go on the front
page. This was done for our second edition, which has to
be ready and off the stone at 10.45 p.m. There was a call to
the office from Rupert Murdoch that night. It came to me
first and was then put through to Harold Evans. It should
be noted, however, that the call came about two hours
after the decision to change the position of the story had
been made.

This was entirely correct, if unavoidably incomplete. Murdoch
was not in America as *Panorama* said. At the time he was,
according to *Panorama*, telling me what to do, he was in
Concorde on his way to London. He flew in to join a group of
Times staff on the morning of 11 December for a visit and
private talk I had arranged with the US Defence Secretary,
Caspar Weinberger. The first and only time he came on the
phone that evening was after he had received the first edition of
the paper at his home at Eaton Place and it would not have got
there earlier than 10.45 p.m.

The *Panorama* lie, which went uncorrected, came from within
the editorial department of *The Times*, but it was endemic in
Murdoch's way of working. It thrived on the suspicion and fear
to which Parry-Jones rightly referred. It accused me of acquiesc-
ing in the very thing I was resisting.

At this critical point Douglas-Home handed me a letter:

Dear Harry,
    In the separate notes I am sending you on the exercise in
reduced manpower you will see that I have recommended
merging the home and foreign departments and putting

them under the deputy editor, saving two assistant editors. I have not done this with myself in mind since I want to apply for redundancy.

I won't go into the many reasons which have brought me to this decision and would not dream of walking out on you at this critical time. The accountant says it would be better for me to stay until the start of the new financial year in April and that would also enable you to have a holiday after this crisis is over in March.

So I would like to work about six weeks of my eighteen months' notice period and then take cash in lieu of the remaining notice along with my redundancy for seventeen years' service.

A sad but necessary decision. We had some good times together, for which thanks.

Yours sincerely,

Charlie

My eyes lingered on the final sentence: 'We had some good times together, for which thanks.' I had not imagined that our recent difficulties merited this. I asked him to withdraw his application and resignation with it. *The Times* was in turmoil with its threatened closure. We were fighting for survival. I understood how attractive a new life might be compared to the stresses of Gray's Inn Road, but this was not the time, I thought, to be rocking the boat still more. I asked him to hold his letter; Murdoch seemed close to winning his fight with the clerical union – he did – and everything might look different quite soon. If not, I would see to it that he could still take redundancy. He agreed to put his resignation on ice and not say anything to anyone. I got on with editing the newspaper.

Two days later, on the morning of a memorial service for Lady Pamela Hartwell, I was asked by Long to stay behind in his office after the executive committee meeting.

'Aren't you unhappy?' he asked, pursing his lips. 'We have been together for a year. Rupert is thinking of changes, fresh beginnings. I'll be having a change myself.'

It was my cue, I suppose, to say that I was so miserable I would like a change too. I felt not the slightest inclination to put my foot on this escalator to a vacant lot. I told him, over his raised eyebrows, that I relished editing *The Times*, but that I did not like the way I was being 'frozen out'. I knew Thatcherite politics were involved and I was not shy about arguing politics robustly. In some things, I said, to demonstrate the infinite possibility of debate, I might be to the right of Rupert Murdoch. Long looked incredulous, as well he might. Half an hour later I saw a gaunt Murdoch across the aisle in St Margaret's, Westminster. In the afternoon there was a note from him. He wrote: 'I don't see why we should be writing notes to each other when my door is always open to you. Gerry Long has told me of his talk with you this morning and we must have a serious talk as soon as we get through the present troubles.' There was a PS: 'The sports pages look terrific.'

I had decided I must consult the national directors. Two weeks previously I had written memoranda for them on the threats to *The Times*, instancing Murdoch's harassments and my lack of a budget. I held back sending them to Robens, Roll, Greene and Dacre, because I was due to see Robens at a long-arranged lunch and I thought it better to take his counsel first. With the threat now to my own position as well as to the guarantees, I invited Robens, as the leader of the original four, to come to my office. I took pleasure in showing him how we had displayed in the editorial offices the paintings of *Times* men which Long had banished from the sixth floor. I would have been glad to have Douglas-Home in on the conversation because of the challenges to *The Times*, but Robens gently took my arm in a dissuasive gesture and we went into my room. Under the benevolent gaze of Henri de Blowitz, who always had a way of eavesdropping on news, I told Robens what had been happening. 'Oh, that's his game, is it?' he said. The political pressure was news to him and we talked for a little while about politics: there was very little difference between us, not least on monetarism, as I knew from previous talks, and he had anyway an appreciation of the issue of independence. He was enormously sympathetic. He had no time for Murdoch's methods, 'the way they carry on here'. This was all uplifting, marred only for a few moments by an imperfect understanding of our constitution. Robens had not appreciated that the national directors could refuse to approve the dismissal of an editor. He was under the impression that their power was restricted to the right of approving a newly-nominated editor and hence only in a filibuster. I showed him the Articles of Association. He said that I must not let Murdoch and his men get me down. The first thing was for me to meet for dinner with all four of the original directors – 'not Pickering, mark you'.

I decided I should put the fifth national director on his mettle; a sixth had not then been appointed to take Denis Hamilton's place. Edward Pickering represented Murdoch on the board of the publishing house of Collins, which was owned 42 per cent by Murdoch. Hamilton had said at the time that the other national directors at *The Times* raised an eyebrow, but Murdoch had defended it as a journalistic charity: Pick needed the money. Pickering is not a man of vivid affections and is slow and heavy in speech, but we had always had friendly relations. He was a Middlesbrough boy who had been a sub-editor on my beloved *Northern Echo* under Reg Gray. When I came to London, we had lunch at the Garrick and he happily reminisced about those days and his less happy editorship of the *Daily Express* under Lord Beaverbrook. I met him later, after he had retired from IPC, when we were all trying to rouse the Government to resist the moves in UNESCO that would inhibit the development of a free press in the Third World.

I was surprised to find him in *The Times* a great deal after his appointment. He always seemed to be wandering around. I did not ask him what he was up to. I feared he might buttonhole me about UNESCO. He saw the dummy pages in Edwin Taylor's office during the redesign exercises the previous spring and suggested that, instead of photographs of MPs on the parliamentary page, we should have caricatures, a bright idea but also a stratagem to ruin me for ever in Hickey's eyes. Then I learned that Murdoch had given him an office. Except on one occasion, when he wondered if there were any books I could put Collins's way, he never asked to see me. But recently he had taken Douglas-Home to dinner at the Garrick and there he endorsed a definition of Murdoch's ideal editor. Douglas-Home had reported it to me with stunning casualness. 'What you are saying,' Douglas-Home said to Pickering, 'is that Murdoch wants as editor of *The Times* someone who is technically competent but politically compliant.' Pickering replied: 'That sums it up.'

When Pick came into my office, a stooping, unwrinkled man in his seventieth year with a hippodrome of a bald head, I said I'd heard he thought the news pages were too featureish. Had he anything in mind? He washed his hands loosely. 'That paper is fine, fine,' he said in his heavy voice. I hoped he would tell me directly if he had any criticisms. 'Of course, Harry.' He was uncomfortable. I put it to him straight: 'What protection can I expect from you as a national director against improper pressures?'

His big, round eyes looked at me through his big, round spectacles. He smiled faintly.

'You have to remember,' said the fifth independent national director, 'that I worked for Beaverbrook ... that's the way things are.'

●

The party faithful

JOHN RANELAGH

Margaret Thatcher was the first female Prime Minister of the UK. Thatcher replaced Edward Heath as Conservative Party leader in 1975, having previously served under him as Minister of Education. In John Ranelagh's book, *Thatcher's People*, the former Attorney

General, Peter Rawlinson, describes how Heath used to get very annoyed with her in Cabinet. 'He used to begin tapping the table, because, although she talked sense, she did talk too much. On one occasion when Thatcher, who made a practice of speaking about matters other than Education in Cabinet meetings, was thus engaged, Heath's patience snapped. Never the most receptive of men, Heath leaned forward (Thatcher was along the side of the table, out of his sight) and shouted down at her, "Shut up! Shut up!" That sort of experience leaves a lasting mark.' In this extract Ranelagh, formerly a member of the Conservative Research Department, the Party's think-tank, describes how Heath was not the only former Tory leader who came to hate Mrs Thatcher.

Edward Heath and Harold Macmillan were the two men who hated Thatcher, and the two men she played off: Heath explicitly and Macmillan implicitly. Heath was the one unsuccessful outsider that the Conservative Party has had as leader. He hated her because she did what he thought he was going to do, and he let himself down after 1975 by bluntly making his feeling public. Macmillan was less straightforward, making his view of Thatcher known in asides and jokes. The historian and television interviewer Ludovic Kennedy was once interviewing Macmillan when, after a morning's filming, they were to drive to lunch. 'Which car are we going in?' Macmillan asked. 'Are we going in Mrs Thatcher?' Seeing Kennedy's expression, he explained, 'This car makes a noise if you don't fasten your seat-belt, and a light starts flashing if you haven't closed the door. It's a *very bossy* car.' Macmillan thought that he had brought about a synthesis of Tory men and Whig measures; that he was being genuinely conservative, preserving free enterprise while ensuring that the poor prospered. But he presided over the progressive decline of British competitiveness without apparently noticing. He hated Thatcher because she effectively repudiated his record and his view of Britain, which, until she came to power, had not been seriously challenged. It never occurred to Thatcher that Britain was not one nation. She never felt the need to search for existential connections between the working class and the upper class, and she never thought that the hereditarily advantaged were distinguished. Unlike so many of her colleagues, and so many people in academia and the media, she did not regret the distinctions between the classes, and she had no romance about the working class.

The ultimately overriding feeling that unions should be appeased was buoyed by idealistic social engineers and by romance. In the thirty years after 1945, there was a general sense that the working class had borne the brunt of the killing in the First World War, of the Depression of the 1930s and of the distress of the Second World War, and deserved 'fair' treatment. This was very much Harold Macmillan's view. Public school men often seemed fearful of, or deferential to, the working classes. In 1970, soon after he became Prime Minister, and after he had announced plans to curb union power, Heath gave a dinner party at Chequers for Harold Macmillan. At the end of dinner, Macmillan spoke. 'The words of the speech flickered like the lights from the flames of the fire around our splendid young leader's prematurely silvered head,' recorded Peter Rawlinson, one of the few people present. 'We must remember, said the sage, that the men from Stockton and the Yorkshire coalfields had fought and died with him at Ypres and Passchendaele and he had seen their sons march past their Sovereign in triumph in the great parade after victory in North Africa. Here the orator flicked away what appeared by the gesture to be the ghost of an inconvenient tear. Happily only temporarily overcome, he went on gravely to reflect that we had at last become as a nation truly one people. No one and indeed no organization of our people must be crushed. Caution, he counselled, staring into the fire, caution and, above all, restraint.'

Macmillan was voicing the Old Guard's view that Heath, by attempting to 'break the mould of British politics' in challenging the unions, was breaking the post-war consensus. 'It was a stern, paternal warning,' reflected Rawlinson, 'against dividing the One Nation which the past quarter-century had at last created, and it demonstrated how in 1970 the mould of the "Butskellite" era was far tougher and harder to crack than it would be a decade later after the defeat of Ted and the second, raffish reign of Harold Wilson, when the unscrupulous exploitation of power by the trade-union bosses had finally brought the nation to the end of its toleration of their holding the nation to ransom.'

There were plenty of Conservatives who were against the Butskellism of Macmillan and Heath. There was also a great degree of discontent within the Conservative Parliamentary Party at the way in which Heath managed it. For whatever reason, he came across to many of his backbenchers as arrogant and uncaring of their problems and their opinions. He had, said John Biffen who was a backbencher from 1961 to 1975, 'a glacial personality'. An MP might find he had a problem with a policy proposal, and privately attempt to secure some changes. All too often he or she would be told by the political officials around Heath: 'We had a Policy Group on this issue some time ago. Why didn't you make your views known then? Now it's too late: the policy has been agreed.' It was a sign that Heath had really diminished: a Chief Whip type should be acutely aware of what is not said, and should have an exceptional sense of micro politics and backbench feeling. After losing two elections on the trot in 1974, Ted Heath could not escape the consequences.

Heath had developed a number of enmities in the Party. Drawing a distinction between Tories and Conservatives, Tories never liked him; at most they found him useful. Conservatives – hard-headed business types who felt no organic Toryism in their bones – did not like him because he had betrayed Selsdon Man. The largest body of enmity towards him consisted of backbench MPs who would follow any leader who did not appear to be compromising the nation's interests. They were people who made a temperamental – not a class or an operational – critique of Ted. They were not like the Conservatives, angry about his U-turn, or like the Tories, pursing their lips about his rough self-presentation. They were simply in the ordinary field of politics observing that they might well be killed in an attack their general did not believe was coming.

•

Blood on the Gucci tie

GERALD McKNIGHT

In the early years of the twentieth century, Guccio Gucci founded the family leather business that grew to become one of the greatest names in luxury goods. But in the years since, feuds and even bloodshed have marred the family's success, as Guccio's four grandsons fought each other for power. In the words of one woman, 'Being married to the Guccis is worse than dining with the Borgias.'

Giuseppe Bandini, driver of a taxi dropping a fare in the via Tornabuoni, was probably the first to see it happen. One hot day in July 1982 he had pulled into the side of the fashionable Florentine street, site of some of the most elegant and expensive shops in the western world, in full view of the palatial Gucci establishment spread across two buildings. Giuseppe was fumbling for change when a small, dapper man clasping a blood-stained handkerchief to one side of his head came running out of the heavy glass Gucci doors.

As the astonished taxi-driver watched, the injured signor jumped into a car. It drove off at speed in the direction, as Giuseppe later told his wife, of the hospital.

The man looked just like one of the Gucci family. Perhaps one of the sons of the great Gucci *Presidente* himself, Dr Aldo Gucci. There had been rumours circulating in Florence and in the gossip columns of the world press for some time about bad blood in the family, but this, as Giuseppe told his wife that evening, beat everything.

Blood was running down one side of the man's face and no doubt – he chuckled – staining his Gucci tie, his Gucci shirt and only the Heavenly Father knew what other items of expensive excellence. Whoever he was, the man was shouting in English at a party of American women who had just got out of a chauffeur-driven limousine and were entering the shop: 'You see? You see what happens when the Gucci board of directors meet! The blue bloods are no different from us!'

In the car, Paolo Gucci's mind was far from such egalitarian considerations. His face under the bandage smarted painfully, but the bruise to his pride hurt more. What possible right did his father, Aldo, his cousin Maurizio and his two brothers Giorgio and Roberto, have to assault him? The last few moments in the boardroom came back in a montage of outraged glimpses.

Someone had seized him from behind. He had been tussling with Giorgio over the tape-recorder. He had just told them all – the enraged faces of his family and the other board directors, mainly lawyers, flowed into his mind – how, if they persisted in refusing to hear, or minute, his questions he would put them on record using the tape-recorder he had brought for the purpose.

Giorgio was seated opposite him, on the other side of the long boardroom table. Paolo saw him jump up and run round in his direction. He pushed down the recording button just as his brother tried to grab the machine. Whilst they both tugged at the instrument an arm came round his neck from behind his back like an iron clamp. It must have been then, too, that he felt the sting of whatever it was that had cut his face and seen the first spatters of blood on his jacket.

With his own doctor, hastily summoned, beside him and the driver racing them towards the doctor's clinic, Paolo had time to reflect that what had just happened could and with any luck would grow into an international scandal. This fracas would, for the first time, shatter the mask of superior breeding and refinement which had stamped Gucci behaviour in public for half a century. No more would his father be able to pretend to the world that the quality and excellence of any of their 'GG' embossed products, from tie-clips to the hallmarked leather trim of a Cadillac, was a reflection of personal family character.

He was glad.

The scene that had startled the taxi-driver was certainly not going to pass unnoticed. Newspapers and radio and television in every capital city ran the story. On the breakfast tables of the rich and famous it caused more than a mild frisson of astonishment and amusement. Fancy the Guccis falling out! This gossip was rich enough to keep the tittle-tattle going for several days. In the world's most expensive hairdressers' salons the warm air driers vibrated with it.

For shopkeepers to quarrel and fight, in the Medici's Florence, was understandable. For a Gucci, well, that was an altogether more appetizing titbit of scandal. From New York Jacqueline Kennedy Onassis cabled one word to Paolo's father, an old acquaintance who had helped her spend uncounted thousands of dollars in his discreet Fifth Avenue *galleria*. It expressed potently what the fashionable, deliciously titillated world felt about the brawl. Jackie's cable simply read, 'Why?'

America's ex-queen of opulent chic was only giving succinct voice to society's universal cry of alarm. From Monaco Prince Rainier telephoned the Florence headquarters to express sorrowful condolence. The prince had long esteemed Gucci's galaxy of tooled leather and gold symbols. At his wedding to Grace Kelly on 19 April 1956 he reportedly had ordered Gucci scarves by the gross, and presented each female guest with one to signify his delight at having at last won a woman who was the pinnacle of glamour. The world press did nothing to suppress the general feeling of astonishment. In America, *People* magazine headlined a three-page, illustrated report 'Move over *Dallas*; Behind the Glittering Façade, a Family Feud Rocks the House of Gucci'.

In fact, the shock waves radiating out from Florence's via Tornabuoni were threatening to destroy a reputation for punctilious service to the mighty which had taken three generations of

Guccis infinite pains and labour to create. Certainly this was no backstreet incident. The via Tornabuoni has a permanent air of Fifth Avenue elegance unmatched in all but a few of Europe's shopping thoroughfares. A hundred years or so ago, English and American diplomats sauntered in and out of their consulates at number 14 and 10 respectively. Wealthy English tourists have been a common sight since the days when they banked their Victorian sovereigns at number 5, the premises of Maquay Hooker & Co, 'bankers to the gentry'.

When the reasons for it became known, it was soon clear that this was no sudden emotional storm which would blow away on the Mediterranean breeze. Behind the explosion, the assault and mauling of fifty-one-year-old Paolo, was a long fuse which had been spluttering and burning for over ten years.

It was known, of course, that the Guccis had been suffering serious differences of opinion over how to run their multi-million dollar empire of shops and boutiques around the world, and that they were anything but a united and happy family. Passionate, deeply loyal in their own way, they were also known to be true to the ancient traditions of this northern Italian city of Florence which had given them birth, where vendettas and family feuds flourish like weeds. But until now their most curious family traits and characteristics had lain discreetly hidden.

For example, the illiberal measure that no Gucci on the distaff side could inherit any part of the business: this had been an iron rule of the family since its origin. As with most Florentine dynasties the male line was all important, and histori-cally it had been as natural for a male Gucci to dominate his women as for him to expect total and absolute obedience from his children and lesser relatives. Persuaders, seducers and miraculous salesmen though they were, when opposed or forced to make conditions any Gucci would switch (as Paolo had discovered) from warm-hearted camaraderie to threats and violence in a snap of fingers.

Yet, as history showed, they had absolutely no equals when it came to weaving the magical spells under which the richest, most powerful people allowed themselves to be bewitched into signing away small fortunes for the luxury and esteem of that cherished 'GG' symbol. Commercially, the Guccis had established an unrivalled key to status. Hermès in Paris, perhaps, came a close second. In England, whom could one compare them with? Aspreys? There were few other dynasties.

How had they done it? If one believes their press agents, the family were aristocratic saddle-makers to royalty for centuries before they became humble leather merchants. As a family they could (and their press agents did) claim direct descent from titled, landed nobles related to the Medicis, with their own coat of arms. The less glamorous truth is that the great Gucci corporation grew quite recently from a waiter's dream.

The first step into a realm of 24-carat marketing was taken by Guccio Gucci who, having stoked coal to come to England during the last days of Queen Victoria and found work washing dishes at the new and glamorous Savoy Hotel, was elevated to a waiter. He was struck by the opulence and ostentation of the hotel's wealthy patrons. Their taste for expensive, elegant leather astonished him. When he returned to work in a leather-goods store in Florence to pick up a trade, the dream of one day supplying this luxury stayed in his mind.

It became a reality mainly because Guccio's vision satisfied a universal craving. A longing, especially among the *nouveau riche*, to demonstrate wealth and class, whether or not it was actually possessed. And because the woman he married shared his dream and had as much drive as he had, if not more. They both sensed that between the wars a new, socially aspiring class had emerged and was judging and being judged by its shoes and luggage. These 'puppies' of the twenties wanted a hallmark to indicate their good taste and readiness to spend lavishly on what was out of reach of the masses.

In much the same way as a royal enclosure ticket at Ascot or an Ivy League fraternity pin, Gucci offered a recognizable badge, the discreet symbol of an élite club. By personalizing the high cost of quality, his goods came to signify the status of the wearer, or owner. To achieve this, to rise from a humble leather-goods shop to a symbol of the highest quality, required an extraordinary blend of psychological talent and industry.

More than once Guccio found himself in financial difficulties. Only the fact that he possessed both natural ability, doggedness and an epicurean sense of good taste gave him his remarkable edge in a viciously competitive trade.

Thus, nurturing impeccably fine quality had become a carefully protected Gucci asset which Paolo's scandalous episode threatened to destroy. His grandfather would have been furious at the damage it could do to the reputation he had taken such great care to establish. And Paolo's sensational disclosure of the family's internal war was all the more outrageous in that it threatened a multi-million dollar livelihood for them all.

It had been widely assumed that Guccio had passed on to his three sons and their offspring the same sense of discipline and respect for appearances that he and his wife Aida shared. If the Savoy had not managed to recognize it, the wealthy tourists of the years between Europe's two wars unfailingly had done so. So who could explain this grandson's astonishing behaviour?

Never before had there been a flagrant breach of this sort. The stories whispered about the womanizing antics of the male Guccis were no more than enjoyably risqué asides by comparison. Could it be, malicious tongues asked, that fame and eminence were at last expanding the Guccis' heads? After Paolo's 'dastardly assault' the London *Daily Express* reported 'nothing but fireworks from the world-wide multi-million business which is run with all the chaos of a Rome pizza parlour'. It was well known that Paolo's father, the founder's son Aldo, claimed to have been awarded a doctorate by the city's university for his 'distinguished service to the economic life of Florence'. A report in the *New York Times* referring to his son's assault as 'a climactic move' suggested that a medical doctorate would have been more appropriate.

The oldest living Gucci, Guccio's daughter Grimalda, aged

in 1987 eighty-four, knows only too well what such a scandal would have cost her father. She and her husband gained least of any in the family from the Gucci success story, but she was deeply distressed by the conflict between her nephews. Even more so by the publicity which followed Paolo's assault, and horrified that it showed her family to be so fiercely divided.

In her eyes the bloodstained Paolo Gucci being whisked away in the speeding car was as responsible as any for the years of struggle and conflict. It was he who had provoked more scenes and squabbles than any of his relations – always, let it be said, in the righteous belief that his creative plans for the company were being unfairly rejected, his position in it treacherously undermined.

This grandson of the founder believed that he was being violently baulked in trying to assert his professional, let alone his native rights. Beside him in the car a Dr Nepi was making reassuring noises. Telling him that the cut on his face was little more than a deep graze. But that was not the wound that bothered Paolo Gucci. To be first of all denied authority as a director of his family company, then to have his only recourse to the record snatched at, as if wresting a toy from a naughty child, was his bitterest injury. And then to be physically assaulted, and by his own flesh and blood! The insult, the indignity, the sheer impotence of his position, would have been no less unbearable had he been slain.

Well, there was one course of action open to him. He had used it before and was no stranger to its ways. If the days of daggers in the night were no more, at least the law was like a sharp weapon in Paolo's hand. He would sue.

In New York, Paolo Gucci's lawyer Stuart Speiser well knew his client's recourse to legal action. Speiser is a disarmingly mild man who manages to create a feeling of comfort and security for even those among his clients who have the least hope of winning their actions. Paolo's suit against his family charged breach of contract, infliction of severe emotional stress, and assault and battery. It followed other equally internecine actions the attorney had fought for him in the recent past. If the Guccis could grow fat on the fruits of their commercial flair, Speiser felt no reluctance in taking on the legal pillow-fights of this warring clan. All the more grist to an already opulent practice which, seen from his suite of luxurious offices in the Park Avenue Pan Am building in Manhattan, gave him daily satisfaction.

An unashamed airplane buff and legal aviation expert, Speiser's collection of trophies, pictures and ephemera from the early days of seat-of-the-pants flying is of considerable worth. The walls of his office give an impression of an exclusive flying club. Close to retirement, he now devotes as much of his time to his hobby as he can spare from the writing of books on tort and some of the more interesting cases he has handled in his long and lucrative career.

In a preface to one of his books Speiser quotes his favourite legal wit, Ambrose Bierce, whose *Devil's Dictionary* is famous for its pertinent definitions. 'Litigation,' Bierce wrote in 1911, is 'a machine which you go into as a pig and come out as a sausage'. The only sure impunity, he suggests, is wealth. And a litigant is one who is 'about to give up his skin for the hope of retaining his bones'.

Paolo Gucci had not seen himself as fodder for a sausage machine, but there was little doubt that he had paid dearly for his legal fencing with the family. In Speiser's opinion a conservative estimate of the costs to date of the Guccis' legal adventures would be in the order of $5 million, or £3¼ million. For their part, the Guccis one and all appeared to regard lawsuits as no more disturbing than buzzing insects or stinging nettles. Stuart Speiser referred to them, indeed to all litigious punters, with philosophical detachment.

Even so, when Paolo faced him with details of the boardroom battle, Speiser was surprised at the intensity of feeling which lay under his client's expensively accoutred surface. 'The Guccis don't seem to know how to compromise,' he explained later. In all dealings with the family it was to become his watchword.

Paolo wanted blood. He knew Speiser's firm, Speiser & Krauze, would advise him how best to hit back at his hostile family. The case Speiser prepared would certainly do that if successful. It claimed that the attack on Paolo had been unprovoked and unexpected, that having been fired from the family business but remaining a shareholder, his client was merely trying to exercise his right to question the board's 'conspiratorial and malicious conduct' in running the company.

By introducing papers into a previous lawsuit, Paolo had already laid bare a number of swindles which involved Panamanian companies set up by his father and uncle in Hong Kong to siphon off monies which should by rights have been declared as taxable income in the United States. With Speiser, he now contrived to bring these to the attention of the American tax authorities, the Internal Revenue Service. It was done, Paolo says, only to try and force his father's hand and never with the intention of letting the incriminating papers stay on file in the case. But when Aldo refused to withdraw the company's objection to Paolo trading under his own name, which he regarded as his right after he had been fired from the company, the damage was done. The court refused to return the papers and Aldo had to face trial.

Ironically, Paolo's action was subsequently dismissed by the New York State Supreme Court for lack of material evidence. But the damning papers remained. And if his father's sentence did nothing else, it clearly showed how suicidal the family could be, and the deep rift dividing the house of Gucci. As a result of Paolo's vindictive action, in September 1986 his eighty-one-year-old father was jailed for a year and a day, heavily fined, and ordered to repay over $7 million in back taxes.

At his trial in a Manhattan court Aldo Gucci wept openly, while admitting that fraudulent 'devices' had been used to divert income from his family's international chain of shops to accounts he and his brother controlled outside the United States. Aldo pleaded that he was not personally guilty of tax evasion. The frauds, he said, had been perpetrated without his knowledge or consent by an accountant for the firm, Edward H. Stern, who in the meantime (conveniently) had died. And, as part of a plea-bargaining agreement, Paolo's distressed and penitent father handed over a cheque for $1 million (nearly £700,000), towards his tax arrears. A further $6 million was offered.

It was a cruel thrust by his son's legal dagger, and from the dock Aldo showed that he understood all too well who had aimed it. 'Some of my sons,' he cried, 'have done their duty. But some sought revenge and only God may judge them. I forgive anybody who wanted me here today.' No one doubted that the old man had left a valediction that would sting like a curse.

But the Guccis can smite one moment and kiss the next. When Aldo's brother Rodolfo had died three years before the sentence and his nephew Maurizio presided over Aldo's dismissal from the company's presidency – the man who had done more than any of his generation to build the business to its present $500 million a year turnover – it became clear then that a gulf the size of the Grand Canyon was splitting the two factions, the descendants of the two brothers Aldo and Rodolfo. Paolo's boardroom scuffle was only a symptom of the rift.

To the onlooker, it seemed farcical. Every male Gucci already had more wealth than most men could earn in a dozen lifetimes. The hidden mainspring was their lust for power, for supremacy. If it was a quality more common in the televised fictions of Florida, it was no less dramatic or deadly in Florence. To be the grand panjandrum of Gucci world-wide, the totem around which the whole machinery of the business rotated, was a sufficient motive, apparently, for each of the family shareholders to wage war on his most intimate relatives, even when he had held nothing but love and admiration for them all his life.

It had merely come to a head on that July day in Florence. 'They went berserk,' Paolo says in retrospect. 'My own family shouted me down. Ask your father, they screamed at me, as if I was still a child. What nonsense was that, I wanted to know? I don't have to go to my father to ask these things. I am a director and shareholder of the company! It was then that I saw that the secretary taking the minutes was not making a note of what was going on and I pulled out my tape-recorder.'

In doing so, he had opened the eyes of the world to a Gucci family crisis which was threatening to ruin their billion dollar business and destroy their world-famous name. It may be exaggerating to say that pride and lust for power alone had brought the Guccis to this bitter clash, and it would certainly be nonsense to suggest that such conflicts do not flourish behind the nameplates of many equally successful merchant families. But the vigour and venom of the Gucci battle was truly astonishing.

Perhaps the old English saying 'clogs to clogs in three generations' was familiar to Guccio Gucci. He might have heard it during his months in the kitchen of the Savoy Hotel. But he cannot then have known that he was destined to make one of the world's greatest commercial fortunes. Or that his descendants, down to the third generation, would fight over it like medieval barons. If he had had even the slightest suspicion of the trouble that would follow the realization of his dreams, would he not have tried to prevent it in his lifetime?

•

Gentlemen-at-arms

TAKI

New York: I witnessed a terrible fight last week, one that left me longing for the days when gentlemen settled their differences in a chivalrous way, with lances, swords, pistols, even whips. I was with my friend Chuck Pfeiffer, a very tough ex-Green Beret captain who won the Silver Star in Vietnam, and we were dining in one of the trendiest restaurants down in Greenwich Village. The fight started suddenly, and to our amazement involved three men, all perfectly respectable and seemingly well-educated. But it was vicious and two people got badly hurt. Chuck stopped it while I covered his back, as he yelled for me to do. The restaurant owner sent over a bottle of champagne to thank us but I was no longer in the mood. I guess I'm getting old and no longer enjoy fights.

Long ago, it could never have happened. One weapon that was rarely used by angry or insulted folk was the human fist. Satisfaction was usually had after a little bloodletting, although at times things did tend to get out of hand – no pun intended – and severe injury occurred. Duelling separated the patricians from the plebeians and also ensured a certain decorum and standard of behaviour among the upper classes, an unheard of phenomenon among today's moneyed classes.

Duelling might seem a senseless custom today, but it did manage to keep society extremely polite. A few hasty words might mean a challenge, and more often than not, one or both of the combatants had reason to regret his loss of temper. Although it was illegal to fight duels, the law was seldom enforced. Usually there was a trial only after one of the duellists had been killed. The survivor, generally, was charged with manslaughter and given a very light sentence. The unwritten rule was that if one happened to kill one's adversary, especially if the victor had issued the challenge, he would exile himself for a decent interval. After that, everything would return to normal.

Sometimes the dying loser would not only forgive his adversary with his last breath but might even accept the blame. Such was the case in a famous duel between Colonel Richard Thornhill and Sir Cholmley Dering, which took place in 1711 and resulted in the latter's death. Thornhill had insisted on the duel after Sir Cholmley had stepped on his foot after a long bout of drinking. As Sir Cholmley lay dying he said that the duel was of his own seeking. Thornhill never served a day.

His dying gesture was recognized as typical gentlemanly behaviour. Some of the most famous duels have been fought over differences of opinion that would be barely noticed in today's permissive and certainly dishonourable times, when vanity is more important than pride. I will not dwell on the famous duels that have been fought in the past. They are well-known and I haven't the space. I will, however, mention a few that have taken place since the Second World War. The best-known was fought by two men I knew. It was an artistic duel in more ways than one. It took place in Paris in 1958, between the Marquis de Cuevas, of ballet fame, and Serge Lifar, the Russian-born choreographer. Cuevas was 72 at the time and Lifar 53. Lifar had flung his scented handkerchief at Cuevas during the intermission at the Black and White ballet. They met at an estate 50 miles from Paris, and after a lot of weaving and bobbing, Cuevas pricked Lifar in the arm. Then Cuevas burst into tears and collapsed. The bleeding Lifar consoled him. They embraced and it was all over.

There have been at least seven duels at Oxford and Cambridge since the war, employing sabres, rapiers, umbrellas, even champagne corks. The most unusual was fought by – who else – Anthony Haden-Guest. He was challenged by a Greek schoolmate while at Gordonstoun. The Greek insisted on javelins at 50 paces, however. Both missed, although Anthony's javelin was embedded in a nearby plane tree.

Duelling would work wonders if it came back today. At the very least, it would restore a touch of dignity to late-night proceedings in Manhattan bars and allow one to finish a meal in peace. Only two days after Pfeiffer and I had witnessed that bad brawl downtown, we saw another one, this time in a place that was far more chic. A man lost his temper with two gays who were making fun of him and decided to slap one of them. He missed and hit a girl who was with them. The two gays scratched him and called him names. Pfeiffer and I let that one go on.

•

Clash of the colas

DOUGLAS K. RAMSEY

The feud between America's two leading soft-drinks companies, Coca-Cola and Pepsi-Cola, has been going since 1893. In one advertising campaign after another each company attempted to steal an advantage over its rival, such as which cola tastes better, or which diet cola tastes better. And then, in 1985, Coca-Cola decided that it would replace the old Coke with a smoother, better-tasting cola that was second to none. The $4 million in market research promised that it was 'the surest thing' the company had ever done. Pepsi saw things a little differently.

At headquarters Pepsi-Cola USA's president, Roger Enrico, was jubilant. Tipped off two days earlier, Enrico ordered his New York sales staff to arrange a free Pepsi giveaway and taste test just outside the Coliseum. Two days later he placed full-page advertisements in newspapers around the country to claim victory. 'Coca-Cola is withdrawing their product from the marketplace, and is reformulating brand Coke to be "more like Pepsi"', the ads boasted. 'Maybe they finally realized what most of us have known for years: Pepsi tastes better than Coke . . . After 87 years of going at it eyeball to eyeball, the other guy just blinked.' With that, Enrico declared the following Friday a company holiday. 'Victory is sweet,' the copy concluded, 'and we have earned a celebration . . . Enjoy!'

Enrico's ebullience was partly cosmetic. Given the results of Coke's marketing research, Pepsi could only assume that its archrival had come up with a formula that would, at the very least, make it difficult to count on taste tests and the Pepsi Challenge as a bulwark of the company's marketing strategy in the future. From the start, therefore, Enrico knew that Pepsi's response would have to be targeted at the reason behind

Coca-Cola's move – and its apparent admission of what Pepsi had claimed all along: consumers prefer the taste of Pepsi.

On that Tuesday in April, however, neither Enrico nor [Roberto] Goizueta [Coca-Cola's CEO] fully appreciated the extent or nature of public response to the switch. Over the next ten weeks, 150 million Americans tried New Coke, and the company's surveys indicated that 75 percent of them were going to buy it again. But for a vociferous minority, Coca-Cola's decision to discard its ninety-nine-year-old secret formula amounted to betrayal, and their reaction was immediate. Some began hoarding bottles of 'old' Coke. In Seattle, a retired hotel owner formed Old Cola Drinkers of America to lobby for the return of 7X [old Coke].

At first the reaction was anticipated. Goizueta knew there would be a sentimental backlash. But once consumers had a chance to taste the new Coke, he felt, they would go with the change, and Pepsi drinkers, tempted by all the hoopla, would taste the new formula and possibly switch. Blind taste tests, carried out on a weekly basis through the spring, confirmed Goizueta's gut feeling. New Coke beat both old Coke and Pepsi by even wider margins than it had prior to the product's introduction. Four weeks after New Coke's debut, Dyson continued to harp on the company's optimistic expectations and newfound willingness to take risks. 'We're not following the lead of others, we're setting the pace,' he told bottlers. 'We are on the front lines of change.'

Two months later, however, it was clear that the controversy wouldn't go away. The furor continued to make headlines and had become a staple of TV coverage. By mid June operators at Coke's headquarters in Atlanta were recording fifteen hundred calls daily, almost all demanding the return of old Coke. Some bottlers reported that their deliverymen were being harassed by retailers and shoppers. In a few markets shipments of New Coke were down 15 percent after the May surge. Supermarket surveys every Thursday showed that the tide had changed: in June, more than half of those responding didn't like New Coke, and the ranks of the disenchanted appeared to be growing daily. At a regional meeting of Coke bottlers in Dallas on June 18, disgruntled bottlers signed a petition asking Atlanta to bring back old Coke. Goizueta got the same advice from a fellow Atlanta businessman, Ted Turner. 'You don't cancel a winner,' Turner would say later, recounting the meeting with Goizueta, 'just because you are bringing out a new product.'

On the first Wednesday of July, Roberto Goizueta and Don Keough met with senior executives from Coke's five biggest bottlers. The meeting went badly. If the barrage of bad publicity continued, the bottlers claimed, Coke – by whatever name – risked losing market share overnight to Pepsi, a share that would be that much harder to regain. Goizueta promised to have a decision by the following Monday.

To all intents and purposes, Goizueta had already decided that Coca-Cola would have to change tactics dramatically. Going back to work the following day, he ordered all departments to prepare for the return of old Coke. Even the bottlers agreed that New Coke should remain the standard, given the amount of publicity and consumer awareness generated by the controversy. Old Coke would therefore be aimed at die-hard fans of the original formula, New Coke at younger consumers and Pepsi drinkers. That decision taken, Keough ordered the research department to test several possible names for the old Coke, among them Original Coke, Coke I, Coke 1886, or, simply, Old Coke.

On Monday morning Sergio Zyman argued against Goizueta and Keough's decision. He felt that the company was caving in too quickly. The marketer was still convinced that the furor would subside as quickly as it arose and the red-and-silver 'New' banner was removed from Coke cans. But Goizueta and Keough had made up their minds. Dyson agreed, especially after a meeting early Monday morning with bottlers who were urging the company to cut its losses and do it quickly. It was the last straw. Goizueta made the decision official and ordered Zyman to call Alvin Schechter in New York.

Schechter, who had designed the Diet Coke can, was given forty-eight hours to come up with a package design for Coca-Cola Original, one of the names that had tested best among those used in surveys taken over the weekend. Working late into the night, Schechter devised half a dozen styles, all using the same basic red motif that runs through all of Coke's cola offerings. The next morning a colleague flew to Atlanta with the drawings, returning the same afternoon. Coke executives asked for minor changes in one of the drawings, and one big one: instead of Coca-Cola Original, Goizueta wanted to go with the more alliterative Coca-Cola Classic, which had also tested well.

The next day, Schechter shipped the final version to Atlanta: a can wrapped in a distinctive red wrapper, *Coca-Cola* in the company's bold, white, Spencerian script, the word *Classic* in capital letters, also in white, floating just below. With no time to devise a sophisticated advertising campaign to accompany the stunning reversal in Coke's plans, Zyman asked McCann-Erickson to send a TV crew to Atlanta and booked a local studio to tape an announcement by Keough. With the New Coke and dummy Coca-Cola Classic cans on a desk, Keough sitting behind it, the thirty-second spot began with Coca-Cola's president thanking 'the millions' of consumers who had made New Coke a success. He also apologized to 'the millions' who preferred the taste of old Coke. Then he announced that the old Coke was coming back in a new can labeled Coke Classic. Several takes were required before getting a good version on tape.

Keough returned from the studio to pandemonium at Coke headquarters. Rumors that it was bringing back old Coke were awash on Wall Street, and the company's public relations office was flooded with calls from reporters around the country. Plans were already under way for a press conference in Atlanta the next day, Thursday, but Goizueta and Keough decided to end the confusion before it got out of hand. Late in the afternoon they ordered Zyman to contact the sales departments at all three major broadcasting networks and asked for last-minute time on the evening newscasts. The final thirty-second spot – shot in one continuous take with no editing – was beamed to New York via satellite, with only minutes to spare before the first 6:30 p.m. newscasts.

At Coca-Cola headquarters, the decision to bring back the old formula as Coke Classic radically altered the downbeat mood that had been building. 'Thank you for bringing old Coke back,' read the letter from a sixty-eight-year-old woman. 'The only thing better is sex!' Within days Coca-Cola was flooded with calls, telegrams, even bouquets of flowers. Overhead an airplane trailed a banner that read THANK YOU, ROBERTO!

By Roberto Goizueta's own admission, it would take months to assess whether the decision to market two Coca-Colas was the right one. But he refused to call the original launch of New Coke a mistake. 'Consumers were so mad, but they were not reacting against the taste of New Coke,' he told a reporter after the Coke Classic announcement. 'It was the idea that "somebody took away my soft drink".' Don Keough readily admitted that the events of the past three months were not, as some skeptics conjectured, a finely tuned strategy to hype the introduction of New Coke. 'Some critics will say Coca-Cola made a marketing mistake; some cynics will say that we planned the whole thing,' Keough told reporters the day after his thirty-second spot announcing the change was beamed into millions of American homes. 'The truth is, we are not that dumb – and we are not that smart.'

In fact, Coca-Cola was that dumb *and* that smart. Goizueta admitted that the company knew all along that it could reintroduce the old formula, without actually expecting to have to do so. But once public sentiment shifted decisively away from New Coke, for whatever reason, Goizueta was quick to change course. Coca-Cola had proved once again and this time successfully that, under its new leadership, it could adapt quickly to the marketplace.

The payoff was almost immediate. Despite three months of

bad press, the awareness of Coke's advertising around the country had hit an all-time high. Retailers began stocking their shelves with Coke Classic alongside New Coke. Had the company opted to introduce New Coke the way it had Diet Coke, without scrapping Tab, retailers may have been less willing to carry the new product. In the end, Coca-Cola got the best of both worlds – a product to satisfy Coke's die-hard fans, and a product to meet the Pepsi Challenge. By September Coca-Cola was reporting that sales of its three sugared colas, including Cherry Coke, were running 10 percent higher than Coke sales a year earlier, when Coke was growing by only 3 percent. And an *Advertising Age* survey the same month showed that the company's overall market share was up almost two points; Pepsi's was *down* just under a point.

●

Explaining the Nazi hatred of the Jews
PRIMO LEVI

In 1943 Primo Levi joined a partisan group in northern Italy, was captured and transported to Auschwitz. It was his knowledge as a chemist that saved his life. His camp was liberated in 1945 and Levi worked as a writer and chemist until his retirement in 1975. He committed suicide in 1987. In his books *If This is a Man* and *The Truce* he records his experiences in the death camp. In an afterword to these books, Levi provides some answers to his readers' questions regarding the Holocaust.

How can the Nazis' fanatical hatred of the Jews be explained?

It can be said that anti-Semitism is one particular case of intolerance; that for centuries it had a prevailingly religious character; that in the Third Reich it was exacerbated by the nationalistic and military predisposition of the German people and by the 'differentness' of the Jewish people; that it was easily disseminated in all of Germany – and in a good part of Europe – thanks to the efficiency of the Fascist and Nazi propaganda which needed a scapegoat on which to load all guilts and all resentments; and that the phenomenon was heightened to paroxysm by Hitler, a maniacal dictator.

However, I must admit that these commonly accepted explanations do not satisfy me. They are reductive; not commensurate with, nor proportionate to, the facts that need explaining. In rereading the chronicles of Nazism, from its murky beginnings to its convulsed end, I cannot avoid the impression of a general atmosphere of uncontrolled madness that seems to me to be unique in history. This collective madness, this 'running off the rails', is usually explained by postulating the combination of many diverse factors, insufficient if considered singly, and the greatest of these factors is Hitler's personality itself and its profound interaction with the German people. It is certain that his personal obsessions, his capacity for hatred, his preaching of violence, found unbridled echoes in the frustration of the German people, and for this reason came back to him multiplied, confirming his delirious conviction that he himself was the Hero prophesied by Nietzsche, the Superman redeemer of Germany.

Much has been written about the origin of his hatred of the Jews. It is said that Hitler poured out upon the Jews his hatred of the entire human race; that he recognized in the Jews some of his own defects, and that in hating the Jews he was hating himself; that the violence of his aversion arose from the fear that he might have 'Jewish blood' in his veins.

Again, these explanations do not seem adequate to me. I do not find it permissible to explain a historical phenomenon by piling all the blame on a single individual (those who carry out horrendous orders are not innocent!). Besides, it is always difficult to interpret the deep-seated motivations of an individual. The hypotheses that have been proposed justify the facts only up to a point, explain the quality but not the quantity.

I must admit that I prefer the humility with which some of the most serious historians (among them Bullock, Schramm, Bracher) confess to *not understanding* the furious anti-Semitism of Hitler and of Germany behind him.

Perhaps one cannot, what is more one must not, understand what happened, because to understand is almost to justify. Let me explain: 'understanding' a proposal or human behavior means to 'contain' it, contain its author, put oneself in his place, identify with him. Now, no normal human being will ever be able to identify with Hitler, Himmler, Goebbels, Eichmann, and endless others. This dismays us, and at the same time gives us a sense of relief, because perhaps it is desirable that their words (and also, unfortunately, their deeds) cannot be comprehensible to us. They are non-human words and deeds, really counter-human, without historic precedents, with difficulty comparable to the cruelest events of the biological struggle for existence. The war can be related to this struggle, but Auschwitz has nothing to do with war; it is neither an episode in it nor an extreme form of it. War is always a terrible fact, to be deprecated, but it is in us, it has its rationality, we 'understand' it.

But there is no rationality in the Nazi hatred: it is a hate that is not in us; it is outside man, it is a poison fruit sprung from the deadly trunk of Fascism, but it is outside and beyond Fascism itself. We cannot understand it, but we can and must understand from where it springs, and we must be on our guard. If understanding is impossible, knowing is imperative, because what happened could happen again. Conscience can be seduced and obscured again – even our consciences.

For this reason, it is everyone's duty to reflect on what happened. Everybody must know, or remember, that when Hitler and Mussolini spoke in public, they were believed, ap-plauded, admired, adored like gods. They were 'charismatic leaders'; they possessed a secret power of seduction that did not proceed from the credibility or the soundness of the things they said but from the suggestive way in which they said them, from their eloquence, from their histrionic art, perhaps instinctive, perhaps patiently learned and practiced. The ideas they proclaimed were not always the same and were, in general, aberrant or silly or cruel. And yet they were acclaimed with hosannahs and followed to the death by millions of the faithful. We must remember that these faithful followers, among them the diligent executors of inhuman orders, were not born torturers, were not (with a few exceptions) monsters: they were ordinary men. Monsters exist, but they are too few in number to be truly dangerous. More dangerous are the common men, the functionaries ready to believe and to act without asking questions, like Eichmann; like Hoss, the commandant of Auschwitz; like Stangl, commandant of Treblinka; like the French military of twenty years later, slaughterers in Algeria; like the Khmer Rouge of the late seventies, slaughterers in Cambodia.

It is, therefore, necessary to be suspicious of those who seek to convince us with means other than reason, and of charismatic leaders: we must be cautious about delegating to others our judgment and our will. Since it is difficult to distinguish true prophets from false, it is as well to regard all prophets with suspicion. It is better to renounce revealed truths, even if they exalt us by their splendor or if we find them convenient because we can acquire them gratis. It is better to content oneself with other more modest and less exciting truths, those one acquires painfully, little by little and without shortcuts, with study, discussion, and reasoning, those that can be verified and demonstrated.

It is clear that this formula is too simple to suffice in every case. A new Fascism, with its trail of intolerance, of abuse, and of servitude, can be born outside our country and be imported into it, walking on tiptoe and calling itself by other names, or it can loose itself from within with such violence that it routs all defenses. At that point, wise counsel no longer serves, and one must find the strength to resist. Even in this contingency, the memory of what happened in the heart of Europe, not very long ago, can serve as support and warning . . .

In these books there are no expressions of hate for the Germans, no desire for revenge. Have you forgiven them?

My personal temperament is not inclined to hatred. I regard it as bestial, crude, and prefer on the contrary that my actions and thoughts, as far as possible, should be the product of reason; therefore I have never cultivated within myself hatred as a desire for revenge, or as a desire to inflict suffering on my real or presumed enemy, or as a private vendetta. Even less do I accept hatred as directed collectively at an ethnic group, for example, all the Germans; if I accepted it, I would feel that I was following the precepts of Nazism, which was founded precisely on national and racial hatred.

I must admit that if I had in front of me one of our persecutors of those days, certain known faces, certain old lies, I would be tempted to hate, and with violence too; but exactly because I am not a Fascist or a Nazi, I refuse to give way to this temptation. I believe in reason and in discussion as supreme instruments of progress, and therefore I repress hatred even within myself: I prefer justice. Precisely for this reason, when describing the tragic world of Auschwitz, I have deliberately assumed the calm, sober language of the witness, neither the lamenting tones of the victim nor the irate voice of someone who seeks revenge. I thought that my account would be all the more credible and useful the more it appeared objective and the less it sounded overly emotional; only in this way does a witness in matters of justice perform his task, which is that of preparing the ground for the judge. The judges are my readers.

All the same I would not want my abstaining from explicit judgment to be confused with an indiscriminate pardon. No, I have not forgiven any of the culprits, nor am I willing to forgive a single one of them, unless he has shown (with deeds, not words, and not too long afterward) that he has become conscious of the crimes and errors of Italian and foreign Fascism and is determined to condemn them, uproot them, from his conscience and from that of others. Only in this case am I, a non-Christian, prepared to follow the Jewish and Christian precept of forgiving my enemy, because an enemy who sees the error of his ways ceases to be an enemy.

●

The Wapping factor

PETER CHIPPENDALE AND CHRIS HORRIE

Owned by Rupert Murdoch, the *Sun* is the biggest selling newspaper in the English language. At its headquarters in Wapping, the *Sun*'s foul-mouthed editor Kelvin MacKenzie presides over a rabid tabloid that has been called the Rottweiler of British journalism. But it is not always public figures who find themselves the target of the *Sun*'s hatred. Sometimes the *Sun* turns on one of its own.

A strange malaise had also begun to grip the office which soon became known as the 'Wapping Factor'. Some of the hacks, although they only realized it afterwards, had begun unconsciously to reject Wapping as a workplace. There was no single cause they could pin down, but much of the reason was thought to be claustrophobia from the low ceilings, now exacerbated by the loss of the only window.

The Wapping Factor seemed to hit the features department first and a number of experienced female writers began looking around for new jobs. But there were others who were not so sure of their job prospects elsewhere, and yet others who appeared to be barnacles, stuck on the bottom of the good ship Wapping for ever. MacKenzie's pillorying of all these different types stepped up when the pickets had left, as they had all feared. Nobody was actually fired, but some were told to their face they had no future in the place. They were given impossible jobs to do and heaped with huge workloads. Their expenses were slashed, they were personally insulted and told they were useless, and subjected to one of MacKenzie's favourite tactics.

He would come up to their desks, put his face close to theirs and say: 'You still 'ere, then, eh? Haven't you gone yet, eh?' Nerves started jangling.

The hacks had always known that people who cravenly agreed with MacKenzie only subjected themselves to more abuse. He had seemed to get a particular needle with Stuart Higgins, a minion on the newsdesk who was always eager to please his colleagues. Higgins was a small, plump individual who other hacks joked had dropped out of the rat race to join the mouse race. He was personable enough, but there were divided opinions about his curious habit at parties of dropping on all fours and going round barking like a dog, pretending to bite women's ankles.

MacKenzie used to get intensely irritated by Higgins's habit of just smiling at him however severe the bollocking, and he would be driven to new heights of abuse and denigration. 'You smarmy c***, Higgy, you take it all, don't you, eh?' MacKenzie raged at him one day in front of the desk. 'You just sit there soaking it all up, don't you, eh? Know what you're like, don't you? You're like a sponge. A fucking human sponge.'

Hacks watching this performance saw MacKenzie stop as though a lightbulb had gone on in his head. He scurried off into his office and the hacks heard demonic cackling. Higgy soaked it up so much the readers were about to be invited to join MacKenzie in having a go. It was a public pillorying ranking at least equal with that arranged for Mike Terry, the hapless Bingo Bungler.

The next morning on page 5 a library mugshot of Higgins smiling and holding a telephone appeared next to the strapline: 'Want someone to yell at? Scream at? Fume at? – RING HIGGY THE HUMAN SPONGE, HE'LL SOAK IT UP.' The copy was a public version of a MacKenzie bollocking, shorn of the swear words.

Are you mad enough to make a life miserable? Is something driving you k-k-k-krazy? Do you feel like a villain looking for a victim?

Well . . . GREAT NEWS! You've found him! Presenting

the *Sun*'s very own happy, soothing voice of reason . . . HIGGY THE HUMAN SPONGE.

He LOVES loudmouths. Can't LIVE without a tongue-lashing. A week without being called a wally – or worse – is a week wasted in his book. So pick up the phone and fume, folks. His Wimpishness is waiting for your calls with a silly-billy grin on his face and honeyed words of love in his heart . . . the fool!

Printed in large type was the number of Higgins's direct line on the newsdesk. Higgins, who still had to do his normal work, was bombarded with calls from inside the paper as well as outside as the hacks joined in by posing as readers and ringing from their extensions. The next day the results were published under the headline 'WE HATE HIGGY!' 'Screaming hordes of *Sun* readers took advantage of Higgy the Human Sponge yesterday . . .' A thirteen-year-old schoolboy told him he 'must feel a right pratt sitting there' and a 'well-spoken woman from Essex' said: 'My God. You're so ugly. I've never seen anyone so ugly in my life.'

In all, the paper claimed, hapless Higgins received more than 1,000 calls but, true to form, was still smiling at the end of the day. The most popular caller with the hacks was the one who said he would like to do something to him with 'the rough end of a pineapple'. Higgins did soak it all up, as predicted, but from that time on the divide in the office was even clearer.

•

Spoiling for a fight
PETER CHIPPENDALE AND CHRIS HORRIE

For twenty years, since Sir Larry Lamb edited the newspaper, the *Sun* has had a feud with one other newspaper jostling for position nearest the top of the gutter, the *Daily Mirror*. Spoiling tactics are common enough in Fleet Street, but between the *Sun* and the *Mirror* they are quite commonly matters of the most bitter enmity.

Hand in hand with lifting went 'spoiling', another long-accepted practice which Lamb had specialized in. This involved throwing together a garbled and inferior (and free) version of a rival's major exclusive like a series or book serialization. The 'spoiler' was designed to fool punters glancing at the headlines into believing they were getting the real thing. It was a practice which Robert Maxwell, apparently unaware that the paper he had bought had been doing it for years, was now determined to stamp out.

Still fuming from the way in which the *Sun* had spiked his guns over the £1 million bingo game, Maxwell decided to teach MacKenzie a lesson by taking recourse to the courts. In May 1985 the *Mirror* bought the expensive serialization rights to a book called *The Killing of the Unicorn*, which told the steamy story of the murder of model Dorothy Stratten, who had been nicknamed the Unicorn and had been the lover of Hugh Hefner, the head of the *Playboy* empire. Maxwell knew MacKenzie would attempt to spoil it.

Five days before the *Mirror*'s *Unicorn* exclusive was due to start on Monday, 10 May, Maxwell's lawyers sent MacKenzie a letter threatening an immediate High Court injunction if he made any attempt to lift it. The next day MacKenzie, spurred by this challenge, announced that the *Sun* would also be carrying 'the full story'. Maxwell's injunction arrived in Bouverie Street at once, putting the *Sun* in the theoretical position of facing a substantial bill for costs and criminal action for contempt of court if it continued with its promised action.

MacKenzie ignored the injunction and published his 'spoiler', pushed together from rehashed old interviews and cuttings. Maxwell's lawyers crawled over the *Sun*'s text and concluded that one passage consisting of nineteen words had been directly lifted from the book. Clutching this damning evidence Maxwell triumphantly rushed to the High Court, where he accused the

Sun of being run by 'thieves and kleptomaniacs'. Magnanimous-
ly, he informed the judge that he did not want to see MacKenzie
behind bars (contempt carries a potential jail sentence), but he
did demand that News International be punished.

The judge, Mr Justice Hirst, was singularly unimpressed.
'The very virulence of this attack', he intoned, 'might suggest
that the proverbial adage about people who live in glasshouses
is not entirely inapposite.' He could not see how the inclusion
of nineteen words from a book of 200 pages amounted to
breach of copyright and, rejecting Maxwell's plea, advised the
Sun and the *Mirror* to call a 'truce'. MacKenzie boomed back:
'There will be no truce.' The verdict, he said, was 'a great
victory for the *Sun*'.

MacKenzie had played for high stakes during the *Unicorn*
affair and had won. 'Spoiling is a legitimate part of tabloid
journalism,' he announced triumphantly. As he saw it, the fun
of being an editor was all about taking outrageous risks. He
knew that Murdoch agreed. So long as the *Sun* did not get
caught out . . .

Maxwell's attempt to teach the 'thieves and kleptomaniacs' of
the *Sun* a legal lesson over the *Unicorn* saga may have looked
ludicrous, but it had a more serious side to it. The *Mirror*
naturally had the most to gain from castigating the *Sun* for
stealing stories and constructing second-hand 'spoilers'. Many
hacks on the Street thought it was just the pot calling the
kettle black. But an earlier *Mirror* leader headed 'LIES,
DAMNED LIES AND SUN EXCLUSIVES' had slammed another *Sun*
'lift' which had gone much further than rivalry between the two
papers and caused both disgust and alarm in Fleet Street.

In Lamb's period, when the *Sun* could be written off as a tits
and bums paper, nobody in journalism took it seriously; its
excesses could be explained as having little to do with the rest
of the industry. All editors knew that their paper practised
journalistic dishonesty of some sort, about which the first rule
was not to be caught. But when MacKenzie started flying

wildly about, transferring loose journalistic morals across the range from showbiz to deadly serious news stories, it was a different matter. And when he made the cardinal error of being caught at it, the Street began to wake up. The paper was dragging the whole profession down in the eyes of the public, and the dust-up between MacKenzie's *Sun* and the *Star* had given a whole new layer to the bottom of the barrel.

The *Mirror*'s 'LIES' editorial had been written about the *Sun*'s most notorious invention to date – a so-called 'WORLD EXCLUSIVE' interview with Mrs Marica McKay, the widow of Sergeant Ian McKay, a hero of the Falklands. The 'interview', under the headline 'PRIDE AND HEARTBREAK OF TWO VCS' WIDOWS', was published after the public announcement that Ian McKay and Lieutenant-Colonel H. Jones were being awarded the Victoria Cross posthumously. In fact Mrs McKay had never spoken to the *Sun* – despite the paper using every weapon in its armoury to get her to.

Sergeant McKay's widow was an intelligent and sensible woman who had been deeply affected by her husband's death. She did not want any publicity herself, and had been extremely reluctant to talk to any of the papers. Forced to accept the inevitable, she had consented to a joint proposal by the *Mirror* and Independent Television News to 'protect' her from the pack in return for exclusive interviews. The *Mirror* had accordingly installed her in the Howard Hotel, at the back of the Strand in London's West End, with a vast team of hacks standing guard round the clock.

The *Mirror*'s deal was like a red rag to a bull for MacKenzie. He marshalled his heaviest team to get to Mrs McKay at the hotel, leading to what was euphemistically described at the later Press Council hearing as 'an unpleasant scene' as the two sets of hacks clashed on the premises. Meanwhile 'Commander' Petrie had sent out a 'red alert' mobilization order to *Sun* hacks all over the country, ordering them to scour their region for anyone they could find. The paper hit gold when a hack interviewed Mrs McKay's mother-in-law, Mrs Freda McKay, and obtained a full report of what her daughter-in-law had told her about the VC award. The resulting screeds of copy were filed to Bouverie Street, other hacks on the mob-handed job got their hands on unscreened parts of an ITN interview and further quotes to throw into the mix were gleaned from older stories in the *Mail* and the *Express*.

The tricky job of assembling this disparate material into one piece to provide a classic spoiler was handed to reporter John Kay ... Kay had ... matured into the paper's best writer, commanding awed respect from the subs for his speed, accuracy and ability to compose stories in such perfect *Sun*-ese they could just be dropped into the paper without alteration. Kay was also extraordinarily skilled at the black Fleet Street art of sailing as close to the wind as possible when rehashing old material. He knew the line which turned a lift from a classic piece of allowed 'journalistic licence' into a fundamental dishonesty.

However, the *Sun*'s version of the Marica McKay interview crossed that line with a vengeance. It began: 'VC's widow Marica McKay fought back her tears last night and said: "I'm so proud of Ian. His name will remain a legend in the history books forever."' The story continued: 'Hugging her two children at their home in Rotherham, she said: "I'm proud of Ian's Victoria Cross – but I'd exchange all the medals in the world to have him back."'

Mrs McKay had indeed said all of these things at various times, and Kay had never written that she had said them directly to the *Sun*. But what had changed as the story went through the paper's system was that her mother-in-law, to whom remarks had been attributed, had disappeared. And, crucially, there had been a terrible error at the subbing stage. Kay had been extremely careful not to date the quotes. But an inexperienced sub working on the story was not aware what was going on. He had noticed the omission – a serious one on a paper where news was continuously hyped as having happened 'last night' unless it was dated 'recently' which was tabloidese for anything up to five years ago. The sub dutifully wrote in the key words 'last night', nobody noticed this unstitching of Kay's painstaking needlework, and the whole delicate exercise was then put completely over the top by MacKenzie's wild addition of the 'WORLD EXCLUSIVE' tag as a deliberate two fingers to the *Mirror*.

The *Mirror* fired back at the time with a *Sun*-bashing leader entitled 'THE SUN SINKS EVEN LOWER', branding its rival as a 'lying newspaper'. The *Mirror* could prove beyond doubt that Mrs McKay had never spoken to the *Sun* that night. She had been locked up with them in the Howard Hotel. That was as far as the matter looked like going and normally it would have been forgotten as just another Fleet Street lift – the sort of thing that took place all the time.

But the *Observer*'s Pendennis diarist, Peter Hillmore, a leading Unpopular hack in the game of *Sun*-sniping, was disgusted. He determined that the *Sun* should be reported to the Press Council. But the obvious person to make the complaint, Mrs McKay, had returned home with nothing but a deep desire to forget the whole episode and wanted nothing to do with it. So Hillmore asked his secretary to make the complaint in her name, using her private address in Essex. Reluctantly, Mrs McKay then consented to play her part by confirming that she had never spoken to the *Sun*. Nine months later, after grinding through the Press Council bureaucracy, the complaint was upheld, the *Sun* censured, and the *Mirror* printed its 'LIES, DAMN LIES' editorial, using the Council's verdict that the *Sun* had perpetrated 'A DEPLORABLE, INSENSITIVE DECEPTION ON THE PUBLIC' as the subsidiary headline.

Murdoch hit the roof. Although MacKenzie was not personally responsible for the slip which had given the game away, as editor he had to shoulder the blame. This time the stew really had boiled over and MacKenzie's minder, editorial director Peter Stephens, later mildly summarized the ensuing huge row as 'the boat rocking a little'. For whatever excuses could be made for the rest of it, the WORLD EXCLUSIVE tag was impossible to explain away. The hacks had been amazed to see it when everybody knew Mrs McKay was going to be all over the *Mirror* the next morning. But hacks who admired MacKenzie saw it just as his form of naughtiness. He was overseeing the whole thing and he just didn't give a fuck.

•

Cold-blooded murder in Nagorno-Karabakh
HEDRICK SMITH

Karabakh is an island of Christian Armenians engulfed in a surrounding sea of Azerbaijanis, who are Islamic in their culture and religion. Historically this area of the Caucasus has seen unending conflict, as has the neighbouring province of Nakhichevan. Azerbaijan was awarded control over Nagorno-Karabakh by Stalin in 1921. As Hedrick Smith reports, a few Armenians suspect Stalin of having acted with satanic purpose, knowing the Karabakh issue would rile the Armenians and keep these two nationalities forever at dagger points. And when Gorbachev's *glasnost* lifted the political lid, the Armenians were the first people to seize aggressively on the new openness.

It was almost immediately after Gorbachev's accession to power in 1985 that Armenians began bombarding the new leadership with appeals to return Karabakh and Nakhichevan. In 1987, the Karabakh Committee was formed to lobby Moscow and organize public support in Armenia. That fall Armenia became the site of the first large public demonstrations of the Gorbachev era, the central issues being Karabakh and industrial pollution. But the real explosion of public protest came in early 1988, after the Armenians felt they had been deceived by Gorbachev, triggering a campaign that would force the ouster of Communist leaders in both Armenia and Azerbaijan and set Armenia once again on the path to war with its neighbors.

The Armenians had high hopes that Gorbachev, with his

democratic approach, would let the Armenian majority in
Karabakh determine its own destiny and rejoin Armenia. After
lengthy private negotiations with the Communist Party Central
Committee in Moscow, there was great excitement in Armenia
at a December 1987 report in the French Communist newspaper
L'Humanité. The paper quoted Armenian economist Abel
Aganbegyan, an adviser to Gorbachev, as telling the Armenian
community in Paris that Moscow – presumably meaning
Gorbachev – had decided to settle the issue of the Nagorno-
Karabakh situation, and to return the province to Armenia.
Aganbegyan's statements, repeated in the Soviet press, hit like
thunder in the Azerbaijani capital of Baku.

The Azerbaijani leadership warned Moscow that any change
on Karabakh would not only bring hundreds of thousands of
Azerbaijanis into the streets, but would inflame all of Soviet
Central Asia. This was an ominous threat to the Kremlin, and
many Soviet officials, for fear of opening up a Pandora's box,
opposed any change in territorial arrangements in the Caucasus.
Across the country, there were at least thirty-five significant
territorial disputes; a change in one area was sure to invite
pressures on other disputed territories, a nightmare for Moscow.
None the less, the Armenians were on the offensive, and on
February 20, 1988, the regional soviet, or council, of Nagorno-
Karabakh, dominated by Armenians, called for transferring the
region to Armenian control. The Soviet Politburo immediately
rejected and condemned this move as an 'extremist' action.
Yerevan reacted with an eruption of demonstrations more massive than the Soviet Union had seen since the Bolshevik Revolution. On February 25, between half a million and a million
people assembled in downtown Yerevan, carrying banners that
proclaimed KARABAKH IS PART OF ARMENIA! AND KARABAKH
IS A TEST CASE FOR *PERESTROIKA*!

In Azerbaijan, emotions flamed out of control, and on February 27, a mob of young Azerbaijani toughs went on a bloody
rampage against Armenians in Sumgait, a city about thirty miles
from Baku. After three days of looting and murder, thirty-two

people were dead, hundreds were wounded, and tens of thousands had fled for their lives.

When I visited Sumgait, Azerbaijani officials admitted to me that it is a breeding ground for violence – a tough industrial town with high unemployment, inadequate housing, terrible pollution from thirty-two chemical plants and other heavy industry, and what officials called 'criminal elements' – meaning ex-convicts legally barred from living in Baku.

On each of the three terrible days, Azerbaijani rallies charged with emotion had been held in Lenin Square, in front of Sumgait City Hall, and city leaders took part. Armenian refugees told me later that the mobs had been sent out by official leaders in Sumgait to hunt Armenians. After the violence, Sumgait's mayor and Party boss were fired for incompetence, but their successors insisted to me that the old officials had not fomented the violence. They acknowledged that those officials had been slow and ineffective in controlling police and city authorities; but they contended that emotions had been fired up, not by local officials, but by the accusations of Azerbaijanis, who had come to Sumgait with stories of having been chased out of Armenia and Karabakh.

The bloodbath in Sumgait changed the dynamics of the Karabakh dispute: It was a nightmare, publicized worldwide, and, in sharpening hostilities on both sides, it propelled both into an escalating cycle of violence.

In Sumgait, I talked with Azerbaijanis who had given shelter to terrified Armenians, and outside Yerevan, I talked with Armenian survivors, who described the carnage. One young woman, Irina Melkunyan, who had hidden for hours in a neighbor's bathtub, told of hearing the mob breaking down doors, hurling furniture out the windows, starting bonfires. She had married into a family in which five people, including her husband, were murdered: mother, father, daughter, and two sons. A middle-aged woman, Asya Arakelyan, told me how she had tried to escape into the apartment of a Russian woman across the hall, but had been chased down by a gang wielding bicycle chains, knives, and hatchets.

'The Azerbaijanis came, all dressed in black,' she said, trying to control her terror as she relived the trauma. 'They went through every building, looking for Armenians and shouting slogans – "Death to Armenians," "We'll annihilate all the Armenians. Get them out of here."

'They broke down our apartment door and my husband and I escaped. Our Russian neighbor took us to her place. They smashed and burned everything in our place, and then came, with a bullhorn, and told us to come out in the name of the law. I was close to the door and they hit me first with their crowbar. They grabbed me and started pulling me downstairs, outside, to the courtyard. They threw me down, ripped my dress, and started wildly beating me with anything they could lay their hands on. And those axes and knives – it was terrible. They had a big knife and they threatened to cut my head off. When I looked up, I understood they were about to kill me. So I raised my arm in self-defense, and they slashed open my arm with their huge knife.'

She showed me how she had shielded her head, exposing a terrible scar, nearly a foot long, a slice all across the soft flesh of her underarm. We were sitting knee-to-knee in a tiny room, and I could feel her begin to cry. When I reached out to comfort her, she seized my hand, telling me through her tears that the Azerbaijani mob, taking her for dead, had thrown a rug over her.

'Then they dumped some gasoline over my body and burned me,' she said. 'I didn't know that, right next to me, they had gone at my husband. They hacked him with an ax and burned his body. Practically next to me. Only I did not know it then.'

She glanced at a nearby dresser, where she had a framed portrait of her husband, a nice-looking man in his fifties, dressed in a business suit. The sight of him was too much to bear. She broke into sobs, her body throbbing.

'I was there for hours, losing consciousness,' she went on haltingly. 'Rain started. It stopped the fire . . . When I came to, it was dark. I was bleeding. My back was all burned . . . Finally, my younger son came to me. "Mama, Mama, what happened to you?" I lifted my head with difficulty and told him to run: "Go away or else they will kill you." He asked me not to move and went for an ambulance. There were Azerbaijani cars all around. He asked them to take him to the ambulance, but they wouldn't help . . . Later, much later, the boy came back with a truck.'

Considering it a miracle that Asya Arakelyan was alive, the Armenians called her the 'Madonna' of Sumgait.

For some, the bloodbath at Sumgait was a modern reenactment of the Turkish massacre of 1915. A journalist named Armen Oganesyan, a trim, steely, violently passionate Armenian nationalist, said:

'If you know Armenian history, you should know that Armenians were always victims – always paying with their lives, with their lands, with their possessions, going through endless genocides, endless manslaughters, endless bloodshed.' As Armen spoke, his brown eyes were burning. 'Right now you see a so-called minigenocide, because Azerbaijanis are like Turks, and their pan-Turkic ideology sees Armenia as the big obstacle to their unity, to achieving the goals of pan-Turkism. People want to present all this as Christians against Muslims and vice versa. I have nothing against Islam, but when someone wants to use religious fanaticism as a political weapon, causing the death of children and old people, it becomes a crime.'

I saw Armen several times; he took me to other groups of refugees, showed me his articles about Sumgait, explained his desperate attempts to see justice done, seethed with raw fury that only a few minor punishments had been meted out against the Azerbaijani perpetrators. His pain was understandable, but to me he seemed a fanatic who was nursing and spreading hatred. Ashot Manucharyan was trying to turn the pain and passion of Karabakh toward reform, whereas Armen Oganesyan was turning it toward revenge. He said to me that his ethic was Old Testament: an eye for an eye.

Sadly, it was easy to find victims on the other side. By the summer of 1989, when I reached the Caucasus, about 200,000

Armenians had fled from Azerbaijan, and about 160,000 Azerbaijanis had fled from Armenia. Most of these Azerbaijani refugees were concentrated in Baku, where their anger fueled the already heightened tensions. There were still about 200,000 Armenians living in Azerbaijan, but virtually all of the Azerbaijanis cleared out of Armenia as a result of waves of Armenian violence and intimidation, especially in October and November 1988.

In a very plain Baku apartment, I talked with an Azerbaijani family, the Guliyevs, whose twenty-eight-year-old son, Magaran, had been attacked by Armenians in Massis, a city about twenty miles from Yerevan, and not far from their former village of Zangiler, where there had been periodic violence. By the family's account, Magaran Guliyev's murder was as brutal, savage, and cold-blooded as that of Asya Arakelyan's husband.

As tensions had risen in Armenia through the summer of 1988, the Guliyev family, like many Azerbaijanis, had begun preparing to move to Baku. Coming back from Baku, their older son, Magaran, was set upon at the Massis railroad station by Armenians, who attacked him and his uncle with hammers, axes, and screwdrivers.

'They were hiding, a group of them,' Mrs Guliyev said she was told by the uncle, who somehow survived. 'My son got off the train and they attacked him and my brother. My brother fell down; they thought he was dead. So they beat my son, hammered him several times, and threw his body in some water [near the station]. It was sort of a swamp. A soldier found him, saw him still breathing, and brought him to the hospital. In three days, they called us from the hospital and said: "There's a dead man here. Come and take him."'

The victim's body was buried immediately, but after a couple of weeks his family decided to take his body with them to Azerbaijan, and they had his body exhumed. 'There were many Armenians around, including the heads of the local militia, Babahanyan and Iskandaryan, and many soldiers,' said Mushtur Guliyev, the surviving son. 'They were all saying, "All the

Turks should be killed ... All the Azerbaijanis should be caught and killed this way – have their heads cut off."'

The family was sitting around a rough wooden table in the courtyard of their apartment building – mother, father, brother, two sisters, wife, and small child. Their grief hung in the summer air, thick and heavy. The father, a gray-haired work-man, was crying openly, as were the women.

'When I went to get my son's body, there was a militiaman, named Makhachiyan, who asked me: "Why are you crying? Is this not enough for you? We should have annihilated all of your kind, as we did this one."'

•

Right-hand man

JEFFREY BERNARD

Last Saturday afternoon I went with a friend into the Mecca betting shop in Greek Street to listen to a race commentary. I had a financial interest in the event and was anxious to hear how my money would run. I heard very little of the race thanks to a man who was making a lot of noise watching a football match from Germany on television. I remonstrated with him, pointing out to him that a betting shop was primarily a place for horse and greyhound racing punters and not one for football freaks and yobs. At that he asked me to to step outside and I did.

That was my first mistake. You should never accept such an invitation or make it. Either you walk away from the situation or you hit your man immediately and as hard as you can. It would be understating the case to say that I am a trifle ring-rusty. I am on the scrap-heap. But I went outside on to the pavement with him noting that he was probably two pounds lighter than a cart-horse. The second mistake was to think. It is amazing how many things you can think of in a split second and in a split second I was mulling over matters concerning street fights. It occurred to me that if I began by jabbing a left on to his nose it might disconcert him somewhat and bring tears to his eyes, putting me into soft focus. It was during these considerations that he caught me flush on the chin with a right-hander. I have been hit harder. The punch didn't matter. What did was my head hitting the pavement. It made a sickening noise like two coconuts being banged together and the pain nearly made me vomit. I thought I might lie there for three weeks.

Now I have seen a lot of the police in my time, usually an unwelcome sight, but on this occasion they appeared quite miraculously out of the blue. Shades of the US Cavalry in the last reel. There was a uniformed policeman and an unmarked squad car which must have been cruising Soho on the look-out for drug dealers. My opponent was bundled into the car and was nicked. My head hurt so much I thought of taking it to hospital for an X-ray but it recovered slowly over a couple of drinks in the Ming Chinese restaurant. All that hurts now after four days is a pelvic bone, seeing as how my flesh now no longer acts as a cushion. My friend went off to Vine Street police station to make a statement and I kept hearing echoes of the skull hitting the pavement. The manager of the betting shop, I heard later, had telephoned for the police at the 'off' and so thanks to him. I would not fancy his job. There are some dodgy customers in that shop but he can't help that. But the man who put me on the pavement was, I am pretty sure, a stranger on the manor. He looked like one of those people who can start a fight in an empty room and I wonder what he got when he came up to face the beak on Monday.

I had resolved shortly after being lifted to my feet to fight only women and children from now on, but something much more frightening than the man with the right hand marched into the Coach and Horses the following day. A gang – that is the only word – a gang of 12 lesbians walked in throwing out challenging glances at us poor men nursing fractured skulls or hangovers. I find lesbians really rather frightening. They do actually *hate* you whereas men like the right hand merely want to duff you up. That is pretty mindless of them but it is not as awesome as hate. Not much is.

In a strange way I would quite like a return with the right hand if I was equipped with a large spanner or a car starting handle which was a favourite weapon in the 1950s. No, I wouldn't. He might just possibly be okay and I know how nasty I can be in circumstances which involve something as trivial but irritating as asking someone to switch off the television or turn it down. I could have hit the Colonel over the head with the television set in the day room of the hospital last week if he had looked as though he would live to see the *News at Ten*.

Well, to be a mite realistic I don't think that Saturday was the last occasion on which I shall be whacked but at least I shall bob and weave a bit the next time I come out of this unlucky corner. And to think that 30 years ago I liked to hear the call 'seconds out' followed by the bell. Both the bell and the bell for last orders are to be dreaded now.

●

Men who hate women and why

SUSAN FORWARD

Nobody in his right mind would stay with someone in my condition. The only reason Jeff stays is because he loves me.

When Nancy first came to see me she was sixty pounds overweight and had an ulcer. She wore old, baggy jeans and a shapeless smock; her hair was stringy, her fingernails were bitten down to the quick, and her hands shook. When she had married Jeff, four years before, she had been a fashion coordinator for a major Los Angeles department store. In her work she had traveled through Europe and the Orient selecting designer clothes for the store. She had always dressed in the latest fashions and dated fascinating men; she had been written about in a number of articles on successful women in the Los Angeles area – and she had accomplished this before she was 30. Yet, when I first saw her, at age 34, she was so ashamed of how she looked and felt about herself that she seldom left home.

The decline of Nancy's self-esteem seemed to have begun when she married Jeff. Yet, when I questioned her about her husband, she began with a long list of superlatives.

> He's a wonderful man. He's charming and witty and dynamic. He's always doing little things for me – he sent me flowers to commemorate the anniversary of the first night we'd made love. Last year he bought two surprise tickets to Italy for my birthday.

She told me that Jeff, a busy and successful entertainment lawyer, always found time to spend with her, and that despite her current appearance he still wanted her along for all his business dinners and outings.

> I used to love going out with him with his clients because we'd still hold hands like high-school lovers. I'm the envy of all my friends because of him. One friend said, 'You've got the special one, Nancy.' And I know he is. But look at me! I don't understand what's happened. I feel so low all the time. I've got to get myself back together or I'm going to lose him. A man like Jeff doesn't have to lug around a wife like me. He can have anyone he wants, including movie stars. I'm lucky he's hung in as long as he has.

As I listened to Nancy and observed her appearance, I asked myself, 'What's wrong with this picture?' There was a basic contradiction here. Why would a competent and effective woman, in a loving relationship, get so ground down? What had happened to her in the four years of her marriage to make such a marked change in both her appearance and her sense of self-worth?

I pressed her to tell me more about her relationship with Jeff, and bit by bit a fuller picture emerged.

I guess the only thing that really bothers me about him is how much he flies off the handle.

'What do you mean by "fly off the handle"?' I asked. She laughed a little.

He does what I call his King Kong imitation, yelling and making lots of noise. He also puts me down a lot, like he did the other night when we were having dinner with friends. He was talking about a play and I interjected something and he just snapped at me, 'Why don't you shut up?' Then he said to our friends, 'Don't pay any attention to her. She's always got some stupid thing to say.' I was so humiliated I felt like sinking into the upholstery. I could hardly swallow my food afterwards.

Nancy began to cry as she recalled several other humiliating scenes in which Jeff had called her stupid, selfish, or thoughtless. When enraged, he would often yell at her, slam doors, and throw things.

The more I questioned her, the clearer the picture became. Here was a woman trying desperately to figure out how to please a husband who was often angry and intimidating as well as charming. Nancy said she often fell asleep long after he did with his cruel words stinging in her ears. During the day, she had fits of crying for no apparent reason.

It was at Jeff's insistence that Nancy had quit her job when they married. Now she felt incapable of returning to her career. As she described it:

Now I wouldn't even have the nerve to go on an interview, much less a buying trip. I don't feel like I could make the decisions anymore because I've lost confidence in myself.

Jeff made all the decisions in their marriage. He insisted on total control of every aspect of their life together. He oversaw all spending, selected the people with whom they socialized, and even made decisions about what Nancy should do while he was at work. He derided her for any opinion she had that differed from his, and he yelled at her, even in public, whenever he was displeased. Any deviation on her part from the course he had set for them resulted in a hideous scene.

I told Nancy we had a lot of work to do, but I assured her she would begin to feel less overwhelmed. I told her we would take a hard look at her relationship with Jeff and that the self-confidence she thought she'd lost was not really gone, only misplaced. Together, we would get it back again. When she left that first session, she felt a little steadier and less lost. But I began to feel shaky.

Nancy's story had hit me very hard. I knew that as a therapist, my reactions to a client were important tools. I make emotional connections with the people I work with, which helps me understand more quickly how they are feeling. But this was something else. After Nancy left my office, I felt very uncomfortable. This was not the first time a woman had come to see me with this type of problem, nor was it the first time I had reacted so strongly. I could no longer deny that what was affecting me was the fact that Nancy's situation was too close to my own.

On the outside, I appeared confident, fulfilled – a woman who truly had it all. All day long, at my office, at the hospital and the clinic where I practiced, I worked with people to help them find confidence and a renewed sense of their own strength. But at home, it was another story. My husband, like Nancy's, was charming, sexy, and romantic, and I had fallen madly in love with him almost immediately after we met. But I soon discovered that he had a great deal of anger inside him and that he had the power to make me feel small, inadequate and off-balance. He insisted on being in control of everything I did, believed, and felt.

The Susan who was a therapist could say to Nancy, 'Your husband's behavior doesn't sound loving. In fact, it sounds as if there's a lot of psychological abuse going on.' But what was I saying to myself? The Susan who went home at night twisted herself into a pretzel trying to keep her husband from yelling at her. That Susan kept telling herself that he was a wonderful man, that he was exciting to be with, and that, therefore, if something went wrong, it must be her fault.

Over the next few months, I looked more closely at what was going on both in my own marriage and in the relationships of my clients who appeared to be in similar situations. What was really happening here? What were the patterns? Although it was the women who usually sought my help, it was the behavior of the men that claimed my attention. As their partners described them, they were often charming and even loving, but they were able to switch to cruel, critical, and insulting behavior on a moment's notice. Their behavior covered a wide spectrum, from obvious intimidation and threats to more subtle, covert attacks which took the form of constant put-downs or erosive criticism. Whatever the style, the results were the same. The man gained control by grinding the woman down. These men also refused to take any responsibility for how their attacks made their partners feel. Instead, they blamed their wives or lovers for any and every unpleasant event.

I knew from my experience in working with couples that every marriage has two sides. However, it's easy for therapists to over-identify with the client when we only hear one side of the story. Certainly each partner contributes to whatever turmoil and conflict exists in a relationship. But once I began seeing some of my clients' male partners in counseling, I realized that they did not suffer nearly as much as they caused their partners to suffer. It was the women who were in pain. All of them had dramatic losses of self-esteem, and many had additional symptoms and reactions. Nancy had ulcers, was overweight, and had let her appearance go; others had severe problems with drug and/or alcohol abuse, migraines, gastrointestinal complaints, eating disorders, and sleeping disorders. Their job performance had often suffered. Their once-promising careers had declined. Previously successful and competent women found themselves doubting their skills and their judgment. They experienced depressions, crying spells, and anxiety with alarming frequency. In every case, these problems had begun to appear during the partnership or marriage.

As I realized that I was seeing a distinct pattern in these relationships, I began to discuss it with my colleagues. They were all familiar with the type of man I described; each had treated women who either had been married to, had been in love with, or were the daughters of men who fit my description. What was so surprising to me was that while the type of behavior was so familiar to all of us, no one had yet described it in a cohesive way.

At this point I started reviewing the psychological literature. Because of the man's lack of sensitivity to the pain he was causing his partner, I first re-examined character disorders. People with character disorders have little capacity for guilt, remorse, or anxiety. These emotions are uncomfortable but necessary monitors of our ethical and moral interactions with other people.

I knew that there were two major types of recognized character disorders. First, there are the narcissists. These are people who are totally self-obsessed. They tend to make relationships primarily in order to be reassured of their own specialness in the world. Men who fall into this category often flit from one relationship to another in search of love and admiration. Some familiar names for this type of man are Peter Pans and Don Juans. They have been called 'the people who cannot love'.

The men in the relationships I was looking at were different. They appeared to love intensely, and in many cases they had been in a long-term relationship with one partner. Also, their primary need differed from that of the narcissist in that they seemed to need to *control* more than they needed to be *admired*.

At the other end of the character-disorder spectrum were the more extreme and dangerous sociopaths. These are people who create a whirlwind of chaos in their lives. They use and exploit anyone who comes into their orbit. Lies and deception are second nature to them. They can range from common criminals to prominent and successful professionals who are chronically involved in white-collar crime. The most striking feature about sociopaths is their total lack of conscience.

But the man I was attempting to define was often genuinely responsible and competent in his dealings with society. His destructive behavior was not generalized, as was that of the sociopath. In fact, it was very focused. Unfortunately, it was focused almost exclusively on his partner.

He used for weapons his words and his moods. While he tended not to physically abuse the woman in his life, he systematically wore her down through psychological battering, which in the end is every bit as emotionally devastating as physical violence.

I wondered whether these men got some sort of perverse pleasure out of the pain and suffering they were causing their partners. Were they, in fact, sadists?

After all, many of the people I discussed my discoveries with assured me that the women involved with these men were classic textbook masochists. This made me angry. I knew that the labeling of women in unhealthy relationships as masochistic – that is, seeking and enjoying suffering – has long been standard practice in my profession and in our culture. This is a convenient but highly dangerous way of attempting to explain why so many women fall into self-denying, submissive behavior with men. In reality, women learn these behaviors early, and are consistently rewarded and praised for them. The paradox here is that the behaviors that make a woman vulnerable to mistreatment are the very ones she has been taught are feminine and lovable. The concept of masochism is particularly dangerous because it serves to justify aggression against women – it confirms that 'that's what women really want'.

As I talked more extensively with the couples I was counseling, I found that neither of these terms applied. Rather than getting emotional or sexual pleasure from his partner's pain, as the sadist does, the man I was attempting to define felt both *threatened* and *enraged* by his partner's suffering. The woman was no more a masochist than the man was a sadist. She did not get any hidden sexual or emotional pleasure from her partner's abusive treatment of her. Instead, it severely demoralized her. Once again I found that the psychological categories and terminology were not adequate to describe what I was seeing in these relationships. The man I was attempting to define did not appear in the literature.

He was not a clear-cut sociopath, narcissist, or sadist, although some of these elements were often present in his character. The most dramatic difference between this man and those described in the psychological literature was that he was capable of engaging in a long-term relationship with one woman. In fact, his love seemed particularly hot and intense. The tragic part was that he did everything he could to destroy the woman he professed to love so deeply.

I know as a therapist that the words 'I love you' don't necessarily indicate what is going on in a relationship. I know that it is behavior, not words, that defines reality. As I listened to my clients, I asked myself: Is this the way you treat someone you really love? Isn't this in fact the way you treat someone you hate?

•

That's football

BILL BUFORD

During the 1980s, Bill Buford, an American living in Britain, editor of
the literary magazine *Granta*, travelled with English football supporters, recording his first-hand impressions of soccer hooligans. He
witnessed many scenes of fighting on, and off, the football terraces,
one of which is described here.

A December match against Chelsea. All morning long, the
supporters have been gathering at the Lion and Lamb, a red-
brick Irish pub near Euston Station, arriving, once again,
according to a calculatedly staggered schedule – by hired coaches
arranged during the week, vans and minibuses that have avoided
the major motorways, private cars. Both rooms of the pub are
crowded – steamy and sweaty and unpleasant – and the floor is
covered with a gooey mix of beer and mud and wetness. It is
impossible to move. I try briefly to get a drink but never reach
the bar. At around one-thirty, the principal figures accounted
for, the group sets off, the manner of its leaving by now a ritual
known even to me. The pub is evacuated, glass breaking as
pints of beer are simply dropped, and a crush of people
instantaneously fills up the small street outside, a preposterous
number in a preposterous hurry – no one wanting to be left
behind – and then turns into the main Euston Road, spreading
out, kerb to kerb, blocking the traffic in both directions,
everyone organized and united and feeling the high energy and
jubilant authority of suddenly being a crowd.

They avoid the Underground at Euston Station (too many
police) and march to the next one, Euston Square, entering it as
one – placards, posters, stools being picked up and swept along
en route, no barricade or turnstile an impediment – everyone
chanting now, the group's euphoria building, no one buying a

ticket, no one being stopped or challenged, and board the train
that happens to be waiting at the bottom of the escalator,
holding open the doors to prevent its leaving until everyone is
inside.

But the train does not move.

The doors close finally, but the train remains at the platform.
It is waiting; the driver is waiting – for something; for some
sign; in all likelihood, for the police. Every carriage, front to
back, is filled with supporters. Every seat is filled; every aisle,
entrance or bit of space – for standing, sitting, squatting,
holding on – has been taken. This is rush-hour closeness, an
intolerable number of people pressed tightly together. The train
has become hot and unbearably uncomfortable. Someone pushes
the button to open the doors but they don't open. The supporters start shouting. They pound the windows. They try rocking
the carriage from side to side.

And then the train starts and rapidly attains full speed. It
passes through the first Underground station, Great Portland
Street, without stopping. It passes through Baker Street and
through the next one, Edgware Road, and it is apparent that the
train is not going to stop, and that, with all other traffic cleared
off the line, the train is going straight to Chelsea (*if* that's where
it is going). I watch the faces of two passengers, a couple in
their late fifties, modestly dressed, the man in a duffel coat,
shopping bags at their feet, whose Saturday outing was ruined
the moment they made the mistake of boarding this particular
train. They appear too uncomfortable to make themselves conspicuous by objecting to where they are being taken, and sit
anxiously looking side to side. Notting Hill Gate appears and
disappears in a blur.

The train finally stops at Fulham Broadway, the station near
the ground, and there is, despite the preparation – the elaborate
routes into London, the expensive hire vehicles, the strategies
of evasion – nothing to see but members of the Metropolitan
Police. There are rows and rows of them. They are the only
people on the platform; they have taken over the station. They

appear, once we finally reach the top of the stairs, to be the only people waiting outside as well, but then, amid the police and the horses – a helicopter is noisily overhead – the pushing and the jostling, I hear someone say that he sees 'their lads'.

In the confusion around the entrance to the ground, the police line momentarily falls apart, and I notice a short, red-haired lad from Chelsea has slipped in among the Manchester supporters. He is following one, walking closely behind him, stride for stride. He taps him on the shoulder and, as the supporter turns round, fells him by an act of decisive violence: a heavy object, an iron bar or a weight that the red-haired fellow is holding in both his fists, is raised so suddenly, rammed with such force into the supporter's Adam's apple, that he is lifted off his feet, rising several inches into the air, and then falls backwards and collapses. When I look for the Chelsea supporter, he is gone, disappeared into the crowd.

Inside the ground, the policing continues but at a distance: there is a line of police along the bottom of the terraces, on the other side of the perimeter fence; there is another line at the top, along the uppermost row, looking down; and there are clusters on either side, in the stands left empty to provide a buffer between the home and visiting supporters. The police, it would appear, are happy to keep the area surrounded but reluctant to enter it themselves. Inside it, Chelsea supporters have 'infiltrated' and, like the little urban terrorist who surprised the United fan from behind, are conducting a discreet campaign of highly targeted violence – most of it unobserved by the police. I suspect, in fact, that the police are happy to 'unobserve' the violence: there is the sense that anything that occurs within the perimeters of the net they have formed is tolerable provided it doesn't slip through and get out into the open; but there is also the sense that anyone who gets hurt probably deserves it – for being there.

The effect is unpleasant. The experience of the whole match is unpleasant – nasty, unsettling. It is cold and windy: there is grit in my eyes, and I can feel it in my hair and underneath my clothes. There is constant movement: too many people have been admitted – a familiar ploy, to get them off the streets – which makes it difficult to do more than try to remain upright and fight for a view of the match. Every now and then, there is another little *snap*-violent disturbance effected by one of these runt-like infiltrators: everyone cranes his neck to have a look at the thing that has happened; you can never quite see it. Moments later, there is another incident somewhere else, and everyone cranes his neck in that direction. And so it goes on. Someone has taken to throwing spark plugs, and a supporter near me is struck in the head by one, slicing his forehead. It is uneasy and claustrophobic. There is mention of a stabbing, but I don't see it, and it would be in keeping that there would be one, but also that there wouldn't be one, that it would have simply felt appropriate that someone should have been stabbed by now.

Towards the end of the match I spot the red-haired Chelsea supporter. I had thought that he would be among those who had infiltrated the visitors' stands. I watch him. His face, even though cheerfully freckled, is hard and unforgiving. He has the familiar crescent cheek, the encrusted scar from being knifed. He is small – he comes about half-way up my chest – but his smallness is not a liability or a weakness: it serves only to make him compact and spring-like and immediately menacing. He is an unhappy thing to look at, a little entrepreneurial machine of small-time violence. When he comes closer, working his way through the terraces, and passes in front of me – he is an arm's length away – I feel an urge to take him from behind by the neck and squeeze him until his breathing stops. The urge is a real one, I am convinced, and not a violent fantasy, and as he walks out of my reach, I regret I have done nothing.

By the end of the match, everyone is restless and frustrated; the 'atmosphere' is charged in some manner, as though by electricity or some kind of pressure in the air. I have grown irritated. I want to be warm. I want to be home. I am tired of standing and of the policing and have got a chill from the cold and damp of the night air, and am unhappy about the prospect of being held back, crushed up against lads smelling of bad food and bad drink and the bad indigestion that is the result, while waiting for the streets to be cleared of rival supporters. I resolve that I will figure out a way of slipping through the police line.

A policeman reaches out for me, looking as though he wants to stop me, but then lets me pass. I am on the other side. I am free to go. I am very relieved.

I recognize the person walking next to me; he is a Manchester supporter. I surmise that he must have done what I just did: he, too, has slipped through the police line, by himself, looking very solemn and very thoughtful – the last person in the world who could cause trouble.

I carry on. I spot Robert. How did Robert, of all people, succeed in getting past the police?

Behind Robert is another lad. This one, also by himself, is also terribly serious in manner: preoccupied, distracted. This is suspicious. Then there is another, until finally it occurs to me that they are all emerging from the ground in the same manner, having separated so that they can sneak through the police line one by one. There is a momentary indecisiveness and then they start down the Fulham Road, not wanting to hang about, not walking too fast, everyone maintaining the I-am-on-my-own-and-not-about-to-start-trouble look. I can't tell how much of this has been planned; the feeling is of overwhelming spontaneity. A crowd is forming, and the effect is of something coming alive. I can see more people joining up, attracted by the familiar, powerful magnetism of numbers, but they don't seem like additions: they don't seem to come from the outside, but from within the crowd itself. You can feel it growing, as though this crowd, this thing, this creature were some kind of biological entity, multiplying in the way cells multiply, expanding from the centre.

I follow, not wanting to miss out. I don't know why they are going in this particular direction but I am determined to be there – wherever 'there' might turn out to be. I have forgotten that a moment ago I was ready to go home. I am no longer

tired or irritable or cold, but, like everyone around me, alive to
the possibility that something is going to happen.

There are faces I haven't seen before – older faces, supporters
in their mid-thirties and early forties, veterans of violence, old
hands who have turned up because it is a match against Chelsea.
The experience is manifestly so familiar to them that they have
an eerie ease and knowingness. They are canny and savvy and
know not to say a word.

The group – still fairly disparate, unhurried, deliberately
casual – strolls silently round the Fulham Broadway, going
behind the Underground station by way of a side street. The
police, concentrated near the entrance, have dogs and horses
and a small fleet of vans. Everyone knows that, having got this
far, he must not be detected. It is a ludicrous effect: as if a
thousand people, having just burgled the back of a house, are
now leaving on tiptoe through the living-room, while the
owner sleeps in front of the television. It would take only one
policeman to spot what is going on. But no policeman notices.
Each step increases the expectation that they're going to get
away with it. I catch sight of a street name – Vanston Place. I
don't know the area and find that I am looking for reference
points. Everyone bears to the right. I follow. And then they
turn sharply to the left, a quick left. They have done it: the
Fulham Broadway is behind us.

I don't see any Chelsea supporters. But I understand enough
to know that I don't see any police either. *That* is what matters:
that the police are behind us, receding with each step, mistakenly
positioned on every Underground platform between here and
Euston Station, waiting for the violent supporters who will
never appear. The realization is intoxicating. Nobody says a
thing – the silence of the group is uncompromising – but you
can see it in the faces.

We are free, the faces are saying.

We have got past the police, the faces believe.

We cannot be stopped now.

All day long a crowd has been trying to form, and all day

long it has been prevented from doing so. It has been cribbed and frustrated and contained. The experience of the day has been one of being boxed in: the pub in the morning; the train at Euston Square; the platform at Fulham Broadway where everyone was frisked, scrutinized, surrounded and then escorted to the ground. They were boxed in during the match – literally a box, its sides made of the heavy steel fences of the enclosed terraces. Throughout, the containment has been absolute. At every moment, there have been limits.

And now there is none.

The pace picks up. I can feel the pressure to go faster, an implicit imperative, coming from no one in particular, coming from everyone, a shared instinct for the heat and the strength of feeling, knowing that the faster the group goes the more coherent it becomes, the more powerful, the more intense the sensations. The casual stroll becomes a brisk walk and then a jog. Everyone is jogging in formation, tightly compressed, silent.

I am enjoying this. I am excited by it. Something is going to happen: the crowd has an appetite, and the appetite will have to be fed; there is a craving for release. A crowd, already so committed, is not going to disperse easily. It has momentum: unstoppable momentum.

I catch sight of a street name – Dawes Road. I press on, going a little faster, wanting to get to the very front, while repeating the name of the street as I run. I recognize the familiar high-street businesses – a Ladbrokes, a Lloyds Bank, a building society, a shop selling fruit and vegetables – but they could be anywhere. I could be anywhere.

It is getting congested. I am on the pavement, which is filled with supporters, and I am having difficulty getting any closer to the front. There are more supporters on the other side of the street as well, on the opposite pavement, and some running between the cars.

For the first time I hear shouting, although it is some distance away. It is a football chant, but I can't make out what is being said. I am surprised by the sound. Someone says: 'Their lads.' These words seem slightly intrusive – *their lads* – and they echo round in my head. The shouting, I then understand, comes from Chelsea supporters. What does this mean? That we are being chased by Chelsea supporters? I find the idea thrilling. The crowd has a purpose: the Chelsea supporters have provided one. Actually I find many things in the idea. I also find it frightening: there are no police; this is about to become ugly. And I find it confusing. How, at this point, can the Chelsea supporters be *behind* us? I look back but see little: only members of the Manchester crowd, who seemed to have swelled now, a bloated presence, filling the full width of Dawes Road. I can't see beyond them. I can't tell if anyone is chasing us, but I hear them. Yes, the chanting is definitely Chelsea's.

Yes, someone else says, it's their lads.

I press forward. I don't want to get caught from behind in a fight, but to get any closer to the front I have to push people out of the way. I inadvertently make someone stumble, but he doesn't fall. He swears at me, and I mumble an apology, and when I look up again I see the most astonishing sight: it is Sammy. Sammy is at the front of the group. Where did he come from?

I remember Sammy in the pub in that morning, but I haven't seen him since. It seems fitting that as this crowd came into being he would emerge out of it, pushed up to the front, created by the crowd. I feel reassured seeing him. I watch him. He is jogging steadily, his little lieutenants by his side. He has noted that the Chelsea supporters are behind us – he turns his head every three or four steps – but the prospect does not disturb him. Sammy does not look unhappy. Something is going to happen – that's his look; he knows it's going to go off.

Even so, I still don't understand: where have the Chelsea supporters come from? It is as if they have materialized out of our footprints. There was the police barrier; the police at Fulham Broadway; the quick route through the back streets. But nowhere were there Chelsea supporters. Something is missing. Is it possible that the United supporters set out in this direction knowing they were going to be followed? But how could they have known that? Were the Chelsea supporters in hiding, waiting for them to pass? Did I miss them?

I continue watching Sammy – in control, still checking behind him, judging how close the Chelsea supporters are. Everything, his manner suggests, is going to plan. And then the thought occurs to me: yes, it *is* going to plan. It is an improbable notion, but it makes sense of everything. It has been planned. Riots are meant to be spontaneous and sudden: you don't control the uncontrollable. Crowd violence is never planned – or is it? Is it possible to have a riot by appointment?

I want to ask, but things are moving very fast. Sammy, having been offered control, is exercising it. The pace quickens. I am running hard, too hard to catch sight of anything. There are shops, but they are unfamiliar. I don't even recognize the high street standards. It is a strange sensation: I feel as though I am running in a tunnel. Along the peripheries of my vision is a blurry darkness, the light – from a sign or a window or a headlamp from a car – is intermittent and unfocused. I am having to concentrate on the back of Sammy's head; I have hooked my gaze there so that I can be dragged along by it, so that I won't stumble or fall. The chanting of the Chelsea supporters is louder – progressively louder. They are getting closer.

Someone says: They are on our tails.

Sammy presses on. Stay together, he calls out; it is the first thing he has said. Stay close together, he repeats.

I still can't see any Chelsea supporters, but I believe that I can *feel* them. They are just behind the last members of the Manchester crowd, keeping pace but also distance, maintaining a buffer.

Streets start appearing rapidly on our right. I catch the name of one, but then forget it. There are more streets. For some reason, there are many. Every fifteen or twenty yards, it seems, there is another one. I notice Sammy noticing them. He seems to be looking for a particular one. There is a strategy at work but I am not understanding it. Sammy then shouts something –

he has discovered the street he wants – and the crowd, sprinting now, runs with him. He leads us round the first corner. Then a quick right: after ten yards, there is another corner. And, surprisingly, another quick right. Three small streets, and then we are back to where we started from, except in one crucial respect: before we were being chased; now, having looped round, we are the ones chasing.

Later, looking at a map, I will discover that Dawes Road passes through the area at an angle, cutting diagonally across the other streets, breaking them into small residential triangles, making it possible for Sammy to run round one rapidly enough to be able to re-emerge directly behind the Chelsea supporters.

It is the first time I have seen them, but it is, I think, only the younger ones I see, the ones hanging back, at the rear of the crowd, bouncing in and out of my vision. I can take in little more than vague figures, the occasional face, a look of panic as someone turns round to see what is chasing him down from behind. The pavement ends, we enter the street, cross it, the pavement begins. I see this because I am watching my feet, everyone pressed so closely together and moving so fast that I don't want to fall. But I don't know how many streets we have passed. I perceive them not as facts, but as symptoms of movement. Where is the traffic?

It goes on. I was convinced that, having looped round, the momentum would carry us straight into the violence, but it doesn't. It is a chase, and the chase continues, pressing against this barrier, this threshold, the act of transgression moments away, but no one prepared to undertake it: on and on and on and nothing is happening. I am being held back, restricted, leashed. The buildings around me, although hardly discernible, have a weightiness about them: they are shadowy and dark and oppressive. I find that I am noticing them – more than I am noticing the supporters. I want the buildings not to be there. It is as if the street were no longer wide or large enough for me. The buildings have become aggressive physical facts, constricting and overbearing. Something has got to give way, something has got to give.

And when it does, it is property.

There is glass breaking: it is a window. I hear it, I don't see it, but the effect is sensational – literally sensational: it fills the senses, reverberates inside me, as though a blast of voltage has passed through my limbs. Something has burst, erupted. There is another sound: the soft, crushed sound of a windscreen shattering. The sensation of hearing this is intensely gratifying. There is another muted crash, another windscreen. And then everywhere, glass is breaking. It is property that is being destroyed first, in order to help us across this barrier: *property*, the symbol of shelter, the fact of the law.

And then they are gone. They go over the crest. There is the roar, and then everyone flies – as though beyond gravity – into violence. They are lawless. Nothing will stop them except the physical force of the police. Or incapacitating injury.

·

Bloody Nora

JOHN OSBORNE

John Osborne describes his reaction on hearing of the suicide of his former wife, the actress Jill Bennett.

Notebook, 7 October 1990: Nora Noel Jill Bennett committed suicide yesterday. Except, of course, that she didn't, merely perpetrating a final common little deceit under the delusion that it was an expression of 'style', rather than the coarse posturing of an overheated housemaid.

Reading through the glib newspaper cant of today, it appears that only I know what should have been apparent to even the most crass journalist: that she was a woman so demoniacally possessed by Avarice that she died of it. How many people have died in such a manner, of Avarice? Of pride, sloth, gluttony and, most publicly, of lust. But to die of Avarice takes driving of the will, some low, scheming ingenuity. However, there it is,

she did actually contrive to polish herself off with the deadly
draught. This final, fumbled gesture, after a lifetime of glad-
rags borrowings, theft and plagiarism, must have been one of
the few original or spontaneous gestures in her loveless life.

I don't think she would have been too pleased with her
notices this morning, in spite of the corn-drivel phrases from
the lady hacks, who are simply relieved to find that they're a bit
more on top of their own plundering avidity. But she would
have been satisfied with the poor Silly-Jilly gush spewed up by
the gay faithful and hairy show-biz sob-sisters. The power of
popular sentimentality does wonders with invention.

B. A. (Freddie) Young tootles on in the *Financial Times* (she
deserved a rave review there – money was her undisputed
reason for living): 'Petite [he can't even remember what she
looked like] and charming, she was always an active outdoor
woman.' He must have been at the Garrick port a little too late
in the afternoon. Something's certainly fevered his muddy old
remembrance. She could have tucked little Freddie under her
'glitzy, up-market armpits' (*Daily Express*).

During the nine years I lived beneath the same roof with her,
she spent half the day in bed. There was a short period when
she took dressage lessons, that most intensive course in aids to
severe narcissism, but in an *in*door school. She *was* intermittently
athletic. She could throw a weighty punch or kick, *and* sustain it
for hours on end. My friends can give you a guided tour of the
scars around my head.

'At the Court, she played the Russian Countess in *A Patriot
for Me*, a part she adorned beyond its proper worth.' Wrong,
Freddie. Petite and charming as a rattle-snake before breakfast,
she got the part by default, and it was later truly 'adorned' with
considerable power, grace and charm by Sheila Gish and June
Ritchie in the 1983 revival. Apart from their superior gifts, they
managed to speak the text without sounding like a puppy with a
mouthful of lavatory paper.

During the long nights of hearing her lines, which only laziness
prevented her from getting down unassisted, I did everything I

could to scrub up her diction, but it never improved. Indeed, after we separated and she was consigned to lesser parts, it became even worse. During a television series in which she stooged to Maria Aitken, lamentable even by the pier-cnd standards of sit-com, she was quite incomprehensible and cried out for sub-titles.

Perhaps it was Tony's declaration that she was the 'worst actress in England' and Anthony Page's capitulation to little Jilly's tiresome refusal to give a reading that persuaded me to give her the Countess nod. For once, Mary McCarthy was uncommonly perceptive when she pronounced the performance 'common and strident'. It was straight from life.

More of today's 'tributes': 'Former screen sex symbol' (the *Sun*, couldn't remember who she was); 'Tempestuous, ritzy star' (*Express*, again). Star she never was, even by the saloon-bar tally of the *TV Times*. All those lies she fed out *ad nauseum* are here again: of J.O. having gone off with her 'best friend', who was never more than a lunchtime acquaintance; of *her* sheepdog – mine – which *I* had destroyed. I loved him and saved him from her vicious neglect. And so on – the perpetuation of this whole rotting body of lies and invention which was her crabbed little life.

At least some of them have rumbled her real age. Poor Willis had years of grilling with immigration officials infuriated by her amateurish efforts to change her birth date. As so often, the provincial papers were on to it first.

> Marguerite Vernon, 81, of Sidford in East Devon, was Jill's cousin, and closest surviving relative. 'When she became famous, contact was broken. We went to see some of her plays but were fairly coldly received. [I'll bet.] She was a good actress, but extrovert, noisy and loud.' [Come, Mrs Vernon, don't you mean 'witty and vulnerable, warm-hearted, feline, wonderfully droll and naughty, instinctive and hard to please'?] Mr Vernon is also convinced that Jill, who won best actress award in 1968 for her part in John Osborne's *Time Present*, kept a secret of her real age.
>
> *Western Morning News*

But what of her 'diamond sparkle which made her so irresistible and so wonderful in *Hedda Gabler*' (Patrick Procktor, painter of her portrait and a friend of twenty-five years)? Well, he didn't have to hump her through her lines. Wasn't it her 'essential quality of intelligence and lack of sentimentality which made her Hedda so remarkable' (Anthony Page)? Sentimentality she had in abundance; feeling none.

'She was eighteen years younger than my wife,' Mr Vernon continues, 'which would make her sixty-three and not fifty-nine as she claimed.' No matter, Mr Vernon. The producer Thelma Holt recalls her 'wit and larky sense of fun. Even in recent times, when her career and personal life were sometimes in the doldrums, she maintained her essential elegance and stoic brightness.' I remember the tragic actress's stoic brightness very well, Ms Holt. I remember the shit and the vomit on the sheets and calling out my friend Patrick Woodcock every other month with his little black bag. I know how carefully she knew the practical drill of suicide and how many times she rehearsed it:

> ESSENTIALS Thirty or forty sleeping pills of maximum strength. 30mg Carbitol, for instance. At least half bottle of brandy. Half a loaf of moist brown bread. Most important: make sure that you will not be accidentally disturbed. An anonymous, second-rate hotel, booked in on Friday with the Do Not Disturb notice put up at once. The Cumberland at Marble Arch is ideal.

My cheap joke about calling her 'Adolf' has followed her to Putney Vale. Even those who might consider themselves her admirers took to using it.

How do I know that Adolf didn't intend to kill herself? Very simple. Her body contained hardly a trace of alcohol. She was relying on someone 'coming on her' sufficiently comatose for a good night's sleep but not enough to feel the brush of angels' wings. But her dog-walker failed to return and the millionaire

Dogs home left £½m by actress

By A J McIlroy

THE ACTRESS Jill Bennett, former wife of John Osborne, the playwright, left more than £500,000 to Battersea Dogs Home in her will.

Miss Bennett, who died last October, left estate valued at £582,530 net (£596,978 gross). The will bequeathed the residue of her estate to her mother but stipulated it should go to the dogs home should her mother die before her.

There were bequests of £5,000 each to the Theatrical Ladies Guild of Charity and her long-standing secretary and companion Mrs Linda Drew. Had her mother not died the dogs home would also have received £5,000.

Jill Bennett: always had dogs around

Daily Telegraph, 27 May 1991

stockbroker whose bed — and fortune — she coveted, was on business in Hungary and could not be summoned.

The sound of 'I left my heart in San Francisco' will waft across Putney Vale, and that distinguished film director Michael Winner will pronounce: 'She was a bit of a sexpot. One of the kindest, nicest people you could ever meet!'

Notebook, 27 May 1991: Adolf has left half a million to Battersea Dogs' Home. She never bought a bar of soap in all the time she lived with me. Always she cried poverty. 'Poor Jilly, she's got no money.' All the time she was bursting with krugerrands, cast-iron stocks and bond she inherited from her wise old dad, Randle, to say nothing of the £157,000 old mother Nora left her. Ever since those days in 1947 when I used to pass her front-of-house photograph outside the Vaudeville in the Strand on my way from Benn Brothers to pick up Renee, she had been piling up the heftiest assets of any actress since Lily Langtry.

I must have been more profitably 'touched' than most, but all her gay boyfriends, clamouring for AIDS charities, can't be well pleased. She left them only her contempt. Half a million pounds. To the Dogs' Home.

It is the most perfect act of misanthropy, judged with the tawdry, kindless theatricality she strove to achieve in life. She had no love in her heart for people and only a little more for dogs. Her brand of malignity, unlike Penelope's, went beyond even the banality of ambition. It had its roots deep in a kind of bourgeois criminality. Her frigidity was almost total. She loathed men and pretended to love women, whom she hated even more. She was at ease only in the company of homosexuals, whom she also despised but whose narcissism matched her own. I never heard her say an admiring thing of anyone. Her contempt was so petty and terrible. Everything about her life had been a pernicious confection, a sham.

I have only one regret remaining now in this matter of Adolf. It is simply that I was unable to look down upon her open coffin and, like that bird in the Book of Tobit, drop a good, large mess in her eye.

•

Beat the Yids and save Russia
VITALI VITALIEV

The Russian journalist, Vitali Vitaliev, himself a Jew, describes the origins of anti-Semitism as it currently exists in Russia.

Jews have been living on the territory of the present-day Soviet Union since time immemorial. The arrival of the Jews is linked with the exile of the Ten Tribes (720 BC) or with the Destruction of the First Temple (586 BC). Greek inscriptions in the Black Sea area testify to the presence of Jews in the early centuries of the Common Era (Anno Domini). Since that time they have also settled in Central Asia and the Caucasus. There were Jews in Kievan Rus in the tenth century and in the Crimea in the thirteenth.

The Russian tsars fell over themselves to keep Jews out of their territories. In 1727, all Jews were expelled from the country, and ten years later from the Ukraine and Belorussia. Much of the adverse feeling towards the Jews originally stemmed from Christian beliefs that they had killed Christ. 'From the enemies of Christ I wish neither gain nor profit!' Tsarina Elizabeth declared in the eighteenth century, banning Jewish merchants from trading in the Ukraine. After Polish partition in 1772 thousands of Polish Jews found themselves under Russian rule. They were confined to live and work in special restricted areas – the so-called 'Pale of Settlement' – and were banned from dwelling in major Russian cities and towns. The period before 1917 was alternately characterized by repression and relaxation. The early twentieth century was marked by the appearance of the so-called Black Hundreds, predecessors of the present-day Pamyat, the fascist Memory Society. They organized pogroms directed against Jews and members of the progressive intelligentsia. 'Beat the Yids and save Russia!' became their slogan. The authorities tended to ignore the pogroms and Tsar Nicholas II even thanked the Black Hundreds for their support.

There were five million Jews living in the Russian empire on the eve of the 1917 revolution. It was not by chance that they became one of Bolshevism's main driving forces: no other national minority was oppressed by the tsarist regime as much as they. Jews occupied leading posts in the first Bolshevik government led by Lenin. They fought in the Red Army in the 1917–22 Civil War. During the twenties and the early thirties a certain revival of Jewish culture was observed in the Soviet Union. In 1927 the country had 509 Jewish schools teaching 107,000 pupils.

Strange as it may seem, it was the end of the Second World War that brought about a big rise in anti-Semitic feeling. People were looking for a scapegoat to be blamed for the hunger and devastation and Stalin helped them to find one. On his orders Solomon Mikhoels, a famous Jewish actor and stage director, was murdered in the street in Minsk by state security agents in 1948. After the killing, a truck was driven over his corpse to give the impression of an accident. In 1952 the members of the Jewish Anti-Fascist Committee were shot on Stalin's instructions and the 'doctors' plot' continued the vicious anti-Semitic campaign.

Under Khrushchev and Brezhnev public anti-Semitism went into hiding, but its ugly face could be seen in the secret 'enrollment norms' for Jewish high-school students which were observed to the letter, in the ignominious virtually complete banning of Jews from government posts, diplomacy, security, defence industries, the army, the militia, the executive Party jobs. Strict norms for showing Jewish faces on TV and for mentioning Jewish names by the press were introduced. In 1967 *The Commissar*, a brilliant feature film directed by Alexander Askoldov, was banned simply for presenting a Jewish family in a sympathetic light. It was genocide all right, but a hidden, cowardly and covert one which made it even more repugnant. As to the popular, unofficial anti-Semitism, it was contained as well as any other nationalistic trend in which the rulers were inclined to see an immediate threat to themselves and their powers.

What happened with the ascent of Gorbachev was that official anti-Semitism was slightly curbed, though all the norms and percentages remain in force. It has simply become more cunning, less obvious and was technically no longer officially encouraged. But it was not discouraged either.

What was and is being encouraged is so-called 'unofficial anti-Semitism', which has always been very easy for the rulers to manipulate. During Gorbachev's reign it has reached unseen dimensions and triggered an unprecedented exodus of Jewish people from the Soviet Union at a rate of 200,000 a year.

It all started in 1986–7 with the formation of Pamyat, an anti-Semitic, fascist organization. The leader of Pamyat, a mediocre former actor called Dmitri Vassilliev, introduced a special uniform – black T-shirts with a picture of a tolling bell on them and black knee-length boots. Masking themselves with claims that they were 'saving Russian culture', they gradually unleashed the biggest anti-Semitic campaign in the Soviet history.

It is interesting to note that Pamyat was the first unofficial organization to hold an unsanctioned rally in the centre of Moscow, shortly after its formation in 1987. The officials treated the rally with unusual restraint. They didn't disperse the demonstrators with truncheons, as they used to do with tiny groups of political dissenters. Pamyat members were even received by Boris Yeltsin, then First Secretary of the Moscow Party Committee, although this was the first and last Pamyat meeting with an official of this rank.

Pamyat agitators were sent all round the country. I saw one in the main street of Krasnodar, Caucasus. He was distributing leaflets covered with figures specifying the number of Jews in the first Bolshevik government, in Cheka (Lenin's secret police) and so on. The point was simple: the Bolshevik revolution was part of the Zionist conspiracy to destroy mother Russia. Now that destruction is complete – which incidentally is true – the Jews, having finished their historic mission, are fleeing to Israel. With all the antediluvian primitivism of this declaration, it did manage to strike a responsive chord among the Russian people, driven to extreme despair by unending shortages and growing unrest: they are eager to find culprits, even if imaginary ones . . .

The farther in, the deeper. Soon it became common knowledge that Pamyat was conducting a census of the country's Jewish population. To become a Pamyat member, one had to provide the addresses of five Jewish families (or of three Jews with Russian names) as an entrance fee. There were also numerous cases of physical violence against Jews. People were appealing to the government and to Gorbachev to do something to curb anti-Semitism. There was no reaction.

It was becoming clearer and clearer that some powerful force
was standing behind Pamyat, whose members were systematically breaking not only the constitution but also the Criminal
Code by disseminating nationalistic information and spreading
racial hatred – but not one of them had even been detained! In
fact officialdom gave Pamyat the support of several fully official
and highly circulated publications – *Nash Sovremenik, Molodaya
Gvardiya, Kuban, Literaturnaya Rossiya* and *Sovietskaya Rossiya.*
(The last one, by the way, has a circulation of about ten million
copies and is the official organ of the Communist Party Central
Committee!) These newspapers and magazines took up openly
pro-Pamyat anti-Semitic positions, insulting and cursing Jews
in every issue, but the authorities stubbornly turned a blind eye
while *Molodaya Gvardiya* asserted: 'No, we do not like Jews in
the USSR and we can't be forced to like them.'

In May 1989 Lord Nicholas Bethell visited Moscow and met
the leaders of Pamyat. The harrowing account of this meeting
was published in the *Mail on Sunday* under the heading 'I meet
the Soviet Nazis': 'They claim support running into several
million. They have branches in thirty cities. During the meeting
I was openly filmed by a young man with a video camera, an
expensive Sony of a type not normally on sale in the Soviet
Union. "Anti-Russian forces have captured our press, radio and
TV," Vassilliev told me. "The white nations are being driven
out of Europe." As he rambled on, I sat hardly believing that I
was listening to the language of Hitler and Oswald Mosley in a
Moscow flat.'

Lord Bethell's fear is shared by numerous Western observers.
'Pamyat people believe that the Jews killed Christ and Tsar
Nicholas II. They say Jews organized the Bolshevik Revolution,
and masterminded Stalin's Terror. They see glasnost and
perestroika as a conspiracy to allow Jewish capitalists to regain
control of the country,' Carroll Bogert wrote in *Newsweek.*

Here's the sad, though incomplete, chronicle of other Pamyat
'achievements': anti-Semitic leaflets sent to many of Moscow's
progressive newspapers and magazines; threats and pogroms;

anti-Jewish rallies; raids on dachas belonging to the Jewish intelligentsia; harassing of anti-Pamyat parliamentary deputies; murders of several Jewish activists; arson attacks on flats of non-Jewish Pamyat opponents; scuffles on Moscow's Pushkin Square where people with 'suspicious faces' were severely beaten; pogrom in the Moscow Writers' Club, the appearance of an article entitled 'Russophobia' in *Nash Sovremenik* where the author, academician Igor Shafarevich, wrote of 'small people' (a euphemism for Jews) dominating 'big people' (i.e. Russians).

On 21 March 1990, five radical Russian nationalist groups formed a coalition under the umbrella title the Popular Orthodox Movement of Russia Pamyat. They published a manifesto saying that Russia has become 'the appendage of the world Zionist oligarchy', that the murder of Tsar Nicholas II and his family was 'a brutal Jewish ritual killing', that Russia is being systematically robbed by 'international usurious Zionist capital'. Thus Pamyat has become a real political force.

At the beginning of May 1990, two men with white bags over their heads burst into the flat of a non-Jewish Moscow writer and journalist, who was very anti-Pamyat and had more than once delivered tough speeches against it on the Russian service of the Munich-based Radio Liberty. At the time he was abroad and his flat was occupied by the family of his friend Steve Crawshaw, the newly arrived Moscow correspondent of the *Independent* who hadn't been provided with his own flat yet. Steve was in the office and his wife Eva had just put their little daughter Ania to sleep.

The hooded invaders were brandishing knives. They kicked Eva into the kitchen and slammed the door. One of them held the knife at her throat. 'Svolotch!' – 'bitch,' he said in Russian. A rag was thrust into Eva's mouth to prevent her crying out. She started struggling. The masked attacker smashed her against the furniture, wall and door. One of her fingers was sliced through with the knife and her entire body was cut and bruised. They would certainly have killed her had a neighbour not overheard Eva's muffled screams and rung the doorbell. The intruders panicked and fled. They were not found.

That was clearly the hand of Pamyat: Klu Klux Klan hoods, two untouched wallets, ignored by the attackers, and the fact that only two weeks before petrol had been spilt on the threshold outside the flat's door. This last detail is especially convincing, since more than once Pamyat has spilt petrol on the doorsteps of Jewish activists in Leningrad as a warning: if you don't move out, we'll set fire to your flat. And on many occasions they have carried out this threat.

The flat of Vladimir Pribilovski, a member of the *Panorama* editorial board, was set on fire on the night of 23 August 1990 while he was on holiday. The fire followed the newspaper's publication of an article critical of Pamyat. Three months earlier, on 16 May, the flat of *Panorama*'s editor was burnt. The arson attack occurred the day after another article in the same paper exposing Pamyat. Many *Panorama* journalists used to get threatening letters signed by 'Russian patriots'. The arsonists remain unknown even now.

In August 1990, Konstantin Smirnov-Ostashvili, the Pamyat activist and bigot responsible for the pogrom in the Writers' Club in January when many Jewish authors were insulted and beaten up, was brought to trial under pressure of public opinion. He was sentenced to two years' imprisonment, but his trial was used by Pamyat to propagate their ideas. Suddenly Ostashvili, a drunkard and a hooligan, became a martyr. He was showered with flowers in the courtroom and he solemnly promised to continue his struggle with Jews even in jail. Outside the courtroom Ostashvili's supporters carried banners saying 'Zionist genocide against the Russian people is continuing' and 'Democracy in Russia is for Jews only'. One of the demonstrators shouted: 'Russian villages are dark and hungry while the Jews get rich. Who is making our gas and benzene disappear? The answer is as obvious as the sun in the sky!' A leaflet distributed outside the courtroom said: 'Zionists want to throw Smirnov-Ostashvili into prison because he told the truth. It is no coincidence that this trial is taking place at the exact moment when our anti-people government moves to a so-called market economy – which really means the conversion of our state into a colony of multi-national corporations. The Zionists seek to use this trial to divert attention from the crimes being perpetrated against the Russian people.' Again the authorities didn't make even a meek attempt to curb this anti-Semitic manifestation.

On 19 September 1990, Alexander Men', a Russian Orthodox priest, a theologian and a people's deputy, was killed with an axe on the way to his church in the Moscow region. Father Alexander was a baptised Jew. In his sermons he preached the ideas of peace, tolerance and national reconciliation. He taught Christianity in a Moscow school and was spiritual teacher to many human rights activists. Again the assassins were not found. In the first days of 1991 Hegumen Lazar, a member of the church commission set up to investigate Father Men's murder was killed in his home: he must have found a trail.

So why are Pamyat's activities being stubbornly ignored by the ruling élite? They would say that it is because of pluralism. But pluralism accepts anything but attacks on pluralism itself. The real reason is that at this stage of the country's development, the rulers can retain power only in an atmosphere of social unrest, instability and mutual hatred, with the population fragmented into many small warring factions. There's no more certain way of doing this than to offer them a scapegoat. Why are the shops empty? Because of cunning Jewish cooperators. Why is crime rocketing? Because of Jewish journalists teaching the underworld how to rob poor Soviet people. They have ruined our country and now they are fleeing to Israel. Kill them! Try them before they leave! 'We won't let you flee this time like Trotsky: we'll kill you here in Russia!' one of the letters to *Ogonyok* said. 'We must try every Jew for his or her crimes against the Russian people. Even children! Let capitalist bankers pay us at least 100,000 roubles for every emigrating Jew!' Ostashvili said in one of his interviews.

Or let's look at the protocols of the Sixth Plenum of the

Board of the Russian Federation Writers' Union, 13–14 November 1989, where, according to tradition, high-ranking members of the CPSU Central Committee were present as guests. Here's what the so-called writers said from the rostrum with the tacit approval and applause of the Party leaders:

Anatoly Builov: Let's talk about the Jews. The Jews are evidently the only national group interested in breeding strife amongst us. Some time ago I didn't know anything about this Jewish subject. But why are they everywhere where there's a smell of profit? I was told they're clever. But why have they led us down a blind alley? [*Applause*] Let's also speak about those who've changed their names and nationalities from their Jewish ones, and whose number is three times larger than the official figure.

Tatyana Glushkova: There is an argument between Zionism – the worst form of world fascism – and humanity. We shouldn't conceal the fact that everyone who speaks out like me is risking her neck like the Palestinians or those protesting against the apartheid regime in South Africa. How long will Russian writers, the legitimate sons of the Russian land, the Russians with roots, languish under the heel of the oppressors and usurpers?

Vladimir Sharikov: I'll say a few words about the oft-cited decree of the Council of People's Commissars of 25 July, 1918, 'On the Prevention of Anti-Semitism and Jewish Pogroms'. I believe it's high time to make a thorough study of the reasons behind that decree, under which practically every citizen of Russia could become an outlaw for pronouncing a not-too-well-thought-of word. The label 'anti-Semite' has been stuck to such world-famed names as Cicero, St John Chrysostom, Tacitus, Seneca, Shakespeare, Dickens, Fichte, Hegel, Kant, Gogol, Dostoyevsky. Generally this label could be stuck to almost the whole culture of the world.

Vassily Bielov: I am surprised that the Secretariat of the Russian Federation Writers' Union has allowed Moscow and Leningrad writers of Jewish nationality to lead it by the nose for many years. I am ready to repeat this opinion of mine anywhere.

Two other rampant anti-Semites – Valentin Rasputin and Veniamin Yarin – were appointed by Gorbachev to his Presidential Council, the country's main ruling body. Valentin Rasputin, actually a talented writer, hasn't written anything noteworthy since he joined the anti-Semites. 'The foundation of anti-Semitism has always been mediocrity,' said Nikolai Berdiayev, the well-known Russian religious philosopher. Rasputin does however often accompany Gorbachev on his visits abroad.

Gorbachev's only public mention of anti-Semitism at the Twenty-First Annual Congress of Komsomol on 11 April 1990 was demagogic and rather vague: 'We must do everything to prevent the spread of anti-Semitism and all other isms,' he stated. What did he mean by 'all other isms'? Zionism? Internationalism? No one knows, but it is clear that he could stop the exodus of Jews and 'the spread of anti-Semitism' by simply saying publicly just once: 'Don't leave! We need you! We'll protect you!' He has never said this and he never will.

This refusal to act gives reassurance to the fascists themselves. 'Our struggle is supported by official Soviet organs and healthy forces in the KGB, the MVD [the Interior Ministry – VV], the army and the Presidential Council,' Pamyat states cynically in its manifesto. And they seem to be right.

Alexandr Yakovlev, the former Politburo member, answering the question of why no criminal prosecutions had been brought against those spreading national hatred, said: 'I myself asked the Procurator General this question more than once. But it looks like even the Procurator General can't bring himself to institute such proceedings. Some powerful pressure from the top does not allow the law to be applied.'

Mikhail Chlenov, a leader of the Moscow Jewish community, commented: 'The trouble is that the authorities have never condemned anti-Semitism openly. Gorbachev's attitude is to be silent in the face of our problems. Perhaps the leadership is frightened of being accused of being pro-Zionist. Or maybe they would far rather we all left the country, once and for all.'

Oleg Gordievsky, a former KGB officer, said: 'The anti-Semitic campaign is being pursued with the evident connivance of some authorities in the Party and it would appear that there are even some members of the Politburo sympathetic to chauvinism.'

G. Shatalov, a Soviet journalist from Baku, complained: 'I think that our statesmen have a certain interest in being lenient to extremists and very rough towards their victims.'

Zeev Ben-Shlomo, the London *Jewish Chronicle* Eastern Europe correspondent, wrote: 'A top Russian Communist has been named in a Soviet TV report as a supporter of anti-Semitic organisations. Mr Ivan Polozkov, head of the Russian Federation Communist Party, was named by Mr Andrei Makarov, public prosecutor in the trial of Pamyat activist Konstantin Smirnov-Ostashvili. During the trial Mr Makarov said: "Serious forces are behind Pamyat."'

While progressive public figures both in the Soviet Union and in the West are looking for the sources of 'the powerful pressure from the top' which supports 'Pamyat comrades', anti-Semitism keeps growing. The percentage norms for quotas of Jewish applicants have been reintroduced at some faculties of the Moscow University. Anti-Semitic assaults, beatings and insults are becoming more and more frequent. Many schools in Moscow and Leningrad are dominated by Pamyat and it is no longer unusual for schoolteachers to call any boy or girl whose nose seems to be of a suspicious shape a dirty Jewess, Yid or Kike. A Moscow synagogue had to open a special school for the Jewish kids thrown out of ordinary schools. There are more than eighty children there.

In summer 1990 *Moscow News* carried the results of an opinion poll conducted among Muscovites by the Moscow Institute of open research in conjunction with Houston University: 27.7 per cent of those polled were of the opinion that 'given a choice between people and money Jews will take the money'; 26.6 per cent claimed that they would be unhappy 'if a Jew were to become a member of their family'. 'Thus,' concludes the newspaper, 'about 25 per cent of us are rabid anti-Semites.'

But the most eloquent development occurred on 1 February 1990, when Goskomtrud (the USSR State Committee for Labour Resources) issued instruction N56–9 as an addition to the USSR Council of Ministers decree of 6 October 1989, N825, 'On Giving War Veterans' Benefits to Former Prisoners of the Fascist Concentration Camps'. This was a long-awaited decree. Since Stalin's times, prisoners of the German labour camps have been officially treated as traitors. Now, after forty-five years – at last! – justice triumphed. But not for everyone. In the above-mentioned Goskomtrud instruction it is written in black and white: 'Citizens of Jewish nationality, who were imprisoned in fascist ghettos during the Great Patriotic War, are exempt from the benefits provided under the decree N825.'

I'd like to leave the last word on anti-Semitism in the Soviet Union to the letters of relatives of some of my new friends, recent Soviet emigrants to Australia.

I don't understand Jewish communities in Western countries. It looks as if they are interested in having us victimized by the fascist mongrels. Or maybe they are waiting for the 'final solution'? I am reading yours and mum's letters from Australia and my eyes are filled with tears. I think that we are the most unfortunate nation in the world – eternally harassed and persecuted. We'll probably go mad before we get an answer from the embassy. *Minsk, February 1990*

We want to tell you that we are still alive and are just holding out, though, frankly, we don't know whether we want to. We've lost all faith in the future. The situation here is very troublesome, and we were promised a night of terror by anti-Semites on May 5. If God helps us survive, then goodbye. If not, then farewell to you! Don't think that I have gone mad. It's simply that we are living on a powder keg. *Kiev, February 1990*

We were preparing to celebrate the Day of Atonement. My daughter and grandson came to visit us from Kishinev. While my daughter and wife were busy in the kitchen, two unknown men in black masks burst into our flat. They announced that they didn't need anything from us Jews, but our lives. They left my daughter alone only after they had split her head open and she was bleeding to death. My wife, trying to save us, led them to the neighbouring room and there they dealt with her, stabbing her three times. She died on the spot. We were the last remaining Jewish family in our town. *Moldavia, October 1990*

The situation in our town of Bershad' is very critical. Many Jewish people are leaving. Two days ago a distant relative was killed. She lived alone and was eighty-two years old. She was brutally murdered: her arms and legs were twisted, her breasts were cut off – this was something unheard of. Now Jewish people are scared of going out in the evening. One man, a Jew, did go out, and was beaten up. 'We'll give you Jews a roasting!' they told him. This is all our news. *Ukraine, November 1990*

•

Petty feuds in journalism
RORY KNIGHT BRUCE

In this piece, taken from the *Spectator*, Rory Knight Bruce, editor of the *Evening Standard*'s Londoner's Diary column, argues that petty feuding is damaging serious journalism. Well, he should know.

The week before this year's [1991] Tory party conference the telephone rang for me at the *Evening Standard*. It was Jeffrey Archer. 'People in Cabinet have told me that you are fair, but I have not found you so. I have got a file on you, and I am ringing to tell you that you are not invited to my party at Blackpool this year.'

I had not thought about Archer until that moment since the day that I went to his party in Brighton last year. It brought back the recollection of how Archer, at about two in the morning, had marched up to me, in front of several Cabinet ministers, and told me to leave. It did not matter that I had been invited along by other guests in a private capacity and had no intention of writing about the evening. I only did write about his behaviour because he threatened that I would be dismissed from my job in the morning.

Vendetta, feud or simple campaigns of social attrition are by no means rare between politicians and journalists. But often, and at more senior levels, the deteriorated relationship between politician and journalist rages without the general public being aware of it.

One such current tussle is that between Andrew Neil, editor of the *Sunday Times*, and the Chancellor of the Exchequer, Norman Lamont. Neil has consistently attacked Lamont's performance. Then Lamont finally struck back, labelling the *Sunday Times* a 'pretty squalid paper'.

This may be deemed the behaviour of immaturity, but behind it lies a deep-seated social and cultural antipathy between the two, based on class, power and sexuality. Neil – for his part, well documented in the court case with Peregrine Worsthorne – is a Paisley grammarian of the Y-fronts and white Ford variety. For all his achievements – most recently the purchase of a ridiculous publication for hillwalkers and fly-tiers, but with the all-important title of *Country Gentleman's Association* magazine – he is still unsettled by a man like Lamont. Lamont was educated at Loretto and Cambridge, and is a successful minister of the Crown. One has a sneaking feeling that there is more to it than this. Not only is he a happily married man, but he is much admired by the ladies. Neil, on the other hand, spent last Christmas in Barbados hanging around with the diaspora of the racing set, enthusiastically listening to their tales of female conquests.

If there is something rather seedy in this, there is a more serious observation to be made of such public vendettas. They distort the true emphasis of news and fail to serve the readers. And whilst it is admirable to be outside the establishment, as Neil claims to be, it must be desperate to be an outsider – like an urchin with its nose permanently pressed against the window of Harrods – seething with envy.

Britain is stuffed to the blighted gills with people who, from a casual meeting or through a loss in love, wage silent war against their foes. Auberon Waugh never fails to gang people against Lord Gowrie because of his Oxford successes with the ladies – one of whom Waugh coveted. Former Labour Foreign Secretary Tony Crosland's sister, Eve, takes her opportunities to turn opinion against his widow, Susan. 'Her columns have stripped the name of all credibility and dignity,' she said recently of Susan's offerings in 'that squalid paper'.

Personal vendetta is a sign of insecurity. It suggests an inability to argue issues without drawing in personalities. It admits to a paucity of judgment, and an inability to separate feeling from thought. More seriously, it self-confesses moral ineptitude.

Of course, in the 18th century, the practice of lampoon and satire, stretching as it did far beyond the restrictive libel laws today, was a common and colourful practice. But it was precisely because no punches were pulled. Sides were defined and taken. From Pope to Byron, satire was recognizable and literally made fools of people in public. Today it is the public who are fooled by the petty eddies, ripples and sniggers masquerading as serious journalism.

Those cases of mutual loathing which are cast widely abroad, Goldsmith against Ingrams, Thatcher against Heath, even Anna Ford tossing wine over Jonathan Aitken over the handling of TV-am, leave all parties stained long after the wine has dried.

I have lately been exposed to that master of the vendetta, John Osborne, having been asked to write a feature on him to coincide with his second volume of memoirs, *Almost a Gentleman*. Having had lunch with me in the summer, he promised me an interview in October. However, when I turned up as planned, I found he had already given the interview to – you may have already guessed – a 'squalid Sunday paper'. So I wrote the feature anyway to pre-empt the *Sunday Times*. Osborne was incensed. I received letters from him and his Shropshire neighbours telling me to leave the valley where he and I have houses. 'Go and pat sheep and patronize people elsewhere,' said one. Osborne himself was more direct. 'The safest place for wee Rory is in a cosy padded cell,' he concluded to my editor.

But of all the practitioners of vendetta, Osborne is the one most worthy of respect. He is a man with a talent for abuse. He is direct, and has the energy for a sustained campaign, long enough to outlive the victims, particularly if they are ex-wives. When I thought the embers of his ire were cooling, I received another letter. 'I am giving a small party for my friends. Someone suggested you might come and give your views on life in Salop. There'll be about a hundred or less, but I'm sure you would cope with great *élan*. Don't disappoint them. They'll be in a sportive mood.' Never before have I received an invitation with menaces.

But against the tawdry spats of Neil and Lamont, Osborne's hatred against his fellow thespians, and even against a modest journalist, are truly majestic. Would I mount a campaign against him? Only if it got him a knighthood.

Sources

Adams, Samuel Hopkins, *Alexander Woollcott*, Hamish Hamilton, 1946

Addison, Joseph, *The Spectator* No. 99, 1711

Agate, James, 'Likes and Dislikes', in A *Book of English Essays*, Penguin, 1980

Anonymous, *Duelling in Great Britain and Ireland*, in J. G. Millingen, *The History of Duelling*, Richard Bentley, 1841

Bergman, Ingmar, *The Magic Lantern*, Penguin, 1988

Bernard, Jeffrey, 'Right-hand man', in the *Spectator*, 25 June 1988

Booker, Christopher, *The Seventies: Portrait of a Decade*, Penguin, 1980

Boswell, James, *The Life of Samuel Johnson*, J. M. Dent & Sons, 1791

Boyd, Brian, *Vladimir Nabokov: The American Years*, Chatto & Windus, 1991

Boyle, Jimmy, *A Sense of Freedom*, Pan, 1977

Brown, Mick, *Richard Branson: The Inside Story*, Michael Joseph, 1988

Buford, Bill, *Among the Thugs*, Secker & Warburg, 1991

Chippendale, Peter, and Chris Horrie, *Stick It Up Your Punter*, Heinemann, 1990

Chitty, Susan, *The Beast and the Monk*, Hodder & Stoughton, 1975

Clarke, Gerald, *Capote: A Biography*, Simon & Schuster, 1988

Cockerell, Michael, *Life from Number 10*, Faber, 1988

Cody, William F., *The Life of Buffalo Bill*, 1878

Coleman, Ray, *John Lennon*, Futura, 1985

Considine, Shaun, *Bette and Joan: The Divine Feud*, Hutchinson, 1989

Crisp, Quentin, *The Naked Civil Servant*, Flamingo, 1985

de Valbourg, Misson, *Memoirs and Observations in England*, 1719

Desmond, Adrian and James Moore, *Darwin*, Michael Joseph, 1991

Dillon, Martin, *The Shankill Butchers*, Hutchinson, 1989

Ellmann, Richard, *Oscar Wilde*, Hamish Hamilton, 1987

Evans, Harold, *Good Times, Bad Times*, Coronet, 1984

Foot, Michael, *Aneurin Bevan*, Vol. II, Davis-Poynter, 1973

Forward, Susan, *Men Who Hate Women and the Women Who Love Them*, Bantam, 1988

Gide, André, *If It Die*, Secker & Warburg, 1951

Gluckman, Max, *Custom and Conflict in Africa*, Blackwell, 1956

Hayman, Ronald, *Proust*, Minerva, 1991

Hazlitt, William, *On the pleasure of hating*, in *Selected Writings*, ed. Ronald Blythe, Penguin, 1970

Herskowitz, Mickey, with Alfred de Marigny, *A Conspiracy of Crowns*, Bantam, 1990

Hitler, Adolf, *Mein Kampf*, Hutchinson, 1969

Hurt, Henry, *Reasonable Doubt*, Sidgwick & Jackson, 1986

Kelley, Kitty, *His Way*, Bantam, 1986

Kingsmill, Hugh, *More Invective*, Eyre & Spottiswoode, 1930

Knight Bruce, Rory, *Spectator*, 30 November 1991

Knox, John, *First Blast of the Trumpet*, in Hugh Kingsmill, *More Invective*, Eyre & Spottiswoode, 1930

Lacey, Robert, *Ford: The Man and the Machine*, Heinemann, 1986

Levi, Primo, *If This is a Man*, Abacus, 1987

Lynd, Robert, 'Why we hate insects', in *A Book of English Essays*, Penguin, 1980

Macaulay, Lord Alfred, *Essays*, Methuen, 1903

Machiavelli, Niccolò, *The Prince*, translated by N. H. T., Kegan, Paul, Trench & Co., 1882

McKay, Peter, *Inside Private Eye*, Fourth Estate, 1989

McKnight, Gerald, *Bitter Legacy*, Bantam, 1987; *Gucci: A House Divided*, Sidgwick & Jackson, 1987

Malcolm X, *The Autobiography of Malcolm X*, Penguin, 1965

Melville, Lewis, and Reginald Hargreaves, *Famous Duels and Assassinations*, Jarrolds, 1929

Naifeh, Stephen and Gregory White Smith, *Jackson Pollock: An American Saga*, Barrie and Jenkins, 1990

The New York Times, 'Hemingway Slaps Eastman in the face', 14 August 1937

Orwell, George, *Homage to Catalonia*, Penguin, 1938

Osborne, John, *Almost a Gentleman*, Faber, 1991

Parton, James, *Life and Times of Aaron Burr*, Houghton, Mifflin & Co., 1884

Pearson, John, *The Profession of Violence*, Panther Books, 1973

Percy, Sholto and Reuben, *The Percy Anecdotes*, Original and Select, 1823

Plimpton, George, *Shadow Box*, Simon & Schuster, 1989

Plutarch, *The Fall of the Roman Empire*, Penguin, 1958

Ramsey, Douglas K., *The Corporate Warriors*, Grafton, 1988

Ranelagh, John, *Thatcher's People*, Harper Collins, 1991

Rockstro, W. S., *Life of Handel*, Macmillan, 1883

Schlesinger, Arthur M., Jr, *Robert Kennedy and His Times*, André Deutsch, 1978

Simmons, Ernest J., *Pushkin*, Oxford University Press, 1937

Smith, Hedrick, *The New Russians*, Hutchinson, 1991

Smollett, Tobias, *Travels Through France and Italy*, 1766, in *Works*, Vol. XI, Constable, 1900

Stuart, Charles (ed.), Lord Reith, *The Diaries*, Collins, 1975

Swift, Jonathan, *A Letter to Pope*, 1725, in *Works*, Constable, 1824

Taki, *High Life*, Viking, 1989

Theoharis, Athan G., and John Stuart Cox, *The Boss: J. Edgar Hoover and the Great American Inquisition*, Harrap, 1989

Thompson, Hunter S., *Hell's Angels*, Penguin, 1967

Thornton, Michael, *Royal Feud*, Michael Joseph, 1985

Tolstoy, Leo, *Childhood, Boyhood and Youth*, Penguin, 1964; and *A Confession*, Penguin, 1987

Twain, Mark, *Life on the Mississippi*, Penguin, 1984

Van der Water, Frederic F., 'Rudyard Kipling's Vermont Feud', from *Rudyard Kipling: Interviews and Recollections*, ed. Harold Orel, Macmillan, 1983

Vitaliev, Vitali, *Dateline Freedom*, Hutchinson, 1991

Whistler, James, *The Gentle Art of Making Enemies*, Heinemann, 1890

Wright, William, *Lillian Hellman; The Image, the Woman*, Sidgwick & Jackson, 1987

Acknowledgements

We would like to thank all the authors, publishers and literary representatives who have given permission to reprint copyright material included in this anthology.

Samuel Hopkins Adams: to A. M. Heath & Co. Ltd, and Brandt & Brandt, Inc. for an extract from *Alexander Woollcott* (Hamish Hamilton, 1946). Copyright, 1945 by Samuel Hopkins Adams. Renewed 1973 Hester Adams and Katherine Adell

Ingmar Bergman: to Hamish Hamilton Ltd for an extract from *The Magic Lantern* (Penguin Books, 1988)

Jeffrey Bernard: to the author for 'Right-hand Man' from the *Spectator* (25 June 1988)

Christopher Booker: to Curtis Brown Ltd for an extract from *The Seventies: Portrait of a Decade* (Penguin Books, 1980)

Brian Boyd: to Random Century Group and Princeton University Press for extracts from *Vladimir Nabokov: The American Years* (Chatto & Windus, 1991). Copyright © 1991 by Princeton University Press

Jimmy Boyle: to Canongate Publishing Ltd for extracts from *A Sense of Freedom* (Pan Books, 1977)

Mick Brown: to Michael Joseph Ltd for extracts from *Richard Branson: The Inside Story* (Michael Joseph, 1985)

Bill Buford: to Octopus Publishing Group Library for an extract from *Among the Thugs* (Secker & Warburg, 1991)

Peter Chippendale and Chris Horrie: to Octopus Publishing Group Library for extracts from *Stick It Up Your Punter* (William Heinemann, 1990)

Susan Chitty: to Curtis Brown Ltd for an extract from *The Beast and the Monk* (Hodder & Stoughton, 1975)

Gerald Clarke: to Hamish Hamilton Ltd and Simon & Schuster, Inc. for extracts from *Capote: A Biography* (Simon & Schuster, 1988)

Michael Cockerell: to Faber & Faber Ltd for an extract from *Life from Number 10* (Faber, 1988)

Ray Coleman: to Sidgwick & Jackson Ltd, a division of Pan Macmillan, and MCA Music Ltd for an extract from *John Lennon* (Futura Books, 1985)

Shaun Considine: to Random Century Group and E. P. Dutton, an imprint of New American Library, a division of Penguin Books USA, Inc. for an extract from *Bette and Joan: The Divine Feud* (Hutchinson, 1989). Copyright © 1989 Shaun Considine

Quentin Crisp: to Harper Collins Publishers for an extract from *The Naked Civil Servant* (Flamingo Books, 1985)

Adrian Desmond and James Moore: to Michael Joseph Ltd for extracts from *Darwin* (Michael Joseph, 1991)

Martin Dillon: to Random Century Group for an extract from *The Shankill Butchers* (Hutchinson, 1989)

Richard Ellmann: to Hamish Hamilton Ltd and Alfred A. Knopf, Inc. for extracts from *Oscar Wilde* (Hamish Hamilton, 1987). Copyright © 1987 by the Estate of Richard Ellmann

Harold Evans: to George Weidenfeld & Nicolson Ltd for an extract from *Good Times, Bad Times* (Coronet Books, 1984)

Michael Foot: to Reg Davis-Poynter on behalf of the author for an extract from *Aneurin Bevan*, Volume II (Davis-Poynter, 1973)

Susan Forward and Joan Torres: to Bantam Books, Inc., a division of Bantam Doubleday Dell Publishing Group, Inc. for an extract from *Men Who Hate Women and the Women Who Love Them* (Bantam, 1988). Copyright © 1986 by Susan Forward and Joan Torres

André Gide: to Octopus Publishing Group Library for an extract from *If It Die*, translated by Dorothy Bussy (Secker & Warburg, 1951)

Max Gluckman: to Blackwell Publishers Ltd for an extract from *Custom and Conflict in Africa* (Blackwell, 1956)

Ronald Hayman: to Peters Fraser & Dunlop Group for extracts from *Proust* (Minerva, 1991)

Mickey Herskowitz and Alfred de Marigny: to Transworld Publishers Ltd and Adler Publishing Co. for extracts from *A Conspiracy of Crowns* (Bantam Books, 1990)

Adolf Hitler: to Random Century Group for an extract from *Mein Kampf*, translated by Ralph Mannheim (Hutchinson, 1969)

Henry Hurt: to Sidgwick & Jackson, a division of Pan Macmillan, for an extract from *Reasonable Doubt* (Sidgwick & Jackson, 1986)

Kitty Kelley: to Bantam Books, Inc., a division of Bantam Doubleday Dell Publishing Group, Inc. for extracts from *His Way: The Unauthorized Biography* (Bantam Books, 1986). Copyright © 1986 by H. B. Productions, Inc.

Hugh Kingsmill: to Octopus Publishing Group Library for extracts from *More Invective* (Eyre & Spottiswoode, 1930)

Rory Knight Bruce: to the *Spectator* for 'Masters of the Public Vendetta' from the *Spectator* (30 November 1991)

Robert Lacey: to Curtis Brown Ltd for an extract from *Ford: The Man and the Machine* (William Heinemann, 1986)

Primo Levi: to Random Century Group for extracts from *If This is a Man* (The Bodley Head)

Robert Lynd: to Peter Wheeler and Jack Gaster, on behalf of the Estate of Robert Lynd, and Octopus Publishing Group Library for 'Why We Hate Insects' from *A Book of English Essays* (Penguin Books, 1980)

Peter McKay: to Fourth Estate Ltd for an extract from *Inside Private Eye* (Fourth Estate, 1989)

Gerald McKnight: to Transworld Publishers Ltd for an extract from *Bitter Legacy* (Bantam Books, 1987). Copyright © Gerald McKnight, 1987; and Sidgwick & Jackson, a division of Pan Macmillan, for an extract from *Gucci: A House Divided* (Sidgwick & Jackson, 1987)

Malcolm X: to Random Century Group for an extract from *The Autobiography of Malcolm X* (Penguin Books, 1965)

Stephen Naifeh & Gregory White Smith: to Random Century Group and Clarkson N. Potter, Inc. for an extract from *Jackson Pollock: An American Saga* (Barrie & Jenkins, 1990)

George Orwell: to A. M. Heath & Company on behalf of the estate of the late Sonia Brownell Orwell and Martin Secker & Warburg for an extract from *Homage to Catalonia* (Penguin Books, 1938)

John Osborne: to Faber & Faber Ltd for an extract from *Almost a Gentleman* (Faber, 1991)

John Pearson: to Harper Collins Publishers for extracts from *The Profession of Violence* (Panther Books, 1973)

George Plimpton: to Simon & Schuster, Inc. for extracts from *Shadow Box* (Simon & Schuster, 1989)

Plutarch: to Penguin Books Ltd for an extract from *The Fall of the Roman Empire*, translated by Rex Warner (Penguin Classics, 1958). Copyright © Rex Warner, 1958

Douglas Ramsey: to Harper Collins Publishers and Houghton Mifflin, Co. for an extract from *The Corporate Warriors* (Grafton Books, 1988). Copyright © 1987 by Douglas Ramsey

John Ranelagh: to Harper Collins Publishers for an extract from *Thatcher's People* (Harper Collins, 1991)

Arthur Schlesinger Jr: to André Deutsch Ltd and Houghton Mifflin Co. for an extract from *Robert Kennedy and His Times* (Deutsch, 1978)

Ernest J. Simmons: to Harvard University Press for extracts from *Pushkin* (Oxford University Press, 1937). Copyright © 1937 by the President and Fellows of Harvard College

Hedrick Smith: to Random Century Group and Random House, Inc. for an extract from *The New Russians* (Hutchinson, 1991). Copyright © 1990 by Hedrik Smith

Charles Stuart (ed.): to Harper Collins Publishers for an extract from *Lord Reith: The Diaries* (Harper Collins, 1975)

Taki: to Dieter Klein Associates for 'Gentlemen-at-Arms' from *High Life* (Viking, 1989)

Athan G. Theoharis and John Stuart Cox: to Temple University Press for an extract from *The Boss: J. Edgar Hoover and the Great American Inquisition* (Harrap Publishers, 1989)

Hunter S. Thompson: to Penguin Books Ltd and Random House, Inc. for an extract from *Hell's Angels* (Penguin Books, 1967). Copyright © Hunter S. Thompson, 1966, 1967

Michael Thornton: to Michael Joseph Ltd for an extract from *Royal Feud* (Michael Joseph, 1985)

Frederic F. Van de Water: to The Countryman Press, Inc. for 'Rudyard Kipling's Vermont Feud' from *Rudyard Kipling: Interviews and Recollections*, ed. Harold Orel (Macmillan, 1983)

Vitali Vitaliev: to Random Century Group for an extract from *Dateline Freedom* (Hutchinson, 1991)

William Wright: to Sidgwick & Jackson, a division of Pan Macmillan, for extracts from *Lillian Hellman: The Image, the Woman* (Sidgwick & Jackson, 1987)

Every effort has been made to contact all copyright holders. The publishers will be pleased to make good in future editions any errors or omissions brought to their attention.